ORGANIZATIONAL TRUST

A Reader

Edited by

Roderick M. Kramer

UNIVERSITY PRESS

OXFORD
UNIVERSITY PRESS

Great Clarendon Street, Oxford OX2 6DP

Oxford University Press is a department of the University of Oxford.
It furthers the University's objective of excellence in research, scholarship,
and education by publishing worldwide in

Oxford New York

Auckland Cape Town Dar es Salaam Hong Kong Karachi
Kuala Lumpur Madrid Melbourne Mexico City Nairobi
New Delhi Shanghai Taipei Toronto

With offices in

Argentina Austria Brazil Chile Czech Republic France Greece
Guatemala Hungary Italy Japan Poland Portugal Singapore
South Korea Switzerland Thailand Turkey Ukraine Vietnam

Oxford is a registered trade mark of Oxford University Press
in the UK and in certain other countries

Published in the United States
by Oxford University Press Inc., New York

The various contributors 2006

British Library Cataloguing in Publication Data

Data available

Library of Congress Cataloging in Publication Data

Organizational trust : progress and promise in theory and research / edited by Roderick M. Kramer.
p. cm.
Includes index.
ISBN-13: 978–0–19–928850–2 (alk. paper)
ISBN-10: 0–19–928850–X (alk. paper)
ISBN-13: 978–0–19–928849–6 (alk. paper)
ISBN-10: 0–19–928849–6 (alk. paper)
1. Organizational behavior–Moral and ethical aspects. 2. Trust–Social aspects. 3. Integrity. I. Kramer,
Roderick Moreland, 1950-HD58.7.O74644 2006
302.3′5–dc22

Typeset by SPI Publisher Services, Pondicherry, India
Printed in Great Britain
on acid-free paper by
Biddles Ltd., King's Lynn, Norfolk

ISBN 0–19–928849–6   978–0–19–928849–6
ISBN 0–19–928850–X (pbk.)   978–0–19–928850–2 (pbk.)
1 3 5 7 9 10 8 6 4 2

Contents

Contents

Acknowledgements

R. Hardin, 'The Street-level Epistemology of Trust', reprinted from *Analyse & Kritik*, 14 (1992). Copyright © Russell Hardin, reproduced with kind permission of the author.

O. E. Williamson, 'Calculativeness, Trust, and Economic Organization', *Journal of Law and Economics*, 34 (1993), published by The University of Chicago. Copyright 1993 by The University of Chicago. All rights reserved.

R. C. Mayer, J. H. Davis, and F. D. Schoorman, 'An Integrative Model of Organizational Trust', *Academy of Management Review*, 20 (1995). Copyright © 1995 The Academy of Management. Reprinted with permission.

D. H. McKnight, I. L. Cummings, and N. L. Chervany, 'Initial Trust Formation in New Organizational Relationships', *Academy of Management Review*, 23 (1998). Copyright © 1998 The Academy of Management. Reprinted with permission.

E. M. Whitener, S. E Brodt, A. Korsgaard, and J. M. Werner, 'Managers as Initiators of Trust: An Exchange Relationships Framework for Understanding Managerial Trust worthy Behavior', *Academy of Management Review*, 23 (1998). Copyright © 1998 The Academy of Management. Reprinted with permission.

P. Kollock, 'The Emergence of Exchange Structures: An Experimental Study of Uncertainty, Commitment, and Trust', *American Journal of Sociology*, 100 (1994), published by The University of Chicago. Copyright 1994 by The University of Chicago. All rights reserved.

J. H. Dyer and W. Chu, 'The Role of Trustworthiness in Reducing Transaction Costs and Improving Performance: Empirical Evidence from the United States, Japan, and Korea'. Reprinted from *Organization Science*, 14 (2003). Copyright © 2003 INFORMS.

R. S. Burt and M. Knez, 'Kinds of Third-Party Effects on Trust', *Rationality and Society*, 7 (3), pp. 255–92, copyright 1995 by Sage Publications Inc., Reprinted by Permission of Sage Publications Inc.

M. Sako, 'Does Trust Improve Business Performance?'. Reprinted from *Trust Within and Between Organizations: Conceptual Issues and Empirical Applications*, edited by C. Lane and R. Bachmann, Oxford University Press, 1998.

S. B. Sitkin and N. L. Roth, 'Explaining the Limited Effectiveness of Legalistic "Remedies" for Trust/Distrust'. Reprinted from *Organization Science*, 4 (1993). Copyright © 1993 INFORMS.

Acknowledgements

S. Robinson, 'Trust and Breach of the Psychological Contract', *Administrative Science Quarterly*, 41 (1996), pp. 574–99. Copyright © Cornell University, Johnson Graduate School of Management. Reprinted with permission.

A. Fenigstein and P. A. Vanable, 'Paranoia and Self-consciousness', *Journal of Personality and Social Psychology*, 62 (1992), pp. 129–38. Copyright © 1992 by the American Psychological Association. Reprinted with permission.

G. Fine and L. Holyfield, 'Secrecy, Trust, and Dangerous Leisure: Generating Group Cohesion in Voluntary Organizations'. Copyright © 1996 by the American Sociological Association.

D. Meyerson, K. Weick, and R. M. Kramer, 'Swift Trust in Temporary Groups', *Trust in Organizations: Frontiers of Theory and Research* edited by R. M. Kramer and T. R. Tyler, pp. 166–95, copyright 1996 by Sage Publications Inc., Reprinted by Permission of Sage Publications Inc.

R. Bachmann, 'Trust, Power, and Control in Trans-organizational Relations'. Reproduced with permission from *Organization Studies*, Copyright © SAGE Publications 2001, by permission of Sage Publications Ltd.

List of Contributors

Reinhard Bachmann, Management Department, Birkbeck College, University of London

Susan E. Brodt, Queen's School of Business, Queen's University

Ronald S. Burt, The University of Chicago Graduate School of Business

Norman L. Chervany, Carlson School of Management, University of Minnesota

Wujin Chu, College of Business Administration, Seoul National University

Larry L. Cummings, formerly of the University of Minnesota

James H. Davis, Mendoza College of Business, University of Notre Dame

Jeffrey H. Dyer, Marriott School of Management, Brigham Young University

Allan Fenigstein, Department of Psychology, Kenyon College

Gary Alan Fine, Department of Sociology, Northwestern University

Russell Hardin, Wilf Family Department of Politics, New York University

Lori Holyfield, Department of Sociology & Criminal Justice, University of Arkansas

Marc Knez, The University of Chicago Graduate School of Business

Peter Kollock, Department of Sociology, University of California, Los Angeles

M. Audrey Korsgaard, Moore School of Business, University of South Carolina

Roderick M. Kramer, Stanford Graduate School of Business, Stanford University

Roger C. Mayer, College of Business Administration, The University of Akron

D. Harrison McKnight, The Eli Broad College of Business, Michigan State University

Debra Meyerson, School of Education, Stanford University

Sandra L. Robinson, Sauder School of Business, University of British Columbia

Nancy L. Roth, School of Communication, Information, and Library Studies, Rutgers University

Mari Sako, Saïd School of Business, University of Oxford

F. David Schoorman, Krannert School of Management, Purdue University

Sim B. Sitkin, Fuqua School of Business, Duke University

Peter A. Vanable, Kenyon College

Karl E. Weick, Ross School of Business, University of Michigan

Jon M. Werner, College of Business and Economics, University of Wisconsin-Whitewater

Ellen M. Whitener, formerly of the University of Virginia

Oliver E. Williamson, Walter A. Haas School of Business, University of California, Berkeley

Introduction

Organizational Trust: Progress and Promise in Theory and Research

Roderick M. Kramer

Over the past two decades, the topic of trust moved from bit player to center stage in organizational theory and research. Whereas previously it often had been treated as a mediating variable in empirical studies—a variable of secondary interest, at best—trust emerged in the 1990s as a subject deemed important and worthy of study in its own right. Illustrative of the new significance afforded trust as a serious and central subject for the organizational sciences is a series of special journal issues (Bachmann and Van Witteloostuijn 2003; Bachmann, Knights, and Sydow 2001; McEvily, Perrone, and Zaheer 2003; Rousseau et al. 1998) and edited volumes (Cook 2001; Falcone, Singh, and Tan 2001; Hardin 2004; Kramer and Cook 2004; Kramer and Tyler 1996; Lane and Bachmann 1998) devoted exclusively to the subject. These contributions were complemented by several scholarly integrations and critical assessments of this rapidly burgeoning literature (Creed and Miles 1996; Hardin 2002; Hollis 1998; Kramer 1999; Misztal 1996; Sztompka 1999).

Another indication of the intense interest in the topic was the number of popular books on trust which appeared during this same period. These treatments included attempts to think through the managerial implications of trust (Shaw 1997; Whitney 1994; Zand 1997) and also the problems of trust within organizational contexts (e.g. Kanter and Mirvis 1989). There were also attempts to explore the relevance of trust to political institutions (Brown 1994; Carnevale 1995; March and Olsen 1989, 1994; Orren 1997; Porter 1995). Finally, there were a number of books that attempted to discuss in more general terms the problems associated with trust in the context of close personal relationships

(Brothers 1995; Govier 1998; Janoff-Bulman 1992), societal relations (Seligman 1997; Solomon and Flores 2001), and international relations (Lane and Bachmann 1998; Pharr 1997; Yamagishi and Yamagishi 1996).

Recognizing its growing importance, trust researchers left few stones unturned, exploring both the diverse determinants of trust and its varied benefits (e.g. Fukyuma 1995; Putnam 1993, 2000; Sztompka 1999). Scholarly attention turned as well to the myriad problems and dilemmas associated with attempts to secure those benefits (e.g. Brothers 1995; Janoff-Bulman 1992; Seligman 1997). As a result of this industrious enterprise, empirical evidence regarding the antecedents and consequences of trust accumulated at a rapid rate. This empirical progress was matched by impressive strides on the theoretical front (see Hardin 2002 and Sztompka 1999 for particularly important and original formulations).

Despite evidence of impressive progress on these various fronts, many questions remained unanswered as to the origins and foundations of trust, as well as the causes of "shortfalls" in trust evident in a variety of domains (see e.g. critical and insightful discussions by Hardin 2002; Inglehart 1997; Lawrence 1997; Mansbridge 1997; Nye and Zelikow 1997; Seligman 1997). Before proceeding further, accordingly, it might be helpful to provide a brief overview of the state of trust theory and research. I begin by noting some of the diverse ways in which trust has been characterized in the organizational sciences.

Emerging Conceptions of Organizational Trust

Although social scientists afforded considerable attention to the problem of defining trust (e.g. Barber 1983; Luhmann 1988; Mayer, Davis, and Schoorman 1995), a universally accepted definition has remained elusive. As a consequence, the term *trust* continues to be used in a variety of distinct, and not always compatible, ways within the social sciences. At one end of the spectrum are formulations that highlight ethical and moralistic facets of trust. For example, Hosmer (1995) characterized trust as "the expectation ... of ethically justifiable behavior—that is, morally correct decisions and actions based upon ethical principles of analysis" (p. 399). Other conceptions emphasize the strategic and calculative dimensions of trust within organizational and institutional settings. Thus, for example, Burt and Knez (1996) defined trust simply as "anticipated cooperation" (p. 70), arguing that the "issue isn't moral .... It is office politics" (p. 70).

Despite divergence with respect to such particulars, most trust theorists did seem to agree that, whatever else its essential features, trust is fundamentally a psychological state (see Hardin 2002 for a particularly lucid discussion of definitional issues).

When conceptualized as a psychological state, trust was most often defined in terms of several interrelated cognitive processes and orientations. First and foremost, it was generally assumed that trust entails a state of perceived vulnerability or risk related to individuals' uncertainty regarding the motives, intentions, and prospective actions of others on whom they depend. For example, Lewis and Weigert (1985) characterized trust as the "undertaking of a risky course of action on the confident expectation that all persons involved in the action will act competently and dutifully" (p. 971). Similarly, Robinson (1996) defined trust as a person's "expectations, assumptions, or beliefs about the likelihood that another's future actions will be beneficial, favorable, or at least not detrimental to one's interests" (p. 576).

Other influential definitions construed trust as a more general attitude or expectancy about other people and/or the social systems in which they are embedded (Garfinkel 1963; Luhmann 1988). For example, Barber (1983) characterized trust as a set of "socially learned and socially confirmed expectations that people have of each other, of the organizations and institutions in which they live, and of the natural and moral social orders that set the fundamental understandings for their lives" (p. 164–5).

Although acknowledging the importance of these cognitive components of trust, other researchers argued that trust needed to be conceptualized as a more complex, multidimensional psychological state that includes, at the very least, consideration of its affective and motivational components (Cummings and Bromiley 1996; Kramer, Brewer, and Hanna 1996; Lewis and Weigert 1985; McAlister 1995; Tyler and Degoey 1996). As Fine and Holyfield (1996) noted along these lines, although cognitive models of trust provided a necessary understanding of trust-related phenomena, they do not provide a sufficient one. For example, trust clearly embodied also, they suggested, aspects of the "world of cultural meanings, emotional responses, and social relations ... one not only thinks trust, but feels trust" (p. 25).

Concerned about the conceptual morass into which the trust literature had devolved, several organizational researchers argued the usefulness of conceptualizing trust in terms of individuals' choice behavior when confronting various kinds of trust dilemma situations (Arrow 1974; Hollis 1998; Kreps 1990; Miller 1992). One advantage of conceptualizing trust in terms of choice is that such decisions are observable behaviors. Another is that organizational theorists possessed a well-developed conceptual armamentarium for pursuing the theoretical and empirical implications of trust-as-choice (Hollis 1998; March 1994).

Within this rich and rapidly growing literature, two contrasting images of choice gained particular prominence, one which construed choice in relatively rational, calculative terms, and another which afforded more weight to the social and relational underpinnings of choice in trust dilemma situations. The first perspective, termed the *rational choice perspective*, was imported largely from sociological (Coleman 1990), economic (Williamson 1993), and political (Hardin 1992, 2002) theories. It remains to this day one of the more influential conceptions of trust within organizational science. From the perspective of rational choice theory, decisions about trust are similar to other forms of risky choice: individuals are presumed to be motivated to make rational, efficient choices (i.e. choices that maximize expected gains or minimize expected losses from their transactions). Such models posit further, as Schelling (1960) noted, that choice is motivated by a "conscious calculation of advantages, a calculation that in turn is based on an explicit and internally consistent value system" (p. 4).

Hardin's conception of *encapsulated trust* (1992, 2002) articulated many of the essential features of this view. A rational account of trust, he noted, includes two central elements. The first is the knowledge that enables a person to trust another. The second is the incentives of the person who is trusted (the trustee) to honor or fulfill that trust. Individuals can trust someone, Hardin proposed, if they have adequate grounds for believing it will be in that person's interest to be trustworthy "in the relevant way at the relevant time" (p. 153). This notion of trust, he observed further, is predicated not on individuals' narrow contemplation of their own interests but is enfolded instead in a sophisticated understanding of the other party's interests. "You can more confidently trust me," Hardin (1991) posited, "if you know that my own interests will induce me to live up to your expectations. Your trust then encapsulates my interests" (p. 189).

Given its prominence as a conceptual platform from which much recent organizational theory and research on trust proceeded, it is worth noting some of the concerns that have been raised about rational choice perspectives. First, although the approach has proven enormously useful in terms of clarifying how individuals should, from a normative or prescriptive standpoint, make decisions about trust, its adequacy as a descriptive account of how people actually do make such decisions has been questioned on several grounds. Most notably, a large and robust literature on behavioral decision-making suggests that many of the assumptions of rational choice models are empirically untenable. Specifically, the extent to which decisions about trust, or any other risky decision for that matter, are products of conscious calculation and internally consistent value systems must be regarded as highly suspect. As March (1994) cogently noted in summarizing such research, rational model of choice overstate decision-makers' cognitive capacities, the degree to which they engage in conscious calculation, and the extent to which they possess stable values and orderly preferences.

Introduction: Progress and Promise in Theory and Research

From a psychological perspective, another limitation of conceptions of trust grounded in presumptions regarding the rationality of choice is that they are too narrowly cognitive. Such conceptions, critics noted, afford too little role to emotional and social influences on trust decisions. As Grannovetter (1985) aptly observed in this regard, these conceptions provided, at best, an under-socialized conception of trust. At a more fundamental level, March and Olsen (1989) took exception to the idea that notions of rational expectation and calculation were even central to the phenomenon of trust. The core idea of trust, they proposed, is that it is not based on an expectation of its justification. "When trust is justified by expectations of positive reciprocal consequences it is simply another version of economic exchange, as is clear from treatments of trust as reputation in repeated games" (p. 27).

In response to these limitations and concerns, a number of scholars suggested that an adequate theory of organizational trust must incorporate more systematically the social and relational underpinnings of trust-related choices (Mayer, Davis, and Schoorman 1995; McAlister 1995; Tyler and Kramer 1996). According to these arguments, trust needs to be conceptualized not only as a calculative orientation toward risk, but also a social orientation toward other people and society as a whole.

The initial impetus for these relational models, it should be noted, was sociological theory and research on the impact of social embeddedness on economic transactions (Grannovetter 1985). The development of relational conceptions of trust was further fueled by research implicating a variety of "macrolevel" structures, including networks and governance systems, in the emergence and diffusion of trust within and between organizations (Burt and Knez 1995; Coleman 1990; Kollock 1994; Powell 1996).

Subsequent psychological research extended this initial work by elaborating on the cognitive, motivational, and affective underpinnings of relational trust (Shapiro, Sheppard, and Cheraskin 1992; Sheppard and Tuchinsky 1996). Within social psychology, there were attempts to develop systematic frameworks for conceptualizing the nature, determinants, and consequences of relational trust. In some instances, these approaches took as a point of departure either social identity theory (Kramer, Brewer, and Hanna 1996) or the group-value model (Tyler and Degoey 1996; Tyler and Lind 1992). A common feature of these models was their broader emphasis on social rather than purely instrumental (resource-based) motives driving trust behavior, including consideration of how actors' self-presentational concerns and identity-related needs and motives influence trust-related cognition and choice.

Rational choice and relational perspectives on trust projected, of course, fundamentally different images of trust and tended to push empirical research in quite different directions. To a large extent, however, the ongoing tensions between these perspectives should be construed as owing more to their distinct disciplinary origins, rather than to inherent features of the organizational phenomenon they sought to explain.

To reconcile these diverse views of trust, it is helpful to avoid thinking of the disparity between them as reflecting a conflict between mutually incompatible models of choice (i.e. that trust either *is* instrumental and calculative *or* social and relational). Rather, a more useful approach would be to move in the direction of developing a *contextualized* account that acknowledges the role of both calculative considerations and social inputs in our trust-related judgments and decisions. In other words, what is needed is a conception of organizational trust that incorporates calculative processes as part of the fundamental "arithmetic" of trust, but that also articulates how social and situational factors influence the salience and relative weight afforded to various instrumental and non-instrumental concerns in such calculations.

Hardin (1992, 2002) has provided one promising way of moving beyond this conceptual impasse. It is useful, he argued, to conceptualize trust as a three-part relation involving properties of a *truster*, attributes of a *trustee*, and a specific *context* or domain over which trust is conferred. From this perspective, strategic, calculative, and instrumental considerations would be expected to exert a dominant influence in some organizational contexts (e.g. transactions involving comparative strangers). However, in other contexts (such as those involving members of one's own group), relational considerations might be more salient and exert more influence over how trust is construed. Fully elaborated, a three-part theory of trust would thus afford adequate attention to both the calculative and relational underpinnings of trust.

In the present volume, an effort has been made to sample broadly from these diverse conceptions of trust and to draw out some of their implications.

Tracing the Ascent of Trust

The rise of trust as a major focus of organizational theory and research during the 1990s was hardly accidental. Its increasing importance reflected, in no small measure, at least two converging developments. The first development was a growing appreciation of the substantial and varied benefits that accrue when high levels of trust are in place within organizations. The affirmative case for trust as a vital and generative organizational resource was boldly laid out in several influential books and articles. Perhaps foremost in this regard were Putnam's provocative findings (1993) implicating trust as a critical factor in civic engagement and the emergence of stable, cooperative regimes. Putnam's seminal contribution was quickly followed by Fukuyama's impressive survey of empirical findings (1995) documenting the extent to which trust matters within organizational and societal settings. If Putnam's and Fukuyama's pioneering treatments laid an impressive foundation for an affirmative case for trust, Sztompka's (1999) and Putnam's (2000) subsequent overviews of additional evidence helped solidify it. Viewed in aggregate, these works demonstrated the extent to which trust constitutes an important source of *social capital* within organizations and social systems *writ large*.

Although framing the merits of trust in terms of the concept of social capital provided a fresh, powerful, and compelling lens through which to appreciate its myriad benefits, the intellectual moorings of that argument itself were not entirely new, at least from a historical perspective. Many of the virtues of trust had been long recognized and carefully elaborated by numerous scholars across the spectrum of the social sciences (see e.g. Barber 1983; Fox 1974; Gambetta 1988; Luhmann 1979; Zucker 1986).

Within organizational settings, these virtues had been discussed primarily on three levels. The first was the constructive effects of generalized trust on reducing transaction costs within organizations. When trust was in place, it was clearly less essential to negotiate and formalize the terms of exchange. The second was the role trust plays in fostering various forms of spontaneous sociability and cooperation among organizational members. Trust, from this perspective, provides a generative "expectational backdrop" against which organizational actors can more freely and easily engage in actions that promote their joint outcomes without worrying so much about the risks attending such exposure. The third was the role of trust in facilitating adaptive or appropriate forms of deference to organizational authorities. When high levels of trust exist between leaders and followers or managers and subordinates, for instance, compliance and commitment become less problematic.

The second and somewhat parallel influence affecting the emergence of trust as a major topic of organizational theory and research was growing appreciation of the fact that, however desirable trust might be, it was often an elusive and fragile resource. However much leaders might desire to create high levels of trust within their organizations, for instance, it was often evident they lacked the skills needed to do so. The challenges associated with creating and sustaining high levels of trust, were more substantial and difficult it seemed than they first looked. Moreover, discovering the optimal organizational structures and processes that create and sustain such trust were not so obvious either (Creed and Miles 1996). Indeed, within many organizations, distrust and suspicion remain enduring and seemingly intractable problems (Hardin 2004; Kramer 2002). More often than not, the evidence suggested, trust was hard won and easily lost.

....

An Emerging Crisis in Trust?

If the seemingly clear and unconditional benefits associated with high levels of organizational and social trust provided much of the initial impetus for the study of trust in the 1990s, there were more troubling currents that were also fueling interest in the topic. Specifically, there was a growing body of other research which examined the pressing problem of distrust in organizations, including both public and private institutions (Brown 1994; Carnevale 1995; Nye, Zelikow, and King 1997). As Pfeffer (1997) noted generally, from the moment we are born and until we die, public and private institutions exert a profound impact on the quality of our lives. Their ability to do so, however, depends in no small measure upon public trust in them, including trust in both their competence and integrity (Barber 1983; Brown 1994; Hardin 2002).

Unfortunately, substantial evidence developed in the 1990s indicated that trust in both public and private institutions had been declining for several decades (e.g. Carnevale 1995; Coleman 1990; Nye, Zelikow, and King 1997; PEW 1996, 1998). For example, although 75 percent of Americans said they trusted the federal government in 1964, only 25 percent express comparable levels of trust by the end of the 1990s. Similarly, trust in universities had fallen from 61 to 30 percent, medical institutions from 73 to 29 percent, and journalism from 29 to 14 percent (Nye 1997) during this same period. Major private companies fare no better, trust in them having fallen from 55 to 21 percent over this same period (Nye 1997). Another indication of the pervasiveness of institutional distrust and suspicion was provided by data regarding the frequency with which many Americans endorsed various conspiracy theories and abuses of trust involving public institutions (Butler, Koopman, and Zimbardo 1995; Goertzel 1994; Harrison and Thomas 1997; Pipes 1997). Putnam's updated assessment (2000) provided few grounds for greater optimism regarding positive changes in these trends. Americans were not only bowling alone, they were looking over their shoulders while doing it.

Although data regarding the prevalence of the problem was unequivocal, the sources of institutional distrust and suspicion remained much less clear from this research. Researchers advanced many different explanations for the decline in institutional trust, ranging from historical, economic, organizational, psychological, and sociological factors (see Harrison and Thomas 1997 and Nye, Zelikow, and King 1997 for overviews). A number of studies highlighted the importance of unmet or violated expectancies in explaining why public trust in institutions has eroded. Nye (1997), for instance, noted that the decline of public trust in government might be attributed, at least in part, to its perceived failure to solve a variety of social ills. According to this hypothesis, government had promised to remedy urgent social problems (e.g. to eradicate poverty, racial injustice, and catastrophic illnesses), and these promises had led to heightened expectations that government would solve these problems. As these expectations went unfulfilled, so trust diminished.

Assuming unmet expectations and generally negative beliefs about public institutions did contribute to the erosion of trust, other researchers pursued the possible sources of those negative expectations and beliefs. Cappella and Jamieson (1997) made major contributions in this area, assembling a strong body of evidence implicating the media in the growing distrust and cynicism of the public toward its institutions. The *framing* of news, they argued, directly affected the public's mistrust of institutions. In particular, they demonstrated that news stories that adopted *strategic frames* (i.e. frames that emphasized themes of "winning and losing and the self-interest implied by that orientation," and that activated, in turn, negative actor traits such as those indicative of "artifice, pandering, deceit, staging, and positioning for advantage" (p. 85) tended to promote greater mistrust and cynicism than more neutral, issue-oriented frames. To investigate this hypothesis, they conducted a series of carefully controlled experiments in which news involving public leaders and institutions was systematically framed in either strategic terms or in terms of more neutral, issue-pertinent frames. The results from these studies supported their argument that strategic frames produce greater mistrust and cynicism.

Although these studies left little doubt that distrust of private organizations and public institutions had declined substantially over the past several decades, the implications of this trend were far less evident than sometimes assumed. First, as Cappella and Jamieson (1997) cogently pointed out, it was not clear whether the high-observed levels of distrust and suspicion reflected *unwarranted* cynicism regarding the state of contemporary organizations or institutions—or was, in fact, just a reasonably veridical portrait. Second, even if real, the tangible (behavioral) implications of such distrust and suspicion were far from clear. As the Pew Report (1996) concluded, although "a general distrust of others is an obvious social ill ... its direct relevance to the way people act is unclear" (p. 7). Finally, although it was often portrayed in the popular press and social science literature largely in negative terms, distrust and suspicion could be viewed as constituting appropriate and even adaptive stances toward institutions—especially if those institutions did in fact lack trustworthiness, a point Hardin (2002) compellingly hammered home. Vigilance and wariness regarding institutions, from this perspective, could be construed as constituting essential components of healthy and resilient organizations and societies—and especially for those institutions charged with oversight and accountability (Barber 1983; March and Olsen 1994; Shapiro 1987).

Another emerging area of organizational research related to concerns about trust, and one that has become increasingly important within just the past few years, concerns the relationship between technology and trust. Enthusiasm over technological remedies to trust-related problems was, throughout the 1990s, considerable, as evidenced by the rapid infusion into the workplace of surveillance systems and other forms of electronic monitoring of employee performance. For example, over 70,000 US companies purchased surveillance software between 1990–2, at a cost of more than $500 million dollars (Aiello 1993). Organizations typically adopted such technological remedies, it should be noted, in the hope of enhancing employee trustworthiness (e.g. assuring compliance with regulations and deterring misbehavior). Ironically, however, evidence was accumulating that such systems could actually undermine trust and might even elicit the very behaviors they were intended to suppress or eliminate.

In reviewing this evidence, Cialdini (1996) identified several reasons why monitoring and surveillance might actually diminish trust within an organization. First, when people think their behavior is under the control of extrinsic motivators, intrinsic motivation might be reduced. According to this argument, surveillance might undermine individuals' motivation to engage in the very behaviors such monitoring was intended to induce or ensure. For example, innocent employees who were subjected to compulsory polygraphs, drug testing, and other forms of mass screening designed to deter misbehavior, might instead become less committed to internal standards of honesty and integrity in the workplace.

To some extent all of these concerns regarding the reliability and resilience of trust were dramatically heightened—and given new urgency—shortly after the beginning of the new millennium. A cascade of tragic and stunning events necessitated a reappraisal of trust as a virtue. In particular, there was a discernible movement away from an almost uncritical embrace of trust as organizational and social panacea to a more sobering appreciation of the dangers of misplaced or naive trust (Sievers 2003). Perhaps most importantly, the events of September 11, 2001 demonstrated the potentially catastrophic costs of such naive or misplaced trust in those institutions and individuals upon whom our welfare and security ultimately depend.

Subsequent revelations regarding major breaches of trust by heretofore admired corporations such as Enron, Worldcom, and Parmalata served to further underline how dangerously thin were the security nets under us. These breaches of trust were compounded, of course, by the equally unexpected and stunning failure of those institutions (such as Arthur Andersen), to do their due diligence. Such institutions were, in a very real sense, our Centurions at the gate. Instead of vigilantly standing guard over our welfare, however, the public discovered those Centurions were either asleep or, worse yet, had their eyes averted and their hands out. As all of these examples served to remind us, although trust may be desirable in the abstract, it really makes sense only when those trustees on whom people depend are deserving of that trust. On top of these highly visible and much discussed abuses of trust was a more subtle but no less insidious erosion of confidence in trust as a mechanism for achieving desired organizational outcomes.

There have been some thoughtful attempts, it should be noted, to put the problem of trust in broader and deeper perspective (see, e.g. Hardin 2004; Gambetta 1988; Govier 1998; Larson 2004; Seivers 2003; Westwood and Clegg 2003). A particularly skeptical, yet constructively probing, critique was offered by Sievers (2003). "I do agree that trust constitutes an important source of social capital within organizations," he conceded (p. 357). However, he went on to argue, "It appears to me the apparent lack of trust in organizations, the inflation of its necessity and its occasional bankruptcy, is too often neglected" (p. 358). Westwood and Clegg (2003) were even sharper in expressing their skepticism. "It is hard to countenance a new rhetoric of trust in organizations," they proclaimed, "within the same discursive (and material) space as structural unemployment, layoffs, the new social contract of individual responsibility for jobs, skills, and career, downsizing and other human resource and organizational design strategies that signal the precariousness of people's place in organizations" (p. 340). This "new rhetoric of trust," they accordingly concluded, "rings hollow in a climate in which such managerial strategies are made manifest in the name of *economic rationalism*" (p. 340). In terms of Hardin's conception of trust (2002) as encapsulated interests, one might ask just whose interests were, in the end, being encapsulated in the new organizational order.

In summary, there has been a great deal of work focusing on the conceptualization of trust, its bases, and its problems. In many respects, this prior work provides the backdrop and foundation for the present volume, the intent and scope of which I discuss next.

Taking Stock: Intent and Scope of the Present Volume

Even granting the clear importance of the topic, the reader might ask, "Why compile a reader on trust and why now?" A first and foremost answer is that there is clearly a need for such a resource. Despite the obvious importance of the topic, to date no single volume currently exists that provides the interested reader with a sound introduction or reasonable overview of this rapidly growing, widely dispersed, and inherently multi-disciplinary literature. Indeed, some of the most influential, foundational pieces remain scattered in relatively obscure journals or books, some of which are not easily found or—in some instances, no longer even in print. Thus the individual scholar hoping to come up to speed with this literature currently has nowhere to turn. One of the primary aims of this volume, accordingly, is to provide trust scholars and researchers with a handy reference volume. The volume is also intended as a broad reader for graduate students hoping to understand and possibly contribute to this significant and growing literature. There remain many fundamental and important questions about the nature of trust and its foundations. Moreover, we have only begun to chart the benefits of trust and the best ways to obtain those benefits. Finally, this reader is intended to provide a resource for teachers and students at the undergraduate level, in the hope of stimulating interest in this major topic in undergraduate anthropology, economics, political science, psychology, organizational sciences, and sociology courses. The development of trust theory and its application to real-world social problems will depend upon the efforts of future scholars who are just embarking on their scholarly careers.

Plan and Organization of the Book

With all of these concerns and considerations in mind, I have brought together in this volume some of the most interesting, influential, and provocative ideas regarding organizational trust. Assembling these diverse pieces in a single volume will, I hope, foster a greater appreciation of some of the important and nuanced distinctions in the conceptualization of trust scattered across disciplinary boundaries. The selections illustrate also the many differing ways that creative researchers have explored the bases and benefits of trust across organizational contexts. Finally, both by what they examine and what they omit, they point directly and indirectly to some of the still unresolved issues that future trust researchers might address. The papers assembled for this volume engage all of these central concerns in contemporary trust theory. They are, each in their own way, distinctive with respect to the contribution they make, and breathtaking in their scope, originality, and thoughtfulness.

The volume begins, appropriately enough, with foundational concerns. What is trust? What is its essential nature? The chapters in the First Section offer some original and provocative perspectives on these questions. In the Second Section, attention shifts to an examination of what we know about the development and maintenance of trust. The third section continues with an examination of the bases and benefits of organizational trust. In particular, it reviews what we know about the psychological, social, and organizational underpinnings of trust. The papers in this section also articulate what we know about the positive consequences of trust.

The fourth section of the volume focuses on the fragility of organizational forms of trust. A comprehensive account of trust should enlighten us not only about the bases and benefits of trust, but also provide insight into the conditions that contribute to the erosion and destruction of trust. In the fifth and final section, attention is turned to exploring some of the subtle differences in the manifestations of trust—especially its distinctive antecedents and consequences across different organizational contexts. Although social scientists often express the desire for a universal conception of some construct and strive to find robust prescriptions, a sensible reading of the trust literature reminds us of the extent to which the manifestations of trust—its concrete antecedents, its particular benefits, and the specific problems associated with securing those benefits heavily depend on organizational context. If trust is, among other things, largely about individuals' positive expectations, codings of interaction histories, and attributions regarding others' trustworthiness on the basis of those codings, then the organizational context in which such expectations, histories, and attributions are embedded obviously matters—and matters a great detail. For any theory of organizational trust, the devil is in the details, and the details are in the context. For that reason, the present volume affords particular attention to the contextual determinants of trust-related cognitions and behaviors.

It is my hope that putting the pieces together in this way helps provide an orientation to this intellectually vibrant and challenging enterprise—an enterprise characterized by considerable progress already, but one filled with immense promise as well. There is an old saying that wishes us that we might live in interesting times. These are certainly interesting times for trust researchers. Following the cataclysmic events of 9/11 and the moral meltdowns in the private sector, trust theorists confront daunting conceptual challenges. Putting trust and distrust in their proper perspectives remains an ongoing task. It is hoped that the present volume provides the reader with a basis for engaging such challenges intelligently and perhaps even a foundation for finding sensible answers to them.

References

Aiello, J. R. (1993). 'Computer-based Monitoring: Electronic Surveillance and Its Effects', *Journal of Applied Social Psychology*, 23: 499–507.

Arrow, K. (1974). *The Limits of Organization*. New York: Norton.

Bachmann, R., and van Witteloostuijn, A. (2003). 'Networks, Social Capital, and Trust,' *International Studies of Management and Organization*, 33, whole issue.

Bachmann, R., Knights, D., and Sydow, J. (2001). 'Special Issue: Trust and Control in Organizational Relations', *Organization Studies*, 22, whole issue.

Roderick M. Kramer

Barber, B. (1983). *The Logic and Limits of Trust*. New Brunswik, NJ: Rutgers University Press.

Brothers, D. (1995). *Falling Backwards: An Exploration of Trust and Self Experience*. New York: Norton.

Brown, P. G. (1994). *Restoring the Public Trust*. Boston: Beacon.

Burt, R. and Knez, M. (1995). 'Kinds of Third-Party Effects on Trust', *Journal of Rational Choice 7*, pp. 255–92.

—— —— (1996). 'Third-Party Gossip and Trust,' in R. M. Kramer and T. R. Tyler (eds.), *Trust in Organizations*. Thousand Oaks, CA: Sage.

Butler, L. D., Koopman, C., and Zimbardo, P. G. (1995). 'The Psychological Impact of Viewing the Film JFK: Emotions, Beliefs, and Political Behavioral Intentions,' *Political Psychology*, 16: 237–57.

Cappella, J. N. and Jamieson, K. H. (1997). *Spiral of Cynicism: The Press and the Public Good*. New York: Oxford University Press.

Carnevale, D. G. (1995). *Trustworthy Government: Leadership and Management Strategies for Building Trust and High Performance*. San Francisco: Jossey Bass.

Cialdini, R. (1996). 'The Triple Tumor Structure of Organizational Behavior,' in D. M. Messick and A. E. Tenbrunsel (eds.), *Codes of Conduct*, New York: Russell Sage.

Coleman, J. (1990). *Foundations of Social Theory*. Cambridge, MA: Harvard University Press.

Cook, K. S. (2001). *Trust in Society*. New York: Russell Sage Foundation.

Creed, W. E., and Miles, R. E. (1996). 'Trust in Organizations: A Conceptual Framework Linking Organizational Forms, Managerial Philosophies, and the Opportunity Costs of Controls,' in R. M. Kramer and T. R. Tyler (eds.), *Trust in Organizations: Frontiers of Theory and Practice*, pp. 1–15. Thousand Oaks, CA: Sage.

Cummings, L. L., and Bromiley, P. (1996). 'The Organizational Trust Inventory: Development and Validation', in R. M. Kramer and T. R. Tyler (eds.), *Trust in Organizations: Frontiers of Theory and Practice*. pp. 302–30. Thousand Oaks, CA: Sage.

Falcone, R., Singh, M., and Tan, Y. (2001). *Trust in Cyber-Societies*. Berlin: Springer.

Fine, G. and Holyfield, L. (1996). Secrecy, Trust and Dangerous Leisure: Generating Group Cohesion in Voluntary Organizations, *Social Psychology Quarterly*, 59: 22–38.

Fox, A. (1974). *Beyond Contract: Power and Trust Relations*. London: Faber & Faber.

Fukuyama, F. (1995). *Trust: The Social Virtues and the Creation of Prosperity*. New York: Free Press.

Gambetta, D. (1988). 'Can We Trust Trust?', in D. Gambetta (ed.), *Trust: Making and Breaking Cooperative Relationships*. pp. 213–37. Cambridge: Basil Blackwell.

Garfinkel, H. (1963). 'A Conception of, and Experiments with, Trust as a Condition of Stable Concerted Actions', in O. J. Harvey (ed.), *Motivation and Social Interaction: Cognitive Determinants*. New York: Ronald.

Goertzel, G. (1994). 'Belief in Conspiracy Theories', *Political Psychology*, 15: 731–42.

Govier, T. (1998). *Dilemmas of Trust*. Montreal: McGill-Queen's University Press.

Granovetter, M. (1985). 'Economic Action and Social Structure: The Problem of Embeddedness', *American Journal of Sociology*, 91: 481–510.

Hardin, R. (1991). 'Trusting Persons, Trusting Institutions', in R. J. Zeckahuser (ed.), *Strategy and Choice*. Cambridge, MA: MIT Press.

—— (1992). 'The Street-Level Epistemology of Trust', *Analyse & Kritik*, 14: 152–76.

—— (2002). *Trust and Trustworthiness*. New York: Russell Sage Foundation.

—— (2004). *Distrust*. New York: Russell Sage Foundation.

Harrison, A. A., and Thomas, J. M. (1997). The Kennedy Assassination, Unidentified Flying Objects, and other Conspiracies: Psychological and Organizational Factors in the Perception of "Cover-Up" ?', *Sys. Res. Behavioral Science*, 14: 113–28.

Hollis, M. (1998). *Trust Within Reason*. Cambridge, UK: Cambridge University Press.

Hosmer, L. T. (1995). 'Trust: The Connecting Link Between Organizational Theory and Ethics', *Academy of Management Review*, 20: 379–400.

Ingelhart, R. (1997). 'Postmaterialist Values and the Erosion of Institutional Authority', in J. S. Nye, P. D. Zelikow, and D. C. King (eds.), *Why People Don't Trust Government* pp. 217–36. Cambridge, MA: Harvard University Press.

Janoff-Bulman, R. (1992). *Shattered Assumptions: Toward a New Psychology of Trauma*. New York: Free Press.

Kanter, D. L., and Mirvis, P. H. (1989). *The Cynical Americans: Living and Working in an Age of Discontent and Disillusion*. San Francisco, CA: Jossey-Bass.

Kollock, P. (1994). 'The Emergence of Exchange Structures: An Experimental Study of Uncertainty, Commitment and Trust', *American Journal of Sociology*, 100: 313–45.

Kramer, R. M. (1999). 'Trust and Distrust in Organizations: Emerging Perspectives, Enduring Questions', *Annual Review of Psychology*, 50: 569–98.

—— (2002). 'Organizational Paranoia: Origins and Dynamics', in B. M. Staw and R. Sutton (eds.), *Research on Organizational Behavior*, vol. 23, pp. 1–42. New York: Elsevier Science.

—— and Cook, K. S. (2004). *Trust and Distrust Within Organizations: Dilemmas and Approaches*. New York: Russell Sage Foundation.

—— and Tyler, T. (1996). *Trust in Organizations: Frontiers of Theory and Research*. Thousand Oaks, CA: Sage.

—— Brewer, M. B., and Hanna, B. (1996). 'Collective Trust and Collective Action in Organizations: The Decision to Trust as a Social Decision,' in R. M. Kramer and T. R. Tyler (eds.), *Trust in Organizations*. Thousand Oaks, CA: Sage.

Kreps, D. M. (1990). 'Corporate Culture and Economic Theory', in J. Alt and K. Shepsle (eds.), *Perspectives on Positive Political Economy*. New York: Cambridge University Press.

Lane, C., and Bachmann, R. (1998). *Trust Within and Between Organizations: Conceptual Issues and Empirical Applications*. Oxford, UK: Oxford University Press.

Larson, D. W. (2004). 'Distrust: Prudent, If Not Always Wise', in R. Hardin (ed.), *Distrust*. New York: Russell Sage Foundation.

Lawrence, R. Z. (1997). 'Is It Really the Economy Stupid?', in J. S. Nye, P. D. Zelikow, and D. C. King (eds.), *Why People Don't Trust Government*. pp. 111–32. Cambridge, MA: Harvard University Press.

Lewis, J. D. and Weigert, A. (1985). 'Trust as a Social Reality', *Social Forces*, 63: 967–85.

Luhmann, N. (1979). *Trust and Power*. Chichester, UK: Wiley.

—— (1988). 'Familiarity, Confidence, Trust: Problems and Alternatives', in D. Gambetta (ed.), *Trust: Making and Breaking Cooperative Relations*, pp. 94–108. Cambridge, MA: Oxford University Press.

Mansbridge, J. (1997). 'Social and Cultural Causes of Dissatisfaction with U. S. Government', in J. S. Nye, P. D. Zelikow, and D. C. King (eds.), *Why People Don't Trust Government*. pp. 237–52. Cambridge, MA: Harvard University Press.

March, J. G. (1994). *A Primer on Decision Making*. New York: Free Press.

—— and Olsen, J. P. (1989). *Rediscovering Institutions: The Organizational Basis of Politics*, New York: Free Press.

—— and Olsen, J. P. (1994). *Democratic Governance*. New York: Free Press.

Mayer, R. C., Davis, J. H., and Schoorman, F. D. (1995). 'An Integrative Model of Organizational Trust', *Academy of Management Review*, 20: 709–34.

McAlister, D. J. (1995). 'Affect- and Cognition-based Trust as Foundations for Interpersonal Cooperation in Organizations', *Journal of Academy Management*, 38: 24–59.

McEvily, B., Perrone, V., and Zaheer, A. (2003). Special Issue: Trust an an (?) Organizational Context, *Organization Science*, 14, whole issue.

Miller, G. J. (1992). *Managerial Dilemmas: The Political Economy of Hierarchies*. New York: Cambridge University Press.

Misztal, B. A. (1996). *Trust in Modern Societies: The Search for the Bases of Social Order*. New York: Polity Press.

Nye, J. S. (1997). 'The Decline of Confidence in Government', in J. S. Nye, P. D. Zelikow, and D. C. King (eds.), *Why People Don't Trust Government*. Cambridge, MA: Harvard University Press.

—— and Zelikow, P. D. (1997). 'Reflections, Conjectures, and Puzzles', in J. S. Nye, P. D. Zelikow, and D. C. King (eds.), *Why People Don't Trust Government*. pp. 253–82. Cambridge, MA: Harvard University Press.

—— —— and King, D. C. (1997). *Why People Don't Trust Government* Cambridge, MA: Harvard University Press.

Orren, G. (1997). Fall from Grace: The Public's Loss of Faith in Government, in J. S. Nye, P. D. Zelikow, and D. C. King (eds.), *Why People Don't Trust Government*, pp. 77–108. Cambridge, MA: Harvard University Press.

Pew Research Center for the People and the Press (1996). *Trust and Citizen Engagement in Metropolitan Philadelphia: A Case Study*. Washington, DC: Pew.

—— (1998). *Deconstructing Distrust: How Americans view Government*. Washington, DC: Pew.

Pfeffer J. (1997). *New Directions in Organizational Theory: Problems and Prospects*. New York: Oxford University Press.

Pharr, S. J. (1997). 'Public Trust and Democracy in Japan', in J. S. Nye, P. D. Zelikow, and D. C. King (eds.), *Why People Don't Trust Government*. pp. 237–52. Cambridge, MA: Harvard University Press.

Pipes, D. (1997). *Conspiracy*. New York: Free Press.

Porter, T. M. (1995). *Trust in Numbers: The Pursuit of Objectivity in Science and Public Life*. Princeton, NJ: Princeton University Press.

Powell, W. (1996). 'Trust in Governance Structures', in R. M. Kramer and T. R. Tyler (eds.), *Trust in Organizations*. Thousand Oaks, CA: Sage.

Putnam, R. D. (1993). *Making Democracy Work: Civic Traditions in Modern Italy*. Princeton, NJ: Princeton University Press.

—— (2000). *Bowling Alone: The Collapse and Revival of American Community.* New York: Simon & Schuster.

Robinson, S. L. (1996). 'Trust and Breach of the Psychological Contract', *Administrative Science Quarterly,* 41: 574–99.

Rousseau, D. M., Sitkin, S. B., Brut, R. S., and Camerer, C. (1998). 'Special Topic Forum on Trust in and Between Organizations', *Academy of Management Review,* 23, whole issue.

Schelling, T. C. (1960). *The Strategy of Conflict.* New Haven, CT: Yale University Press.

Seligman, A. B. (1997). *The Problem of Trust.* Princeton, NJ: Princeton University Press.

Shapiro, S. (1987). 'Policing Trust', in C. D. Shearing and P. C. Stenning (eds.), *Private Policing.* Thousand Oaks, CA: Sage.

Shapiro, D. L., Sheppard, B. H., and Cheraskin, L. (1992). 'Business on a Handshake', *Journal of Negotiation,* 8: 365–77.

Shaw, R. B. (1997). *Trust in the Balance.* San Francisco: Jossey-Bass.

Sheppard, B. H., and Tuchinsky, M. (1996). 'Micro-OB and the Network Organization', in R. M. Kramer and T. R. Tyler (eds.), *Trust in Organizations.* Thousand Oaks, CA: Sage.

Sievers, B. (2003). '"Fool'd with Hope, Men Favour the Deceit," or Can We Trust in Trust?', in R. Westwood and S. Clegg (eds.), *Debating Organization: Point-Counterpoint in Organization Studies.* pp. 356–67. Oxford, UK: Blackwell.

Solomon, R. C. and Flores, F. (2001). *Building Trust in Business, Politics Relationships, and Life.* New York: Oxford University Press.

Sztompka, P. (1999). *Trust: A Sociological Theory.* Cambridge, UK: Cambridge University Press.

Tyler, T. R. and Degoey, P. (1996). 'Trust in Organizational Authorities: The Influence of Motive Attributions on Willingness to Accept Decisions', in R. M. Kramer and T. R. Tyler (eds.), *Trust in Organizations.* Thousand Oaks, CA: Sage.

—— and Kramer, R. M. (1996). 'Whither Trust?', in R. M. Kramer and T. R. Tyler (eds.), *Trust in Organizations.* Thousand Oaks, CA: Sage.

—— and Lind, E. A. (1992). 'A Relational Model of Authority in Groups', in M. Snyder (ed.), *Advances in Experimental Social Psychology.* 25, pp. 115–92. New York: Academic Press.

Westwood, R. and Clegg, S. (2003). 'Trust: Organizational Psychosis Versus the Virtues of Trust', in Westwood and S. Clegg (eds.), *Debating Organization: Point-Counterpoint in Organization Studies.* p. 338–40. Oxford, UK: Blackwell.

Whitney, J. (1994). *The Trust Factor.* New York: McGraw-Hill.

Williamson, O. (1993). 'Calculativeness, Trust, and Economic Organization', *Journal of Law Economics,* 34: 453–502.

Yamagishi, T. and Yamagish, M. (1996). 'Trust and Commitment in the United States and Japan', *Motivation and Emotion,* 18: 129–66.

Zand, D. E. (1997). *The Leadership Triad: Knowledge, Trust, and Power.* New York: Oxford University Press.

Zucker, L. G. (1986). 'Production of Trust: Institutional Sources of Economic Structure, 1840–920', *Research in Organizational Behavior,* 8: 53–111.

I. FOUNDATIONS FOR ORGANIZATIONAL TRUST THEORY

1

The Street-Level Epistemology of Trust

Russell Hardin*

Trust as Encapsulated Interest

A widely held view is that trust and distrust are essentially rational. For example, James Coleman bases his account of trust on complex rational expectations.[1] There are two central elements in applying a rational choice account of trust: incentives of the trusted to fulfill the trust and knowledge to allow the truster to trust (or to recommend distrust). The knowledge at issue, of course, is that of the potential truster, not that of the theorist or social scientist who observes or analyzes trust. Hence we require an account of the epistemology of individual knowledge or belief, of street-level epistemology, to complete the rational theory of trust.

A full statement of the rational theory, including the incentive and knowledge effects, would be roughly as follows. First, you trust someone if you have

* In writing this article, I have benefited from discussions with David Blau, Joan Rothchild Hardin, Josh Hardin, Daniel Kahneman, Robert K. Merton, Alejandro Portes, Sarah Rosenfield, Andrei Shleifer, and especially from the students in my seminar on trust at the University of Chicago, Spring 1992; from research assistance by Paul Bullen and the research staff of the Russell Sage Foundation, especially Pauline Rothstein and Camille Yezzi; and from general support from the Mellon Foundation and the Russell Sage Foundation. This article was first published in *Analyse & Kritik*, vol. 14, pp. 152–76. Reprinted by permission.

adequate reason to believe it will be in that person's interest to be trustworthy in the relevant way at the relevant time.[2] One's trust turns not on one's own interests but on the interests of the trusted. It is encapsulated in one's judgment of those interests. Some accounts do not specifically include reference to the trusted's interest in being trustworthy, but merely require an expectation that the trusted will fulfill.[3] Adequate reason for such an expectation will typically turn on past experience to a large extent and on likely future incentives. Annette Baier is concerned with the trusted's motivation toward the truster, but it is unclear whether she would equate that to the incentive of the trusted to fulfill on the trust.[4] Coleman implicitly includes the trusted's incentives when he notes that a reciprocal trusting relationship is mutually reinforcing for each truster.[5] Why? Because each person now has additional incentive to be trustworthy. I trust you because it is in your interest to do what I trust you to do. If there is some residue beyond rational expectations on one-way trust, there is less role for that residue in this straight, likely self-interested exchange.

The encapsulated interest account backs up a step from a simpler expectations account to inquire into the reasons for the relevant expectations. Perhaps the prototypical case at the individual level involves an interaction that is part of a long sequence of interactions between the same parties. Each exchange is simply the resolution of a prisoner's dilemma.[6] A sequence of exchanges is therefore an iterated prisoner's dilemma with, perhaps, variation in the stakes at each exchange. Hence the incentive that one faces in a particular exchange in which one is trusted by the other is the potential benefit from continuing the series of interactions. As discussed further below, this is the usual model for the thick relationship in which the parties know one another well and have strong incentives for trustworthiness from their relationship itself. But we may also have incentives to be trustworthy that are grounded in other than a thick relationship directly with the person whose trust we fulfill.

Baier thinks the prisoner's dilemma is overemphasized in discussions of moral philosophy, and that this is especially a mistake for discussion of trust. But she has a formal view of the prisoner's dilemma as inherently fitted to contracts and fixed payoffs.[7] It is because many relations have the prisoner's dilemma structure that trust is at issue in them. Moreover, the prisoner's dilemma need not represent anything vaguely approaching equality of the parties. Baier says trust is quite different from promise keeping "in part because of the very indefiniteness of what we are counting on them to do or not to do." She holds that contracts are at one extreme of trust, infant trust at the other extreme. "Trust in fellow contractors is a limit case of trust, in which fewer risks are taken, for the sake of lesser goods."[8]

Luhmann seemingly opposes the encapsulated interest account. "It must not be that the trusted will toe the line on her own account, in the light of her interests," he writes.[9] This unexplicated obiter dictum runs counter to his own general account, according to which the overriding consideration is that the two parties in a trust relation are typically going to meet again[10]—presumably in an iterated prisoner's dilemma in which a strong reason for trustworthiness is one's interest in keeping the iteration going.

Trust is a three-part relation: A trusts B to do X.[11] Typically, I trust you to do certain kinds of things. I might distrust you with respect to some other things and I may merely be skeptical or unsure with respect to still other things. To say "I trust you" seems almost always to be elliptical, as though we can assume some such phrase as "to do X" or "in matters Y." Only a small child, a lover, Abraham speaking to God, or a rabid follower of a charismatic leader might be able to say "I trust you" without implicit modifier. Even in their cases, we are apt to think they mistake both themselves and the objects of their trust.

As virtually all writers on trust agree, trust involves giving discretion to another to affect one's interests. This move is inherently subject to the risk that the other will abuse the power of discretion. As Hume said, "Tis impossible to separate the chance of good from the risk of ill."[12] Also, most writers at least implicitly suppose that potentially trust is *by far the more productive option*. Distrust leads to forgone opportunities, trust can lead to successful and mutually beneficial interactions. More generally, it leads to greater variance in piecemeal outcomes because it offers both greater potential gains and greater potential losses. Coleman says misplaced trust entails a large loss, while forgone trusts entails only a small loss.[13] But forgone trust entails enormous losses if it blocks establishing a longer-term relationship.[14] Distrust produces an aggregate of lost opportunities, each one regular and predictable. Trust leads to an aggregate of some real losses plus some real gains. In the aggregate, the gains may far outweigh the losses, so that the gains from trust far outweigh the savings from distrust.

....

The Epistemology of Trust

The philosophy of knowledge and belief is a highly developed inquiry. Much of it focuses on particular beliefs or types of belief and the criteria for truth or justified true belief. For the understanding of trust (and other behaviors as well), we require not a philosophically general epistemology of knowledge, but a street-level epistemology. The economic theory of belief focuses on the individual believer, not on the matter of belief (e.g., the height of Mont

Blanc), on the costs and benefits to the individual in coming to have various beliefs.[15] In such theory we cannot speak of the justification of belief X *tout court*; rather we must speak of the justification of belief X by person A. For this we require a theory that focuses on the individual and on the ways the individual comes to know or believe relevant things, such as how trustworthy another person is.

In addition, we require a theory of how to act on relevant street-level knowledge. I will presume that this theory of decision is roughly a common-sense version of Bayesianism, perhaps an instinctive Bayesianism. You may start with such limited information about me that you can only estimate the likelihood that the typical person in my position would be trustworthy with respect to what you might entrust to me. You might even have such limited information about me that you can only assess from your past experience whether trust paid off in similar circumstances. Suppose it did and now you trust me. (This is not to say you *choose* to trust me. Rather, gambling on me seems to you the rational thing to do. That simply means you trust me to some extent). You either gain or lose from your trust, and this experience is added to your Bayesian evidence on trustworthiness for future occasions. If I am some-how a new kind of person in your experience, your initial estimate may be very unstable and my behavior might tilt your Bayesian assessment heavily for or against my kind in future encounters.

If we wish to understand trust for real people, what we will have to understand are the capacities for commitment and trust, which must largely be learned. Hence we must understand trust from the commonsense epistemology of the individual in a position to trust or distrust. One cannot simply start trusting people as of tomorrow unless the people one deals with are suddenly and credibly different in relevant ways as of tomorrow. When I meet someone new with whom I wish or have to deal, I may start with considerable skepticism. But my skepticism will not primarily be directed at the new person in particular. I may not yet know enough about the person to judge her or his trustworthiness or her or his rationality in being trustworthy. I make my skeptical judgment largely by generalization from past encounters with other people. In that sense, my degree of trust in the new person has been learned.

My prior experiences with trust may have been so charmed that I optimistically trust this new person. Or they may have been so disastrous that I pessimistically distrust her or him. The new person is no different in the two cases; my alternative experiences, unrelated to this person, are the source of difference. Experience molds the psychology of trust. If my past experience too heavily represented good grounds for trust or poor grounds, it may now take a long run of contrary experience to correct my assessments and, therefore, my actual psychological capacities. Those capacities will reflect a commonsense but likely unarticulated Bayesianism. My capacity is constrained by the weight of past experience with all of the Bayesian reassessment and updating that this experience has stimulated. Trust has to be learned, just like any other kind of generalization.[16] Insofar as my trust is a generalization in the face of new persons, this merely means that the capacity to trust, the optimistic Bayesian estimate of trustworthiness, is learned from perhaps long experience.

Raymond Chandler's cynical, distrusting movie mogul ruefully says, "I'm going to find myself doing business with a man I can trust and I'm going to be just too goddamn smart to trust him."[17] In his milieu, unfortunately, he is probably as smart as he ought to be and part of the cost of being so smart is the occasional error on the side of failing to cooperate. The less-smart person who would cooperate with the trustworthy man would, alas, also cooperate with some others who were not trustworthy. Perhaps the movie mogul trusted at the optimal level. Epistemologically, one can do no better.

Because a high capacity for trust—that is, general optimism about the trustworthiness of others—enables us to enter mutually beneficial relations, we might readily conclude that a utilitarian should encourage trust. It does not follow that the utilitarian should be more trusting, however, because a person's degree of trust is determined by the street-level epistemology of trust. All that the utilitarian should do is encourage pessimistic distrusters to trust up to the level that the utilitarian thinks is justified in the relevant population. In the model discussed below (Figure 1), one might go somewhat further and say that

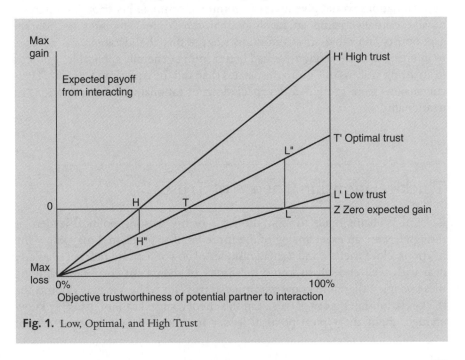

Fig. 1. Low, Optimal, and High Trust

the utilitarian should encourage people to trust more than what the utilitarian, on present expectations, thinks correct, because the more trusting person will have greater opportunity to learn from experience than the less trusting person. Hence erring on the optimistic side is more readily corrected than erring on the pessimistic side.

Note the nature of the beliefs one must have about another to trust that other. In the encapsulated interest account, one must know something about the incentives the other has to fulfill the trust. Consider an oddly important but simple case. During the recently ended cold war, rabid anti-Communists in the United States proclaimed, "You can trust the Communists." What does this mean? It did not mean you could trust them to follow their clear incentives. It meant you could trust them to act from their more or less malevolent ideology. Why would anyone follow such an ideology? Those who thought you could trust the Communists could only answer this question with "I don't know, it's crazy that anyone would follow that ideology, which is contrary to human interests, and which certainly violates the interest structure of Smithian economic and social theory." These trusters had to be true believers about the true believership of the Communists, that is, they had to be true believers in what they took to be the continuing stupidity of the Communists. That is an odd stance. One might well wonder how their beliefs were established.

Many market economists long asserted that eventually the people of the Eastern nations would give up on Communist command economics. Interests must eventually trump an ideology that ran counter to interests. Market economists and rabid anti-Communists agree that the ideology was counter to interests. But the economists had better (more generally applicable) grounds for trusting citizens of Communist states than did the American far right. Their conclusions were grounded in expectations of rationality, not expectations of irrationality.

....

Thick-relationship Theory of Trust

Bernard Williams tends to view the issue of my trusting political leaders as though it were an exact analog of the more familiar problem. I may know my relations, close friends, and a small number of coworkers and others I regularly deal with well enough to know the limits of their trustworthiness. Among these people I therefore know whom I can trust for what. We may call this the thick-relationship theory of trust. On this theory, since I cannot plausibly know enough about the typical political leader to trust her or him, trust cannot handle this relationship in general.[18] But this conclusion is partly wrong. What I can know reasonably well is that the incentives someone in office faces are in the right direction. For my close relations, I may think their incentives are to give various supports to me in particular, so that I can trust them for that reason. The political office holder has no particular interest in me, need not even know about me, but may have a strong interest in supporting people in my position in relevant ways. On Williams's account, as well as Geoffrey Hawthorns's and sometimes Luhmann's, it is virtually a matter of the logic of large numbers and the impossibility of thick relations with very many people that political leaders cannot be trusted. Luhmann says trust is still vital in personal relations, but participation in functional systems such as the economy or politics is no longer a matter of personal relations. It requires confidence, but not trust.[19] As an anthropological observer of very small societies, F. G. Bailey speaks of trust in political leaders achieved through devices of familial style plus unique capacities, such as intuition.[20]

Against the view of Williams, Hawthorn, Luhmann at times, perhaps Bailey, and others, the correct way to see the role of thick relationships is as *one possible source of knowledge* for the truster about the trustworthiness of another and *one possible source of incentives to the trusted* to be trustworthy. The first of these is essentially an epistemological role. But, obviously, thick relationships yield only a part of the knowledge we have of others. They are one among many possible epistemological considerations. Why should our theory stop with only the thick-relationship class of epistemological considerations? In practice, this class may often have priority among our sources in our face-to-face interactions. But this descriptive fact does not give it conceptual or theoretical priority. A fully articulated theory will include this class as a part, not as the whole story, of the epistemology of trust. There is unlikely to be any quarrel with the view that knowledge of another's trustworthiness can come from many sources other than thick relationships.

Similarly, a thick relationship with another is only one of many possible ways to give that other the incentive to be trustworthy. A thick relationship with the truster gives the trusted incentives to be trustworthy through the workings of an iterated prisoner's dilemma of reciprocal cooperation, and this must be a very important effect on trustworthiness among familiar relations.[21] But one may also have incentive to attend to reputational effects, institutional rewards and sanctions, other third-party effects,[22] and other considerations.

In sum, if we have a general incentive-to-be-trustworthy theory of trust, the thick-relationship theory must be merely a special case of it. In particular, the thick-relationship theory is wholly subsumed by the encapsulated interest theory.

Related to the thick-relationship theory of trust is the quick blurring of individual and institutional problems, which is one of the most common mistakes in all of the writing on trust. It may be more common in the writings of philosophers, least in those of sociologists. But writers in all disciplines occasionally succumb to the easy analogy from individual to institutional issues that abstracts from the institutional constraints. For some theories of trust and how it can work, Williams's conclusion that trust cannot generalize beyond the small scale may well follow. For other theories, it may be easy to see how individual-level and institutional-level trust are conceptually related, even though different kinds of data or evidence might go into functional variables in applications at different levels. In any theory, the restriction to small-scale thick relationships must follow from other principles. Going back to those principles is a first step in generalizing the theory.

Oddly, Williams is writing metatheory. He does not present a theory of trust or criticize any actual theories. He tries simply to outline some constraints on any theory of trust. But his metatheoretical claims are muddied by an implicit theory or trust—the thick-relationship theory. But again, that theory, which is based on a thick relationship between the trusted and the one who trusts, may be merely a special case of some larger theories. Partha Dasgupta's example of the bravery of the Gurkhas is a compelling instance of the possibility of my trusting someone without my having any relationship at all with that person.[23] Why might I trust a Gurkha to do certain things? On the epistemological side, perhaps I know an enormous lot about their behavior on various occasions and that behavior was consistent. On the incentive side, perhaps I trust the effectiveness of the social constraints on the behavior of the typical Gurkha.

John Dunn and others clearly wish to speak of trust even in large-number contexts, as in politics. Although Luhmann seems to agree with Williams that trust tends to apply only to small-number contexts, on the model of cooperation in iterated prisoner's dilemma,[24] in his earlier, greater contribution on trust, he explicated what he called system trust.[25] Locke was concerned with trust in those who govern. The more complex and the more economically differentiated the society in question, the more likely he thought trust was to be absent.[26] Much of his view seems to imply need for something like face-to-face interactions, which implies small society only. A central appeal of the Anti-Federalist vision during the constitutional era in the United States was to representation by one's own kind. Why? They can be trusted to share one's interests on various legislative matters. In this respect, today's communitarians agree with the Anti-Federalists and Dunn's Locke. Bailey similarly argues that people are more inclined to like those whom they see as like themselves.[27] This may depend on nothing more than that we are merely better at predicting the behavior of those most like ourselves.

Trust and Trustworthiness

Many discussions of trust run trust and trustworthiness together, with claims about trust that might well apply to trustworthiness but that seem off the mark for trust. In particular, writers often transfer to trust the moral approbation that might be thought applicable to trustworthiness. Independently of whether there is something moral about being trustworthy or untrustworthy, however, trust might be fully explicable as a capability or as a product of rational expectation without any moral residue. I treat trust as an unmoralized notion, as Coleman and many others commonly do. Most of the argument would have some force even in a moralized account of trust, in which the potential truster is held morally accountable for a failure to trust. The argument would be of special interest in the moralized account insofar as it is about constraints on the capacity to anticipate trustworthiness.

Surprisingly much of the literature on trust hardly mentions trustworthiness, even though much of it is primarily about trustworthiness, not about trust. Under the guise of discussing trust, Williams[28] gives an account of the possibilities of general trustworthiness, from which trust is merely inferred. Similarly, Roland McKean ostensibly addresses the economics of trust,[29] but his actual problem is that of trustworthiness. It is not trust per se that is the collective good in his account, but trustworthiness. Creating institutions that help secure trustworthiness thus helps to support or induce trust.

Where there is trust that is justified, there are increased possibilities for experience and action. Luhmann says trust constitutes a more effective form of complexity reduction.[30] This seems to be a very elliptical claim. Trust by itself constitutes nothing. Presumably Luhmann is saying that we cannot handle enormous complexity without others acting de facto on our behalf. But if we cannot count on their acting in our interest, we may therefore be reluctant to empower them or to follow their advice. Hence whatever can secure their trustworthiness enough for us to trust them will help us manage complexity. That is to say, again, the focal problem is trustworthiness, not trust.

In his novel, *The Remains of the Day*, Kazuo Ishiguro portrays Mr. Stevens, an aging butler rethinking his life with his late master. In an imagined debate with another servant, Stevens says, "the likes of you and I will never be in a position to comprehend the great affairs of today's world, and our best course will always be to put our trust in an employer we judge to be wise and honourable, and to devote our energies to the task of serving him to the best of our ability."[31] He slowly revalues his master in the light of the views of others, who detested the lord's reprehensible and foolish politics. Stevens says, "at least he had the privilege of being able to say at the end of his life that he made his own mistakes. ... I cannot even claim that. You see, I *trusted*. I trusted in his lordship's wisdom. All those years I served him, I trusted I was doing something worthwhile. I can't even say I made my own mistakes. Really—one has to ask oneself—what dignity is there in that?"[32] Trust can finally be stupid and even culpable. Merely trusting per se obviously need not help in managing complexity well—it could lead to dismal results, including quick destruction. Again, the core of Luhmann's account of the role of trust must be an account of the importance of trustworthiness. If it really commends trust, it elevates Steven's culpable stupidity. Trust led Stevens not to manage complexity so much as to fall victim to it.

The Learned Capacity to Trust

Some writers speak of the greater ability to trust. Typically they run the likely state of the world—whether those who are trusted will prove trustworthy—into this ability. But there is a genuine problem in whether I can trust independent of the outside world I now face, that depends only on my capacities as developed up to this moment. Suppose there is a reasonable degree of trustworthiness in my present community. Now, if I have an adequate capacity to trust, I will benefit. Someone who lacks such capacity will be a relative loser. More generally, we can give a literal meaning to McKean's claim: "Greater ability to trust each other to stick with agreed-upon rules would save many costs and make life much pleasanter."[33] Or as Dasgupta says, trust is important because "its presence or absence can have a strong bearing on what we choose to do and in many cases what we *can* do."[34]

The best condition for humans is an environment in which they are fortunate enough to have well-founded confidence.[35] This is not an individual-level problem, but is a collective problem. For me to rely on not locking up my home or shop would require that I have trust in almost everyone. The individual-level problem here is to judge rightly what the collective behavior on trustworthiness is.

Being an optimistic truster opens up the opportunity of great loss and of great gain, neither of which might be possible without risking trust. If optimistic trusting does lead to good returns on average, then trust contributes value. Indeed, an individual might gain more from increased trusting than from increased trustworthiness, and the external effects of greater trusting might outweigh the external effects of greater trustworthiness. There is no a priori reason to suppose that either trust or trustworthiness is the dominant consideration in general. Teaching our children to be trustworthy is likely to be good for them. But teaching them to trust—for example, by being trustworthy and supportive of their trust in our dealings with them and giving them many opportunities to test our trustworthiness—may be even better for them. In this sense, trust is, as Gambetta says, a result rather than a precondition of cooperation,[36] although of course it is both a result of past cooperation and typically the condition for attempting future cooperation. In a Hobbesian view, trust must be a precondition of cooperation, and trust is underwritten by a strong government to enforce contracts and to punish theft. Without such a government, cooperation would be nearly impossible and trust would be irrational.

If the rough account of infant trust and the later capacity to be optimistically trusting is right,[37] two plausibly large groups are at a cruel disadvantage: those whose early years are spent in fractured conditions of caprice and neglect, as in the case of many children of American inner-city communities wrecked by poverty, drugs, and broken families; and those, perhaps especially women, who have suffered substantial abuse in their early years from the very persons who might have provided the first experience of trustworthiness.

The sense that the upper-middle class have tremendous social advantages over others may have some of its grounding in the greater propensity of their children to trust, to risk relations that could be beneficial to them. This propensity may have been learned from the apparently justified trusting of family, friends, and others while infants and children. The terrible vision of a permanent underclass in American city ghettos may have its grounding in the lesson that the children of the ghetto are taught, all too successfully, that they cannot trust others, 'especially not outsiders or strangers but also not even closer associates. Providing opportunities of educational and economic mobility does not equalize prospects for the ingrained distruster, who cannot optimistically trust enough to take full advantage of opportunities that entail risks of betrayal.

Similarly, the many adults who were abused as very young children, often by parents and other very close relations, may have been deprived of the normal evidence that trust is justified. For them, it too often was not. Their incapacity to enter relations with others—as the woman who was sexually abused as a child may find it hard to be sexually at ease or even close to anyone as an adult—is merely a well-learned distrust. That ingrained distrust may exact a severe additional cost of the earlier abuse if the distrust is no longer justified by the conditions of the world she has grown into.[38] Substantial additional experience would be required to update the Bayesian assessment of general untrustworthiness.

On this account, in some societies trust must be a benefit—or rather, it must lead to benefits. It would be in one's interest therefore to cultivate it. And it would be in the interests of one's children for one to teach them optimistic trust. Trust cannot be produced at will,[39] although it can be willfully instilled, as in children. Moreover, as-if trust can be willed[40] repeatedly so that one may slowly develop optimistic trust, just as Pascal said one may willfully set about following religious practices in order to come to believe. In many potentially iterated prisoner's dilemma interactions, one should open with a cooperative move in the hope of engaging the other also to be cooperative. This is not merely a moral injunction. It is a rational claim of self-interest.[41] One should open with cooperation when the expected long-run benefits of iterated co-operation outweigh the short-term risk of loss.

But optimistic trust can be beneficial only if the general social conditions the optimistic truster faces are relatively favorable, so that statistically the acts of trust will be rewarded by trustworthiness. The huge genre of post-apocalypse films and novels of our time portray conditions in which trust is generally not justified. Life is impoverished beyond measure, with the demands of survival and struggle preempting almost all else. To have optimistic trust in these conditions might be to risk suicide. A central issue for optimistic trust is how well past experience corresponds to future opportunities.

In his account of the so-called state of nature, Hobbes portrays a situation in which trusting to any significant extent would be self-destructive and even suicidal. Hobbes's actual view may be relatively modest, despite his violent vision of the state of nature. He supposes that, without enforcement, the few who would take adverse advantage of others would finally drive others to be too defensive to enter into beneficial relations that they could readily have sustained without the threat of the few. In essence, his argument is that the potential costs of misplaced trust overwhelm the potential advan-tages of well-placed trust if there is no political order to secure reliability of certain kinds. Hence trust is virtually irrational in a Hobbesian state of nature.

The psychological development of a propensity to trust involves extensive investment, *especially by others, such as parents*. If there has been little invest-ment during early years, far greater investment may be required in later years to compensate. As in Robert Frank's understanding of the role of the emotions in such actions as trusting,[42] I may now find it very hard to act as if I trust when I do not. Early trust may be rewarded enough to stimulate its further development and reinforcement. Because relevant investments were made in my development, I may have optimistically trusted enough times to begin to learn fairly well when trust is warranted and when it is not, so that I use trust very well. If relevant investments were not made, I may have so pessimistically distrusted or at best been so wary that I have little or no learning of the value of trust. I may seldom have put it to test. The failure of investment by my parents need not correlate with the untrustworthiness of my associates in later life. But it might. The very fact that I have a hard time trusting even those who would turn out to be trustworthy may mean that I fail to establish ongoing cooperative relations with such people and therefore disproportionately face short-term relations with people who, on average, are less trustworthy, thus reinforcing my attitude of distrust or wariness. Trusters and the trustworthy may interact chiefly with each other, leaving distrusters and the untrustworthy with reduced opportunities for successful interactions.

A behavioral learning account of development, such as that of Erik Erikson, supplies an essential part of an economic or rational account of trust. It is about how particular expectations develop from experience. Such expectations are, of course, central to the rational account. "The firm establishment of enduring patterns for the solution of the nuclear conflict of basic trust versus basic mistrust in mere existence is the first task of the ego, and thus first of all a task of maternal care." What is needed is not simply quantities of food and so on, but the quality of the maternal relationship. "Mothers create a sense of trust in their children by that kind of administration which in its quality combines sensitive care of the baby's individual needs and a firm sense of personal trustworthiness."[43]

If trust is learned from experience, there is little sense in the claim of some that trust is a more or less consciously chosen policy for handling the freedom of other human agents or agencies.[44] I just do or do not trust; I do not, in an immediate instance, *choose* to trust. Trusting need not be purposive.[45] I do not trust you in order to gain from interacting with you. But, because I do trust you, I can expect to gain from interacting with you if a relevant opportunity arises. That is all it means to say I trust you. I might choose to take a risk on someone that goes beyond what I would trust of that person. But my level of trust is defined, either fairly accurately from experience with that person or vaguely by Bayesian generalization from my, perhaps very limited, experience of others.

On a reasonable view of the epistemology of trust, it also follows that common claims that trust is a gamble or risky investment are at least elliptical and perhaps confused. Baier says that trusting someone is always a risk "given the partial opaqueness to us of the reasoning and motivation of those we trust and with whom we cooperate."[46] Trust is not a risk or a gamble. It is, of course, risky to put myself in a position to be harmed or benefited by another. But I do not calculate the risk and then additionally decide to trust you; my estimation of the risk is my degree of trust in you. Again, I do not typically choose to trust and therefore act; rather, I do trust and therefore choose to act. The degree of trust I have for you is just the expected probability of the dependency working out well. On Luhmann's general account, trust is a way of dealing with the risks inherent in complexity. To say, on top of this, as he does, that trust is itself a risk is to compound the single risk at stake.[47]

....

Low and High Capacity for Trust

On a Bayesian learning account, those who start life badly are disadvantaged by the continuing loss of welfare in forgone opportunities from low capacity for trust. The disadvantage must continue until they have enough experience to update their estimates of the general trustworthiness. Consider how devastating the early abuse and development of low trust is in the Bayesian account. Suppose that, in our society, trust at reasonable levels usually pays off. If I was so heavily abused as a very young child that I now expect almost no interaction to pay off, I will enter into very few of the potential interactions I face. I will suffer from what former President Jimmy Carter calls "hopelessness based on sound judgment."[48] I am objectively wrong in my assessments, but my assessments make eminently rational sense given the perverse experience I have had.

As a commonsense Bayesian, I may eventually correct my earlier assessment of how poor the prospects are. To do so, I would have to have many interactions that typically paid off well, so that my aggregate experience, from early to recent, begins to approach the average experience. But, because I have such low expectations, I am willing to test very few interactions. If you had a generally good experience of the benefits from trusting, you would readily enter into far more of these interactions. It therefore would take me longer to gain data to recommend changing my pessimistic assessments. All the while, I also enter fewer interactions and therefore benefit less than you do as you enter many which, on average, pay off well. If we start with similar levels of welfare, you soon outdistance me.

Suppose, on the other hand, that I started life with such a charmed existence that I now am too optimistic about trusting others, so that I often overdo it and get burned. Because I am trusting, I enter into many interactions and I collect data for updating my Bayesian estimates very quickly. My aggregate experience soon approaches the aggregate average and I reach an optimal level of trust that pays off well in most of my interactions, more than enough to make up for the occasions when I mistakenly overrate the trustworthiness of another. Oddly, therefore, if parents are to err on one side or the other in instilling a belief that others are trustworthy, a strictly Bayesian account suggests that they should err on the side of instilling greater optimism in others than they think is objectively warranted.

Modeling Bayesian trust. The alternative conditions of high and low capacity for trust may be modeled simply as in the model in Figure 1. To simplify the problem, make the following assumptions.

1. Suppose the objective world that we now face is one in which the distribution of trustworthiness is linear from 0 percent to 100 percent trustworthy.

2. We are all competent to assess the *relative* trustworthiness of people, but we may have different mean estimates of how trustworthy they are *absolutely*. That is, you and I would both rank the same kinds of people as most trustworthy and the same kinds as most untrustworthy. But you might optimistically expect all people to be more likely trustworthy than not, while I pessimistically expect all to be more likely untrustworthy than trustworthy.

3. There is a net, positive payoff from trusting someone who fulfills the trust and a loss from trusting someone who defaults on the trust.

4. The objective value of the potential loss and gain is the same for all potential partners to interaction, but the probability of getting the gain ranges from 0 percent to 100 percent. Hence, the (objective) expected payoff will be lower for trusting the (objectively) less trustworthy than for trusting the more trustworthy.

There is an objective break-even point at which the average return from trusting a person of that degree of trustworthiness is neither gain nor loss. The difference between a very optimistic truster and a very pessimistic distruster is that the latter supposes this break-even point is reached only for interactions with (objectively) very trustworthy people, while the former supposes it is reached already at significantly lower levels of (objective) trustworthiness. One who trusts at the optimal level for this population supposes the break-even point is where it is objectively.

For the person of low trust in Figure 1, the break-even point occurs (in the subjective estimate of the low truster) at L, or about 85 percent objective trustworthiness. For the optimal truster, it occurs at T, or about 50 percent, and for the high truster at H, or about 30 percent trustworthiness. All three will trust only above the respective break-even point and will not trust below it. The distruster will therefore trust relatively seldom, only in the range L to Z. The excessively optimistic truster will trust very often, but will lose in the range from H to T. These losses will be offset by gains from trusting in the range T to Z. The optimal truster will trust in the range T to Z and will have an expected net gain throughout that range.

The optimal truster will have the largest actual payoff from risking trust, as represented by the large triangle TZT′ (the right-hand cross-hatched triangle in Figure 2). The distruster has the much smaller expected payoff represented by the small triangle LZL′, but the larger actual payoff represented by the trapezoidal area LZT′ L″ under the optimal-trust line to the right of L. The high truster has an expected payoff of the very large triangle HZH′, but the smaller actual payoff that is the optimal trust payoff less the loss represented by the small triangle HTH″ (the left-hand cross-hatched triangle in Figure 2). The

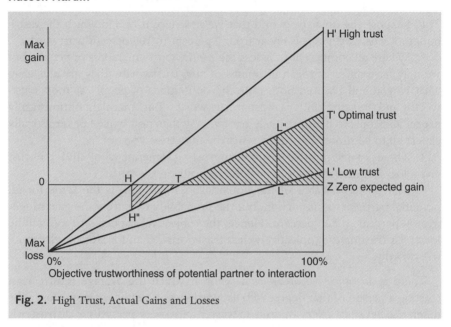

Fig. 2. High Trust, Actual Gains and Losses

latter triangle area represents the losses from too optimistically trusting those who are too unlikely to be trustworthy. The difference in payoffs for the three conditions of trust could be enormous, with the optimal truster several times better off than the distruster. For the values given in Figure 1, the optimal truster's payoff is somewhat larger than that of the high truster and about two and a half times that of the low truster.

Finally, note that the excessive truster will enter far more interactions than will the distruster and will therefore have many more direct opportunities to correct her or his judgment of the break-even point and the actual distribution of trust-worthiness. The distruster will have far fewer direct opportunities to correct her or his judgment and will lose even in comparison to someone who entered the society as an idealized Bayesian who guesses that the average person would cooperate at, say, the 50 percent level.

Great distrust essentially implies an expected loss from most interactions, as represented by the large triangle defined by the segment OL and the point at the lower left. The area of this triangle is very much larger than the expected gain, area LZL', for the low truster. Total distrust would seemingly lead to no interactions, resulting in zero payoff with neither gains or losses. As Dunn artfully remarks, "Determination to avoid being a sucker, if generalized to the human race, would subvert human sociality more or less in its entirety."[49] It would be worse than that: It would utterly subvert individual existence as well. With a complete absence of trust, one must be catatonic, one could not even get up in the morning.[50]

Luhmann says that neither trust nor distrust is feasible as a universal attitude.[51] This follows as an analytical claim for distrust. For trust, however, the claim is empirical and wrong. Trust as a universal attitude could pay off for someone in a very benign world in which the level of trustworthiness is quite high. There have surely been such worlds, although Luhmann's claim is likely true for most people in modern industrial states. Even in only modestly supportive worlds, however, adopting an attitude of optimism toward trusting others may be beneficial. It is risky, but the gains might outweigh the losses. Or perhaps one should speak not of adopting an attitude of optimism but of adopting the behavior of an optimistic truster. That behavior opens up the possibility of discovering the trustworthy.

Great trust implies expected gain from most interactions, as in the triangle HZH'. If the optimal-trust line crosses break even at 50 percent, then never trusting and always trusting have the same net payoff of no gain or loss. But the 100 percent truster has many interactions from which to learn better about the world; the 0 percent truster has none. The high truster does the equivalent of as-if testing; the distruster does not. Suppose we wish to correct the deficiencies with which low trusters face the world. *Simply providing equal opportunity will not accomplish this end.* In Figure I and throughout this discussion, the various trusters are assumed to face identical opportunities as of the time of their current interactions. The low truster nevertheless loses ground and suffers severe relative welfare losses. An equal opportunity program cannot stop that morose trend.[52] The losses are not merely of opportunities, but of the capacity to capitalize on opportunities.

There may be other correlates of high and low capacities for trust from early learning. For example, one may develop a capacity for spontaneity from being able to trust people not to react badly, even to react positively, to one's odd experiments or ways. Narcissists are also characteristically spontaneous—yet they do not get that way from supportive experience. Indeed, the source of narcissistic personality disorder is thought to be severe neglect rather than abuse. If parents and other caretakers are neglectful, perhaps because of alcoholism or severe illness, during the first year or two of a child's life, the child may learn not to take others into account, neither to trust nor to distrust.[53]

Shortcomings of the model. There are many complications that are not captured in the model of Figure 1. These include the stated simplifying assumptions such as, for example, the linearity of distribution of objective and expected trustworthiness. In addition, note the following.

First, the model ignores the relative size of loss and gain at risk. If the downside of risking an interaction is extremely bad compared to the benefit of a successful interaction, one will require much higher probability of gain to offset the occasional losses. The break-even point would move to the right in Figure 1. In experiments on the iterated prisoner's dilemma, as the sucker's payoff (the loss from cooperating with another player who defects) increases, rates of cooperative play decrease, and eventually there is no cooperation. This shortcoming can easily enough be accommodated in the model.

Second, in a point that is related to the first limit of the model, the model ignores the possibility of varied weights of potential interactions. Such variety is implicit in the claim that trust is a three-part relation: A trusts B to do X. In one interaction I might merely trust you to put a quarter in my parking meter while in another I might hope to be able to trust you to take care of my small child. I might loan you a dollar or a thousand dollars. If there were no correlation between the scale of what is to be trusted with the likelihood of any person's trustworthiness in fulfilling the trust, this issue would not matter. But it seems generally implausible that there is no such correlation. Everyone is likely to be a lower truster for high stakes than for low stakes.

Third, the model ignores strategic effects such as as-if trust behavior to test the trustworthiness of people of a particular kind and, more generally, the incentive effects of iterated interaction with the same person. It seems likely that one will tend initially to trust a new person only in limited ways and will trust on more important matters only after building up to them.[54] Swinth found as-if testing less important than one might think in his experimental tests.[55]

Fourth, the model has the shortcoming of Cournot models of economic processes in that it assumes strategic calculation by the potential truster of whether to enter into interactions but does not attribute any sophistication to the potentially trusted person. The model is only half strategic.

Fifth, the model ignores the complexity of possible ways of learning. One might learn indirectly from others' experiences as well as directly from one's own experiences. In the light of the second problem of the model noted above, we may note that learning might be quite cheap with minor risks and grievously expensive with major risks. And there is greater value from learning in contexts of likely iteration of interactions.

Sixth, the model may not accommodate complex skews in trusting people, such as the trust many automatically put in a managerial of professional person, even in matters outside their professional competence (Coleman discusses various intermediary effects).[56] This shortcoming may, however, be easily addressed within the simplified Bayesian model.

The worst of these shortcomings for an account of trust as encapsulated interest are the failures to accommodate strategic considerations, especially incentive effects in iteration (either directly or through reputational effects). Some of the other problems may be easily addressed in the more general encapsulated interest account of trust. And some may be easily fitted into the model of Figure 1. Even with its shortcomings, the simple model implies most of Julian Rotter's standard conclusions about interpersonal trust. Rotter finds that high trusters are more likely to give others a second chance (this sounds almost definitional), and they are less likely to be unhappy and more likely to be liked by others.[57] If they are in an environment in which trust leads more, on balance, to gain than to losses, they should be less unhappy. And their openness to trusting others should lead others to select them as partners in various activities.

Further Implications of Bayesian Trust

Note some other important implications of the Bayesian account of learned trust. First, a newcomer to a community may similarly be disadvantaged in ways that are perversely reinforcing. Second, enforcement and sanctions may have a strong positive effect on capacity for trust in contexts well outside the coverage of the sanctions. Finally, the Bayesian learning account undercuts conceptual claims that trust is a form of human capital.[58]

The outsider. Consider the condition of an outsider or new immigrant to a community. The outsider may initially seem untrustworthy to others in the community. This could follow merely from a Bayesian guess, a judgment of that person as less likely to be trustworthy than those who are long well-known. Until more knowledge of trustworthiness is generated, that person is given fewer opportunities to demonstrate trustworthiness. Hence it may take depressingly long for that person to become trusted. Since again the combination of trusting and being trusted conveys benefits in various kinds of exchange and mutual aid, the outsider faces greater difficulties getting ahead and may begin to seem less able and worthy. Superficially, we might suppose a group that held off from trusting an outsider for a long time was prejudiced in a racist or related sense. But the rational prejudice of the Bayesian might be sufficient to explain the community's attitude.

Alejandro Portes and Julia Sensenbrenner describe an informal financial system in the Cuban immigrant community in Miami in the 1960s after Fidel Castro came to power. Newly arrived immigrants with no collateral could obtain so-called "character loans" based on the entrepreneurial reputations they had in Cuba. Reputedly, these loans, ranging from $10,000 to $30,000 were invariably repaid and their recipients often went on to great prosperity.[59]

These loans involved trust by the Latin bankers who made them. Portes and Sensenbrenner call that trust enforceable. Why? Because the Cuban exiles were virtually trapped. They could prosper in the transplanted Cuban community only if they proved reliable in repaying their loans. But there was nowhere else for them to go where they could prosper. They could not return to Cuba, and there was no welcoming community elsewhere. There was no other community of people who had natural access to their reputations and who could have trusted them in the sense of having good reason to believe that their incentive to be trustworthy was compelling, even overpowering. They were an unusual case: outsiders with almost insider status in one exclusive community on which they were fully dependent. The availability of that status was brief. By 1973, character loans ended because the newly arriving Cubans were no longer known to the local banking community, and they might also have had little or no entrepreneurial success in Cuba on which to ground a reputation.

Many of us, of course, might start by trusting newly encountered people or people in newly undertaken areas. Even then we would not trust in very important matters without a substantial prior history of trustworthiness. If we were outsiders, we might be open to as-if trust in order to get started. But if we were fully outsiders or if we had other communities to turn to, we might readily prove to be untrustworthy in the face of large burdens. Hence we could not be trusted as readily as the 1960s Cubans in Miami.

Sanctions and trust. Sociologists writing on trust are generally concerned with social mechanisms that generate trust.[60] Luhmann supposes that the structure of trust relations requires that calculation of risk remain latent. Yet contractual relations may require such calculation to be overt and present and may therefore introduce an atmosphere unfavorable to trust. When such interdependence already exists so that the risks are openly known to all without need of specific present discussion, mutual understanding and trust may be enhanced.[61]

This merely means that the transition from informal to formal regulation of relations may be uneasy, as the street-level Bayesian should expect. New conditions that have ill-defined prior expected probabilities attached generally introduce initial instability. But the results of successfully completing that transition may be to enhance trust.

Coleman says development of norms with sanctions enhances cooperation.[62] This is also Hobbes's theory: Creation of strong sanctions to protect each makes all better off. In Hobbes's account of the need for a powerful state, what is mainly needed for most people is merely enough security to be able to enter into exchange relations with others without fear of being killed for what one has or merely preemptively.[63] Without the background of police protection, I may be wary of you altogether. With police protection, I may readily engage with you in varied activities for mutual benefit. If I no longer need distrust you for possibly having very violent motives against me, I can begin to trust your minor motivations to gain from mutual interaction.

At the more mundane level of daily life, we may note, with Bernard Barber,[64] that trust can be enhanced by making distrust and devices for social control more effective. How can trust be enhanced by enforceable contract (or by audits with the threat of sanction)? The contract or audit may protect a relationship against the worst of all risks it might entail, thereby enabling the parties to cooperate on less-risky matters. Without the threat of sanctions, they might have been able to do none of these. Recall the problem of prisoner's dilemma games with large sucker's payoffs, as mentioned above. If you and I can arrange to have the worst possible payoffs blocked—by legal sanction if necessary—we can go on to cooperate to our mutual advantage. McKean thinks we value enforcement mechanisms partly because we recognize "how costly life would be without trust, even if the basis has to be created in part by such enforcement mechanisms."[65]

Consider a particularly interesting case. Under foreign (Habsburg) rule, Sicilians and southern Italians were able to trust neither the fairness nor the protection of the law.[66] Theirs was not a fully Hobbesian state of nature, but it had Hobbesian tendencies. In such conditions as theirs, distrust plausibly breeds distrust and today, long after the Habsburgs have left the stage, distrust continues. Not being able to trust the state leads to not being able to trust other individuals.[67] People do not cooperate when it would be mutually beneficial; they compete in harmful ways; they refrain from competing in those instances in which they could all gain from competition.[68] They engage in the promotion and selective exploitation of distrust.[69] A stronger regime, capable of coercively overriding the influence of the mafia, could enhance the grounds for trust. Most Sicilians would not be coerced by law that coerced the mafia. Rather, they would be freed of coercion by the mafia if such law worked.

Sanctions need not come from legal authorities, of course. They commonly are built in from iteration and expectation of continued gain that outweighs momentary gain from defection. The incentive to cooperate (or to fulfill a trust) and the sanction not to do so are one and the same. They are the benefits of future interaction that ride on present trustworthiness. For an apparently extreme case, Coleman discusses a £200,000 spot loan from the Hambros merchant bank in London to a foreign shipper, negotiated almost instantly over the telephone and delivered immediately. He says that the loan was made with nothing more substantial than the ship owner's intention to repay and the Hambros man's belief in both the ship owner's honesty and his ability to repay.[70] It seems unlikely that this was really true. There was some threat (surely left unstated) of suit and court enforcement. Even if enforcement was not guaranteed, suit could be initiated and, once undertaken, was likely to have reputational consequences that would have been costly to the ship owner in the future. But even this sanction is largely informal.

To fully judge the Hambros loan, we must back off from the instant case and consider the question whether it is in the interest of such bankers to do what Hambros did. The answer seems likely to be yes if a sufficiently high degree of trustworthiness can be assured through legal, reputational, or other incentives. Trusting opens up opportunities for doing business.

Trust as capital. One might speak of trust or the capacity for trust as a form of human capital. But it is an odd form. For much of what is called human capital, we assume direct investment in its creation in the face of opportunity costs of other things not done. The capacity for trust could come about through the deliberate investment of someone in the development of a child. Much of the time, however, the capacity for trust must seem more nearly like an accidental by-product of activities that give the child experience of rewarded trust but that were not undertaken for that purpose. Trust must be learned, but the most important learning is apt to be inadvertent. Hence high capacity for trust is a by-product of fortunate experience. As in the joke about life more generally, trust or distrust is what happens to us while we're making other plans. Yet Luhmann, Dasgupta, and others refer to trust as a kind of human capital.[71] That is a misleading way to characterize it, perhaps grossly misleading.

Let us spell this out. Contrary to the wording of the previous paragraphs, investment may be the wrong term altogether for what leads a typical infant and child to have a capacity for trust. The parent may do things for the child out of love or instant pleasure in the child, not out of a deliberate program to put so much time into the development of the child's capacity to trust. (A woefully misdirected Kantian or utilitarian might put in time with a child only to help it develop.) That capacity is therefore not a full analog to standard notions of human capital. A typical Olympic swimmer has great human capital from giving up inordinately many hours to train, sometimes in the water, sometimes in the weight room. A child might grow up loving to swim and spending many hours in the pool and might therefore be quite good. But the child might have sacrificed nothing to become a better swimmer; the child might have preferred swimming over every other available activity at the time. For the Olympic swimmer, swimming or weight lifting might often have been an ordeal. Because the child enjoyed, even preferred, the activity of swimming while doing it, the de facto training and development that came from the swimming had little or no opportunity costs. The development was just a fortuitous by-product of taking the pleasure.

Development of a capacity to trust, either in infancy or in later life, has more in common with the development of the non-Olympic child's swimming capacity than with the arduous training of the Olympian. It is just a fortuitous by-product of activities undertaken in one's own right. Indeed, it is even more fortuitous than that. It is very much the by-product of experiences over which the individual may have had little control, experiences which the individual did not even undertake. For example, you may have a great capacity for trust because you grew up in a wonderfully supportive family and because your later life has been in a society in which optimistic trust pays off handsomely. You are accountable for little or none of your capacity, you are merely its beneficiary. Any actual instance of your trusting someone will depend on this past experience and also, of course, on the apparent future incentives of the trusted to do what you trust her or him to do.

Concluding Remarks

In many accounts of trust, including Coleman's strictly rational account,[72] one might suppose that those who are to trust are all interchangeable in the following sense. Given the same incentives (potential objective payoffs), we would all trust to the same degree. But there is an important prior element that some might think of as psychological: We may have different capacities for trust. This issue should not be treated as psychological in the sense of irrational or not rationally justifiable but, rather, as essentially epistemological, and hence as pragmatically rational. The sometime claim that there is a psychological dimension of trust that is different from the cognitive or calculative or rational[73] may be little more than nascent recognition of this epistemological problem.

A problem with the encapsulated interest account of trust is that it is inherently subjective in the following sense. *What it is sensible for a given individual to expect depends heavily on what* that individual *knows, both about the past and the future of the person or other party to be trusted.* Obviously, assessments of the future matter for an expectations analysis. But why the past? Partly for reputational reasons. But also because the past reveals the other's capacity to trust and be trustworthy. To a very large extent, this is merely the capacity to judge the likely risks and benefits of entering trust relationships.

These retrospective and prospective views imply that there are two, perhaps causally related, kinds of knowledge about another that play a role in assessments of trustworthiness. First, there is simple inductive knowledge of the kind that goes into reputation. The American anti-Communists, discussed earlier, had some inductive knowledge on which they based their conclusions. The second kind of knowledge is theoretical. Economists had theoretical knowledge about people in general and about the working of centrally determined and market-determined economic outcomes. Many economists thought that their theoretical knowledge must eventually trump inductive knowledge about loyalty to Communist ideology.

A general problem with inductive knowledge, if it is completely atheoretical, is that it cannot justify a claim that what has always happened before must happen again. Most of us are willing to live with inferences that various things will continue to happen in the ways they always have happened so far. But we are apt to suppose that there are reasons for this, merely that we do not know the reasons. The economists' theoretical knowledge about economic product-ivity gave an explanation (perhaps wrong) of why the trend of loyalty to Communism must eventually end. A relevant answer to the economists would have to be grounded in an alternative theoretical claim. The anti-Communists generally proposed no alternative theory, they merely asserted the certainty of the Communists' continuing irrationality.

A full account of rational trust must be grounded in reasons for expecting another to fulfill a trust and in reasons for holding general beliefs about trustworthiness. These are addressed, respectively, by the incentive account of trustworthiness that justifies and explains trust and by the commonsense Bayesian account of learned trust. The commonsense Bayesian is little more than an inductivist who generalizes from the past to the future, as in the model of Figure 1. To break the hold of a bad and misleading past, the Bayesian requires a lot of new experience or a bit of theory that runs counter to prior experience. The model of Figure 1 suggests that correcting the pessimistic Bayesian estimates of trustworthiness merely by amassing better experience may be very slow, so that these misestimates produce a long string of lost opportunities. Understanding that others will be trustworthy when their incen-tives are right, as in the encapsulated interest account of trust, may hold greater, quicker promise for grasping those opportunities. This requires seeing the choices of others from their perspective to comprehend their incentives. Then trust becomes fully strategic. It is no longer merely induction on senseless facts.

Notes

1. James S. Coleman, *Foundations of Social Theory* (Cambridge, MA: Harvard University Press, 1990), ch. 5.
2. Russell Hardin, "Trusting Persons, Trusting Institutions," in Richard Zeckhauser, ed., *The Strategy of Choice* (Cambridge, MA: MIT Press, 1991), 185–209.
3. Bernard Barber, *The Logic and Limits of Trust* (New Brunswick, NJ: Rutgers Univer-sity Press, 1983); Diego Gambetta, ed., *Trust: Making and Breaking Cooperative Relations* (New York and Oxford: Blackwell, 1988), 217–18; Partha Dasgupta, "Trust As a Commodity," in Gambetta, *Trust*, 49–72.

4. Annette Baier, "Trust and Antitrust," *Ethics* 96 (1986): 231–60.

5. Coleman, *Foundations of Social Theory,* 177–80.

6. Russell Hardin, "Exchange Theory on Strategic Bases," *Social Science Information* 21 (1982): 251–72.

7. Baier, "Trust and Antitrust," 252.

8. Ibid., 251.

9. Niklas Luhmann, *Trust: A Mechanism for the Reduction of Social Complexity,* in Luhmann, *Trust and Power* (New York: Wiley, 1980), 4–103, at 42; also see Lars Hertzberg, "On the Attitude of Trust," *Inquiry* 31 (1988): 307–22.

10. Luhmann, *Trust,* 37.

11. Baier, "Trust and Antitrust," 236; Luhmann, *Trust,* 27.

12. David Hume, *A Treatise of Human Nature,* edited by L. A. Selby-Bigge and P. H. Nidditch, 2nd edn. (Oxford: Oxford University Press, 1978 [1739–40]), 497.

13. Coleman, *Foundations of Social Theory,* 101.

14. Erik H. Erikson, *Childhood and Society,* 2nd edn. (New York: Norton, 1963), 247–51.

15. Russell Hardin, "The Economics of Knowledge and Utilitarian Morality," in Brad Hooker, ed., *Rationality, Rules, and Utility: Essays on Richard Brandt's Moral Philosophy* (Boulder, CO: Westview, 1993: 127–47).

16. Luhmann, *Trust,* 27.

17. Coleman, *Foundations of Social Theory,* 100.

18. Bernard Williams, "Formal Structures and Social Reality," in Gambetta, *Trust,* 3–13; also see Geoffrey Hawthorn, "Three Ironies in Trust," in Gambetta, *Trust,* 111–26.

19. Niklas Luhmann, "Familiarity, Confidence, Trust: Problems and Alternatives," in Gambetta, *Trust,* 94–107, at 102. As noted below, Luhmann earlier wrote of "system-trust," which must transcend interpersonal (thick) relations (Luhmann, *Trust,* 22, 30).

20. F. G. Bailey, "The Creation of Trust," in Bailey, *Humbuggery and Manipulation"* (Ithaca, NY: Cornell University Press, 1988), 82–99, at 85–86, 91.

21. Hardin, "Trusting Persons, Trusting Institutions."

22. Coleman, *Foundations of Social Theory,* 180–85.

23. Dasgupta, "Trust As a Commodity."

24. Luhmann, "Familiarity, Confidence, Trust."

25. Luhmann, *Trust,* 22 and 30.

26. John Dunn, "Trust and Political Agency," in Gambetta, *Trust,* 73–93, at 83.

27. Bailey, "The Creation of Trust," 85.

28. Williams, "Formal Structures."

29. Roland N. McKean, "Economics of Trust, Altruism, and Corporate Responsibility," in Edmund S. Phelps, ed., *Altruism, Morality, and Economic Theory* (New York: Russell Sage, 1975): 29–44.

30. Luhmann, *Trust,* 8.

31. Kazuo Ishiguro, *The Remains of the Day* (New York: Vintage, 1990 [1989], 201.

32. Ibid., 243.

33. McKean, "Economics of Trust," 29. In context, this seems to be a claim about the trustworthiness of those we might trust.

Russell Hardin

34. Dasgupta, "Trust As a Commodity," 51, also 64; George Akerlof, "The Market for 'Lemons': Qualitative Uncertainty and the Market Mechanism," *Quarterly Journal of Economics* 84 (1970): 488–500; Kenneth J. Arrow, *The Limits of Organization* (New York: Norton, 1974).
35. Dunn, "Trust and Political Agency," 84.
36. Gambetta, *Trust*, 225.
37. Baier, "Trust and Antitrust"; Hardin, "Trusting Persons, Trusting Institutions."
38. The incidence of severe post-traumatic stress disorder (PTSD) may be extremely high among those abused at very young ages. A recent Dutch study found that 62% of women who were victims of childhood incest suffered PTSD. A control group of women with "ordinary negative life events" in childhood suffered no PTSD (Francine Albach and Walter Everaerd, "Posttraumatic Stress Symptoms in Victims of Childhood Incest," *Psychotherapy and Psychosomatics* 57 [1992]: 143–52). PTSD, first well studied in soldiers with grim combat experiences, now seems likely to afflict abused children and women even more heavily. For example, multiple personality disorder is thought to be a severe form of post-traumatic stress disorder after childhood abuse. A central problem of effective therapy is establishing trust with patients who do not readily trust ("Post-Traumatic Stress: Part II," *Harvard Mental Health Letter* 7, no. 9 [March 1991]: 1–4).
39. Gambetta, *Trust*, 230.
40. Ibid., 232.
41. Hardin, "Trusting Persons, Trusting Institutions," 187–88.
42. Robert Frank, "A Theory of Moral Sentiments," in Jane J. Mansbridge, ed., *Beyond Self-Interest* (Chicago: University of Chicago, 1990), 71–96.
43. Erikson, *Childhood and Society*, 249. John Bowlby and his co-workers have assumed that the child faces ethological constraints during development. For example, if language is not learned before a certain young age, it cannot be learned thereafter. So too, there might be developmental stages in attachment (Inge Bretherton, "The Origins of Attachment Theory: John Bowlby and Mary Ainsworth," *Development Psychology* 28 [1992]: 759–75, at 762) and trusting.
44. Dunn, "Trust and Political Agency," 73, 80; Luhmann, *Trust*, 19.
45. Baier, "Trust and Antitrust," 235.
46. Annette Baier, "What Do Women Want in a Moral Theory?" *Nous* 19 (1985): 53–64, at 61: also see Gambetta, *Trust*, 235.
47. Luhmann, *Trust*, 24.
48. Jimmy Carter's remarks at the Russell Sage Foundation, New York, September 24, 1992, during a brief account of an Atlanta project to reach the very poor.
49. Dunn, "Trust and Political Agency," 85; also see Luhmann, *Trust*, 88.
50. Luhmann, *Trust*, 4.
51. Luhmann, *Trust*, 72.
52. Perhaps this is the sense of Luhmann's (*Trust*, 74) claim that distrust is self-reinforcing: It does not generate enough information for the distruster to correct her or his view of possibilities.
53. This may be another ethological constraint on development (see n. 43 above).

54. This is a common theme in the trust literature, especially the social psychological literature. For example, see Robert L. Swinth, "The Establishment of the Trust Relationship," *Journal of Conflict Resolution* 11 (1967): 335–44.

55. Swinth, "Establishment of the Trust Relationship," 343.

56. Coleman, *Foundations of Social Theory*, 180–85.

57. Julian B. Rotter, "Interpersonal Trust, Trustworthiness, and Gullibility," *American Psychologist* 35 (1980): 1–7.

58. Other learning accounts might have similar implications.

59. Alejandro Portes and Julia Sensenbrenner, "Embeddedness and Immigration: Notes on the Social Determinants of Economic Action," *American Journal of Sociology* 98 (May 1993): 1320–50.

60. For example, Luhmann, "Familiarity, Confidence, Trust," 95.

61. Luhmann, *Trust*, 36.

62. Coleman, *Foundations of Social Theory*, 114.

63. Russell Hardin, "Hobbesian Political Order," *Political Theory* 19 (1991): 156–80.

64. Barber, *Logic and Limits of Trust*, 170.

65. McKean, "Economics of Trust," 31.

66. Anthony Pagden, "The Destruction of Trust and Its Economic Consequences in the Case of Eighteenth-Century Naples," in Gambetta, *Trust*, 127–41; see also, 162.

67. Gambetta, *Trust*, 163.

68. Ibid., 158.

69. Ibid., 159. There are other factors that further burden Sicilian society. For example, economic backwardness produces little opportunity for advancement. A standard way to advance is to prevail over others in one's own society—hence, advancement is a positional good (ibid., 163).

70. Coleman, *Foundations of Social Theory*, 92.

71. Luhmann speaks of trust as capital in a passage in which his subject seems not to be trust but, rather, trustworthiness (*Trust*, 64). One could straightforwardly invest in becoming trustworthy or in a reputation for trustworthiness. The appearance of trustworthiness may therefore be a capital asset in some cases. But to treat trust as human capital is confusing.

72. Coleman, *Foundations of Social Theory*.

73. For example, John L. Aguilar, "Trust and Exchange: Expressive and Instrumental Dimensions of Reciprocity in a Peasant Community," *Ethos* 12 (1984): 3–29.

2

Calculativeness, Trust, and Economic Organization*

Oliver E. Williamson

My main purpose in this article is to explicate what Diego Gambetta has referred to as "the elusive notion of trust."[1] As the literature on trust reveals, and as developed here, "trust" is a term with many meanings. The relentless application of calculative economic reasoning is the principal device that I employ to define and delimit the elusive notion of trust.

The calculative approach to economic organization is sketched in Section I. The concept of "calculative trust," which enjoys widespread and growing acceptance but with which I take exception, is examined in Section II. Societal trust, which works through the institutional environment and takes a series of hyphenated forms, is briefly treated in Section III. Nearly noncalculative uses of trust of a personal kind are developed in Section IV. Concluding remarks follow in Section V.

Calculativeness

As compared with the other social sciences, the economic approach to economic organization is decidedly more calculative. That is widely regarded as

* Presented at the John M. Olin Centennial Conference in Law and Economics at the University of Chicago Law School, April 7–9, 1992. The author is Transamerica Professor of Business, Economics, and Law, University of California, Berkeley. This article has benefitted from comments from the participants at the Institutional Analysis Workshop at the University of California, Berkeley, and at the Research Conference on Industrial Organization in Toulouse. The helpful comments of James March, Claude Menard, and Vai-Lam Mui are also acknowledged, as are those of my two discussants, Richard Craswell and Lars Stole, and the conference participants at Chicago.

both the distinctive strength and the Achilles' heel of economics. A failure to appreciate the limits of calculativeness purportedly gives rise to excesses, as a consequence of which economists are prone to make mistaken assessments of many economic phenomena.

I do not disagree, but I contend that the excesses to which calculativeness is sometimes given are usually remediable. I furthermore contend that the analytical reach of the calculative approach to economic organization is *extended rather than diminished by admitting to these limitations.* Once the excesses to which calculativeness is given are displayed and understood, the distortions can be anticipated and can thereafter be folded in at the design stage. A (more farsighted) calculative response to the (myopic) excesses of calculativeness thereby obtains. Provided that bounds on rationality are respected, calculativeness opens the door to a deeper understanding of economic organization.

Economics and the Contiguous Disciplines[2]

Applications of economic analysis and economic reasoning to the contiguous social sciences—principally law, political science, and sociology—have increased considerably in the past thirty years. To be sure, John R. Commons deserves credit for his early recognition that "law and economics" was a combined enterprise.[3] The institutional economics program with which he was involved enjoyed only limited success,[4] however, and the first concerted applications of economics to the law were mainly concentrated on antitrust.[5] That quickly changed after 1960 with the publication of Ronald Coase's "Social Cost" article[6] and Guido Calabresi's related work on torts.[7] Economics has since made its way into virtually every field of legal scholarship.[8]

The joinder of economics and political science has also undergone a significant transformation. Kenneth Arrow's work on social choice,[9] Anthony Downs's treatment of an economic theory of democracy,[10] Mancur Olson's logic of collection action,[11] and James Buchanan and Gordon Tullock's work on constitutions[12] were all implicated in this transformation. As recent conference volumes in the *Journal of Law, Economics, and Organization* make clear,[13] the use of economic reasoning to examine politics and political institutions has become widespread and, for some issues, even essential.

Economics and sociology bear a more distant relation to each other,[14] although this too has been changing, especially as the "rational choice" approach to sociology[15] has been taking shape. A wide gulf between them nevertheless needed to be bridged. Thus, Paul Samuelson distinguished economics and sociology in terms of their rationality orientations, with rationality being the domain of economics and nonrationality being relegated to sociology.[16] James Duesenberry subsequently quipped that economics was preoccupied with how individuals made choices, whereas sociology maintained that individuals did not have any choices to make.[17] Both George Homans[18] and Herbert Simon[19] protested that sociology had a stake in rationality analysis and could not accept this division of labor, but such a division persisted.

What, it might be asked, is behind the successes of economics in moving into law, political science, and sociology? Coase observes that what binds a group of scholars together is "one or more of the following: common techniques of analysis, a common theory or approach to a subject, or a common subject matter."[20] Although, in the short run, the use of certain techniques or a distinctive approach may provide the means by which economists are able to move successfully into another field,[21] Coase argues that the subject matter is decisive in the long run: "What economists study is the working of the social institutions which bind together the economic system: firms, markets for goods and services, labor markets, capital markets, the banking system, international trade, and so on. It is the common interest in these social institutions which distinguishes the economics profession."[22] He subsequently remarks, however, that it is because economists "study the economic system as a unified whole, ... [that they] are more likely to uncover the basic interrelationships within a social system than is someone less accustomed to looking at the working of a system as a whole. ... [Also, the] study of economics makes it difficult to ignore factors which are clearly important and which play a part in all social systems [such as relative prices]."[23]

These last remarks seem to me to be more an endorsement of the economic approach than of the economic subject matter. Be that as it may, the economic approach, rather than the subject matter, is what I emphasize here. Calculativeness is the general condition that I associate with the economic approach and with the progressive extension of economics into the related social sciences. (I view it as the strategy that Gary Becker[24] has applied so widely and effectively.)[25] Note in this connection that calculative economic reasoning can take several forms—of which price theory, property rights theory, agency theory, and transaction cost economics are all variants.[26]

Transaction Cost Economics

Institutional Economics. Institutional economics works at two levels of analysis. The macro variant, which is especially associated with the work of Douglass

North,[27] deals with the institutional environment. The micro variant deals with the institutions of governance. Lance Davis and North[28] distinguish between these two as follows (emphasis in original):

> The *institutional environment* is the set of fundamental political, social and legal ground rules that establishes the basis for production, exchange and distribution. Rules governing elections, property rights, and the right of contract are examples. . . .
>
> An *institutional arrangement* is an arrangement between economic units that governs the ways in which these units can cooperate and/or compete. It . . . [can] provide a structure within which its members can cooperate . . . or [it can] provide a mechanism that can effect a change in laws or property rights.

The way that I propose to join these two is to treat the institutional environment in which a transaction (or a related set of transactions) is embedded as a set of shift parameters, changes in which elicit shifts in the comparative costs of governance.[29] These issues are developed further in Section III below. My main purpose here is to examine the rudiments of governance.

Governance. Although hyperrationality has been responsible for some of the truly deep insights of economics, there is a need, at some stage, to describe "man as he is, acting within the constraints imposed by real institutions."[30] What are the key attributes of economic actors?

Opportunism and bounded rationality are the key behavioral assumptions on which transaction cost economics relies.[31] Bounded rationality is a cognitive assumption, according to which economic agents are "*intendedly* rational, but only *limitedly* so."[32] An immediate ramification of bounded rationality is that impossibly complex forms of economic organization (such as complete contingent-claims contracting)[33] are infeasible. Standing alone, that is a negative result. But there is more to it than that. If mind is a scarce resource,[34] then economizing on bounded rationality is warranted. This expands, rather than reduces, the range of issues to which the economic approach can be applied. Among other things, the "conscious, deliberate, purposeful" use of organization as a means by which to economize on bounded rationality is made endogenous.[35]

Opportunism is a self-interest-seeking assumption. By contrast with simple self-interest seeking, according to which economic agents will continuously consult their own preferences but will candidly disclose all pertinent information on inquiry and will reliably discharge all covenants, opportunistic agents are given to self-interest seeking with guile. Whether economic agents will tell the truth, the whole truth, and nothing but the truth and will reliably self-enforce covenants to behave "responsibly" are therefore problematic. Accordingly, "contract as promise" is fraught with hazards. Although that too is a negative result, again there is a positive research agenda.

The lessons of opportunism can be construed broadly or narrowly. The myopic construction is associated with Machiavelli, who advised his prince that he both could and should breach contracts with impunity.[36] By contrast, transaction cost economics advises that, once alerted to the *systematic hazards* of opportunism, the wise (farsighted) prince will both give and receive credible commitments. That more deeply calculative response permits superior deals to be made than could otherwise be supported.[37] Machiavellian grabbing is not implied if economic agents have a more farsighted understanding of the economic relation of which they are a part than myopic Machiavellianism ascribes to them.

Note, moreover, that the idea of credible commitments is a thoroughly hardheaded one. Contracts that have no need for added support (the "ideal" contracts of both law and economics)[38] will not be provided with them. More generally, contracts will be provided with added supports only in the degree to which these are cost-effective. Calculativeness is thus pervasive.

Taken together, the lessons of bounded rationality and opportunism lead to the following combined result: organize transactions so as to economize on bounded rationality while simultaneously safeguarding them against the hazards of opportunism. Not only do credible commitments arise when incomplete contracts are examined in their entirety, but complaints over obsessive calculativeness, truncated calculativeness, and anticalculativeness are mitigated as well.

Purported Excesses of Calculativeness

Obsessive Calculativeness. A calculative approach to economic organization can and sometimes does result in obsessive demands for control. One of the prescient lessons of sociology is that demands for control can have both intended and unintended effects and that unintended effects often have dysfunctional consequences.[39]

One possible response to this finding is to argue that the economic approach is flawed because of its preoccupation with intended effects to the neglect of unintended effects. But that assumes that the economic approach is unable or unwilling to take into account all relevant regularities whatsoever. If the deeper lesson is to design control systems with reference to all consequences—both those that are intended and those that were (originally) unanticipated—and if economics can implement this deeper lesson, then the claim that the economic approach is mindlessly given to obsessive calculativeness is overdrawn. The correct view is that a naive application of calculativeness can be and sometimes is given to excesses but that this is often remediable. On being informed about added consequences, these will be factored into the design exercise from the outset. (A calculative response to the excesses of calculativeness thereby obtains.)

Truncated Calculativeness. Many models of economic organization work out of truncated logic, according to which economic actors are assumed to be myopic. Aspects of the Keynesian macro model work out of a myopic logic. The same is true of the cobweb cycle,[40] barriers to entry arguments,[41] and the resource dependency approach to economic organization.[42]

Transaction cost economics responds to all of these conditions identically: although complex contracts are unavoidably incomplete, a farsighted approach to contract is often feasible. Many of the problems associated with truncated contracting are relieved in the process.

The differences between the resource dependency and credible commitment approaches to economic organization are illustrative. The resource dependency approach is concerned with power disparities that arise when contractual dependency comes as an unwanted surprise. That occurs frequently if myopic agents are unable to project and make provision for the Fundamental Transformation—according to which a large-numbers bidding situation at the outset is (sometimes) transformed into a small-numbers supply relation during contract execution and at the contract renewal interval.[43] If this transformation is unforeseen, then one of the parties may find itself at a power disadvantage in relation to the other after the initial contract has been agreed to.

Transaction cost economics employs an efficiency perspective and treats dependency as a (broadly) foreseeable condition. In the degree, therefore, to which asset specificity (which is responsible for bilateral dependency) yields benefits (added revenues and/or production cost savings) that are not more than offset by the added governance costs, added asset specificity is deliberately incurred. Accordingly, farsighted parties purposefully create bilateral dependency and support it with contractual safeguards, but only in the degree to which the associated investments are cost-effective. Because price, asset specificity, and contractual safeguards are all determined simultaneously, calculativeness is the solution to what would otherwise be a problem (unwanted resource dependency).

Anticalculativeness: Voice. Yet another view is that the calculative approach to economic organization emphasizes exit (the traditional economic means by which to express dissatisfaction) to the neglect of voice (which is associated with politics and is purportedly less calculative).[44] Transaction cost economics is sometimes held to be especially reprehensible.[45]

My response is twofold. First, if voice in the absence of an exit option is relatively ineffective, which evidently it is,[46] then voice really does have a calculative aspect. Second, voice works through mechanisms, and those mechanisms are often carefully designed.

Karl Llewellyn's view of contract as framework,[47] as against contract as legal rules, is pertinent (emphasis added): "[The] major importance of legal contract is to provide a framework for well-nigh every type of group organization and for well-nigh every type of passing or permanent relation between individuals and groups … a *framework highly adjustable*, a framework which almost never accurately indicates real working relations, but which affords a rough indication around which such relations vary, an occasional guide in cases of doubt, and a norm of *ultimate appeal* when the relations cease in fact to work."

Plainly, Llewellyn provides for voice: parties to a (bilaterally dependent) contract will try to work things out when confronted by unanticipated disturbances. Within a broad range, the contract serves as framework. Llewellyn nevertheless observes that the contract serves also as a norm of ultimate appeal if the parties are unable to reconcile their differences. An exit option is thereby preserved, but court ordering of the contract serves to delimit threat positions. Bargaining through voice is thus greatly influenced by knowledge that the terms of exit are defined by the contract.

But there is more to it than that. The voice mechanics are often defined by the terms of the contract. Consider the provisions in the thirty-two-year coal supply agreement[48] between the Nevada Power Company and the Northwest Trading Company:

In the event an inequitable condition occurs which adversely affects one Party, it shall be the joint and equal responsibility of both Parties to act promptly and in good faith to determine the action required to cure or adjust for the inequity and effectively to implement such action. Upon written claim of inequity served by one Party upon the other, the Parties shall act jointly to reach an agreement concerning the claimed inequity within sixty (60) days of the date of such written claim. An adjusted base coal price that differs from market price by more than ten percent (10%) shall constitute a hardship. The Party claiming inequity shall include in its claim such information and data as may be reasonably necessary to substantiate the claim and shall freely and without delay furnish such other information and data as the other Party reasonably may deem relevant and necessary. If the Parties cannot reach agreement within sixty (60) days the matter shall be submitted to arbitration.

Plainly, the procedures through which voice is expected to work are laid out in advance. Again, therefore, calculativeness is implicated in the design of ex post governance (voice).

As previously remarked, moreover, transaction cost economics maintains that ex post governance is aligned with the needs of transactions in a discriminating way. Some, but not all, transactions are provided with voice mechanisms. Specifically, classical transactions in which each party can go its own way without cost to the other will not be supported with voice.

The upshot is that calculativeness, albeit of a much richer and more varied kind than the orthodox exit-without-voice approach contemplates, applies throughout. The importance of voice is not in the least discredited. Instead, voice is encompassed within the extended calculative perspective.

Calculative Trust[49]

My purpose in this and the next two sections is to examine the aforementioned "elusive notion of trust."[50] That will be facilitated by examining a series of examples in which the terms trust and risk are used interchangeably—which has come to be standard practice in the social science literature—after which the simple contractual schema out of which transaction cost economics works is sketched. As set out there, transaction cost economics refers to contractual safeguards, or their absence, rather than trust, or its absence. I argue that it is redundant at best and can be misleading to use the term "trust" to describe commercial exchange for which cost-effective safeguards have been devised in support of more efficient exchange. Calculative trust is a contradiction in terms.

Trust as Risk

"Trust" is a good word. So is "risk." Social scientists have begun to describe situations of trust as "a subclass of those involving risk. They are situations in which the risk one takes depends on the performance of another actor."[51] According to this formulation, trust is warranted when the expected gain from placing oneself at risk to another is positive, but not otherwise. Indeed, the decision to accept such a risk is taken to imply trust.[52]

This theme is repeated throughout the influential seminar series organized by Gambetta and published under the title *Trust: Making and Breaking Coopera- tive Relations*. That volume closes with the following unifying observation:[53] "[T]here is a degree of convergence in the definition of trust which can be summarized as follows: trust ... is a particular level of the subjective prob- ability with which an agent assesses that another agent or group of agents will perform a particular action. ... When we say we trust someone or that someone is trustworthy, we implicitly mean that the probability that he will perform an action that is beneficial or at least not detrimental to us is high enough for us to consider engaging in some form of cooperation with him." Jeffrey Bradach and Robert Eccles expressly embrace this view in their recent treatment of "Price, Authority, and Trust" in the *Annual Review of Sociology*.[54]

As discussed below, David Kreps[55] and Partha Dasgupta[56] employ similar notions in their game theoretic treatments of trust. The upshot is that trust is purportedly made more transparent and operational by treating calculated trust as a subset of calculated risk.

James Coleman's chapter on "Relations of Trust" develops the rational choice approach to trust through three examples.[57] The first involves a Norwegian shipowner who is urgently seeking a £200,000 loan, thereby to release a ship of his that had undergone repairs in Amsterdam. The second involves the arrival of a farmer to a new area and the unexpected breakdown of his equipment. The third is that of an immigrant high school girl who lacked companionship in her new surroundings.

Confronted by the unwillingness of the Amsterdam shipyard to release his ship, the Norwegian shipowner telephoned his merchant banker, Hambros, in the City of London to arrange a loan. Within three minutes, the Hambros banker had arranged for an Amsterdam bank to deliver the money, whereupon the shipowner was told that his ship would be released. Coleman summarizes this case as follows:[58]

This case clearly involves trust. The manager of the Norwegian department at Hambros placed trust in the Norwegian shipowner who telephoned him—trust to the extent of £200,000 of Hambros's money. There was no contract signed, no paper involved in the transaction, nothing more substantial than the shipowner's intention to repay the money and the Hambros man's belief in both the shipowner's honesty and his ability to repay. Similarly, the bank in Amsterdam trusted Hambros to the extent of £200,000, again merely on the basis of a verbal request over the telephone. It committed £200,000 of its money on the assumption that Hambros would, on Monday morning, repay the sum.

The farmer example involves the breakdown of a hay baler and the prospect that the crop would be ruined by rain. This was avoided by a neighbor's offer to use his baler and to help bale the hay without charge. When the farmer who had received the assistance asked what was needed in return, he was told "all he wants is the gasoline it took to bale the hay." Coleman interprets this as the "placement of trust by the second farmer in the first—trust that in a situation of need or time of trouble, when he might call on the first farmer, that farmer would provide help, as he had in this case."[59]

The third example begins with the assent by a high school girl to be walked home by a boy. She further assented, at his request, to take a shortcut through the woods. He then made a sexual advance, which she resisted. She was thereupon roughed up and sexually assaulted. Coleman interprets this as "a special case of a special circumstance involving trust" in which weaker women place themselves at hazard where "[s]ometimes, as in this episode, that trust is misplaced."[60]

Another example that is widely believed to reflect trust is that of diamond dealers in New York City. Yoram Ben-Porath describes the relationship as one in which major deals are "sealed by a handshake."[61] Such deals would not be possible were it not for the prevalence of trust within the Jewish community. Interestingly, those conditions of trust are said to be undergoing a change. An elderly Israeli diamond dealer has described the changes as follows: "[W]hen I first entered the business, the conception was that truth and trust were simply the way to do business, and nobody decent would consider doing it differently. Although many transactions are still consummated on the basis of trust and truthfulness, this is done because these qualities are viewed as good for business, a way to make a profit."[62]

James Henlin's account of the decisions by cab drivers to pick up a fare or not is used by Craig Thomas[63] to illustrate "characteristic-based trust": "Since cabbies do not know anything specific about the prospective passenger based through past experiences with that person, they must make their decision to stop based on what they can infer from the setting, the physical appearance of the person, and the manner in which the person presents himself. Henlin ... argues that trust consists of an actor offering a definition of herself, and an audience choosing either to interact with (trust) or not to interact with (distrust)."

Recent game theoretic treatments of economic organization routinely refer to trust, usually in the context of parties engaged in sequential, repeated games. David Kreps's description of the game is typical. The basic setup is a one-sided version of the Prisoner's Dilemma game in which there is a sequence of two moves on every play of the game. First, Party X decides whether to put himself at hazard ("trust Y") or not ("do not trust Y"). If Party X accepts the hazard, then Party Y decides whether to take advantage of X ("abuse X's trust") or not ("honor X's trust"). The payoffs are such that the joint gain is maximized by the trust/honor outcome. But since Y's immediate gains are maximized if he abuses X's trust, the no-trust/no-play result will obtain if presented as a one-shot game.

Kreps thereupon converts the relation to a repeated game in which there is a high probability that each round will be followed by another. This changes the analysis "dramatically."[64] Say, for example, X tells Y, "I will begin by trusting you, hoping that you will honor that trust. Indeed, I will continue to trust you as long as you do not abuse that trust. But if ever you abuse that trust, I will never again trust you." If Y hears and believes that statement, and if the game is played repeatedly (with high probability), then the honor-trust arrangement is self-enforcing.[65] The commercial context notwithstanding, trust and honor are evidently what this game is all about.

Probably the most expansive treatment of trust in a gaming context is Partha Dasgupta's chapter on "Trust as a Commodity." He begins with the claim that "[t]rust is central to all transactions and yet economists rarely discuss the notion."[66] He elaborates as follows:[67] "For trust to be developed between individuals they must have repeated encounters, and they must have some memory of previous experiences. Moreover, for honesty to have potency as a concept there must be some *cost* involved in honest behavior. And finally, trust is linked with reputation, and reputation has to be acquired." Dasgupta further remarks that "[i]f the incentives are 'right,' even a trustworthy person can be relied upon to be untrustworthy."[68]

The Simple Contractual Schema

Risk entails exposure to probabilistic outcomes. If a gamble has two outcomes, good and bad, the utility valuation of each is G and B, respectively, and if the probability of a good outcome is q, then the expected utility of the gamble can be expressed as $V = qG + (1 - q)B$.

Actions can sometimes be taken to mitigate bad outcomes and/or enhance good outcomes. I will define competent calculativeness as a situation in which the affected parties (1) are aware of the range of possible outcomes and their associated probabilities, (2) take cost-effective actions to mitigate hazards and enhance benefits, (3) proceed with the transaction only if expected net gains can be projected, and, (4) if X can complete the transaction with any of several Ys, the transaction is assigned to that Y for which the largest net gain can be projected.[69]

Parties to such transactions understand a great deal about the contractual relation of which they are a part and manage it in a calculative way.[70] The simple contractual schema to which transaction cost economics makes repeated reference describes exchange as a triple (p, k, s), where p refers to the price at which the trade takes place, k refers to the hazards that are associated with the exchange, and s denotes the safeguards within which the exchange is embedded. The argument is that price, hazards, and safeguards are determined simultaneously.

The schematic and the values that each element in the vector take on are shown in Figure 1. As shown, Node A involves no hazards. The good or service in question is completely generic. Goods or services are exchanged now for prices paid now. This is the classical market exchange that Ian Macneil has described as "sharp in by clear agreement; sharp out by clear performance."[71]

It will facilitate comparisons to assume that suppliers are competitively organized and are risk neutral. The prices at which product will be supplied therefore reflect an expected break-even condition. The break-even price that is associated with Node A is p. There being no hazards, $k = 0$. And since safeguards are unneeded,[72] $s = 0$.

Node B is more interesting. The contractual hazard here is $\bar{k}$. If the buyer is unable or unwilling to provide a safeguard, then $s = 0$. The corresponding break-even price is $\bar{p}$.

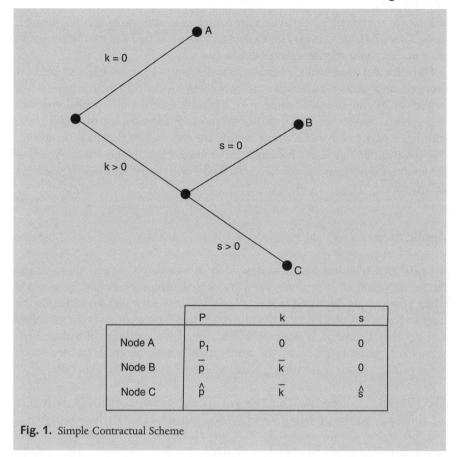

Fig. 1. Simple Contractual Scheme

Node C poses the same contractual hazard, namely, $\bar{k}$. In this case, however, a safeguard in amount $\hat{s}$ is provided. The break-even price that is projected under these conditions is $\hat{p}$. It is elementary[73] that $\hat{p} < \bar{p}$.

In the language of the Section above, Node A poses no risk, hence trust is unneeded. Nodes B and C, by contrast, do pose a risk. In the language of trust, Node B is the low-trust and Node C is the high-trust outcome.

Note that Bradach and Eccles contend that "mutual dependence [i.e., $k > 0$] between exchange partners ... [promotes] trust, [which] contrasts sharply with the argument central to transaction cost economics that ... dependence ... fosters opportunistic behavior."[74] What transaction cost economics says, however, is that because opportunistic agents will not self-enforce open-ended promises to behave responsibly, efficient exchange will be realized only if dependencies are supported by credible commitments. Wherein is trust implicated if parties to an exchange are farsighted and reflect the relevant hazards in the terms of the exchange? (A better price ($\hat{p} < \bar{p}$) will be offered if the hazards

Oliver E. Williamson

$(k > 0)$ are mitigated by cost-effective contractual safeguards $(s > 0)$.) Indeed, I maintain that trust is irrelevant to commercial exchange and that reference to trust in this connection promotes confusion.

Note further that while credible commitments deter breach and support more efficient exchange, breach is not wholly precluded. On the contrary, if it is inefficient to supply under some state realizations, then an optimal contract will project breach for those states. Whereas *efficient breach* of commercial contract is easy to reconcile with a calculative approach to contract, the notion that trust can be efficiently breached experiences considerable strain. Much of the contract law literature would be clarified if trust were consistently used in a delimited way.

Applications

If calculative relations are best described in calculative terms, then diffuse terms, of which trust is one, that have mixed meanings should be avoided when possible. As discussed below, all of the above examples save one can be interpreted in terms of efficiency and credibility. (The exception is the assaulted girl, but that, I contend, is not properly described as a condition of trust either.) Were my arguments to prevail, the word "trust" would hereafter be used much more cautiously—at least among social scientists, if not more generally.

The Norwegian Shipowner. The Norwegian shipowner required a loan. Let q_1, q_2, and q_3 be the probabilities of a good outcome (timely loan repayment and profitable future business) that are projected by the shipyard, the Amsterdam bank, and the London merchant banker (Hambros), respectively. Let G_1, G_2, and G_3 be the corresponding gains and B_1, B_2, and B_3 be the corresponding losses that each associates with dealing with the Norwegian shipowner directly. The expected net gains are then given by $V_i = q_i G_i + !(1 - q_i)B_i$. As I interpret Coleman, the reason why the Hambros deal went through, while the other two did not, is because $V_3 < 0$ (the merchant banker trusts) and $V_1 < 0$, $V_2 < 0$ (the shipyard and Amsterdam bank distrust). But that is not necessary. As a matter of good business practice, the Hambros deal should go through if $V_3 > 0$ and $V_3 > V_1$ and V_2.

On my interpretation, (1) all parties were calculative, (2) the loan was made by the party that projected the largest expected net gain, and (3) no trust is implied. That the merchant banker was best suited to bear the risk is, I conjecture, because it had the most knowledge of the shipowner and the best prospect of future business. Indeed, the Amsterdam shipbuilder may have the policy of never releasing ships without payment. That is not because he always projects a net negative outcome. Instead, his policy is one of efficient decision making in the context of the *system* of which shipbuilding is a part.[75] Shipbuilders know shipbuilding but have much less experience with and knowledge of clients' financial conditions, have less assurance of repeat business, and have less competence to pursue their claims for unpaid debts in court. Since the merchant banker is more well-suited in all of these respects, the shipbuilder adopts a policy whereby production is specialized to one party and financial risk is specialized to another.

Even assuming, arguendo, that the merchant banker in London was better suited than the Amsterdam bank or the shipbuilder to bear the risk, might not trust come in through knowledge possessed by the London banker of the personal integrity of the Norwegian shipowner? That is, in addition to the objective features mentioned above, might idiosyncratic knowledge of personal integrity also favor running the transaction through London? Is trust then implicated after all?

I would argue that the London banker's deep knowledge of the personal integrity of the Norwegian shipowner merely permitted him to improve his estimate of integrity. That the London banker has a better estimate, in this sense, does not imply that he has a more favorable estimate of the Norwegian shipowner's integrity. (Indeed, the London banker may refuse the loan because he knows the Norwegian shipowner to be a crook.) More generally, if N shipowners approach Hambros with the same request and only $M < N$ are approved, what are we to infer? I submit that calculativeness is determinative throughout and that invoking trust merely muddies the (clear) waters of calculativeness.

The Hay Baler. The hay baler case is one where issues of informal organization are posed. If accidents occur with stochastic regularity and if there is a great deal of indeterminacy in setting the price for emergency aid, then there are advantages to embedding these transactions in an institutional form in which quick responsiveness on nonexploitative terms will obtain. An informal, reciprocal aid mechanism is one possible institutional response.

Cheating is nevertheless a hazard. Sanctions are needed lest opportunistic farmers abuse informal supports. Thus, although almost all requests for emergency aid elicit quick and favorable responses, failures to reciprocate are not forgotten or forgiven and, if they persist, will elicit moral suasion and, eventually, sanctions—such as ostracism and refusals of assistance. The efficacy of informal organization thus turns on calculative supports. If almost-automatic and unpriced assistance is the most efficient response, provided that the practice in question is supported by sanctions and is ultimately made contingent on reciprocity, then calculativeness obtains and appeal to trust adds nothing.

The proviso that "the practice in question is supported by sanctions" is, however, crucial. In regions where informal organization delivers very weak sanctions, deferred payment schemes that rely on a reciprocal sense of responsibility will be less viable. Less "spontaneous" cooperation will therefore be observed and/or immediate payment will be expected (demanded) on providing emergency assistance.

Diamond Dealers. The appearance of trust among diamond dealers is deceptive. As Mark Granovetter observes, these transactions are "embedded in a close-knit community of diamond merchants who monitor one another's behavior closely."[76] Lisa Bernstein[77] elaborates:

What is unique about the diamond industry is not the importance of trust and reputation in commercial transactions, but rather the extent to which the industry is able to use reputation/social bonds at a cost low enough to be able to create a system of private law which enables most transactions to be consummated and most contracts enforced completely outside of the legal system. . . . This is accomplished in two main ways: (1) through the use of reputation bonds; (2) through a private arbitration system whose damage awards are not bounded by expectancy damages, and whose judgments are enforced by both reputation bonds and social pressure.

Put differently, Node C "trust relations" do not obtain because the diamond industry had the good luck to be organized by an ethnic community in which trust is pervasive. On the contrary, the Jewish ethnic community that organized this market succeeded because it was able to provide cost-effective sanctions more efficiently than rivals. Until recently, moreover, the efficacy of those sanctions[78] depended on restrictive entry: In the past, Jews formed a cohesive geographically concentrated social group in the countries in which they lived. Jewish law provided detailed substantive rules of commercial behavior, and the Jewish community provided an array of extralegal dispute resolution institutions. Non-Jews to whom the sanctions for rule violation were weak—hence, would follow the rules only if that suited their convenience—could not be admitted without jeopardy to the Node C condition.[79]

The organization of this industry has nevertheless been changing in response to new information and monitoring technologies. (Conceivably, the efficacy of ethnic sanctions may be weakening, too.) Despite resistance by "older dealers accustomed to dealing primarily with friends and long standing business acquaintances,"[80] new governance structures[81] are making headway: "Among the proposals currently being considered by the World Federation of Diamond Bourses are: setting up an international computer database with reports of arbitration judgments from all member bourses in an attempt to foster international uniformity in trade customs, and a rule requiring that every bourse be equipped with a fax machine for rapid transmission of credit worthiness information. Also under consideration, although staunchly opposed by many dealers, is the creation of an international computer database describing goods available for sale worldwide."

The change is akin to a new technology, where the need for learning-by-doing is reduced by the appearance of a standardized machine. In the diamonds case, a new information technology makes it possible to support greater dealer diversity. To be sure, ethnic identity within markets may still have value. But ethnic disparity between markets is now easier to support. To describe the earlier arrangement as a high-trust condition and the emerging arrangement as a low-trust condition confuses rather than illuminates. Both reflect calculativeness.

Put differently, it is a mistake to suppose that commercial trust has supplanted real trust. Rather, the basis for commercial trust has become more transparently calculative as new communication technologies have made inroads into this small trading community by making it possible to track commercial reputation effects in larger trading networks. As a consequence, the diamond market has become larger and more faceless.[82]

Cab Drivers. Cab drivers need to decide whether to pick up a fare or not. Although the probability assessment out of which they work is highly subjective (it reflects risk attitudes, knowledge of particular circumstances, and prior own—and indirect—experience), this is an altogether calculative exercise. There is no obvious value added by describing a decision to accept a risk (pick up a fare) as one of trust.

Game Theory. The "dramatic" change in the games described by Kreps comes about on moving from a one-shot game (where refusal to play was the rational choice) to a game that is repeated with high probability. Given the behavioral rules stipulated by Kreps, reputation effects relentlessly track those who breach contracts. Trading hazards are thus mitigated by embedding trades in networks in which reputation effects are known to work well.

Again, that can be interpreted as a Node C outcome. The parties have examined alternative trading scenarios and have opted for one in which the immediate gains of breach are deterred by the prospective loss of future business. To be sure, some markets are better able to support reputation effects than others. Reputation effects can and sometimes do break down[83] and are not therefore a trading panacea. Calculative assessments of the efficacy of reputation effects are, however, properly included within the efficient contracting exercise. Reference to trust adds nothing.

Oliver E. Williamson

Kreps might agree, but he could argue that this misconstrues his enterprise. What Kreps is really concerned with is the evolution of trading relationships— these being the product of learning, social conditioning, corporate culture, and the like. His use of the word "trust" is merely incidental. The intertemporal mechanisms are the key.

I am not only sympathetic with this line of argument, but I would call attention to the fact that the static schema in Figure 1 oversimplifies, in that it takes these types of intertemporal effects as given. I submit, however, that Kreps's use of the term "trust," especially as stated in the behavioral rules that he employs, obscures rather than illuminates these mechanisms. More micro-analytic attention to the *processes* through which trading relationships evolve[84] is indeed a rewarding research enterprise.

The Assaulted Girl. Consider finally the case of the assaulted girl and suppose that the matter is put to her in the abstract: should she take shortcuts through the woods with ostensibly friendly boys of slight acquaintance? I submit that the girl in question would assign a nontrivial probability to a bad outcome $(1 - q)$, and a large negative value to B. Even for large values of G, the expected net gain from such walks would commonly be negative. Posed therefore as an abstract policy decision, the rational choice result is this: do not walk in the woods with strangers.

People, however, often cross bridges when they come to them rather than develop an abstract policy in advance. Still, why did she make the "wrong" decision when faced with the particulars?

One possibility is that she did not have the time to work out the calculus. Another possibility is that she had the time but got rattled. Still another possibility is that there is a dynamics to the situation which complicated matters. She cannot simply say no but needs a reason, otherwise her negative response to a "friendly" invitation will appear to be antisocial. Lacking a previously prepared response such as "I am sorry but I cannot walk in the woods because my hay fever is bothering me," and not wanting to appear unfriendly, she takes a chance.

This last involves a two-stage net benefit calculus. The first stage is as described earlier and, if the expected net gain comes out positive, the person assents and events thereafter unfold. If, however, the first stage comes out net negative, then the issue of tactful refusal must be faced. If a tactful refusal quickly presents itself, then the first stage calculus rules. But if a tactful refusal cannot be devised, then a choice between two net negatives needs to be made. Is a blunt refusal, which gives offense and/or results in a reputation for unfriendliness, more or less negative than the projected net loss from accepting the invitation (taking the risk)? Expressed in this way, the assaulted girl was caught up in a coercive situation. She was confronted with a contingency for which she was not prepared, and the social forces coerced her into taking a risky choice.

Situations that are mainly explained by bounded rationality—the risk was taken because the girl did not get the calculus right or because she was not clever enough to devise a contrived but polite refusal on the spot—are not illuminated by appealing to trust.[85]

Hyphenated Trust

Opportunism and bounded rationality are the key behavioral assumptions on which transaction cost economics relies. That parsimonious description is suitable for some purposes. But if man, after all, is a "social animal," then socialization and social approvals and sanctions are also pertinent. How can these be accommodated?

My response is suggested, if not evident, from my discussions of embeddedness and the institutional environment above. The Norwegian shipowner was part of a network, the farmer and diamond dealers are part of a community, and the assaulted high school girl is presented with a coercive situation. More generally, the argument is that trading hazards vary not only with the attributes of transaction but also with the trading environment of which they are a part.

Although the environment is mainly taken as exogenous, calculativeness is not suspended but remains operative. That is because the need for transaction-specific safeguards (governance) varies systematically with the institutional environment within which transactions are located. Changes in the condition of the environment are therefore factored in—by adjusting transaction-specific governance in cost-effective ways. In effect, institutional environments that provide general purpose safeguards relieve the need for added transaction-specific supports. Accordingly, transactions that are viable in an institutional environment that provides strong safeguards may be nonviable in institutional environments that are weak—because it is not cost-effective for the parties to craft transaction-specific governance in the latter circumstances.

One should not, however, conclude that stronger environmental safeguards are always better than weaker. Not only can added environmental sanctions be pushed to dysfunctional extremes in purely commercial terms, but the environment can be oppressive more generally. My purpose here is merely to describe some of the contextual features with respect to which transaction-specific governance is crafted, rather than to prescribe an optimal institutional environment. Embeddedness attributes of six kinds are distinguished: societal culture, politics, regulation, professionalization, networks, and corporate culture.[86] Each can be thought of as institutional trust of a hyphenated kind: "societal-trust," "political-trust," and so forth.

Societal Culture

Culture applies to very large groups, sometimes an entire society, and involves very low levels of intentionality. The degree of trading trust in Japan, for example, is said to be much higher than in Great Britain.[87] By contrast, the villages in southern Italy described by Edward Banfield[88] are characterized by very low trading trust outside of the family.

The main import of culture, for purposes of economic organization, is that it serves as a check on opportunism. Social conditioning into a culture that condones lying and hypocrisy limits the efficacy of contract in three respects. First, social sanctions against strategic behavior (such as contrived breach) are weak. Second, court enforcement is problematic—since bribery is widespread. Third, individuals feel slight remorse when they behave in opportunistic ways. Given the added hazards, transactions will tend to be of a more generic (Node A, spot market) kind in societies where cultural checks on opportunism are weak, ceteris paribus.

Politics

Legislative and judicial autonomy serve credibility purposes. As Harold Berman observes, credibility will be enhanced if a monarch who has made the law "may not make it arbitrarily, and until he has remade it—lawfully—he is bound by it."[89] Self-denying ordinances and, even more, inertia that have been crafted into the political process have commitment benefits.[90]

That this had not fully registered on Eastern Europe and the Soviet Union is suggested by the following remarks of Mikhail Gorbachev (advising U.S. firms to invest quickly in the Soviet Union rather than wait): "Those [companies] who are with us now have good prospects of participating in our great country ... [whereas those who wait] will remain observers for years to come—*we will see to it*."[91] That the leadership of the Soviet Union "will see to it" that early and late movers will be rewarded and punished, respectively, reflects conventional carrot-and-stick incentive reasoning. What it misses is that ready access to administrative discretion is the source of contractual hazard. The paradox is that fewer degrees of freedom (rules) can have advantages over more (discretion) because added credible commitments can obtain in this way. Effective economic reform thus requires that political reneging options be foreclosed if investor confidence is to be realized.

Regulation

As Victor Goldberg[92] and Lynne Zucker[93] have explained, regulation can serve to infuse trading confidence into otherwise problematic trading relations. The creation and administration of a regulatory agency are both very intentional acts—although that is not to say that regulation does not have a (spontaneous) life of its own.[94] Provided that the regulation in question is "appropriate," both parties to the transaction—the regulated firm and its customers—will be prepared to make investments in specialized assets on better terms than they would in the absence of such regulation.

Professionalization

The obligation to fulfill the definition of a role is especially important for professionals—physicians, lawyers, teachers, and so on. Although these roles generally arise in a spontaneous (evolutionary) manner, they are thereafter supported by entry limitations (such as licensing), specific ethical codes, added fiduciary obligations,[95] and professional sanctions. Such support features are highly intentional. They can have the effect of infusing trading confidence into transactions that are characterized by costly information asymmetries, although sometimes the (intentionality) purposes served are strategic.[96]

Networks

The diamond dealers described above are an example of a trading network. So are the network forms of organization that have recently appeared in northern Italy.[97] Other ethnic trading groups also qualify.[98] Although many of these networks have spontaneous origins, the maintenance of these networks depends on the perfection of intentional trading rules, the enforcement of sanctions, and the like. Credibility turns on whether these reputation effects work well or poorly.

Corporate Culture

The above-described features of the institutional environment are popula-tion-level effects, mainly of a spontaneous kind. Corporate culture displays both spontaneous and intentional features and works mainly within particular organizations. Informal organization[99] is one example; the use of focal points[100] is another.

Barnard argued that formal and informal organization always and everywhere coexist[101] and that informal organization contributes to the viability of formal organization in three significant respects: "One of the indispensable functions of informal organizations in formal organizations ... [is] that of communication. ... Another function is that of maintaining the cohesiveness in formal organizations through regulating the willingness to serve and the stability of objective authority. A third function is the maintenance of the feeling of personal integrity, of selfrespect, and independent choice."[102] That has turned out to be a productive formulation. Economic activity will be better organized where there is an appreciation for and intentional use of informal organization.

Internal effects spill over, moreover, onto external trade if firms take on distinctive trading reputations by reason of the corporate culture through which they come to be known and evaluated.[103] Whether added corporate culture is warranted, however, varies with the circumstance: "In general, it will be crucially important to align culture with the sorts of contingencies that are likely to arise."[104] Accordingly, calculativeness characterizes even such apparently "soft" notions as corporate culture, of which Japanese economic organization is an example.[105]

Nearly Noncalculative Trust

Just as it is mind-boggling to contemplate hyperrationality of a comprehensive contracting kind, so is it mind-boggling to contemplate the absence of calculativeness. That is not to say that calculativeness cannot be suppressed or to deny that some actions or individuals are more spontaneous than others. Indeed, I shall argue that it is sometimes desirable to suppress calculativeness. If, however, the decision to suppress calculativeness is itself purposive and calculative, then the true absence of calculativeness is rare if not nonexistent.[106]

Unable to foreclose some shred of calculativeness in the personal trust relations described here, I describe personal trust as nearly noncalculative. The argument proceeds in two stages. Discrete structural analysis, with special reference to the economics of atmosphere, is discussed first. Personal trust is then examined.

Discrete Structural Analysis

A colleague noted that the economics of atmosphere plays a larger role in *Markets and Hierarchies*[107] than in *The Economic Institutions of Capitalism*[108] and asked about the de-emphasis. I replied that I thought atmosphere at least as important to an understanding of economic organization in 1985 as I had in 1975. Not having made more headway, however, I had little to add.

One of the lessons of the economics of atmosphere is that calculativeness can be taken to dysfunctional extremes. That can show up within governance structures as well as between them. The employment relation is one such context.

Suppose that a job can be split into a series of separable functions. Suppose further that differential metering at the margin is attempted with reference to each. What are the consequences?

If functional separability does not imply attitudinal separability, then piecemeal calculativeness can easily be dysfunctional. The risk is that pushing metering at the margin everywhere to the limit will have spillover effects from easy-to-meter onto hard-to-meter activities. If cooperative attitudes are impaired, then transactions that can be metered only with difficulty, but for which consummate cooperation is important, will be discharged in a more perfunctory manner. The neglect of such interaction effects is encouraged by piecemeal calculativeness, which is to say by an insensitivity to atmosphere.

A related issue is the matter of externalities. The question may be put as follows: ought all externalities to be metered that, taken separately, can be metered with net gains? Presumably, this turns partly on whether secondary effects obtain when an externality is accorded legitimacy. All kinds of grievances may be "felt," and demands for compensation made accordingly, if what had hitherto been considered to be harmless by-products of normal social intercourse are suddenly declared to be compensable injuries. The transformation of relationships that will ensue can easily lead to a lower level of felt satisfaction among the parties than prevailed previously—at least transitionally and possibly permanently.

Part of the explanation is that filing claims for petty injuries influences attitudes toward other transactions. My insistence on compensation for A leads you to file claims for B, C, and D, which induces me to seek compensation for E and F, and so on. Although an efficiency gain might be realized were it possible to isolate transaction A, the overall impact can easily be negative. Realizing this to be the case, some individuals would be prepared to overlook such injuries. But everyone is not similarly constituted. Society is rearranged to the advantage of those who demand more exacting correspondences between rewards and deeds if metering at the margin is everywhere attempted. Were the issue of compensation to be taken up as a constitutional matter, rather than on a case-by-case basis, a greater tolerance for spillover would commonly obtain.[109]

Also pertinent is that individuals keep informal social accounts and find the exchange of reciprocal favors among parties with whom uncompensated spillovers exist to be satisfying.[110] Transforming these casual social accounts into exact and legal obligations may well be destructive of atmosphere and lead to a net loss of satisfaction between the parties. Put differently, pervasive pecuniary relations impair the quality of "contracting"—even if the metering of the transactions in question were costless.[111]

The argument that emerges from the above is not that metering ought to be prohibited but that the calculative approach to organization that is associated with economics can be taken to extremes. An awareness of attitudinal spillovers and nonpecuniary satisfactions serves to check such excesses of calculativeness. Consider now a more extreme possibility: there are some transactions for which the optimal level of *conscious* metering is zero.[112]

The idea here is that conscious monitoring, even of a low-grade kind, introduces unwanted calculativeness that is contrary to the spirit of certain very special relations and poses intertemporal threats to their viability. Not only can intendedly noncalculative relations be upset by a Type I error, according to which a true relation is incorrectly classified as false, but calculativeness may be subject to (involuntary) positive feed-back. Intendedly noncalculative relations that are continuously subject to being reclassified as calculative are, in effect, calculative.

Issues akin to those examined by Robert Nozick in his discussion of "Love's Bond" are implicated.[113] Nozick contends that the idea of "trading up" is inimical to a loving relationship: "The intention in love is to form a *we* and to identify with it as an extended self, to identify one's fortunes in large part with its fortunes. A willingness to trade up, to destroy the *we* you largely identify with, would then be a willingness to destroy yourself in the form of your own extended self" (emphasis in original).[114] If entertaining the possibility of trading up devalues the relation, a discrete structural shift that disallows trading up, which is a variety of calculativeness, is needed.

Personal Trust

John Dunn's recent treatment of "Trust and Political Agency"[115] raises many of the pertinent issues. Thus, Dunn distinguishes between trust as a "human passion" and trust as a "modality of human action," where the latter is "a more or less consciously chosen policy for handling the freedom of other human agents or agencies."[116] He subsequently remarks that "trust as a passion is the confident expectation of benign intentions by another agent," but as a "modality of action, ... trust is ineluctably strategic."[117] He also contends that "the twin of trust is betrayal"[118] and avers that "human beings need, as far as they can, to economize on trust in persons and confide instead in well--designed political, social, and economic institutions."[119]

Trust as a passion versus trust as a modality corresponds in my treatment to personal trust and calculative trust, respectfully. Moreover, Dunn's characterization of calculative trust as strategic, whereas personal trust is not, is exactly right. But whereas Dunn contends that the twin of trust is betrayal, I would reserve betrayal for personal trust and would use breach of contract to describe calculative relations. As hitherto remarked, breach of contract is sometimes efficient, even in a commercial contract that is supported by perfect safeguards.[120] By contrast, betrayal of a personal trust can never be efficient. Betrayal is demoralizing.

Also, although I subscribe to the notion of economizing on trust, I would put the issue somewhat differently. Trust, I submit, should be concentrated on those personal relations in which it really matters, which will be facilitated by the use of "political, social, and economic institutions" to govern calculative relations.[121]

If calculativeness is inimical to personal trust, in that a deep and abiding trust relation cannot be created in the face of calculativeness, and if preexisting personal trust is devalued by calculativeness, then the question is how to segregate and preserve relations of personal trust.[122] I will take it that X reposes personal trust in Y if X (1) consciously refuses to monitor Y, (2) is predisposed to ascribe good intentions to Y when things go wrong, and (3) treats Y in a discrete structural way. Conditions 1 and 3 limit calculativeness. Under condition 2, "bad outcomes" are given a favorable construction: they are interpreted by X as stochastic events, or as complexity (Y didn't fully understand the situation), or as peccadillos (Y was inebriated).

To be sure, there are limits. An event where Y unambiguously violates the trust that X reposes in him threatens the relationship. Also (and here is where calculativeness creeps back in), a succession of minor violations may jeopardize the condition of trust. What further distinguishes personal trust, however, is that X insists that Y "reform" rather than merely "do better." That is because experience rating with continuous updating of the trustworthiness of Y places X in a calculative relation to Y. That degrades the relationship. Rather than do that, X elevates the relationship by placing it on all-or-none terms. Should Y refuse to make a discrete structural break with his past, then X will no longer trust him.[123] If instead Y agrees to reform, then trust will be renewed.

Personal trust is therefore characterized by (1) the absence of monitoring, (2) favorable or forgiving predilections, and (3) discreteness. Such relations are clearly very special. Although some individuals may have the natural instincts to behave noncalculatively, others will need to figure it out—to look ahead and recognize that calculativeness will devalue the relation, which is a farsighted view of contract. It does not, moreover, suffice merely to figure it out, in that some of those who do may be unable to shed calculativeness—because calculativeness (or fear) is so deeply etched by their experience.[124] Be that as it may, trust, if it obtains at all, is reserved for very special relations between family, friends, and lovers. Such trust is also the stuff of which tragedy is made. It goes to the essence of the human condition.[125]

Concluding Remarks

Linguistic and Conceptual Tools

A case can be made, and I will assume here, that a science of organization is in progress.[126] The development of "specialized vocabularies" and "new languages" commonly attend such a project.[127]

The development of a science of administration,[128] which was Simon's objective in *Administrative Behavior*,[129] posed exactly those needs. Given the deep insights afforded by Chester Barnard's path-breaking book *The Functions of the Executive*,[130] how could that project be advanced? Simon observed in this connection that "we do not yet have, in this field, adequate linguistic and conceptual tools for realistically and significantly describing even a simple administrative organization—describing it, that is, in a way that will provide the basis for scientific analysis of the effectiveness of its structure and operation."[131] The need, as he saw it, was to "be able to describe, in words, exactly how an administrative organization looks and how it works. . . . I have attempted to construct a vocabulary which will permit such a description."[132]

Calculativeness

The way in which human actors are described and the processes through which contracting is perceived to work are both crucial to the development of a science of organization. Human actors are described here as boundedly rational and opportunistic, while the contracting process entails "incomplete contracting in its entirety."[133] This last views the governance of contractual relations broadly, including an examination of the systems context within which contracts are embedded. A very calculative orientation to commercial contracting is the result.

Such a farsighted approach to contract (in which credible commitments, or the lack thereof, play a key role) collides with sociological views on power and trust. As James March has observed, power is a diffuse and disappointing concept.[134] I contend that the same is true of trust. The recent tendency for sociologists and economists alike to use the terms "trust" and "risk" interchangeably is, on the arguments advanced here, ill-advised.

Not only is "calculated trust" a contradiction in terms, but user-friendly terms, of which "trust" is one, have an additional cost. The world of commerce is reorganized in favor of the cynics, as against the innocents, when social scientists employ user-friendly language that is not descriptively accurate—since only the innocents are taken in. Commercial contracting will be better served if parties are cognizant of the embeddedness conditions of which they are a part and recognize, mitigate, and price out contractual hazards in a discriminating way.[135]

Categories of Trust

Without purporting to be exhaustive, trust differences of three types are distinguished: calculative trust, personal trust, and institutional (or hyphenated) trust. For the reasons given above, calculative relations should be described in calculative terms, to which the language of risk is exactly suited. The practice of using "trust" and "risk" interchangeably should therefore be discontinued.

Personal trust is made nearly noncalculative by switching out of a regime in which the marginal calculus applies into one of a discrete structural kind. That often requires added effort and is warranted only for very special personal relations that would be seriously degraded if a calculative orientation were "permitted." Commercial relations do not qualify.[136]

Institutional trust refers to the social and organizational context within which contracts are embedded. In the degree to which the relevant institutional features are exogenous, institutional trust has the appearance of being noncalculative. In fact, however, transactions are always organized (governed) with reference to the institutional context (environment) of which they are a part. Calculativeness thus always reappears.[137]

Should these arguments prevail, trust will hereafter be reserved for noncalculative personal relations (and, possibly, in a hyphenated form, to describe differences in the institutional environment). Although this is a long article to reach such a modest result, the literature on trust is truly enormous, and the confusions associated with calculativeness are growing. The incipient science of organization needs common concepts and language as the productive dialogue between law, economics, and organization takes shape. The irony is that the limits on calculativeness are realized by examining user-friendly terms—of which "trust" is one—in a thoroughly calculative way.

Notes

1. Diego Gambetta, Can We Trust Trust? in Trust: Making and Breaking Cooperative Relations, at p. ix (Diego Gambetta ed. 1988).
2. The heading is borrowed from Ronald Coases's article on this subject, Economics and Contiguous Disciplines, 7 J. Legal Stud. 201 (1978).
3. See John R. Commons, Legal Foundations of Capitalism (1924); and John R. Commons, Law and Economics, 34 Yale L. J. 371 (1925).
4. The most significant contribution to law and economics stemming from the Commons's tradition is his book Legal Foundations of Capitalism, *supra* note 3. Albeit important, older-style institutional economics became embroiled in methodological controversy and failed to develop a research agenda to rival orthodoxy (see George Stigler's remarks appearing in Edmund W. Kitch, The Fire of Truth: A Remembrance of Law and Economics at Chicago, 1932–1970, 26 J. Law & Econ. 163, 170 (1983)). Some concluded, too harshly I think, that the work of American institutionalists "led to nothing ... [since] without a theory, they had nothing to pass on" (Ronald H. Coase, The New Institutional Economics, 140 J. Inst. & Theor. Econ. 229, 230 (1984)).
5. Richard A. Posner, The Chicago School of Antitrust Analysis, 127 U. Pa. L. Rev. 925 (1979).
6. Ronald H. Coase, The Problem of Social Cost, 3 J. Law & Econ. 1 (1960).
7. Guido Calabresi, Some Thoughts on Risk Distribution and the Law of Torts, 70 Yale L. J. 499 (1961).
8. Richard A. Posner, Economic Analysis of Law (1977).
9. Kenneth J. Arrow, Social Choice and Individual Values (1951).
10. Anthony Downs, An Economic Theory of Democracy (1957).
11. Mancur Olson, The Logic of Collective Action (1965).
12. James Buchanan & Gordon Tullock, The Calculus of Consent (1964).
13. The 1990 conference volume is entitled "The Organization of Political Institutions," while the 1992 conference volume deals with "The Economics and Politics of Administrative Law and Procedures."
14. Much of the distance between economics and sociology appears to be attributable to the need for sociology, as a new discipline, to define itself in such a way as to avoid confrontation with economics, from which it had been spun off. See Richard Swedberg, Economic Sociology: Past and Present, 35 Current Soc. 1 (1987).
15. See James Coleman, Foundations of Social Theory (1990); Siegwart Lindenberg, Homo Socio-oeconomicus: The Emergence of a General Model of Man in the Social Sciences, 146 J. Inst. & Theor. Econ. 727 (1990); and Michael Hecter, Principles of Group Solidarity (1987).
16. Paul Samuelson, Foundations of Economic Analysis (1947).
17. James Duesenberry, An Economic Analysis of Fertility: Comment, in Demographic and Economic Change in Developed Countries 233 (1960).
18. George Homans, Social Behavior as Exchange, 62 Am. J. Social. 597 (1958).

19. Herbert Simon, Rationality as Product and Process of Thought, 68 Am. Econ. Rev. 1 (1978).

20. Coase, *supra* note 2, at 204.

21. *Id.*

22. *Id.* at 206–7.

23. *Id.* at 209–10.

24. Gary Becker. The Economic Approach to Human Behavior (1976).

25. Note that there are real differences between the incomplete contracting approach out of which transaction cost economics works, in which bounded rationality is featured, and the optimality setup out of which Becker works. Herbert Simon, however, takes exception with both. Becker is scored for excesses of hyperrationality (Simon, *supra* note 19, at 2), while I am scored for using an incomplete contracting setup for which empirical support is purportedly lacking (Herbert Simon, Organization and Markets, 5 J. Econ. Persp. 25, 26–27 (1991)). Becker is his own best agent. As for myself, I would observe that empirical work in transaction cost economics is much greater than Simon indicates (see Oliver E. Williamson, The Economic Institutions of Capitalism (1985), ch. 5; Paul Joskow, Asset Specificity and the Structure of Vertical Relationships: Empirical Evidence, 4 J. L. Econ. & Org. 95 (1988); Paul Joskow, The Role of Transaction Cost Economics in Antitrust and Public Utility Regulatory Policies, 7 J. L. Econ. & Org. 53 (1991); and Howard Shelanski, Empirical Research in Transaction Cost Economics: A Survey and Assessment (unpublished manuscript, Univ. California, Berkeley 1991)) and is growing exponentially. Joskow concludes that the empirical research in transaction cost economics "is in much better shape than much of the empirical work in industrial organization generally" (The Role of Transaction Cost Economics, *supra*, at 81)—to which, however, he quickly adds that more and better theoretical and empirical work is needed: "[T]here is no rest for the weary" (*id.* at 82). I concur.

26. Note in this connection is that the massive expansion of economic reasoning out of antitrust law into the law more generally had transaction cost economics origins (Coase, *supra* note 6). Many of the initial applications of economic reasoning to economic organization also rely, directly and indirectly, on transaction cost arguments (Arrow, *supra* note 9; Kenneth J. Arrow, The Organization of Economic Activity: Issues Pertinent to the Choice of Market versus Nonmarket Allocation, in 1 U.S. Joint Economic Committee, 91st Cong., 1st Sess., The Analysis and Evaluation of Public Expenditure: The PPB System 59 (1969); Oliver E. Williamson, Markets and Hierarchies: Analysis and Antitrust Implications (1975); Armen Alchian & Harold Demsetz, Production, Information Costs, and Economic Organization, 62 Am. Econ. Rev. 777 (1972); and Michael Jensen & William Meckling, Theory of the Firm, 3 J. Fin. Econ. 305 (1976)).

27. Douglass North, Institutions, 5 J. Econ. Persp. 97 (1991).

28. Lance E. Davis & Douglass C. North, Institutional Change and American Economic Growth 6–7 (1971).

29. Oliver E. Williamson, Comparative Economic Organization: The Analysis of Discrete Structural Alternatives, 36 Admin. Sci. Q. 269 (1991).

30. Coase, *supra* note 4, at 231.
31. The aspect of bounded rationality that is most frequently emphasized is that of limited cognitive competence, on which account irrationality or satisficing are often thought to be implied. Intended (but limited) rationality, however, is a broader concept. Not only are intendedly rational agents attempting effectively to cope, whence irrationality (except, perhaps, for certain pathological cases) is not implied, but satisficing is merely one manifestation of coping. The satisficing approach, which appeals to psychology and works out of an aspiration level mechanics, has not found wide application within economics (Robert Aumann, What Is Game Theory Trying to Accomplish? in Frontiers of Economics 35 (Kenneth Arrow & Seppo Honkapohja eds. 1985)). Also see Kenneth Arrow, Reflections on the Essays, in Arrow and the Foundations of the Theory of Economic Policy 734 (George Feiwel ed. 1987).
32. Herbert Simon, Administrative Behavior, at p. xxiv (2nd edn. 1957).
33. Roy Radner, Competitive Equilibrium under Uncertainty, 36 Econometrica 31 (1968).
34. Simon, *supra* note 19, at 12.
35. Chester Barnard, The Functions of the Executive 4 (15th printing 1962) (1st printing 1938).
36. Niccolò Machiavelli, The Prince 92–93 (1952).
37. See Oliver E. Williamson, Credible Commitments: Using Hostages to Support Exchange, 73 Am. Econ. Rev. 519 (1983). The remarks of Richard Dawkins about conscious foresight, expressed in the context of selfish genes, are pertinent (Richard Dawkins, The Selfish Gene 215 (1976)):

    One unique feature of man ... [is] his capacity for conscious foresight. Selfish genes ... have no foresight.

    [Thus] even if we look on the dark side and assume that individual man is fundamentally selfish, our conscious foresight ... could save us from the worst selfish excesses of the blind replicators. We have at least the mental equipment to foster our long-term selfish interests rather than merely our short-term selfish interests. We can see the long-term benefits of participating ... and we can sit down to discuss ways of making ... [agreements] work.

38. Ian Macneil, The Many Futures of Contract, 47 S. Cal. L. Rev. 691 (1974), at 738.
39. See Robert Merton, The Unanticipated Consequences of Purposive Social Action, I Am. Social. Rev. 894 (1936); James G. March & Herbert Simon, Organizations (1958).
40. Ronald H. Coase & Ronald Fowler, Bacon Production and the Pig Cycle in Great Britain, 2 Economica 142 (1935).
41. George Stigler, The Organization of Industry (1968).
42. See Jeffrey Pfeffer & Gerald Salancik, The External Control of Organizations (1978); and Jeffrey Pfeffer, Power in Organizations (1981).
43. Williamson, *supra* note 25, at 61–63.
44. Albert O. Hirschman, Exit, Voice and Loyalty (1970).
45. See Mark Granovetter, Economic Action and Social Structure: The Problem of Embeddedness, 91 Am. J. Sociol. 481 (1985); and Mark Granovetter, The

Sociological and Economic Approaches to Labor Market Analysis, in Industries, Firms, and Jobs (George Farkas & Paula England eds. 1988).

46. Hirschman, *supra* note 44.

47. Karl N. Llewellyn, What Price Contract? An Essay in Perspective, 40 Yale L. J. 704, 736–37 (1931).

48. Reproduced from Williamson, *supra* note 25, at 164–65.

49. There is an enormous literature on trust. Some of that will be apparent from the discussion. For a more expansive survey, see Craig Thomas, Public Trust in Organizations and Institutions: A Sociological Perspective (1991).

50. Gambetta, *supra* note 1, at ix.

51. Coleman, *supra* note 15, at 91.

52. *Id.* at 105.

53. Gambetta, *supra* note 1, at 217.

54. Jeffrey Bradach & Robert Eccles, Price, Authority, and Trust, 15 Am. Rev. Sociol. 97 (1989).

55. David M. Kreps, Corporate Culture and Economic Theory, in Perspectives on Positive Political Economy (James Alt & Kenneth Shepsle eds. 1990).

56. Partha Dasgupta, Trust as a Commodity, in Gambetta ed., *supra* note 1, at 49.

57. Coleman, *supra* note 15.

58. *Id.* at 92.

59. *Id.* at 93.

60. *Id.* at 94.

61. Yoram Ben-Porath, The F-Connection: Families, Friends, and Firms and the Organization of Exchange. 6 Population & Dev. Rev. 1 (1980).

62. Quoted in Lisa Bernstein, The Choice between Public and Private Law. (Discussion paper No. 70, Harvard Law School, Program in Law and Economics, 1990), at 38.

63. Thomas, *supra* note 49, at 22.

64. Kreps, *supra* note 55, at 102.

65. *Id.* at 103.

66. Dasgupta, *supra* note 56, at 49.

67. *Id.* at 59.

68. *Id.* at 54.

69. This may appear to be indistinguishable from maximizing—at least if due allowance is made for (1) the incompleteness of contracting, (2) the crude quality of information, and (3) discrete choices. For a discussion of satisficing versus maximizing, see Oliver Williamson, Transaction Cost Economics and Organization Theory, 2 Indus. & Corp. Change 165 (1993).

70. Pervasive calculativeness notwithstanding, the rhetoric of exchange often employs the language of promises, trust, favors, and cooperativeness. That is understandable, in that the artful use of language can produce deals that would be scuttled by abrasive calculativeness. If, however, the basic deal is shaped by objective factors, then calculativeness (credibility, hazards, safeguards, net benefits) is where the crucial action resides.

71. Macneil, *supra* note 38, at 738.

72. Another way of putting it is that (transition problems aside) each party can go its own way without cost to the other. Competition provides a safeguard.

73. For a more systematic development, see Williamson, *supra* note 37. For related empirical work, see Scott Masten & Keith Crocker, Efficient Adaptation in Long-Term Contracts: Take or Pay Provisions for Natural Gas, 75 Am. Econ. Rev. 1085 (1985), and the surveys reported by Paul Joskow, *supra* note 25.

74. Bradach & Eccles, *supra* note 54, at 111.

75. The main systems argument is in the text. But there is another possibility. Shipbuilders (or, more generally, businessmen—as opposed to bankers) are optimistic fellows, on which account they project subjective probabilities for good outcomes that exceed the objective conditions. Refusing to release ships may be a good policy for bringing such excesses of optimism under control. An important but little remarked purpose of having "firm but arbitrary" policies is to protect parties against idiosyncratic appeals.

76. Granovetter, Economic Action and Social Structure, *supra* note 45, at 492.

77. Bernstein, *supra* note 62, at 35–36.

78. *Id.* at 41.

79. The question of endgames sometimes arises. If Jews do not defect on the last play, does that imply that trust is operative after all? I would respond negatively if retired Jews remain in their community (in which event they would be subject to sanctions) or have active religious consciences. The contrast between a retiring Jew who remains within the community and the illicit deal related by Dostoyevsky in *The Brothers Karamozov* is instructive. Russell Hardin (Trusting Persons, Trusting Institutions, in Strategy and Choice 185 (Richard J. Zeckhauser ed. 1991)) retells that event as follows:

> [A] lieutenant colonel ... managed substantial sums of money on behalf of the army. Immediately after each periodic audit of his books, he took the available funds to the merchant Trifonov, who soon returned them with interest and a gift. In effect, both the lieutenant colonel and Trifonov benefited from funds that would otherwise have lain idle, producing no benefit for anyone. Because it was highly irregular, theirs was a secret exchange that depended wholly on personal trust not backed by the law of contracts. When the day came that the lieutenant colonel was to be abruptly replaced in his command, he asked Trifonov to return the last sum, 4,500 rubles, entrusted to him.
>
> Trifonov replied, "I've never received any money from you, and couldn't possibly have received any."

Although Hardin describes the relation between the lieutenant colonel and Trifonov as "personal trust," I submit that Trifonov did view (and the lieutenant colonel should have viewed) the relation calculatively—as a self-enforcing contract to which no legal or social sanctions apply (Lester Telser, A Theory of Self-enforcing Agreements, 53 J. Bus. 27 (1981)).

80. Bernstein, *supra* note 62, at 42.

81. *Id.* at 43.

82. Ethnic groups that greatly prefer continued trading within an identifiable membership, but whose costs are great in comparison with the new alternative, may need to accept lower compensation to be competitively viable, ceteris paribus.

83. See Kreps, *supra* note 55; Bernard Williams, Formal Structure and Social Reality, in Gambetta ed., *supra* note 1, at 14; Oliver E. Williamson, Economic Institutions: Spontaneous and Intentional Governance, 7 J. L. Econ. & Org. 159 (1991).

84. See Kenneth J. Arrow, Uncertainty and the Welfare Economics of Medical Care, 53 Am. Econ. Rev. 941 (1963); Kreps, *supra* note 55 (and see Section IIIF below); and John Orbell & Robyn Dawes, A "Cognitive Miser" Theory of Cooperators' Advantage, 85 Am. Polit. Sci. Rev. 515 (1991).

85. To be sure, individuals trapped in coercive situations are attempting to cope. Is it really useful, however, to interpret a bad outcome from a coercive event as a bad draw? It is more instructive, I submit, to regard coercive events as a special class of problems that "invite" people to make risky choices from which they should be shielded (for example, by protecting them against exposure to coercive situations—possibly through training, possibly through draconian penalties against those who contrive coercion). Becker's recent treatment of addiction affords a somewhat different perspective—see Gary Becker, Habits, Addictions, and Traditions (unpublished manuscript, Univ. Chicago 1991).

86. For more expansive discussions of the institutional environment, see Lynne Zucker, Production of Trust: Institutional Sources of Economic Structure, 1849–1920, 6 Res. Org. Behav. 53 (1986); Susan Shapiro, The Social Control of Impersonal Trust, 93 Am. J. Sociol. 623 (1987); and Thomas, *supra* note 49.

87. Ronald Dore, Goodwill and the Spirit of Market Capitalism, 39 Brit. J. Soc. 459 (1983).

88. E. C. Banfield, The Moral Basis of a Backward Society (1958).

89. Harold Berman, Law and Revolution (1983).

90. Douglass North & Barry Weingast, Constitutions and Commitment: The Evolution of Institutions Governing Public Choice in 17th Century England, 49 J. Econ. Hist. 803 (1989).

91. Quoted from the International Herald Tribune, June 5, 1990, at 5; emphasis added.

92. Victor Goldberg, Toward an Expanded Economic Theory of Contract, 10 J. Econ. Issues 45 (1976).

93. Zucker, *Supra* note 86.

94. Marver Bernstein, Regulating Business by Independent Commission (1955).

95. Fiduciary obligations arise in the context of information asymmetries where the less informed party is exposed to serious losses by failures of "due care."

96. Arrow, *supra* note 84.

97. S. Mariotti & G. Cainara, The Evolution of Transaction Governance in the Textile-Clothing Industry, 7 J. Econ. Behav. & Org. 351 (1986).

98. Janet T. Landa, A Theory of the Ethnically Homogeneous Middleman Group: An Institutional Alternative to Contract Law, 10 J. Legal Stud. 349 (1981).

99. Barnard, *supra* note 35.

100. Kreps, *supra* note 55.

101. Barnard, *supra* note 35, at 20.

102. *Id*. at 122.

103. Kreps, *supra* note 55.
104. *Id.* at 128.
105. Oliver E. Williamson, Strategizing, Economizing, and Economic Organization, 12 Strategic Mgt. J. 75 (1991).
106. Conceivably, some situations are so complicated that we decide to throw darts or examine entrails. But we are attempting to cope nonetheless. My discussion assumes that noncontingently selfless behavior of a Good Samaritan kind is the exception.
107. Williamson, *supra* note 26.
108. Williamson, *supra* note 25.
109. Thomas Schelling, Micromotives and Macrobehavior (1978).
110. A. W. Goulder, Industrial Bureaucracy (1954).
111. The buying of "rounds" in English pubs is an example. Would a costless meter lead to a superior result? Suppose that everyone privately disclosed a willingness to pay and that successive bids were solicited until a break-even result was projected. Suppose that the results of the final solicitation are either kept secret or posted, depending on preferences, and that rounds are thereafter delivered to the table on request. Monthly bills are sent out in accordance with the break-even condition. How is camaraderie effected?
112. Unconscious or subconscious metering is another problem. Observations that are not consciously processed may be processed by the subconscious nonetheless, and their ramifications may insistently intrude on consciousness.
113. Robert Nozick, An Examined Life (1988), ch. 8, Love's Bond.
114. *Id.* at 78.
115. John Dunn, Trust and Political Agency, in Gambetta ed., *supra* note 1, at 73.
116. *Id.* at 73.
117. *Id.* at 74.
118. *Id.* at 81.
119. *Id.* at 85.
120. Williamson, *supra* note 37.
121. Dennis Robertson's remark is pertinent: "[I]f we economists mind our own business, and do that business well, we can, I believe, contribute mightily to the economizing, that is to the full but thrifty utilization, of that scarce resource Love—which *we* know, just as well as anybody else, to be the most precious thing in the world" (Dennis Robertson, What Does the Economist Economize? in Economic Commentaries 154 (1976)).
122. There is nonetheless a sense in which incomplete contracts are continuously calculative, and that is in relation to reputation effects. If one party cannot make significant commercial moves without notice of the other—even moves that have no direct bearing on the immediate contract but involve different contracts with different trading partners—then continuous Bayesian updating may "ineluctably" obtain. In that event, reputation effects are pervasive (Kreps, *supra* note 55).
123. That does not mean that X will no longer have anything to do with Y. If, however, the relation continues, X will thereafter treat Y in a calculative way.

Note in this connection that any shred of calculativeness does not imply that the relation is calculative. Rather, calculativeness needs to cross some (rather low) threshold before the relation is classified as calculative. The line is drawn—that is, a discrete structural break occurs—where X asks Y to reform.

124. Joseph Raz makes a related argument: some people "fail to see that personal relations cannot be valued in terms of commodities" (Joseph Raz, The Morality of Freedom 353 (1986)).

125. See Nozick, *supra* note 113. Note that to repose trust in someone does not imply confidence in their judgment. Rather, as Dunn (*supra* note 115) has put it, to trust is to ascribe benign intent. Selective delegation is consistent with trust if the judgment of the trusted delegatee is believed to be better in some contexts than in others.

126. See Oliver E. Williamson, Chester Barnard, and the Incipient Science of Organization, in Organization Theory (Oliver Williamson ed. 1990); as well as Williamson, *supra* note 29; and the special issue on The New Science of Organization, 7 J. L. Econ. & Org. 1 (1991).

127. Thomas S. Kuhn, The Structure of Scientific Revolutions 203–4 (1970).

128. A science of organization deals with markets, hybrids, hierarchies, bureaucracies, and the like, whereas the science of administration is preoccupied with internal organization.

129. Simon, *supra* note 32, at 44, 248–53.

130. Barnard, *supra* note 35.

131. Simon, *supra* note 32, at xlv.

132. Id.

133. This phrase is my own.

134. James G. March, Decisions and Organizations 6 (1988).

135. This is not to deny the excesses of calculativeness that sociologists (for example, Merton, *supra* note 39) and contract law specialists (for example, Stewart Macauley, Noncontractual Relations in Business, 28 Am. Soc. Rev. 55 (1963)) have forcefully called to our attention. Transaction cost economics takes a farsighted view of contract in which "feasible" calculativeness is featured.

136. I subscribe to the proposition that "[t]he core idea of trust is that it is not based on an expectation of its justification. When trust is justified by expectations of positive reciprocal consequences, it is simply another version of economic exchange" (James March & Johan Olsen, Rediscovering Institutions 27 (1989)).

137. Also, the parties to a transaction sometimes influence the context, the capture (Bernstein, *supra* note 94) or precapture (George Stigler, The Theory of Economic Regulation, 2 Bell J. Econ. 3 (1971)) of regulation being examples.

3 An Integrative Model of Organizational Trust

Roger C. Mayer, James H. Davis, and
F. David Schoorman

The topic of trust is generating increased interest in organizational studies. Gambetta (1988) noted that "scholars tend to mention [trust] in passing, to allude to it as a fundamental ingredient or lubricant, an un-avoidable dimension of social interaction, only to move on to deal with less intractable matters" (unnumbered foreword). The importance of trust has been cited in such areas as communication (Giffin, 1967), leadership (Atwater, 1988), management by objectives (Scott, D., 1980), negotiation (Bazerman, 1994), game theory (Milgrom & Roberts, 1992), performance appraisal (Cummings, 1983), labor-management relations (Taylor, 1989), and implementation of self-managed work teams (Lawler, 1992).

Although a great deal of interest in trust has been expressed by scholars, its study in organizations has remained problematic for several reasons: problems with the definition of trust itself; lack of clarity in the relationship between risk and trust; confusion between trust and its antecedents and outcomes; lack of specificity of trust referents leading to confusion in levels of analysis; and a failure to consider both the trusting party and the party to be trusted. The purpose of this article is to illuminate and resolve these problems in the presentation of a model of trust of one individual for another. Through this model we propose that this level of trust and the level of perceived risk in the situation will lead to risk taking in the relationship.

Need for Trust

Working together often involves interdependence, and people must therefore depend on others in various ways to accomplish their personal and organizational goals. Several theories have emerged that describe mechanisms for minimizing the risk inherent in working relationships. These theories are designed to regulate, to enforce, and/or to encourage compliance to avoid the consequences of broken trust. In order to avoid self-serving behaviors as well as potential litigation, many firms utilize control mechanisms and contracts, and they alter their decision-making processes, internal processes, reward systems, and structures (Jensen & Meckling, 1976; Meyer, 1983; Sitkin & Bies, 1994; Williamson, 1975). Legalistic remedies have been described as weak, impersonal substitutes for trust (Sitkin & Roth, 1993), which may bring organizational legitimacy, yet often are ineffective (Argyris, 1994; Donaldson & Davis, 1991; Granovetter, 1985; Sitkin & Roth, 1993).

Current trends in both workforce composition and the organization of the workplace in the United States suggest that the importance of trust is likely to increase during the coming years. One important trend in workforce composition is the increase in diversity. Jamieson and O'Mara (1991) projected that the minority share of the workforce will grow from 17 percent in the late 1980s to over 25 percent by the year 2000. Jackson and Alvarez (1992) pointed out that increases in workforce diversity necessitate that people with very different backgrounds come into contact and deal closely with one another. A diverse workforce is less able to rely on interpersonal similarity and common background and experience to contribute to mutual attraction and enhance the willingness to work together (Berscheid & Walster, 1978; Newcomb, 1956). In this context, the development of mutual trust provides one mechanism for enabling employees to work together more effectively.

Another trend related to changes in the organization of work also will lead to an increased interest in the study of trust. Lawler (1992) cited continuing changes in the workplace in the direction of more participative management styles and the implementation of work teams. A recent survey indicates that 27 percent of American companies are implementing self-directed work teams in some part of the organization (Wellins, Byham, & Wilson, 1991). The emergence of self-directed teams and a reliance on empowered workers greatly increase the importance of the concept of trust (Golembiewski & McConkie, 1975; Larson & LaFasto, 1989) as control mechanisms are reduced or removed and interaction increases.

The trends just cited suggest that the development of a model of trust in organizations is both timely and practical. In the use of self-directed teams, trust must take the place of supervision because direct observation of employees becomes impractical. Further, a clear understanding of trust and its causes can facilitate cohesion and collaboration between people by building trust through means other than interpersonal similarity. In spite of the growing importance of trust, a number of institutions that measure trust have witnessed diminishing trust among employees (Farnham, 1989).

One of the difficulties that has hindered previous research on trust has been a lack of clear differentiation among factors that contribute to trust, trust itself, and outcomes of trust (Cook & Wall, 1980; Kee & Knox, 1970). Without this clear distinction, the difference between trust and similar constructs is blurred. For example, many researchers have agreed with Deutsch (1958) that risk, or having something invested, is requisite to trust. The *need* for trust only arises in a risky situation. Although numerous authors have recognized the importance of risk to understanding trust (Coleman, 1990; Giffin, 1967; Good, 1988; Lewis & Weigert, 1985; Luhmann, 1988; March & Shapira, 1987; Riker, 1974; Schlenker, Helm, & Tedeschi, 1973), no consensus on its relationship with trust exists. It is unclear whether risk is an antecedent to trust, is trust, or is an outcome of trust. This key issue of how risk fits with trust must be resolved, and it is dealt with later in this article. The model developed in this article complements the risk literature by clarifying the role of interpersonal trust in risk taking. A parsimonious model (James, Mulaik, & Brett, 1982; Runkel & Mc-Grath, 1972) with a manageable number of factors should provide a solid foundation for the empirical study of trust for another party.

Each of the essential trust issues that have just been described will be explored as a model of dyadic trust is developed. Although there is a growing body of literature in social psychology that examines trust in dating and other such relationships (e.g., Larzelere & Huston, 1980), the nature and bases of such relationships may be different from those in organizations. Thus, the model developed here is designed to focus on trust in an organizational setting involving two specific parties: a trusting party (trustor) and a party to be trusted (trustee) (Driscoll, 1978; Scott, C. L., 1980). The model explicitly encompasses factors about both the trustor and the trustee, which previous models have neglected. This relationship-specific boundary condition of our approach is important, because a number of authors have dealt with trust for generalized others (e.g., Rotter, 1967) and trust as a social phenomenon (e.g., Lewis & Weigert, 1985). Even though such approaches help provide a general sense of the considerations involved in trust, they do not clarify the relationship between two specific individuals and the reasons why a trustor would trust a trustee. Further, the failure to clearly specify the trustor and the trustee encourages the tendency to change referents and even levels of analysis, which obfuscates the nature of the trust relationship.

In the following sections, the definition of trust developed from our research is presented, and it is differentiated from similar constructs. Next, characteristics of both the trustor and the trustee, which affect the amount of trust the trustor has for the trustee, are considered. Following that, the relationship of trust and risk is considered. Finally, the effects of context as well as the long-term development of trust are considered.

Definition of Trust

Johnson-George and Swap (1982: 1306) asserted that "willingness to take risks may be one of the few characteristics common to all trust situations." Kee and Knox (1970) argued that to appropriately study trust there must be some meaningful incentives at stake and that the trustor must be cognizant of the risk involved. The definition of *trust* proposed in this research is the *willingness of a party to be vulnerable to the actions of another party based on the expectation that the other will perform a particular action important to the trustor, irrespective of the ability to monitor or control that other party.* This definition of trust is applicable to a relationship with another identifiable party who is perceived to act and react with volition toward the trustor. This definition parallels that of Gambetta (1988), with the critical addition of vulnerability. Being vulnerable (Boss, 1978; Zand, 1972) implies that there is something of importance to be lost. Making oneself vulnerable is taking risk. Trust is not taking risk *per se*, but rather it is a *willingness* to take risk. This distinction will be further explored in a later section.

Several terms have been used synonymously with trust, and this has obfuscated the nature of trust. Among these are *cooperation, confidence,* and *predictability.* The sections that follow differentiate trust from these constructs.

Cooperation

One conceptual difficulty with studying trust is that it has often been confused with cooperation (Bateson, 1988). For instance, Gambetta (1988: 217) asserted that trusting someone means "the probability that he will perform an action that is beneficial or at least not detrimental to us is high enough for us to consider engaging in some form of cooperation with him." The distinction of trust from cooperation is unclear.

Although trust can frequently lead to cooperative behavior, trust is not a necessary condition for cooperation to occur, because *cooperation does not necessarily put a party at risk.* An employee could cooperate with and, indeed, even appear to act like he or she trusts another employee who he or she does not trust. However, the reason for the cooperation may be due to a powerful manager who is clearly expected to punish the other employee for any act that damages the focal employee's interests. The focal employee may cooperate with and appear to trust the other employee, but his or her actions are due to a lack of perceived risk. Such means as control mechanisms and lack of available alternatives may lead a party to cooperate, even in the absence of trust. As Gambetta stated, "As the high incidence of paranoid behaviour among dictators suggests, coercion can be *self-defeating*, for while it may enforce 'cooperation' in specific acts, it also increases the probability of treacherous ones: betrayal, defection, and the classic stab in the back" (1988: 220).

Kee and Knox (1970) also concluded that there were a number of reasons why individuals may be observed to act in cooperative or competitive fashions that are not reflective of the level of trust in the relationship. For example, a person may not be able to avoid a situation structured like the prisoner's dilemma. His or her behavior may appear to be trusting, but it is based on other motives or rationales.

Even though trust and cooperation have at times been treated as synonymous, it is important to distinguish between them. You can cooperate with someone who you don't really trust. If there are external control mechanisms that will punish the trustee for deceitful behavior, if the issue at hand doesn't involve vulnerability to the trustor over issues that matter, or if it's clear that the trustee's motives will lead him or her to behave in a way that coincides with the trustor's desires, then there can be cooperation without trust. In each of these cases, vulnerability is minimal or absent.

Confidence

The relationship between confidence and trust is amorphous in the literature on trust. For example, Deutsch (1960) considered the reasons why one person would trust another person to produce some beneficial events. The "individual must have *confidence* that the other individual has the ability and intention to produce it" (Deutsch, 1960: 125). Cook and Wall (1980: 39) defined *trust* as "the extent to which one is willing to ascribe good intentions to and have *confidence* in the words and actions of other people." A number of other authors have not clearly distinguished between the two (e.g., Coleman, 1990; Frost, Stimpson, & Maughan, 1978; Jones, James, & Bruni, 1975).

Luhmann (1988) proposed a distinction that helps to differentiate trust from confidence. He asserted that both concepts refer to expectations that may lead to disappointment. Luhmann argued that trust differs from confidence because it requires a previous engagement on a person's part, recognizing and accepting that risk exists. Although Luhmann suggested that both confidence and trust may become routine, the distinction "depends on perception and attribution. If you do not consider alternatives (every morning you leave the house without a weapon!), you are in a situation of confidence. If you choose one action in preference to others in spite of the possibility of being disappointed by the action of others, you define the situation as one of trust" (1988: 102).

Luhmann's differentiation between trust and confidence recognizes that in the former risk must be recognized and assumed, and such is not the case with confidence. The trustor's explicit recognition of risk within our model precludes the conceptual ambiguity present in the research just cited.

Predictability

There is clearly a relationship between predictability and trust, but, again, the association is ambiguous. Both prediction and trust are means of uncertainty reduction (Lewis & Weigert, 1985). However, much of the literature tends to equate predictability with trust. For example, Gabarro (1978: 294) cited several definitions of trust, including "the extent to which one person can expect predictability in the other's behavior in terms of what is 'normally' expected of a person acting in good faith." Several other theorists have defined trust in ways that also appear to overlap substantially with predictability (Dasgupta, 1988; Gambetta, 1988; Good, 1988; Rotter, 1967).

To be meaningful, trust must go beyond predictability (Deutsch, 1958). To equate the two is to suggest that a party who can be expected to consistently ignore the needs of others and act in a self-interested fashion is therefore trusted, because the party is predictable. What is missing from such an approach is the willingness to take a risk in the relationship and to be vulnerable. One can believe such a trustee to be predictable in a situation in which the trustee influences resource distribution between the trustee and the trustor but also be unwilling to be vulnerable to that trustee.

Another party's predictability is insufficient to make a person willing to take a risk. If a person's superior always "shoots the messenger" when bad news is delivered, the superior is predictable. However, this predictability will not increase the likelihood that the individual will take a risk and deliver bad news. On the contrary, predictability can reduce the likelihood that the individual will trust and therefore take actions that allow vulnerability to the superior.

Predictability might best be thought of as influencing cooperation. If one expects that a party will predictably behave positively, one will be disposed to cooperate with the party. However, the reason for that predictability may be external to the party, such as strong control mechanisms (Friedland, 1990).

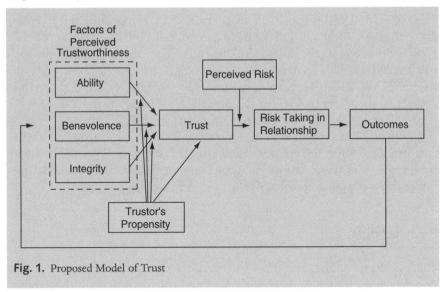

Fig. 1. Proposed Model of Trust

Without those mechanisms, a person may be unwilling to be vulnerable to the party. Thus, predictability is insufficient to trust.

The previous section dealt with the nature of trust itself, differentiating it from similar constructs. The following sections of this paper deal first with factors concerning the trustor and then the trustee that lead to trust. These components of the model can be seen in Figure 1.

Characteristics of the Trustor

One factor that will affect the trust one party has for another involves traits of the trustor. Some parties are more likely to trust than are others. As discussed in this section, several authors have considered trust from the perspective of a person's general willingness to trust others.

Among the early trust theorists was Rotter (1967: 651), who defined *interpersonal trust* "as an expectancy held by an individual or a group that the word, promise, verbal or written statement of another individual or group can be relied upon." Although his definition appears to suggest the author is speaking of trust for a specific referent, Rotter's widely used measure focuses on a generalized trust of others—something akin to a personality trait that a person would presumably carry from one situation to another. For example, typical items in his scale are "In dealing with strangers one is better off to be cautious until they have provided evidence that they are trustworthy" and "Parents usually can be relied upon to keep their promises."

Several other authors have discussed trust in similar ways. For example, Dasgupta's treatment of trust includes generalized expectations of others; for example, "Can I trust *people* to come to my rescue if I am about to drown?" (1988: 53; emphasis added). Similarly, Farris, Senner, and Butterfield (1973: 145) defined trust as "a personality trait of people interacting with peripheral environment of an organization." In this approach trust is viewed as a trait that leads to a generalized expectation about the trustworthiness of others. In the proposed model this trait is referred to as the *propensity to trust*.

Propensity to trust is proposed to be a stable within-party factor that will affect the likelihood the party will trust. People differ in their inherent propensity to trust. Propensity might be thought of as the *general willingness to trust others*. Propensity will influence how much trust one has for a trustee prior to data on that particular party being available. People with different developmental experiences, personality types, and cultural backgrounds vary in their propensity to trust (e.g., Hofstede, 1980). An example of an extreme case of this is what is commonly called blind trust. Some individuals can be observed to repeatedly trust in situations that most people would agree do not warrant trust. Conversely, others are unwilling to trust in most situations, regardless of circumstances that would support doing so.

Some evidence exists that this dispositional approach is worth pursuing. For example, using Rotter's (1967) measure, Conlon and Mayer (1994) found the willingness to trust others was significantly related to the behavior and performance of persons working in an agency simulation. Other researchers also have found this dispositional trust factor to be related to behaviors of interest in organizational research (e.g., Moore, Shaffer, Pollak, & Taylor-Lemcke, 1987; Sabatelli, Buck, & Dreyer, 1983). Propensity should contribute to the explanation of variance in trust if used as a part of a more complete set of variables.

Propensity to trust is similar to Sitkin and Pablo's (1992) definition of propensity in their model of the determinants of risk behavior. They define *risk propensity* as "the tendency of a decision maker either to take or avoid risks" (1992: 12). However, our approach differs in that propensity to trust others is viewed as a trait that is stable across situations, whereas according to Sitkin and Pablo's approach, risk propensity is more situation specific, affected both by personality characteristics (i.e., risk preference) and situational factors (i.e., inertia and outcome history).

Proposition 1. The higher the trustor's propensity to trust, the higher the trust for a trustee prior to availability of information about the trustee.

Even though an understanding of trust necessitates consideration of the trust propensity of the trustor, a given trustor has varied levels of trust for various trustees. Thus, propensity is by itself insufficient. To address this variance, in the next section we examine the characteristics of the trustee.

Characteristics of the Trustee: The Concept of Trustworthiness

One approach to understanding why a given party will have a greater or lesser amount of trust for another party is to consider attributes of the trustee. Ring and Van de Ven (1992) argued that because of the risk in transactions, managers must concern themselves with the trustworthiness of the other party. A number of authors have considered why a party will be judged as trustworthy.

Some of the earliest research on characteristics of the trustee was conducted by Hovland, Janis, and Kelley (1953) in the famous Yale studies on communication and attitude change. According to these researchers, credibility was affected by two factors: expertise and trustworthiness. Trustworthiness was assessed as the motivation (or lack thereof) to lie. For example, if the trustee had something to gain by lying, he or she would be seen as less trustworthy.

In more recent work, Good (1988) suggested that trust is based on expectations of how another person will behave, based on that person's current and previous implicit and explicit claims. Similarly, Lieberman (1981) stated that trust in fiduciary relationships is based on a belief in the professional's competence and integrity. Examination of the items in Johnson-George and Swap's (1982) measure of trust reveals that they reflect inferences about the trustee.

All of these authors have suggested that characteristics and actions of the trustee will lead that person to be more or less trusted. These characteristics are important if researchers are to understand why some parties are more trusted than others. In the remainder of this section, three characteristics of the trustee that determine trustworthiness are examined. Although they are not trust per se, these variables help build the foundation for the development of trust.

The Factors of Trustworthiness

Conditions that lead to trust have been considered repeatedly in the literature. Some authors identify a single trustee characteristic that is responsible for trust (e.g., Strickland, 1958), whereas other authors delineate as many as 10 characteristics (e.g., Butler, 1991). A review of factors that lead to trust is summarized in Table 1. Even though a number of factors have been proposed, three

Table 1. Trust Antecedents

Authors	Antecedent Factors
Boyle & Bonacich (1970)	Past interactions, index of caution based on prisoners' dilemma outcomes
Butler (1991)	Availability, competence, consistency, discreetness, fairness, integrity, loyalty, openness, promise fulfillment, receptivity
Cook & Wall (1980)	Trustworthy intentions, ability
Dasgupta (1988)	Credible threat of punishment, credibility of promises
Deutsch (1960)	Ability, intention to produce
Farris, Senner, & Butterfield (1973)	Openness, ownership of feelings, experimentation with new behavior, group norms
Frost, Stimpson, & Maughan (1978)	Dependence on trustee, altruism
Gabarro (1978)	Openness, previous outcomes
Giffin (1967)	Expertness, reliability as information source, intentions, dynamism, personal attraction, reputation
Good (1988)	Ability, intention, trustees' claims about how (they) will behave
Hart, Capps, Cangemi, & Caillouet (1986)	Openness/congruity, shared values, autonomy/feedback
Hovland, Janis, & Kelley (1953)	Expertise, motivation to lie
Johnson-George & Swap (1982)	Reliability
Jones, James, & Bruni (1975)	Ability, behavior is relevant to the individual's needs and desires
Kee & Knox (1970)	Competence, motives
Larzelere & Huston (1980)	Benevolence, honesty
Lieberman (1981)	Competence, integrity
Mishra (In press)	Competence, openness, caring, reliability
Ring & Van de Ven (1992)	Moral integrity, goodwill
Rosen & Jerdee (1977)	Judgment or competence, group goals
Sitkin & Roth (1993)	Ability, value congruence
Solomon (1960)	Benevolence
Strickland (1958)	Benevolence

characteristics of a trustee appear often in the literature: ability, benevolence, and integrity. As a set, these three appear to explain a major portion of trustworthiness.[1] Each contributes a unique perceptual perspective from which to consider the trustee, while the set provides a solid and parsimonious foundation for the empirical study of trust for another party.

Ability

Ability is that group of skills, competencies, and characteristics that enable a party to have influence within some specific domain. The domain of the ability is specific because the trustee may be highly competent in some technical area, affording that person trust on tasks related to that area. However, the trustee may have little aptitude, training, or experience in another area, for instance, in interpersonal communication. Although such an individual may be trusted to do analytic tasks related to his or her technical area, the individual may not be trusted to initiate contact with an important customer. Thus, trust is domain specific (Zand, 1972).

A number of theorists have discussed similar constructs as affecting trust, using several synonyms. Cook and Wall (1980), Deutsch (1960), Jones, James, and Bruni (1975), and Sitkin and Roth (1993) all considered *ability* an essential element of trust. Others (e.g., Butler, 1991; Butler & Cantrell, 1984; Kee & Knox, 1970; Lieberman, 1981; Mishra, In press; Rosen & Jerdee, 1977) used the word *competence* to define a similar construct. In the Yale studies described previously, *perceived expertise* was identified as a critical characteristic of the trustee. Similarly, Giffin (1967) suggested expertness as a factor that leads to trust. Finally, Gabarro (1978) identified nine bases of trust, including functional/specific competence, interpersonal competence, business sense, and judgment. All of these are similar to *ability* in the current conceptualization. Whereas such terms as *expertise* and *competence* connote a set of skills applicable to a single, fixed domain (e.g., Gabarro's interpersonal competence), *ability* highlights the task- and situation-specific nature of the construct in the current model.

Benevolence

Benevolence is the extent to which a trustee is believed to want to do good *to the trustor*, aside from an egocentric profit motive. Benevolence suggests that the trustee has some specific attachment to the trustor. An example of this attachment is the relationship between a mentor (trustee) and a protégé (trustor). The mentor wants to help the protégé, even though the mentor is not required to be helpful, and there is no extrinsic reward for the mentor. Benevolence is the perception of a positive orientation of the trustee toward the trustor.

A number of researchers have included characteristics similar to benevolence as a basis for trust. Hovland and colleagues (1953) described trustworthiness in terms of the trustee's motivation to lie. This idea is clearly consistent with the view that perceived benevolence plays an important role in the assessment of trustworthiness, in that high benevolence in a relationship would be inversely related to motivation to lie. Several authors have used the term *benevolence* in their analyses of trust, focusing on the specific relationship with the trustor (Larzelere & Huston, 1980; Solomon, 1960; Strickland, 1958). Others have considered intentions or motives as important to trust (e.g., Cook & Wall, 1980; Deutsch, 1960; Giffin, 1967; Kee & Knox, 1970; Mishra, in press). Although these authors reflect a belief that the trustee's orientation toward the trustor is important, the terms *intentions* and *motives* can include wider implications than the orientation toward the trustor (e.g., the trustee's profit motives). Benevolence connotes a personal orientation that is integral to the proposed model. Also, in a similar vein, Frost, Stimpson, and Maughan (1978) suggested that altruism contributes to the level of trust. Butler and Cantrell (1984) identified loyalty among their determinants of dyadic trust. Jones, James, and Bruni (1975) suggested that confidence and trust in a leader are influenced in part by the extent to which the leader's behavior is relevant to the individual's needs and desires. Rosen and Jerdee (1977) considered the likelihood that the trustee would put organizational goals ahead of individual goals. Thus, all of these researchers used some construct similar to benevolence, as defined in our model.

Integrity

The relationship between integrity and trust involves the trustor's perception that the trustee adheres to a set of principles that the trustor finds acceptable. McFall (1987) illustrated why both the adherence to and acceptability of the principles are important. She suggested that following some set of principles defines *personal integrity*. However, if that set of principles is not deemed acceptable by the trustor, the trustee would not be considered to have integrity for our purposes (McFall called this *moral integrity*). The issue of acceptability precludes the argument that a party who is committed solely to the principle of *profit seeking at all costs* would be judged high in integrity (unless this principle is acceptable to the trustor). Such issues as the consistency of the party's past actions, credible communications about the trustee from other parties, belief that the trustee has a strong sense of justice, and the extent to which the party's actions are congruent with his or her words all affect the degree to which the party is judged to have integrity. Even though a case could be made that there are differentiable reasons why the integrity of a trustee could be perceived as higher or lower (e.g., lack of consistency is different from acceptability of principles), in the evaluation of trustworthiness it is the perceived level of integrity that is important rather than the reasons why the perception is formed.

Integrity or very similar constructs have been discussed as antecedent to trust by a number of theorists. Lieberman (1981) included integrity per se as an important trust factor. Sitkin and Roth's (1993: 368) approach utilizes a similar but more constrained construct of *value congruence*, which they defined as "the compatibility of an employee's beliefs and values with the organization's cultural values." Their approach compares the trustee's values with those of an organizational referent, rather than a judgment of the acceptability of the trustee's values to the trustor. Integrity and consistency were trust determinants in Butler and Cantrell's (1984) model. Likewise, Butler (1991) included consistency, integrity, and fairness as conditions of trust. Although a lack of consistency would cause one to question what values a trustee holds, being consistent is insufficient to integrity, as the trustee may consistently act in a self-serving manner. Gabarro (1978) suggested that three bases of trust were commonly mentioned by their interviewees, one of which was *character*. He contended that character includes integrity. Hart, Capps, Cangemi, and Caillouet's (1986) analysis of 24 survey items revealed three factors, one of which was openness/congruity (i.e., the integrity, fairness, and openness of management). Inclusion of integrity in the proposed model is well grounded in previous approaches to trust.

It is apparent from the previous discussion that the three factors of ability, benevolence, and integrity are common to much of the previous work on trust. Earlier models of trust antecedents either have not used the three factors together or have expanded into much larger sets of antecedents (e.g., Butler, 1991; Gabarro, 1978). These three factors appear to explain concisely the within-trustor variation in trust for others.

Proposition 2. Trust for a trustee will be a function of the trustee's perceived ability, benevolence, and integrity and of the trustor's propensity to trust.

Interrelationship of the Three Factors

Ability, benevolence, and integrity are important to trust, and each may vary independently of the others. This statement does not imply that the three are unrelated to one another, but only that they are separable.

Consider the case of an individual and would-be mentor. Ideally, the individual would want the mentor to be able to have the maximum positive impact on the protégé's career and to help and guide the protégé in any way possible. To what extent would the protégé trust the mentor? The mentor would need to be knowledgeable about the profession, have a thorough knowledge of the company, be interpersonally and politically astute, and so on. All of these attributes would contribute to the protégé's perception that the mentor has the ability to be helpful. This perception, alone, would not assure that the mentor *would* be helpful; it would mean only that the possibility exists.

Previous positively viewed actions of the mentor in his or her relationships with others, compatibility of the mentor's statements and actions, and credible communications from others about honorable actions by the mentor would build the assessment of the mentor's integrity. However, even if the individual is deemed to have high integrity, he or she may or may not have the knowledge and capabilities to be a helpful mentor. Thus, integrity by itself will not make the individual a trusted mentor.

But what about the person whose integrity is well known and whose abilities are stellar? Would this potential mentor be trusted? Perhaps not—this individual may have no particular attachment to the focal employee. Would the focal employee trust this person enough to divulge sensitive information about mistakes or shortcomings? If the manager also were benevolent toward the employee, he or she may try to protect the employee from the possible ramifications of mistakes. A manager who is less benevolent to the focal employee may be more disposed to use the information in a way that helps the company most, even at the possible expense of the employee. However, benevolence by itself is insufficient to cause trust. A well-intentioned person who lacks ability may not know who in the organization should be made aware of what. Aside from not being helpful, the person could actually do significant harm to the employee's career. Thus, it is possible for a perceived lack of any of the three factors to undermine trust.

If ability, benevolence, and integrity were all perceived to be high, the trustee would be deemed quite trustworthy. However, trustworthiness should be thought of as a continuum, rather than the trustee being either trustworthy or not trustworthy. Each of the three factors can vary along a continuum. Although the simplest case of high trust presumes a high level of all three factors, there may be situations in which a meaningful amount of trust can develop with lesser degrees of the three. Consider the case in which a highly able manager does not demonstrate high integrity (e.g., in dealings with others) but forms an attachment to a particular employee. The manager repeatedly demonstrates strong benevolence toward the employee, providing resources even at others' expense. Will the employee trust the manager? On one hand, it can be argued that if the employee strongly believes in the benevolence of the manager, the employee has no reason to doubt how the manager will behave in the future. On the other hand, if the manager's integrity is questionable, can the employee help but wonder how long it will be until the manager betrays her or him as well? Whether or not the employee will trust the manager depends in part upon the employee's propensity to trust. In addition to propensity affecting trust when there are no data on characteristics of the trustee, propensity can enhance the effect of these factors, thereby producing a moderating effect on trust. The point is that the employee may or may not trust the manager in such a scenario. Clearly, if all three factors were high, the employee would trust, but how low can some of the three factors be before the employee would not trust the manager? In what situations is each of the three factors most sensitive or critical? These questions clearly deserve investigation.

The proposed model can explain trust (based on propensity) before any relationship between two parties has developed. As a relationship begins to develop, the trustor may be able to obtain data on the trustee's integrity through third-party sources and observation, with little direct interaction. Because there is little information about the trustee's benevolence toward the trustor, we suggest that integrity will be important to the formation of trust early in the relationship. As the relationship develops, interactions with the trustee allow the trustor to gain insights about the trustee's benevolence, and the relative impact of benevolence on trust will grow. Thus, the development of the relationship is likely to alter the relative importance of the factors of trustworthiness.

Proposition 3. The effect of integrity on trust will be most salient early in the relationship prior to the development of meaningful benevolence data.

Proposition 4. The effect of perceived benevolence on trust will increase over time as the relationship between the parties develops.

Each of these three factors captures some unique elements of trustworthiness. Previously we suggested that as a set, ability, benevolence, and integrity appear to explain a major portion of trustworthiness while maintaining parsimony. Each element contributes a unique perceptual perspective from which the trustor considers the trustee. If a trustee is perceived as high on all three factors, it is argued here that the trustee will be perceived as quite trustworthy.

Even though there are many conceptualizations of which factors of trustworthiness are important, ability, benevolence, and integrity appear to encompass the major issues. Using three of the most current models available, Table 2 illustrates that factors of trustworthiness from earlier models are subsumed within the perceptions of these three factors. For example, Mishra's (In press) conceptualization includes competence, openness, caring, and reliability. Competence and ability are clearly similar, whereas caring parallels benevolence. A lack of trustee reliability as Mishra conceptualizes it would clearly damage the perception of integrity in the current model. Mishra's openness is measured through questions about both the trustee's general openness with others and openness with the trustor, which could be expected to be related to either integrity or benevolence, respectively. Likewise, if a trustor perceived that a trustee were low on any one of Butler's (1991) 10 factors of trustworthiness, that perceived deficiency would also lower the perception of one of three factors in our current model. Specifically, if a trustor perceived a trustee to be deficient on any of Butler's loyalty, openness, receptivity, or availability factors, it wold also lower the perception of the trustee's benevolence in the current model. Butler's factors of consistency, discreetness, fairness, integrity, and promise fulfillment are encompassed within the current conceptualization of integrity. If a trustor were concerned with a trustee's competence in Butler's

Table 2 Apparent Overlap of Recent Models

Authors	No. of Factors	Similar Factors Included			
		Propensity	Ability	Benevolence	Integrity
Butler (1991)	10	No	Competence	Loyalty, openness, receptivity, availability	Consistency, discreetness, fairness, integrity, promise fulfillment
Mishra (in press)	4	No	Competence	Caring, openness	Reliability, openness
Sitkin & Roth (1993)	2	No	Ability	No	Value congruence

model, those concerns would be reflected in the perception of ability in our model. Like the current model, Sitkin and Roth's (1993) model includes ability. Their definition of value congruence parallels the considerations encompassed in integrity. Thus, the factors of trustworthiness described in earlier, more complex models are accounted for in the current approach while gaining the advantage of parsimony (James, Mulaik, & Brett, 1982; Runkel & McGrath, 1972).

In the preceding sections, characteristics of a trustor and a trustee that lead to trust were examined. The distinction between a trustor's characteristics and trustee's characteristics is important. Perceptions of ability, benevolence, and integrity of another party leave a considerable amount of variance in trust unexplained, because they neglect between-trustor differences in propensity to trust. Likewise, understanding the propensity to trust does not include the trustworthiness of a given trustee. In sum, to understand the extent to which a person is willing to trust another person, both the trustor's propensity to trust and the trustor's perceptions of the trustee's ability, benevolence, and integrity must be discerned.

The above presentation dealt with characteristics of the trustor and trustee that lead to trust. What follows is a consideration of risk and its relationship with engaging in trusting actions.

Risk Taking in Relationship

It was argued previously that risk is an essential component of a model of trust. It important for researchers to understand the role of risk. There is no risk taken in the *willingness* to be vulnerable (i.e., to trust), but risk is inherent in the *behavioral manifestation* of the willingness to be vulnerable. One does not need to risk anything in order to trust; however, one must take a risk in order to engage in trusting action. The fundamental difference between trust and trusting behaviors is between a "willingness" to assume risk and actually "assuming" risk. Trust is the willingness to assume risk; behavioral trust is the *assuming* of risk. This differentiation parallels Sitkin and Pablo's (1992) distinction in the risk-taking literature between the *tendency* to take risks and risk *behavior*. This critical differentiation highlights the importance of clearly distinguishing between trust and its outcomes.

Trust will lead to risk taking in a relationship, and the form of the risk taking depends on the situation. For example, a supervisor may take a risk by allowing an employee to handle an important account rather than handling it personally. The supervisor risks repercussions if the employee mishandles the account. Likewise, an employee may trust a manager to compensate for exceptional contributions that are beyond the scope of the employee's job. If the employee allows performance on some aspects of his or her formal job description to suffer in order to attend to a project that is important to the supervisor, the employee is clearly taking a risk. If the supervisor fails to account for the work on the project, the employee's performance appraisal will suffer. In both examples, the level of trust will affect the amount of risk the trustor is willing to take in the relationship. In the former case, trust will affect the extent to which the supervisor will empower the employee; in the latter case, trust will affect the extent to which the employee will engage in organizational citizenship behavior. Even though the form of the risk taking depends on the situation, in both cases the amount of trust for the other party will affect how much risk a party will take.

Thus, the outcome of trust proposed in this article is risk taking in relationship (RTR). RTR differentiates the outcomes of trust from general risk-taking behaviors because it can occur only in the context of a specific, identifiable relationship with another party. Further, RTR suggests that trust will increase the likelihood that a trustor will not only form some affective link with a trustee, but also that the trustor will allow personal vulnerability. The separation of trust from RTR is illustrated in Figure 1 by the inclusion of a box representing each construct.

Trust is not involved in all risk-taking behavior. For example, when a farmer invests time and resources into planting crops, the farmer is taking a risk that sufficient rain will fall during the critical times of the growing season so that there will be a profitable crop to harvest. Although this behavior involves risk, it does not involve trust as defined in this theory, because there is no relationship with an identifiable "other party" to which the farmer would make himself or herself vulnerable. Even though proponents of a sociological approach might argue that this is an example of trust because there is a system that produces meteorological forecasts, it is important to remember that the meteorologists do not control the weather—they merely provide data about the likelihood of various weather scenarios. Perceptions of meteorologists' accuracy would affect risk perception (Sitkin & Pablo, 1992). Thus, the farmer does not trust the weather but takes a risk on what the weather will do (Deutsch, 1958).

Assessing the risk in a situation involves consideration of the context, such as weighing the likelihood of both positive and negative outcomes that might occur (Bierman, Bonini, & Hausman, 1969; Coleman, 1990). If a decision involves the possibility of a negative outcome coupled with a positive outcome, the aggregate level of risk is different than if only the possibility of the negative outcome exists. Thus, the stakes in the situation (i.e., both the possible gains and the potential losses) will affect the interpretation of the risk involved. In an integrative review of risk behavior, Sitkin and Pablo (1992) identified a number of other factors that influence the perception of risk, such as familiarity of the domain of the problem, organizational control systems, and social influences.

It is important that we clarify what is meant by the perception of risk in this model, because it extends the risk literature in its meaning. In our model, the perception of risk involves the trustor's belief about likelihoods of gains or losses *outside of considerations that involve the relationship with the particular trustee*. Current approaches to perceived risk implicitly incorporate knowledge of the relationship with the trustee with non-relational reasons for assessments of risk, and, therefore, they do not clarify how trust for a given trustee is related to risk behavior. For example, Sitkin and Pablo (1992: 10) defined risk as "a characteristic of decisions that is defined here as the extent to which there is uncertainty about whether potentially significant and/or disappointing outcomes of decisions will be realized." In our model of trust, the decision to which Sitkin and Pablo refer is the RTR, wherein the trustor takes action. Two categories of factors influence the assessment of the likelihood of significant and/or disappointing outcomes: the relationship with the trustee (i.e., trust) and factors outside the relationship that make the decision significant and uncertain. In sum, to understand how trust actually affects a person's taking a risk, one must separate trust from other situational factors that *necessitate* trust (i.e., perceived risk in the current model).

We propose that the *level* of trust is compared to the level of perceived risk in a situation. If the level of trust surpasses the threshold of perceived risk, then the trustor will engage in the RTR. If the level of perceived risk is greater than the level of trust, the trustor will not engage in the RTR.

In sum, trust is a willingness to be vulnerable to another party, but there is no risk involved with holding such an attitude. Trust will increase the likelihood of RTR, which is the behavioral manifestation of trust. Whether or not a specific risk will be taken by the trustor is influenced both by the amount of trust for the trustee and by the perception of risk inherent in the behavior.

Proposition 5. RTR is a function of trust and the perceived risk of the trusting behavior (e.g., empowerment of a subordinate).

Early in this article it was argued the placement of risk in a model of trust was important, and this section clarifies that issue. Two other issues warrant exposition: the effects of context and the evolution of trust.

The Role of Context

The preceding discussion of risk-taking behavior makes a clear argument for the importance of the context in which the risk is to be taken. Even though the level of trust (as determined by ability, benevolence, integrity and propensity to trust) may be constant, the specific consequences of trust will be determined by contextual factors such as the stakes involved, the balance of power in the relationship, the perception of the level of risk, and the alternatives available to the trustor.

Similarly, the assessment of the antecedents of trust (ability, benevolence, and integrity) are affected by the context. For example, in the previous discussion of ability we noted that ability was domain specific—high ability at one task does not necessarily imply high ability at another task. Furthermore, perceived ability will change as the dynamics of the situation in which the task is to be performed change. For example, a protégé may believe that the mentor is able to advance his or her career, but a change in top management's philosophy may change the situation. Although the mentor's skills are constant, the context in which those skills will be utilized has changed. The net result of the change in context (i.e., politics) has decreased the protégé's perception of the mentor's ability.

Perceived levels of benevolence also are influenced by context. For example, if an employee perceives that a new supervisor has attitudes and preferences similar to his or her own, the employee will perceive higher levels of benevolence from that supervisor (Berscheid & Walster, 1978; Newcomb, 1956). The context of the situation (i.e., perceived similarity) helps to determine the perceived level of benevolence that the supervisor has for the employee.

The context of a party's actions affects the perception of integrity as well. A middle manager may make a decision that appears to be inconsistent with earlier decisions. Knowing nothing else about the situation, employees may question the manager's integrity. However, if the employees learn that the manager's actions were in response to orders from those higher in the organization, the manager's integrity will no longer be questioned. The manager's actions are seen as unavoidable given the context, and they are not deemed to be his or her fault. Thus, the perception of integrity can be influenced by the context of the actions.

In sum, the trustor perception and interpretation of the context of the relationship will affect both the need for trust and the evaluation of trustworthiness. Changes in such factors as the political climate and the perceived volition of the trustee in the situation can cause a reevaluation of trustworthiness. A strong organizational control system could inhibit the development of trust, because a trustee's actions may be interpreted as responses to that control rather than signs of trustworthiness. A clear understanding of trust for a trustee necessitates understanding how the context affects perceptions of trustworthiness.

Long-Term Effects

Up to this point, in the proposed model we have described trust at a given point in time. A more complete understanding of trust would come from consideration of its evolution within a relationship (Boyle & Bonacich, 1970; Kee & Knox, 1970). The level of trust will evolve as the parties interact. Several factors that affect the process by which trust evolves have been explored in the literature and are discussed next.

Strickland's (1958) analysis of monitoring and employee locus of motivation provides an interesting insight into the evolution of trust. He suggested that low trust will lead to a greater amount of surveillance or monitoring of work progress. Kruglanski (1970: 215) suggested that a frequently monitored employee might interpret the supervisor's surveillance as illustrating distrust for the employee. The employee may react in retaliation by "double-crossing the supervisor whenever the opportunity arises. The supervisor's anticipation of such an effect might lead him to continue his surveillance of the subordinate."

A number of researchers have suggested that the emergence of trust can be demonstrated in game theory as a reputation evolves from patterns of previous behavior. For example, Solomon (1960) described effects of reputation on trust utilizing a prisoner's dilemma. He asserted that an individual who receives cooperation from another develops a liking for that individual, increasing the likelihood of the person's behaving in a trustworthy fashion. Boyle and Bonacich described the dynamic interplay between experiences and trust. They argued that "a Cooperative move by Opponent will increase Player's trust in him, while a Noncooperative move will decrease Player's trust" (1970: 130). Other researchers have used a repeated decision game to show how trust emerges in a transaction between two parties (e.g., Butler, 1983; Dasgupta, 1988; Davis, Helms, & Henkin, 1989; Milgrom & Roberts, 1992).

Our proposed model incorporates the dynamic nature of trust. This is represented in Figure 1 by the feedback loop from the "Outcomes" of RTR to the perceived characteristics of the trustee. When a trustor takes a risk in a trustee that leads to a positive outcome, the trustor's perceptions of the trustee are enhanced. Likewise, perceptions of the trustee will decline when trust leads to unfavorable conclusions. Boyle and Bonacich (1970) have suggested that the outcomes of engaging in a trusting behavior will affect trust directly. We propose that the outcome of the trusting behavior (favorable or unfavorable) will influence trust indirectly through the perceptions of ability, benevolence, and integrity at the next interaction. For example, a manager empowers an employee to deal with a task that is critical to the manager's performance. If the employee's performance of the task is very good, the manager's perception of the employee's trustworthiness will be enhanced. Conversely, if the employee performs poorly and damages the manager's reputation, the manager's perception of the employee's trustworthiness is diminished. The manager may attribute the employee's high or low performance to ability, benevolence, and/ or integrity, depending upon the situation.

Proposition 6. Outcomes of trusting behaviors (i.e., RTR) will lead to updating of prior perceptions of the ability, benevolence, and integrity of the trustee.

Conclusions and Future Directions

This article raises a number of issues for the study of trust in organizations. Each is considered and dealt with in the development of a model of dyadic trust in an organizational context. The model proposed in this article is the first that explicitly considers both characteristics of the trustee as well as the trustor. The model clearly differentiates trust from factors that contribute to it, and it also differentiates trust from its outcome of risk taking in the relationship. The current approach defines trust in a way that distinguishes trust from other similar constructs (cooperation, confidence, predictability), which often have been confused with trust in the literature. Likewise, the critical role of risk is clearly specified in this model. This article develops a versatile definition of trust and a parsimonious set of determinants.

The differentiations between factors that cause trust, trust itself, and outcomes of trust are critical to the validation of this model. All three must be measured in order to fully test the model. Measures of the perceptions of a trustee's ability, benevolence, and integrity must be developed that are consistent with the definitions provided. Behaviors that are characterized by vulnerability and the lack of ability to monitor or control can be assessed to operationalize RTR. RTR must be measured in terms of actual behavior, not willingness to engage in behavior. Such behaviors as monitoring are examples of a lack of risk taking in relationship. Dealing with these behaviors from a measurement perspective requires a reverse scoring of the measure of their occurrence. The extent of perceived risk involved in engaging in the trusting behavior should be assessed either directly (e.g., through survey items) or controlled for, such as structuring a simulation wherein the subjects have a limited number of possible responses that clearly vary in the amount of risk they involve. The most problematic component of the model from the standpoint of measurement is trust itself. Because trust is a willingness to be vulnerable, a measure that assesses that willingness is needed. Even though trust is conceptually easy to differentiate from perceived ability, benevolence, and integrity of the trustee, separating the *willingness* to be vulnerable from *actually* being vulnerable constitutes a finer distinction. To measure trust itself, a survey or other similar methodology that taps into the person's *willingness* to be vulnerable to the trustee is needed, because this is distinct from observable RTR.

The question "Do you trust them?" must be qualified: "trust them to do what?" The issue on which you trust them depends not only on the assessment of integrity and benevolence, but also on the ability to accomplish it. Thus, if a party is trusted on one task, will that increase the trust on another unrelated task, even in the absence of data on the party's ability on the new task? Consistent with the arguments of Sitkin and Roth (1993), this model suggests that assessments of ability may not generalize across dissimilar tasks or situations.

Several limitations of the proposed theory should be recognized. First, its focus is limited to trust of a specific trustor for a specific trustee. Thus, its contribution to understanding trust in a social system (e.g., Barber, 1983; Lewis & Weigert, 1985) is beyond the scope of this model. Second, trust as considered in this model is unidirectional: from a given trustor to a given trustee. In its present form it is not designed to examine the development of mutual trust between two parties. Third, this model is focused on trust in an organizational relationship, and its propositions may not generalize to relationships in other contexts. Finally, the labels for the constructs in this model were selected from several options used earlier in the trust literature. To us, these labels most clearly reflected the constructs as defined in the proposed model; however, in some cases this necessitated that the definitions vary somewhat from some of the prior uses of the same terms.

In addition to model-specific hypotheses, a number of other avenues of research should be pursued. For example, the process by which trust develops needs further exploration. We propose that the need for trusting behavior often arises while there is still a lack of data regarding some of the three factors. For instance, an employee may not have had enough interaction with a given manager to be able to assess the manager's benevolence toward him or her. In order to gather such data, the employee first may have to be vulnerable (i.e., to trust the manager) to see how the manager deals with the vulnerability. In this instance, the employee may have to display a type of trust similar to blind faith. Depending on how the manager responds to the vulnerability, the employee will develop more or less trust.

A number of theorists have suggested that trust evolves over time based on a series of observations and interactions. A critical issue is the process by which trust evolves, given the framework of our model. Further research should investigate the relationship between trust and cooperation. Game theorists tend to equate cooperation and trust, suggesting that over time a pattern of cooperative behavior develops trust (Axelrod, 1984). To what extent does cooperation that can be attributed to external motivations develop trust? This idea also suggests the need to test the feedback loop in the proposed model.

There are many areas in organizational studies in which trust has been cited as playing a key role. Further development and operationalization of the model proposed in this article would benefit the study of organizations through an increased understanding of such topics as employee-organization linkages, negotiation, and the implementation of self-managed teams.

Acknowledgement

We would like to thank Edward Conlon, Robert Vecchio, and four anonymous reviewers for their helpful comments.

Notes

1. It is interesting to note that Aristotle's *Rhetoric* suggests that a speaker's ethos (Greek root for ethics) is based on the listener's perception of three things: intelligence; character (reliability, honesty); and goodwill (favorable intentions toward the listener). These bases provide an interesting parallel with the factors of ability, integrity, and benevolence, respectively.

References

Argyris, C. A. 1994. Litigation mentality and organizational learning. In S. B Sitkin & R. J. Bies (Eds.), *The legalistic organization*. Thousand Oaks, CA: Sage.

Atwater, L. E. 1988. The relative importance of situational and individual variables in predicting leader behavior. *Group and Organization Studies*, 13: 290–310.

Axelrod, R. 1984. *The evolution of cooperation*. New York: Basic Books.

Barber, B. 1983. *The logic and limits of trust*. New Brunswick, NJ: Rutgers University Press.

Bateson, P. 1988. The biological evolution of cooperation and trust. In D. G. Gambetta (Ed.), *Trust*: 14–30. New York: Basil Blackwell.

Bazerman, M. H. 1994. *Judgment in managerial decision making*. New York: Wiley.

Berscheid, E., & Walster, E. H. 1978. *Interpersonal attraction* (2nd ed.). Reading, MA: Addison-Wesley.

Bierman, H., Jr., Bonini, C. P., & Hausman, W. H. 1969. *Quantitative analysis for business decisions* (3rd ed.). Homewood, IL: Irwin.

Boss, R. W. 1978. Trust and managerial problem solving revisited. *Group and Organization Studies*, 3: 331–342.

Boyle, R., & Bonacich, P. 1970. The development of trust and mistrust in mixed-motive games. *Sociometry*, 33: 123–139.

Butler, J. K. 1983. Reciprocity of trust between professionals and their secretaries. *Psychological Reports*, 53: 411–416.

Butler, J. K. 1991. Toward understanding and measuring conditions of trust: Evolution of a conditions of trust inventory. *Journal of Management*, 17: 643–663.

Butler, J. K., & Cantrell, R. S. 1984. A behavioral decision theory approach to modeling dyadic trust in superiors and subordinates. *Psychological Reports*, 55: 19–28.

Coleman, J. S. 1990. *Foundations of social theory*. Cambridge, MA: Harvard University Press.

Conlon, E. J., & Mayer, R. C. 1994. *The effect of trust on principal-agent dyads: An empirical investigation of stewardship and agency*. Paper presented at the annual meeting of the Academy of Management, Dallas, TX.

Cook, J., & Wall, T. 1980. New work attitude measures of trust, organizational commitment, and personal need nonfulfillment. *Journal of Occupational Psychology*, 53: 39–52.

Cummings, L. L. 1983. Performance-evaluation systems in context of individual trust and commitment. In F. J. Landy, S. Zedrick, & J. Cleveland (Eds.), *Performance measurement and theory*: 89–93. Hillsdale, N.J.: Earlbaum.

Dasgupta, P. 1988. Trust as a commodity. In D. G. Gambetta (Ed.), *Trust*: 49–72. New York: Basil Blackwell.

Davis, J., Helms, L., & Henkin, A. B. 1989. Strategic conventions in organizational decision making: Applications from game theory. *International Review of Modern Sociology*, 19: 71–85.

Deutsch, M. 1958. Trust and suspicion. *Journal of Conflict Resolution*, 2: 265–279.

Deutsch, M. 1960. The effect of motivational orientation upon trust and suspicion. *Human Relations*, 13: 123–140.

Donaldson, L., & Davis, J. H. 1991. Stewardship theory or agency theory: CEO governance and shareholder returns. *Australian Journal of Management*, 16(1): 49–64.

Driscoll, J. W. 1978. Trust and participation in organizational decision making as predictors of satisfaction. *Academy of Management Journal*, 21: 44–56.

Famham, A. 1989. The trust gap. *Fortune*, Dec. 4: 56–78.

Farris, G., Senner, E., & Butterfield, D. 1973. Trust, culture, and organizational behavior. *Industrial Relations*, 12: 144–157.

Friedland, N. 1990. Attribution of control as a determinant of cooperation in exchange interactions. *Journal of Applied Social Psychology*, 20: 303–320.

Frost, T., Stimpson, D. V., & Maughan, M. R. C. 1978. Some correlates of trust. *Journal of Psychology*, 99: 103–108.

Gabarro, J. 1978. The development of trust, influence, and expectations. In A. G. Athos & J. J. Gabarro (Eds.), *Interpersonal behavior: Communication and understanding in relationships*: 290–303. Englewood Cliffs, NJ: Prentice Hall.

Gambetta, D. G. (Ed.). 1988. Can we trust trust? In D. G. Gambetta (Ed.), *Trust*: 213–237. New York: Basil Blackwell.

Giffin, K. 1967. The contribution of studies of source credibility to a theory of interpersonal trust in the communication department. *Psychological Bulletin*, 68: 104–120.

Golembiewski, R. T., & McConkie, M. 1975. The centrality of interpersonal trust in group processes. In C. L. Cooper (Ed.), *Theories of group processes*. New York: Wiley.

Good, D. 1988. Individuals, interpersonal relations, and trust. In D. G. Gambetta (Ed.), *Trust*: 131–185. New York: Basil Blackwell.

Granovetter, M. 1985. Economic action and social structure: The problem of embeddedness, *American Journal of Sociology*, 91: 481–510.

Hart, K. M., Capps, H. R., Cangemi, J. P., & Caillouet, L. M. 1986. Exploring organizational trust and its multiple dimensions: A case study of General Motors. *Organization Development Journal*, 4(2): 31–39.

Hofstede, G. 1980. Motivation, leadership, and organization: Do American theories apply abroad? *Organizational Dynamics*, 9(1): 42–63.

Hovland, C. I., Janis, I. L., & Kelley, H. H. 1953. *Communication and persuasion*. New Haven, CT: Yale University Press.

Jackson, S. E., & Alvarez, E. B. 1992. Working through diversity as a strategic imperative. In S. Jackson (Ed.), *Diversity in the workplace*: 13–29. New York: Guilford Press.

James, L. R., Mulaik, S. S., & Brett, J. M. 1982. *Causal analysis: Models, assumptions, and data*. Beverly Hills, CA: Sage.

Jamieson, D., & O'Mara, J. 1991. *Managing workforce 2000: Gaining the diversity advantage*. San Francisco: Jossey-Bass.

Jensen, M. C., & Meckling, W. H. 1976. Theory of the firm: Managerial behavior, agency costs and ownership structure. *Journal of Financial Economics*, 3: 305–360.

Johnson-George, C., & Swap, W. 1982. Measurement of specific interpersonal trust: Construction and validation of a scale to assess trust in a specific other. *Journal of Personality and Social Psychology*, 43: 1306–1317.

Jones, A. P., James, L. R., & Bruni, J. R. 1975. Perceived leadership behavior and employee confidence in the leader as moderated by job involvement. *Journal of Applied Psychology*, 60: 146–149.

Kee, H. W., & Knox, R. E. 1970. Conceptual and methodological considerations in the study of trust. *Journal of Conflict Resolution*, 14: 357–366.

Kruglanski, A. W. 1970. Attributing trustworthiness in supervisor-worker relations. *Journal of Experimental Psychology*, 6: 214–232.

Larson, C. E., & LaFasto, F. M. J. 1989. *Teamwork: What must go right/what can go wrong*. Newbury Park, CA: Sage.

Larzelere, R., & Huston, T. 1980. The dyadic trust scale: Toward understanding interpersonal trust in close relationships. *Journal of Marriage and the Family*, 42: 595–604.

Lawler, E. 1992. *The ultimate advantage: Creating the high-involvement organization*. San Francisco: Jossey-Bass.

Lewis, J., & Weigert, A. 1985. Trust as a social reality. *Social Forces*, 63: 967–985.

Lieberman, J. K. 1981. *The litigious society*. New York: Basic Books.

Luhmann, N. 1988. Familiarity, confidence, trust: Problems and alternatives. In D. G. Gambetta (Ed.), *Trust*: 94–107. New York: Basil Blackwell.

March, J. G., & Shapira, Z. 1987. Managerial perspectives on risk and risk taking. *Management Science*, 33: 1404–1418.

McFall, L. 1987. Integrity. *Ethics*, 98: 5–20.

Meyer, J. W. 1983. Organizational factors affecting legalization in education. In J. W. Meyer & W. R. Scott (Eds.), *Organizational environments: Ritual and rationality*: 217–232. San Francisco: Jossey-Bass.

Milgrom, P., & Roberts, J. 1992. *Economics, organization and management*. Englewood Cliffs, NJ: Prentice Hall.

Mishra, A. K. In press. Organizational responses to crisis: The centrality of trust. In R. M. Kramer & T. Tyler (Eds.), *Trust in organizations*. Newbury Park, CA: Sage.

Moore, S. F., Shaffer, L. S., Pollak, E. L., & Taylor-Lemcke, P. 1987. The effects of interpersonal trust and prior common problem experience on common management. *Journal of Social Psychology*, 127: 19–29.

Newcomb, T. M. 1956. The prediction of interpersonal attraction. *American Psychologist*, 11: 575–586.

Riker, W. H. 1974. The nature of trust. In J. T. Tedeschi (Ed.), *Perspectives on social power*: 63–81. Chicago: Aldine.

Ring, S. M., & Van de Ven, A. 1992. Structuring cooperative relationships between organizations. *Strategic Management Journal*, 13: 483–498.

Rosen, B., & Jerdee, T. H. 1977. Influence of subordinate characteristics on trust and use of participative decision strategies in a management simulation. *Journal of Applied Psychology*, 62: 628–631.

Rotter, J. B. 1967. A new scale for the measurement of interpersonal trust. *Journal of Personality*, 35: 651–665.

Runkel, P. J., & McGrath, J. E. 1972. *Research on human behavior: A systematic guide to method*. New York: Holt, Rinehart, & Winston.

Sabatelli, R. M., Buck, R., & Dreyer, A. 1983. Locus of control, interpersonal trust, and nonverbal communication accuracy. *Journal of Personality and Social Psychology*, 44: 399–409.

Schlenker, B., Helm, B., & Tedeschi, J. 1973. The effects of personality and situational variables on behavioral trust. *Journal of Personality and Social Psychology*, 25: 419–427.

Scott, C. L., III. 1980. Interpersonal trust: A comparison of attitudinal and situational factors. *Human Relations*, 33: 805–812.

Scott, C. L. 1980. The causal relationship between trust and the assessed value of management by objectives. *Journal of Management*, 6: 157–175.

Sitkin, S. B., & Bies, R. J. 1994. The legalization of organizations: A multitheoretical perspective. In S. B Sitkin & R. J. Bies (Eds.), *The legalistic organization:* 19–49. Thousand Oaks, CA: Sage.

Sitkin, S. B., & Pablo, A. L. 1992. Reconceptualizing the determinants of risk behavior. *Academy of Management Review*, 17: 9–38.

Sitkin, S. B., & Roth, N. L. 1993. Explaining the limited effectiveness of legalistic "remedies" for trust/distrust. *Organization Science*, 4: 367–392.

Solomon, L. 1960. The influence of some types of power relationships and game strategies upon the development of interpersonal trust. *Journal of Abnormal and Social Psychology*, 61: 223–230.

Strickland, L. H. 1958. Surveillance and trust. *Journal of Personality*, 26: 200–215.

Taylor, R. G. 1989. The role of trust in labor-management relations. *Organization Development Journal*, 7: 85–89.

Wellins, R. S., Byham, W. C., & Wilson, J. M. 1991. *Empowered teams: Creating self-directed work groups that improve quality, productivity, and participation.* San Francisco: Jossey-Bass.

Williamson, O. E. 1975. *Markets and hierarchies: Analysis and antitrust implications.* New York: Free Press.

Zand, D. E. 1972. Trust and managerial problem solving. *Administrative Science Quarterly*, 17: 229–239.

II. TRUST DEVELOPMENT AND MAINTENANCE

4

Initial Trust Formation in New Organizational Relationships

D. Harrison McKnight, Larry L. Cummings, and Norman L. Chervany

Several trust theorists have stated that trust develops gradually over time (e.g., Blau, 1964; Rempel, Holmes, & Zanna, 1985; Zand, 1972), but when contrasted with some recent empirical findings, their theories present an interesting paradox. By positing that trust grows over time, these trust theorists implicitly assume that trust levels start small and gradually increase. Some researchers, then, expecting this, have been surprised at how high their subjects' early trust levels were—both in survey and experimental studies (e.g., Berg, Dickhaut, & McCabe, 1995; Kramer, 1994). For example, economics-based researchers Berg et al. (1995) expected subjects to exhibit low to medium trust in each other when faced with a trust dilemma. Instead, their subjects frequently exhibited high trust—passing to a second subject dollars they were given during the first part of the experiment, without any reason to expect their generosity to be reciprocated. Another example is Kramer's (1994) survey of MBAs who were previously unknown to each other. Because the MBAs had no interaction history, one would have expected them to have low trust levels; however, surprisingly, Kramer found high trust levels among these individuals.

Theoretical Background

The Paradox of High Initial Trust Levels

High initial trust findings are paradoxical because, as we stated above, several trust theorists predict low initial trust. By "initial" we mean when parties first meet or interact. An example of initial trust predictions is provided by economics- or *calculative-based* trust researchers (e.g., Coleman, 1990; Williamson, 1993), who theorize that individuals make trust choices based on rationally derived costs and benefits (Lewicki & Bunker, 1995; Shapiro, Sheppard, & Cheraskin, 1992). Thus, calculative-based trust theorists would predict that the lack of incentives (benefits) of subjects in Berg et al. would result in low levels of trusting behavior among them. However, the results in Berg et al. do not agree with this prediction. As another example, *knowledge-based* trust theorists propose that trust develops over time as one accumulates trust-relevant knowledge through experience with the other person (Holmes, 1991; Lewicki & Bunker, 1995). From this perspective, Kramer's study participants would require time and an interaction history to develop a high level of trust in each other. However, Kramer's results directly contradict this. Thus, studying initial trust formation is important, because the results from such studies require an explanation beyond what calculative-based and knowledge-based trust theories provide.

In this article we argue that the paradox of high trust in initial relationships may be explained by identifying "hidden" factors and processes that enable trust to be high when people in organizations first meet. We develop a model of initial trust formation to explain why trust may be high when members of organizations barely know each other.

Increasingly Common New Work Relationships

In today's work environment, interacting with a new manager or with new coworkers is becoming commonplace. Such a situation involves initial trust, because the parties have not worked together long enough to develop an interaction history. Initial trust situations occur naturally, when an employee or manager is newly hired or transferred, when cross-functional teams are formed, when salespeople or consultants call, when mergers bring two sets of employees together, or when a new joint venture begins.

These situations are becoming more common because of increased mergers or acquisitions and because widespread corporate restructuring and reduced employee loyalty have increased the typical turnover rate of organizational workers and managers (e.g., Evans, Gunz, & Jalland, 1996). The nature of tasks is also increasing new work encounters, as temporary task teams or project engagements become the norm in organizations. Meyerson, Weick, & Kramer (1996) explain that such environmental factors as outsourcing and labor/skill shortages have increased the number of temporary task teams. Further, communication technology now enables millions of people (Henry & Hartzler, 1997) to work on virtual task teams (Lipnack & Stamps, 1997), in which participants are often new to each other.

Because working together well requires some level of trust (Bromiley & Cummings, 1995), increasingly common new work encounters demand that the parties come to trust each other quickly (Meyerson et al., 1996). Thus, the need exists for a model of how trust initially forms.

A Model of Initial Trust Formation

Initial trust between parties will not be based on any kind of experience with, or firsthand knowledge of, the other party. Rather, it will be based on an individual's disposition to trust or on institutional cues that enable one person to trust another without firsthand knowledge. Figure 1 depicts the initial trust formation model. The model applies only to new encounters between people. Therefore, it excludes experiential processes (e.g., observing the trustees' behavior), but it does include cognitive processes and factors that lead to initial trust. As we explain in the next section, the model uses constructs from four trust research streams.

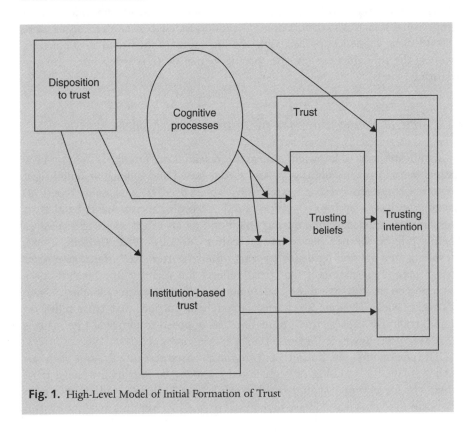

Fig. 1. High-Level Model of Initial Formation of Trust

We define "trust" to mean that one believes in, and is willing to depend on, another party (e.g., Mayer, Davis, & Schoorman, 1995). This high level trust concept can be broken into two constructs: (1) trusting *intention*, meaning that one is willing to depend on the other person in a given situation (e.g., Currall & Judge, 1995), and (2) trusting *beliefs*, meaning that one believes the other person is benevolent, competent, honest, or predictable in a situation (Mayer et al., 1995).

Distinguishing two constructs that constitute trust is important, because the word "trust" is so confusing (Shapiro, 1987a) and broad (Williamson, 1993) that it almost defies careful definition (e.g., Gambetta, 1988). The distinction between trusting beliefs and trusting intention follows the Fishbein & Ajzen (1975) typology separating constructs into *beliefs*, attitudes, *intentions*, and behaviors. We exclude attitudes and behaviors here so we can focus the article on cognitive concerns.

At a summary level, the model (Figure 1) implies that trust forms because of one's disposition to trust, one's institution-based trust, and two cognitive processes we discuss later. "Disposition to trust" refers to a tendency to be willing to depend on others. "Institution-based trust" means that one believes impersonal structures support one's likelihood for success in a given situation. To avoid the vagueness of discussing the formation of the broad trust concept, we use the model to explore the specific formation of trusting intention and trusting beliefs.

Theoretical Foundations for the Initial Trust Model

A significant body of knowledge from five research streams sheds light on how initial trust forms. In addition to knowledge-based and calculative-based trust research, three other research streams have been used: (1) personality based, (2) institution based, and (3) cognition based. According to *personality-based* trust researchers, trust develops during childhood as an infant seeks and receives help from his or her benevolent caregiver (Bowlby, 1982; Erikson, 1968), resulting in a general tendency to trust others (Rotter, 1967). *Institution-based* trust researchers maintain that trust reflects the security one feels about a situation because of guarantees, safety nets, or other structures (Shapiro, 1987a; Zucker, 1986). *Cognition-based* trust researchers purport that trust relies on rapid, cognitive cues or first impressions, as opposed to personal interactions (Brewer, 1981; Lewis & Weigert, 1985b; Meyerson et al., 1996).

The personality-, institution-, and cognition-based research streams each can help explain the paradox of high initial trust levels. Personality-based trust theorists, for example, would say that subjects in Kramer's study with a high disposition to trust would have high initial trust. However, this may not explain the overall high level of trust, because it is unlikely that nearly all of Kramer's subjects had high disposition-to-trust levels. Institution-based theorists would argue that the structure of the classroom situation supported high levels of initial trust by enabling subjects to feel secure in the situation (e.g., Lewis & Weigert, 1985a; Shapiro, 1987a). Kramer himself used a cognitive explanation for his results, attributing high trust levels to the favorable views the MBAs had toward those of their own kind.

Each of these three trust research streams can partially explain high initial trust, but if we focus on only one of the three, we face the danger of the other two acting as hidden confounds. The danger of hidden confounds exists because, in a given context, all three types of factors—personality, institutional, and cognitive—may be present. Sitkin and Pablo (1992) demonstrated this with respect to the prediction of risk behavior; they identified a hidden personality-related construct (risk propensity) that explained the paradoxical empirical results researchers found when predicting risk behavior with situational and organizational variables. By identifying the hidden construct, Sitkin and Pablo were able to specify more fully the antecedents of risk behavior.

To explain the paradox of high initial trust, we will justify the initial trust formation model (Figure 1), based on the detailed constructs and processes in Figure 2. The detailed model's constructs and processes come from four of the five research streams mentioned above (see Figure 2): (1) personality (faith in humanity), (2) institutional (institution-based trust), (3) calculative (trusting stance), and (4) cognitive (categorization processes and illusions of control process). Trusting beliefs and trusting intention come from more than one research stream. The fifth research stream—knowledge-based trust—assumes that the parties have firsthand knowledge of each other, based on an interaction history. Because "initial relationships," by definition, have no interaction history, firsthand knowledge-based trust does not apply to them. Hence, firsthand knowledge-based trust formation processes lie outside the scope of this article. We address second-hand knowledge, such as reputation, as a categorization process.

We chose the model's four trusting beliefs because they are the most commonly used trusting beliefs in the literature (e.g., Mayer et al., 1995). Each trusting belief is proposed to be more highly correlated with other trusting beliefs than with the model's other constructs, indicating a type of convergent validity. The constructs in institution-based trust and disposition to trust also display convergent validity. Trusting beliefs are proposed to be more highly related to trusting intention than they are to institution-based trust and disposition to trust, as reflected by the box grouping them together as a composite trust concept.

We define the model's constructs at the individual level of analysis. Hence, the model's constructs are internally consistent, even though one set of constructs (institution-based trust) reflects group- or organization-level phenomena. In limiting the article's scope to the individual level of analysis, we are

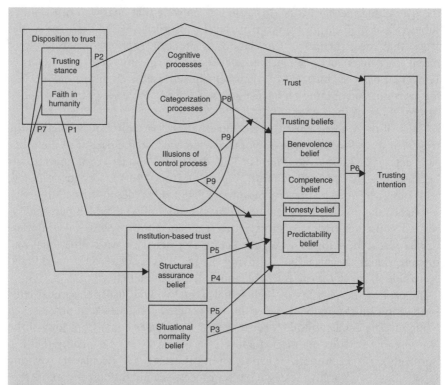

Fig. 2. Detailed Model of Initial Formation of Trust[α]

[α] Boxes containing other boxes are not measurable constructs but are categories of constructs or "second-order" constructs (see Hunter & Gerbing, 1982). Arrows directed into/out of the trusting beliefs category box represent individual relationships with each of the four trusting beliefs. Some subset of the four trusting beliefs could be used in empirical work, or a combination of them could be used as a second-order construct. Also, each could be used on its own. Processes are pictured in oval shape to distinguish them from constructs.

not disallowing social and organizational effects. In fact, we believe organizational-level constructs affect trust. However, these lie outside the scope of the article.

Our primary contribution is in creating a model that explains why trust can be high initially. But the model also addresses a second paradox. Although trust frequently has been termed "fragile" (e.g., Worchel, 1979), it has also been described as "robust" (e.g., Luhmann, 1979). An added contribution is that we discuss the model's implications for understanding why trust is considered both fragile and robust. We include research implications for the model in the last section of the article.

A Model Explaining the High Initial Trust Paradox

Disposition to Trust Affects Trusting Beliefs and Trusting Intention

A person exhibits a disposition to trust to the extent that she or he demonstrates a consistent tendency to be willing to depend on others across a broad spectrum of situations and persons—a personality construct that builds on the work of Erikson (1968) and Rotter (1967, 1971, 1980). In contrast to others, we distinguish between two types of disposition to trust, each of which affects trusting intention in a different way: (1) faith in humanity and (2) trusting stance. Reflecting the traditional view of personality-based trust, "faith in humanity" means that one believes that others are typically well-meaning and reliable (e.g., Rosenberg, 1957; Wrightsman, 1991). "Trusting stance" means that one believes that, regardless of whether people are reliable or not, one will obtain better interpersonal outcomes by dealing with people as though they are well-meaning and reliable. Because it reflects a conscious choice, trusting stance derives from the calculative-based trust research stream (e.g., Riker, 1971). As an example of trusting stance, one of the authors asked a respondent if she trusted her new manager, who had just been hired from outside the company. She replied "yes," explaining that she generally trusts new people until they give her some reason not to trust them. Hence, she exhibited a personal strategy to trust newcomers. Both faith in humanity and trusting stance are "dispositional," which refers to personal tendencies, not traits, because they reflect tendencies that apply across various situations.

Mixed empirical findings. Researchers have experienced mixed results when using disposition to trust to predict trust. From their research, Johnson-George and Swap conclude that constructs like disposition to trust "do not accurately determine an individual's trust in another under particular circumstances" (1982: 1307). In contrast, others have found disposition-related constructs to be important predictors. For example, Goldsteen, Schorr, and Goldsteen (1989) found that disposition-related trust had a statistically significant effect on peoples' mistrust of federal nuclear plant authorities whom they did not know personally. Mayer et al. (1995) reviewed additional evidence that disposition-based trust is important to other trust constructs. However, Holmes (1991) declares that although researchers assume disposition to trust is a contributor to the development of relationship-specific trust, this link has not been proven.

Resolving the research findings. We can resolve these mixed results by using our initial trust model. The time frame of the relationship is important in predicting the effects of disposition to trust. Although other variables will swamp the effects of a person's trusting tendency in *ongoing* relationships, disposition to trust likely will have a significant effect on a person's trusting beliefs and trusting intention in *new* organizational relationships. Johnson-George and Swap cite evidence that disposition to trust predicts what they call "trusting behavior" only when parties are new to each other in "highly ambiguous, novel, or unstructured situations, where one's generalized expectancy is all one can rely on" (Johnson-George & Swap, 1982: 1307; cf., Rotter, 1980). A transferred worker's relationship with a new manager in an unfamiliar area exemplifies such a situation, because roles and relationships are not yet clear. Goldsteen et al.'s (1989) finding—that dispositional trust was related to specific trust of federal authorities individuals had never met—supports the idea that dispositional trust is salient when people do not know each other.

Faith in humanity effects. Because faith in humanity reflects the extent to which one believes that nonspecific others are trustworthy, this characteristic will probably affect one's initial trusting beliefs (Kramer, 1994). Already-developed patterns of thinking about relationships in general tend to transfer to a specific initial relationship. This is particularly true if an individual cannot draw on other reasons (e.g., trusting beliefs or institution-based trust), because the situation, the type of relationship, and the type of other person are new. In other words, if no more specific situational information is available, one will rely on one's basic beliefs about human nature (Wrightsman, 1991), as reflected in faith in humanity. This is similar to the argument, presented by Mullins and Cummings, that "weak situations" display ambiguity in terms of the meaning of the situation (in press). In weak situations the person's disposition will be more salient than the situation. Initial trust-related situations may be ambiguous because the parties' roles or task may be new. Rotter (1971) has said that the novelty of the situation affects how salient dispositional trust will be. In a novel situation, then, faith in humanity will enable trusting beliefs to be high.

Proposition 1: In the initial relationship, to the extent the situation is novel and ambiguous, faith in humanity will lead to trusting beliefs.

Trusting stance effects. Trusting stance influences one to be intentionally willing to depend on another, regardless of beliefs in the other. An individual with high trusting stance probably believes that things turn out best when one is willing to depend on others, even though others may or may not be trustworthy. Thus, trusting stance does not lead to beliefs about the other person; rather, it directly supports one's willingness to depend on that person.

Proposition 2: In the initial relationship, trusting stance will lead to trusting intention. The effects of trusting stance on trusting intention will not be mediated by trusting beliefs.

Institution-Based Trust Affects Trusting Intention

Institution-based trust means that one believes the necessary impersonal structures are in place to enable one to act in anticipation of a successful future endeavor (e.g., Shapiro, 1987a; Zucker, 1986). Trusting intention at the beginning of a relationship may be high because of high institution-based trust levels. In the literature two types of institution-based trust are discussed: (1) situational normality, defined as the belief that success is likely because the situation is normal, and (2) structural assurances, defined as the belief that success is likely because such contextual conditions as promises, contracts, regulations, and guarantees are in place. Later, we discuss the effects of institution-based trust on trusting beliefs. In this section we look at direct effects on trusting intention.

Situational normality belief effects. Situational normality belief stems from the appearance that things are normal (Garfinkel, 1963: 188) or "customary" (Baier, 1986: 245), or that "everything seems in proper order" (Lewis & Weigert, 1985a: 974). Situational normality involves a properly ordered setting that appears likely to facilitate a successful interaction. For example, a person who enters a bank tends to expect a setting conducive to both customer service and fiduciary responsibility that is reflected in the workers' professional appearance, the prosperous and secure physical setting, and the friendly, yet safe, money-handling procedures. The individual's belief that the situation is normal helps that person feel comfortable enough to rapidly form a trusting intention toward the other party in the situation.

Garfinkel's experiments, in contrast, demonstrated that when people face inexplicable, abnormal situations, trust between them breaks down. For example, one subject told the experimenter he had a flat tire on the way to work. The experimenter responded, "What do you mean, you had a flat tire?" (1963: 221). At this point trust broke down because of the experimenter's illogical question.

Situational normality also can relate to one's comfort with one's own roles and the other person's roles in that setting (Baier, 1986). Socially constructed roles create a shared understanding among members of the social system that facilitates trusting intention among them.

Proposition 3: In the initial relationship, situational normality belief will lead to trusting intention.

Structural assurance belief effects. Shapiro refers to structural safeguards in terms of institutional "side bets" (1987b: 204), such as regulations, guarantees, and legal recourse.

- *Regulations* enable people to feel assured about their expectations of the other party's future behavior (e.g., Sitkin, 1995). For example, a company subcontracting the construction of metric-sized engine parts relies on the other party to use the same measures the company itself uses since they are specified by well-accepted metric standards makers.
- *Guarantees* mitigate the perceived risk involved in forming trusting intention. Hence, structural assurance belief leads to trusting intention, as evidenced by Zaheer, McEvily, and Perrone's (in press) finding that structure-based trust is positively related to interpersonal trust.
- *Legal recourse* (i.e., regarding contracts or promises) is related to trusting intention for two reasons (Baier, 1986). First, the trustor feels comfortable that the promise has the type of significance in the particular setting so that the trusted person will make every effort to fulfill it, or risk reaping sanctions through social disapproval or legal action (e.g., Sitkin, 1995). Second, the trustor feels comfortable that the trusted person, out of either socially learned behavior patterns or fear of sanctions, will act according to the norms surrounding promise in the social setting.

Structural assurance belief will be more influential in the initial relationship than it will later, because information about the other person is very incomplete when the relationship begins, making situational information quite salient.

Proposition 4: In the initial relationship, structural assurance belief will lead to trusting intention.

Structural Assurance Belief and Situational Normality Belief Affect Trusting Beliefs

Structural assurance belief is likely to affect trusting beliefs for three reasons, the last two of which are shared by situational normality belief. First, believing that a situation is bounded by safeguards enables one to believe that the individuals in the situation are trustworthy. For example, a new employee can better believe in the boss's benevolence if the employee believes the workplace has procedures that punish abusive managerial treatment. Also, an employee is more likely to believe a new coworker is competent if that individual believes the department's hiring process is sound.

Second, the institutions in the situation reflect the actions of the people involved; therefore, beliefs about the institutions will help form beliefs about the people who are involved in the institutions. For example, within the bounds set by corporate practices and procedures, the boss is the chief administrator of fairness in the workplace. Thus, one's belief about the structures supporting fairness in the workplace will support one's belief in the boss's benevolence. Similarly, a situational normality belief implies that the people in the situation will act normally and can therefore be trusted.

Third, based on many studies of cognitive consistency (Abelson et al., 1968), we believe that structural assurance and situational normality beliefs will probably stay consistent with related beliefs, such as trusting beliefs. Cognitive consistency is probably even more salient during the initial relationship, before beliefs about the other person and the situation become highly differentiated through experiential knowledge (Sitkin & Roth, 1993).

Proposition 5: In the initial relationship, the trusting beliefs will be a function of structural assurance belief and situational normality belief.

Trusting Beliefs Affect Trusting Intention

Evidence for the link between trusting beliefs and trusting intention is reviewed elsewhere (Mayer et al., 1995). Dobing (1993) also found a strong relationship between his trusting beliefs and trust (willingness to depend) constructs. Logically, if one believes that the other party is benevolent, competent, honest, and predictable, one is likely to form a trusting intention toward that person. Therefore, trusting beliefs will positively impact trusting intention.

At a more general level, the literature that links beliefs to intentions supports this relationship (e.g., Davis, 1989; Fishbein & Ajzen, 1975). Ajzen (1988) discusses evidence that beliefs and intentions tend to stay consistent. They should be especially consistent at first, when one has no experiential basis *not* to believe the other person is trustworthy.

Proposition 6: In the initial relationship, trusting intention will be a function of benevolence belief, competence belief, honesty belief, and predictability belief.

Faith in Humanity and Trusting Stance Affect Structural Assurance Belief

Faith in humanity reflects one's lifelong experiences with others (e.g., Rotter, 1967). A person who believes in the honesty and benevolence of people generally will probably have stronger beliefs in the security afforded by human institutions. Stated another way, one's structural assurance belief is probably partly based on how one feels about people in general, because people play roles that relate to how secure the situation is. Hence, one's feelings about people in general will likely influence one's structural assurance belief. This is more likely to be true at the beginning of a relationship, when beliefs about the situation are based more on assumptions than on facts.

Trusting stance also will affect initial structural assurance belief. An individual with high trusting stance believes that trusting others facilitates success, regardless of his or her beliefs about specific people. This assumption is consistent with a perception that safeguards or safety nets will protect the individual involved from bad consequences other people cause. In other words, developing a high level of structural assurance belief is facilitated when one has a high level of trusting stance. When parties first meet, the person's already-formed high level of trusting stance will tend to encourage a corresponding high level of structural assurance belief. Over time, the relationship between these constructs may be reciprocal, but at the initial meeting, a person will rely on his or her prior tendencies, in terms of trusting stance, to form structural assurance belief.

Proposition 7: In the initial relationship, faith in humanity and trusting stance will lead to structural assurance belief.

Categorization Processes Enable High Levels of Trusting Beliefs

In a new relationship a person may use three types of categorization processes to develop trusting beliefs: (1) unit grouping, (2) reputation categorization, and (3) stereotyping. "Unit grouping" means to put the other person in the same category as oneself. "Reputation categorization" means that one assigns attributes to another person based on second-hand information about the person. "Stereotyping" means to place another person into a general category of persons.

Unit grouping. Because those who are grouped together tend to share common goals and values, they tend to perceive each other in a positive light (Kramer,

Brewer, & Hanna, 1996). Hence, one group member will be more likely to form trusting beliefs toward another group member. For example, Zucker, Darby, Brewer, and Peng (1996) found that being a member of the same organization generated the trust needed for scientists to collaborate on research. In their study Brewer and Silver (1978) found that people perceived in-group members to be more trustworthy than out-group members. These studies provide evidence that unit grouping quickly leads to high levels of trusting beliefs. As an example of the rapid effects of unit grouping, in studying prospective dating couples who had never met, Darley and Berscheid (1967) found that the knowledge that one would be paired with the other tended to enhance the former's beliefs about the latter's characteristics. Applied to a new task team, unit grouping would enable one member to immediately form trusting beliefs about another team member.

Reputation categorization. Those with good reputations are categorized as trustworthy individuals. Reputation may reflect professional competence (Barber, 1983; Powell, 1996) or the other trusting beliefs: benevolence (Dasgupta, 1988), honesty, and predictability. A person may be perceived as a competent individual because she or he is a member of a competent group (Dasgupta, 1988) or because of her or his actions. Therefore, if the individual has a good reputation, one will quickly develop trusting beliefs about that individual, even without firsthand knowledge.

Stereotyping. Stereotyping may be done either on a broad level, such as gender (e.g., Orbell, Dawes, & Schwartz-Shea, 1994), or on a more specific level, such as prejudices for or against occupational groups (e.g., used-car salespeople). At their first meeting, parties may form stereotypes about each other, based on voice (e.g., male/female or domestic/foreign; Baldwin, 1992) or physical appearance (Dion, Berscheid, & Walster, 1972; Riker, 1971). By positive stereotyping, one can quickly form positive trusting beliefs about the other by generalizing from the favorable category into which the person was placed.

Proposition 8: In the initial relationship, categorization processes that place the other person in a positive grouping will tend to produce high levels of trusting beliefs.

Illusions of Control Process: Interactive Effects That Elevate Trusting Beliefs

Here we explain why the illusions of control process will interact with categorization processes, faith in humanity, and structural assurance belief to produce high levels of trusting beliefs. People in an uncertain situation will take small actions to try to assure themselves that things are under their personal control (Langer, 1975). This results in unrealistically inflated perceptions of personal control (Taylor & Brown, 1988), which Langer (1975) terms "illusions of control." Illusions, obviously, involve perceptions that differ from reality, and considerable evidence demonstrates the presence of illusion in cognitive processing (e.g., Fiske & Taylor, 1984).

The illusions of control process that helps build trusting beliefs may be similar to the process by which people become overconfident of their judgments, as reported by Langer (1975) and Paese and Sniezek (1991). First, one forms a tentative belief, and then one watches for clues that confirm the belief. Even without evidence, the effort of watching tends to overinflate confidence in one's judgment (Davis & Kotteman, 1994). Similarly, even a slight effort at confirming one's tentative trusting beliefs in another may overinflate one's confidence that high levels of trusting beliefs are warranted.

Token control efforts. People may make an initial effort to think about another person's trustworthiness, or they may, upon meeting a person, immediately attempt to gauge whether or not they can influence that person in some small way (e.g., make them smile). We term such actions "token control efforts." One individual is not trying to categorize the other but, rather, is testing his or her ability to deal with the other individual successfully.

Initially, a person is likely to use token control efforts because she or he does not know from experience whether or not the other has the attributes needed to be considered trustworthy. After making such small control efforts, the individual may form an unjustifiably strong confidence that one's positive categorization, faith in humanity, and structural assurance beliefs are correct and, therefore, that the other person is trustworthy. Langer (1975), for example, in a study of overconfidence, found that token control efforts to improve one's chances in a lottery (i.e., by choosing their own lottery ticket) made one very overconfident of winning.

Trust theorists have posited that trust building involves illusion (Holmes, 1991; Meyerson et al., 1996). The results of one empirical trust study support this position. Kramer (1994) found that ruminating for a few minutes about others' motives and intentions increased a person's confidence in the accuracy of his or her judgments of the others. Mental assessments tend to increase one's confidence because, as Langer (1975) found, they move a task further from the realm of chance and closer to the realm of a skill-based judgment task. Hence, token control efforts can support a person's confidence in trust-related beliefs.

Interactive effects. We propose that token control efforts will interact with categorization processes, faith in humanity, and structural assurance belief, strengthening an individual's capacity to form trusting beliefs. Token control efforts will give a person the illusion that his or her positive faith in humanity can apply to the particular other party by convincing the individual that he or she is applying skill—not just chance—to a trust-related judgment of the other party. Similarly, token control efforts will (1) build confidence that one's positive categorization of the other person is correct, and (2) bolster confidence that structural safeguards make the environment secure and, by association, the people involved trustworthy.

Proposition 9: In the initial relationship, token control efforts will strengthen the tendency of categorization processes, faith in humanity, and structural assurance belief to produce high levels of trusting beliefs.

....

Model Implications for Trusting Intention Fragility/Robustness

Paradoxically, although trust often has been termed "fragile" (e.g., Worchel, 1979), it has also been described as "robust," in that it progresses in upward spirals (e.g., Zand, 1972) or becomes more fully developed over time (Gabarro, 1978; Sitkin & Roth, 1993). Our model of initial trust development improves our understanding of how initial trusting intention, the model's ultimate consequent, may be either fragile or robust under different conditions.

Conditions Under Which Initial Trusting Intention is Likely to be Fragile

Initial trusting intention is likely to be fragile under three conditions: (1) inadequate support from Figure 2's antecedent constructs, (2) the tentative and assumption-based nature of the antecedent constructs, and (3) high perceived risk. *Fragile* refers to a trusting intention level that is likely to undergo large changes during a given time frame. That is, as time passes and conditions change, to what extent is the level of trusting intention likely to change? Although researchers' use of the term "fragile" typically refers to a high trust level suddenly becoming low, we define the term so that it could apply to either high or low trust levels. At high levels, fragile trust is subject to rapid decreases, whereas at low levels, fragile trust is subject to rapid increases. In either case fragile trust is unstable, quickly changeable, or easily influenced.

Robust (the opposite of fragile) refers to a trusting intention level that does not change dramatically during a given time frame. As an example of the difference between robust and fragile, if a trusting intentions level were to move downward dramatically, we would call it fragile rather than robust.

Inadequate antecedent support. Intuitively, the more highly positive antecedents trusting intention has, the less fragile it will be; a weak combination of trusting intention antecedents will result in a fragile trusting intention. That is, if trusting intention is associated with only one highly positive antecedent, it is likely to change downward soon after the initial period of a relationship.

For example, suppose a home buyer with a low disposition to trust and low trusting beliefs in the home builder enters into a contract to have a house built, based on the belief that the legal processes will provide a safety net (structural assurance belief). Further, the home buyer has no cues by which to categorize the home builder positively. In this situation the only highly positive antecedent of trusting intention is structural assurance belief. In such cases, Dasgupta remarks that the trust one person has in another to fulfill a contract rests precariously upon the power of the agencies that are able to enforce contracts: "If your trust in the enforcement agency falters, you will not trust persons to fulfill their terms of an agreement and thus will not enter into that agreement. . . . It is this inter-connectedness which makes trust such a fragile commodity" (1988: 50). However, if the home buyer's structural assurance belief is accompanied by trusting beliefs in the home builder, he or she may be able to maintain trusting intention even when his or her structural assurance belief wavers.

In general, then, when any particular antecedent of trusting intention is the only one at a high level, trusting intention most likely will be fragile. For example, the home buyer's honesty belief is an antecedent of trusting intention that can crumble quickly (Dasgupta, 1988), if the buyer's experience with the builder indicates that the belief is mistaken. We previously discussed how disposition to trust may be a weak trusting intention antecedent in the presence of a strong situation. The home buyer's high disposition to trust will not hold up if he or she has reason to believe that structural assurances are missing or that the home builder may be dishonest. Situation- or person-specific beliefs supporting trusting intention quickly become stronger than dispositional support as the buyer gains experience with the situation.

Tentative, assumption-based antecedents. Trusting intention will be fragile at the start of a relationship because of the tentative and assumption-based nature of its antecedents (Figure 2). Initial trust is not based so much on evidence as on lack of *contrary* evidence (Gambetta, 1988). Illusions of control are almost completely assumption based. If the illusion crumbles, the constructs bolstered by it can decrease rapidly, negatively affecting trusting intention. Riker points out that stereotyping categorization is tentative because "only rarely do [the applied categories] effectively discriminate between the trustworthy and the untrustworthy" (1971: 78). Hence, trusting beliefs (leading to trusting intention) produced by categorization are subject to abrupt corrections. Initial institution-based trust, founded on assumptions about the situation, is subject to rapid deterioration as facts become known. One's disposition to trust assumes things will work out successfully, and will only be salient until situational or personal facts are uncovered (Johnson-George & Swap, 1982).

Experience supplies facts that can quickly displace illusions and assumptions. Fazio and Zanna (1981) point out two reasons for this. First, people consider behavioral experience information to be more reliable than indirectly obtained information. Further, more reliable information reduces uncertainty, making it highly desirable (Smith, Benson, & Curley, 1991). Second, an individual's direct experience in forming an attitude or judgment makes that attitude more readily accessible in his or her memory (cf., Riker, 1971: 78).

High perceived risk. Some risk is perceived even when people trust each other (e.g., Mayer et al., 1995). High levels of perceived risk make it more likely that the trustor will pay attention to the other's behavior, seeking validating information. Kramer (1996) found this to be true in relationships between students and faculty members. The more one attends to new information about the other person, the more likely it is that contrary evidence will be found, negatively affecting trusting intention.

Proposition 10: In the initial relationship, high trusting intention is likely to be very fragile when it is supported by only one or two antecedents, when it relies almost exclusively on assumptions, and when perceived risk is high.

Several of the above fragility examples demonstrate that the interdependent nature of the model constructs is itself a reason trusting intention may be fragile. When one construct's level is reduced, it is likely to negatively affect a related construct. For example, whereas a decrease in trusting stance directly affects trusting intention, it also affects institution-based trust. Also, while institution-based trust will have a direct effect on trusting intention, it will also affect trusting intention through trusting beliefs. Hence, the model portrays the possibility that trusting intention is like the roof on the proverbial "house of cards," which collapses when one structurally key antecedent slips.

Conditions Under Which Trusting Intention Is Likely to Be Robust

Trusting intention is likely to be robust for three reasons: (1) adequate antecedent support, (2) belief-confirming cognitive mechanisms, and (3) social mechanisms.

Adequate antecedent support. Given our model, the most obvious reason trusting intention will continue to be high is that, in many cases, several of the antecedents shown in Figure 2 will exist at high levels. Further, it is more probable that the antecedents will exist at a consistently high level rather than in a combination of high and low levels. Researchers of cognitive consistency have found evidence that related beliefs tend to stay consistent with each other because people keep their various cognitions reconciled (Abelson et al., 1968; Luhmann, 1979). Hence, for a given subject, we expect to find relatively consistent levels among trust constructs, especially as the relationship begins. A consistently high set of antecedents will be less likely to cause a trusting intention dissolution than will an inconsistently high set.

For example, in a classroom setting it is likely that, because of past experiences, students feel comfortable with their own and the instructor's roles (institution-based trust). Hence, the students probably have formed structural assurance beliefs within class situations generally. Hopefully, they have heard enough about the instructor's reputation so that, along with early cues, they can categorize her or him as having trustworthy attributes (e.g., competence), thus forming one or more of the trusting beliefs. Under these circumstances, the students are likely to have high initial trusting intention toward the instructor. This trusting intention probably will prove stable, given it is likely supported by trusting beliefs and institution-based trust. Unless the instructor does something to seriously violate the positive expectations a student develops from the initial class interaction, the student's trusting intention is likely to endure throughout the course. But trusting intention is even more likely to stay high if the student also has high disposition to trust, which will reinforce his or her institution-based trust and trusting beliefs. A person with a high disposition to trust is more likely to see good points and to overlook flaws in another person or situation that would threaten high trusting intention levels by lowering trusting beliefs or institution-based trust.

Belief-confirming cognitive mechanisms. Attentional cognitive processes play a role in sustaining initial trust. Not all information is attended to, and unless it is, it will not affect trust-related constructs. Indeed, peoples' beliefs and preconceived notions tend to filter the information they heed. Good (1988) remarks that evidence contrary to one's beliefs is seldom sought and often ignored, citing psychological experimental evidence (e.g., Mitroff, 1974; Tajfel, 1969; Wason, 1960) for this confirmation bias effect. Similarly, Taylor and Brown cite evidence that people "generally select, interpret, and recall information to be consistent with their prior beliefs or theories (see Fiske & Taylor, 1984; Greenwald, 1980; Taylor & Crocker, 1981, for reviews)" (1988: 202). The authors apply this effect to positive illusion-based beliefs: "Consequently, if a person's prior beliefs are positive, cognitive biases that favor conservatism generally will maintain positive illusions more specifically" (Taylor & Brown, 1988: 202). They cite additional evidence that peoples' preconceptions guide which information they consider relevant and, therefore, to which information they attend (Howard & Rothbart, 1980; Nisbett & Ross, 1980).

Researchers conducting empirical studies have confirmed that much counterbelief evidence is simply ignored. An example is provided by Starbuck and Milliken's (1988) study of the 1986 NASA Challenger disaster. The authors found that NASA and Morton-Thiokol managers ignored or explained away evidence that rocket booster O-rings would erode in a low-temperature takeoff. Contrary evidence is especially ignored when people perceive things to be going well. Sitkin, for example, states that "small successes may unintentionally induce low levels of attention and reduced information search" (1992: 232). In contrast, "The greater the incidence of small prior failure, the more attention will be paid to and the more deeply will [be] the processing of information about potential problems" (Sitkin, 1992: 240).

The tendency to ignore counterbelief evidence should be true of trusting beliefs as well as other beliefs. However, in the initial relationship, the desire to feel assured through experiential evidence (Fazio & Zanna, 1981) will, to some extent, mitigate this cognitive bias. This desire will be heightened by low levels of disposition to trust or institution-based trust or by high levels of perceived risk, because the person will require additional assurances that his or her initial beliefs are accurate.

When people do attend to information that disconfirms their views, they often discount it as inaccurate or uninformative (Markus, 1977; Ross & Anderson, 1992; Swann & Read, 1981; Taylor & Brown, 1988), or they reinterpret it positively (Holmes, 1991; Robinson, 1996). Ross and Anderson point out that "beliefs ... are remarkably resilient in the face of empirical challenges that seem logically devastating" (1982: 144). People tend to accept belief-supportive information uncritically, but slowly acknowledge disconfirming evidence (Tetlock, 1985). Ross and Anderson (1992) posit that people subject disconfirming evidence to considerable scrutiny but do not go back and update or re-evaluate evidence relevant to their beliefs based on disconfirming evidence. People also search their memories to find ways of explaining their existing beliefs (Ross & Anderson, 1982).

Similarly, Kahneman and Tversky (1973) found significant evidence that people will interpret ambiguous or incomplete information in a way that agrees with their pre-existing beliefs. If one has a high level of trusting intention toward another, for example, then one can view specific trust violations as isolated exceptions or as a personal quirk (Sitkin & Roth, 1993; Zucker, 1986), with no resulting negative effect on trusting beliefs. High faith in humanity provides another reason to ignore or discount such behavior, because it assumes that most people are basically good. Having high faith in humanity will facilitate quick forgiveness of trust violations.

Good (1988) has suggested that another reason for this "cognitive inertia" is the "set effect," which refers to the continued use of mentally stored procedures to handle a situation, even when the situation changes. That is, once people have developed a situational strategy, they tend to continue to use it, even when it does not work. Applied to trust, this means that an individual will continue to trust another, even when the latter breaches the former's trust—at least for a while. Good (1988) uses the set effect to reinterpret some of the results of experimentalists who studied trust with such procedures as the Trucking Game. Note the interactive effect of this cognitive tendency with the model's constructs: high institution-based trust and high disposition to trust jointly encourage a person to believe such a course of action is not very risky.

Luhmann (1979) offers a related reason for why trust may be resilient, stating that people build up mechanisms to handle refutations of their trust decisions. This is especially true when the felt security associated with trusting intention is not strong:

Insecure expectations, however paradoxical it may at first appear, are psychologically more stable [than secure ones].... [They are] normalized, stereotyped and thus in various ways immunized against the refutation. Explanations of disappointment are built into [them] in such a way that a particular case of disappointment presents no problem but rather confirms the structure of the expectation as a whole. (Luhmann, 1979: 79)

Hence, it appears that people develop mechanisms enabling them to absorb disappointments as part of their expectation of the other person, thus reducing the effect of the disappointment on trusting intention. We speculate that individuals with high levels of disposition to trust will absorb disappointments better than those with low levels.

Proposition 11: In the initial relationship, high trusting intention is likely to be robust when (1) a combination of several of its antecedents encourages the trustor to ignore, rationalize, or absorb the negative actions of the other and (2) continued success or low perceived risk of failure consequences cause little critical attention to be paid to the other's behavior. Subjects with high disposition to trust or institution-based trust levels are likely to pay even less critical attention.

Social mechanisms. Good (1988) notes that being around another person generally will increase an individual's favorable beliefs about that person. This occurs because the interpersonal cues from the other person generally are harder to misconstrue face to face and because the pair can more easily go beyond surface information to more substantive levels of mutual understanding. Hence, high levels of trusting intention likely will be sustained as people interact in cooperative ways. If the individuals hold positive beliefs about each other, they are not likely to decrease interaction (Darley & Fazio, 1980). Therefore, the trusting cycle becomes self-sustaining.

Social interaction also will tend to uphold early trusting intention, because people in social situations tend to confirm their beliefs about themselves (Swann, 1983) and about each other. For example, one who trusts another will tend to express that trust in actions toward the other. Because initially extended trust is usually reciprocated (e.g., Burt & Knez, 1996), the other party will also express trust. This confirms the first party's trusting beliefs, as Dasgupta (1988) notes, which, in turn, supports continued high levels of trusting intention.

Social interaction also upholds early trusting intention because of reputation effects. A person's reputation spreads gradually (Dasgupta, 1988), through social interaction (Burt & Knez, 1996). One party remembers the other party's previous encounters. This interactional history cumulates, along with information about the person's background (Dasgupta, 1988), and is transmitted to others. When many people perceive that an individual has a good reputation, it is harder for a negative event to significantly reduce a high level of trusting beliefs in that individual.

We believe that social interaction also sustains trusting intention through institution-based trust. When parties interact in a cordial way, they establish a feeling and appearance that everything is normal or in proper order (Lewis & Weigert, 1985a). Hence, social interaction sustains situational normality belief. Through situational normality belief, the parties' interaction strengthens trusting intention. If one has high levels of situational normality belief, one is also likely to believe that structural assurances will operate properly in the situation. Structural assurance will, in turn, positively influence trusting beliefs and trusting intention, as discussed above.

Proposition 12: In the initial relationship, high trusting intention is likely to be robust when (1) the parties interact face to face, frequently in positive ways, or (2) the trusted party has built a widely known good reputation. Social interaction affects trusting intention by its positive effects on trusting beliefs and institution-based trust.

Research Implications and Conclusion

Future Research Implications

The interplay between trusting intention and its antecedents helps explain the paradox of high trust in new relationships and situations (e.g., Kramer, 1994), but our model also can help explain "disturbing" results in game theory research (Baxter, 1972: 100)—a well-spring for trust theory historically. In Baxter's review of the two-person game theory research, he indicates that researchers had found no solid link between trusting personality and trusting behavior in the Prisoner's Dilemma game. Because our model ties dispositional variables to beliefs and intentions, it suggests that personality variables may be too distal from behaviors to be predictive. Our model's time boundary suggests that disposition-related trust will only be salient when the parties first meet in an ambiguous situation. Further, the institution-based trust constructs help explain why no solid link was found by game theorists.

Whereas game theorists assume that the game context effectively restricts the effects of situational variables (Baxter, 1972), our model's use of institution-based trust suggests that what a subject believes about the situation is an empirical question that should be measured as a potential confound (e.g., Erez, 1992), rather than being assumed away. Over 25 years ago, Kee and Knox recommended that Prisoner's Dilemma research should include "continuous" measures of subjects' cognitions in addition to their behavioral choices (1970: 365). Very little trust research has been done in this manner. Our model's constructs provide a reasoned theoretical basis for doing so. We suggest that researchers replicate early behavioral experiments while measuring our constructs. This will enable researchers to reinterpret historical results.

Significant empirical work is needed in order to obtain evidence regarding the propositions we make in this article. First, researchers should develop reliable and valid instruments reflecting the constructs in this article, and they should then use them to test various subsets of the model through questionnaire studies. For example, Propositions 1 and 2 and 4 through 7 could be tested in one study by measuring trusting intention, faith in humanity, trusting stance, structural assurance belief, and benevolence belief.

Second, researchers should test our categorization and illusion propositions in laboratory settings, incorporating disposition to trust and institution-based trust constructs as control variables.

Third, researchers should test the model's interactive effects. For example, scholars should test whether disposition to trust constructs moderate the effects of categorization on trusting beliefs. Based on Proposition 1, one could test whether or not structural assurance belief moderates the link between faith in humanity and trusting beliefs. Trusting stance and institution-based trust may also have an interactive effect on trusting intention. The combination of a high situational normality belief and a high structural assurance belief would probably produce higher trusting beliefs than either would alone.

Finally, the fragility/robustness of initial trust should be tested, based on our propositions, in which we argued that initial trust may be either fragile or robust under certain conditions. For example, one could test, through longitudinal laboratory experiments, the extent to which social interaction increases the robustness of trusting intention when (1) the relationship is successful/unsuccessful or (2) risk is high or low. Many more conditions could be posited.

Our distinction between trust *levels* and trust *fragility/robustness* raises important issues that merit further conceptual and empirical work. For example, a high initial level of trusting intention may be quite fragile (subject to change), whereas a low initial level of trusting intention may not be very fragile. Thus, an interesting research question is under what conditions are low initial levels of trusting intention less fragile than high initial levels of trusting intention?

Conclusion

Our primary contribution in this article is explaining the high initial trust paradox by synthesizing a model of constructs and processes from diverse trust research streams. Because initial trusting intention is not always high, our model resolves the paradox by pointing out why it could be high initially but may not be high because of the situation or the persons involved. Thus, the model is predictive based upon specified conditions related to the antecedents of trusting intention.

This model, along with our discussion of the conditions producing fragile versus robust initial trust, should generate significant amounts of research. The delineation of two specific types of institution-based trust and disposition to trust constructs provides researchers construct definitions that lend themselves to consistent empirical measurement. By using both higher-level constructs (e.g., trusting beliefs) and lower-level constructs (e.g., honesty belief), we have helped organize the "confusing potpourri" (Shapiro, 1987a: 625) of trust construct definitions researchers must grapple with.

Our model integrates different aspects of trust that have not been linked previously, and it does so within a specific time parameter. Some have called for more integrative models that simultaneously address dispositional and situational constructs (Davis-Blake & Pfeffer, 1989; Sitkin & Pablo, 1992). We have answered this call, creating a model that brings together dispositional, situational, and interpersonal constructs from four divergent research streams.

Poole & Van de Ven (1989) remark that by adding the temporal dimension, one can improve theories. In this article we explain that the processes by which trust forms initially are not the same as those by which it forms later. In particular, a model of continuing trust will emphasize experiential knowledge while de-emphasizing assumptions and dispositions. In this way, the model's temporal lens highlights the unique aspects of how trust forms at the earliest stage of an organizational relationship.

....

Acknowledgement

We express our appreciation to Ellen Berscheid, Shawn Curley, Fred Davis, Gerald Smith, and Aks Zaheer for their helpful reviews and comments on earlier versions of this article. Special thanks go to Special Issue Editor Sim Sitkin and the anonymous reviewers of *AMR*.

....

References

Abelson, R. P., Aronson, E., McGuire, W. J., Newcomb, T. M., Rosenberg, M. J., & Tannenbaum, P. H. (Eds.). 1968. *Theories of cognitive consistency: A sourcebook.* Chicago: Rand-McNally.

Ajzen, I. 1988. *Attitudes, personality, and behavior.* Chicago: Dorsey Press.

Baier, A. 1986. Trust and antitrust. *Ethics,* 96: 231–260.

Baldwin, M. W. 1992. Relational schemas and the processing of social information. *Psychological Bulletin,* 112: 461–484.

Barber, B. 1983. *The logic and limits of trust.* New Brunswick, NJ: Rutgers University Press.

Baxter, G. W. 1972. Personality and attitudinal characteristics and cooperation in two-person games: A review. In L. S. Wrightsman, J. O'Connor, & N. J. Baker (Eds.), *Cooperation and competition: Readings on mixed-motive games:* 97–103. Belmont, CA: Wadsworth.

Berg, J., Dickhaut, J., & McCabe, K. 1995. *Trust, reciprocity, and social history.* Unpublished working paper. University of Minnesota, Minneapolis.

Blau, P. M. 1964. *Exchange and power in social life.* New York: Wiley.

Bowlby, J. 1982. *Attachment and loss. Volume It Attachment.* New York: Basic Books.

Brewer, M. B. 1981. Ethnocentrism and its role in interpersonal trust. In M. B. Brewer & B. E. Collins (Eds.), *Scientific inquiry and the social sciences:* 214–231. San Francisco: Jossey-Bass.

Brewer, M. B., & Silver, M. 1978. Ingroup bias as a function of task characteristics. *European Journal of Social Psychology*, 8: 393–400.

Bromiley, P., & Cummings, L. L. 1995. Transactions costs in organizations with trust. In R. Bies, B. Sheppard, & R. Lewicki (Eds.), *Research on negotiations in organizations*, vol. 5: 219–247. Greenwich, CT: JAI Press.

Burt, R. S., & Knez, M. 1996. Trust and third-party gossip. In R. M. Kramer & T. R. Tyler (Eds.), *Trust in organizations: Frontiers of theory and research*: 68–89. Thousand Oaks, CA: Sage.

Coleman, J. S. 1990. *Foundations of social theory*. Cambridge, MA: Harvard University Press.

Currall, S. C., & Judge, T. A. 1995. Measuring trust between organizational boundary role persons. *Organizational Behavior and Human Decision Processes*, 64: 151–170.

Darley, J. M., & Berscheid, E. 1967. Increased liking as a result of anticipation of personal contact. *Human Relations*, 20: 29–40.

Darley, J. M., & Fazio, R. H. 1980. Expectancy confirmation processes arising in the social interaction sequence. *American Psychologist*, 35: 867–881.

Dasgupta, P. 1988. Trust as a commodity. In D. Gambetta (Ed.), *Trust: Making and breaking cooperative relations*: 47–72. New York: Basil Blackwell.

Davis, F. D. 1989. Perceived usefulness, perceived ease of use, and user acceptance of information technology. *MIS Quarterly*, 13: 319–340.

Davis, F. D., & Kotteman, J. E. 1994. User perceptions of decision support effectiveness: Two production planning experiments. *Decision Sciences*, 25: 57–77.

Davis-Blake, A., & Pfeffer, J. 1989. Just a mirage: The search for dispositional effects in organizational research. *Academy of Management Review*, 14: 385–400.

Dion, K. K., Berscheid, E., & Walster, E. 1972. What is beautiful is good. *Journal of Personality and Social Psychology*, 24: 285–290.

Dobing, B. 1993. *Building trust in user-analyst relationships*. Unpublished doctoral dissertation. University of Minnesota, Minneapolis.

Erez, M. 1992. Reflections on the Latham/Erez/Locke Study. In P. J. Frost & R. E. Stablein (Eds.), *Doing exemplary research*: 155–164. Newbury Park, CA: Sage.

Erikson, E. H. 1968. *Identity: Youth and crisis*. New York: Norton.

Evans, M. G., Gunz, H. P., & Jalland, R. M. 1996. The aftermath of downsizing: A cautionary tale about restructuring and careers. *Business Horizons*, 39: 61–66.

Fazio, R. H., & Zanna, M. P. 1981. Direct experience and attitude-behavior consistency. In L. Berkowitz (Ed.), *Advances in experimental social psychology*, vol. 14: 162–202. New York: Academic Press.

Fishbein, M., & Ajzen, I. 1975. *Belief, attitude, intention and behavior: An introduction to theory and research*. Reading, MA: Addison-Wesley.

Fiske, S. T., & Taylor, S. E. 1984. *Social cognition*. Reading, MA: Addison-Wesley.

Gabarro, J. J. 1978. The development of trust, influence, and expectations. In A. G. Athos & J. J. Gabarro (Eds.), *Interpersonal behavior: Communication and understanding in relationships*: 290–303. Englewood Cliffs, NJ: Prentice-Hall.

Gambetta, D. 1988. Can we trust trust? In D. Gambetta (Ed.), *Trust: Making and breaking cooperative relations*: 213–237. New York: Basil Blackwell.

Garfinkel, H. 1963. A conception of, and experiments with, "trust" as a condition of stable concerted actions. In O. J. Harvey (Ed.), *Motivation and social interaction:* 187–238. New York: Ronald Press.

Goldsteen, R., Schorr, J. K., & Goldsteen, K. S. 1989. Longitudinal study of appraisal at Three Mile Island: Implications for life event research. *Social Science and Medicine,* 28: 389–398.

Good, D. 1988. Individuals, interpersonal relations, and trust. In D. Gambetta (Ed.), *Trust: Making and breaking cooperative relations:* 31–48. New York: Basil Blackwell.

Greenwald, A. G. 1980. The totalitarian ego: Fabrication and revision of personal history. *American Psychologist,* 35: 603–618.

Henry, J. E., & Hartzler, M. 1997. Virtual teams: Today's reality, today's challenge. *Quality Progress,* 30(5): 108–109.

Holmes, J. G. 1991. Trust and the appraisal process in close relationships. In W. H. Jones & D. Perlman (Eds.), *Advances in personal relationships,* vol. 2: 57–104. London: Jessica Kingsley.

Howard, J. W., & Rothbart, M. 1980. Social categorization and memory for ingroup and outgroup behavior. *Journal of Personality and Social Psychology,* 38: 301–310.

Hunter, J. E., & Gerbing, D. W. 1982. Unidimensional measurement, second order factor analysis, and causal models. In B. M. Staw & L. L. Cummings (Eds.), *Research in organizational behavior,* vol. 4: 267–320. Greenwich, CT: JAI Press.

Johnson-George, C., & Swap, W. C. 1982. Measurement of specific interpersonal trust: Construction and validation of a scale to assess trust in a specific other. *Journal of Personality and Social Psychology,* 43: 1308–1317.

Kahneman, D., & Tversky, A. 1973. On the psychology of prediction. *Psychological Review,* 80: 237–251.

Kee, H. W., & Knox, R. E. 1970. Conceptual and methodological considerations in the study of trust and suspicion. *Journal of Conflict Resolution,* 14: 357–366.

Kramer, R. M. 1984. The sinister attribution error: Paranoid cognition and collective distrust in organizations. *Motivation and Emotion,* 18: 199–230.

Kramer, R. M. 1998. Divergent realities and convergent disappointments in the hierarchic relation: Trust and the intuitive auditor at work. In R. M. Kramer & T. R. Tyler (Eds.), *Trust in organizations: Frontiers of theory and research:* 216–245. Thousand Oaks, CA: Sage.

Kramer, R. M., Brewer, M. B., & Hanna, B. A. 1996. Collective trust and collective action: The decision to trust as a social decision. In R. M. Kramer & T. R. Tyler (Eds.), *Trust in organizations: Frontiers of theory and research:* 357–389. Thousand Oaks, CA: Sage.

Langer, E. J. 1975. The illusion of control. *Journal of Personality and Social Psychology,* 32: 311–328.

Lewicki, R. J., & Bunker, B. B. 1995. Trust in relationships: A model of trust development and decline. In B. B. Bunker & J. Z. Rubin (Eds.), *Conflict, cooperation and justice:* 133–173. San Francisco: Jossey-Bass.

Lewis, J. D., & Weigert, A. J. 1985a. Trust as a social reality. *Social Forces.* 63: 967–985.

Lewis, J. D., & Weigert, A. J. 1985b. Social atomism, holism, and trust. *The Sociological Quarterly,* 26: 455–471.

Lipnack, J., & Stamps, J. 1997. *Virtual teams: Reaching across space, time and organization with technology.* New York: Wiley.

Luhmann, N. 1979. *Trust and power.* New York: Wiley.

Markus, H. 1977. Self-schemata and processing information about the self. *Journal of Personality and Social Psychology,* 35: 63–78.

Mayer, R. C., Davis, J. H., & Schoorman, F. D. 1995. An integrative model of organizational trust. *Academy of Management Review,* 20: 709–734.

Meyerson, D., Weick, K. E., & Kramer, R. M. 1996. Swift trust and temporary groups. In R. M. Kramer & T. R. Tyler (Eds.), *Trust in organizations: Frontiers of theory and research:* 166–195. Thousand Oaks, CA: Sage.

Mitroff, I. I. 1974. *The subjective side of science.* Amsterdam: Elsevier Science Publications.

Mullins, J. W., & Cummings, L. L. In press. Situational strength: A framework for understanding the role of individuals in bringing about proactive strategic change. *Journal of Organizational Change Management.*

Nisbett, R. E., & Ross, L. 1980. *Human inference: Strategies and shortcomings of social judgments.* Englewood Cliffs, NJ: Prentice-Hall.

Orbell, J., Dawes, R., & Schwartz-Shea, P. 1994. Trust, social categories, and individuals: The case of gender. *Motivation and Emotion,* 18: 109–128.

Paese, P. W., & Sniezek, J. A. 1991. Influences on the appropriateness of confidence in judgment: Practice, effort, information, and decision-making. *Organizational Behavior and Human Decision Processes,* 48: 100–130.

Poole, M. S., & Van de Ven, A. H. 1989. Using paradox to build management and organization theories. *Academy of Management Review,* 14: 562–578.

Powell, W. W. 1996. Trust-based forms of governance. In R. M. Kramer & T. R. Tyler (Eds.), *Trust in organizations: Frontiers of theory and research:* 51–67. Thousand Oaks, CA: Sage.

Rempel, J. K., Holmes, J. G., & Zanna, M. P. 1985. Trust in close relationships. *Journal of Personality and Social Psychology,* 49: 95–112.

Riker, W. H. 1971. The nature of trust. In J. T. Tedeschi (Ed.), *Perspectives on social power:* 63–81. Chicago: Aldine.

Robinson, S. L. 1996. Trust and breach of the psychological contract. *Administrative Science Quarterly,* 41: 574–599.

Rosenberg, M. 1957. *Occupations and values.* Glencoe, IL: Free Press.

Ross, L., & Anderson, C. A. 1982. Shortcomings in the attribution process: On the origins and maintenance of erroneous social assessments. In D. Kahneman, P. Slovic, & A. Tversky (Eds.), *Judgment under uncertainty: Heuristics and biases:* 129–152. Cambridge, England: Cambridge University Press.

Rotter, J. B. 1967. A new scale for the measurement of interpersonal trust. *Journal of Personality,* 35: 651–665.

Rotter, J. B. 1971. Generalized expectancies for interpersonal trust. *American Psychologist,* 26: 443–452.

Rotter, J. B. 1980. Interpersonal trust, trustworthiness, and gullibility. *American Psychologist,* 35: 1–7.

Shapiro, S. P. 1987a. The social control of impersonal trust. *American Journal of Sociology,* 93: 623–658.

Shapiro, S. P. 1987b. Policing trust. In C. D. Shearing & P. C. Stenning (Eds.), *Private policing:* 194–220. Newbury Park, CA: Sage.

Shapiro, D. L., Sheppard, B. H., & Cheraskin, L. 1992. Business on a handshake. *Negotiation Journal*, 3: 365–377.

Sitkin, S. B. 1992. Learning through failure: The strategy of small losses. In B. Staw & L. L. Cummings (Eds.), *Research in organizational behavior*, vol. 14: 231–266. Greenwich, CT: JAI Press.

Sitkin, S. B. 1995. On the positive effect of legalization on trust. In R. Bies, B. Sheppard, & R. Lewicki (Eds.), *Research on negotiations in organizations*, vol. 5: 185–217. Greenwich, CT: JAI Press.

Sitkin, S. B., & Pablo, A. L. 1992. Reconceptualizing the determinants of risk behavior. *Academy of Management Review*, 17: 9–38.

Sitkin, S. B., & Roth, N. L. 1993. Explaining the limited effectiveness of legalistic "remedies" for trust/distrust. *Organization Science*, 4: 367–392.

Smith, G. F., Benson, P. G., & Curley, S. P. 1991. Belief, knowledge, and uncertainty: A cognitive perspective on subjective probability. *Organizational Behavior and Human Decision Processes*, 48: 291–321.

Starbuck, W. H., & Milliken, F. J. 1988. Challenger: Finetuning the odds until something breaks. *Journal of Management Studies*, 25: 319–340.

Swann, W. B., Jr. 1983. Self-verification: Bringing social reality into harmony with the self. In J. Suls & A. G. Greenwald (Eds.), *Social psychology perspectives*, vol. 2: 33–66. Hillsdale, NJ: Lawrence Erlbaum Associates.

Swann, W. B., Jr., & Read, S. J. 1981. Self-verification processes: How we sustain our self-conceptions. *Journal of Experimental Social Psychology*, 17: 351–370.

Tajfel, H. 1969. Cognitive aspects of prejudice. *Journal of Social issues*, 25: 79–97.

Taylor, S. E., & Brown, J. D. 1988. Illusion and well-being: A social psychological perspective on mental health. *Psychological Bulletin*, 103: 193–210.

Taylor, S. E., & Crocker, J. 1981. Schematic-bases of social information processing. In E. T. Higgins, C. P. Herman, & M. P. Zanna (Eds.), *Social cognition: The Ontario Symposium*, vol. 1: 89–134. Hillsdale, NJ: Lawrence Erlbaum Associates.

Tetlock, P. 1985. Accountability: The neglected social context of judgment and choice. In L. L. Cummings & B. M. Staw (Eds.), *Research in organizational behavior*, vol. 7: 297–332. Greenwich, CT: JAI Press.

Wason, P. C. 1960. On the failure to eliminate hypotheses in a conceptual task. *Quarterly Journal of Experimental Psychology*, 12: 129–140.

Williamson, O. E. 1993. Calculativeness, trust, and economic organization. *Journal of Law and Economics*, 34: 453–502.

Worchel, P. 1979. Trust and distrust. In W. G. Austin & S. Worchel (Eds.), *The social psychology of intergroup relations:* 174–187. Monterey, CA: Brooks/Cole Publishing.

Wrightsman, L. S. 1991. Interpersonal trust and attitudes toward human nature. In J. P. Robinson, P. R. Shaver, & L. S. Wrightsman (Eds.), *Measures of personality and social psychological attitudes. Volume 1: Measures of social psychological attitudes:* 373–412. San Diego: Academic Press.

Zaheer, A., McEvily, B., & Perrone, V. In press. Does trust matter? Exploring the effects of interorganizational and interpersonal trust on performance. *Organizational Science.*

Zand, D. E. 1972. Trust and managerial problem solving. *Administrative Science Quarterly*, 17: 229–239.

Zucker, L. G. 1986. Production of trust: Institutional sources of economic structure, 1840–1920. In B. M. Staw & L. L. Cummings (Eds.), *Research in organizational behavior*, vol. 8: 53–111. Greenwich, CT: JAI Press.

Zucker, L. G., Darby, M. R., Brewer, M. B., & Peng, Y. 1996. Collaboration structure and information dilemmas in biotechnology: Organizational boundaries as trust production. In R. M. Kramer & T. R. Tyler (Eds.), *Trust in organizations: Frontiers of theory and research:* 90–113. Thousand Oaks, CA: Sage.

5

Managers as Initiators of Trust: An Exchange Relationship Framework for Understanding Managerial Trustworthy Behavior

Ellen M. Whitener, Susan E. Brodt,
M. Audrey Korsgaard, and Jon M. Werner

Imagine driving into work one day and hearing over the radio that your employer had agreed to merge with a rival firm and that the combined company would probably employ at least 10 percent fewer workers. Ciba Geigy employees experienced this scenario in 1996, when they were surprised to learn about their company's planned merger with Sandoz.

In a perfect world, this would never happen. Good news or bad, employees could trust management to give it to them straight, to mean what it said, and always to follow through on promises. But corporate America in 1996 is far from perfect. Management has lost credibility, employees are scared, and organizational trust has hit rock bottom. (Caudron, 1996: 20)

At the same time that trust in organizations has hit "rock bottom," researchers have shown that interpersonal trust has significant relationships with many organizational variables, such as the quality of communication (e.g., Muchinsky, 1977; Roberts & O'Reilly, 1974a, b; Yeager, 1978), performance (Earley, 1986), citizenship behavior (McAllister, 1995), problem solving (Zand, 1972), and cooperation (Axelrod, 1984; Deutsch, 1962). Moreover, trust has long been considered fundamental to cooperative relationships (Blau, 1964; Deutsch, 1958).

In recent reviews scholars have summarized common elements of the many different definitions of interpersonal trust (Hosmer, 1995; Mayer, Davis, & Schoorman, 1995). Drawing on these reviews and the work of others (Deutsch, 1962; Gambetta, 1988; Zand, 1972), we use a definition that reflects three facets. First, trust in another party reflects an expectation or belief that the other party will act benevolently. Second, one cannot control or force the other party to fulfill this expectation—that is, trust involves a willingness to be vulnerable and risk that the other party may not fulfill that expectation. Third, trust involves some level of dependency on the other party so that the outcomes of one individual are influenced by the actions of another.

With these components, trust can be viewed as an attitude held by one individual—the trustor—toward another—the trustee (Robinson, 1996). This attitude is derived from the trustor's perceptions, beliefs, and attributions about the trustee, based upon his or her observations of the trustee's behavior. Not surprisingly, most research on the antecedents of trust has focused on trustor perceptions and beliefs, such as trustors' perceptions of trustees' competence, benevolence, and integrity, that appear to be critical conditions for trust (Butler, 1991; Mayer et al., 1995). These insights into trustors' perceptions help identify how trust arises and suggest that managers can have considerable impact on building trust. Indeed, we will argue that managers' actions and behaviors provide the foundation for trust and that it is actually management's responsibility to take the first step and initiate trusting relationships. However, little is known about what causes managers to behave in a trustworthy manner and, consequently, what managers can do to build trust.

Our purpose in this article is to analyze the types of behavior managers may engage in that build trust, which we label "managerial trustworthy behavior," and to present a framework for understanding the antecedents of this behavior in organizations. To complement existing research on trustors' perceptions, we focus on trustees' behavior and the complex motivational context in which it occurs. By focusing on behavior, we go beyond factors that merely create the perception or impression of trust to what supports or constrains actions that promote trust. We use an exchange theory lens to identify and analyze organizational, relational (exchange), and individual factors that encourage or constrain trustworthy behavior in organizations. In doing so, we provide insight into how organizations can create an environment that supports trustworthy behavior. We also place the concept of interpersonal trust in a different context: trust is not merely an attitude held by one party toward another but exists in the parties' relationship.

The article consists of five sections. We begin by briefly reviewing agency and social exchange theories and discussing implications for trust formation.

Second, we propose a taxonomy of five dimensions of trustworthy behavior derived from research on antecedents of trust. Third, we present our framework representing the organizational, relational, and individual antecedents of trustworthy behavior. Fourth, we delve more deeply into the challenge of trust initiation and discuss what organizations can do to support managerial trustworthy behavior. We conclude the article with a discussion of implications and avenues for future research and practice.

The Manager-Employee Exchange Relationship

Many theories of trust are grounded in social exchange theory (Blau, 1964), which assumes that trust emerges through the repeated exchange of benefits between two individuals. Because it addresses the process of initiating and expanding social exchanges, this theory provides a useful lens for examining the motivational mechanisms underlying the initiation of trustworthy behavior. However, managers and employees are also involved in an economic exchange relationship. Theories of economic exchange, like agency theory (Eisenhardt, 1989), place little emphasis on trust, but they do offer explanations for managerial behavior, such as monitoring and control, that are commonplace in organizations and that affect employees' perceptions of trust. They also capture the economic context in which social exchange relationships develop. Therefore, we use both theories to analyze the motivation to engage in trustworthy behavior.

Agency Theory

Agency theorists describe the structuring of economic exchange relationships between two parties (Eisenhardt, 1989; Jensen & Meckling, 1976; Noorderhaven, 1992). A principal–agent relationship exists when one party—the principal—contracts with another party—the agent—to perform a task involving delegation of decision making in exchange for compensation. Agency theorists examine how principals and agents attempt to structure the relationship to protect their own interests. Applying agency theory to manager-employee dyads, we can consider the employee to be an agent and the manager to represent the interests of the principal.[1]

This perspective assumes self-interest—meaning that individuals strive to maximize individual utility and that both parties seek to minimize risks associated with the relationship. Agents bear risk as a function of how they are compensated. To the extent that their compensation is based on outcomes that are beyond their control, the risk to them is greater. In contrast, the principal faces the risk of opportunism and incompetence on the part of agents. The risk of opportunism is greater when the principal lacks information about agents' actions (i.e., information asymmetry) and when competing incentives or goals (i.e., goal incongruence) for agents motivate them to engage in actions other than what was contracted by the principal. For example, when employees are contracted to perform a job that the manager cannot directly observe, the manager faces the risk that the employees may shirk their duty. To minimize agency risk, principals generally either monitor agents' behavior to ensure contract compliance or base agents' compensation on task outcomes to align the agents' goals with the principals'.

Social Exchange Theory

Although the formal or contractual relationship in employment is economically driven, a social element to such relationships typically evolves. Social exchange theory (Blau, 1964) helps to explain the dynamics of such exchanges. In a social exchange one individual voluntarily provides a benefit to another, invoking an obligation of the other party to reciprocate by providing some benefit in return. Proving oneself trustworthy may be problematic when one is initially forming such social exchange relationships. Blau argues, however, that trust may be generated through two means: (1) through the regular discharge of obligations (i.e., by reciprocating for benefits received from others) and (2) through the gradual expansion of exchanges over time.

Social exchanges differ from economic ones in several fundamental ways (Blau, 1964). First, social exchanges may involve extrinsic benefits with economic value (e.g., information and advice) or intrinsic benefits without any direct objective economic utility (e.g., social support). Further, extrinsic benefits often are expressions of support and friendship and, thus, have intrinsic value as well. Therefore, exchanges that have little or unclear economic benefit can have a strong impact on the social dimension of a relationship.

Second, whereas benefits in economic exchanges are formal and often contracted explicitly, such benefits are rarely specified a priori or explicitly negotiated in social exchanges (Blau, 1964). Thus, providing benefits is a voluntary action.

Finally, because such behavior is voluntary, there is no guarantee that benefits will be reciprocated or that reciprocation will result in receipt of future benefits. The exchange of benefits involves uncertainty, particularly in early stages of the relationship, when the risk of non-reciprocation is relatively high.

Consequently, relationships evolve slowly, starting with the exchange of relatively low-value benefits and escalating to higher-value benefits as the parties demonstrate their trustworthiness (Blau, 1964).

Taken together, agency theory and social exchange theory expand the picture of trust formation in organizations. An agency theory lens highlights the formal economic context and self-interest motive, as well as the behavioral consequences. It also delineates factors that contribute to the risk of opportunism and identifies how the exchange relationship can be structured to minimize this risk. Although implying how relationship context contributes to risk, agency theory takes a relatively static view of relationships.

A social exchange theory lens, however, highlights dynamic elements of the exchange relationship. It emphasizes the exchange process, including its development over time, and indicates that successful social exchanges should influence perceptions of risk of nonreciprocation (i.e., opportunism) and trust. This lens also helps us identify when, under conditions of agency risk, an individual is likely to trust another party, rather than impose greater controls. For example, imagine two managers each working with a subordinate who telecommutes. From an agency theory perspective, information asymmetry is high in both cases and, therefore, agency risk (i.e., risk of opportunism) is high. However, the manager who forms a strong social bond with his or her subordinate through the process of successful social exchanges should perceive less risk of opportunism, despite equal levels of information asymmetry.

In summary, our agency theory lens identifies relatively static, contextual factors associated with the risk of opportunism in economic exchanges. It is under these circumstances of agency risk that social exchange theory is particularly relevant, for it helps us examine when one party is willing to trust another rather than impose control on the other. Specifically, our social exchange theory lens suggests that, by habitually discharging one's obligations, trust develops that may mitigate the risk of opportunism inherent in the organizational context. Therefore, managers may reduce the risk of opportunism by engaging in trustworthy behavior. In the following section we define trustworthy behavior and describe its dimensions.

Dimensions of Trustworthy Behavior

Managerial behavior is an important influence on the development of trust in relationships between managers and employees. We define *managerial trustworthy behavior* as *volitional actions and interactions performed by managers that are necessary though not sufficient to engender employees' trust in them.* This behavior occurs in a social and economic exchange context, in which managers initiate and build relationships by engaging in trustworthy behavior as a means of providing employees with social rewards. Managers who engage in this behavior will increase the likelihood that employees will reciprocate and trust them, providing a necessary, but not sufficient, foundation for employees' "trust-in-supervisors."

Five categories of behavior capture the variety of factors that influence employees' perceptions of managerial trustworthiness:

1. behavioral consistency,
2. behavioral integrity,
3. sharing and delegation of control,
4. communication (e.g., accuracy, explanations, and openness), and
5. demonstration of concern.

These categories are similar to those proposed by previous researchers (Butler, 1991; Clark & Payne, 1997). For example, Butler (1991) describes ten conditions that lead individuals to trust in another person, including consistency, discreetness, fairness, integrity, loyalty, and openness. However, these conditions primarily reflect qualities attributed to the trustee by the trustor. Because we turn the tables and examine trustees' behavior, our analysis provides a unique perspective on the dimensions of trustworthy behavior.

Behavioral Consistency

Behavioral consistency (i.e., reliability or predictability) is an important aspect of trust (Butler, 1991; Gabarro, 1978; Jennings, 1971; Johnson-George & Swap, 1982; Robinson & Rousseau, 1994). As we noted previously, trust reflects the willingness to be vulnerable to the actions of another party and the willingness to take risks (Johnson-George & Swap, 1982; Mayer et al., 1995). If managers behave consistently over time and across situations, employees can better predict managers' future behavior, and their confidence in their ability to make such predictions should increase. More important, employees become willing to take risks in their work or in their relationship with their manager. Predictable, positive behavior reinforces the level of trust in the relationship (Graen & Uhl-Bien, 1995).

Behavioral Integrity

Employees observe the consistency between managers' words and deeds and make attributions about their integrity, honesty, and moral character. Dasgupta

(1988) has identified two behaviors—(1) telling the truth and (2) keeping promises—as key behavioral antecedents to attributions of integrity: attributions that affect employees' trust in their managers (e.g., Butler, 1991; Gabarro, 1978; Giffin, 1967; Larzelere & Huston, 1980; Mayer et al., 1995; Ring & Van de Ven, 1992).

Although behavioral consistency and behavioral integrity have some similarities, they are distinct dimensions. Both reflect a consistency that serves to reduce employees' perceived risk in trusting their managers. However, on the one hand, behavioral consistency reflects the reliability or predictability of managers' actions, based on their past actions. Behavioral integrity, on the other hand, refers to the consistency between what the manager says and what he or she does.

Sharing and Delegation of Control

Research on trust perceptions has indicated that sharing control, including participation in decision making and delegating control, are key components of trustworthy behavior. Managers vary in the extent to which they involve employees in decision making. Involvement may range from having no employee input at all into decisions to full discussion and input—even to the point of everyone coming to a consensus (Driscoll, 1978; Vroom & Yetton, 1973). The extent to which managers involve employees influences the development of trust. Driscoll (1978), for example, has found that employees' trust is higher when they are satisfied with their level of participation in decisions; it is also higher when employees can determine their work roles (Deci, Connell, & Ryan, 1989). Even when control is limited to the process of decision making, such as in having the opportunity to voice opinions, it is positively associated with trust in managers (Alexander & Ruderman, 1987; Folger & Konovsky, 1989; Korsgaard & Roberson, 1995).

Managerial sharing and delegation of control may promote trust because of the interplay between economic and social factors. When managers involve employees in decision making, employees have greater control over decisions that affect them and, therefore, can protect their own interests. In agency terms this control by employees reduces the risk of opportunism on the part of the manager and increases the likelihood of favorable outcomes for the employee.

Even more important to our understanding of trust, however, is the symbolic value sharing and delegation of control are likely to have for employees. When managers share control, they demonstrate significant trust in and respect for their employees (Rosen & Jerdee, 1977). Employees value being involved in decision making, because it affirms their standing and worth in the organization (Tyler & Lind, 1992). In the language of social exchange theory, sharing and delegation of control are social rewards, in the form of approval or respect that the manager grants to the subordinate. To the extent that this reward represents an initiation or escalation of exchange of social benefits between a manager and employee, the employee's trust in the manager is likely to increase, especially when coupled with enhanced outcomes for the employee.

Communication

Communication researchers identify three factors that affect perceptions of trustworthiness; (1) accurate information, (2) explanations for decisions, and (3) openness. In many studies accuracy in information flow has had the strongest relationship with trust-in-supervisor when compared with other variables (e.g., desire for interaction, summarization, gatekeeping, and overload; Mellinger, 1956; Muchinsky, 1977; O'Reilly, 1977; O'Reilly & Roberts, 1974, 1977; Roberts & O'Reilly, 1974a, b, 1979; Yeager, 1978). Employees see managers as trustworthy when their communication is accurate and forthcoming. In addition, adequate explanations and timely feedback on decisions lead to higher levels of trust (Folger & Konovsky, 1989; Konovsky & Cropanzano, 1991; Sapienza & Korsgaard, 1996). Evidently, managers who take the time to explain their decisions thoroughly are likely to be perceived as trustworthy. Finally, open communication, in which managers exchange thoughts and ideas freely with employees, enhances perceptions of trust (Butler, 1991; Farris, Senner, & Butterfield, 1973; Gabarro, 1978; Hart, Capps, Cangemi, & Caillouet, 1986).

The emphasis in communication is on sharing and exchanging ideas. This dimension is more limited than the previous dimension that focuses on sharing and relinquishing control. However, both dimensions build employees' trust in their managers.

Demonstration of Concern

Benevolence (Mayer et al., 1995)—demonstrating concern for the welfare of others (McAllister, 1995; Mishra, 1996)—is part of trustworthy behavior and consists of three actions; (1) showing consideration and sensitivity for employees' needs and interests, (2) acting in a way that protects employees' interests, and (3) refraining from exploiting others for the benefit of one's own interests. These actions on the part of managers may lead employees to perceive them as loyal and benevolent. Researchers have shown such evidence of managerial loyalty to be an important condition that leads to trust between mentors and protégés (Butler, 1991; Jennings, 1971).

From the justice literature we know that managers can promote trust by showing concern for employees' needs and interests (Lind, 1997), by respecting others' rights, and by apologizing for unpleasant consequences (Greenberg, 1993; Konovsky & Pugh, 1994). Managers demonstrating concern also show that they "do good" for their employees, apart from any egocentric or opportunistic motives (Mayer et al., 1995; Mishra, 1996). That is, their behavior connotes a genuine interest in an employee's welfare and may imply some attachment to the employee.

Finally, this dimension reflects behavioral restraint—that is, managers who could take advantage of their employees' vulnerability "stay their hand," choosing not to behave opportunistically (Bromiley & Cummings, 1995). For example, managers could use confidential or personal information about employees to their personal or organizational advantage, could present an employee's innovative idea as their own, or could engage in other similar "cunning" (Pettit, 1995) or "dark-side" (Kramer, Brewer, & Hanna, 1996) behavior that takes advantage of employees' vulnerability. Employees may not always observe managerial restraint, for it may involve the absence of action. However, if they are aware that their manager refrained from exploiting them, they are more likely to perceive their manager as trustworthy.

Antecedents of Trustworthy Behavior

Earlier, we discussed how the combination of agency and social exchange theories integrates structural (economic) factors and social processes and helps us understand the development of trust. These theories also address the determinants of the sorts of behavior, discussed above, that build trust.

Viewed from the lens of agency theory, trustworthy behavior, such as sharing control, communicating openly, and demonstrating concern, includes actions that may conflict with a manager's ability to directly control an employees' actions. Agency theorists would suggest that contextual factors, such as organizational characteristics, influence the degree to which managers tighten control and closely monitor employees and, therefore, inhibit them from engaging in trustworthy behavior.

Viewed from the lens of social exchange theory, trustworthy behavior, such as sharing and delegation of control, may be experienced by the subordinate as a social reward: it represents a form of approval extended to the subordinate by the manager. Social exchange theorists would imply that the nature of work

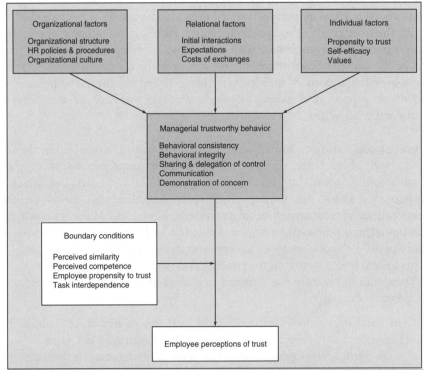

Fig. 1. Exchange Framework of Initiating Managerial Trustworthy Behavior

Note: The focus of the framework is to identify factors that affect trustworthy behavior. Thus, the white boxes (boundary conditions and employee perceptions of trust) are beyond the scope of our propositions but are addressed in the discussion.

relationships influences managers' willingness to initiate and escalate the exchange of such rewards.

These theoretical lenses lay the foundation for our framework for organizing the antecedents of managerial trustworthy behavior. As we show in Figure 1, this framework identifies major sets of variables at the organizational, relational and individual level that we believe support or encourage managerial trustworthy behavior. We also suggest some general propositions for future research.

Organizational Factors

According to R. Hardin (1996), organizations can be designed to enhance trustworthiness by creating structures that make trusting successful; however,

Hardin falls short in recommending specific structures to accomplish this goal. From an agency theory perspective, the critical issue seems to be the extent to which the organization requires high control and close monitoring of employees. Organizational attributes, such as structure, policies, and culture, may dictate the degree of control managers—acting in the role of principal—should exert over the actions of their employees. In doing so, these attributes may inhibit or support the extent to which managers engage in a variety of trustworthy behaviors.

Organizational structure. Investigating the role of trust in organization theory, Creed and Miles (1996) propose different trust requirements of varying organizational forms. By turning their approach around, we can develop propositions about the impact of different organizational forms on the development of trustworthy behavior. Indeed, Creed and Miles acknowledge that managerial philosophies can be defined to include an orientation toward trustworthy behavior and can evolve over time as a response, in part, to "operational forces"—that is, the strategy and structure of the organization.

These authors review five different organizational forms that vary along a continuum of control:

1. In the *owner-managed entrepreneurial form* the owner exerts control by exercising direct supervision over employees and making all decisions.

2. In a *vertically integrated functional organization* managers balance the delegation of operating responsibilities to functional specialists with tight guidelines, budgets, and schedules.

3. In a *diversified, divisionalized firm* divisions organized around products, service, or geography accept controls and direction from the corporate office but operate autonomously in their specific markets.

4. In a *mixed-matrix form* organizations combine stable functional departments and temporary project groups, and they create mechanisms to allocate and control resources through joint planning and negotiation.

5. In the *network form organizational* members share control, recognize their mutual dependence, and pursue common goals.

On the one end of the continuum, the control imposed by an entrepreneur constrains the development of trustworthy behavior, and on the other, the codependence required by network organizations necessitates the development of trustworthy behavior. Creed and Miles conclude that high-control organizations, with a high degree of centralization and formalization and a primary focus on efficiency, will constrain or impede the development of trustworthy behavior, such as delegation and open communication. Low-control organizations, however, with greater decentralization, lower formalization, and a focus on effectiveness, should make managers more likely to delegate decisions and communicate openly.

Proposition 1: Organizations that are highly centralized, formalized, hierarchical, and focused on efficiency will be less likely to generate managerial trustworthy behavior—in particular, communication and delegation of control—than will organizations that are decentralized, less formal, less hierarchical, and focused on effectiveness.

Human resource policies and procedures. Creed and Miles (1996) also suggest that the design of human resource (HR) policies and procedures should affect perceptions of trust. Therefore, such HR systems as reward, control, and performance appraisal practices may facilitate or inhibit managerial trustworthy behavior. Research indicates that the extent to which performance appraisal procedures follow principles of procedural justice has a positive impact on employees' trust in their manager (Folger & Konovsky, 1989; Korsgaard & Roberson, 1995).

Performance evaluation policies, then, may be one way to encourage such behavior. For example, Taylor, Tracy, Renard, Harrison, and Carroll (1995) found that when an appraisal system was modeled on due-process principles, managers communicated more openly and allowed more employee participation than did managers following a traditional appraisal process. Thus, by developing appraisal and reward procedures on principles of due process, such as adequate notice, fair hearing, and judgment based on evidence (Folger, Konovsky, & Cropanzano, 1992), it may be possible to stimulate trustworthy behavior. In addition to increasing communication, the establishment of procedurally fair HR policies should encourage managers to behave consistently toward all subordinates.

Proposition 2: The more an organization's HR policies and procedures incorporate (procedural) justice principles into performance appraisal and reward systems (e.g., regular and timely feedback and mechanisms for employee input into performance appraisal), the more likely it will be that managerial trustworthy behavior, especially communication and behavioral consistency, will occur.

Organizational culture. Organizational culture is a unit- or organizational-level phenomenon derived from social interactions among members of the unit or organization (Rousseau, 1990). It consists of "the set of shared, taken-for-granted implicit assumptions that a group holds" (Schein, 1996: 236) and influences how the members of the group understand and respond to their environment. The "content" of culture—the specific assumptions, norms, and values of the culture—shapes members' patterns of behavior (Rousseau, 1990) and creates an environment in which certain behaviors are encouraged and receive support.

Through social learning processes, culture may directly influence managerial trustworthy behavior. Managers observe how their organizations respond to others and learn what behavior is rewarded and punished; moreover, they experience social rewards when they behave in a manner that is consistent with cultural values and norms (O'Reilly & Caldwell, 1985; Thompson & Luthans, 1990).

Also, culture may indirectly encourage (or discourage) managerial trustworthy behavior through the structuring of general patterns of communication, coordination, and decision making. That is, certain cultural values and norms, more than others, are likely to engender managerial trustworthy behavior. Rousseau's (1990) taxonomy of cultural values and norms helps us identify values that encourage trustworthy behavior. For example, cultures that value risk taking (a task-related value) will reward and support managers who take such risks as sharing or delegating control to a subordinate, regardless of the outcome. Similarly, cultures that share such interpersonal values as inclusiveness, open communication, and valuing people will reward managers for collaborating, sharing information, explaining decisions, discussing issues openly, and showing concern. Hence, cultures that support these behaviors will also encourage and reward trustworthy behavior.

Proposition 3: Organizations with cultures characterized by risk taking, inclusiveness, open communication, and valuing people will show greater trustworthy behavior, particularly delegating control, communicating openly, and showing concern, than will organizations with cultures that do not share these values or norms.

Relational Factors

Research on leader–member exchange suggests that high-quality exchange relationships between managers and their subordinates are characterized by the very types of behavior we have identified as engendering trust. Specifically, high-quality exchange relationships involve showing mutual respect and concern and sharing of decision control (Dienesch & Liden, 1986; Liden & Maslyn, 1993). From a social exchange perspective, managers may exhibit such behavior to provide social rewards to employees and to elicit various prosocial or pro-organizational benefits from the employee, such as compliance and loyalty (Graen & Scandura, 1987; Marcus & House, 1973). Managers' motivation to engage in such behavior is thus related to the value of the benefits received from the employee and the costs of engaging in such behavior.

Research on leader-member exchange and related areas, such as social dilemmas, indicates three exchange factors that influence this cost-benefit analysis and, ultimately, its consequences for trustworthy behavior: (1) initial interactions, (2) expectations, and (3) costs of exchanges.

Initial interactions. One of the factors that contributes to establishing a strong relationship is managers' impressions of new employees' capabilities, based on the employees' initial responses to the role expectations for the job (Graen & Scandura, 1987). Based on their impressions, managers then provide "negotiating latitude" to employees who fulfill expectations and demonstrate their capability (Docker & Steiner, 1990; Graen & Scandura, 1987; Graen & Uhl-Bien, 1995). Negotiating latitude includes two-way communication between manager and employee, and delegation—both important dimensions of trustworthy behavior. In addition, favorable initial interactions are likely to enhance the quality of the relationship, which will lead managers to show concern and respect. These findings imply that employees' initial role performance will encourage trustworthy behavior.

Proposition 4: The more effective an employee is in initially meeting role requirements, the greater the likelihood will be that the manager will engage in trustworthy behavior, particularly sharing control, communicating openly, and showing concern.

Expectations. The tenuous nature of reciprocation in social exchange puts the manager in a sort of trust dilemma. When a manager initiates trustworthy behavior, he or she runs the risk of realizing no return on such overtures. Research on social dilemmas indicates that expectations of another party's willingness to cooperate are positively correlated with an individual's decision to take risks and cooperate with the other party (Dawes, 1980). This finding implies that a manager's willingness to initiate or escalate such exchanges will be predicated on his or her expectations and beliefs about whether the employee will reciprocate.

Proposition 5: The greater a manager's expectations are concerning an employee's willingness to reciprocate, the greater the likelihood will be that the manager will engage in trustworthy behavior, particularly sharing control and communicating openly.

Costs of exchanges. Expectancy theorists (Porter & Lawler, 1968) tell us that both the expectancy that certain actions will lead to certain outcomes and the valence of those outcomes influence motivation. In Proposition 5 we examined managers' expectations about reciprocation; here, we examine the valence of outcomes—specifically, the negative valence associated with an employee's failure to reciprocate or costs of exchanges.

The social dilemma paradigm suggests that a related problem involving the initiation of exchanges is the potential for exploitation (Kramer et al., 1996). That is, the employee may take advantage of benefits provided by the manager without reciprocating. Indeed, managers may bear substantial cost by extending certain rewards associated with trustworthy behavior if the employee does not reciprocate. For example, delegating control of a highly visible project can have substantial negative repercussions for the manager if the employee does not reciprocate with loyalty and compliance, because delegation allows employees greater freedom to behave opportunistically. In contrast, delegation of minor or less visible tasks poses far fewer costs if the employee fails to reciprocate.

Proposition 6: The higher the costs associated with unreciprocated exchanges, the lower the likelihood will be that managers will engage in trustworthy behavior, particularly sharing control.

Individual Factors

As we discussed above, social exchange suggests that managers engage in exchanges of rewards based, in part, on their expectation of reciprocation and the perceived cost of nonreciprocation. Although the quality of the interpersonal relationship should factor strongly into whether managers exchange rewards, characteristics of the manager may also influence these expectations. We propose that three individual factors—(1) propensity to trust, (2) self-efficacy, and (3) values—will influence managers' beliefs and expectations regarding the likelihood of successful social exchange and, hence, their propensity to engage in trustworthy behavior.

Propensity to trust. Such researchers as Rotter (1967), Farris et al. (1973), and Mayer et al. (1995) have argued that some individuals are more dispositionally trusting than others. In his scale, for example, Rotter conceptualizes trust as a trait that is stable over time and across situations. Individuals endorse statements like "Parents usually can be relied upon to keep their promises," indicating a generalized belief that others, as well as oneself, exhibit such trustworthy behavior as promise keeping and other indicators of behavioral integrity. In part, this propensity stems from one's expectations about how others are likely to behave. Managers who have a high propensity to trust expect their employees to reciprocate. According to our exchange framework, this expectation should influence their motivation to engage in trustworthy behavior.

Proposition 7: The greater a manager's propensity or disposition to trust is, the greater the manager's expectation of reciprocation will be, and the greater the likelihood will be that the manager will engage in trustworthy behavior, particularly behavioral integrity.

Self-efficacy. In addition to personality characteristics or traits, individual factors also include managers' self-efficacy regarding their knowledge, skills, and ability (KSA; Gist & Mitchell, 1992). For example, managers who have low self-efficacy regarding their ability to delegate control will find it difficult to use participative management processes. Similarly, individuals who have low self-efficacy in their conflict management skills may be reluctant to engage employees in two-way communication.

Mishra (1996) provides examples from the auto industry, showing how competence or the lack thereof could undermine one's best attempt at acting in a trustworthy manner. If managers believed they lacked the basic knowledge, skills, and ability, their low self-efficacy either hampered their motivation to initiate trust or led to poor performance and unsuccessful attempts to establish trusting relationships.

Proposition 8: Managers who lack efficacy regarding their knowledge, skills, and abilities to perform trustworthy behavior (e.g., delegating control or communicating openly) will be unlikely to engage in trustworthy behavior.

Values. Managers' values influence their motivation to display trustworthy behavior. Individual values consist of definable goals, varying in importance, that motivate and guide people's choices, attitudes, and behaviors (Rokeach, 1973; Schwartz, 1992, 1994). Schwartz (1992) found, for example, that values cluster into distinct types that serve different motivational purposes, several of which may provide a value-based foundation for trustworthy behavior. Most relevant is the distinction between values that reflect "self-transcendence," such as universalism and benevolence, versus "self-enhancement," such as achievement, hedonism, and power.

Managers with self-transcendent values may be more likely to engage in trustworthy behavior. More specifically, managers with universalist values (understanding, appreciation, and protection of the welfare of all people) may be more likely to demonstrate concern for employees than might be managers with power values (control or dominance over people). Similarly, managers who value benevolence (the enhancement of the welfare of others) may be more likely to keep promises and tell the truth (behave with integrity) than might be managers who value hedonism (self-gratification). In sum, the values held by managers are likely to provide the primary "internal compass" that promotes several dimensions of trustworthy behavior, including demonstrating concern, behaving consistently, and behaving with integrity.

Proposition 9: Managers whose values are self-transcendent will be more likely to engage in trustworthy behavior, such as demonstration of concern and behavioral integrity, than will those whose values are self-enhancing.

The Challenge of Trust Initiation

Using agency theory and social exchange theory lenses and prior organizational research, we have examined key antecedents of managerial trustworthy behavior. Upon closer examination, we believe these lenses also highlight unique challenges to initiating the social exchanges that ultimately build trust. To establish trust through the reciprocal exchange of social benefits, someone must make the first move. From the manager's perspective, initiating involves engaging in trustworthy behavior preemptively, perhaps before the subordinate has demonstrated his or her worthiness. Managers may be reluctant to do so, preferring instead to impose tight control or to monitor behavior. To reap the organizational benefits of trust, however, managers must be encouraged to make the first move. Initiating this process, then, is the challenge to, and arguably the responsibility of, management.

Our purpose in this section is to discuss three potential impediments to trust initiation—(1) the motivational complexity of exchange relationships, (2) social dilemmas and the nature of interdependence, and (3) the role of cultural values—and to suggest ways of overcoming them. Suggestions come directly from our framework and, as such, provide implications and extensions of our propositions.

Motivational Complexity

As we noted previously, agency theory and social exchange theory create a complex motivational dynamic for managers. On the one hand, agency theory highlights managers' motivation to minimize risk exposure—for example, via the imposition of tight control mechanisms and close behavioral monitoring (Eisenhardt, 1989). On the other hand, social exchange theory suggests that if managers want to create relationships built on the voluntary discharge of reciprocal obligations, this should lead them to relax control and promote trust.

The juxtaposition of these lenses highlights a fundamental tension between building a relationship based on trust and reducing the risk of opportunism that could potentially preempt trust initiation. As suggested by Proposition 1, however, judicious design of organizational factors may mitigate this problem and encourage trust initiation. For example, low-control organizations, with greater decentralization and lower formalization, shoulder (or at least share) the risk of opportunism by creating a context that essentially requires managers to initiate trustworthy behavior, such as delegation of control and open communication. The organization's design supports delegation of control and encourages trust initiation.

Social Dilemmas

Social exchange theories contain inherent conflicts related to trust initiation. For example, similar to theories of economic exchange, theories of social exchange presume individual self-interest—that is, people are motivated to maximize their individual rewards (e.g., money, status, or respect) and minimize their individual costs (e.g., embarrassment or loss of self-esteem). Complicating the situation is the fact that managers often find themselves in situations where the interdependence of individuals' outcomes creates a conflict between self-interest and the collective good.

These situations, called social dilemmas, occur when individuals' outcomes are maximized as they act in their own self-interest, regardless of what others do. But their actions actually create negative outcomes for everyone involved. The classic example of such a dilemma is G. Hardin's (1968) "The Tragedy of the Commons," a study of how individual cow herders' self-interested behavior (i.e., increasing the size of one's herd) leads to overgrazing of the public pasture, which undermines the collective good. Two types of social dilemmas complicate trust initiation for managers who find themselves in these situations: the classic Prisoner's Dilemma and the Volunteer Dilemma.

In the Prisoner's Dilemma (see Kormorita & Parks, 1994; Rapoport & Chammah, 1965), individuals who cannot communicate with each other face a conflict between maximizing individual interests by not trusting each other (i.e., defecting) versus maximizing collective welfare by trusting and cooperating. By initiating a social exchange and not knowing whether it will be reciprocated, a manager in this situation runs the risk of being exploited and ending up with a "sucker's payoff" (e.g., embarrassment or poor leadership). Managers often face such dilemmas and exhibit this fear; concerns about gullibility and embarrassment often underlie managers' reluctance to trust (Rotter, 1980).

In the Volunteer Dilemma (Diekmann, 1985) one person must make a sacrifice so that the entire group benefits. Typically, the cost of self-sacrifice is uncertain or highly negative in the short term. For example, a manager might be asked to take a pay cut so that his or her group will have additional resources to complete a project—for which the entire group benefits. If the manager fails to take this first step, the group, including the manager, will not succeed. This situation leads to potentially tragic outcomes for organizations wanting to encourage volunteerism for the collective good; the call to create a "trusting organization," for example, may never be fulfilled because of the reluctance on the part of managers, as well as employees, to volunteer to initiate the process.

Drawing on our framework, especially Propositions 5 and 6, we see that from a relational perspective, these dilemmas reflect the nature of outcome interdependence between individuals (e.g., the payoffs for cooperating or not), the expectations about others' behavior (e.g., expectation of cooperation), and the costs associated with unreciprocated exchanges. To mitigate this situation, our framework suggests that changing the nature of the interdependence will encourage managers in dilemma situations to initiate trust. For example, reward structures could be changed to foster cooperation by making greater use of equity-, team-, or organization-based incentives. Such systemic changes would provide greater alignment between employee and organizational interests (Wilson, 1995).

As this example points out, such solutions are often beyond the control of the manager-subordinate dyad. Changing the nature of the outcome interdependence between managers and their subordinates is ultimately an issue for the organization as a whole. Our framework also suggests that decreasing the perceived cost associated with unreciprocated exchanges encourages managers to initiate trust.

Cultural Values

The variety of cultural values that exist around the world influences individual behavior (Brodt & Seybolt, 1997; Hofstede, 1980; Lind, Tyler, & Huo, 1997) and potentially complicates managerial trust initiation. Cultural values reflect a social group's shared ways of understanding and behaving. Although reflecting a group's understanding, we will conceptualize cultural values at an individual level—that is, cultural values as represented in an individual manager's beliefs and behavior.

Depending on the particular cultural values, trust initiation may be helped or hindered. For example, individualistic cultures that emphasize self-interest (e.g., the United States) may make salient the dilemmas discussed above. Managers in these cultures face a conflict between managing agency risk (risk of opportunism) and building a trusting relationship. As suggested by our framework, particularly Proposition 7, these managers will perceive the possibility of unreciprocated trust to be too great and the costs of unrequited trust to be too high to justify initiating trust. In contrast, a manager whose cultural values are less individualistic and less focused on self-interest (e.g., a Japanese manager) may experience little or no conflict in an identical managerial situation. This manager's cultural values (and practices) may reflect a propensity to cooperate, which will encourage him or her to initiate trust and engage in many trustworthy behaviors (e.g., behavioral consistency, demonstrating concern, and behavioral integrity).

Discussion

Vulnerability and risk are inherent in exchange relationships in organizations. Managers and employees may face different types of risks and vulnerabilities, but risk is an issue for all parties involved in a social or economic exchange. Individuals and organizations can, and generally do, look for ways to manage these risks. Managers, in particular, often use monitoring and control mechanisms, as depicted by agency theory (see Horwitz, 1994, for an example of electronic monitoring in an organization that processes donations for charities). Such mechanisms minimize the need to trust employees to act in organizationally desirable ways (Hosmer, 1995).

However, high levels of performance are less likely when organizations rely on such "weak" forms of trust (Barney & Hansen, 1994). Moreover, mutual dyadic trust may be essential for organizational survival and growth. As Handy recently stated in discussing new organizational forms, "Trust is the heart of the matter" (1995: 44). We share Gambetta's (1988) concern, however, that, even though trust is important, it has appeared nebulous and seemingly intractable for study. For this reason we draw from diverse bodies of literature to spell out major dimensions of managerial trustworthy behavior. We also shift the research focus from the question, "How can managers influence employees' perceptions of managerial trustworthiness?" to the question. "What is trustworthy behavior, and what can organizations do to support such behavior?" This shift from trustors' perceptions to managerial behavior is important, because managers can exert the greatest degree of volitional control over their own actions.

Finally, our exchange relationship framework of managerial trustworthy behavior embeds the question of trust in the organizational context; organizational, relational, and individual factors influence a manager's motivation to exhibit trustworthy behavior. Although similar to leader-member exchange theory (e.g., Graen & Uhl-Bien, 1995), our framework is distinct in several ways. First, we make trust the primary focus of our framework, rather than positing trust as one aspect of leader-member exchange. Second, we analyze the dynamics of managerial trustworthy behavior using two different exchange lenses: an economic exchange lens and a social exchange lens. This broader exchange lens makes it possible to describe more completely the sets of variables, such as the role of organizational structure and policies that influence trustworthy behavior. Finally, whereas Graen and Uhl-Bien (1995) also argue that managers should initiate exchange relationships, our framework provides considerably more detail and direction concerning why and how this initiation process should take place. Overall, we believe that our dimensions of trustworthy behavior, as well as the framework we have laid out, make a unique contribution to our understanding of managerial trustworthy behavior and advance both theory and practice concerning trust in exchange relationships.

Implications for Research

Our emphasis on managerial behavior serves to complement the current emphasis in the interpersonal trust literature on trust perceptions. Employee trust perceptions are clearly crucial and have been emphasized heavily in recent research. However, our fear is that an emphasis on trust perceptions can lead researchers and managers to focus exclusively on managing impressions of managerial trustworthiness. Such an emphasis without a genuine display of trustworthy behavior can cultivate a belief that managers merely need to display the *appearance* of trustworthiness (Greenberg, 1990) to create trusting relationships. In addition to possible ethical difficulties, such tactics may be counterproductive, if they are perceived as insincere (Greenberg, 1990), and also may be difficult to sustain over time.

However, impression management attempts need not be manipulative or insincere (Goffman, 1959; Liden & Mitchell, 1988). Indeed, a focus on behavior calls attention to what organizations can do to initiate and manage trustworthy behavior and to engender and support trusting relationships that are self-perpetuating and sustainable. In the spirit of our change of focus, future research is needed regarding our typology of managerial trustworthy behavior, as well as elements of our framework and propositions concerning the antecedents of such behavior. Researchers might also investigate additional dimensions of trustworthy behavior and possible other factors that affect trust initiation.

A second avenue to pursue concerns the robustness of trustworthy behavior, including information about the boundary conditions around these behaviors. We have proposed that trustworthy behavior is necessary but not sufficient to influence employees' perceptions of trust. Individual factors (e.g., perceived similarity, competence, and propensity to trust) and situational factors (e.g., task interdependence) may limit the extent to which managerial trustworthy behavior affects employees' perceptions of trust.

First, as we depict in Figure 1, two cognitive processes influence employees' perception of managerial trustworthiness: (1) perceived similarity and (2) competence. Trust often builds between two people as they are attracted to each other and perceive that they have similar characteristics (e.g., Creed & Miles, 1996; Giffin, 1967; Larzelere & Huston, 1980; McAllister, 1995; Zucker, 1986). In addition, perceived ability (Cook & Wall, 1980; Mayer et al., 1995; Sitkin & Roth, 1993) or its corollary—competence (Butler, 1991; Mishra, 1996)—may be essential elements of trust. Without the judgments that one' manager possesses the competence or ability to fulfill the managerial role, an employee is unlikely to develop trust in that manager. Although neither of these judgments automatically engenders trust between managers and employees, each lays a perceptual foundation that increases the likelihood that employees will react positively to trustworthy behavior on the part of the manager.

Second, employee characteristics may also influence reactions to managerial trustworthy behavior. Specifically, employees may observe their managers' trustworthy behavior but may be unlikely to trust if they lack a general predisposition to trust others (Luhmann, 1979; Mayer et al., 1995). That is, the extent to which managers' trustworthy actions lead to perceptions of trust may perhaps be moderated by employees' propensity to trust. We argued earlier that managers' predispositions to trust will influence their behavior; similarly, employees' propensity to trust may influence their responsiveness to managers' trustworthy behavior.

Research is also needed on other contextual factors that may influence managers' propensity to engage in trustworthy behavior and employees' reactions to such behavior. For example, the nature of the task—specifically, the degree of interdependence—may make trust more or less relevant. Because performance on interdependent tasks requires cooperation, trust may be critical to performing effectively on such tasks. Thompson's (1967) conceptualization of intensive technology, where goods and services flow between various organizational members, as well as team settings in which tasks, goals, and rewards are highly interdependent (Campion, Medsker, & Higgs, 1993), are good examples. Because there is a greater need to build trust on interdependent tasks, managers may be willing to initiate trustworthy behavior. However, dependency is a necessary but not sufficient condition for trust (Hosmer, 1995).

Implications for Practice

Our analysis has several practical implications for managers. First, as indicated above, we provide concrete guidance for managers and organizations concerning how to "get the ball rolling."

Second, we identify several ways to overcome the potentially challenging conflicts and uncertainties in this process. For example, individuals should adopt a sophisticated understanding of the coupling between their own fate and that of the collective to reduce the conflict between short-term individual gain and long-term benefit for the collective. In this way organizations and individuals develop a "collective trust" that is conceptually similar to other types of shared resources (Kramer et al., 1996).

In addition, organizational systems can help managers overcome the potential barriers to initiating trust. Such systems might include coordinating reward structures between managers and employees, rewarding managers who initiate trust and employees who reciprocate, requiring certain managers to take the lead, and providing invisible "safety nets" and evidence that the sucker's payoff is not as economically or psychologically painful as one might expect.

Organizations also can provide training and educational opportunities to enable and enhance managerial trustworthy behavior. Training and development opportunities can enhance managers' competencies, skills, and capabilities, especially in the areas of leadership, participation in decision making, delegation, communication, and fairness. As managers increase the specific skills associated with trustworthy behavior through training and development opportunities, they are more likely to initiate and exercise it (Caudron, 1996).

Finally, trustworthy behavior may provide a source for competitive advantage (Barney & Hansen, 1994). Evironmental and competitive pressures are pushing organizations toward more fluid or network forms, and there has been increased attention to process reengineering—that is, dramatically redesigning the processes used to achieve organizational objectives. Hammer and Champy (1993), for example, describe organizations of the future as flat and team oriented forms, in which workers will perfom multidimensional work with the autonomy to make decisions. These changes will only come about, however, with greater monitoring and control, increased trust between employees and management, or some combination of the two. Given the limits of employee monitoring (Grant, 1992), high levels of mutual trust between managers and employees seem to be critical in order for reengineering efforts to be successful. Organizations that successfully attain high levels of managerial trustworthiness should be at a competitive advantage in the marketplace, compared to those that do not (Barney & Hansen, 1994). More important, companies that anticipate these changes, designing themselves and encouraging their managers to initiate and establish trusting relationships, will be well positioned for the future. The irony here is that trust is often criticized by managers as a "soft" and seemingly intractable concept, yet it may a necessary condition for attaining the competitive advantage associated with strategic and structural innovations.

Conclusion

R. Hardin notes that "the best device for creating trust [may be] to establish and support trustworthiness" (1996: 29). We propose that managers and organizations interested in establishing trust must take the first step, by designing organizations in ways that encourage managers to initiate trusting relationships, and by rewarding employees for reciprocating, management can establish a foundation for a trusting organization. In light of theorists' visions of the future, such designs and management practices stand to enhance organizational effectiveness and viability.

Notes

1. Agency theory typically has been applied to relationships in which the principal is an owner of the firm and the employees are the agents of the owners. Because managers are not necessarily owners, they may serve in the role of agents *relative* to the owners of the company. Regardless of their level of ownership, however,

managers serve the role of principal *relative to* the role of their subordinates in that they hire or engage the subordinate "to perform some service on their behalf which involves delegating some decision making authority to the agent" (Jensen & Meckling, 1976: 308).

....

References

Alexander, S., & Ruderman, M. 1987. The role of procedural justice and distributive justice in organizational behavior. *Social Justice Research*, 1: 177–197.

Axelrod, R. 1984. *The evolution of cooperation*. New York: Basic Books.

Barney, J. B., & Hansen, M. H. 1994. Trustworthiness as a source of competitive advantage. *Strategic Management Journal*, 15: 175–190.

Blau, P. M. 1964. *Exchange and power in social life*. New York: Wiley.

Brodt, S., & Seybolt, P. 1997. *Culture and conflict: The role of national conflict and performance feedback in understanding interpersonal conflict in global organizations*. Unpublished manuscript, Duke University, Durham, NC.

Bromiley, P., & Cummings, L. L. 1995. Transaction costs in organizations with trust. In R. Bies, B. Sheppard, & R. Lewicki (Eds.), *Research on negotiations in organizations*, vol. 5: 219–247. Greenwich, CT: JAI Press.

Butler, J. K., Jr. 1991. Towards understanding and measuring conditions of trust: Evolution of a conditions of trust inventory. *Journal of Management*, 17: 643–663.

Campion, M. A., Medsker, G. J., & Higgs, A. C. 1993. Relations between work group characteristics and effectiveness: Implications for designing effective work groups. *Personnel Psychology*, 46: 823–850.

Caudron, S. 1996. Rebuilding employee trust. *Training and Development Journal*, 50(8): 19–21.

Clark, M. C., & Payne, R. L. 1997. The nature and structure of workers' trust in management. *Journal of Organizational Behavior*, 18: 205–224.

Cook, J., & Wall, T. D. 1980. New work attitude measures of trust, organizational commitment and personal need non-fulfillment. *Journal of Occupational Psychology*, 53: 39–52.

Creed, W. E. D., & Miles, R. E. 1996. Trust in organizations: A conceptual framework linking organizational forms, managerial philosophies, and the opportunity costs of controls. In R. M. Kramer & T. R. Tyler (Eds.), *Trust in organizations: Frontiers of theory and research*: 16–38. Thousand Oaks, CA: Sage.

Dasgupta, P. 1988. Trust as a commodity. In D. Gambetta (Ed.), *Trust: Making and breaking cooperative relations*: 49–72. Cambridge, MA: Basil Blackwell.

Dawes, R. M. 1980. Social dilemmas. *Annual Review of Psychology*, 31: 169–193.

Deci, E. L., Connell, J. P., & Ryan, R. M. 1989. Self-determination in a work organization. *Journal of Applied Psychology*, 74: 580–590.

Deutsch, M. 1958. Trust and suspicion. *Conflict Resolution*, 2: 265–279.

Deutsch, M. 1962. Cooperation and trust: Some theoretical notes. In M. R. Jones (Ed.), *Nebraska Symposium on Motivation*: 275–317. Lincoln: University of Nebraska Press.

Diekmann, A. 1985. Volunteer's dilemma. *Journal of Conflict Resolution*, 29: 605–610.

Dienesch, R. M., & Liden, R. C. 1986. Leader-member exchange model of leadership: A critique and further development. *Academy of Management Review*, 11: 617–634.

Docker, T. M., & Steiner, D. D. 1990. The role of initial interactions. *Group and Organization Studies*, 15: 395–413.

Driscoll, J. W. 1978. Trust and participation in organizational decision making as predictors of satisfaction. *Academy of Management Journal*, 21: 44–56.

Earley, P. C. 1986. Trust, perceived importance of praise and criticism, and work performance: An examination of feedback in the United States and England. *Journal of Management*, 12: 457–473.

Eisenhardt, K. M. 1989. Agency theory: An assessment and review. *Academy of Management Review*, 14: 57–74.

Farris, G., Senner, E., & Butterfield, D. 1973. Trust, culture and organizational behavior. *Industrial Relations*, 12: 144–157.

Folger, R., & Konovsky, M. A. 1989. Effects of procedural and distributive justice on reactions to pay raise decisions, *Academy of Management Journal*, 32: 115–130.

Folger, R., & Cropanzano, R. 1992. A due process metaphor for performance appraisal. In B. M. Staw & L. L. Cummings (Eds.), *Research in organizational behavior*, vol. 14: 129–177. Greenwich, CT: JAI Press.

Gabarro, J. J. 1978. The development of trust influence and expectations. In A. G. Athos & J. J. Gabarro (Eds.), *Interpersonal behavior: Communication and understanding in relationships*: 290–303. Englewood Cliffs, NJ: Prentice-Hall.

Gambetta, D. 1988. Can we trust trust? In D. Gambetta (Ed.), *Trust: Making and breaking cooperative relations*: 213–237. Cambridge, MA: Basil Blackwell.

Giffin, K. 1967. The contribution of studies of source credibility to a theory of interpersonal trust in the communication process. *Psychological Bulletin*, 68: 104–120.

Gist, M., & Mitchell, T. 1992. Self-efficacy: A theoretical analysis of its determinants and malleability. *Academy of Management Review*, 17: 183–211.

Goffman, E. 1959. *The presentation of self in everyday life*. Garden City, NY: Doubleday.

Graen, G. B., & Scandura, T. B. 1987. Toward a psychology of dyadic organizing. In B. M. Staw & L. L. Cummings (Eds.), *Research in organizational behavior*, vol. 9: 175–208. Greenwich, CT: JAI Press.

Graen, G. B., & Uhl-Bien, M. 1995. Relationship-based approach to leadership: Development of leader-member exchange (LMX) theory of leadership over 25 years; Applying a multi-level multi-domain perspective. *Leadership Quarterly*, 6: 219–247.

Grant, R. A. 1992. Work monitored electronically. *HR Magazine*, May: 81–86.

Greenberg, J. 1990. Looking fair vs. being fair: Managing impressions of organizational justice. In B. M. Staw & L. L. Cummings (Eds.), *Research in organizational behavior*, vol. 12: 111–157. Greenwich, CT: JAI Press.

Greenberg, J. 1993. The social side of fairness: Interpersonal and informational classes of organizational justice. In R. Cropanzano (Ed.), *Justice in the workplace*: 79–103. Hillsdale, NJ: Lawrence Erlbaum Associates.

Hammer, M., & Champy, J. 1993. *Re-engineering the corporation: A manifesto for business revolution.* New York: HarperBusiness.

Handy, C. 1995. Trust and the virtual organization. *Harvard Business Review,* May-June: 40–50.

Hardin, G. 1968. The tragedy of the commons. *Science,* 162: 1243–1248.

Hardin, R. 1996. Trustworthiness. *Ethics,* 107: 26–42.

Hart, K. M., Capps, H. R., Cangemi, J. P., & Caillouet, L. M. 1986. Exploring organizational trust and its multiple dimensions: A case study of General Motors. *Organization Development Journal,* 4(2): 31–39.

Hofstede, G. 1980. *Culture's consequences: International differences in work related values.* Beverly Hills, CA: Sage.

Horwitz, T. 1994. Mr. Edens profits from watching his workers' every move. *The Wall Street Journal,* December 1: A1, A9.

Hosmer, L. T. 1995. Trust: The connecting link between organizational theory and philosophical ethics. *Academy of Management Review,* 20: 379–403.

Jennings, E. E. 1971. *Routes to the executive suite.* New York: McGraw-Hill.

Jensen, M. C., & Meckling, W. C. 1976. Theory of the firm: Managerial behavior, agency costs, and ownership structure. *Journal of Financial Economics,* 3: 305–360.

Johnson-George, C., & Swap, W. C. 1982. Measurement of specific interpersonal trust: Construction and validation of a scale to assess trust in a specific other. *Journal of Personality and Social Psychology,* 43: 1306–1317.

Konovsky, M. A., & Cropanzano, R. 1991. Perceived fairness of employee drug testing as a predictor of employee attitudes and job performance. *Journal of Applied Psychology,* 78: 698–707.

Konovsky, M. A., & Pugh, S. D. 1994. Citizenship behavior and social exchange. *Academy of Management Journal,* 37: 656–669.

Kormorita, S., & Parks, C. 1994. *Social dilemmas.* Madison, WI: Brown and Benchmark.

Korsgaard, M. A., & Roberson, L. 1995. Procedural justice in performance evaluation. *Journal of Management,* 21: 657–699.

Kramer, R. M., Brewer, M. B., & Hanna, B. J. 1996. Collective trust and collective action: The decision to trust as a social decision. In R. M. Kramer & T. R. Tyler (Eds.), *Trust in organizations: Frontiers of theory and research:* 357–389. Thousand Oaks, CA: Sage.

Larzelere, R. E., & Huston, T. L. 1980. The dyadic trust scale: Toward understanding interpersonal trust in close relationships. *Journal of Marriage and the Family,* 42: 595–604.

Liden, R. C., & Maslyn, J. M. 1993. *LMX-MDM: Scale development for a multidimensional measure of leader-member exchange.* Paper presented at the annual meeting of the Academy of Management, Atlanta, GA.

Liden, R. C., & Mitchell, T. R. 1988. Ingratiatory behavior in organizational settings. *Academy of Management Review,* 13: 572–587.

Lind, E. A. 1997. Litigation and claiming in organizations: Antisocial behavior or quest for justice? In R. A. Giacalone & J. Greenberg (Eds.), *Antisocial behavior in organizations:* 150–171. Thousand Oaks, CA: Sage.

Lind, E. A. Tyler, T., & Huo, Y. 1997. Procedural context and culture: Variation in the antecedents of procedural justice judgments. *Journal of Personality and Social Psychology,* 73: 787–780.

Luhmann, N. 1979. *Trust and power.* New York: Wiley.

Marcus, P. M., & House, J. S. 1973. Exchange between superiors and subordinates in large organizations. *Administrative Science Quarterly,* 18: 209–222.

Mayer, R. C., Davis, J. H., & Schoorman, F. D. 1995. An integrative model of organizational trust. *Academy of Management Review,* 20: 709–734.

McAllister, D. J. 1995. Affect- and cognition-based trust as foundations for interpersonal cooperation in organizations. *Academy of Management Journal,* 38: 24–59.

Mellinger, G. D. 1956. Interpersonal trust as a factor in communication. *Journal of Abnormal and Social Psychology,* 52: 304–309.

Mishra, A. K. 1996. Organizational responses to crisis: The centrality of trust. In R. M. Kramer & T. R. Tyler (Eds.), *Trust in organizations: Frontiers of theory and research*: 261–287. Thousand Oaks, CA: Sage.

Muchinsky, P. M. 1977. An intraorganizational analysis of the Roberts and O'Reilly organizational communication questionnaire. *Journal of Applied Psychology,* 62: 184–188.

Noorderhaven, N. G. 1992. The problem of contract enforcement in economic organization theory. *Organization Studies,* 13: 292–243.

O'Reilly, C. A., III. 1977. Supervisors and peers as information sources, group supportiveness, and individual decision-making performance. *Journal of Applied Psychology,* 62: 632–635.

O'Reilly, C. A., & Caldwell, D. R. 1985. The impact of normative social influence and cohesiveness on task perceptions and attitudes: A social information processing approach. *Journal of Occupational Psychology,* 58: 193–206.

O'Reilly, C. A., III, & Roberts, K. H. 1974. Information filtration in organizations: Three experiments. *Organizational Behavior and Human Performance,* 11: 253–285.

O'Reilly, C. A., III, & Roberts, K. H. 1977. Task group structure, communication, and effectiveness in three organizations. *Journal of Applied Psychology,* 62: 674–681.

Pettit, P. 1995. The cunning of trust. *Philosophy and Public Affairs,* 24: 202–225.

Porter, L. W., & Lawler, E. E., III. 1968. *Managerial attitudes and performance.* Homewood, IL: Irwin.

Rapaport, A., & Chammah, A. 1965. *Prisoner's dilemma.* Ann Arbor, MI: University of Michigan Press.

Ring, P. S., & Van de Ven, A. H. 1992. Structuring cooperative relationships between organizations. *Strategic Management Journal,* 13: 483–498.

Roberts, K. H., & O'Reilly, C. A., III. 1974a, Failures in upward communication in organizations: Three possible culprits. *Academy of Management Journal,* 17: 205–215.

Roberts, K. H., & O'Reilly, C. A. 1974b. Measuring organizational communication. *Journal of Applied Psychology,* 59: 321–326.

Roberts, K. H., & O'Reilly, C. A. 1979. Some correlates of communication roles in organizations. *Academy of Management Journal,* 22: 42–57.

Robinson, S. L. 1996. Trust and breach of the psychological contract. *Administrative Science Quarterly*, 41: 574–599.

Robinson, S. L. & Rousseau, D. M. 1994. Violating the psychological contract: Not the exception but the norm. *Journal of Organizational Behavior*, 15: 245–259.

Rokeach, M. 1973. *The nature of human values*. New York: Free Press.

Rosen, B., & Jerdee, T. H. 1977. Influence of subordinate characteristics on trust and use of participative decision strategies in a management simulation. *Journal of Applied Psychology*, 62: 628–631.

Rotter, J. B. 1967. A new scale for the measurement of interpersonal trust. *Journal of Personality*, 35: 615–665.

Rotter, J. B. 1980. Interpersonal trust, trustworthiness, and gullibility. *American Psychologist*, 35: 1–7.

Rousseau, D. M. 1990. Assessing organizational culture: The case for multiple methods. In B. Schneider (Ed.), *Organizational climate and culture*: 153–192. San Francisco: Jossey-Bass.

Sapienza, H. J., & Korsgaard, M. A. 1996. Managing investor relations: The impact of procedural justice in establishing and sustaining investor support, *Academy of Management Journal*, 39: 544–574.

Schein, E. H. 1996. Culture: The missing concept in organization studies. *Administrative Science Quarterly*, 41: 229–240.

Schwartz, S. H. 1992. Universals in the content and structure of values: Theoretical advances and empirical tests in 20 countries. In M. Zanna (Ed.), *Advances in experimental social psychology*, vol. 25: 1–65. San Diego: Academic Press.

Schwartz, S. H. 1994. Beyond individualism/collectivism: New cultural dimensions of values. In U. Kim, H. C. Triandis, C. Kagitçibasi, S. Choi, & G. Yoon (Eds.), *Individualism and collectivism: Theory, method, and applications*: 85–119. Thousand Oaks, CA: Sage.

Sitkin, S. B., & Roth, N. L. 1993. Explaining the limited effectiveness of legalistic remedies for trust/distrust. *Organization Science*, 4: 367–392.

Taylor, M. S., Tracy, K. B., Renard, M. K., Harrison, J. K., & Carroll, S. J. 1995. Due process in performance appraisal; A quasi-experiment in procedural justice. *Administrative Science Quarterly*, 40: 495–523.

Thompson, J. D. 1967. *Organizations in action: Social science bases of administrative theory*. New York: McGraw-Hill.

Thompson, J. D. & Luthans, F. 1990. Organizational culture: A behavioral perspective. In B. Schneider (Ed.), *Organizational climate and culture*: 319–344. San Francisco: Jossey-Bass.

Tyler, T. R., & Lind, E. A. 1992. A relational model of authority in groups. In M. Zanna (Ed.), *Advances in experimental social psychology*, vol. 25: 115–191. New York: Academic Press.

Vroom, V. H., & Yetton, P. 1973. *Leadership and decision making*. Pittsburgh: University of Pittsburgh Press.

Wilson, T. B. 1995. *Innovative reward systems for the changing workplace*. New York: McGraw-Hill.

Yeager, S. J. 1978. Measurement of independent variables which affect communication: A replication of Roberts and O'Reilly, *Psychological Reports*, 43: 1319–1324.

Zand, D. E. 1972. Trust and managerial problem solving. *Administrative Science Quarterly*, 17: 229–239.

Zucker, L. G. 1986. Production of trust: Institutional sources of economic structure, 1840–1920. In B. M. Staw & L. L. Cummings (Eds.), *Research in organizational behavior*. vol. 8: 53–111. Greenwich, CT: JAI Press.

6

The Emergence of Exchange Structures: An Experimental Study of Uncertainty, Commitment, and Trust[1]

Peter Kollock

Introduction

The emergence of social structure has been a chronically underexamined topic across all areas in sociology (Coleman 1986). In particular, the feature of social structure that is examined here—the emergence of stable exchange relationships—has received very little empirical attention. The purpose of this study is to begin to explore this issue experimentally, examining the effects of a crucial variable—uncertainty—on the patterns of exchange that emerge. A further goal is to examine the role of reputation as an important factor related to the formation of stable exchange relations and to examine some of the consequences of different patterns of exchange—in particular, how different exchange conditions lead to different levels of trust among trading partners.

This project brings together elements from two research traditions: social exchange theory and work on social dilemmas.[2] While the majority of research to date in these traditions has examined the effects of preexisting social structures on exchange and cooperation, this experiment is directed toward studying the *emergence* of different kinds of exchange structures. In addition, this project examines exchange situations in which deceit and opportunism are possible (in contrast to most work in social exchange theory) and where actors can move into and out of different exchange relations (in contrast to most work on social dilemmas).

A particularly evocative example of the kind of situation I wish to investigate is given in the work of Siamwalla (1978) and Popkin (1981) on the structure of commodity exchange in Thailand. Two contrasting cases are highlighted. The first is the market for rubber. Rubber is an interesting commodity in that at the time of sale it is impossible to determine its quality. It is not until months later, after extensive processing, that the buyer can determine whether the grower took the extra time and expense to insure a high-quality crop. Within this situation the buyers are not motivated to pay a high price for goods of unknown quality and the growers are not motivated to produce high quality goods as there is no simple, objective way of displaying the care they took. The participants are faced with a type of Prisoner's Dilemma that is the result of asymmetric information. Further, there are no regulatory agencies to monitor and sanction the actions of each exchange partner.

It is a difficult situation and one possible conclusion is that the buyers and sellers could not escape their fate, that is, cooperation would not emerge and the market would "fail" in that only low-quality goods would be bought and sold despite the fact that everyone could earn more buying and selling high-quality goods. And yet the growers and buyers of rubber have escaped this fate. Not because they decided to trust each other blindly or because they managed to create an institution to monitor and sanction themselves, but because they abandoned the anonymous exchange of the market for personal, long-term exchange relationships between particular buyers and sellers. Within this framework it is possible for the growers to establish reputations for fairness and trustworthiness.

In contrast, if the uncertainty regarding the good is low, the need for commitment and the concern over reputation will be lower. An example is the market for rice (Siamwalla 1978; Popkin 1981). Unlike rubber, the quality of rice can be ascertained directly and at essentially no cost by rubbing a few grains together between blocks of wood. In this situation, exchange more closely resembles the neoclassical model of the market: "Since quality is easy to assess instantaneously, rice markets are generally auction markets: immediate, relatively impersonal transactions. Or what Adam Smith thought all capitalism was like—information easily and readily ascertainable, easy switching of buyers, little reason for loyalty to any marketer or to any buyer. The grower's reputation matters relatively little since direct quality assessments are so easy to perform" (Popkin 1981, pp. 72–73).

This pair of examples captures the key points of this article. In essence, the goal was to create experimental analogs of the rubber and rice markets in order to examine the effects of uncertainty on the emergence of commitment and trust, as well as the importance of reputation in these settings.[3]

Commitment in Exchange Relations

Social exchange theory has a long and fruitful history of examining the *effects* of different exchange structures (networks of various shapes) on patterns of interaction, but very little research has investigated the emergence of these networks. Within a given network structure, researchers have sometimes had something to say about which pairs of actors are likely to trade (e.g., Bienenstock and Bonacich 1993; Cook, Emerson, Gillmore, and Yamagishi 1983; Markovsky, Willer, and Patton 1988). Of particular importance is an early experiment by Cook and Emerson (1978), who developed a measure of commitment as part of a study on power use in two four-person networks. I use the term *commitment* in the same sense they do to refer to *behavioral* patterns of exchange—that is, who trades with whom and to what extent. Because their focus was on power, they did not study patterns of commitment per se but rather the mediating effects of commitment on power use. One of the very few studies that has experimentally examined commitment is Lawler and Yoon (1993). This research focused on dyads, with each member of the dyad having a single, less attractive (i.e., less profitable) alternative. Their results indicated that the distribution of power, and whether a bargaining situation is zero sum or is not zero sum, can indirectly affect the frequency of trading between two exchange partners.[4]

However, in each of these studies the researchers created particular network structures within which subjects interacted. The question addressed here—What pattern of committed exchange relations emerges in a situation where anyone might interact with anyone else?—has received almost no empirical attention.[5]

A second limitation in current work within social exchange theory is the neglect of deceit and opportunism in exchange relations. That is, in the typical exchange experiment actors bargain over the price of their goods or how to divide a set number of points, but there is never the possibility of lying about the value of what one has, receiving a good without paying the agreed price, or backing out of a contract after it has been agreed upon. In other words, the typical social exchange experiment guarantees the terms of the exchange. In one sense this is an understandable feature of an experimental paradigm if one wishes to study, for example, the dynamics of power in a controlled way, but in another sense it sidesteps much that is crucial in actual interaction (concerns of uncertainty, risk, and being taken advantage of) and thus much that may be central in explaining why social structure in the form of networks of commitment exists.

If actors are not required to trade "in good faith," the interaction can have the structure of a social dilemma in that (like the rubber market) individuals gain by being deceitful, but all are hurt if all choose this course of action. Work on social dilemmas thus treats as its central concern the kind of deceit and uncertainty (caused by the tension between individual and collective rationality) that is usually ignored in exchange theory. The emergence of social structure, however, has also been taken for granted in much of the literature on social dilemmas.

In some of the best known work on the emergence of cooperation in the face of social dilemmas (e.g., Axelrod 1984; Hardin 1982; Taylor 1987), the structural property that is doing most of the work in these analyses—the fact that transactions occur repeatedly with the same actors—is fixed by assumption. Said another way, these scholars provide no mechanism to explain commitment to an exchange partner or group: commitment is fixed and unvarying across actors and time. Each actor is forced to interact with every other actor and is unable to choose partners or to leave unsatisfactory exchange relations. This is troubling because according to these theorists conditional cooperation occurs only because of iterated transactions with identifiable others; yet there is no explanation of how a longitudinal exchange relation is established or maintained or what pattern those networks of relations might take.

Recent work has begun to relax some of these stringent assumptions. Studying the emergence of committed exchange requires that actors be able to move into and out of relationships, and Schuessler (1989) as well as Orbell and Dawes (1991) have conducted computer simulations of groups of actors playing an iterated Prisoner's Dilemma game. In this work, actors had the option of exiting, that is, leaving their current partner for a new one, after each round. Because these researchers wished to study whether cooperation could emerge under very harsh conditions, in both cases the models assumed that actors could not recognize each other. Thus, issues such as commitment and reputation were irrelevant.

Research on social dilemmas in which actors can recognize each other as well as exit from the relationship includes computer simulations by Vanberg and Congleton (1992) and Yamagishi, Hayashi, and Jin (1992), and experimental work by Marwell and Schmitt (1975), Orbell, Schwartz-Shea, and Simmons (1984), and Yamagishi (1992). In each case, however, the focus was on the level of cooperation; the emergence of committed exchange relationships was not studied.

Peter Kollock

Uncertainty and Trust

As I discussed above, an important limitation in current work in social exchange theory is the absence of deceit or opportunism in experimental designs. Yet situations in which we can be taken advantage of are pervasive in every realm of our lives. The motivations of those we interact with can be inferred but never known directly and the quality of goods and services we are offered is often unknown or known only approximately. In the language of game theory, we are often faced with *information asymmetries:* you and I have different bundles of information. This lack of information about the motivations of others and the quality of what is exchanged can open one up to serious risks and lead to unfortunate outcomes.[6]

A classic example of this sort of situation is the market for "lemons" (i.e., used cars of poor quality) analyzed by Akerlof (1970). The problem faced by the buyer of a used car is that he or she often cannot know the true quality of a car until after the car has been purchased and driven for a time. The car seller often does have a good idea of the car's quality, but there is no simple means of conveying this information in a believable way. The buyer realizes that the seller is motivated to describe the car as reliable regardless of the true nature of the car and that the seller stands to make an especially large profit if a "lemon" can be sold as a reliable car. According to Akerlof's analysis, because of this risk a buyer will be unwilling to purchase a used car at a high price. If the seller cannot get a high price the seller will be motivated to sell only lemons. The pessimistic conclusion is that in the absence of other factors only low-quality cars will be bought and sold at a low price. Both buyers and sellers are hurt by this outcome, and so the situation has the structure of a social dilemma in that individually rational behavior leads to a collectively irrational outcome.[7]

Faced with a situation in which one can be taken advantage of, a natural response is to restrict one's transactions to those who have shown themselves to be trustworthy (i.e., becoming committed to particular exchange partners). This is not a possibility in Akerlof's original analysis because he assumes the purchase of a used car between a particular buyer and seller is a one-time transaction. In contrast, the market for rubber involves the same problem of information asymmetries but in a situation in which buyers and sellers might encounter each other from one season to the next. The possibility of repeated exchanges means commitment can be used as a response to the risks that derive from information asymmetries.

As sellers and buyers repeatedly trade with each other it will be possible for trust to develop. As I use the term here, an action demonstrates *trust* if it "increase[s] one's vulnerability... to another whose behavior is not under one's control. [It refers to] the conscious regulation of one's dependence on another"

(Zand 1972, p. 230; cf. Deutsch 1962).[8] Thus, the development of high levels of trust requires more than just ongoing interaction. Some level of risk must also be present so that there is a *test* of trust (Dasgupta 1988). As Kelley and Thibaut (1978, p. 237) observe in a discussion of the development of exchange relations:

If the [situation] is extremely correspondent [i.e., what is good for one actor is good for the other], there is . . . no basis for the development of trust, for there is nothing to risk, hence no test of willingness to take risks: cooperative overtures will be attributed to the structure of the situation rather than to dispositional . . . properties of the participants. Therefore it is in the middle regions of the continuum of outcome correspondence, in which elements of both conflict and cooperation are present as temptations, that attributions of trust have their origins.

The implication is that trust is likely to be higher among actors who manage to establish successful exchange relations in situations such as the rubber market (where information asymmetries introduce significant risks), as opposed to actors in situations similar to the rice market (where more information is available and the risks are significantly lower). Of course, risk creates a breeding ground not only for trust but for exploitation as well. It may be then that in looking at the trust actors have for each other in a risky exchange situation one will find extremes of both trust and distrust. This will be one of the issues explored in the experiment.

Granovetter (1985) has also argued that ongoing experience within a network of exchange relationships is likely to be a key source of trust. Indeed, his claim is that this may be the most important source:

The widespread preference for transacting with individuals of known reputation implies that few are actually content to rely on either generalized morality *or* institutional arrangements to guard against trouble. . . . [Instead] social relations, rather than institutionalized arrangements or generalized morality, are mainly responsible for the production of trust in economic life. (pp. 490–91; emphasis in original)

His comment also raises the issue of reputation. A *reputation*, as defined by Robert Wilson (1985, pp. 27–28), is a "characteristic or attribute ascribed to one person . . . by another (e.g., 'A has a reputation for courtesy'). Operationally, this is usually represented as a prediction about likely future behavior (e.g., 'A is likely to be courteous'). It is, however, primarily an empirical statement (e.g., 'A has been observed in the past to be courteous'). Its predictive power depends on the supposition that past behavior is indicative of future behavior." If actors encounter each other repeatedly in a risky situation, reputation is likely to be an important concern, both in terms of establishing a particular reputation for oneself as well as making some judgment about the reputation of one's potential exchange partners.

In recent years there has been a great deal of theoretical work in game theory and microeconomics on the important effects of reputations in situations with information asymmetries (Kreps and Wilson 1982; Kreps et al. 1982; Milgrom and Roberts 1982; Shapiro 1982; Wilson 1985).[9] This research has argued that "differences in the information available to participants make their strategies acutely sensitive to their beliefs and expectations" (Wilson 1985, p. 59), and hence actors will be concerned about both their own and their partners' reputation. A further conclusion is that this concern will vary depending upon the amount of risk in the exchange, with situations characterized by a high degree of uncertainty (such as the rubber market) leading to a greater concern for reputation.

There have also been theoretical discussions of the importance of reputation in the literature on social dilemmas (e.g., Axelrod 1984) as well as in the rational choice tradition within sociology (e.g., Coleman 1990; Raub and Weesie 1990). Curiously, the concept of reputation has been all but absent in social exchange theory.[10] Exchange theory has focused on the flow of tangible resources through an exchange network, but the work that has been done on reputation suggests that the flow and management of information will likely be as important a determinant of exchange processes and structures.[11]

In sum, this discussion suggests that variations in the initial structural constraints that affect the availability of information should have predictable effects on the strategies of exchange that actors adopt in their transactions and therefore on the structure of the exchange networks that emerge. Specifically, if the uncertainty regarding a good that is exchanged is high, actors will enter into committed exchange relations with those partners who have shown themselves to be trustworthy. In this setting commitment will be high, actors will be very concerned about reputations, and trust is likely to be high (at least among committed exchange partners). It will be a system of exchange marked by a network of personalized, long-term exchange relations. In contrast, the example of the market for rice implies that when uncertainty is low, commitment will be low, actors will not be as concerned about reputations, and the level of trust between exchange partners will be lower. These are the hypotheses that will be explored in the experiment. Thus, at least in a limited way both sides of the micro–macro relationship are brought in: I investigate how the initial structural conditions of exchange affect interaction which in turn reproduces or reforms the exchange structure.

Method

Design

I created two experimental conditions. The single factor varied (between subjects) was the information subjects had about the quality of goods they were trading. In the first condition the quality of the goods being sold was public knowledge. In the second condition buyers discovered the quality of the goods they had purchased only after the sale was made. It is important to note that the unit of analysis is the group as a whole. This is necessary both because the key dependent variable of interest (the degree of commitment in the exchange system) is a property of the group as a whole and because actors within a given group are of course interdependent, making statistical tests at the individual level inappropriate.

Subjects

The experiment was run during the spring of 1991. Subjects were recruited from undergraduate social science courses at the University of California, Los Angeles, during the winter of 1990–91 and at the beginning of spring. Recruitment was based solely on the opportunity to earn money, and prospective subjects were told they could earn from $10 to $30 (depending on their performance in the experiment) for two hours of their time. A total of 80 subjects participated in groups of eight.[12] The subjects ranged from 18 to 33 years of age, with a mean age of 21.5 years.

Procedure

Subjects were scheduled in groups of eight. Four subjects were randomly assigned the role of seller and four were assigned the role of buyer. The experiment took place in a room with a divider so that sellers could not see buyers and vice versa. At the front of the room, in view of all of the subjects, was a large erasable board on which were recorded the subjects' offers to buy and sell. Subjects made offers and accepted them by writing messages on small individual boards; talking was prohibited. Thus buyers and sellers could neither see nor hear each other and were identified only on the basis of a letter each had been assigned. They were also explicitly told that they would not see each other after the experiment was over.

Subjects read a set of instructions and went through a training period before the experiment began. In both experimental conditions, buyers and sellers traded goods of different qualities in order to earn points (which were converted to money at the end of the experiment). In the uncertain-quality condition (as in the rubber market), buyers did not discover the quality of what they had purchased until after the sale, and the quality was disclosed only to that particular buyer, not to the group as a whole. In the certain-quality condition (as in the rice market), the quality of the goods being sold was public knowledge.

In the uncertain-quality condition, the instructions read by the subjects were as follows:

For sellers.—During each trading period you will have an opportunity to sell *one* shipment of "goods" to one of the buyers. The shipment you sell can vary in terms of its quality. There are three levels of quality (low, regular, super) and the higher the quality the more it will cost you to produce a shipment (a low costs 20 points, a regular costs 60 points, and a super costs 100 points). You will be asked at the beginning of each trading period what quality of goods you wish to produce. The higher the quality, the more the shipment is worth to a buyer. However, *at the time you sell the shipment the buyer will not know the quality.* After the purchase the buyer will be told the quality of the shipment he or she just bought from you.

For buyers.—During each trading period you will have an opportunity to buy *one* shipment of "goods" from one of the sellers. The value of a shipment to you depends on its quality. There are three levels of quality (low, regular, super) and the higher the quality, the higher its value to you (this value is known as the "redemption value"). A low is worth 40 points, a regular is worth 120 points, and a super is worth 200 points. *At the time you buy the shipment you will not know the quality* but after the purchase you will be told the quality of the shipment you bought.

In the certain-quality condition, the instructions informed the subjects that the quality of goods being sold would be public knowledge. The value of the goods for buyers and sellers was designed to create a situation that had two key characteristics. First, the higher the quality, the greater the cost to produce, but the higher the value to buyers; second, the higher the quality, the more profit there was to split up. Subjects were aware of these two features, which were emphasized during the training period. Subjects did not know, however, the exact value of the goods for the people with whom they were trading. That is, buyers did not know exactly how much it cost sellers to produce a good and sellers did not know the exact redemption value of a given quality of goods for buyers.

While actual quality was unknown in the uncertain-quality condition, sellers were allowed to advertise if they wished; that is, they could claim the shipment they were trying to sell was of a particular grade. It was emphasized (and buyers quickly discovered this) that sellers were under no obligation to advertise truthfully.

Each trading period lasted a maximum of five minutes, during which buyers and sellers could make as many offers and counteroffers as they wished (though they could complete only one trade during a given period). These offers and counteroffers were listed on the large board at the front of the room and so could be seen by all subjects.[13] There were two types of offers that could be made: *public* offers, which could be accepted by anyone, or *private* offers, which were directed toward a particular person and could be accepted only by that person. This feature allowed subjects to enter into restricted trading relations if they so desired.

Buyers and sellers were free to accept or not to accept an offer at any time. Once an offer was accepted it became binding. In the uncertain-quality condition, the buyer was then privately informed of the quality of the good he or she had just purchased (of course, this information was already known to the buyer in the certain-quality condition). Once the sale was made, the relevant information was recorded on a data sheet, and the subjects calculated their profits for the round. In order to eliminate endgame effects, the number of trading periods was varied and subjects did not know which period would be their last. All groups traded for at least 20 rounds.

After the experiment, subjects were given a questionnaire that contained (1) items designed to serve as manipulation tests, (2) questions regarding demographic characteristics, (3) items designed to measure how concerned they were about their own and their partners' reputation and how likely they were to switch partners, and (4) ratings of others in the group on a variety of dimensions.

The Measurement of Commitment

The key dependent variable of interest is commitment. The variable will be defined and measured at the behavioral level; that is, the question will be, Who traded with whom and to what extent? Even when the variable is defined strictly in behavioral terms, there are a number of complexities that emerge in designing a measure of commitment.

One possibility for assessing commitment would be to compare the number of trades two actors engaged in to the total number of trades. That is, if A and B trade seven times out of 15 possible trades, one could compute a commitment measure that is simply the ratio of trades completed to total trades possible (a score of .467 in this case). Such "pair-based" measures, however, are local measures that examine only one relationship at a time. This can lead to counterintuitive results in which actors might be given the same commitment score despite very different patterns of exchange.[14]

The alternative would be a measure that took into account the entire set of possible exchange relationships each actor faced. Such a measure (which can be termed "network-based" rather than "pair-based") was developed by Cook and Emerson (1978). For each actor, this measure compares the number of trades made with different partners. That is, it contrasts each possible exchange relationship with every other possible exchange relationship in which an actor might take part.

Peter Kollock

A revised version of their measure will be used here. Specifically, for an exchange system in which each actor has four potential trading partners, the level of commitment for actor I with potential partners J, K, L, and M, after t trading periods will be defined as

$$(C_i)_l = [(T_{ij} - T_{ik})^2 + (T_{ij} - T_{il})^2 + (T_{ij} - T_{im})^2 + (T_{ik} - T_{il})^2 + (T_{ik} - T_{im})^2 + (T_{il} - T_{im})^2]/[3(t^2)], \tag{1}$$

where T_{ij} signifies the number of trades I completed with J. The commitment measure has a maximum value of 1.0 when an actor has completed a trade every round and always with the same partner, and a minimum value of 0.0 when trades are evenly distributed among all possible trading partners. As Cook and Emerson (1978, p. 735) point out, while each person in the group "can have a different commitment score, the [eight] scores are obviously interdependent. To the extent that any person becomes committed, others, losing 'choice' in partner selection, become structurally committed of necessity."

As the term is used here, commitment also implies that an actor will resist at least some levels of temptation (e.g., a better price from another potential partner). The implication is that once a committed exchange relationship forms, actors will not abandon the relationship the moment a slightly better alternative presents itself. To tap into this possibility, on the postexperimental questionnaire subjects were asked to report how often they kept trading with a buyer/seller even when they could get a better price from someone else.[15]

Other Measures

On the postexperiment questionnaire, subjects were also asked a variety of questions designed to serve as manipulation tests, including how realistic they felt the study was, how clear the instructions were, how strongly motivated they were to earn as much as possible, and how much they enjoyed the experiment.

In addition to the question concerning commitment, subjects were asked how concerned they were about both their own and their partners' reputation for being fair in their trades.[16]

Finally, the postexperiment questionnaire allowed subjects to evaluate each person the subject might have traded with (i.e., the four buyers if a seller was answering the questionnaire, and the four sellers if the subject had been a buyer) on 12 bipolar scales. Of particular importance is the scale which asked subjects to rate how untrustworthy/trustworthy each of their potential trading partners was.[17]

Hypotheses

Note that the sellers and buyers in the uncertain-quality condition are not exposed to the same level of risk. The seller does face some risk (producing a costly, high-quality good and then not being able to get a high price for it), but the risks for the buyer are much greater. The seller makes a trade with full information about the quality of the good and the price being paid. In contrast, the buyer must trade blindly, knowing the price but learning the quality only after the exchange is consummated. The experiment was designed with this structure for two reasons: first, this structure models a great many empirical situations; and second, for some variables this allows one to make hypotheses not simply about differences between the two conditions (certain vs. uncertain quality), but also about differences between the role subjects played in the experiment (seller vs. buyer).

Seven hypotheses will be investigated. Based on the discussion above, the key prediction is the effect of uncertainty on commitment:

Hypothesis 1.—*Commitment will be greater in the uncertain-quality condition.*

Related to this prediction is the hypothesis concerning subjects' response to tempting offers by other exchange partners:

Hypothesis 2.—*Subjects will be more likely to report staying with an exchange partner even when they could get a better price from someone else in the uncertain-quality condition.*

The second variable of interest is trust. As discussed above, developing high levels of trust requires that there be some test of trust, that is, risk. Assuming buyers and sellers establish successful exchange relations in both conditions, the prediction is:

Hypothesis 3.—*Subjects will rate their partners as significantly more trustworthy in the uncertain-quality condition.*

The uncertain-quality condition could produce extremes of both trust (for one's favored trading partner) and distrust (for other partners, who perhaps tried to take advantage of the subject). This possibility will be investigated by examining not just the overall level of trust within the group, but the average trustworthiness rating for one's most trusted and least trusted trading partner as well. Because of the asymmetric risk in the uncertain-quality condition, I also expect that the trustworthiness ratings made by buyers will be more "extreme" than those made by sellers. Specifically:

Hypothesis 4.—*Within the uncertain-quality condition, the trustworthiness rating of one's most trusted partner will be higher for buyers than sellers, and the trustworthiness rating for one's* least *trusted partner will be lower for buyers than sellers.*

The reason for this prediction is that, since buyers face much greater risk in their trading, they will have particularly strong evidence about the trustworthiness or untrustworthiness of their partners. One should also expect to find a relationship between commitment and trust in that there should be higher trust among partners who frequently trade with each other. Hence:

Hypothesis 5.—*The trustworthiness rating for one's most frequent exchange partner will be greater than the rating for one's least frequent exchange partner.*[18]

A positive relationship between commitment and trust should definitely be found in the uncertain-quality condition. I also expect to find this relationship in the certain-quality condition despite the absence of significant risk. Previous research (Homans 1961; Lawler and Yoon 1993; Molm 1991) has suggested that frequent exchange is sufficient in itself to produce positive evaluations of one's partner. However, while commitment and trust are likely to be related in both conditions, the average level of trust should be higher in the uncertain-quality condition.[19]

The final variable of interest is concern for reputation, and it is expected that greater risk leads to greater concern for reputation. Hence:

Hypothesis 6.—*Subjects will be significantly more concerned about both their own and their partners' reputation in the uncertain-quality condition.*

Here, as with trust, I expect a difference between buyers and sellers in the uncertain-quality situation, and for a similar reason. Because buyers face a much greater risk—being exploited by a seller—the prediction is that buyers will be particularly concerned about the reputation of sellers and sellers will be especially concerned about their own reputation. Hence:

Hypothesis 7.—*Within the uncertain-quality condition, the concern for one's partners' reputation will be higher for buyers than sellers, and the concern for one's own reputation will be higher for sellers than buyers.*

Results

Analysis of the postexperimental questionnaire provides evidence that the subjects were highly motivated to earn as much as possible (mean = 6.01,

SD = 0.38; seven-point scale), rated the instructions they received as very clear (mean = 6.28, SD = 0.38), found the study realistic (mean = 4.89, SD = 0.30), and greatly enjoyed participating in the experiment (mean = 6.16, SD = 0.41). Only one of these scores differed significantly between the two experimental conditions (the question concerning the motivation to earn as much as possible; this result is discussed below).

The results will be grouped according to the dependent variables, beginning with the measures of commitment, then reporting on the level of trust in the groups, variables relevant to concerns about reputation, and finally a section on other findings that were not explicitly predicted. Because the group is the unit of analysis, all variables consist of group averages.

Commitment

Figure 1 displays the average level of commitment across time for both experimental conditions. The trading rounds were grouped into five blocks of four rounds each. The effect of uncertainty on commitment was significant and in the direction hypothesized; commitment was significantly greater in the uncertain-quality condition ($F_{1,8} = 5.46$; $P < .05$), supporting hypothesis 1.

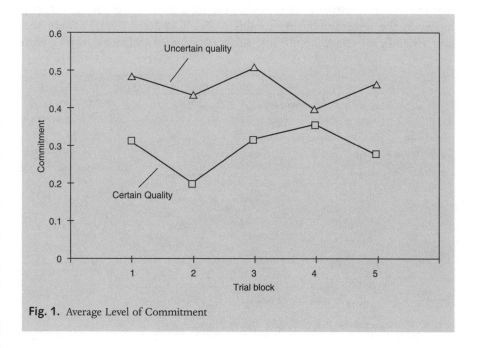

Fig. 1. Average Level of Commitment

There were no significant differences across blocks of trading rounds ($F_{4,32} = 0.72$; $P = .581$), nor was the interaction of uncertainty × blocks significant ($F_{4,32} = 0.73$; $P = .577$).[20]

Consistent with the hypothesis 2, subjects in the uncertain-quality condition were significantly more likely to report that they sometimes kept trading with a particular partner even when they could get a better price from someone else. (Mean = 2.68, 3.98 for the certain- and uncertain-quality conditions, respectively; $P < .05$. Means are based on a seven-point scale with a higher score indicating a greater tendency to remain with one's partner.)

Trust

The average trust rating for all potential partners was significantly higher in the uncertain-quality condition, supporting hypothesis 3. (Mean = 4.08, 4.62 for the certain- and uncertain-quality conditions, respectively; $P < .01$.)

Because this overall average could be masking extremes of both trust and distrust, the average trustworthiness ratings of subjects' most and least trusted partner were examined separately. Figure 2 displays the trustworthiness rating of subjects' *most* trusted partner for sellers and buyers in both experimental conditions.

There is a very strong main effect for the influence of uncertainty, indicating that the level of trustworthiness for one's most trusted partner is significantly higher in the uncertain-quality condition ($F_{1,8} = 41.26$; $P < .001$). There was also a significant effect for the role subjects occupied (seller vs. buyer), with

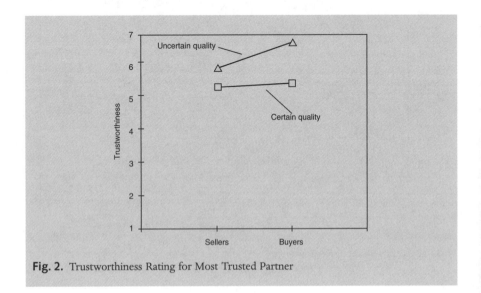

Fig. 2. Trustworthiness Rating for Most Trusted Partner

buyers on average rating their most trusted partner higher than sellers ($F_{1,8} = 9.26$; $P < .05$; role is treated as a repeated measure). However, this effect is largely the result of the difference between sellers and buyers in the uncertain-quality condition; sellers and buyers do not differ significantly in the certain-quality condition. This results in a significant interaction effect between uncertainty (certain vs. uncertain quality) and role (seller vs. buyer; $F_{1,8} = 5.60$; $P < .05$). Note that subjects in the uncertain condition rated their most trusted partner higher than did subjects in the certain-quality condition and that the buyers in the uncertain condition rated their most trusted partner exceptionally high (mean = 6.80 on a seven-point scale).

Figure 3 displays the trustworthiness rating of subjects' *least* trusted partner. The main effect for uncertainty was not significant ($P = .918$), but the effect for role was significant ($F_{1,8} = 13.68$; $P < .01$). Once again, this effect is due to the difference between sellers and buyers in the uncertain-quality conditions, a difference that results in a significant interaction effect ($F_{1,8} = 11.36$; $P < .01$). In this case sellers in the uncertain-quality condition rated their least trustworthy partner higher than other experimental subjects, whereas buyers in the uncertain-quality condition rated their least trusted partner lower than other subjects.

Looking at both Figures 2 and 3, one can see that buyers in the uncertain condition rated their most trusted partner higher than sellers in the uncertain condition and they rated their least trusted partner lower than sellers, all of which supports hypothesis 4. Note also that in the certain-quality condition there is essentially no difference between buyers and sellers in their ratings of their partners' trustworthiness.

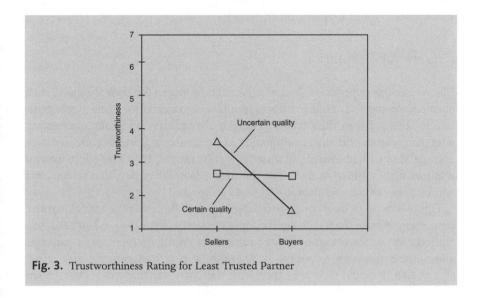

Fig. 3. Trustworthiness Rating for Least Trusted Partner

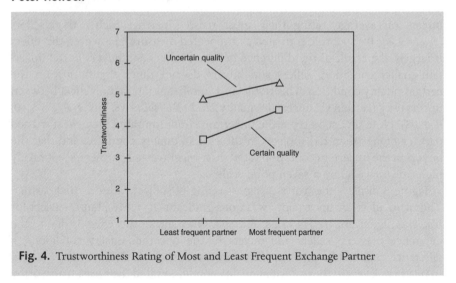

Fig. 4. Trustworthiness Rating of Most and Least Frequent Exchange Partner

One should also expect to find a relationship between trust and commitment. Figure 4 displays the trustworthiness rating of subjects' most and least frequent trading partner for the two experimental conditions.

As predicted by hypothesis 5, the difference between the trustworthiness rating of subjects' least and most frequent exchange partner is significant in both conditions, with subjects rating their most frequent partner as more trustworthy ($F_{1,8} = 10.35$; $P < .05$). The effect for uncertainty is also significant, indicating that subjects in the uncertain-quality condition on average rated their trading partners as more trust-worthy ($F_{1,8} = 20.24$; $P < .01$). The interaction effect was not significant ($P = .365$).

Concern for Reputation

The remaining hypotheses deal with subjects' concern for their own and their partners' reputation. Figure 5 displays subjects' concern for their *own* reputation for being fair in their trades. There is a significant effect for uncertainty, with subjects in the uncertain-quality condition being more concerned on average about their own reputation ($F_{1,8} = 20.17$; $P < .01$). The effect for role was not significant ($P = .693$), but the interaction effect between uncertainty and role was nearly significant ($F_{1,8} = 4.76$; $P = .061$).

Figure 6 displays how concerned subjects were about their potential *partners'* reputation. Again, there is a significant uncertainty effect ($F_{1,8} = 6.07$; $P < .05$). Subjects in the uncertain-quality condition on average were more concerned about their partners' reputation. There is a nearly significant role effect ($F_{1,8} = 3.68$; $P = .091$). As was true with the trust variables, this effect is the

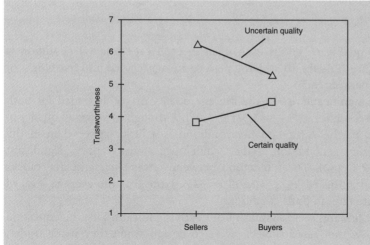

Fig. 5. Concern for *Own* Reputation for Being Fair

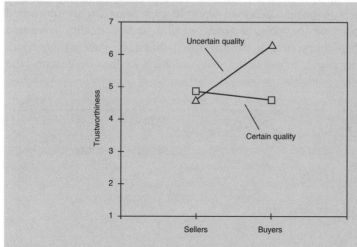

Fig. 6. Concern for *Partners'* Reputation for Being Fair

result of the difference between sellers and buyers in the uncertain-quality condition, which results in a significant interaction effect ($F_{1,8} = 6.66$; $P < .05$).

In each case subjects in the uncertain-quality condition were on average significantly more concerned about both their own and their potential partners' reputation, confirming hypothesis 6. In addition, within the uncertain-quality condition, sellers were more concerned about their partners' reputation. In other words, subjects in the uncertain condition were especially concerned about sellers' reputation. This finding confirms hypothesis 7.

Other Findings

The average quality of goods exchanged in each experimental condition is shown in Figure 7. Again, the trading periods are aggregated into five blocks of four trading periods each.

There is a significant rise in the average quality of goods traded for both experimental conditions ($F_{4,32} = 5.33$; $P < .01$). Although the over-all quality of goods traded in the certain-quality condition is a little higher than in the uncertain-quality condition, the difference was not significant ($F_{1,8} = 2.14$; $P = .182$). The interaction between uncertainty and trial blocks was also not significant ($F_{4,32} = 0.80$; $P = .533$). Note that the average level of quality is quite high in both conditions.

Four other findings were significant or nearly significant. First, in a question that asked how motivated subjects were to be fair when they made trades, the average level of motivation for being fair was significantly higher in the uncertain-quality condition (mean $= 4.18$, 5.58 on a seven-point scale for the certain- and uncertain-quality conditions, respectively; $P < .01$). Second, although subjects in both conditions reported they were highly motivated to earn as much as possible, subjects in the *certain* quality condition had significantly higher scores on this measure—that is, they were more motivated to earn as much as possible (mean $= 6.28$, 5.75 for the certain- and

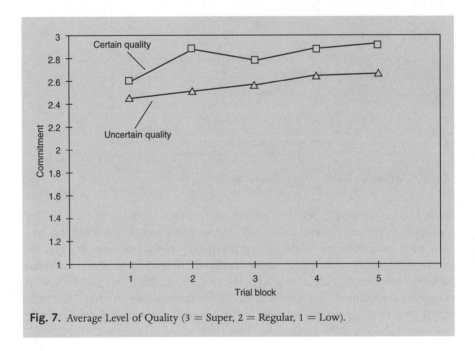

Fig. 7. Average Level of Quality ($3 =$ Super, $2 =$ Regular, $1 =$ Low).

uncertain-quality conditions, respectively; $P < .05$). Third, an unanticipated finding was that when subjects were asked their impression of how rational their potential trading partners were, the overall rationality rating was significantly higher in the uncertain-quality condition (mean = 4.29, 4.81 for the certain- and uncertain-quality conditions, respectively; $P < .01$). Finally, it seems that subjects in the uncertain-quality condition attributed more "extreme" personality characteristics (whether in the positive or negative direction) to their trading partners than did subjects in the certain-quality condition. By "extreme" I mean the extent to which ratings on the bipolar personality scales departed from the midpoint. A measure was constructed that summed the absolute value of each rating minus four points (the midpoint). The average departure from the midpoint was greater for the uncertain-quality condition (mean = 1.103, 1.455 for the certain- and uncertain-quality conditions, respectively; $P = .056$).

Discussion

All the hypotheses were supported by the results. Commitment, the reported tendency to remain with a partner despite a better offer, the average level of trust, and concern for one's own and others' reputation were all significantly higher in the uncertain-quality condition.

Although commitment, as operationalized by the Cook and Emerson measure, was significantly higher in the uncertain-quality condition, observations of subjects' trading behavior suggest a more complex definition of commitment may be needed. In some cases, sellers were observed advertising truthfully when trading with some buyers and trying to exploit others. For example, in one case a seller established a trading relationship with one favored buyer within which the seller always advertised truthfully and sold the goods at a reasonable price. When interacting with other buyers however, the seller tried to pass on low-quality goods as high-quality goods. When trying to sell a "lemon," the seller was very careful to shut out the favored buyer by making only private offers and only to the other three buyers. In that way the favored buyer could not inadvertently buy the shipment thinking it was a high-quality good (which would damage the relationship the seller had carefully nurtured).[21]

This example demonstrates the kind of sophisticated strategic behavior that some subjects engaged in. It also illustrates a different way of thinking about commitment. Intuitively, it seems reasonable to say that this seller was committed to the favored buyer. Yet simply looking at the number of trades the seller made and with whom would not uncover the kind of commitment expressed here. While the Cook and Emerson measure clearly taps into an important behavioral pattern, future work would likely benefit from using a more complex operational definition of commitment.

It is also important to note that the difference in commitment between the two experimental conditions was relative rather than absolute—commitment was definitely present in the certain quality condition. This suggests that commitment will be present to some degree in any exchange system. Indeed, Baker (1984) has shown that even in exchange situations that have been designed to eliminate quality uncertainty and transaction costs as much as possible, such as the Chicago Options Exchange, commitment between particular buyers and sellers emerges.

Trust was significantly higher on average in the uncertain-quality condition, though this general result ignores interesting interaction effects. As I discussed above, sellers and buyers both face risks in the uncertain condition, but buyers face much greater risks—they are always in danger of being exploited by sellers because of their lack of knowledge about the quality of the good being sold. This means that sellers face a particularly severe test of their trustworthiness, and so it is not surprising to see that, in the uncertain-quality condition, buyers' most trusted partners were ranked exceptionally high in trustworthiness and their least trusted partners were ranked exceptionally low (Figs. 2 and 3). Buyers' ratings of their least trusted partner was the one case in which the level of trust was lower in the uncertain condition. It is noteworthy that there were no differences between sellers and buyers in the certain-quality condition. This is understandable given that sellers and buyers are in equivalent situations in that each has full information about quality and price.

The other finding regarding trust was the relationship between commitment and trust (Fig. 4), and as expected the results demonstrate that subjects rank their most frequent exchange partner as more trustworthy than their least frequent partner. This relationship held in both conditions, although the level of trustworthiness was once again significantly higher in the uncertain-quality condition. The fact that the relationship between trading frequency and trust also existed in the certain-quality case is interesting. It seems that ongoing interaction, even in the absence of significant uncertainty, can lead to an increase in trust. Note, however, that the level of trust for subjects' *most* frequent partner in the certain-quality condition was still lower than the trust rating for subjects' *least* frequent partner in the uncertain condition.

Concern about reputation was also significantly higher in the uncertain-quality condition. Once again, this general finding ignores a variety of interesting interaction effects that can be seen once sellers and buyers are examined individually. In the uncertain-quality condition sellers had the opportunity to exploit buyers, and so it is understandable that buyers in this condition were especially concerned about sellers' reputation for being fair and sellers were especially concerned about their own reputation for being fair

(Figs. 5, 6). This concern about fairness in the uncertain-quality condition is also reflected in the finding that subjects in this condition were more likely to report that they were motivated to be fair in their trades with others.

The finding that subjects' impressions of each other's rationality was higher in the uncertain-quality condition was unexpected, and I am not certain how to interpret the result. One tentatively offered possibility is that the greater challenge of completing successful trades under conditions of uncertainty required sophisticated strategies and decision making, and so when subjects looked back on the actions of their trading partners they were inclined to rate them as quite rational. As for the finding that subjects in the uncertain-quality condition attributed more "extreme" personality characteristics to their trading partners, a possible interpretation is that trading under conditions of risk leads to subjectively more secure assessments of others' characteristics. Whatever the case, it is interesting that different structural conditions of exchange can lead to significantly different attributional patterns about individuals' underlying dispositions and capacities.

Observations of subjects' trading behavior in the uncertain-quality condition also revealed interesting details about their approach and reactions to risky exchange. Subjects seemed to follow a number of different strategies in trying to make successful trades. In the uncertain-quality condition there were some buyers who started off selling high-quality goods from the beginning and never tried to take advantage of buyers. Although no communication was permitted between subjects and the quality of the good was disclosed only to the buyer, because subjects had an opportunity to trade with each other over a number of rounds, those sellers who were reliable sources of high-quality goods were quickly discovered, and buyers often bid each other up in price for the opportunity of trading with the trusted seller. Indeed, the prices buyers were willing to pay for goods from a particular seller and the rush by some buyers to complete a trade with particular sellers seemed to be sources of information for other buyers—if other buyers were eager to trade with seller X, then perhaps they should be too. In this way sellers who established a reputation for selling high-quality goods could demand a premium for their goods because of the identity they had established for themselves.

Other sellers in the uncertain-quality condition tried to get away with all they could, sometimes stringing a buyer along with a few good trades and then exploiting them by passing on a low-quality good that they advertised as a high-quality good. Still other sellers, as was illustrated in the commitment example above, were always fair with some buyers (to the extent that they advertised truthfully) while not hesitating to exploit other buyers.

Also noteworthy was the exceptional involvement of subjects in the experiment and a moral element that seemed to color the experience. Those buyers in the uncertain-quality condition who were betrayed by a seller (having been sold low-quality goods that were advertised as high-quality goods) appeared very disturbed and often wrote notes in the margins of their data sheets such as "Never trade with C again!" Conversely, when successful exchange relations were established under conditions of risk, subjects reacted very positively. In two groups in the uncertain-quality condition, a pair of subjects formed exclusive trading relations (all trades were completed with only one partner) that were also highly successful (only high-quality goods were traded). The outcome was very interesting: although subjects were told they would not meet each other afterward and would not be able to identify each other, in these two cases the trading partners sought each other out, asking subjects as they left the experiment what position they held. When they found each other they greeted one another as old friends even though they had not known each other prior to the experiment (and of course knew each other during the experiment simply by an identifying letter, their only source of information about the other being their trading behavior). They congratulated each other, praised each other, exchanged "high-fives," and in one case even made plans to meet for lunch the next day. It is also noteworthy that exclusive exchange relations never developed in the certain-quality condition.

Risk, Regulation, and Trust

It is possible to think about the *certain*-quality condition as an exchange system in which a third party (the experimenter) served as a regulatory agency to insure the terms of the transaction. Indeed, it was an ideal regulatory system in that it operated perfectly (no seller could misrepresent the quality of his or her goods, and no one could back out of a contract once it had been made) and at no cost to the participants.

The quality of goods traded in the certain condition was a little higher than the goods traded in the uncertain condition, which suggests the advantage of a formal regulatory system. Yet this difference was not significant and, given that there was a significant increase in quality over time in both conditions, it may be that even this small difference would disappear. Further, the results indicated that there may be some drawbacks to a system that relies on an outside party to provide guarantees even when the monitoring system works perfectly. The average level of interpersonal trust was significantly lower in the certain-quality condition compared to the uncertain-quality condition. To the extent this finding is robust, one implication is that in some situations an external, formal regulatory system might work against the emergence of trust within a group or result in the atrophy of already existing trust. This possibility has been discussed by a number of theorists. At the most general level, Taylor (1987, p. 168) has argued that "the more the state intervenes ... the more 'necessary' (on this view) it becomes, because positive altruism and voluntary cooperative behavior *atrophy* in the presence of the state and *grow* in its absence. Thus, again, the state exacerbates the conditions which are supposed to make it necessary. We might say that the state is like an addictive drug: the more of it we have, the more we 'need' it and the more we come to 'depend' on it" (emphasis in original).

Hirschman (1984, p. 93) makes a similar point, stating that trust and other "moral resources" are "resources whose supply may well increase rather than decrease through use; these resources do not remain intact if they stay unused; like the ability to speak a foreign language or to play the piano, these moral resources are likely to become depleted and to atrophy if *not* used" (emphasis in original).

An interesting empirical example that is consistent with these views comes from research by Light, Kwuon, and Zhong (1990). Their research contrasts the effects of rotating credit associations with bureaucratized financial institutions as a source of capital in a Korean-American community. Rotating credit associations are informal lending circles that often involve a significant risk (the possibility that one of the participants will default). They argue that these informal exchange systems can actually encourage trust and solidarity within the community:

Like ethnic business generally, [Korean rotating credit associations] encourage the ethnic solidarity they require. In short, social trust reciprocally shapes credit institutions and is shaped by them, being helped to persist where credit institutions require a high level of social solidarity in the user population, and damaged where general social (not economic) life undermines the requisite solidarity. This result supports the claim that bureaucratized financial institutions accelerated the atomization of the population rather than having, as previously thought, served the otherwise intractable needs of already atomized people. (Light et al. 1990, p. 48)[22]

While the links between these larger issues of social order and the experiment are speculative, the results do indicate that the presence of uncertainty in the form of information asymmetries can promote high levels of interpersonal trust.[23] It is conceivable that the higher levels of trust that emerged in this condition could serve as a form of "social capital" (Coleman 1988), making possible various actions that might otherwise not be successful (e.g., contributing toward the provision of some public good or managing a commons). Messick et al. (1983), for example, have demonstrated empirically that individuals who rated their exchange partners as trustworthy were more likely to cooperate in an N-person social dilemma (by reducing their own "harvest" in a commons type of collective dilemma).

This would be a very interesting route to solving group-level dilemmas because it would not require a formal control system. Undoubtedly, formal controls will often be needed, but there is an argument to be made against the inevitable *necessity* of formal controls as a solution to *N*-person social dilemmas. It is possible that endogenous solutions to *dyadic* dilemmas based on such features as commitment and reputation (as demonstrated in this experiment) could create the trust and solidarity necessary to solve *collective* dilemmas. An empirical test of these ideas is currently being designed.

Stable versus Optimal Outcomes

While the emergence of commitment, trust, and successful trading relations are possible results of an exchange system resembling the uncertainquality condition, in no way are they inevitable results. I do not assume that the effects of commitment and reputation will always solve such problems as trading under conditions of uncertainty. That is, I wish to avoid a functionalist or "adaptionist" (Gould and Lewontin 1984) argument that would assume exchange systems inevitably converge on one optimal outcome.

That more than one stable outcome is possible is suggested by the pretrials that were run for this experiment. In the first pretrials, sellers in the uncertainquality condition were not allowed to advertise. Under this condition two different groups reached different stable outcomes: for one group the transactions resembled the ones reported here (high-quality goods being exchanged), while in the other group the market "failed" in that after a short length of time only low-quality goods were being sold at low prices (and so resulting in low profits for everyone). It seemed that the first few trades subjects made had a great effect on subsequent transactions. In the group where the first few moves were trusting (producing high-quality goods, and offering a high price in buying goods), these actions seemed to encourage a trend toward high prices and high quality, but in the group where the first few moves were exploitative (trying to get a high price for low-quality goods), low-quality goods were soon the only ones available in the group.[24]

One possible interpretation is that although sellers were not required to be truthful in their advertising, it still served to communicate information that had a beneficial impact on trading. To put it differently, restricting the flow of information seemed to increase the sensitivity to initial conditions (i.e., the first few trades subjects made). Again, these are not established results, merely impressions from the pretrials, but the implications are certainly important enough to warrant future research, and they do make the point that an outcome of high quality and high profits is not inevitable.[25]

Thus, the kind of model of exchange and the emergence of social structure I have in mind is a contingent, "multiple equilibrium" one. In contrast, "in less contingent arguments—including most neoclassical economic work, many versions of Marxism or population ecology, and functionalism of all varieties—outcomes are predicted without the necessity of looking closely at the historical background of particular settings, the preexisting economic institutions, or the social structure and collective action of individuals" (Granovetter 1990, p. 106). While unique predictions might not be possible, "such multiple equilibrium models, even if underdetermined, are far from the historicist argument that every case is unique and anything is possible" (Granovetter 1990, p. 107). The challenge then is to specify the crucial parameters and the outcomes that will follow.

If uncertainty is too high, the risks too large, or perhaps the temptations of exploitation too great, high trust and successful exchange relations may not emerge. On the other hand, the quote from Kelley and Thibaut (1978, p. 237) in the introduction makes the point that if there is no risk in an exchange situation, exploitation will not occur, but neither will high levels of trust develop. Thus, one way of thinking about this experiment is as an investigation into the *structural* origins of trust in a system of exchange, rather than treating trust as an individual personality variable (e.g., Messick et al. 1983; Yamagishi 1986). It seems that it is in the broad middle range of risk and uncertainty that both the emergence of trust and the possibility of endogenous solutions to the problem of risky trade emerge. Here we see such possibilities as commitment and reputation as social solutions to uncertainty in exchange relations.

Conclusions

The results clearly indicate that it is possible to study experimentally the emergence of different exchange structures as well as the consequences of different patterns of exchange. While this study obviously does not capture all the important processes involved in the emergence of structure and commitment (which might require following groups for weeks or months), it is equally important to note that for at least some important features, this experiment produced stable results and significant differences after 20 periods of exchange.

There are a number of important directions for future research. Using a behavioral measure of trust, perhaps in connection with the provision of a public good, would allow one to test some of the ideas discussed above in the section on risk and regulation. Another variation would be to allow the buyers and sellers to talk among themselves (i.e., buyers with buyers, and sellers with sellers). Presumably this would accelerate the development of reputation and might also lead to organized sanctioning of untrustworthy actors. Increasing the flow of information further by allowing face-to-face interaction of all the subjects would be another interesting variation. Research on social dilemmas (e.g., Messick and Brewer 1983; Orbell and Dawes 1981) and in experimental economics (e.g., Radner and Schotter 1989) has demonstrated that face-to-face communication can promote cooperation and increase bargaining efficiency. The general theme would be to study the effects of variations in the communication network *and* the exchange network (which can vary independently of each other) on the processes and emergent structures of exchange. Other possible modifications to this design include allowing more than one exchange per round or varying the number of buyers and sellers so that the two groups would not be evenly matched. Finally, commitment and trust are not the only important variables in exchange relations, and my future work will examine the effects of sociological variables on price and profit dynamics in risky trading situations.

In sum, this research demonstrates that uncertainty can have significant effects on the emergence of exchange structures, the level of interpersonal trust in a group, and the concern actors have for their own and their partners' reputation. The lessons for social exchange theory include recognizing the important effects of deceit and opportunism on exchange, the need to investigate the emergence of social structure as well as its effects, and the relevance of reputation (and other factors related to the signaling and collection of information) to exchange processes.

Notes

1. Earlier versions of this article were presented at the annual meeting of the American Sociological Association, Pittsburgh, 1992, and at the Fourth Annual International Conference of the Society for the Advancement of Socio-Economics, Irvine, California, 1992. I wish to thank Gerrie Lemus, Elisabeth Schmutzer, and Martin Monto for their help in the design and implementation of this project. I also thank Phillip Bonacich, James Carrier, Harold Kelley, Toshio Yamagishi, Ronald Obvious, and the *AJS* reviewers for comments on earlier drafts. Correspondence may be directed to Peter Kollock, Department of Sociology, University of California, Los Angeles, California 90024–1551. E-mail: kollock@soc.sscnet.ucla.edu.
2. I use the term *social dilemmas* to refer to the broad range of work that has been done in a number of disciplines on situations in which individually rational behavior leads to collectively irrational outcomes. This includes work on the Prisoner's Dilemma, the problem of collective action, public goods and the free-rider problem, etc. For reviews see Messick and Brewer (1983), Orbell and Dawes (1981).
3. Note that the rubber and rice markets are used here simply as examples. The point of the present study is to experimentally examine the emergence of commitment, not to create a detailed simulation of commodity markets in Thailand.
4. While Lawler and Yoon (1993) studied frequency of exchange, as I do, they use the term *commitment* to refer to an *affective* bond. Again, I am using the term here to

refer to *behavioral* patterns of exchange. *Commitment* has also been used to refer to phenomena such as moral obligations or feelings of attachment. For further discussions of these other forms of commitment, see Becker (1960), Johnson (1991), Kanter (1972), Kelley (1983), Leik and Leik (1977), Levinger (1979), Rosenblatt (1977), Rubin and Brown (1973), and Rusbult and Buunk (1993).

5. One study that does address these issues is Podolny (1990). Unfortunately, the experiment in this study is seriously limited, as the author himself acknowledges. Experimental economists (e.g., Fehr, Kirchsteiger, and Riedl 1993; Lynch et al. 1984; Plott 1986) do often examine situations where there are no restrictions on who might exchange with whom, but they are interested in very different issues and so have focused on questions of efficiency, price estimation, etc., rather than studying the emergence of stable exchange relations.

6. There are other sources of uncertainty, but in this article I restrict my attention to uncertainty that is the result of information asymmetries. To define the term more precisely, "In a game of asymmetric information, the information sets of players differ in ways relevant to their behavior. . . . The essence of asymmetric information is that some player has useful *private information*" (Rasmusen 1989, p. 53; emphasis in original). This same situation is sometimes referred to as a game of *incomplete* information (Dasgupta 1988; Kreps 1990). Because this latter term is used inconsistently in the literature I will not use it here. For a detailed analysis that distinguishes perfect, certain, symmetric, and complete information from each other, see Rasmusen (1989, pp. 51–54). Note that he uses these terms in a particular, restricted sense—his usage does not always coincide with common usage, and while I borrow his definition of asymmetries, I do not use such terms as "uncertainty" in the same restricted sense he does. For a discussion of the sources of information asymmetries, see Kollock and O'Brien (1992).

7. There are a variety of institutional arrangements that can help alleviate this kind of risk. Examples include enforceable warranties and contracts (e.g., Heimer 1985) or regulatory agencies (e.g., Zucker 1986). These solutions have their own set of limitations and risks (cf. Coleman 1990; Shapiro 1987).

8. For further elaboration on the concept of trust, see Coleman (1990), Dasgupta (1988), Gambetta (1988), and Yamagishi and Yamagishi (1993).

9. For general overviews of the topic, see Kreps (1990) and Rasmusen (1989).

10. An important exception is the work by Bacharach and Lawler (1981) on bargaining.

11. From a sociological point of view, considering reputation and its effects also brings a dramaturgical element into the study of exchange. To date the possible relevance of research on dramaturgy to work on social exchange has hardly been explored. A more complete analysis of exchange should bring in *both* the structural conditions of exchange and dramaturgical activity to examine the conditions under which such factors as reputation become important. For an extended discussion of the issues of commitment, reputation, and the relevance of dramaturgy to social exchange theory, see Kollock and O'Brien (1992).

12. Because the group is the unit of analysis, although 80 subjects participated in the experiment, for the purpose of tests of statistical significance, $N = 10$.

13. Buyers and sellers could make any offer they desired, subject only to the constraint that they needed to make a profit in order to earn money. Subjects were restricted to making one trade per round in order to be consistent with the important body of work on negatively connected exchange networks (Cook and Emerson 1978; Cook et al. 1983; Markovsky et al. 1988), which imposes the same restriction.

14. For example, in a situation in which an actor has three possible exchange partners and completed 15 trades, consider two possible distribution of trades:

    Case 1   Actor A completes seven trades with B, seven trades with C, and one trade with D;

    Case 2   Actor A completes seven trades with B, four trades with C, and four trades with D.

    Using a pair-based measure, the commitment score for the exchange relation between A and B would be identical in both case 1 and case 2, as will the average level of commitment across partners. Yet A's overall pattern of trade in case 1 (where A is equally committed to both B and C) is very different than case 2 (where B is clearly the partner A is most committed to).

15. Subjects responded on a seven-point scale, ranging from *never* (1) to *always* (7). A direct behavioral measure of such actions would be preferable. However, recording the kind of fine moment-to-moment detail necessary to make such calculations (every offer and counteroffer and the sequence in which they were made) was simply not possible given that data was being recorded with paper and pencil. A future set of studies currently being planned will be run through a computer network, which will allow the recording of every offer and counteroffer through-out the length of the experiment.

16. The questions read, "How strongly were you concerned about your reputation for being a fair seller [buyer]?" and "How strongly were you concerned about the buyers' [sellers'] reputations for being fair in their trades?" As with all question-naire items, subjects responded on a seven-point scale.

17. Subjects were asked to indicate their overall impression of each potential trading partner on the following scales; intelligent/unintelligent, honest/dishonest, reli-able/unreliable, likable/unlikable, irrational/rational, untrustworthy/trustworthy, kind/unkind, incompetent/competent, fair/unfair, unfriendly/friendly, rigid/flexible, and aggressive/unaggressive.

18. Note that in order to test this prediction it is necessary to examine the exchange patterns of particular dyads rather than the group as a whole. Thus for this hypothesis, and only for this hypothesis, a pair-based measure of commitment was used. This measure consists of the ratio of trades completed with a particular partner to total trades possible.

19. I do not make an assumption about the direction of causality between commit-ment and trust, simply that the two will be positively related. Trust and commit-ment are likely to mutually reinforce each other over time. Tracking the fine details of how the two develop (which would require an experimental design that measured trust repeatedly over time) would be an interesting possibility for a future study.

20. Because the commitment measure takes into account the entire group, it is impossible to test for differences between sellers and buyers (the mean score for one subgroup will always equal the mean of the other subgroup). Despite the limitations of a pair-based measure of commitment (i.e., a simple ratio of completed trades to possible trades), statistical tests were run using this measure because it allows comparisons between sellers and buyers. There were no significant or near-significant differences in commitment between sellers and buyers in either experimental condition.

21. These observations were confirmed in a discussion this seller had with the experimenter after the experiment had been completed.

22. And as Taylor (1987, p. 177) notes, "It has often been argued that the choice of the scope and form of social institutions (such as the state) must be based on 'pessimistic' assumptions, so that they will be 'robust' against the worst possible conditions . . . In which they might be required to operate. . . . But if the institutions themselves affect preferences . . . then this approach is inappropriate and may be dangerously misleading."

23. This is not to say that uncertainty *guarantees* high levels of trust. I discuss this issue below.

24. Compare Gamson, Fireman, and Rytina (1982) on the effects of early disagreement in a group on the group's subsequent capacity for collective action.

25. Looking at another possible factor, it is interesting to note that reputations did not seem to provide a solution to a lemons market in a study conducted by Lynch et al. (1984). They believe it is likely that because only two extreme grades of quality were possible (lows and supers), the decision to offer high-quality goods was a very risky one—there was no way to temper one's risk by, for example, offering goods of intermediate quality until trust was established. In addition to the above discussion on advertising and the flow of information, this suggests another situation in which reputation and commitment might not solve the problem of information asymmetries: an exchange system in which the risks to cooperating initially (by offering to buy at a high price or produce a high-quality good) are extreme.

References

Akerlof, George A. 1970. "The Market for 'Lemons': Quality Uncertainty and the Market Mechanism." *Quarterly Journal of Economics* 84:488–500.

Axelrod, Robert. 1984. *The Evolution of Cooperation*. New York: Basic.

Bacharach, Samuel B., and Edward J. Lawler. 1981. *Bargaining: Power, Tactics, and Outcomes*. San Francisco: Jossey-Bass.

Baker, Wayne. 1984. "Floor Trading and Crowd Dynamics." pp. 107–28 in *Social Dynamics of Financial Markets*, edited by Patricia Adler and Peter Adler. Greenwich, Conn.: JAI Press.

Becker, H. S. 1960. "Notes on the Concept of Commitment." *American Journal of Sociology* 66:32–40.

Bienenstock, Elisa, and Phillip Bonacich. 1993. "Game Theory Models for Exchange Networks: Experimental Results." *Sociological Perspectives* 36 (2): 117–35.

Coleman, James S. 1986. "Social Theory, Social Research, and a Theory of Action." *American Journal of Sociology* 91:1309–35.

—— 1988. "Social Capital in the Creation of Human Capital." *American Journal of Sociology* 94 (suppl.): S95–S120.

—— 1990. *Foundations of Social Theory.* Cambridge, Mass.: Harvard University Press.

Cook, Karen S., and Richard M. Emerson. 1978. "Power, Equity and Commitment in Exchange Networks." *American Sociological Review* 43:721–39.

Cook, Karen S., and Richard M. Emerson. Mary R. Gillmore, and Toshio Yamagishi. 1983. "The Distribution of Power in Exchange Networks: Theory and Experimental Results." *American Journal of Sociology* 89:275–305.

Dasgupta, Partha. 1988. "Trust as a Commodity." pp. 49–72 in *Trust: Making and Breaking Cooperative Relations*, edited by Diego Gambetta. New York: Basil Blackwell.

Deutsch, Morton. 1962. "Cooperation and Trust: Some Theoretical Notes." pp. 275–319 in *Nebraska Symposium on Motivation*, edited by M. Jones. Lincoln: University of Nebraska Press.

Fehr, Ernst, Georg Kirchsteiger, and Arno Riedl. 1993. "Does Fairness Prevent Market Clearing? An Experimental Investigation." *Quarterly Journal of Economics* 108 (2): 437–59.

Gambetta, Diego. 1988. "Can We Trust Trust?" pp. 213–37 in *Trust: Making and Breaking Cooperative Relations*, edited by Diego Gambetta. New York: Basil Blackwell.

Gamson, William A., Bruce Fireman, and Steven Rytina. 1982. *Encounters with Unjust Authority.* Chicago: Dorsey Press.

Gould, Stephen Jay, and Richard C. Lewontin. 1984. "The Spandrels of San Marco and the Panglossian Paradigm: A Critique of the Adaptionist Programme." pp. 252–70 in *Conceptual Issues in Evolutionary Biology*, edited by Elliot Sober. Cambridge, Mass.: MIT Press.

Granovetter, Mark. 1985. "Economic Action and Social Structure: The Problem of Embeddedness." *American Journal of Sociology* 91:481–510.

—— 1990. "The Old and the New Economic Sociology: A History and an Agenda." pp. 89–112 in *Beyond the Marketplace: Rethinking Economy and Society*, edited by Roger Friedland and A. F. Robertson. New York: Aldine de Gruyter.

Hardin, Russell. 1982. *Collective Action.* Baltimore: Johns Hopkins University Press.

Heimer, Carol A. 1985. *Reactive Risk and Rational Action: Managing Moral Hazard in Insurance Contracts.* Berkeley and Los Angeles: University of California Press.

Hirschman, Albert O. 1984. "Against Parsimony: Three Easy Ways of Complicating Some Categories of Economic Discourse." *American Economic Review* 74 (2): 89–96.

Homans, George C. 1961. *Social Behavior: Its Elementary Forms.* New York: Harcourt Brace & World.

Johnson, Michael. 1991. "Commitment to Personal Relationships." pp. 117–43 in *Advances in Personal Relationships*, vol. 3. Edited by W. Jones and D. Perlman. London: Jessica Kingsley.

Kanter, R. M. 1972. *Commitment and Community: Communes and Utopias in Sociological Perspective.* Cambridge, Mass.: Harvard University Press.

Kelley, Harold H. 1983. "Love and Commitment." pp. 265–314 in *Close Relationships*, by H. H. Kelley, E. S. Berscheid, A. Christensen, J. Harvey, T. L. Huston, G. Levinger, E. McClintock, L. A. Peplau, and D. R. Peterson. New York: Freeman.

—— and John W. Thibaut. 1978. *Interpersonal Relations: A Theory of Interdependence*. New York: Wiley.

Kollock, Peter, and Jodi O'Brien. 1992. "The Social Construction of Exchange." pp. 89–112 in *Advances in Group Processes*, vol. 9. Edited by E. J. Lawler, B. Markovsky, C. Ridgeway, and H. A. Walker. Greenwich, Conn.: JAI Press.

Kreps, David M. 1990. *A Course in Microeconomic Theory.* Princeton, N.J.: Princeton University Press.

—— Paul Milgrom, John Roberts, and Robert Wilson. 1982. "Rational Cooperation in the Finitely Repeated Prisoners' Dilemma," *Journal of Economic Theory* 27: 245–52.

—— and Robert Wilson. 1982. "Reputation and Imperfect Information." *Journal of Economic Theory* 27:253–79.

Lawler, Edward, and Jeongkoo Yoon. 1993. "Power and the Emergence of Commitment Behavior in Negotiated Exchange." *American Journal of Sociology* 58 (4): 465–81.

Leik, R. K., and S. A. Leik. 1977. "Transition to Interpersonal Commitment." pp. 123–45 in *Behavioral Therapy in Sociology*, edited by R. L. Hamblin and J. H. Kunkel. New Brunswick, N.J.: Transaction.

Levinger, George. 1979. "A Social Exchange View on the Dissolution of Pair Relationships." pp. 169–93 in *Social Exchange in Developing Relationships*, edited by R. Burgess and T. Huston. New York: Academic Press.

Light, Ivan, Im Jung Kwuon, and Deng Zhong. 1990. "Korean Rotating Credit Associations in Los Angeles." *Amerasia* 16 (1): 35–54.

Lynch, Michael, Ross M. Miller, Charles R. Plott, and Russell Porter. 1984. "Product Quality, Information Efficiency, and Regulations in Experimental Markets." Social Science Working Paper no. 528, California Institute of Technology.

Markovsky, Barry, David Willer, and Travis Patton. 1988. "Power Relations in Exchange Networks." *American Sociological Review* 53:220–36.

Marwell, Gerald, and David R. Schmitt. 1975. *Cooperation: An Experimental Analysis*. New York: Academic Press.

Messick, David M., and Marilynn B. Brewer. 1983. "Solving Social Dilemmas." pp. 11–44 in *Review of Personality and Social Psychology*, vol. 4. Edited by L. Wheeler and P. Shaver. Beverly Hills, Calif.: Sage.

—— H. Wilke, M. B. Brewer, R. M. Kramer, P. E. Zemke, and L. Lui. 1983. "Individual Adaptations and Structural Change as Solutions to Social Dilemmas." *Journal of Personality and Social Psychology* 44:294–309.

Milgrom, Paul, and John Roberts. 1982. "Predation, Reputation, and Entry Deterrence." *Journal of Economic Theory* 27:280–312.

Molm, Linda. 1991. "Affect and Social Exchange: Satisfaction in Power-Dependence Relations." *American Sociological Review* 56:475–93.

Orbell, John, and Robyn M. Dawes. 1981. "Social Dilemmas." pp. 37–65 in *Progress in Applied Social Psychology*, vol. 1. Edited by G. Stephenson and J. Davis. New York: Wiley.

—— .1991. "A 'Cognitive Miser' Theory of Cooperators' Advantage." *American Political Science Review* 85 (2): 515–28.

Orbell, John, Peregine Schwartz-Shea, and Randy Simmons. 1984. "Do Cooperators Exit More Readily Than Defectors?" *American Political Science Review* 78: 147–62.

Plott, Charles R. 1986. "Rational Choice in Experimental Markets." *Journal of Business* 59, no. 4, pt. 2: S301–S327.

Podolny, Joel. 1990. "On the Formation of Exchange Relations in Political Systems." *Rationality and Society* 2 (3): 359–78.

Popkin, S. 1981. "Public Choice and Rural Development—Free Riders, Lemons, and Institutional Design." pp. 43–80 in *Public Choice and Rural Development*, edited by C. Russel and N. Nicholson. Washington, D.C.: Resources for the Future.

Radner, Roy, and Andrew Schotter. 1989. "The Sealed-Bid Mechanism: An Experimental Study." *Journal of Economic Theory* 48:179–220.

Rasmusen, Eric. 1989. *Games and Information: An Introduction to Game Theory.* New York: Basil Blackwell.

Raub, Werner, and Jeroen Weesie. 1990. "Reputation and Efficiency in Social Interactions: An Example of Network Effects." *American Journal of Sociology* 96 (3): 626–54.

Rosenblatt, Paul C. 1977. "Needed Research on Commitment in Marriage." pp. 73–86 in *Close Relationship: Perspectives on the Meaning of Intimacy*, edited by George Levinger and Harold L. Raush. Amherst: University of Massachusetts Press.

Rubin, J. A., and Bert R. Brown. 1973. "Becoming Committed." pp. 157–81 in *Liking and Loving*, edited by Z. Rubin. New York: Holt.

Rusbult, Caryl E., and Bram P. Buunk. 1993. "Commitment Processes in Close Relationships: An Interdependence Analysis." *Journal of Social and Personal Relationships* 10:175–204.

Schuessler, Rudolf. 1989. "Exit Threats and Cooperation under Anonymity." *Journal of Conflict Resolution* 33 (4): 728–49.

Shapiro, Carl. 1982. "Consumer Information, Product Quality and Seller Reputation." *Bell Journal of Economics* 13:20–35.

Shapiro, Susan P. 1987. "The Social Control of Impersonal Trust." *American Journal of Sociology* 93:623–58.

Siamwalla, Ammar. 1978. "Farmers and Middlemen: Aspects of Agricultural Marketing in Thailand." *Economic Bulletin for Asia and the Pacific* (June): 38–50.

Taylor, Michael. 1987. *The Possibility of Cooperation*. Cambridge: Cambridge University Press.

Vanberg, Viktor J., and Roger D. Congleton. 1992. "Rationality, Morality, and Exit." *American Political Science Review* 86 (2): 418–31.

Wilson, Robert. 1985. "Reputations in Games and Markets." pp. 27–62 in *Game-Theoretic Models of Bargaining*, edited by Alvin Roth. Cambridge: Cambridge University Press.

Yamagishi, Toshio. 1986. "The Provision of a Sanctioning System as a Public Good." *Journal of Personality and Social Psychology* 51 (1): 110–16.

—— 1992. "Prisoner's Dilemma Networks: Simulations and Experimental Work." Paper presented at the annual meeting of the American Sociological Association, Pittsburgh.

Yamagishi, Toshio, Nahoko Hayashi, and Nobuhito Jin. 1992. "Prisoner's Dilemma Networks: Selection Strategy versus Action Strategy." Paper presented at the Fifth International Conference on Social Dilemmas, Bielfeld, Germany.

Yamagishi, Toshio, and Midori Yamagishi. 1993. "Trust and Commitment as Alternative Responses to Social Uncertainty." Paper presented at the Social Network Conference, Whistler, British Columbia.

Zand, D. E. 1972. "Trust and Managerial Problem Solving." *Administrative Science Quarterly* 17:229–39.

Zucker, Lynne G. 1986. "Production of Trust: Institutional Sources of Economic Structure, 1840–1920." pp. 53–111 in *Research in Organizational Behavior*, edited by B. Staw and L. Cummings. Greenwich, Conn.: JAI Press.

III. BASES AND BENEFITS OF ORGANIZATIONAL TRUST

7

The Role of Trustworthiness in Reducing Transaction Costs and Improving Performance: Empirical Evidence from the United States, Japan, and Korea

Jeffrey H. Dyer and Wujin Chu

The issue of trust in economic exchanges has recently received considerable attention in the academic literature (Barney and Hansen 1994, Mayer et al. 1995, Zaheer et al. 1998) as well as the popular press (*Business Week* 1992, *Economist* 1996, Fukuyama 1995). Trust in exchange relationships has been hypothesized to be a valuable economic asset because it is believed to: (1) *lower transaction costs* and allow for greater flexibility to respond to changing market conditions (Gulati 1995, Barney and Hansen 1994, Uzzi 1997, Dyer 1997) and (2) *lead to superior information sharing* that improves coordination and joint efforts to minimize inefficiencies (Aoki 1988, Clark and Fujimoto 1991, Nishiguchi 1994). Some scholars even claim that national economic efficiency is highly correlated with a high-trust institutional environment (North 1990, Casson 1991, Fukuyama 1995). For example, Fukuyama (1995, p. 7) argues that the economic success of a nation, "as well as its ability to compete, is conditioned by ... the level of trust inherent in the society." Indeed, numerous scholars have suggested that interorganizational trust is a key factor in explaining alliance success (Dyer 1996b, Doz and Hamel 1998). These claims have increased our attention to the important role of trust in economic exchanges.

However, does trust really pay off in hard economic benefits, or does this feel-good approach to economic exchange relationships bring only marginal benefits? Although the theoretical literature on the potential economic value of trust is well developed, empirical research is lacking. In fact, with the exception of some anecdotal, case-study evidence (Dore 1983, Lorenz 1988, Fukuyama 1995) there are virtually no large-sample empirical studies on the relationship between trust and the various activities believed to create economic value in exchange relationships (see Zaheer et al. 1998 for an exception). As Zucker (1986, p. 59) has observed, "For a concept that is acknowledged as central, trust has received very little empirical investigation." For example, Barney and Hansen (1994) argued that trustworthiness reduces transaction costs in exchange relationships and could be a source of competitive advantage, yet empirical studies confirming this hypothesis are essentially nonexistent. One reason for the lack of empirical work examining this important topic is that concepts such as "trust" and "transaction costs" are difficult to operationalize. As Williamson (1985, p. 105) has acknowledged: "A common characteristic of these studies [on transaction costs] is that direct measures of transaction costs are rarely attempted." To date, we are unaware of any other studies that have directly examined the relationship between firm trustworthiness, transaction costs, and firm profit performance.

In this chapter we examine the relationship between trust and performance in a large sample of supplier–buyer exchange relationships. More specifically, we seek to answer the following questions: *Does a high level of supplier trust in a buyer result in: (1) lower transaction costs for the transactors, (2) greater information sharing among the transactors, and (3) better performance for the trustworthy party?* We investigate the relationship between perceived trustworthiness and transaction costs and information sharing in a sample of 344 supplier-automaker relationships in the United States, Japan, and Korea. We also explore the extent to which trustworthiness creates economic value for the automaker by examining whether "trustworthy" automakers incur lower procurement (transaction) costs than "less trustworthy" automakers. In summary, our goal is to examine empirically in a cross-national setting whether trust creates value in exchange relationships in the ways theorized in the academic literature.

....

Theoretical Framework and Hypotheses

Defining Trust

We draw on prior literature in defining trust as *one party's confidence that the other party in the exchange relationship will not exploit its vulnerabilities* (Sako 1991, Ring and Van de Van 1992, Barney and Hansen 1994, Zaheer et al. 1998). This confidence (trust) would be expected to emerge in situations where the "trustworthy" party in the exchange relationship: (1) is known to reliably make good-faith efforts to behave in accordance with prior commitments, (2) makes adjustments (e.g., as market conditions change) in ways perceived as "fair" by the exchange partner, and (3) does not take excessive advantage of an exchange partner even when the opportunity is available (Mayer et al. 1995). Thus, our definition characterizes interfirm trust as a construct based on three related components: reliability, fairness, and goodwill/benevolence. Because the notion of "goodwill" is part of our definition, trust, as defined here, is not based upon contracts but rather on noncontractual mechanisms.

Conceptually, organizations are not able to trust each other; trust is a microlevel phenomenon and has its basis in individuals. Trust can be placed by one individual in another individual or in a group of individuals (e.g., within an organization). However, individuals in an organization may *share an orientation* toward individuals within another organization. From this perspective, *"interorganizational trust describes the extent to which organizational members have a collectively held trust orientation toward the partner firm"* (Zaheer et al. 1998, p. 142).

In this chapter, we consider trust (this collective orientation) by an automotive supplier in its automaker customer (the perceived trustworthiness of the automaker). This was a good research setting because it was important to study a set of transaction relationships in which trust might be important. Many scholars have argued that risk, or having something invested, is requisite to trust. The need for trust only arises in a risky situation (Deutsch 1958, Mayer et al. 1995). Generally speaking, risk would be present, and trust necessary, in settings where transactors make transaction-specific investments and where there is a high degree of environmental uncertainty.

The automobile is a complex product with thousands of components that must work together as a system. Components are often tailored to specific models and, therefore, suppliers must make automaker-specific investments in people, plant, tools, equipment, etc. (Dyer 1996a). Because these investments are not easily redeployable, suppliers are at risk if their automaker customers behave opportunistically. For example, after a supplier has invested in a dedicated asset, the automaker may opportunistically try to renegotiate a contract, threatening to switch to another supplier if the price is not lowered. Furthermore, the auto industry is characterized by a high degree of market uncertainty (Pine 1993), which increases both the risks associated with transacting as well as the importance of information sharing (Lorenz 1988, Aoki 1988). For example, the automaker may expect to sell 100,000 units of a particular model and request that the supplier make the necessary investments to produce parts for 100,000 units. However due to market uncertainty, the automaker may sell only 75,000 units, thereby placing the supplier in the difficult situation of having invested in assets that are not needed. The supplier will lose money on this investment unless it can trust the automaker to help it recoup its investment (or the supplier must anticipate the potential problem and write provisions for it in a legal contract). Unfortunately, many potential problems are impossible to foresee. Thus, an automaker's trustworthiness is of particular importance due to relation-specific investments and market uncertainty that make suppliers vulnerable. Because suppliers are in the vulnerable position, in this study we focus on the buyer as the referent of trust, and the supplier as the "trustor."

Trust and Economic Performance

Trust is of most economic value when it is based on noncontractual, rather than contractual mechanisms.[1] The rationale for the economic value of "non-contractual" trust is straightforward: Trust eliminates the need for formal contracts, which are costly to write, monitor, and enforce (Hill 1995, Barney and Hansen 1994). Thus, trust is believed to reduce transaction costs. Furthermore, some anecdotal evidence suggests that transactors are more likely to share valuable work-related information when they have developed a high level of trust (Sako 1991, Nishiguchi 1994, Uzzi 1997). We examine these proposed relationships in greater detail.

Trust and Transaction Costs. Historically, economists have viewed the firm as a "production function." Consequently, the firm with the most efficient (lowest cost) production function would win in the marketplace. The value chain reflected the combined production functions of all of the firms that engaged in exchanges, from "up-stream" raw materials to "downstream" final assembly. Theoretically, the value chain comprised of firms with the combined "low-cost" production functions would produce the final assembled product at the lowest total cost. However, transaction-cost economics has recognized that the productivity of a value chain is a function of *both production costs and transaction costs* (Williamson 1985). *Transaction costs* involve all of the costs associated with conducting exchanges between firms and can be decomposed into ex ante transaction costs, or search and contracting costs, and ex post contracting costs, or monitoring and enforcement costs (Williamson 1985, Hennart 1993, North 1990). *Search and contracting costs* include the costs of locating a desirable trading partner and then negotiating and writing a mutually acceptable agreement. *Monitoring and enforcement costs* refer to the costs associated with monitoring the agreement and then taking the actions necessary to ensure that each party fulfills the predetermined set of obligations. Most previous studies have lumped these "subtypes" of transaction costs together when discussing transaction costs. However, while together they comprise total transaction costs, they need not be perfectly correlated. In fact, if partners spend more time up front negotiating a mutually acceptable agreement, it is possible that this may reduce ex post monitoring and enforcement costs because all of the expectations and obligations will have been clearly specified during the contracting phase. Consequently, in this study we not only consider the total transaction costs incurred by automakers, we also consider *ex ante contracting costs* separately from *ex post contracting costs*. Transaction costs take many everyday forms—meetings, sales calls, bidding rituals—but their underlying economic purpose is to enable the exchange of goods and services. The sales, procurement, and legal functions within most companies represent a firm's investment in transacting with other parties.

Some scholars claim that transaction costs are significant and have a major impact on economic efficiency (North 1990, Williamson 1991). Indeed, Nobel Prize winner Douglass North (1990) estimates that transaction costs may represent as much as 35–40 percent of the costs associated with economic activity. Similarly, a study by strategy consultant McKinsey & Company (Butler et al. 1997, p. 5) found that "Interactions—the searching, coordinating, and monitoring that people and firms do when they exchange goods services or ideas—account for over a third of economic activity [GDP] in the United States." These studies suggest that firms that achieve the lowest transaction costs are likely to realize efficiency advantages in the marketplace.

Once an exchange partner is identified, trust may reduce transaction costs in a number of ways. First, under conditions of high trust, transactors will spend less time on ex ante contracting because they are confident that payoffs will be fairly divided. As a result, they do not have to plan for all future contingencies because they are confident that equitable adjustments will be made as market conditions change. Thus, trust promotes negotiating efficiency by enabling each party to be more flexible in granting concessions because of the expectation that the exchange partner will reciprocate in the future (Dore 1983). This allows transactors to achieve "serial equity" (equity over a longer period of time) rather than requiring immediate or "spot equity" (Ouchi 1984, Dyer 1997). Consequently, it reduces the need for transactors to invest heavily in ex ante bargaining. In addition, negotiations will likely be more efficient because transactors will have greater confidence that information provided by the other organization is not misrepresented. As observed by Zaheer et al. (1998, p. 144), "Trust reduces the inclination to guard against opportunistic behavior (i.e., deliberate misrepresentation on the part of the exchange partner)." In a study of supplier–buyer relationships in the electrical equipment industry, Zaheer et al. (1998) found support for a negative relationship between interorganizational trust and negotiation costs.

Hypothesis 1. *The greater the supplier trust in the buyer, the lower the ex ante transaction costs (contracting costs) incurred by the exchange partners.*

Trust is also believed to have an inverse relationship with monitoring and enforcement costs for two main reasons. First, under conditions of high trust, trading partners will spend less time and resources on monitoring to see if the other party is shirking or fulfilling the "spirit" of the agreement. If each exchange partner is confident that the other party will not be opportunistic, then both parties can devote fewer resources to monitoring. In contrast, transactors without goodwill trust (who rely only on contract-based trust) will need to invest resources both in monitoring the other party's actions (to ensure compliance with the contract) and in enforcing the contract.

Second, trust may reduce transaction costs by reducing the amount of time and resources that transactors spend on ex post bargaining and haggling over problems that arise in the course of transacting. If trust is high, then each party will assume that the other party is acting in good faith and will interpret behaviors more positively (Uzzi 1997). Consequently, trading partners with high trust will spend less time haggling over problems that have emerged during the course of transacting due to mutual confidence that inequities will be fairly addressed and remedied.

Hypothesis 2. *The greater the supplier trust in the buyer, the lower the ex post transaction costs (monitoring and enforcement costs) incurred by the exchange partners.*

Finally, when we consider Hypotheses 1 and 2 together (the greater the trust, the lower the ex ante and ex post transaction costs), we naturally must conclude that the greater the supplier trust in the buyer, the lower the total transaction costs incurred by the exchange partners. We do not state this as a separate formal hypothesis because it follows directly from the first two hypotheses.

Trust and Information Sharing. We theorize a positive relationship between buyer trustworthiness and supplier information sharing for two primary reasons. First, if the supplier can trust the buyer not to behave opportunistically, it will be more willing to share confidential information, such as on production costs or on product design and process innovations (Aoki 1988, Nishiguchi 1994). However, a supplier will voluntarily share this information only if it trusts the buyer not to steal its ideas and/or share them with competitors or will not attempt to "squeeze" the supplier's profit margins. In the absence of trust, information sharing on costs or new ideas/technologies is unlikely because this information could be "poached" or used opportunistically (Larson 1992, Uzzi 1997).

Second, a lack of trust may cause suppliers to suppress potentially relevant information that would be useful for problem solving. For example, suppliers may be unwilling to share information on production or design problems if they do not trust the buyer to work cooperatively in joint problem solving. In particular, suppliers may be reluctant to share any information that exposes weaknesses in their operations or their cost structure, even though the sharing of such information could result in valuable suggestions from the buyer that could lead to effective solutions. In contrast, high trust may lead to the mechanisms associated with "voice" (i.e., joint problem solving) (Helper 1991) rather than exit (termination of the relationship).

Hypothesis 3. *The greater the supplier trust in the buyer, the more the supplier will share valuable (confidential) work-related information with the buyer.*

Trust, Transaction Costs, and Performance. If trust does indeed lower transaction costs (and increase information sharing) in the ways previously described, then greater trustworthiness on the part of a buyer should reduce the buyer's total costs, thereby increasing profitability. Williamson (1991), among others (see North 1990, Hennart 1993), has argued that firms that are effective at economizing on transaction costs will exhibit superior performance. Indeed, he argues that "strategy is economizing" on transaction costs. Thus, all else being equal, a buyer with a "trustworthy" reputation in exchange relationships should have lower transaction costs, which in turn should translate into better profit performance. Of course, this would be particularly true if transaction costs are as high a fraction of total costs as suggested in the studies by North (1990) and McKinsey & Company (Butler et al. 1997).

Hypothesis 4. *All else being equal, the greater the buyer trustworthiness, the lower the buyer transaction costs and the better the buyer's profit performance.*

Control Variables: Investments in Relation-Specific Assets and Supplier Size. We employ a supplier's investment in relation-specific assets as a variable to control for: (1) the *vulnerability* of the supplier with regard to transaction-specific investments (and hence the need for trust) and (2) the supplier industry, or type of part exchanged. According to TCE, exchanges differ in their need for trust (safeguards) and information sharing. In situations where investments in relation-specific assets are low, trust may be unnecessary. Trust is necessary when transactors have made transaction-specific investments that create appropriable quasi-rents (Klein et al. 1978). Greater asset specificity would also be likely to increase the need for information sharing because idiosyncratic exchanges tend to require greater coordination than standardized exchanges. Thus, we control for asset specificity because any examination of the effects of trust on transaction costs and information sharing must take into account exchange attributes (notably asset specificity) that may influence these constructs.

In addition, asset specificity is a good control for "supplier industry" or type of part. Some suppliers provide commodities such as extruded plastic parts or fasteners, while others provide unique complex parts or subassemblies such as airbags, heating systems, etc. The degree to which parts are customized may change the nature of the relationship between the buyer and the seller. There is currently no consensus on how supplier parts should be grouped together. However, one way to control for type of part is to control for physical and dedicated asset specificity. Because "generic parts" (e.g., fasteners, belts) will have a low level of asset specificity and "highly customized parts" (airbags, heating systems) will have a high level of asset specificity, controlling for physical asset specificity should provide a useful control for "type of part" exchanged.

We also employed a control for supplier size (sales volume to the automaker) because the relationship between automakers and their large and small suppliers may differ. Overall we think that by sampling only "tier one" suppliers, controlling for supplier size, and employing asset specificity controls, we are able to effectively control for supplier industry and size.

We acknowledge that the direction of causality between trust and information sharing is open to debate. For example, one can argue that information sharing leads to high trust rather than vice versa. We expect some degree of reciprocal causality with these variables where trust both influences, and is influenced by, information sharing. However, we have operationalized information sharing as the extent to which the supplier shares *confidential/proprietary information* with the buyer—information that would not be shared without some degree of trust. Of course, after this information is shared (and the other party behaves in a trustworthy manner) this would further increase trust. We explore the issue of reciprocal causality in greater detail in the discussion section.

Sample and Data Collection

We chose a cross-national setting to test our hypotheses for the following reasons. First, Japan has been described as a high-trust environment where interfirm trust is a key factor that facilitates exchange and creates competitive advantages for Japanese firms (Dore 1983, Sako 1991, Hill 1995). Thus, we wanted to empirically examine the extent to which interfirm trust is correlated with valuecreating behaviors (e.g., information sharing, low transaction costs, etc.) in Japan. In contrast, the United States has often been characterized as a low-trust environment relative to Japan (Dore 1983, Sako 1991, Shane 1994). However, Fukuyama (1995) has recently argued that the United States, like

Japan, is a high-trust environment—particularly when it is compared to other less developed countries. Our data allow us to examine whether levels of trust are reported as the same or different, and whether the relationship between trust and performance outcomes holds in both the United States and Japan. Finally, Korea was added because Korea's culture is similar to Japan's, and yet management practices in Korea have been influenced by U.S. firms, particularly in the auto industry where longstanding partner relationships have been formed between Daewoo and General motors (GM owned 50 percent of Daewoo until 1994) and Kia and Ford. Further, adding Korea allowed us to test whether or not the relationship between trust and performance outcomes was robust across numerous institutional environments, including a newly industrializing economy.

The sample consisted of three U.S. (General Motors, Ford, Chrysler), two Japanese (Toyota, Nissan), and three Korean (Hyundai, Daewoo, Kia) automakers and a sample of their Tier I suppliers. These companies represented more than two-thirds of the automotive market in each country. We visited each company's purchasing department and asked the procurement head to select a representative sample of suppliers, which included both partners (i.e., *keiretsu/chaebol* suppliers) and nonpartner (i.e., independent) suppliers. The procurement head also provided us with the total number of individuals employed in procurement for production parts (including management, purchasing agents/buyers, lawyers, and support staff) as well as the total value of goods they procured. This allowed us to develop a measure of automaker transaction costs, expressed as the dollar value of goods (parts) purchased per procurement employee. We interviewed a total of 31 purchasing executives to obtain feedback on the survey and to gain a better understanding of the issues arising in automaker-supplier relations. We also interviewed sales and engineering vice presidents at 70 suppliers (30 U.S., 20 Japanese, 20 Korean), during which a survey was pretested. To minimize key-informant bias and follow the general recommendation to use the most knowledgeable informant (Kumar et al. 1993), we asked the purchasing managers at each automaker to identify the supplier executive who was most responsible for managing the day-to-day relationship.

One may question whether a single informant has sufficient knowledge and ability to assess the collective trust orientation of individuals at her organization towards the automaker organization. Although responses from multiple informants may have been preferred (with a cost of a smaller sample), we believe that our informants were well positioned to make this assessment for the following reasons. First, key informants had been employed at their respective organizations for an average of 16 years; thus they had a long history of working with the automaker. These individuals had primary responsibility for managing the day-to-day relationship with the customer and were well aware of the history of interactions between their, and their customer's, employees. Further, in approximately 15 of our in-person interviews with suppliers, the key informants brought two to three other top supplier executives to the interview who had previously filled out our questionnaire separately from the key informant. During the interview, the group of supplier executives would look at each other's answers and come to a consensus on the "group" answer (we were able to see their individual responses). The degree of similarity in their responses was remarkable; rarely did the responses vary more than one point on a seven-point Likert scale. Consequently, we believe the key informant responses to reliably represent the responses of multiple informants.

Usable responses were obtained from 135 U.S. (66 percent response rate), 101 Japanese (68% response rate), and 108 Korean (55 percent response rate) suppliers. The data collection was done between 1993 and 1994. The U.S. and Japanese data were collected in 1993, reflecting data for 1992, and the Korean data were collected in 1994, reflecting data for 1993. We do not believe this will bias the results because Korean suppliers indicated that their relationship with their largest automaker customer had not changed in any significant ways since 1992.

Operational Measures

Trust. Consistent with previous studies, we operationalized trust (buyer trustworthiness) using multiple scale items designed to measure the extent to which the supplier trusted the automaker not to behave opportunistically[2] (Anderson and Narus 1990, Heide and John 1988, Zaheer and Venkatraman 1995). Trust (TRUST) was operationalized as the sum of the following submeasures that are reflections of a single unidimensional construct:

(1) The extent to which the supplier trusts the manufacturer to treat the supplier fairly;
(2) The extent to which the automaker has a reputation for trustworthiness (following through on promises and commitments) in the general supplier community;
(3) If given the chance, the extent to which the supplier perceives that the automaker will take unfair advantage of the supplier (reverse scored).

Each scale item was measured on a seven-point Likert scale ($1 =$ not at all; $7 =$ to a very great extent). Cronbach's alpha for this construct was 0.84, indicating high reliability.

The Role of Trustworthiness in Reducing Transaction Costs

Transaction Costs. To measure transaction costs, we asked suppliers to estimate: (a) the number of "person-days" of contact between their organization and the automaker during the previous year[3] and (b) what percentage of their face-to-face communication time with automakers involved negotiating a price or contract, or ex post haggling in the form of assigning blame for problems. According to suppliers, face-to-face communication represents the most important, and expensive, form of communication between suppliers and automakers. We consider ex ante transaction costs (negotiating) and ex post transaction costs (haggling) as separate constructs to examine whether trust affects ex ante, and ex post, transaction costs differentially. Thus, ex ante and ex post transaction costs were measured as the number of days per year between the automaker and the supplier that is spent negotiating a price/contract (ex ante contracting) or haggling and assigning blame for problems (ex post haggling). More precisely, these measures are calculated as follows:

Ex ante transaction costs (ExanteTC)
= (total annual "person-days" of face-to-face time spent) × (percent of time spent on price negotiation/contracting) ÷ (supplier sales to the buyer).

Ex post transaction costs (ExpostTC)
= (total annual "person-days" of face-to-face time spent) × (percent of time spent haggling and assigning blame for problems) ÷ (supplier sales to the buyer).

Therefore, our measures represent *transaction cost per dollar of sales.* Because these measures are divided by the supplier's sales to the buyer, we control for supplier sales to the buyer in our model. Our ex ante contracting and ex post haggling constructs capture those activities that by themselves are not value enhancing activities, but rather are activities associated with completing the transaction and ensuring that each party lives up to its part of the agreement.

Supplier Information Sharing. Information sharing was operationalized as the extent to which the supplier shares *confidential/proprietary information* with automaker buyers and engineers (1–7 Likert scale). In particular, the sharing of sensitive information, such as costs and proprietary technology, has been demonstrated to be a critical factor for the successful implementation of automaker and suppliers' joint efforts to minimize costs (Nishiguchi 1994).

Control Variable: Asset Specificity. Asset specificity refers to capital investments in customized machinery, tools, dies, etc. Asset specificity was operationalized as the percent of the supplier's total capital equipment investments that would have to be scrapped if they were prohibited from conducting any future business with the automaker. This percentage was estimated by supplier respondents. Asset specificity was assumed to increase with an increase in the percentage of capital investment that could not be redeployed. Finally, a confirmatory factor analysis was carried out to test the overall fit of the measures with the data.[4]

Model and Data Analysis

The first three hypotheses were tested with data collected from the suppliers (i.e., unit of analysis is the supplier) using the following regressions:

H1: Ex Ante TC = a + (b1) TRUST + (b2) ASSET.SPECIFICITY + e;

H2: Ex Post TC = a + (b1) TRUST + (b2) ASSET.SPECIFICITY + e;

H3: Suppl. Info.Share = a + (b1) TRUST + (b2) ASSET.SPECIFICITY + e.
To examine the relationship between buyer trustworthiness and buyer transaction cost, we tested the following model using data collected at the buyer (automaker) level (i.e., unit of analysis is the automaker).

H4: BUYER TRANSACTION COST = a + (b1) BUYER TRUSTWORTHI-NESS.

The proxy we use for BUYER TRANSACTION COST is the average procurement dollars per person in the purchasing department of the automaker. Automakers incurlower transaction costs as they increase the dollars of goods procured per person. Also, BUYER TRUSTWORTHINESS is the mean trust score for all the suppliers who are associated with the particular automaker.

Results

The simple descriptive statistics for the pooled sample and each country are shown in Table 1. The descriptive statistics indicate that supplier trust is significantly higher in Japan than in Korea or the United States, which have similar levels of supplier trust. The findings from this industrial sector[5] support prior arguments that trust among Japanese transactors is high relative to the United States (Dore 1983, Sako 1991, Shane 1994) and contradict Fukayama's (1995) claims that Japan and the United States have similar levels of trust. The descriptive statistics also show that Japanese suppliers have the lowest expost transaction costs, followed by U.S. suppliers, while comparable measures for Korean suppliers are very high. This is largely because our measure of transaction cost is measured in terms of transaction cost per dollar sales. Because the average Korean supplier is less than one-twentieth in size compared to that of the Japanese and U.S. suppliers, the denominator is very small,

The Role of Trustworthiness in Reducing Transaction Costs

Table 1. Means and Standard Deviations: Pooled Sample and by Country

Variables	Pooled (n=344)	U.S. (n=135)	Japan (n=101)	Korea (n=108)
1. TRUST	14.30	13.63	16.37	13.21
	(3.20)	(2.64)	(2.60)	(3.48)
2. Ex Ante TRANSCOST	3.42	.83	.73	4.8
	(10.51)	(1.62)	(1.04)	(12.72)
3. Ex Post TRANSCOST	1.26	0.20	0.15	1.86
	(3.37)	(0.30)	(0.26)	(4.08)
4. SUPPL. INFOSHARE	4.81	3.57	5.74	5.00
	(1.63)	(1.73)	(1.08)	(1.37)
5. ASSET. SPECIFICITY	0.32	0.16	0.21	0.50
	(0.28)	(0.14)	(0.20)	(0.28)

Note. Standard deviations reported in parentheses.

Table 2. Correlation Matrix

	TRUST	Ex ante TC	Ex post TC	Suppl. Infoshare
Ex ante TC	−0.071			
	(0.369)			
Ex post TC	−0.186	0.433		
	(0.016)	(0.000)		
Suppl. Infoshare	0.322	−0.004	−0.038	
	(0.000)	(0.959)	(0.637)	
Asset.Specificity	−0.040	0.221	0.116	0.129
	(0.547)	(0.006)	(0.156)	(0.050)

Note. Figures in parentheses are significance levels.

resulting in the high transaction costs per dollar of sales. It seems that the high ex ante and ex post transaction cost per dollar of sales for Korean suppliers is more a result of diseconomies of scale, rather than inherent inefficiencies in the way that they conduct their business with the automakers (as we will show later in Figure 2, the percent of face-to-face time that Korean automakers spend on transaction-oriented activities is greater than Japanese automakers, but falls in line with U.S. automakers). The descriptive statistics also indicate that Japanese suppliers share more confidential information than their U.S. and Korean counterparts. Supplier investments in relationspecific assets were found to be highest in Korea, followed by Japan, and the United States. This is not surprising because some studies have found that 72 percent of Korean automotive suppliers supply to only one customer (Oh 1995). The correlation matrix in Table 2 shows that the independent variables used in the regression results do not have multicollinearity problems.

The results of the regression analysis for our first three hypotheses are shown in Table 3.

Table 3. Regression Analysis: Trustworthiness and its Influence on Transaction Costs and Information Sharing

Relationship	Expected Sign	Parameter	T-Value	R^2	F
H1: Trust → Ex ante TC	−	−0.085	−0.241	0.05	4.88***
(Holding Asset.Spec. constant)					
United States:		0.014	0.373	0.00	0.19
Japan:		−0.000	−0.009	0.00	0.00
Korea:		0.062	0.066	0.01	0.61
H2: Trust → Ex post TC		−0.344***	−2.299	0.06	4.49***
(Holding Asset.Spec. constant)	−				
United States:		−0.019***	−2.367	0.05	4.22***
Japan:		−0.003	−.247	0.01	0.51
Korea:		−0.641*	−1.599	0.02	1.29
H3: Trust → Suppl.Infoshare	+	0.088***	3.804	0.19	20.45***
(Holding Asset.Spec. constant)					
United States:		0.034	0.744	0.01	1.14
Japan:		0.068**	1.989	0.04	2.05
Korea:		0.115***	3.069	0.09	4.97***

Note. Size is being controlled for in the transaction cost variables, which include supplier sales to the automaker. The first line represents results for the pooled sample ($N = 344$). The 2nd, 3rd, and 4th lines represent results for United States ($N = 135$). Japan ($N = 101$), and Korea ($N = 108$), respectively.
*** sig. at alpha = 0.01 (one-tailed test).
** sig. at alpha = 0.05 (one-tailed test).
* sig. at alpha = 0.10 (one-tailed test).

First, our data indicate that the relationship between trust and ex post transaction costs is much stronger than the relationship between trust and ex ante transaction costs. Greater supplier trust in the buyer leads to lower ex post transaction costs for the exchange partners in the pooled sample,[6] the United States, and Korea. However, while the sign is in the expected direction, the relationship is short of being significant in Japan. The relationship between trust and ex ante transaction costs falls short of being significant (though the F-statistic for the pooled sample model is significant). It seems that even for hightrusting relationships, it is necessary to spend some effort up-front to make sure that the responsibilities of each party are clearly spelled out (particularly when there is high asset specificity). Overall, Hypothesis 1 is not supported, while Hypothesis 2 receives strong support in the pooled sample and in the United States, and weaker support in Korea ($p < 0.10$).

Second, our analysis suggests a positive relationship between supplier trust and the sharing of confidential work-related information by the supplier. Hypothesis 3 receives strong support in the pooled sample, Japan, and Korea, but is just short of being significant in the U.S. sample.

Finally, to test Hypothesis 4 we examined the correlation between buyer trustworthiness and buyer transaction costs as measured by dollars of goods procured per procurement employee. When we plot relative procurement costs for each automaker, along with the automaker's mean score for trustworthiness, we find a strong positive and significant correlation of $r = 0.66$. The findings indicate that Firm A1, which had low supplier trust, incurred procurement (transaction) costs that were more than twice those of the other U.S. firms, A2 and A3, and almost six times higher than Firm J1. Thus, the data offer support for Hypothesis 4. Finally, to confirm the link between trustworthiness and low transaction costs and financial performance, we examined the correlation between each buyer's trustworthiness and its transaction costs and its average profitability (ROA or pretax profits divided by assets) from 1985–1995. The results indicate a strong correlation between automaker trustworthiness and transaction costs (measured as procurement productivity); see Figure 1. The results also show a strong correlation between automaker trustworthiness and profit performance; see Figure 2. Although there are a number of factors that undoubtedly influence performance differences among automakers, these findings suggest that trustworthiness is a contributing factor because it reduces the automaker's transaction costs, thereby improving automaker profitability.

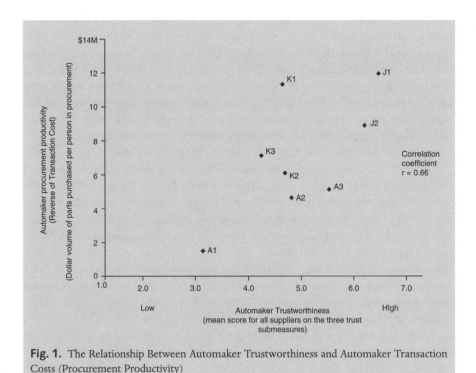

Fig. 1. The Relationship Between Automaker Trustworthiness and Automaker Transaction Costs (Procurement Productivity)

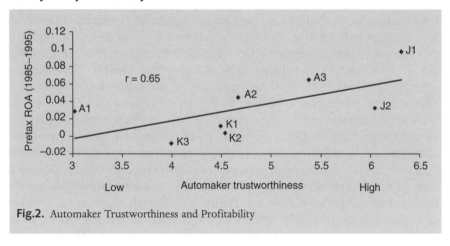

Fig.2. Automaker Trustworthiness and Profitability

Discussion

Our study is one of the first large-sample, cross-national empirical tests of its kind to demonstrate an inverse relationship between trust and transaction costs in supplier–buyer relations. It is also one of the first studies to show a relationship between firm trustworthiness and firm performance. While it is not possible in this research to partition out all of the factors that account for these relative performance differences, the fact that trustworthiness was strongly linked to low transaction costs, and low transaction costs strongly linked to performance, suggests that a reputation for trustworthiness improves performance.

As one of the first cross-national studies on trust, we would like to briefly comment on country-specific differences. First, consistent with prior anecdotal evidence we found supplier trust was universally high in Japan, and there was very low variance on the trust measures. These findings offer empirical support for Dore's (1983) observation that "moralized trading relationships of mutual goodwill" (p. 463) generally pervade Japanese transaction relationships. Moreover, our finding that transaction costs were lower in Japanese transaction relationships confirms the theoretical arguments made by Hill (1995) that Japanese economic relationships are likely to be characterized by low transaction costs for a variety of cultural reasons. In addition, we found greater information sharing among Japanese transactors. The fact that interfirm relationships in Japan were generally characterized by greater trust, lower transaction costs, and greater information sharing may account for the success of Japanese firms in complex product industries (Abbeglen and Stalk 1985, p. 63; Kotler et al. 1985a; Clark and Fujimoto 1991).

The Role of Trustworthiness in Reducing Transaction Costs

We were somewhat surprised to find that trust levels in Korea were much lower than in Japan and even slightly lower than trust levels in the United States. This was surprising because Korean culture is more similar to Japanese culture and because previous research suggests that many Korean suppliers and automakers have an exclusive relationship. One plausible reason for this finding is the Korean government's policy of nurturing large conglomerates (*chaebols*) and its failure to set up laws to protect small-to-medium-sized businesses in their dealings with the powerful *chaebols*. As a result, many small businesses have been at a relative disadvantage in trading with the *chaebols*, which have been in a position to dictate the terms of trading agreements and the relationship in general.

U.S. supplier–automaker relationships were characterized by lower asset specificity and lower information sharing compared to Japanese and Korean relationships. This is consistent with the general desire to minimize dependence in exchange relationships in the United States. Interfirm trust, while lower than in Japan, was actually higher in the United States than in Korea. This is consistent with Fukuyama's argument that interfirm trust in the United States is actually quite high relative to most other countries, especially emerging economies. We should also note, however, strong firm-specific differences within the United States (and indeed within each country), which suggests that institutional environment may be less important than firm-level practices in influencing levels of interfirm trust, transaction costs, and information sharing.

Finally, we want to briefly comment on our finding that trust was positively correlated with information sharing. First, we acknowledge that our measure of information sharing was a single-item measure, which naturally has some validity and reliability concerns. However, we conducted interviews with 70 supplier executives who repeatedly claimed that they were much more likely to bring new product designs and new technologies to "trustworthy" automakers. The following statement by a supplier executive is representative of the comments we heard,

We are much more likely to bring a new product design to [Automaker A3] than [Automaker A1]. The reason is simple. [Automaker A1] has been known to take our proprietary blueprints and send them to our competitors to see if they can make the part at lower cost. They claim they are simply trying to maintain competitive bidding. But because we can't trust them to treat us fairly, we don't take our new designs to them. We take them to [Automaker A3] where we have a more secure long-term future. (Author interview, October 1995)

We caution, however, that due to the cross-sectional nature of the data, we cannot be certain as to the direction of causality. We can only state that we know trust and information sharing are related. Future longitudinal research might more explicitly test the causal relationship between trust and information sharing by examining how a change in trust results in changes in information sharing (or vice versa).

The Distinctiveness of Trust as a Governance Mechanism

In the process of examining the influence of trust on transaction costs and information sharing, we discovered an interesting phenomenon that may explain why trust is particularly valuable as a governance mechanism. This finding emerged as we attempted to determine whether information sharing was an antecedent, or an outcome, of trust. For example, does information sharing lead to trust, or does trust lead to information sharing? Of course, the answer appears to be both—trust and information sharing are subject to mutual causality and each variable is therefore both an antecedent and an outcome of the other. Furthermore, supplier investments in information sharing not only build trust, but also simultaneously create economic value in their own right. To confirm this we ran a regression model to test the relationship between our previous dependent variables (information sharing, transaction costs) and supplier trust (as a dependent variable). We found a significant positive relationship between information sharing and supplier trust (T value $= 4.0$; $p < 0.001$), but not between transaction costs and supplier trust. Thus, trust appears to lead to certain value-creating behaviors (i.e., information sharing) and these value-creating behaviors in turn lead to higher levels of trust.

This phenomenon makes *trust unique as a governance mechanism because the investments that trading partners make to build trust often simultaneously create economic value (beyond minimizing transaction costs) in the exchange relationship.* According to transaction cost theory, the relative attractiveness of each governance mechanism is based on its differential ability to lower transaction costs. Indeed, the theory's focus is almost completely on *cost minimizing* rather than *value creation*. By comparison, trust not only minimizes transaction costs, but also appears to have a mutually causal relationship with information sharing that also creates value in the exchange relationship. This uniqueness may explain why trust has been described as a key factor, and the primary governance mechanism, in most studies of high-performing dyads/networks (Lorenz 1988, Powell 1990, Dyer 1996b). It may also explain why Zaheer et al. (1998) found a direct relationship between interorganizational trust and performance. Zaheer et al. (1998, p. 155) speculate that

The basis for performance enhancement does not appear to be based on efficiencies gained from eased negotiation processes. Rather, we speculate that the enhancement of transaction value (Zajac and Olsen 1993)—such as cooperation in the exploration of new information and coordination technologies, new market opportunities, and product and process innovation—may account for the link between interorganizational trust and exchange performance.

Conclusion

This study validates previous theoretical arguments that trustworthiness lowers transaction costs in exchange relationships (Barney and Hansen 1994). In particular, our findings indicate that trust reduces ex post transaction costs and is correlated with increased information sharing in supplier-buyer relationships. Moreover, the economic value created for transactors, in terms of lower transaction costs, appears to be substantial in the automotive industry. However, we should caution that the validity of the implied causal links of our model is limited by the cross-sectional nature of our research design. We also caution that our findings may only be generalizable to the auto industry or other industries with similar characteristics (i.e., complex-product industries where suppliers are vulnerable because they have made substantial transaction-specific investments). Complex product industries (see Clark and Fujimoto 1991, pp. 10–11) tend to be characterized by a high degree of mutual (reciprocal) interdependence on the part of intermediate component makers and final assemblers. Investments in relation-specific assets are often necessary to coordinate on nonroutine, complex tasks that are reciprocally interdependent. Examples of industries that fit these characteristics include aircraft, heavy machinery, robotics, machine tools, supercomputers, microelectronics, etc.

We believe that trust in supplier-buyer relations may be an important source of competitive advantage in industrial settings in which: (1) transaction costs are expected to be high due to conditions that create transactional difficulties (e.g., environmental uncertainty and high interfirm asset specificity) and (2) there is a high value associated with information sharing (information is a particularly valuable resource due to product complexity and industry uncertainty). Future longitudinal research, and research across multiple industry settings, could shed light on both the validity of the causal links we suggest as well as the generalizability of our findings to other industry settings.

Acknowledgments

The Sloan Foundation, International Motor Vehicle Program at MTT, Global Management Center at Brigham Young University, and Seoul National University Institute of Management of Research are gratefully acknowledged for supporting this research.

Notes

1. Some have argued that it is possible to generate trust contractually (Williamson 1991). However, to do so requires the time and expense associated with writing the contract (which would increase transaction costs).
2. The survey was administered to the suppliers so the measures reflect the perceptions of suppliers regarding the supplier-automaker relationship. However, during our interviews with the automaker purchasing managers we discovered that both the supplier and automaker perceptions regarding the relationship were very similar in specific cases we discussed. There were no instances where the perceptions of suppliers and automakers were dramatically different. Our anecdotal findings are similar to those of Anderson and Narus (1990), who found that suppliers' and buyers' perceptions of levels of trust were quite consistent.
3. This construct includes face-to-face contact between supplier sales personnel and automaker purchasing personnel. We used the identical methodology as Dyer (1996a), where days of contact was calculated by having the supplier's sales vice president identify the number of sales people that worked directly with the particular automaker. Then, s/he indicated the average number of days per week that the typical salesperson would spend having a face-to-face meeting with automaker personnel.
4. We executed confirmatory factor analysis to confirm unidimensionalities of TRUST and to verify the discriminant validity between SUPPL.INFOSHARE, EX ANTE TC, and EX POST TC. Overall fitness of the confirmatory factor analysis model was satisfactory with high goodness of fit and low root mean squared (Chi-squared = 36.97 (d.f. = 16; p = 0.0021), GFI = 0.98, AGFI = 0.94, RMR = 0.021). So, we conclude that our measurement model fits well with the actual data. For TRUST, standardized parameters for each item are sufficiently high to confirm convergent validity so that the individual items are internally consistent measures. (Bagozzi and Yi 1989).
5. Of course, we only have data for this industry so we cannot say definitively that trust levels in the United States as a society are lower than in Japan.
6. In the pooled data, we have included dummy variables for the countries.

References

Abegglen, J. C., & G. Stalk, Jr. 1985. *Kaisha: The Japanese Corporation*. Basic Books.

Anderson, J. C., & J. A. Narus. 1990. A model of distributor firm and manufacturer firm working partnerships. *J. Marketing* **54** 42–58.

Aoki, Masahiko. 1988. *Information, Incentives, and Bargaining in the Japanese Economy*. Cambridge University Press, New York.

Asanuma, Banri. 1989. Manufacturer-supplier relationships in Japan and the concept of relation-specific skill. *J. Japanese and Internat. Economies* **3** 1–30.

The Role of Trustworthiness in Reducing Transaction Costs

Bagozzi, R., & Y. Yi. 1989. On the use of structural equation models in experimental designs. *J. Marketing Res.* **26** (August) 271–284.

Barney, J. B., & M. H. Hansen. 1994. Trustworthiness as a source of competitive advantage. *Strategic Management J.* **15** 175–190.

Business Week. 1992. Learning from Japan. (January 27) 52–60.

Butler, P. T., W. Hall, A. M. Hanna, L. Mendonca, B. Auguste, J. Manyika, & A. Sahay. 1997. A revolution in interaction. *McKinsey Quart.* (1) 3–14.

Casson, Mark. 1990. *Enterprise and Competitiveness: A Systems View of International Business.* Clarendon Press, Oxford, U.K.

Clark, Kim B., & Takahiro Fujimoto. 1991. *Product Development Performance.* Harvard Business School Press, Boston, MA.

Deutsch, M. 1958. Trust and suspicion. *J. Conflict Resolution* **2** 265–279.

Dore, Ronald. 1983. Goodwill and the spirit of market capitalism. *British J. Sociology.* **XXXIV** (4) 459–482.

Doz, Y. L., & G. Hamel. 1998. *Alliance Advantage.* Harvard Business School Press, Boston, MA.

Dyer, Jeffrey H. 1996a. Specialized supplier networks as a source of competitive advantage: Evidence from the auto industry. *Strategic Management J.* **17** (4) 271–292.

—— 1996b. Does governance matter? Keiretsu alliances and asset specialization as sources of competitive advantage. *Organ. Sci.* **7** (6) 649–666.

—— 1997. Effective interfirm collaboration: How firms minimize transaction costs and maximize transaction value. *Strategic Management J.* 18(7) 535–556.

The Economist. 1996. Trust in me. (December 16) 61.

Fukuyama, Francis. 1995. *Trust: The Social Virtues and the Creation of Prosperity.* The Free Press, New York.

Gulati, Ranjay. 1995. Familiarity breeds trust? The implications of repeated ties for contractual choice in alliances. *Acad. Management J.* **38** 85–112.

Heide, Jan B., & G. John. 1988. The role of dependence balancing in safeguarding transaction-specific assets in conventional channels. *J. Marketing* **52** 20–35.

Helper, Susan. 1991. How much has really changed between U.S. automakers and their suppliers. *Sloan Management Rev.* (Summer) 15–28.

Hennart, J. F. 1993. Explaining the swollen middle: Why most transactions are a mix of "market" and "hierarchy." *Organ. Sci.* **4** (4) 529–547.

Hill, Charles W. L. 1995. National institutional structures, transaction cost economizing, and competitive advantage: The case of Japan. *Organization Sci.* **6** (2) 119–131.

Klein, B., R. G. Crawford, & A. A. Alchian. 1978. Vertical integration, appropriable rents and the competitive contracting process. *J. Law and Econom.* **21** 297–326.

Kotler, P., L. Fahey, & S. Jatusripitak. 1985. *The New Competition.* Prentice-Hall, Englewood Cliffs, NJ.

Kumar, N., L. W. Stern, & J. C. Anderson. 1993. Conducting interorganizational research using key informants. *Acad. Management J.* **36** (9) 1633–1651.

Larson, A. 1992. Network dyads in entrpreneurial settings: A study of the governance of exchange relationships. *Admin. Sci. Quart.* **37** 76–104.

Lorenz, Edward H. 1988. Neither friends nor strangers: Informal networks of subcontracting in French industry. D. Gambetta, ed. *Trust: Making and Breaking Cooperative Relations*. Blackwell, New York, 194–210.

Mayer, R. C., J. H. Davis, & F. D. Schoorman. 1995. An integrative model of organizational trust. *Acad. Management Rev.* **20** (3) 709–734.

Nishiguchi, Toshihiro. 1994. *Strategic Industrial Sourcing*. Oxford University Press, New York.

North, Douglass C. 1990. *Institutions, Institutional Change and Economic Performance*. Cambridge University Press, Cambridge, U.K.

Oh, Kyu Chang. 1995. An international comparison of product development and supply systems in the automobile industry. Research Report 364, Korea Institute for Industrial Economics and Trade, Seoul, Korea.

Ouchi, William G. 1984. *The M-Form Society.* Avon Books, New York.

Pine, B. J. 1993. *Mass Customization*. Harvard Business School Press, Boston, MA.

Powell, Walter W. 1990. Neither market nor hierarchy: Network forms of organization. B. Staw and L. Cummings, eds. *Research in Organizational Behavior*, vol. 12. JAI Press, Greenwich, CT, 295–336.

Ring, P. S., & A. H. Van de Ven. 1992. Structuring cooperative relationships between organizations. *Strategic Management J.* **18** 483–498.

Sako, Mari. 1991. The role of "trust" in Japanese buyer-supplier relationships. *Ricerche Economiche* **XLV** (2–3) 449–474.

Shane, S. 1994. The effect of national culture on the choice between licensing and direct foreign investment. *Strategic Management J.* **15** 627–642.

Uzzi, B. 1997. Social structure and competition in interfirm networks: The paradox of embeddedness. *Admin. Sci. Quart.* **42** 35–67.

Williamson, Oliver E. 1985. *The Economic Institutions of Capitalism*. Free Press, New York.

—— 1991. Comparative economic organization: The analysis of discrete structural alternatives. *Admin. Sci. Quart.* **36** 269–296.

Zaheer, A., & N. Venkatraman. 1995. Relational governance as an interorganizational strategy: An empirical test of the role of trust in economic exchange. *Strategic Management J.* **16** 373–392.

—— B. McEvily, V. Perrone. 1998. Does trust matter? Exploring the effects of interorganizational and interpersonal trust on performance. *Organ. Sci.* **9** (2) 141–159.

Zajac, Edward J., & C. P. Olsen. 1993. From transaction cost to transactional value analysis: Implications for the study of interorganizational strategies. *J. Management Stud.* **30**(1) 131–145.

Zucker, Lynne G. 1986. Production of trust: Institutional sources of economic structure, 1840–1920. B. M. Staw and L. Cummings, eds. *Research in Organizational Behavior*, vol. 8. JAI Press, Greenwich, CT, 53–111.

8   Kinds of Third-Party Effects on Trust

Ronald S. Burt and Marc Knez

Trust plays an ambiguous role in contemporary images of organization. Trust is essential to the loose coupling that makes network organizations more adaptive to changing environments. However, the dense relations argued to sustain trust also produce the tight-coupling rigidity for which trust and loose coupling are the cure.

Much of the ambiguity about organizing to produce trust is resolved by focusing on the simplest social conditions for trust, then studying how trust changes as the simple conditions aggregate into social structures. The simplest context for trust is an isolated dyad, two people disconnected from others. Their relationship is the cumulative result of their exchanges, or interaction games, with one another. Their games are private—their behavior displayed only to one another. Trust is by definition interpersonal, but rarely private. The usual context for trust is an embedded dyad, two people surrounded by their various interconnected friends, foes, and acquaintances. The two people play their games in public; a public composed of the third parties surrounding them. What produced trust between two people now involves third parties. The contrast between private and public games sets the empirical question for this article: How does trust vary with the strength of a relationship and its location in social structure?

Trust in Private Games

Exchange theory has trust produced in private games by a simple stimulus-response logic. The theory, rooted in turn-of-the-century British anthropology, is most associated with Homans's (1961) two-party analysis of social behavior, and Blau's (1964) two-party analyses of social exchange (see Ekeh 1974, 81–187, for historical exegesis of the individualistic British-American version of exchange theory contrasted with the French collectivist variant represented by Durkheim and Levi-Strauss). Blau (1964, 112–13) argues that trust develops because social exchange involves unspecified obligations for which no binding contract can be written. When you exchange sensitive information with someone, for example, trust is implicit in the risk you now face that the other person might leak the information. Putting aside Blau's moral obligation aspect of exchange to focus on parameters of cost-benefit calculation (cf. Ekeh 1974, 175), Coleman (1990, ch. 5) captures trust more concretely for his systems of two-party exchange and provides the metaphor for our analysis—trust is committing to an exchange before you know how the other person will reciprocate. Coleman focuses on social factors in the decision to trust (and we will return to his analysis to describe public games), but his crisp definition of trust is also useful for analyzing private games. The essential tension of trust in private games is illustrated by the decision rule in a Prisoner's Dilemma game.

Relations built from private games can be analyzed as the outcome of repeated Prisoner's Dilemma games, each game another cycle of social exchange (see Hardin 1990, 364 ff, on the social exchange substance of the game). Axelrod's (1984) simulation of cooperation in two-person games is intriguing and widely cited evidence for arguments that trust emerges with cooperation in repeated games. Two players choose in each game to cooperate or not. Both players get a high payoff if they both cooperate. Both get a low payoff if both choose not to cooperate. The maximum payoff occurs when one person cooperates and the other does not. The cooperator gets the "sucker's payoff" and the defector gets the maximum payoff. Tension exists because players decide whether to cooperate or not before they know what the other will do. The decision to cooperate is a decision to trust. If you do for the other, will he or she in future do for you or yours? Axelrod's analysis shows how trust can emerge as the dominant form of interaction between a pair of people. Across the spectrum of concepts spanned by Barber's (1983) distinctions between trust as moral order, competence, and obligation, we have reduced trust to a humble level: Trust is anticipated cooperation. We have two reasons. First, we want to keep trust a simple concept to more clearly focus on the complexity of social structural effects. More complex images of trust can emerge from complex structural effects producing trust. Second, anticipated cooperation is much of the trust essential to organization. The issue is not moral. It is office politics. Can you trust me to cooperate with your initiative?

Viewed as anticipated cooperation, trust is twice created by repeated interaction; from the past and from the future. From the past, repeated experience with a person is improved knowledge of the person. Cooperation in today's game is a signal of future cooperation. Across repeated games with cooperative outcomes, you build confidence in the other person's tendency to cooperate. From tentative initial exchanges, you move to familiarity, and more significant exchanges. The gradual expansion of exchanges promotes the trust necessary for them. From past cooperation, you expect future cooperation (cf. Zucker 1986, on process-based trust; Stinchcombe 1990, 164 ff, on the information advantages of current suppliers for building trust). Further, the history of cooperation is an investment that would be lost if either party behaved so as to erode the relationship—another factor making it easier for each party to trust the other to cooperate (see Larson 1992, for discussion and anecdotal evidence on the importance in the long run for trust between firms). Blau (1968, 454) summarizes the process as follows: "Social exchange relations evolve in a slow process, starting with minor transactions in which little trust is required because little risk is involved and in which both partners can prove their trustworthiness, enabling them to expand their relation and engage in major transactions. Thus, the process of social exchange leads to the trust required for it in a self-governing fashion." Where sociological models explain trust emerging from past exchanges, economic models look to the incentives of future exchanges (e.g., Axelrod 1984; Kreps 1990; Gibbons 1992, 88 ff). The expectation that violations of trust will be punished in future games leads players to cooperate even if defection would be more profitable in a single play of the game. From a game-theoretic perspective, the information contained in past experience and the potential for future interactions are inextricably linked. A player's willingness to forego short-term gains is based on the expectation that his or her current behavior will be used to predict his or her behavior in the future.

The prediction for private games is that trust and relation strength are correlated. Repeated cooperation strengthens the relationship between two people, increasing the probability that they "trust" each other. Their strengthened relationship in turn makes future cooperation more likely.

Trust in Public Games

Put the two-person game in a social context of one or more third parties to the game between ego and alter. What was a private game is now public.

Passive Third Parties Watch

With third parties now watching ego's game with alter, ego's behavior affects more than the probability of future alter cooperation—it also affects future cooperation with the third parties. Ego's cooperation signals to the third parties that ego is cooperative, adding to ego's "reputation" for being cooperative. If ego anticipates future interaction with the third parties, then ego has a reputation incentive to cooperate with alter. If ego believes that alter is similarly aware of the third parties, then ego can see alter's incentive to cooperate. Therefore, ego–alter cooperation and trust are more likely with third parties watching ego's game with alter.

This is a small step. Trust is produced by the same stimulus response mechanism that drives private games (e.g., see Blau 1964, 37ff, on impressing others; Kreps 1990, on reputation effects). Players act cooperatively in the short term because future partners use their current behavior to predict their future behavior. In a single interaction between ego and a particular alter, the third parties do not say or do anything. They are passive bystanders whose mere presence as future (active) players affects ego's behavior. By this argument, trust could be created simply by convincing ego that there are third-party witnesses with whom ego and alter will play later (e.g., point video cameras at ego and alter during game play). This model ignores the issue of transmission. Past ego and alter behavior are assumed to be transmitted accurately to every other player. How is transmission affected when it occurs through a network of varyingly accurate third parties?

Active Third Parties Gossip

Let the third parties talk. Even such a minimal assumption of active third parties creates enormous complexity for theoretical analysis because so many conversation topics are possible (e.g., see White's [1992] magisterial work on stories and structure). We focus on one topic: gossip about alter. The third parties have knowledge of alter that they can communicate to ego in stories about games that alter has played.

Third-party gossip is varyingly relevant to two-person games. The social structure of third parties means that some ego-alter pairs of people hear numerous stories about one another while others hear few stories. A strong relation means three things; (a) the connected people have interacted co-operatively in the past, (b) there is some level of trust, and (c) they have some interest in one another (otherwise their tie would be weak). In looking for information on alter, ego turns to trusted contacts with knowledge of alter, and those contacts continue their cooperative relation with ego by sharing what information they have. The people likely to have knowledge of alter, and communicate it to ego, are the people strongly tied to both ego and alter. So, the stronger the indirect connection between ego and alter through mutual friends and acquaintances, the more interaction stories they will hear about one another.

The implication is that indirect connections "lock-in" relationships at positive and negative extremes by making ego more certain of his or her trust in alter. The implication follows whether stories are relayed with full or partial disclosure.

Full Disclosure Gossip Full disclosure has third parties telling complete and accurate stories. Imagine that the stories about alter's interaction games let ego participate vicariously in those games in the sense that vicarious play is in some ways emotionally the same as actual play. The social structure of third parties relaying the stories is like a broadcast system—reaching an audience of ego "armchair quarterbacks." For a game played, signals diffuse in stories about the game to create in ego a feeling of replicated game play. The more third-party indirect connections between ego and alter, the more replicating accounts ego hears about alter—and so the more certain ego is of his or her trust in alter.[1]

Partial Disclosure Gossip Partial disclosure has third parties telling incomplete stories about alter's past behavior. The following assumption provides a rationale for partial disclosure and provides some predictions of its impact through alternative third-party structures. Assume that the third party can strengthen his or her relation with ego by highlighting the similarity of their opinions of other people (a concrete indicator that the third party's values are consistent with ego's). Ego's tentative view of alter is apparent from a variety of cues ranging from the subtle nuance of a raised eyebrow or a skeptical tone when describing alter, to the blatant signal of expressing a positive or negative opinion. To strengthen his or her own relation with ego, the third party relays stories about alter that are consistent with ego's tentative view. If ego seems to trust alter, the third party relays stories of games in which alter cooperated. If ego seems to distrust alter, the third party relays stories in which alter defected. The more third-party indirect connections between ego and alter, the more replicating accounts ego hears that support his or her view of alter. The replicating accounts, like replicating signals from a sequence of actual games with alter, make ego certain that alter is to be trusted (repeated stories of alter cooperating) or distrusted (repeated stories of alter violating trust).[2]

Positive and Negative Effects in Related Work. Economic and sociological analyses disproportionately concern the positive effect of dense networks. The trust likely between two strongly connected people is even more likely when the people are embedded in a network of mutual friends and acquaintances. Examples are numerous (e.g., see Bradach and Eccles 1989; Nohria and Eccles 1992; Swedberg 1993; and several chapters in the Smelser and Swedberg 1994, handbook, esp. Powell and Smith-Doerr 1994). Two widely known arguments for a positive correlation between trust and network density are Coleman's (1990, chs. 5, 8, 12) analysis of trust and social capital, and Granovetter's (1985, 1992) discussion of trust emerging from "structural embeddedness" (trust is more likely between people with mutual friends): "My mortification at cheating a friend of long standing may be substantial even when undiscovered. It may increase when the friend becomes aware of it. But it may become even more unbearable when our mutual friends uncover the deceit and tell one another" (Granovetter 1992, 44). This is a sociology analog to Kreps's (1990) reputation effect. Indirect connections through mutual friends and acquaintances make game behavior more public, which increases the salience of reputation, making ego and alter more careful about the cooperative image they display, which increases the probability of ego-alter cooperation and trust. Here again is the future-past difference between economics and sociology. Where sociologists ensure trust with a dense network of past exchanges, economists look to the incentives of future exchanges with third parties. The difference is not in concept so much as research design. The sociological analysis is keyed to network data, which will let us estimate reputation effects, and so reveal social structural primitives to inform economic analysis.

With scholars focused on when it is safe to trust (dense network), rather than when it is advantageous to trust (sparse network), there is relatively little attention to the dark side of network density.[3] However, the certainty produced by dense indirect connections can be negative or positive. Depending on the frame through which ego sees alter, alter can be trustworthy or treacherous.[4] By the gossip argument, stories from third parties make ego more certain in his or her view of alter. The social process that makes ego more certainly positive can in the same way make for negative certainty.

The central conclusion from the gossip argument is that indirect connections affect trust intensity, not direction. The direction depends on conditions between ego and alter. It is this contingency on existing conditions that makes the gossip argument a rational choice intruder within institutional theory. Ego chooses whether or not to trust alter, but the choice menu is indirectly contingent on existing conditions through the gossip of interested third parties. Where ego has reason to suspect alter, indirect connections through mutual contacts will convey stories that corroborate the suspicion—making ego certain that he or she should distrust alter. Where ego has a strong relation with alter, indirect connections will convey stories that corroborate the strong tie—making ego certain that he or she can trust alter.

Evidence

Our data come from a study of network structure and manager success (Burt 1992, ch. 4). The data are useful here because the manager respondents are a probability sample from a heterogeneous population of senior managers, and the data describe numerous kinds of relations, including indicators of trust and distrust. Here is a brief introduction to the data: The managers operate at the top of one of America's largest high-technology firms (over 100,000 employees at the time of the study). The study population—3,000 people just below vice president—is heterogeneous in the sense of being scattered across regions of the country and corporate functions (sales and service, engineering, production, finance, human resources, marketing, and management) and regions of the country. The stratified probability sample of 284 managers who completed survey questionnaires is an unbiased sample from the population. Managers described their networks of key contacts in and beyond the firm (7 contacts minimum, 22 maximum, 12.6 average). Contacts were identified with nine name generator sociometric questions concerning diverse relations such as informal discussion and socializing, past political support, critical sources of buy-in for projects, authority relations, and so on. (A quick aside on causation: The gossip argument has ego trust emerging from a network of direct and indirect connections. The argument also plays in reverse; trust between ego and alter encourages certain patterns of relations. We discuss our empirical results in the causal language of the argument, but causation remains untested. The data are unusual in describing networks in a probability sample of diverse managers, but they are only a cross-sectional view. We return to the issue of causation in the Discussion section. What our results will establish is the strength and functional form of association between trust and third-party connections.)

Strong and Weak Relations

The 3,584 cited contacts are displayed in Figure 1 by the strength of their relationship with the manager. The networks are a mix of strong and weak relations that show the managers maintaining relations with distant contacts. The most typical relation inside the firm (813 of 2,939 relations) involves infrequent contact (monthly or less) with people known a long time (6 or more years). The left-hand side of Figure 1, labeled Frequency, indicates that managers speak with one fourth of the contacts every day (860 relations, 25 percent), but speak monthly or less often with almost half (48 percent). The center of Figure 1, labeled Duration, indicates that half of the contacts are people the manager has known for

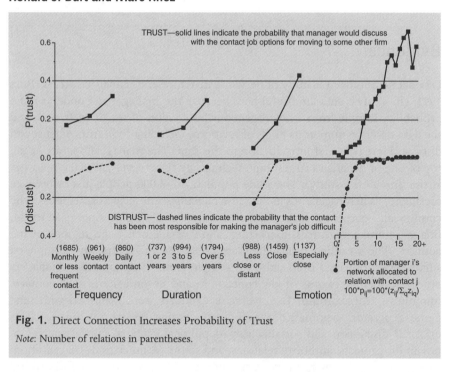

Fig. 1. Direct Connection Increases Probability of Trust

Note: Number of relations in parentheses.

more than 5 years (51 percent), but many are new acquaintances, first met this year or the previous year (21 percent). The right-hand side of Figure 1, Emotion, indicates that one third of the relations are "especially close" (32 percent), but almost another third are at the other extreme of "less close or distant" (28 percent).

The graph to the far right of Figure 1 distinguishes relations by relative strength within each manager's network. Emotional closeness response categories are given quantitative values, then divided by the sum of a manager's relations to indicate the proportion of the manager's network time and energy allocated to each of the manager's contacts. This will be our primary measure of relationship strength. It offers fine-grained distinctions between levels of strength, corresponds to our data on relations between the contacts in a manager's network, provides the strongest association with trust and distrust, and successfully predicts manager success in the original study.[5]

Trust

The main result in Figure 1 is that the data are consistent with a repeated games image of trust. The probability of trust increases up the vertical axis. Reading from left to right, solid lines describe how trust is more likely in stronger relations. Dashed lines describe how distrust is less likely in stronger relations. For example, of the 1,685 relations with contacts met once a month or less often (extreme left of graph), 289 are people cited for trust (solid line is at .172 on the vertical axis), and 176 are people cited for distrust (dashed line is at .105). Trust is more likely with contacts met every day (.172 increases to .322), and distrust is less likely (.105 decreases to .027).

None of the sociometric items are worded in terms of trust ("Who do you trust?" or "Who do you most trust of the people you named?"), but two questions have face and construct validity as indicators of trust. First the face validity, then construct.

Our indicator of trust is discussing job options in other firms: "If you decided to find a job with another firm doing the kind of work you do here, who are the two or three people with whom you would most likely discuss and evaluate your job options? These could be people who work here, or people outside the firm such as friends, family, or people who work at other firms." Managers responded with an average of three names (0 = minimum, 5 = maximum). This is not a comprehensive indicator. Managers probably trust people with whom they would not expect to discuss job options. Job option discussion is nevertheless a trust indicator in this study population. There is a hubris to making it in the firm (as in elite university departments). Employment is more than a contract, it is membership. Moving to another firm repudiates membership—especially for senior managers. Threatening to leave has implications for how you are treated. If word gets around that you want to leave the firm, you are irrelevant to the circulation of opportunities. You become a subject of, rather than a player in, the office gossip that builds solidarity among your colleagues. Your exit creates new opportunities, quickly carved up among your erstwhile colleagues, making it difficult for you not to leave the firm. In short, you do not discuss leaving the firm with just anyone.[6]

The solid lines in Figure 1 show that the probability of discussing job options in other firms increases with the strength of a relationship. It increases with the frequency of contact. It increases sharply if the manager has known the contact for more than 5 years. It increases most clearly with emotional closeness; job option discussion is eight times more likely in especially close relations than in less close or distant relations (.42 vs. .05). The graph to the far right of Figure 1 shows near-zero trust with the most distant contacts, increasing to over .5 with the closest contacts.

Distrust

Our indicator of distrust is a citation in response to asking managers "who has made it the most difficult for you to carry out your job responsibilities?"

Citations are few. The usual response is to cite one person. The wording does not indicate distrust, but managers were asked to explain why they cited the person they did, and their explanations indicate distrust of the repeated-game kind (Burt and Celotto 1992, report the content analysis). The gist of the analysis is that the cited contacts are viewed as uncooperative. All kinds of contacts in the firm were cited. The typical explanation for citing a supervisor is his or her failure to lead: "no support; no coaching, no feedback," "didn't explain the firm's system/culture and advise me," or "egotistical, self-oriented, liar; worst manager I've ever met." Undermining teamwork is the typical explanation for citing a colleague in the manager's own function: "not a team player; does only what is good for himself." The problems are colleagues who pursue their "own agenda" rather than the interests of the group, who are "proprietary" rather than cooperative, who do not "follow through on their commitments," who cannot be "trusted." Typical explanations for citing peers in other functions express frustration over being denied political support: "didn't support my proposals," "had great power and withheld help," "high rank but doesn't open door, in fact he gets in the way," or "tree hugger; do it his way or don't do it at all." In short, the cited contacts are people viewed as routinely uncooperative (cf. Sitkin and Roth 1993).

We expect relations with uncooperative contacts to be weak because managers have little incentive to maintain them. As expected, the dashed lines in Figure 1 show how the probability of distrust decreases with the strength of a relationship. It is most likely with contacts met monthly or less. It is less likely with contacts known for a long time. It is most likely with contacts to whom the manager feels less close or distant—which is not surprising given the opinions quoted above.

Third-Party Effects

In Figure 2, the Figure 1 association between trust and direct connection is displayed for two social contexts: little versus much indirect connection (see Note 5 for the distinction). Thin (bold) lines describe relations embedded in little (much) indirect connection.

The solid lines at the top of Figure 2 show trust amplified within strong relations. The thin and bold lines are similarly close to zero over weak relations. Trust is unlikely in weak relations regardless of indirect connection through third parties. Both lines are higher for stronger relations, with the bold line much higher than the thin over especially close relations. Of 1,039 especially close relations surrounded by little indirect connection, managers cite 41 percent as trustworthy. The odds increase to 61 percent of especially close relations embedded in extensive indirect connection.

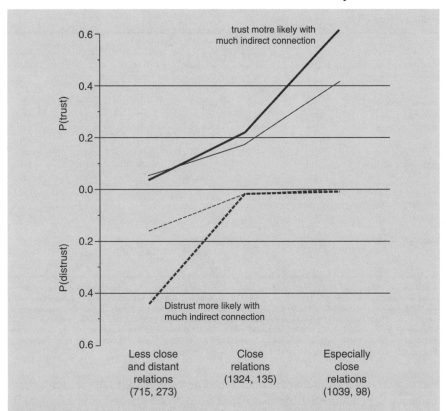

Fig. 2. Trust and Distrust More Likely with Much Indirect Connection

Note: Solid lines show probability of trust, dashed lines show probability of distrust, thin lines describe relations embedded in little indirect connection (private games), bold lines describe relations embedded in much indirect connection (public games), parentheses contain number of relations embedded in (little, much) indirect connection.

The dashed lines at the bottom of Figure 2 show distrust amplified within weak relations. The thin and bold lines are similarly close to zero over close and especially close relations. Distrust is unlikely in strong relations, regardless of indirect connection through third parties. Distrust is more likely in less close and distant relations, especially if the weak relation is embedded in extensive indirect connection. Distrust increases from 16 percent of the weak relations surrounded by little indirect connection, to 44 percent of the weak relations with extensive indirect connection.

Is the amplification statistically significant? Table 1 contains ordinary least squares (OLS) regression results with continuous predictors. The metric coefficients are points of change in trust or distrust associated with a one-point

Table 1. Trust Effects

	Trust		Distrust		Combined	
	All Dyads	Within Firm	All Dyads	Within Firm	All Dyads	Within Firm
Dyads	3,584	3,015	3,584	3,015	3,584	3,015
Multiple correlation	.39	.39	.47	.47	.51	.51
Intercept	−5.55	−12.25	3.25	4.73	−5.03	−9.50
DIRECT connection	2.55	2.67	−1.21	−1.54	1.99	2.28
	(12.0)	(12.6)	(−8.5)	(−8.8)	(12.5)	(13.1)
					[12.1]	[12.8]
INDIRECT connection	0.19	0.58	0.84	0.96	−0.30	−0.18
	(0.9)	(2.9)	(6.3)	(6.1)	(−2.3)	(−1.3)
					[−0.6]	[−0.1]
INDIRECT × STRONG	1.51	1.34			0.60	0.44
	(9.7)	(8.3)			(6.7)	(4.4)
					[5.7]	[3.7]
INDIRECT × WEAK			1.10	0.95	−0.57	−0.47
			(11.0)	(8.2)	(−5.8)	(−4.6)
					[−5.7]	[−4.7]

Note: These are ordinary least squares estimates of regression coefficients with routine *t* tests in parentheses, and *t* tests adjusted for autocorrelation in brackets (see Note 9). TRUST is 100 if the manager trusts the contact, 0 otherwise. DISTRUST is 100 if the manager distrusts the contact, 0 otherwise. COMBINED is 50 if the manager trusts the contact, −50 if the contact is distrusted, 0 otherwise. From manager to a specific contact, DIRECT is 100 times the proportional strength of the direct connection (p_{ij}), INDIRECT is 100 times the portion of relations that lead indirectly to the contact ($\Sigma_q P_{iq} P_{qj}$), STRONG is a dummy variable equal to 1 if the manager is especially close to the contact (0 otherwise), and WEAK is a dummy variable equal to 1 if the manager is less close or distant from the contact (0 otherwise). The metric coefficients are therefore the points of change in trust expected from a one-point increase in direct or indirect connection.

increase in direct or indirect connection. The combined results are for a three-category dependent variable that varies from 50 for trusted contacts, −50 for distrusted contacts, and 0 for relations between the two extremes.[7] The effects are significant, and their significance persists if relations outside the firm are ignored,[8] if we use a logit model,[8] or we control for autocorrelation.[9]

Direct connection predicts trust. Trust is likely in especially close relations (*t* tests = 12.0 and 12.6 in Table 1; $p < .001$), and unlikely in less close or distant relations (*t* tests = −8.5 and −8.8 in Table 1; $p < .001$).

The third-party effects of indirect connection are also apparent. The trust likely in an especially close relation is significantly more likely when the relation is embedded in extensive indirect connection (*t* tests = 3.7 to 6.7 in Table 1; $p < .001$). The trust unlikely in a weak relationship is significantly less likely when the relation is embedded in extensive indirect connection (*t* tests = −4.6 to −5.8 in Table 1; $p < .001$).

The Probability of Trust

Figure 3 provides a better substantive feel for the effects. The graph shows how the probabilities of trust and distrust change as two people get closer—with

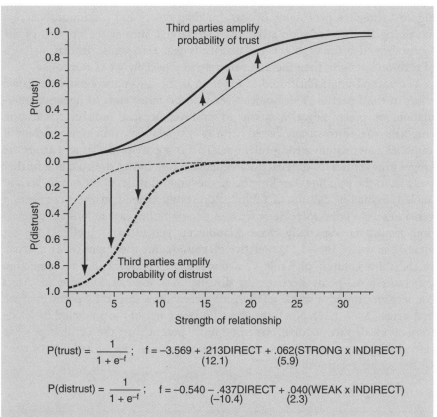

Fig. 3. The Probability of Trust in Private and Public Games

Note: Solid lines show the probability of trust, dashed lines show the probability of distrust, thin lines describe isolated relations (private games), bold lines describe embedded relations (public games), *t* tests are in parentheses.

and without indirect connections through third parties. The horizontal axis is relationship strength measured as in Figure 1 and Table 1 by the proportion of a manager's network invested in the relationship. Relations in our data vary from near-zero ($p_{ij} < .01$) to one third ($p_{ij} = .33$). Based on the displayed logit models, the vertical axis in Figure 3 is the probability of trust (top), and the probability of distrust (bottom). Thin lines show how probabilities change with a strengthening relationship between two people in isolation. Bold lines show the same probabilities—but for people embedded in extensive indirect connection through third parties.[10]

Two substantive points are illustrated in Figure 3. The first is that trust builds incrementally, while distrust is more catastrophic. The solid lines at the top of

Figure 3 show the probability of trust building slowly and continuously across increasing levels of relation strength. The dashed lines at the bottom of the figure show that the probability of distrust is near zero across decreasing levels of relation strength, then increases sharply in especially weak relations.

The second point illustrated in Figure 3 is the disproportionately negative effect of third parties. Third parties seem to be more alert to negative information, or prefer negative gossip to positive, because indirect connection amplifies the distrust associated with weak relations much more than it amplifies trust within strong relations. This is apparent in Figure 3 from the longer gray arrows for distrust. Indirect connection moves the bold line further away from the thin line. Looking back, the larger distrust effect can be seen in Table 1. In the first column of Table 1, a one-point increase in direct connection generates a 2.6-point increase in trust. A one-point increase in indirect connection around an especially close relationship generates a smaller 1.7-point increase in trust (.19 + 1.51). Relative magnitudes are the opposite for distrust. In the third column of Table 1, a one-point increase in direct connection generates a 1.2-point decrease in distrust. A one-point increase in direct connection around a weak relationship generates a larger 1.9-point increase in distrust (.84 + 1.10). Not only do we find evidence of the predicted dark side to network density, it turns out to be more potent than the familiar positive side in which extensive indirect connections increase the probability of trust within strong relationships.[11]

Kinds of Direct Connections

For reasons given with Figure 1, we measure direct connection as a degree of emotional closeness. Popular alternatives are frequency, duration, and social homophily.[12] We find no evidence of frequency affecting trust above and beyond the network variables in Table 1, but duration and homophily do affect trust.[13]

Duration

Duration has a binary association with trust. Trust and distrust are similar across the first 5 years, then trust jumps to continue at a high level, and distrust drops to continue at a low level (see Burt and Knez 1995a). Years known is correlated with the three-category trust variable in Table 1 (.21 correlation), but the correlation is zero across Years 1 to 5 (−.04 correlation), and zero across Years 6 and up (.04 correlation). The years-known correlation is captured with a binary duration variable that distinguishes people known for more than 5 years from people known for fewer years (.20 correlation). People seem to be sorted into two groups after 5 years (a period about equal to two job assignments in this firm); those you trust and with whom you maintain relations versus others you allow to drift away. Adding duration to the regression model in the last column of Table 1 shows that duration is a significant trust factor (t test $= 3.9$ for years known, t test $= 5.0$ for binary duration), but it does not change the conclusions about third-party effects. Indirect connection amplifying trust in strong relations (t test $= 4.4$) remains a strong 3.7, and amplified distrust in weak relations (t test $= -4.6$) remains a strong -4.2.

Homophily

Strong relations tend to connect similar kinds of people. The literature on this topic is extensive. The attributes that most pattern discussion relations between Americans are socioeconomic status (education, occupation, income), age, and race-gender combinations (see Burt 1990, for national probability data; cf. Zucker 1986, on characteristic-based trust). There are income, education, age, race, and gender differences within our study population, but the differences are trivial in comparison to the diversity of the American population. One attribute, however, does affect manager relations: gender. The connection between network structure and success in this firm shows that women are suspect at the senior ranks in the sense that they need a senior sponsor (Burt 1992, 74–8; cf. Ibarra 1992, 1994, for corroborating evidence and literature review). As in many firms, this could be a carryover from earlier times. Describing the firm a decade earlier, Kanter (1984) insightfully notices a variety of ways in which gender is linked with managerial behavior and success. Given the evidence of gender stratification among the managers, we expect trust to be more difficult between men and women.

It is, but in a nonobvious way that further illustrates third-party effects (detailed analysis of the gender effect is available elsewhere; Burt and Knez 1995a). Introducing gender is irrelevant in two senses: Trust is as likely between men and women as between people of the same sex, and third parties significantly amplify trust within all relations regardless of gender. The gender effect concerns the magnitude of third-party effects. Third parties are more important to trust between men and women than they are to trust between people of the same sex. In brief, third parties amplify trust between men and women (t test $= 11.6$) more than they amplify trust between people of the same sex (t test $= 5.7$). Or, stating the effect from the other end, the lack of mutual contacts inhibits trust between men and women. This is to be expected if gender differences inhibit relations. If communication is better between people of the same sex than it is between men and women—as it is in this study population—then gossiping third parties should have more effect on relations between men and women. With poor communication between Susan and Sam, Sam relies more on third parties relaying stories about Susan's past behavior. Without third parties connecting Sam and Susan, trust is difficult because Sam and Susan are uncertain about their respective interpretations of the other's behavior during past interactions with other parties or one another.

Kinds of Indirect Connections

We have shown that the strength of connection through third parties affects trust. The form of the connection also matters. Certain indirect connections increase trust. Certain others decrease trust.

Each row of Table 2 is a different measure of indirect connection predicting trust within strong and weak relations. The entries are t tests for the prediction. The relations are the 3,015 within the firm. (As in Table 1, we get the same pattern of results across all 3,584 relations to contacts inside and outside the firm.) Indirect connection in the first row is the aggregate measure used in

Table 2. Test Statistics for Trust Effects With Kinds of Indirect Connection

Forms of Indirect Connection	Especially Close Relations (n = 712)	Less Close and Distant Relations (n = 971)
1. INDIRECT (aggregate)	3.2	−9.3
Mutual third parties		
2. Σpij through TP1	3.0	3.0
3. Σpij through TP2	2.9	5.1
4. Σpij through TP1 or TP2	3.4	4.1
5. Number (TP1 + TP2)	2.6	4.5
Distant third parties		
6. Σpij through TP3	0.8	3.9
Exclusive third parties		
7. Σpij through TP4	−3.1	−0.4
8. Σpij through TP5	0.3	−3.6
9. Σpij through TP4 or TP5	−3.8	−7.3
10. Number (TP4 + TP5)	−5.0	−5.5

Note: These are routine t tests for ordinary least squares estimates of the row measure predicting three-category trust within column strength relations to people in the firm. INDIRECT is the aggregate measure of indirect connection in Table 1.

Table 1. Indirect connection amplifies trust within strong relations (t test $= 3.2$), and amplifies distrust within weak relations (t test $= -9.3$).

Notice how effects differ between the rows. If all forms of indirect connection were similar conduits for third-party gossip, then the same pattern of positive and negative effects would appear in each row of Table 2. Instead, the rows differ. In rows 2 through 5, indirect connection increases trust within strong and weak relationships. In rows 7 through 10, indirect connection decreases trust within strong and weak relationships. The implication is that the aggregate positive and negative effects of indirect connection reported in the preceding analysis must result from a shifting balance between kinds of third parties around strong and weak relations.

Positive Indirect Connections: Mutual Third Parties

Five kinds of third parties are distinguished in Figure 4. The first two are similar in two ways: they are mutual contacts for ego and alter, and their only effect on trust is positive. The first kind (TP1) is a mutual friend strongly tied to ego and alter. This is the third party usually cited to illustrate sociological analyses of density and trust (e.g., Coleman 1990; Granovetter 1992). Strong ties to ego and alter in Figure 4 are indicated by bold lines.[14] The second kind of third party (TP2) is a close friend of alter's who ego mentions as one of his or her key contacts. Mutual third parties are characteristic of the networks around some managers, but are uncommon in the population. One third of the manager and contact pairs have no mutual friend in common (35 percent), and one quarter have only one mutual friend (26 percent). The white area in the Figure 4 graph quickly disappears at higher levels of indirect connection. In other words, managers frequently have to deal with people they and their closest contacts do not know well. The dense networks of mutual friends characteristic of family and neighborhood life are not characteristic of life at the top of corporate America.

Where mutual third parties do occur, however, they enhance trust. The measure in the second row of Table 2 is the sum of manager relations to TP1 third parties. The measure would be 15, for example, for a relationship where the manager has 5 percent proportional-strength relations to three especially close other people also especially close to the contact. The third row is the sum of proportional relations to TP2 third parties, and the fourth row is the sum to either kind of mutual third party. The proportional strength of manager relations to mutual third parties increases trust within strong relations between employees (t test $= 3.4$) and increases trust within weak relations (t test $= 4.1$). The fifth row of the table measures indirect connection simply by the number of mutual third parties connecting ego and alter. Even this simple count of

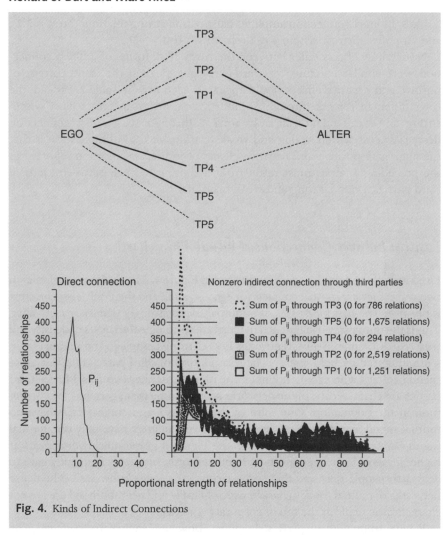

Fig. 4. Kinds of Indirect Connections

mutual third parties is associated with higher trust within strong and weak relationships (*t* tests = 2.6 and 4.5, respectively).

These results are interestingly consistent with the gossip argument. The positive effects of TP1 third parties are not surprising, but TP2 third parties do not have the symmetric ties to ego and alter that in sociological arguments make ego and alter accountable to the same third parties so ego-alter trust is less of a risk. The interests of a TP2 third party—someone distant from ego and especially close to alter—lie more with alter. Stories about alter told to ego by TP2 third parties are more likely to paint a positive than a negative image of alter. Negative stories that ego tells about alter are less likely to find a sympathetic ear from TP2 third parties. Therefore, to the extent that ego's evaluation of alter is affected by stories, trust should increase with indirect connection through TP2 third parties—which is the result in the third row of Table 2. The asymmetry should not be overstated. We only know about the TP2 third parties because the manager counted them among his or her key contacts. Third parties close to alter in our data are in a sense mutual contacts to ego and alter because ego includes them as key contacts. Whether the third party tie to ego is strong (TP1) or weak (TP2), the strong tie to alter means that ego and the third party are more likely to tell one another positive stories about alter, increasing ego's trust in alter.[15]

Negligible Indirect Connections: Distant Third Parties

Third parties weakly connected to ego and alter—TP3 third parties in Figure 4—have no effect on ego-alter trust. They represent low volumes of interaction (dashed line in the graph at the bottom of Figure 4), but occur in large numbers. Four out of five manager relations have at least one mutual distant third party (78 percent), and those with any have an average of 3 (maximum of 15). Although another kind of mutual contact shared by ego and alter, the results in the sixth row of Table 2 show that distant third parties have no association with trust within strong relations between employees (t test $= 0.8$). Distant third parties are associated with higher trust within weak relations (t test $= 3.9$), but are a negligible correlate of trust across relations at all strength levels, $F(3, 3010) = 0.6$ for null hypothesis of no distant third-party effects on trust, $p = .59$. Distant third parties are an innocuous social structural "white noise" around all manager relationships.

Negative Indirect Connections: Exclusive Third Parties

The last two kinds of third parties in Figure 4 amplify distrust. In row 9 of Table 2, indirect connection is measured by proportional relations to either of the two kinds. They significantly decrease trust within strong and weak relations (t tests $= -3.8$ and -7.3, respectively). These are third parties close to ego and distant from alter; contacts more exclusive to ego, confidants on ego's side viewing alter as a distant contact. The TP4 third parties are people especially close to ego and weakly tied to alter. TP5 third parties are people tied in any way to ego and disconnected from alter. In a sense, the TP5 third parties are not intermediaries because they have no connection with alter. But at the top of the firm, everyone is to some degree known to everyone else. We combine TP4 and TP5 third parties into one category of exclusive third parties because they are similarly much closer to ego than to alter; indirect connections through them similarly increase distrust within weak relations, and no other kinds of third parties have that effect. Further, both kinds of third parties tend to be people with whom the manager gets together for informal socializing, and are unlikely to be important work contacts or essential sources of buy-in for the manager's projects (see note 15). These exclusive third parties are the most numerous in this study population. In almost every relationship (99.4 percent), the manager has someone who is his or her friend more than the other person's. The average is eight exclusive third parties per relationship.

By the gossip argument, exclusive third parties should be associated with distrust because they are a more willing conduit for negative stories about alter. When ego has a positive experience with alter, mutual third parties are a receptive audience to stories about the experience because they too have a strong tie to alter. Exclusive third parties are receptive because they wish to preserve their relation with ego.

The two kinds of third parties respond differently to a negative story. Suppose ego has a negative experience with alter. Even between managers who like one another, events can create friction. Mutual friends of the two managers can be expected to blame the event. Alter is usually cooperative. Something must have been odd in this particular ego-alter interaction (see Sitkin and Roth 1993, 371 ff, on attributing a trust violation to event or perpetrator). This is frustrating for ego, who is trying to discharge the irritation of bad interaction with alter by telling stories about it. How much more satisfying to speak of alter's flaws with exclusive third parties. Friends close to one manager and not the other are free to choose between blaming the event or the other manager. By the gossip argument, they will choose as ego chooses, thus reinforcing ego's choice. If ego blames the event that resulted in ego-alter friction, the exclusive third party will relay a story about a similar event. If ego blames alter, the exclusive third party will relay a story about another occasion on which alter created friction. The result of exclusive third parties being more flexible is that negative stories accumulate with them. Distrust will be easier in relationships more surrounded by exclusive third parties—which is the result in rows 9 and 10 of Table 2.

How Mutuals Combine with Exclusives

If mutual third parties consistently increase trust and exclusive third parties consistently decrease trust, then the observed positive and negative amplification of trust at the extremes of direct connection (e.g., Figure 2) must result

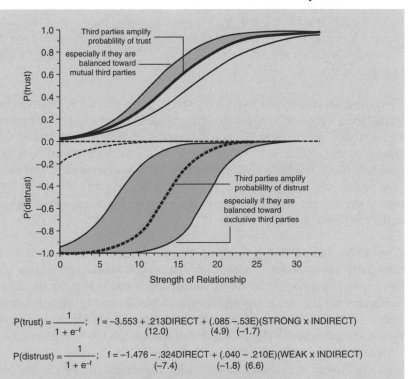

Fig. 5. Trust and Distrust in Mixtures of Mutuals and Exclusives

Note: Solid lines show probability of trust, dashed lines show probability of distrust, thin lines describe isolated relations (private games), bold lines describe embedded relations (public games).

from a shifting balance between mutual and exclusive third parties. We studied trust across relations to see how it changed with specific mixtures of one, or two, or more mutual third parties occurring with one, or two, or more exclusive third parties (Burt and Knez 1995a). The results are summarized in Figure 5.

Figure 5 is a revision of Figure 3. The form is the same: horizontal axis is strength of direct connection, probability of trust is the top of the graph, probability of distrust is the bottom of the graph. The change is that indirect connections through exclusive third parties are distinguished from connections through mutual third parties. There are now three components in the logit functions predicting trust:

$$\alpha + \beta(\text{DIRECT}) + (\gamma_v + \gamma_e E)(\text{STRONG} \times \text{INDIRECT}),$$

which disaggregates the γ indirect connection effect into two parts: γ_v is the effect of the volume of indirect connection, and $\gamma_e E$ is an adjustment for the indirect connection being balanced toward exclusive rather than mutual third parties. Variable E is a fraction measuring the extent to which exclusives outnumber mutuals around the relationship.[16] The graph in Figure 5 illustrates four points that summarize our analysis.

Conclusions About Aggregate Third-Party Effects. First, the two central conclusions from Figure 3 are not changed by the composition distinction between mutual and exclusive third parties. Trust still builds more slowly than distrust (slower change in the lines at the top of Figure 5 than at the bottom), and indirect connection still amplifies distrust within weak relations more than it amplifies trust within strong relations (large difference between the thin and bold dash lines at the bottom of Figure 5 versus the more similar thin and bold solid lines at the top of the figure).

Composition Around Strong Relations. Second, composition matters little for third-party effects within strong relations. Both third-party effects pale in comparison to the effect of direct connection (t test $= 12.0$ for the .213 logit coefficient β), but the composition of third parties around strong relations is sufficiently balanced toward mutuals to make volume alone the significant third-party predictor.[17] The probability of trust at the top of Figure 5 increases with indirect connections between close employees (t test $= 4.9$ for the .085 logit coefficient γ_v), and decreases with the extent to which the indirect connections are through exclusive third parties (t test $= -1.7$ for the $-.053$ logit coefficient γ_e). The composition effect is slight.

The modest composition effect is illustrated by the shaded area around the bold solid line at the top of Figure 5. The bold solid line describes trust in relations embedded in a median balance between mutual and exclusive third parties (median E is .56). The gray area around the bold line describes trust in relations within the interquartile range of observed balances. The bottom of the gray area is trust in relations more embedded in exclusive third parties (.73 is the 75th percentile in the E distribution). The top of the gray area is trust in relations more embedded in mutual third parties (.40 is the 25th percentile of the E distribution). Notice that the gray area is tight around the bold solid line and never much lower than the bold line. In other words, variation in the balance between mutual and exclusive third parties does not much affect trust at a given volume of indirect connection (narrow gray area), nor the difference between public games (bold line) and private games (thin line).

Composition Around Weak Relations. Third, composition matters greatly for third-party effects on distrust. The probability of distrust increases in weak relationships (t test $= -7.4$ for the $-.324$ logit coefficient β), and increases primarily with the balance toward exclusive third parties around the relationship (t test $= 6.6$ for the .210 logit coefficient γ_e, t test $= -1.8$ for the coefficient γ_v). Here, third-party effects are closer to the effect of direct connection, and the balance between mutual and exclusive third parties matters more than the volume of indirect connection.

In Figure 5, the importance of the balance between mutual and exclusive third parties is illustrated by the width of the gray area around the bold dashed line describing the probability of distrust. A balance toward exclusive third parties significantly increases the probability of distrust (bottom of gray area). A balance toward mutuals significantly reduces the probability of distrust (top of gray area). In fact, the extreme of a relation embedded in mutuals without any exclusive third parties is described by the bold, gray, dotted line in Figure 5 ($E = 0$). The dotted line shows a slight increase in distrust within near-zero relations, but can hardly be seen in the printed figure. The probability of distrust is virtually zero within strong and weak relations that are free of exclusive third parties. Between distant people, in other words, mutual third parties can substitute for a strong relation and facilitate trust. This is where their potential lies, in bringing together otherwise distant people.[18]

Trust Potential: Probability of Trust Without Distrust Points two and three together mean that the composition of third parties matters greatly for relations at all levels of direct connection. The fourth point in Figure 5 is that exclusive third parties increase the probability of distrust sufficiently to erode the trust potential of otherwise strong relationships. The gray area at the bottom of Figure 5 shows that exclusive third parties not only increase the probability of distrust within weak relations already sensitive to distrust, they introduce distrust into stronger relationships.

This fourth point is difficult to see in Figure 5 because it asks for a comparison between the probability of trust at the top of the graph and the probability of distrust at the bottom. The graph is complicated by the display of composition effects around both probabilities. The separate probabilities are valuable for understanding third-party effects, but it is their combination that defines the trust potential of a relationship. The issue for managers is not the probability of trust separate from the probability of distrust. It is the probability of a relationship prone to trust and free from distrust. That is the joint probability of trust and a lack of distrust—which in the simplest case is P(trust) from the top of Figure 5, multiplied by one minus P(distrust) from the bottom of Figure 5.[19]

The result is displayed in Figure 6. The thin line in Figure 6 describes how the balance between trust and distrust changes across repeated private games. This is the balance between the solid and dashed thin lines in Figure 5. The two bold lines in Figure 6 describe public games at opposite ends of the interquartile range of third-party composition in the manager data. The upper bold line

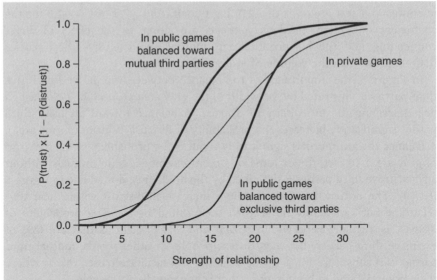

Fig. 6. Probability of Trust Without Distrust

Note: The 25th percentile is balanced toward mutuals, and the 75th percentile is balanced toward exclusives.

compares the top of the gray areas in Figure 5 (composition balanced toward mutual third parties), and the lower bold line compares the bottom of the gray areas in Figure 5 (composition balanced toward exclusive third parties).

Both third-party conditions amplify distrust within weak relations (bold lines lie below the thin at the extreme left of the graph), and amplify trust within strong relations (bold lines lie above the thin at the extreme right of the graph). The difference between them occurs within average relations. The bold line rising above the thin line (at .08 strength relations) shows how a balance toward mutual third parties can increase the trust potential of even a moderate-strength relationship above the level expected from repeated private games, and can continue to amplify trust across stronger relationships. In contrast, the other bold line in Figure 6 stays below the thin line for all but the strongest relations. The bold line does not rise above the thin until relation strength reaches .24 (which is the strongest work relationship in these data). Given a level of trust to be expected from repeated private games between ego and alter (thin line in Figure 6), a balance toward exclusive third parties around ego and alter makes trust almost impossible in weak-to moderate-strength relations (bold line remains near zero until relations reach .12 strength in Figure 6), and erode the trust potential of stronger relations. In sum, exclusive third parties not only increase the probability of distrust within weak relations, already sensitive to distrust, but they also erode the trust potential of otherwise strong relationships.

Summary and Discussion

We have described how trust varies with the strength of a relationship and its location in social structure. The simplest social context for trust is an isolated dyad—two people away from others. Their interaction games are private. The more usual context is two people surrounded by various close friends, foes, and acquaintances. The two people play their games in public; a public composed of the third parties surrounding them. We argue that third-party gossip amplifies both the positive and the negative in a relationship; making ego and alter more certain of their trust (or distrust) in one another. We draw three broad conclusions from an analysis of network data on a probability sample of diverse senior managers:

1. Trust is associated with relation strength, as expected in private games. Figure 1 shows the effect for alternative meanings of a strong relationship.

2. As predicted by the gossip argument for public games, trust is significantly amplified by third parties. Third parties have a positive effect on trust within strong relations, and a negative effect on trust within weak relations. Figure 2 shows the effect, and Figure 3 shows how the probability of trust and distrust are affected by indirect connections at different levels of direct connection.

3. Different forms of indirect connection are responsible for the third-party effects on trust. Connections through mutual third parties (people close to ego and alter) are responsible for the positive effects. Connections through exclusive third parties (people closer to ego than alter) are responsible for the negative effects.

These three broad conclusions obscure significant nuances in the way that positive third-party effects interact with negative effects, but in the limited space remaining we stand back from the analysis to highlight three caveats.

First Caveat

The gossip argument allowing partial disclosure is only feasible if ego is susceptible to third parties selectively reporting information about alter. But why doesn't ego take the third-party gossip with a grain of salt? Gossip is not known for its accuracy. This would be ego dismissing the third-party gossip as "cheap talk" (e.g., Gibbons 1992, 210 ff, on cheap-talk games). Information distortions are certainly feasible within a rational choice framework (e.g., Prendergast 1993), but for the purposes of this introductory analysis, we are comfortable with a simple behavioral assumption about ego's susceptibility: Ego's prior beliefs about alter's trustworthiness are a predisposition to accept third-party gossip consistent with the prior beliefs.

Diverse kinds of evidence can be cited to justify the assumption. Prior beliefs affect how new information is processed (e.g., Hastorf and Cantril 1954; Ross and Anderson 1982). Decisions with no clear empirical referent (e.g., Is alter trustworthy?) are especially susceptible to social influence (e.g., Festinger, Schachter, and Back 1950; Pfeffer, Salancik, and Leblebici 1976; Zucker [1977] 1991; Burt 1982, 1987). How ego perceives relations with and among other people is affected by ego's personal beliefs about the relations (e.g., DeSoto 1960; Freeman, Romney, and Freeman 1987; Krackhardt 1990; Kilduff and Krackhardt 1994).

Further, ego's susceptibility is less of a problem in our analysis than it could be elsewhere. The third parties in our analysis are people that a manager cites as important to his or her work. Relations tend to be positive (72 percent are close or especially close). A manager might suspect individuals among these people to distort information, and the aggregate level of suspicion no doubt varies between managers, but the problem of ego dismissing gossip from these third parties as cheap talk is less than it would be with the many third parties beyond the manager's immediate network.

These justifications notwithstanding, ego's susceptibility is an important question for empirical research. We have presented evidence of strong third-party effects without any controls for personality differences between managers. Our strong results without personality controls, combined with the history of research showing personality differences in susceptibility (Lindzey and Aronson 1985) and research that links network structure to susceptibility (Gartrell 1987; Kilduff 1992), suggest to us that future research will find third-party effects to be interestingly varied across kinds of manager personalities.

Second Caveat

We have only begun the elaboration of third-party effects. Our third parties are simplistic in that they have only one motivation—to strengthen their relation with ego. They listen to stories about ego with alter. They selectively report stories consistent with ego's view of alter. They selectively withhold stories inconsistent with ego's view.

But the third party too has a personal opinion of alter. If the third party has a bad (good) interaction with alter, then one way to punish (reward) alter is to tell ego about the interaction. Consider a less abstract setting. We happen to sit next to one another at the faculty meeting and you wax eloquent about a productive exchange you just had with professor X. I don't want to erode your obvious enthusiasm, and I enjoy being privy to your opinions, but my repeated experience with professor X is such that I wouldn't trust him to carry spit. If I behave as assumed in the preceding analysis, I am expected to communicate to you my positive experiences with professor X even though the balance of my experience is negative.

People often take the easy road of going along with the tone of the conversation, but it is obvious that third parties not only want to strengthen their relation with ego, they also want to convert ego to their opinion of alter. The third party has to make the evaluation of how far he or she can move ego's opinion of alter to the third party's opinion of alter. I dislike professor X, but in your current mood of enthusiasm for professor X, I wait to present my negative opinion and instead offer a positive platitude about X consistent with the moment. The effect on you is corroboration with your current enthusiasm—that is the substance of our gossip argument. But it is also true that I will communicate a more balanced view of professor X in the future when we are discussing an issue on which we have similar views and you have cooled down to a more neutral mood on professor X. Over time, therefore, my negative opinion of professor X is likely to infect your opinion of professor X. In other words, the asymmetry of third-party relations with ego and alter is a clue to the third party's motivation to reinforce or revise ego's opinion of alter.

There is also ego's view of the third party. A more general gossip argument would consider ego and the third party in one another's roles; the third party expressing his or her personal opinion of alter, and ego interested in relaying stories about alter that strengthen ego's relationship with the third party (e.g., network balance theory; Davis 1970). It doesn't seem likely that this more general gossip argument would yield other than our conclusion of third parties reinforcing existing relationships (because the more general model is based on the same process of players telling stories to strengthen their relations by displaying similar orientations to others). Still, the more general gossip argument remains a worthy challenge for future work.

Third Caveat

Our final caveat is about time. Our network data describe a probability sample of heterogeneous managers. That puts us in a much stronger analytical position than is characteristic in structural studies of trust, typically based on nonprobability samples or anecdotal cases. However, what makes our position strong also makes it weak in the sense that we cannot see the dynamic of trust evolving. Our data are a cross-sectional view of the managers. Our correlation between trust and structure could be due to trust emerging from structure, or structure emerging from trust, or both.

Ronald S. Burt and Marc Knez

We discuss our empirical results in the causal language of our argument to present a coherent story, but argument can be made for causation in either direction. Our gossip argument has ego trust emerging from social structure. Trust between two people is encouraged or made difficult by the structure of their relations with others. On the other hand, two people who trust one another can affect the pattern of relations that develops around them. For example: From repeated interaction over time, ego develops stronger beliefs about alter's trustworthiness. Simultaneously, ego and alter develop indirect connections by continuing to be employees in the same firm. Therefore, higher levels of trust or distrust will occur with higher levels of indirect connection even though the indirect connections have no direct effect on trust.

We could also argue that causation is not the issue in our study population that it is in general for cross-sectional network data because third-party connections do not seem to evolve between managers so much as they originate elsewhere (from the broader organization context, or perhaps each manager's characteristic style of bringing third parties into relations; Burt and Knez 1995a). Third-party conditions are independent of the time for which managers have known one another. The years two managers have known each other is correlated .08 with the number of their mutual third parties, $-.04$ with exclusive third parties, and $-.03$ with their strength of indirect connection through third parties. Years known is less significant here than the manager distinction between new versus established relationships. However, the binary duration variable strongly associated with trust shows the same lack of correlation with third-party conditions (.06 with mutual third parties, $-.04$ with exclusive, and $-. 06$ with strength of indirect connection).

We could argue further that causation is not the issue in our analysis that it is in general. Our analysis is less about one variable causing another, than about the general determining the particular. Trust and social structure are not two variables X and Y. They are the same variable on different scales. Trust is social structure; not all of social structure, but by definition a component of social structure. Trust is a kind of relationship, and social structure is the network of other relations in which trust occurs. Our analysis describes how one kind of emotional closeness is associated with the network of varyingly close relations in which it occurs. What we have discussed as trust relations could in other circumstances be discussed as confiding, intimacy, or especially close friendship, which returns us to the problem of data. These alternative labels are possible because we do not have network data designed to measure trust.

In the end, there is no argument that transforms our data into the kind of data now needed. Third-party effects will remain ambiguous until studied under stronger control conditions with respect to time. Time should be monitored in the criterion variable. Trust is a response to exchange with time asymmetry. Our trust variable is a sociometric response to a hypothetical situation (with whom would you discuss moving to another firm). Time should be monitored in the predictor variable. The gossip argument has ego trust affected by third parties telling stories. Our network data describe the residue of working relations accumulated over time. Accurate estimates of third-party effects require knowing when third-party stories are relayed to ego and ego's willingness to trust alter before and after receiving the stories. There are numerous variables in that sentence. It is not clear that the third-party effects are triggered by the story received, or the aggregate of stories received, or the concentration of stories in a brief period of time—all of which is the challenge for future work.

Acknowledgements

Authors' Note: The results reported here were first presented at Rod Kramer and Tom Tyler's May 1994 Stanford University conference on Trust in Organizations. We owe a note of gratitude to the conference participants for the lively debate that sharpened the argument. In particular, discussion with Bob Gibbons sharpened our argument about how third parties amplify trust and distrust, discussion with Rod Kramer sharpened our analysis of cliques and group affiliation effects, and Blair Sheppard's and Bob Bies's comments sharpened our discussion of how distrust builds in indirect connections through exclusive third parties to define the "ambient heat" of an organization.

Notes

1. The full disclosure argument can be stated in terms of full information. No individual knows everyone else. Indirect connections between ego and alter provide alternative communication channels and so increase the probability that ego is fully informed about alter's past behavior. Fully informed means that ego is more certain of his or her trust in alter. Whether the stories relayed through indirect connections improve ego's information on alter, or give ego a feeling of vicarious play in repeated games with alter, the end result is the same—ego is more certain of his or her trust in alter.

2. The step from full disclosure to partial disclosure introduces the complication of predicting what is disclosed and what is not disclosed. We make two key assumptions for this introductory analysis: (a) Ego, accustomed to using third parties as background informants on other people, is similarly affected by full and partial disclosure third-party stories about alter; (b) third parties, to sustain and strengthen their relation with ego, are more likely to disclose to ego experiences with alter that are consistent with ego's opinion of alter. We make these assumptions because we believe they are by and large correct, and our principal analytical concern is to

establish third-party effects, postponing for future research the task of elaborating how third-party effects vary across (a) managers varyingly susceptible to third-party gossip, and (b) third parties who selectively communicate stories consistent with ego's opinion of alter, and strategically communicate stories to revise ego's opinion to be more consistent with the third party's opinion. We return to these issues at the end of this chapter.

3. Although not directly concerned with trust, two lines of work describe a dark side to network density relevant to our analysis of trust. One concerns the extent to which a person is subject to the social pressure of interpersonal influence and sanctions. With interpersonal influence stronger within dense networks, it is easier to impose sanctions within a dense network. This is the subject of a rich literature in political science and sociology, but Coleman's (1990, ch. 11) analysis of social norms is a rational choice exemplar. Small (incremental) sanctions within a dense network can aggregate to a large effect (e.g., pp. 278 ff on negative reputation, and pp. 284 ff on gossip facilitating sanctions by creating or clarifying norms). If distrust is the emotion that accompanies sanction, then dense networks, by intensifying sanctions, intensify distrust. So viewed, our positive and negative density effects on trust merely combine and give functional form to what Coleman has already analyzed, but as separate phenomena; trust strengthened within dense networks and sanctions strengthened within dense networks.

Network theories of competition are a second caveat to our statement about the neglect of density's dark side. Reversing the concerns of the work just described, this line of work concerns the extent to which a person can negotiate the social pressure of interpersonal influence and sanctions. Building on Simmel's ([1922] 1955) and Merton's ([1957] 1968) analyses of conflicting affiliations, network theories of competition describe the information and control advantages of building relations with contacts in disconnected groups (e.g., Burt 1992, 30–6, on structural holes and entrepreneurs). Sparse networks provide broader information access and more opportunities to control exchange relations. Illustrations are Cook and others' (1983) experiments showing how resources accumulate to people at the crossroads in networks, Krackhardt and Stern's (1988) experiments showing higher group performance with cross-group friendships, or Burt's (1992) and Podolny and Baron's (1994) manager surveys showing the promotion advantage of having strong connections to otherwise disconnected groups. Direct application to trust production implies that successful managers build trust in private games (maintaining a sparse network of nonredundant contacts), while less successful managers find themselves in public games (which results in a dense network of mutual friends). Results on the managers studied here are interestingly more complex and available elsewhere (Burt and Knez 1995a).

4. Lindenberg and Frey (1993) discuss more general parameters in ego's rational choice of frame. Our argument is that ego's frame on alter, whatever it is, is reinforced in conversations with third parties. This alleviates the monitoring problem that Hechter (1987; 1990, 243–4) highlights in his argument about dependence and formal control being necessary conditions for group solidarity. Hechter (1987, 73–7) takes issue with Axelrod's (1984, chap. 4) use of the live-and-let-live system of

trench warfare to illustrate the idea that cooperation emerges in even the most difficult circumstances if players anticipate future interaction with one another. Hechter stresses the implicit monitoring necessary to the live-and-let-live system, the difficulty of monitoring even between the two armies, which is analogous to a two-player game, and the implausibility of that monitoring (without formal controls) in games of more than two players. In other words, cooperation is more difficult in larger groups. Hechter's argument presumes the perfect information condition that everyone monitors everyone else, whereupon monitoring is more difficult in larger groups. The gossip argument is less demanding. Everyone is relatively ignorant, but increasingly informed by third parties with increasing indirect connection. All it takes is one third party to relay stories between a pair of people. Systemic properties of amplified trust and distrust emerge from the microsocial context around individual pairs of people. The monitoring problem reduces to realistic proportions. The whole population does not monitor your behavior, just your closest friends and co-workers (cf. Janowitz and Shils [1948] 1991, on why the German Wehrmacht continued to function despite repeated defeats during World WarII—monitoring was between buddies in the squad, and the army was a system of interlocked squads).

5. Let z_{ij} be the intensity of closeness between persons i and j, scaled from the response categories describing relations with and among manager contacts (Burt 1992, 125–6). The proportional strength of manager i's relation with contact j (p_{ij}) is z_{ij} divided by the sum of the manager's relations ($\Sigma_q z_{iq}$). The indirect connection between manager i and contact j is measured as in the original study by the proportion of a manager's network that leads through intermediaries q back to contact j ($\Sigma_q P_{iq} P_{qj}$, q $\neq$ i, j), We multiply the proportional strength measures by 100 to discuss points of change. Direct connection varies from 1 to 25 points with a mean of 7.9, and indirect connection varies from 0 to 32 points around a mean of 11.7 points. To create the dichotomy between little and much indirect connection for Figure 2, we graphed probabilities of trust and distrust across levels of indirect connection. Cutting the data where the lines of trust and distrust cross, we treat less than 15 points of indirect connection as little and above that as much. This justifies our cut point between much and little indirect connection by the shift in its effect on trust. We also ran the analysis with slightly higher and lower cut points, and obtained the same results. We do not want to make too much of the little-much distinction. The point introduced in Figure 2 is supported by the results in Table 1 with continuous measures of indirect connection.

6. Unless you have no future in the firm. The citations to people for job option discussions could be from managers so unhappy in the firm, or so unsuccessful, that they have nothing to lose by talking about moving to another firm. This does not seem to be the case. First, most managers have someone they would turn to. All but three managers cite contacts with whom they would discuss job options. Only 22 limit that discussion to contacts outside the firm. Second, there is no tendency for satisfied or successful managers to cite fewer contacts. Satisfaction is uncorrelated with number of people cited for job option discussion (.02 correlation). Managers are distinguished in Burt (1992, 126–31) by the extent to which they were promoted

early to their current job. This measure of manager success, strongly correlated with network structure, has no correlation with the number of people cited for job option discussion (.05 correlation).

7. Two potential complications turn out to be minor in these data: (a) the assumed equal intervals between trust, neutral, and distrust, and (b) managers who cite a person for both trust and distrust. On issue (b), seven contacts are cited for trust and distrust and the circumstances vary. The one thing consistent across the seven trust-distrust relations is extensive indirect connections. The manager did not trust the contact, but would have to let him know about plans to move to another firm. Taking the distrust component more seriously, we assign the seven trust-distrust relations to the distrust category. This seems a minor issue because we get the same pattern of *t* tests in Table 1 if the seven trust-distrust relations are coded as trust relations, or neutral relations. Discriminant analysis provides a more sophisticated solution to issues (a) and (b). The discriminant function is the linear combination of the four network variables in Table 1 that best predicts two dependent variables: trust and distrust. There is no assumption that the trust-neutral interval equals the interval between neutral and distrust because separate effects are estimated for trust and distrust. The seven trust-distrust relations remain as trust relations in the trust variable and distrust relations in the distrust variable. Most of the effect variation is captured in the first discriminant function (.53 canonical correlation, 82% of the covariance described by the two canonical correlations). Because there is so little overlap between trust and distrust, however, not much is gained with discriminant analysis. The discriminant function scores are correlated .985 with scores for the three-category trust variable predicted from the regression model in Table 1. The Table 1 regression model is simpler, easier to use for significance tests, and yields predictions almost identical to the more sophisticated discriminant function model. We use the Table 1 regression model, but note that collapsing trust and distrust into a single variable will not be reasonable in all study populations.

8. Trust and distrust are extremely skewed binary dependent variables: 791 of the 3,584 contacts are cited for trust, and only 263 are cited for distrust. Logit results for the continuous variables in Table 1 yield the same relative magnitudes of test statistics for trust (*t* test $= 12.3$ for direct connection, *t* test $= 7.8$ for indirect connection around strong relations), and similar test statistics for distrust (*t* test $= -10.6$ for direct connection, *t* test $= 2.6$ for indirect connection around weak relations; and see Burt and Knez 1995b, tab. 1, for similar log-linear results). We focus on ordinary least squares (OLS) results in the text because the metric regression coefficients are more likely familiar to readers, and we reach the same conclusions with logit results. The results for the "combined" variable in Table 1 are valuable because we can take advantage of the ordering between trust and distrust responses to create a less skewed criterion variable more appropriate for OLS estimators.

9. We have 3,584 relationships elicited from 284 managers. The effect estimates are based on the assumption that each relation is an independent observation. The managers are a probability sample, but their relationships are a cluster probability sample (each manager's network a cluster). If relations are autocorrelated within

clusters, the number of independent observations is less than 3,584 and test statistics based on dyad counts are exaggerated. We reestimated the equations predicting the three-category trust variable, adding 283 dummy variables to distinguish managers. There is autocorrelation, but it is concentrated in a minority of managers. There are 70 managers whose dummy variable increases or decreases trust by more than one point. The weakest of these is quite negligible (t test $= 0.1$). We get the bracketed t tests in Table 1 when dummy variables for all 70 managers are included in the model.

10. The displayed logit equations contain effects estimated from the data in Table 1 on relations within the firm. The effects are significant (t tests $= 12.1$ and 5.9 for trust equation, t tests $= -10.4$ and 2.3 for distrust equation; cf. Note 8 for similar tests when effects are estimated from relations within and beyond the firm). To generate the probability of trust and distrust between isolated pairs of people (thin lines in Figure 3), we computed probabilities with INDIRECT set to zero, which means the interaction term drops out of each logit equation (leaving a single predictor, DIRECT, which is $100P_{ij}$). To illustrate amplification through indirect connections (bold lines in Figure 3), (a) we do not know whether relations are especially close or less close, so we let STRONG $=$ pij, WEAK $=$ be a continuous function of relation strength (STRONG $=$ pij, WEAK $= 1 -$ pij), and (b) we set indirect connection to the maximum possible given the proportion of a manager's network allocated to direct connection (INDIRECT $= 100 - 100P_{ij}$).

11. Social structure's different associations with the positive and negative in Figure 3 are suspicious. The different functional forms are consistent with the different measurement criteria in these data. Trust is measured with a criterion of discussing job options. Distrust is measured with a more severe criterion of naming the manager's most difficult co-worker. Tests with more severe trust criteria merely shift the gradually increasing trust function to stronger relations (Burt and Knez 1995b, fig. 3). In other words, the different functional forms for trust and distrust in Figure 3 are not created by the different criteria for positive and negative relationships.

12. There is also the issue of whether emotional closeness should be measured in terms of absolute rather than relative closeness. A proportional strength of .1 could be from a manager especially close to 10 contacts, or less close to 10 contacts. To test for volume, we added the sum of a manager's relations—the denominator for the proportional strength measure—to the all-dyad equation predicting three-category trust in Table 1. Trust is slightly more likely from managers with a higher volume of emotional closeness (t test $= 2.3$), but the effect disappears when autocorrelation is held constant (t test $= 1.7$, see note 9).

13. Strong relations emerge from frequent contact. The more often you bump into the same person in your neighborhood, at social functions, in meetings, the more likely you will eventually say hello and come to know one another. Friendships develop. The process is enhanced by the increased chances that you know some of the same people at these places, which further increases the chances of meeting one another with things in common. Festinger, Schachter, and Back's (1950) study of physical proximity effects on friendship patterns remains the classic empirical

study (with Homans 1950, the related theoretical work). Feld's (1981, 1982) analysis of social foci generalizes the process by linking it to homophily—people with similar socially significant attributes (occupation, age, etc.) are likely to bump into one another in the same places and have mutual friends in those places. We find no evidence of frequency affecting trust above and beyond the factors in Table 1. Figure 1 shows that trust is more likely between people who meet frequently, and distrust more likely when people rarely meet, but the significant zero-order association between contact frequency and the three-category trust variable in Table 1 (t test $= 9.7$), is negligible after direct and indirect closeness are held constant (t test $= 0.1$ for frequency when added to the equation in the last column of Table 1).

14. The data distinguish four levels of manager-contact closeness, three levels between the contacts. Quantitative scores given the levels with an association model of the data make it easy to define relations for Figure 4 (Burt 1992, 287–8). From the manager (ego to third parties), bold lines are especially close or close relationships (closeness scores z_{ij} of 1.0 or .69), and dashed lines are less close or distant relations (z_{ij} of .36 or .01). Between cited contacts (alter and the third parties), bold lines are especially close relations (z_{ij} of 1.0), dashed lines are close (z_{ij} of .34), and missing lines are between people who "do not enjoy one another's company, finding it unpleasant to be together or work together" (z_{ij} of 0.0).

15. To learn more about the people who play each third party role, we recomputed the counts of third parties. Instead of counting third parties between manager and alter, we counted the number of times that alter played each third-party role with respect to each of the manager's other contacts. With these data, we can study the kinds of relations managers have with each kind of third party (see Burt and Knez 1995a, for log-linear results). The two kinds of mutual third parties come from different places. TP1 mutuals are most often contacts outside the firm or colleagues with whom the manager discusses important personal matters and frequently gets together for informal lunch, dinner, home visits, and so on. TP2 mutuals are in the manager's network because they are the manager's boss or essential sources of support for projects.

16. Variable E is the probability that a randomly selected third party to the relationship is exclusive and not mutual: $E = PE(1 - PM)$, where PE is the proportion of third parties around a relationship that are exclusives, and PM is the proportion mutuals (see Burt and Knez 1995a, for detailed analysis of E in terms of the ambient heat of a relationship). For example, consider the relation between one of the managers, call him John, and his boss. John cites 14 important contacts, so there are 13 indirect connections to the boss through other contacts. The 13 indirect connections are 10 through people close to John and the boss, 1 through someone distant from John and his boss, and 2 through people closer to John than his boss. John's relationship with his supervisor is embedded in 77% mutual third parties (10/13) and 15% exclusive third parties (2/13). The balance is away from exclusive third parties (E is .03).

17. Balance toward exclusive third parties is significantly lower around especially close relations than around close, less close, and distant relations (t test $= -7.7$ for mean E in especially close vs. other).

18. This potential animates the facilitator role of consultants. An outsider trustworthy to two groups is brought in to help the two groups cooperate. Sabel's (1993) concept of studied trust is a useful illustration we elaborate elsewhere (Burt and Knez 1995a; cf. Perrow 1992, 461, on network conditions for trust production). The examples also illustrate the importance of having the newly cooperative people take over their cooperative relations as they build in strength. The mutual third party is like the first-stage rocket launching a space vehicle—critical for getting the thing off the ground, best discarded soon thereafter.

19. The product is the joint probability if trust and distrust are independent. We do not believe they are (although there could be an analogy to independent positive and negative affect; Bradburn 1965). The probability of trusting someone is likely contingent on whether there is any reason to distrust the person. This is a subtlety for future research. Joint probability under independent trust and distrust is sufficient to illustrate the points we wish to make here.

References

Axelrod, Robert. 1984. *The evolution of cooperation*. New York: Basic Books.

Barber, Bernard. 1983. *The logic and limits of trust*. New Brunswick: Rutgers University Press.

Blau, Peter M. 1964. *Exchange and power in social life*. New York: Wiley.

—— 1968. Interaction: Social exchange. In *The international encyclopedia of the social sciences*, edited by David L. Sills. New York: Free Press and Macmillan.

Bradach, Jeffrey L., and Robert G. Eccles. 1989. Price, authority, and trust: From ideal types to plural forms. *Annual Review of Sociology* 15:97–118.

Bradburn, Norman. 1965. *Reports on happiness*. Chicago: Aldine.

Burt, Ronald S. 1982. *Toward a structural theory of action*. New York: Academic Press.

—— 1987. Social contagion and innovation: Cohesion versus structural equivalence. *American Journal of Sociology* 92:1287–335.

—— 1990. Kinds of relations in American discussion networks. In *Structures of power and constraint*, edited by Craig Calhoun, Marshall W. Meyer, and W. Richard Scott, 411–51. New York: Cambridge University Press.

—— 1992. *Structural holes: The social structure of competition*. Cambridge: Harvard University Press.

Burt, Ronald S., and Norm Celotto. 1992. The network structure of management roles in a large matrix firm. *Evaluation and Program Planning* 15:303–26.

Burt, Ronald S., and Marc Knez. 1995a. Trust and third parties: The social production of cooperation. Unpublished manuscript, Graduate School of Business, University of Chicago.

Ronald S. Burt and Marc Knez

Burt, Ronald S., 1995b. Trust and third-party gossip. In *Trust in organizations*, edited by Rod Kramer and Tom Tyler. Thousand Oaks, CA: Sage.

Coleman, James S. 1990. *Foundations of social theory.* Cambridge: Harvard University Press.

Cook, Karen S., Richard M. Emerson, Mary R. Gillmore, and Toshio Yamagishi. 1983. The distribution of power in exchange networks: Theory and experimental results. *American Journal of Sociology* 89:275–305.

Davis, James A. 1970. Clustering and hierarchy in interpersonal relations: Testing two graph theoretical models on 742 sociograms. *American Sociological Review* 35:843–52.

DeSoto, Clinton B. 1960. Learning a social structure. *Journal of Abnormal and Social Psychology* 60:417–21.

Ekeh, Peter P. 1974. *Social exchange theory.* Cambridge: Harvard University Press.

Feld, Scott L. 1981. The focused organization of social ties. *American Journal of Sociology* 86:1015–35.

—— 1982. Social structural determinants of similarity. *American Sociological Review* 47:797–801.

Festinger, Leon, Stanley Schachter, and Kurt W. Back. 1950. *Social pressures in informal groups.* Stanford: Stanford University Press.

Freeman, Linton C., A. Kimball Romney, and Sue C. Freeman. 1987. Cognitive structure and informant accuracy. *American Anthropologist* 89:310–25.

Gartrell, C, David. 1987. Network approaches to social evaluation. *Annual Review of Sociology* 13:49–66.

Gibbons, Robert. 1992. *Game theory for applied economists.* Princeton: Princeton University Press.

Granovetter, Mark S. 1985. Economic action, social structure, and embeddedness. *American Journal of Sociology* 91:481–510.

—— 1992. Problems of explanation in economic sociology. In *Networks and organization*, edited by Nitin Nohria and Robert G. Eccles, 25–56. Boston: Harvard Business School Press.

Hardin, Russell. 1990. The social evolution of cooperation. In *The limits of rationality*, edited by Karen S. Cook and Margaret Levi, 358–78. Chicago: University of Chicago Press.

Hastorf, A. H., and H. Cantril. 1954. The saw game: A case study. *Journal of Abnormal and Social Psychology* 49:129–34.

Hechter, Michael. 1987. *Principles of group solidarity.* Berkeley: University of California Press.

—— 1990. On the inadequacy of game theory for the solution of real-world collective action problems. In *The limits of rationality*, edited by Karen S. Cook and Margaret Levi, 240–9. Chicago: University of Chicago Press.

Homans, George C. 1950. *The human group.* New York: Harcourt, Brace and World.

—— 1961. *Social behavior: Its elementary forms.* New York: Harcourt, Brace and World.

Ibarra, Herminia. 1992. Homophily and differential returns: Sex differences in network structure and access in an advertising firm. *Administrative Science Quarterly* 37:422–47.

—— 1994. Untangling the web of interconnections: Pragmatics of gender differences in managerial networks. Harvard University Graduate School of Business Working Paper No. 93–044.

Janowitz, Morris, and Edward A. Shils. [1948] 1991. Cohesion and disintegration in the Wehrmacht in World War II. In *On social organization and social control*, edited by James Burk, 160–75. Chicago: University of Chicago Press.

Kanter, Rosabeth M. 1984. *The change masters: Innovation and entrepreneurship in the American corporation.* New York: Simon & Schuster.

Kilduff, Martin. 1992. The friendship network as a decision-making resource: Dispositional moderators of social influences on organizational choice. *Journal of Personality and Social Psychology* 62:168–80.

Kilduff, Martin, and David Krackhardt. 1994. Bringing the individual back in: A structural analysis of the internal market for reputation in organizations. *Academy of Management Journal* 37:87–108.

Krackhardt, David. 1990. Assessing the political landscape: Structure, cognition, and power in organizations. *Administrative Science Quarterly* 35:342–69.

Krackhardt, David, and Robert N. Stern. 1988. Informal networks and organizational crisis: An experimental simulation. *Social Psychology Quarterly* 51:123–40.

Kreps, David M. 1990. Corporate culture and economic theory. In *Perspectives on positive political economy,* edited by J. Alt and Kenneth Shepsle, 90–143. New York: Cambridge University Press.

Larson, Andrea. 1992. Network dyads in entrepreneurial settings: A study of the governance of exchange relationships, *Administrative Science Quarterly* 37:76–104.

Lindenberg, Siegwart, and Bruno S. Frey. 1993. Alternatives, frames, and relative prices: A broader view of rational choice theory. *Acta Sociologica* 36:191–205.

Lindzey, Gardner, and Elliot Aronson, eds. 1985. *Handbook of social psychology.* Vol. 2, *Special fields and applications.* New York: Random House.

Merton, Robert K., ed. [1957] 1968. Continuities in the theory of reference group behavior. In *Social theory and social structure.* New York: Free Press.

Nohria, Nitin, and Robert G. Eccles, eds. 1992. *Networks and organizations.* Boston: Harvard Business School Press.

Perrow, Charles. 1992, Small-firm networks. In *Networks and organizations*, edited by Nitin Nohria and Robert G. Eccles, 445–70. Boston: Harvard Business School Press.

Pfeffer, Jeffrey, Gerald R. Salancik, and H. Leblebici. 1976. The effect of uncertainty on the use of social influence in organization decision-making. *Administrative Science Quarterly* 21:227–45.

Podolny, Joel M., and James N. Baron. 1994. Make new friends and keep the old?: Social networks, mobility, and satisfaction in the workplace. Unpublished paper, Graduate School of Business, Stanford University.

Powell, Walter W., and Laurel Smith-Doerr. 1994. Networks and economic life. In *The handbook of economic sociology,* edited by Neil J. Smelser and Richard Swedberg, 368–402. Princeton: Princeton University Press.

Prendergast, Canice. 1993. A theory of "yes men." *American Economic Review* 83:757–70.

Ross, Lee, and Craig A. Anderson. 1982. Shortcomings in the attribution process: On the origins and maintenance of erroneous social assessments. In *Judgment under uncertainty: Heuristics and biases*, edited by Daniel Kahneman, Paul Slovic, and Amos Tversky, 129–52. Cambridge: Cambridge University Press.

Sabel, Charles F. 1993. Studied trust: Building new forms of cooperation in a volatile economy. In *Explorations in economic sociology*, edited by Richard Swedberg, 104–44. New York: Russell Sage.

Simmel, Georg. [1922] 1955. *Conflict and the web of group affiliations*. Translated by K. H. Wolff and R. Bendix. New York: Free Press.

Sitkin, Sim B., and Nancy L. Roth. 1993. Explaining the limited effectiveness of legalistic "remedies" for trust/distrust. *Organization Science* 4:367–92.

Smelser, Neil J., and Richard Swedberg, eds. 1994. *Handbook of economic sociology*. Princeton: Princeton University Press.

Stinchcombe, Arthur L. 1990. *Information and organizations*. Berkeley: University of California Press.

Swedberg, Richard, ed. 1993. *Explorations in economic sociology*. New York: Russell Sage.

White, Harrison C. 1992. *Identity and control*. Princeton: Princeton University Press.

Zucker, Lynne G. [1977] 1991. The role of institutionalization in cultural persistence. In *The new institutionalism in organizational analysis*, edited by Walter W. Powell and Paul J. DiMaggio, 83–107. Chicago: University of Chicago Press.

—— 1986. Production of trust: Institutional sources of economic structure, 1840–1920. *Research in Organizational Behavior* 8:53–111.

9

Does Trust Improve Business Performance?*

Mari Sako

Does trust improve business performance? And if so, how can trust be created in business where there is none? These are the two questions which this chapter addresses. The main aim of the chapter is to evaluate various theories which touch on the causes and outcomes of trust, and to provide empirical tests of those theories using a large-scale survey of automotive parts suppliers in the United States, Europe, and Japan.

A growing interest in building trust between organizations stems from the belief that trust enhances business performance. For instance, trust has been identified as an important component which makes partnerships, strategic alliances, and networks of small firms successful (Brusco 1986; Powell 1996; Smitka 1991). Trust is also of great relevance today because the maintenance of consistently high quality, which is an important source of competitiveness, is easier in a high-trust production system than in a low-trust one (Sako 1992). In a similar vein, Fukuyama (1995) attributes national industrial competitiveness to trust as a societal-level cultural norm and a social capital. According to him, people's capacity to institutionalize trust in the realm of work and business accounts for the industrial success in Japan and Germany. By contrast, the "missing middle", namely the absence of intermediate social groups in the area between the family and large, centralized organizations like the Church or the State, accounts for the relative economic backwardness of Latin Catholic countries (like Italy, France, and Spain) and Chinese societies (Fukuyama 1995: 55–6).

* The author acknowledges the funding support of the International Motor Vehicle Program (ZMVP) at MIT which made this study possible. I also thank Susan Helper for entering into a high-trust loose reciprocity research collaboration, in particular for allowing me to use the US data she collected for this paper.

In Fukuyama's (1995) study, as in others, the link between trust and business performance is plausible but not proven. Nevertheless, the idea is so appealing that at the practitioner level, an increasing number of studies exhort business to create trust as an essential component in making partnerships between firms successful (SMMT and DTI 1994; Ingersoll Engineers 1995). In business strategy, recent work on trust between organizations focuses on the possibility of using it to create and maintain competitive advantage (Barney and Hansen 1994; Jarillo 1988). While theoretical explorations on the link between trust and performance abound, empirical studies in this area are rare (exceptions include Mohr and Spekman 1994). This chapter presents evidence which fills this lacuna.

The second, related, question which this paper addresses—how can trust be created when there is none?—has been the subject of much debate. The extreme positions in this debate are held by those who argue that trust can be cultivated intentionally by farsighted parties who recognize the benefits of long-term co-operation (Axelrod 1984), and those who argue that it is a by-product of the embeddedness of parties who share a common cultural or social norm (Granovetter 1985). Both approaches are not very helpful for thinking about how to create trust when there is none. In the former, if the parties are not farsighted enough, or if they are antagonistic from the start, a process of co-operation may never get started. In the latter, those living in communities which are already endowed with high trust can benefit from it, but those without it are doomed to suffer from the adverse consequences of low trust. This chapter examines whether the two extreme views can be reconciled.

The central concept explored in this chapter is mutual trust between a customer and a supplier organization. Trust is an expectation held by an agent that its trading partner will behave in a mutually acceptable manner (including an expectation that neither party will exploit the other's vulnerabilities). This expectation narrows the set of possible actions, thus reducing the uncertainty surrounding the partner's actions. The notion of trust implies that the partner has freedom of choice to take alternative courses of action. Thus, predictability in behavior arises not because of constraints which force the other side to stick to a single possible course of action. Sako (1991, 1992) categorized other reasons for predictability in behavior to distinguish between three types of trust: "contractual trust" (will the other party carry out its contractual agreements?), "competence trust" (is the other party capable of doing what it says it will do?), and "goodwill trust" (will the other party make an open-ended commitment to take initiatives for mutual benefit while refraining from unfair advantage taking?). This three-way distinction will be employed throughout this chapter.

Contractual trust rests on a shared moral norm of honesty and promise-keeping. Competence trust requires a shared understanding of professional conduct and technical and managerial standards. Goodwill trust can exist only when there is consensus on the principle of fairness. Viewed in this way, there seems to be a hierarchy of trust, with fulfilling a minimum set of obligations constituting "contractual trust", and honoring a broader set constituting "goodwill trust". A move from contractual trust to goodwill trust involves a gradual expansion in the congruence in beliefs about what is acceptable behavior. Because of the three-way distinction made in the concept of trust, opportunism, defined as self-interest seeking with guile by Williamson (1985), is not a mere opposite of trust. A precondition for trust of the contractual and goodwill types is the absence of opportunistic behavior. However, lack of opportunism is not a sufficient condition for goodwill trust. For example, a supplier that withholds a vital piece of technical information may not be acting opportunistically according to the strict contractual sense. This amounts to fulfilling the letter, but not the spirit, of the contract. Fulfilling the spirit of the contract, by demonstrating commitment and fair behavior, is close to the notion of goodwill trust.

The chapter is structured as follows. Section 1 reviews various theories which address the issue of whether trust enhances business performance or not. The evidence from a large-scale survey on the impact of trust on supplier performance is reported. Section 2 discusses how trust can be created between organizations particularly when they are in low trust relationships. This section also reports the results of the survey concerning the determinants of trust and opportunism. Section 3 concludes by drawing theoretical and empirical implications of this study.

....

Does Interorganizational Trust Enhance Business Performance?

Interorganizational trust may enhance business performance in a number of ways. This section reviews some of the major works by categorizing them broadly into those which focus on (a) reducing transaction costs, (b) investment with future returns, and (c) continuous improvement and learning. The last subsection presents empirical evidence.

Before doing so, however, a brief word on the link between the notion of interorganizational trust and governance. In organizational studies, it has been common to treat trust either as a determinant of "governance structure" or as a governance structure in itself. "Governance mechanisms" include such formal arrangements as markets, hierarchies, and intermediate modes including long-term contracts, joint ventures and other forms of alliances (Heide and John 1990; Joskow 1988; Walker and Weber 1984; Williamson 1985). Trust or opportunism enter into some of these analyses as one of the determinants of governance structures. For example, trust is a social norm which lessens the need to use hierarchy to attenuate opportunism. Thus, the higher the general level of trust, the less need there is for vertical integration (Williamson 1985). Similarly, the higher the dyadic trust which develops over time, the less need there is to rely on equity-holding (Gulati 1995). Here, trust tends to be conceptualized as a substitute for various governance mechanisms. The notion of governance structure is closely linked to the idea of "safeguards" against opportunistic behavior. Such safeguards, i.e. externally imposed constraints, become unnecessary if actors have an internalized moral norm of behaving in a trustworthy manner. This view of trust as a determinant of governance structures is dominant in the functionalist perspective represented by transaction cost-economics, which argues for an effective alignment of governance structures with transactional characteristics (see below).

An alternative conception is to regard trust as a governance structure, albeit an informal one. "Governance by trust" is an informal control mechanism which enhances the effectiveness of transactions whether they take place in markets or within a hierarchy (Smitka 1991). This conceptualization introduces the possibility that trust may complement, rather than substitute for, hierarchy or market (Bradach and Eccles 1989; Smitka 1992). This paper adopts this "governance by trust" perspective. It posits that trust exists to a varying degree in different types of formal governance structures, be they markets, long-term contracts, or hierarchies. Whatever the formal governance structures, the higher the level of mutual trust, the better the performance is likely to be. While formal governance structures may act as "safeguards" against opportunistic behavior, they are, in themselves, not sufficient to ensure the sort of performance—innovation and learning—which trust induces.

Reducing Transaction Costs

The performance criterion used by transaction-cost economics (TCE) is the minimization of transaction costs. This is achieved by aligning governance structures to the characteristics of the transaction. In particular, whenever the environment is uncertain and specific assets are required in a transaction, both parties have an incentive to behave opportunistically. Depending on the frequency of trading which determines the costs of recontracting, Williamson (1979) prescribes either vertical integration or relational contracting. In this framework, as long as optimal decisions are made, every governance structure is just as efficient as another at the margin.

The TCE paradigm has been so influential that the minimization of transaction costs is taken as a performance objective even in other areas, such as strategic management. Strategic management is about how firms can create and sustain competitive advantage. For instance, it is said that trust enables a network of firms to adapt to unforeseen circumstances, thus reducing transaction costs; in this sense firms can make use of the network strategically (Jarillo 1988). More recently, Barney and Hansen (1994) examine trustworthiness as a source of competitive advantage. They make a distinction among three types of trust: weak form, semi-strong form, and strong form trust. Weak form trust emerges because there are limited opportunities for opportunism. Semi-strong form trust depends on governance devices such as a market for reputation and contracts to safeguard against the threat of opportunism. Strong form trust emerges in response to a set of internalized norms and principles that guide the behavior of exchange partners, and is independent of whether or not specific governance mechanisms exist. (In the three ways employed in this chapter, goodwill trust corresponds roughly to strong form trust, and contractual trust to semi-strong trust.) They argue that only strong form trust leads to competitive advantage. The basis for arguing so is that first, strong form trust is more difficult to imitate than weak form or semi-strong form trust. Second, with strong form trust, less safeguards are needed in the form of governance structures, and therefore it is less costly for the firm.

Investment to Increase Future Returns

This last assertion depends on the time period which is taken into account. Once strong form trust is built and established, firms may enjoy lower costs than those without. But it is quite possible that the process of building trust might have involved a very high initial set-up cost with uncertain or risky returns. A British purchasing manager in a recent interview said that trusting a new supplier requires a leap of faith, even if there are some objective quality standards such as ISO 9000. This is because the formal documentation sought in an initial supplier audit is not revealing about how the quality standard is actually implemented, but the latter is difficult to capture fully in a short visit. Building trust in itself is an investment, and trust between a buyer and a supplier is a "relation-specific skill" (Asanuma 1989). The returns to investment may be in terms of low monitoring and co-ordination costs—the agency costs in principal–agent theory—and it is this aspect which enables such practices as just-in-time delivery and no quality inspection on delivery. However, at any time, a buyer and a supplier which have just begun trading and are in the process of building a high-trust relationship may be incurring a greater set-up cost than other companies in low-trust relationships. This in turn leads to a hypothesis that the older the trading relationship, the greater the gap in performance between high-trust and low-trust supplier relations, assuming that the parties have been following a strategy of developing mutual trust during the whole period of the trading relationship.

Suppliers in a high-trust trading relationship are also willing to invest in customer-specific and general assets because of the assumed long-term commitment in such a relationship. Greater investment in itself may be considered a performance measure. At the same time, asset specialization is likely to increase productivity (Dyer, forthcoming). Following Williamson (1985), specific assets consist not only of physical capital, but also of human capital and location.

Continuous Improvement and Learning

The third and last perspective argues that trust, especially of the goodwill sort, gives rise not only to lower transaction costs or to higher net benefits from investment, but also to more rapid innovation and learning (Sabel 1994). In other words, suppliers in high-trust relations are likely to exploit opportunities to the mutual benefit of both the customer and the supplier, which would otherwise not have been exploited had transactions depended solely on contracts or "incentives". As trust is linked to the notion of "freewill" choice and is seen to obviate the use of "safeguards" or constraints, trust gives that something extra, a positive motivational force which enhances X-efficiency and dynamic efficiency. These outcomes are achieved through an orientation towards joint problem solving to improve quality, to reduce costs, and to innovate production and management methods. Such collaboration between a customer and a supplier leads to learning-by-transacting. This implies that even after trust is built and established, trading partners which are performing well are likely to interact intensively. Thus, unlike in the previous investment perspective, the cost of interaction, if imputed by time spent by all the multifunctional personnel involved in interfacing between suppliers and customers, may be quite high. Trust is therefore like a renewable resource which atrophies with disuse and multiplies with use.

Survey Evidence

The main reason for the relative absence of empirical work to date lies in the characteristics of the relevant theories. In particular, the functionalist approach of TCE asserts that whatever governance structure exists is best for the organization given its environment and circumstances. This has led many researchers to test the determinants of governance structures but not the performance outcomes of these structures. Moreover, all the aforementioned three approaches to linking trust to performance put forward measures which are difficult to quantify, such as transaction costs, net benefit of investment in trust, learning, and innovation. Ideally, also, longitudinal, rather than cross-sectional, studies are necessary in order to unravel the direction of causation between trust building and perform-ance. The survey evidence presented in this chapter does not fully overcome the measurement nor the causation problems, but constitutes an attempt at address-ing the question of whether trust enhances performance.

The data used to explore the links between trust and performance were collected by the author and Susan Helper during 1993 and 1994. The data consist of 1,415 valid responses from first-tier component suppliers in the automotive industry in Japan, the USA, and Europe.

The survey asked respondents to evaluate how much trust they could place on their customer. The items used to measure trust and opportunism in the questionnaire are shown in Table 1. Specifically, the concept of "contractual trust" is operationalized by the reversed statement "We prefer to have every-thing spelt out in detail in our contract"; this preference for detailed formal contracts is presumed to arise from the supplier's distrust that the customer would not stick to promises unless formally spelt out in a contract. The concept of "competence trust" is captured by a reversed statement "The advice our customer gives us is not always helpful". "Goodwill trust" is operationalized by the statement "We can rely on our customer to help us in ways not required by our agreement with them". The survey also asked about suppliers' perception of fairness which is a basis for the sustenance of goodwill trust. Lastly, customer opportunism was captured by the statement "Given the chance, our customer might try to take unfair advantage of our business unit".

In order to examine intercountry differences in trust, the data were divided into the following locations of the responding supplier companies: Japan, the USA, Britain, Germany, and the Latin Catholic countries with caution. But Britain was separated out to examine the supposed similarities with the USA. Germany and the Latin Catholic countries were distinguished in order to examine whether there is any evidence of a contrast between the "spontan-eously sociable" and the "missing middle" countries identified by Fukuyama (1995). The survey asked about interorganizational trust (suppliers' trust of customers). Therefore, we would expect organizational trust in Germany to be higher than in Latin Catholic countries where high interpersonal trust does not extend to trust between organizations.

As shown in Table 1, "contractual trust" is the highest in Germany and Japan, while the suppliers in the Anglo-American and Latin Catholic countries prefer less contractual flexibility. Japanese suppliers exhibit the highest level of "com-petence trust" towards their customer companies, while results for the other countries are mixed, with Latin Catholic suppliers exhibiting a rather high level of "competence trust" in contrast to German suppliers. "Goodwill trust" as measured in the survey is the highest among the Latin Catholic and German suppliers. The expectations about fair customer behavior are most evident among the Japanese suppliers, followed by the German and Latin Catholic

273

Mari Sako

Table 1. Trust and Opportunism in Japan, the USA, and Europe

	Japan (N=472)	USA (N=671)	Britain (N=123)	Germany (N=51)	Latin Catholic Europe (N=52)
Contractual trust (We prefer to have everything spelled out in detail in our contract)	24.03	16.62	15.25	27.45	14.00
Competence trust (The advice our customer gives us is not always helpful)	48.37	31.25	35.51	28.57	39.58
Goodwill trust (We can rely on our customer to help us in ways not required by our agreement with them)	38.81	37.24	42.50	50.00	64.00
Fairness (We can depend on our customer always to treat us fairly)	67.88	42.41	40.00	54.00	54.90
Customer opportunism (Given the chance, our customer might try to take unfair advantage of our business unit)	23.94	55.85	32.50	26.00	26.00

Note: The figures show the percentages responding 4 or 5 on a five-point scale (5=strongly agree; 4=agree; 3=neither agree nor disagree; 2=disagree; 1=strongly disagree). The statements for Contractual trust and Competence trust are reversed, so the figures are the percentages responding 1 or 2.

suppliers, while the majority of Anglo-American suppliers do not expect fair treatment from their customers. Lastly, customer opportunism is more prevalent in the USA and Britain than in Japan, Germany, or the Latin European countries. Although the results are broadly as expected, the anticipated distinction between Germany and the Latin Catholic countries is not evident in the survey.

Next, the impact of suppliers' trust of customers on supplier performance can be examined by looking at the following measures of performance used in the survey: suppliers' costs, profit margins, just-in-time (JIT) delivery, and joint problem solving. The cost measure is in terms of the average annual percentage change in the supplier's total costs for the product it supplied to the customer during the year preceding the survey. The profit measure was in terms of the average annual percentage point change in the supplier's gross margins for the product in the year preceding the survey. The degree of success in implementing JIT was measured by agreement to the statement "Use of JIT has allowed our business unit to increase delivery frequency without increasing costs". Joint problem solving, as an indicator of learning and innovation, was measured by the percentage of contact hours the supplier had with the customer which was for the purpose of "joint efforts to improve the product or process" (other options included 'assigning blame rather than solving problems').

Different types of trust may be presumed to have different impacts on supplier performance. Therefore each type of trust listed in Table 1 was correlated with each of the performance measures. The suppliers were divided into high-trust and low-trust groups, with the former consisting of those who agreed or strongly agreed with each of the statements. The t-test and Kruskal–Wallis test were applied to examine whether suppliers' performance was significantly different between the high-trust and low-trust groups. The five-way locational classification (into Japan, USA, Britain, Germany, and Latin Catholic countries) is applied in this analysis also.

The only type of trust with which the first measure of supplier performance, cost reduction, is associated significantly is goodwill trust. Moreover, when each region is examined separately, it is only in Japan that the high-trust group of suppliers performs significantly better in this respect than the low-trust group (see Figure 1). Although not statistically significant, high goodwill trust is associated with *less* cost reduction in Germany and the Latin Catholic countries. The scope for reducing costs may be considered to depend in part on the starting cost level; that is, the higher the initial cost, the greater the scope for cost reduction, and the lower the initial cost, the more difficult it is to effect further cost reduction at the margin. This argument makes it doubly surprising that Japanese suppliers in the high-trust group, which have been engaging in cost reduction activities for much longer than their counterparts in the USA or Europe, are the ones which have distinguished themselves in reducing costs further.

With respect to changes in suppliers' profit margins, interestingly it is only in the USA that all the five measures of trust (including the reverse of opportunism) listed in Table 1 are significantly associated with better profit margins (in the form of less profit squeeze). In none of the other countries is the profit

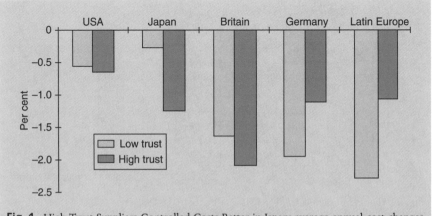

Fig. 1. High-Trust Suppliers Controlled Costs Better in Japan: average annual cost changes 1991/2–1992/3

performance between high-trust and low-trust groups significantly different (see Figure 2 which shows the result for goodwill trust only).

Next, high trust of all types was associated with suppliers being able to increase the frequency of delivery without increasing costs in the USA and Japan. However, in Europe only high goodwill trust significantly enhances JIT delivery in Britain and the Latin European countries (see Figure 3 for results on goodwill trust).

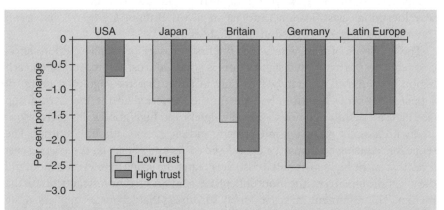

Fig. 2. High-Trust Suppliers Defended their Profit Margins Better in the USA: average annual percentage point change 1993/4

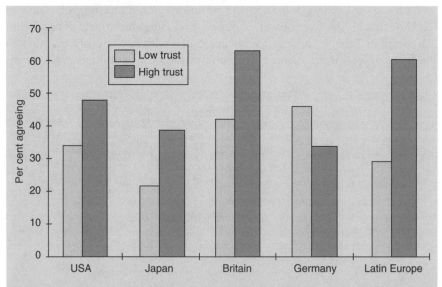

Fig. 3. High-Trust Suppliers Were Better at Just-in-Time Delivery ('Use of JIT has allowed our business unit to increase delivery frequency without increasing costs')

Lastly, high-trust suppliers were significantly more likely to spend a greater proportion of their contact time with customers in 'joint efforts to improve the product or process' in the USA and Japan, according to the measures of competence trust and goodwill trust. On average, suppliers with high goodwill trust in Japan spent 43 per cent of the total contact time in joint problem solving, as compared to 35 per cent for low-trust suppliers; the corresponding figures were 38 per cent and 30 per cent for high- and low-trust suppliers in the USA (see Figure 4). Although some differences exist between high- and low-trust groups in European countries, they were not statistically significant.

Since these are cross-sectional data, it could be that the causation runs the other way, from good performance (in the form of profit margin increase) to trust. However, it seems unlikely that cost reduction by the supplier causes it to increase its trust of customers, nor does it seem likely that better just-in-time delivery in itself increases suppliers' trust of customers.

To summarize the survey results concerning the trust-performance links, there is some support for the hypothesis that trust is conducive to good supplier performance and that this positive link is stronger for goodwill than for other types of trust. As predicted, suppliers spend more of their time in joint problem solving with their customers, the higher the level of goodwill and competence trust placed upon them. However, differences in the nature of the links between specific types of trust and specific performance measures are not fully explainable. In particular, the impact of good will trust on cost reduction is seen only among Japanese suppliers, while profit conditions are better for the high-trust group than for the low-trust.

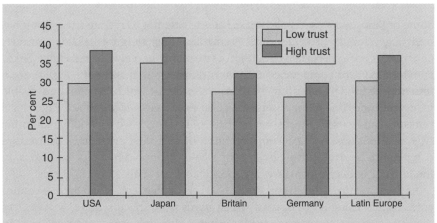

Fig. 4. High-Trust Suppliers are Better at Joint Continuous Improvement: average percentage of time spent on 'joint efforts to improve the product or process'

....

How Can Trust be Created?

Having obtained some evidence that trust in supplier relations is associated with good supplier performance, we will now turn to the question of how trust may be created. More often than not, this question in practice is asked by managers who face low-trust adversarial customer–supplier relationships. They are in a vicious circle of "low-trust dynamics" (Fox 1973), in which low trust generates less open communication (leading to misunderstandings) and tighter control to eliminate any scope for discretion, which in turn reinforces the low-trust attitude. The mutually reinforcing nature of low trust between a customer and a supplier makes both parties reluctant to take the first courageous step to break the vicious circle. Breaking the vicious circle is all the more difficult because a trusting first step—e.g. in the form of disclosing confidential information—increases one's vulnerability to the other's opportunistic behavior.

A number of prescriptions have been offered to break out of the low-trust dynamics in bilateral relationships. The following three sets of approaches are suggested in the existing literature: legalistic remedies including the use of formal contracts, a rational calculative approach, and gift exchange. This section discusses the three approaches, then reviews the relevant institutional environment of bilateral business relationships which is considered to affect the creation and maintenance of trust. The validity of these factors is tested using the survey data.

Favourable and Adversarial Effects of Legalistic Remedies

Some organizations use legalistic measures to attempt to restore trust. But it has been suggested that such legalistic "remedies", including formalizing contracts and rules, work for a certain dimension of trust only, namely task reliability (Sitkin and Roth 1993) or competence trust. According to Sitkin and Roth, legal procedures may be used to substitute for interpersonal trust which may not be available in organizations due to the absence of a history of face-to-face contact. Then, legal remedies can be used to guard against bad contingencies which would undermine trust relationships. A greater formalization of rules and procedures can restore competence trust effectively by fostering co-ordination when past violations, in the form of underperformance, are specific to a particular context or task.

At the same time, Sitkin and Roth (1993) argue that legalistic remedies cannot cure another category of distrust which stems from the absence of a shared set of values between the parties, due for instance to a violation of goodwill trust. In their view, legalistic remedies cannot promote value congruence because the formulation of rules and regulations would only exacerbate the problem of distrust, by maintaining the distance between the parties involved, and by increasing the suspicion that rules are imposed in order to reduce the degree of discretion available to each party. So we may hypothesize that:

H1: Written contracts attenuate customer opportunism and enhance competence trust, but undermine the creation of goodwill trust.

History of Long-term Trading and Rational Calculation

To the extent that trust is built by demonstrating trustworthiness over time, the historical duration and experience of a relationship is said to matter greatly (Sabel 1992). For instance, Zucker (1986) argues that "process-based trust" arises from long-term relationships which have proven to be stable over time. On this basis, some studies (e.g. Gulati 1995) use the duration of trading as a proxy for the level of trust in business relationships. Thus:

H2A: The longer the duration of past trading, the higher is the supplier's trust of its customer.

Expectations of continued trading into the future may be induced by past association. But past association is one of the several ways in which long-term commitment may be made credible (see the next subsection). For those who place importance on the rational calculative basis for creating cooperation, what matters more than the record of long-term trading is the expectation of long-term commitment into the future, what Axelrod calls "enlarging the shadow of the future" (Axelrod 1984; Heide and John 1990).

H2B: The longer the informal commitment made by the customer to continue trading with the supplier, the higher is the supplier's trust for its customer.

Gift Exchange and Credible Commitments

But how can the customer firm create an expectation of informal long-term commitment among its suppliers? One mechanism for creating informal commitment is for the customer to provide technical assistance to a supplier. The customer would receive no return on its investment in training if it fires the supplier. To the extent that the customer demonstrates knowledge and skills by providing technical assistance, it enhances suppliers' competence trust of the customer. Over time, particularly if technical assistance is not fully paid for, suppliers would interpret it as an initiation of "gift exchange" (Akerlof 1982;

Mauss 1966), and it may become a basis for goodwill trust (Sako 1992). In a gift exchange, a long drawn out imbalance of "favors" done and returned sustains the relationship of interdependence. Thus, we may hypothesize that:

> H3A: Technical assistance by customers enhances suppliers' goodwill and competence trust in customers.

Can technical assistance be also a form of credible commitment which attenuates opportunism (Williamson 1985)? In order to test for the difference between credible commitment and gift exchange, the following procedure is adopted in this paper. "Gift exchange" is based on loose reciprocity over time. The purpose of this loose reciprocity is to indebt the other party into doing favours in the future. By contrast, in making credible commitments, both parties give out hostages simultaneously so as to signal to the other party that they are committed because defection is too costly. We interpret the simultaneous provision of suppliers' technical assistance to customers and customers' technical assistance to suppliers as more akin to credible commitment than unilateral assistance. Therefore:

> H3B: Bilateral technical assistance between customers and suppliers reduces customer opportunism.

Another area in which reciprocity may matter is information exchange. Sharing of information facilitates co-ordination between organizations. But disclosing proprietary or confidential information to the other party exposes one's vulnerability. In this situation, a two-way flow of information reduces information asymmetry, and thus reduces any scope for opportunistic behavior (Williamson 1975). However, in order for a customer to develop suppliers' trust in the customer, it must engage in gift exchange, namely the disclosure of its information regardless of whether suppliers also disclose their information at the same time. This mechanism is essential to creating and sustaining trust, which feeds on a loose form of reciprocity over time.

> H4A: The more suppliers' disclosure of information to their customer is matched by the customer's provision of information to suppliers, the lower the supplier's perception of customer opportunism.
>
> H4B: The more customers provide information to their suppliers, the higher the level of suppliers' trust in customers.

Embeddedness

Trust between trading partners may vary not only with the attributes of bilateral transactions but also with the trading environment in which they are a part. Here, societal culture, politics, regulation, professionalization, and national institutions are said to be a relevant set of attributes in which a bilateral relationship may be embedded (Granovetter 1985). This embeddedness approach has led some authors to examine a very broadly defined institutional environment of business relationships, including the industrial environment, the financial system, the national legal tradition, and system, and the systems of industrial relations and skill formation (e.g. Lane and Bachmann 1996). It is beyond the scope of this chapter to review all these factors for all the countries which are covered in the surveys. This subsection focuses, instead, on two aspects of what is meant by embeddedness, namely the importance of path-dependent evolution of societal norms, and the role of intermediate associational networks in moderating competition with co-operation.

In the first sense of embeddedness, Dore (1983) and Sako (1992) provide evidence that Japanese companies are more predisposed to trusting their trading partners than British companies. This is interpreted to be in part due to prevailing business norms, which are determined by societal-level cultural values. Societal norms may be self-reinforcing. Over time, a history of good experience with trusting behavior in Japan may have promoted the diffusion of trust. In fact, cultural norms such as trust can be "the precipitate of history" (Dore 1987: 91). For instance, Japanese suppliers in the automotive industry may trust their customers more today because they have had more customer commitment, more technical assistance, etc., over a much longer period of time than most US suppliers, and their trusting behavior has been honoured by being given growing orders. In contrast, a typical (though more eloquent) US supplier executive asserted that their customer "would steal a dime from a starving grandmother" (Helper 1991). Attempts by US or European companies to imitate the Japanese business norm are costly and difficult because the way in which a network of customer–supplier relations developed in Japan is path-dependent.

In the second sense of embeddedness, Fukuyama (1995) argues convincingly that the density of associational networks at intermediate levels between the State and individual firms accounts for the prevalence of institutionalized trust in certain societies such as Japan and Germany. For example, Smitka (1991) argues that "governance by trust" is more prevalent in the Japanese than in the US automobile industry due to, among other things, the existence of suppliers' associations (*kyoryokukai*) in Japan and their absence in the USA. These are voluntary associations which enhance lateral communication among suppliers, and therefore act as an extra bulwark against customer opportunism (Sako 1996). In Germany, national and regionally based industry associations offer a forum for the exchange of information and the development of common norms and standards, thus creating a favorable environment for the creation and maintenance of trust between firms (Lane and Bachmann 1996). In contrast, trade associations in the US and Britain are relatively weak in their associability and governability (Traxler 1995). While networks of small firms exist in certain parts of the Latin Catholic countries in Europe, they must rely on trust based on common family background, religion, or ethnicity, rather than on institutionally-based trust. This, it is argued by Fukuyama (1995), is due to the relative absence of intermediate associations at the level between the family and the State.

It is expected that there are factors common to all countries which contribute towards creating and maintaining trust between firms. However, because of the above reasons, country-specific institutions, and national history gives rise to a unique level of trust in each country.

Survey Evidence and Discussion

Using the aforementioned datasets, the four sets of hypotheses elaborated above were tested using the ordered probit regression technique. Four measures were chosen as the dependent variables. Customer Opportunism is measured by the statement "Given the chance, our customer might try to take unfair advantage of our business unit". Competence Distrust is measured by "The advice our customer gives us is not always helpful". Goodwill Trust is measured by "We can rely on our customer to help us in ways not required by our agreement with them". Lastly, Fairness, reflecting a shared principle of fairness between the customer and the supplier which is a basis for goodwill trust, is measured by "We can depend on our customer always to treat us fairly". Since all the four scales are ordinal, a response of 4 implies greater agreement than a response of 2, but does not imply twice as much agreement. Thus, the ordered probit regression technique is used. As the correlation matrices in the appendix show, there is no problem with multicollinearity.

First, the datasets are combined to test the hypotheses, while controlling for country differences by dummy variables. In doing so, we focus our analysis on the question of whether determinants are different for different types of trust and opportunism. Next, dummies for the USA, Britain, Germany, and the Latin Catholic countries in Europe are analyzed separately to test the embeddedness hypothesis. Lastly, as is evident in the term "low-trust dynamics" or "high-trust dynamics", the analysis will focus on the possibility of mutual and reverse causation between trust and the main independent variables.

Table 2. Ordered Probit Estimation of Determinants of Trust and Opportunism

Independent variables	Contractual Distrust	Competence Distrust	Goodwill Trust	Fairness	Customer Opportunism
CONTRACT	0.088[c]	−0.000	−0.002	−0.001	−0.001
TRADING	0.000	−0.002	−0.002	−0.004	0.004
COMMIT	−0.001	−0.003[c]	0.004[a]	0.004[b]	−0.005[a]
TECHG	−0.003	−0.087[a]	0.064[a]	0.011	−0.003
TECHDIF	0.001	0.001	−0.003[d]	−0.007[a]	0.004[b]
CUSTINFO	0.020	−0.121[b]	0.222[a]	0.188[a]	−0.182[a]
INFODIF	0.029	0.028	0.001	−0.041[c]	0.047[b]
USA	0.563[a]	0.640[a]	−0.210[b]	−0.866[a]	0.758[a]
UK	0.297[d]	0.330[b]	0.034	−0.485[a]	0.671[a]
GERMANY	0.102	0.562[b]	0.089	−0.345[c]	0.619[a]
LATIN	0.475[b]	0.346[c]	0.417[b]	−0.157	0.552[a]
Log Likelihood	−1627.5815	−1660.8079	−1593.8821	−1600.5942	−1836.0586
Pseudo R^2	0.025	0.037	0.025	0.066	0.059
N	1137	1118	1144	1144	1143

[a] $p < 0.001$
[b] $p < 0.01$
[c] $p < 0.05$
[d] $p < 0.10$

Determinants of Trust and Opportunism

As shown in Table 2, each set of hypotheses is supported to a varying degree.

The first hypothesis, H1, that written contracts (CONTRACT) attenuate customer opportunism and enhance competence trust but reduce goodwill trust, is not supported. It appears that when other mechanisms are present, contract duration in itself fails to be a sufficient enhancer of competence trust or a safeguard to attenuate opportunism.

As hypothesized in H2B, informal commitment (COMMIT) made by the customer enhances all types of trust and reduces customer opportunism. However, contrary to H2A, the length of trading does not have a significant impact on trust. Thus, long-term trading in itself is not sufficient to bring about trust in relationships.

VARIABLES

CONTRACT What is the length of your written contract or purchase order with this customer for this product? (in years)

TRADING Approximately how long has your firm sold products in this product line to this customer?

1 year 2 years 3 years 4 years 5–10 years 11–19 years 20–40 years 41–60 years over 60 years

283

The mid-point of each interval was used; thus the variable takes the value of 1, 2, 3, 4, 7.5, 15, 30, 50.5, or 75.

COMMIT For how long do you think there is a high probability that your business unit will be supplying this or similar item to your customer? (in years)

SUPINFO What types of information does your business unit provide to your customer about the process you use to make the product you listed above? (Please check all that apply.)

- Detailed breakdown of process steps
- Cost of each process step
- Financial information not publicly available
- Production scheduling information
- Type of equipment used
- Your sources of supply
- Detailed information regarding materials you use.

The seven information items were given one point each if checked, and were added.

CUSTINFO Does your customer provide you with any of the following types of information? (Please check all that apply.)

- Warranty or other data from final consumers
- Financial information not publicly available
- Information on how your product is used in their process.

The information items were given one point each if checked, and added.

INFODIF SUPINFO *minus* CUSTINFO

TECHG Over the last four years, what sorts of technical assistance have you received from your customer? (Please check all that apply, and indicate whether 'provided for zero or nominal charge' or 'provided for a fee'.)

- Provided personnel who visited supplier site to aid in implementing improved procedures
- Arranged for training of your personnel at their site
- Provided personnel who worked two weeks or more on your shopfloor to improve your process.

Given a weight of 2 if 'provided for zero or nominal charge' and a weight of 1 if 'provided for a fee', and summed over the three items.

TECHDIF   Approximately what percentage of the contacts with your customer regarding this product were for the following purposes?

Percentage for 'your business unit providing technical assistance to customer' minus percentage for 'customer providing technical assistance to your business unit'.

USA   *A dummy with 1 for US responses, 0 otherwise.*

UK   *A dummy with 1 for UK responses, 0 otherwise.*

GERMANY   *A dummy with 1 for German responses, 0 otherwise.*

LATIN   *A dummy with 1 for responses from France, Italy, or Spain, 0 otherwise.*

As expected, in accordance with H3A, technical assistance by customers (TECHG) enhances goodwill trust and competence trust but does not have a significant impact on opportunism. H3B is also supported. It was hypothesized that due to credible commitments, a smaller gap between suppliers' technical assistance and customers' technical assistance (TECHDIF) would attenuate customer opportunism, and this is the case. At the same time, a greater gap in bilateral technical assistance reduces goodwill trust significantly and also undermines the notion of fair treatment which is a prerequisite for goodwill trust.

The hypotheses H4A and H4B on information sharing are both supported. In particular, the gap between suppliers' provision of information to customers and customers' disclosure of information to suppliers (INFODIF) increases customer opportunism. Moreover, the customer's provision of information (CUSTINFO) in itself has an independent significant effect of enhancing trust and reducing opportunism.

To summarize, the main determinants of goodwill trust are informal customer commitment, customers' technical assistance, and customers' provision of information. The same three factors are significant determinants of competence trust. By contrast, the main determinants of customer opportunism include the information asymmetry between the customer and the supplier, and informal customer commitment. Earlier, it was hypothesized that "gift exchange" enhances trust but does not attenuate opportunism, while "credible commitments" attenuate opportunism but do not enhance trust. The survey data provide some support for this. In particular, customers' technical assistance enhances trust but does not attenuate opportunism. It is the customers' provision of information, regardless of whether suppliers provide information to customers or not, which matters for enhancing trust, while two-way information sharing (which can be interpreted to be credible commitment) is what matters for attenuating opportunism.

Country Differences: a Test of Embeddedness

In order to examine differences in the levels of trust and opportunism among countries, dummy variables were created for suppliers located in the USA, Britain, Germany, and the Latin Catholic countries respectively, using those in Japan as the baseline reference group. These dummies capture the embedded national-specific cultural norms and institutions, after taking account of the factors affecting trust and opportunism, which are common to all suppliers regardless of their country location.

As one might expect, the level of customer opportunism anticipated by suppliers was higher in the USA, the UK, and the continental European countries than in Japan (see Table 2). The level of competence trust was also lower in these three regions than in Japan. For goodwill trust, the level was significantly lower in the USA than in Japan as expected, but surprisingly, significantly higher in the Latin Catholic countries than in Japan. The German suppliers' goodwill trust was not significantly different from that of Japanese suppliers. Lastly, suppliers' perception of fair treatment by customers was lower in the USA, Britain, and Germany as compared to in Japan, but not significantly different between the Latin countries and Japan. These results largely confirm the impressionistic picture given in Table 1, but give a much better indication of the country-specific contribution to raising or undermining different types of trust after controlling for universal factors.

Trust Dynamics and Written Contracts

In order to test for causality, one would ideally require a longitudinal study. As a second best, the survey asked suppliers about the situation now and four years ago in some of the questions, which enables us to conduct cross-lagged tests. The rest of this chapter examines the causation between trust and contract duration. The only measure of trust for "now" and "4 years ago" was the one concerning fair treatment ("We can depend on our customer to treat us fairly"). Therefore, this subsection uses this measure of trust only.

In the analysis above, written contracts were found not to have any significant impact on opportunism or trust. One of the reasons for this may be that when other mechanisms are present, contracts in themselves fail to be a sufficient enhancer of trust or a safeguard to attenuate opportunism. Another possibility is that besides the formal contract duration, other dimensions (such as the actual content of the contract) may matter in affecting opportunism and trust.

Another added complication is that the implicit contract duration may be different from the explicitly agreed contract duration. For example, according to the survey, in Europe, contracts have lengthened from a median of 1 year in 1990 to 3 years in 1994. In the USA also, the median contract duration has increased, though less dramatically, from 1 year in 1989 to 1.5 year in 1993. However, these figures conceal a sharp decrease in contract duration reported by suppliers to one vehicle manufacturer in the USA. In Japan, contracts between companies typically do not contain specific information about the type of products to be supplied. The practice of general framework contracts (without product-specific contracts) prevailed for two thirds of the respondents in both 1989 and 1993. Where there were contracts, the implicit contract in Japan tended to be longer than the basic contract which was renewed annually. Therefore, contract duration alone does not truly reflect differences in customer commitment particularly in Japan.

In spite of the above caveat, the survey data make it possible to examine what were the causes and effects of longer-duration contracts at least in the USA and Europe. In order to test whether changes in the level of trust is causing changes in contract duration or vice versa, cross-lagged tests were applied to each regional dataset. As can be seen in Table 3, the coefficients in both regressions are negative and significant in the USA, implying that a low level of trust has led customers to offer longer-term contracts, which in turn have led to lower levels of trust. In general, lengthening the duration of the contract has not had the intended effect of restoring trust in the USA. Thus, some US automotive supplier relations appear to be suffering from a low-trust dynamics, and the reason may be the inability of legal "remedies" to bring about goal congruence when the existing relationships are adversarial (Sitkin and Roth 1993).

Table 3. Cross-lagged Tests of the Link Between Contract Lengths and Trust

	Japan	USA	Britain	Germany	Latin Catholic Europe
Dependent variable: TRUST NOW					
Independent variable: CONTRACT 4 YEARS AGO	−0.035	−0.087[d]	0.028	−0.142	0.273[c]
Adjusted R^2	−0.001	0.005	−0.008	−0.0001	0.056
N	441	457	121	51	51
Dependent variable: CONTRACT NOW					
Independent variable: TRUST 4 YEARS AGO	0.0395	−0.084[d]	−0.027	−0.016	0.094
Adjusted R^2	−0.0007	0.005	−0.008	−0.022	−0.013
N	441	473	123	47	47

[a] $p < 0.001$.
[b] $p < 0.01$.
[c] $p < 0.05$.
[d] $p < 0.10$.

In Europe overall, the impact of contract duration on trust is positive and significant in countries other than the UK. Thus in the main countries of Germany, France, Italy, and Spain, it appears that automotive customers have been able to enhance suppliers' trust by offering longer-term contracts. When the Latin Catholic countries are separated out from Germany, the positive impact of contract duration on trust is found to be significant; among suppliers in the former only. The German result is not what we expected, but the Latin Catholic countries are seen to share the same civil law tradition with Germany (Arrighetti, Bachmann, and Deakin 1996). In the UK, as in Japan, there has been little change in contract duration, and what little changes there were have had no significant impact on the level of trust among suppliers. This finding, if we contrast the UK with continental Europe, is not inconsistent with Lane and Bachmann's conclusion that (a) adhering to contractual conditions was invariably rated more highly as a trust-creating behavior in Germany than in Britain, and (b) contracts were used in a more varied and adversarial manner in Britain than in Germany (Lane and Bachmann 1996: 385).

To summarize, the empirical evidence presented in this section shows that the determinants of trust are different from the opposite of the determinants of opportunism. The former are such things as technical assistance and customer provision of information to suppliers regardless of whether the suppliers reciprocate or not; these mechanisms were called "gift exchange". The latter include "safeguards" in terms of credible commitments. After taking account of these universal factors, the levels of suppliers' trust and expectations of customer opportunism were found to be significantly different according to their country location. These differences were interpreted to be due to the embeddedness of business relationships in country-specific institutions and history. The impact of one specific institution, the legal framework, was also examined. There is some evidence that the vicious circle of low-trust dynamics (with longer contracts leading to higher distrust which in turn has led to even longer contracts) developed in the US auto industry in the recent past. But for the Latin Catholic countries, the lengthening of the formal contract appears to have contributed towards enhancing trust. Thus, contract lengths have had different effects on trust creation in different countries.

Conclusions

This chapter conceptualized interorganizational trust into "contractual trust", "competence trust", or "goodwill trust", according to the sources of predictability in mutually acceptable behavior. The distinction among the three types of trust has proven to be useful particularly in thinking about the outcomes of trust.

In linking trust to business performance, it was argued that there should be a move away from the framework of minimizing transaction costs towards one with a focus on learning and innovation (see also Goshal and Moran 1996). The main hypothesis was that among the three types of trust, "goodwill trust" would have the strongest impact on performance. This is because the extra edge which "goodwill trust" offers over and above the formal governance structures of contracts or hierarchies is learning and continuous improvement, not merely in making savings in transaction costs. The survey of first-tier automotive suppliers provides evidence that trust is associated with supplier performance particularly in just-in-time delivery and continuous improvement.

In relation to the creation of trust, this paper recommends a move away from a framework which focuses on safeguards against the abuse of trust towards thinking about enhancers of trust. The latter are like "gift exchange" based on loose reciprocity over time. According to the survey evidence, the trust enhancers may take the form of customers' technical assistance to suppliers, which does not function as a safeguard against opportunism. One effective safeguard is information sharing (i.e. two-way flow of information), while the unilateral provision of information by customers, regardless of whether suppliers reciprocated simultaneously or not, was found to enhance trust. Other safeguards, such as legal contracts, were found to have differential effects in different countries, with the USA experiencing a low trust dynamics and the Latin European countries experiencing a positive impact of longer contracts on enhancing trust.

The distinction between "safeguards" and "enhancers" of trust roughly correspond to the difficulty in reconciling the two views on trust alluded to at the beginning of this chapter, namely on regarding trust as an outcome derived from rational calculation and the other equating it with a value traced to culture or social norms. However, "safeguards" are rarely foolproof in business, precisely because trust is more than promise keeping, and contracts are always necessarily open-ended. Thus, while law in certain countries may help jump-start trust relations in business, in the end "goodwill trust" has to be found not by resort to law but through learning-by-interacting to fill in the gap left by incomplete contracts. At the same time, gift exchange as an enhancer of trust, in the form of technical assistance for example, may depend on a social norm of loose reciprocity, but in business, there is no such thing as blind faith. The process of gift exchange may be started, and can only be sustained, by intense communication and monitoring of each other's behavior to find opportunities for continuous improvement, but these are quite different from "safeguards".

References

Akerlof, G. A. (1982), 'Labour Contracts as Partial Gift Exchange', *Quarterly Journal of Economics*, 97: 542–6.

Anderson, E. (1988), 'Transaction Costs as Determinants of Opportunism in Integrated and Independent Sales Forces', *Journal of Economic Behavior and Organization*, 9: 247–64.

—— and Weitz, B. (1989), 'Determinants of Continuity in Conventional Industrial Channel Dyads', *Marketing Science*, 8: 310–23.

Arrighetti, A., Bachmann, R., and Deakin, S. (1996), 'Contact Law, Social Norms and Inter-firm Cooperation', Working Paper no. 36, ESRC Centre for Business Research, University of Cambridge.

Arrow, K. J. (1975), 'Gifts and Exchanges', in E. S. Phelps (ed.), *Altruism, Morality and Economic Theory*. New York: Russell Sage Foundation.

Asanuma, B. (1989), 'Manufacturer–Supplier Relationships in Japan and the Concept of Relation-Specific Skills', *Journal of the Japanese and International Economies*, 3: 1–30.

Axelrod, R. (1984), *Evolution of Cooperation*. New York: Basic Books.

Barney, J. B. and Hansen, M. H. (1994), 'Trustworthiness as a Source of Competitive Advantage', *Strategic Management Journal*, 7: 175–90.

Bradach, J. L. and Eccles, R. G. (1989), 'Price, Authority and Trust: From Ideal Types to Plural Forms', *Annual Review of Sociology*, 15: 96–118.

Brusco, S. (1986), 'Small Firms and Industrial Districts: The Experience of Italy', in D. Keeble and F. Weever (eds.), *New Firms and Regional Development in Europe*. London: Croom Helm.

Cook, J. and Wall, T. (1980), 'New York Attitude Measures of Trust, Organizational Commitment and Personal Need Non-fulfilment', *Journal of Occupational Psychology*, 53: 39–52.

Cook, J. D. et al. (1981), *The Experience of Work: A Compendium and Review of 249 Measures and Their Use*. Orlando: Academic Press.

Cummings, L. L. and Bromiley, P. (1996), 'The Organizational Trust Inventory (OTI): Development and Validation', in R. M. Kramer and T. R. Tyler (eds.), *Trust in Organizations: Frontiers of Theory and Research*. London: Sage.

Deutsch, M. (1958), 'Trust and Suspicion', *Journal of Conflict Resolution*, 2/4: 265–79.

Dore, R. (1983), Goodwill and the Spirit of Market Capitalism', *British Journal of Sociology*, 34: 459–82.

—— (1987), *Taking Japan Seriously*. Stanford: Staniversity Press.

Dyer, J. (forthcoming), 'Does governance matter? Keiretsu alliances and asset specificity as source of Japanese competitive advantage', *Organization Science*.

Fox, A. (1973), *Beyond Contract: Work, Power and Trust Relations*. London: Faber and Faber.

Fukuyama, F. (1995), *Trust: The Social Virtues and the Creation of Prosperity*. London: Hamish Hamilton.

Gambetta, D. (1988) (ed.), *Trust: Making and Breaking Cooperative Relations*. Oxford: Blackwell.

Goshal, S. and Moran, P. (1996), 'Bad for Practice: A Critique of the Transaction Cost Theory', *Academy of Management Review*, 21/1: 13–47.

Granovetter, M. (1985), 'Economic Action and Social Structure: The Problem of Embeddedness', *American Journal of Sociology*, 91: 481–510.

Gulati, R. (1995), 'Does Familiarity Breed Trust? The Implications of Repeated Ties for Contractual Choice in Alliances', *Academy of Management Journal*, 38: 85–112.

Heide, J. B. and John, G. (1990), 'Alliances in Industrial Purchasing: The Determinants of Joint Action in Buyer–Supplier Relationships', *Journal of Marketing Research*, 27: 24–36.

Helper, S. (1991), 'Strategy and Irreversibility in Supplier Relations: The Case of the US Automobile Industry', *Business History Review*, 65: 781–824.

—— and Sako, M. (1995), 'Supplier Relations in the Auto Industry in Japan and the USA: Are they Converging?' *Sloan Management Review* (Spring), 77–84.

Ingersoll Engineers (1995), *Partnership or Conflict? The Automotive-Component Supply Industry: A Survey of Issues of Alignment*. Ruby: Ingersoll Engineers.

Jarillo, J. C. (1988), 'On Strategic Networks', *Strategic Management Journal*, 9: 31–41.

Joskow, P. L. (1988), 'Asset Specificity and the Structure of Vertical Relationships: Empirical Evidence', *Journal of Law, Economics and Organization*, 4/1: 95–118.

Lane, C. and Bachmann, R. (1996), 'Risk, Trust and Power: The Social Construction of Supplier Relations in Britain and Germany', paper presented at the Work, Employment and Society Conference, University of Kent, 12–14 Sept.

Macaulay, S. (1963), 'Non-contractual Relations in Business: A Preliminary Study', *American Sociological Review*, 28/2: 55–67.

Macneil, I. R. (1974), 'Contracts: Adjustment of Long-term Economic Relationship under Classical, Neo-classical, and Relational Contract Law', *Northwestern University Law Review*, 72: 584–906.

Mauss, M. (1966), *The Gift*. London and Henley: Routledge & Kegan Paul.

Mohr, J. and Spekman, R. (1994), 'Characteristics of Partnership Success: Partnership Attributes, Communication Behavior, and Conflict Resolution Techniques', *Strategic Management Journal*, 15: 135–52.

Powell, W. W. (1996), 'Trust-based Forms of Governance', in Kramer and Tyler (eds.), *Trust in Organizations*.

Ring, P. S. and van de Ven, A. H. (1994), 'Developmental Processes of Cooperative Interorganizational Relationships', *Academy of Management Review*, 19: 90–118.

Sabel, C. F. (1992), 'Studied Trust: Building New Forms of Co-operation in a Volatile Economy', in F. Pyke and W. Sengenberger (eds.), *Industrial Districts and Local Economic Regeneration*. Geneva: International Institute for Labour Studies.

—— (1994), 'Learning by Monitoring: The Institutions of Economic Development', in N. J. Smelser and R. Swedberg (eds.), *The Handbook of Economic Sociology*. Princeton: Princeton University Press.

Sako, M. (1991), 'The Role of "Trust" in Japanese Buyer–Supplier Relationships', *Ricerche Economiche*, 45: 449–74.

—— (1992), *Prices, Quality and Trust: Inter-firm Relations in Britain and Japan*. Cambridge: Cambridge University Press.

Sako, M. (1996), 'Suppliers' Associations in the Japanese Automobile Industry: Collective Action for Technology Diffusion', *Cambridge Journal of Economics*, 20/6: 651–71.

Sitkin, S. B. and Roth, N. L. (1993), 'Explaining the Limited Effectiveness of Legalistic "Remedies" for Trust/Distrust', *Organization Science*, 4/3: 356–92.

Smitka, M. (1991), *Competitive Ties: Subcontracting in the Japanese Automotive Industry.* New York: Columbia University Press.

—— (1992), 'Contracting Without Contracts', in S. B. Sitkin and R. J. Bies (eds.), *The Legalistic Organisation*. London: Sage.

Society of Motor Manufacturers and Traders and UK Department of Trade and Industry (1994), *A Review of the Relationships Between Vehicle Manufacturers and Suppliers*. London: SMMT and DTI.

Traxler, F. (1995), 'Two Logics of Collective Action in Industrial Relations?', in C. Crouch and F. Traxler (eds.), *Organized Industrial Relations in Europe: What Future?* Aldershot: Avebury.

Walker, G. and Weber, D. (1984), 'A Transaction Cost Approach to Make-or-Buy Decisions', *Administrative Science Quarterly*, 29: 373–91.

Williamson, O. E. (1975), *Markets and Hierarchies*. New York: Free Press.

—— (1979), 'Transaction-cost Economics: The Governance of Contractual Relations', *Journal of Law and Economics*, 22: 3–61.

—— (1983), 'Credible Commitments: Using Hostages to Support Exchange', *American Economic Review*, 73: 519–40.

—— (1985), *The Economic Institutions of Capitalism*. New York: Free Press.

—— (1993), 'Calculativeness, Trust, and Economic Organization', *Journal of Law and Economics*, 36: 453–86.

Zucker, L. (1986), Production of Trust: Institutional Sources of Economic Structure', *Research in Organizational Behavior*, 8: 53–111.

IV. FRAGILITY OF ORGANIZATIONAL TRUST

10 Explaining the Limited Effectiveness of Legalistic "Remedies" for Trust/Distrust*

Sim B. Sitkin and Nancy L. Roth

Trust is an essential element of all social exchange relations (Barber 1983, Barnard 1938, Blau 1968, Deutsch 1960, Garfinkel 1963) and collective action (Luhmann 1979, Parsons 1951). Organizational scholars have noted that coordination (Cyert and March 1963, Macaulay 1963, Williamson 1975) and control (Arrow 1974, Ouchi 1980) rest upon a foundation of trust. However, in many organizations, the level of interpersonal trust is low—particularly between management and employees (e.g., Golembiewski and McConkie 1975)—leading organizations to adopt control mechanisms (e.g., contracts, bureaucratic procedures, or legal requirements) as substitutes for trust when interpersonal relations are lacking (Fox 1974, Williams 1975). Such "legalistic" mechanisms are typically adopted not only to facilitate administrative coordination (Weber 1947) but also to obtain the symbolic legitimacy that accompanies the use of institutionalized procedures (Edelman 1990, Meyer 1983, Sitkin and Bies 1993, Sitkin and Roth 1993, Yudof 1981) and to restore sufficient levels of trust necessary for activity to continue (Shapiro 1987, Zucker 1986).

Although organizations adopt legalistic remedies (i.e., mechanisms that are institutionalized, mimic legal forms, and exceed legal regulatory requirements) to attempt to restore trust (Meyer 1983, Sitkin and Bies in press-b, Yudof 1981, Zucker 1986), these "impersonal" substitutes for trust are frequently ineffective (Granovetter 1985, Shapiro 1987, Yudof 1981) in that they fail to restore trust

* Accepted by Arie Y. Lewin; received March 18, 1991. This paper has been with the authors for two revisions.

relations. They can also lead to an "inflationary spiral" of increasingly formalized relations, such as when negotiations break down due to haggling over the procedures by which mutually acceptable procedures will be determined.

Extending the existing literature on trust, we will suggest why legalistic "remedies" might have limited effectiveness in addressing trust problems. To do so we will distinguish two aspects of trust that have not been clearly differentiated in the past. We will suggest that in organizations, *trust* rests on a foundation of expectations about an employee's ability to complete task assignments reliably (task reliability), whereas *distrust* is engendered when expectations about the compatibility of an employee's beliefs and values with the organization's cultural values are called into question (generalized value incongruence). We will explain why legalistic mechanisms respond more effectively to the reliability issues that underlie trust violations and why they are less effective in addressing the value congruence issues that underpin the emergence of distrust. To illustrate these ideas, we will focus on organizations with employees with HIV/AIDS—an issue that simultaneously involves both task-specific reliability (due to progressive illness) and value congruence (due to social stigma).

The Production and Reproduction of Trust[1]

Previous Research on Trust

Although scholars have used a variety of definitions and operational measures for trust (see Kee and Knox 1970), nearly all research has at least implicitly accepted a definition of trust as a belief, attitude, or expectation concerning the likelihood that the actions or outcomes of another individual, group or organization will be acceptable (Barber 1983, Garfinkel 1963, Jennings 1971, Lewis and Weigert 1985, Luhmann 1979) or will serve the actor's interests (Deutsch 1962, Kee and Knox 1970, Larzelere and Huston 1980). Anderson and Narus (1990, p. 45) provide a good example of this approach in their study of inter-organizational relationships across distribution channels. They define trust as the "belief that another company will perform actions that will result in positive outcomes for the firm, as well as not take unexpected actions that will result in negative outcomes for the firm." While most scholars implicitly accept the conception of trust as representing a psychological state of positive expectation about another's motives and future actions, research on trust only rarely theorizes about (e.g., Kee and Knox 1970) or empirically examines (e.g., Anderson and Narus 1990) that state directly.

Some scholars distinguish between interpersonal trust (i.e., expectations based on personal experience) and institutional trust (expectations that rely upon formal controls to substitute for interpersonal trust by constraining future behavior) (Barber 1983, Granovetter 1985, Shapiro 1987, Zucker 1986)—and most research focuses on interpersonal trust (e.g., see Golembiewski and McConkie 1975, Zand 1972). Although there is considerable variance in how researchers have operationalized trust-related expectations, four clusters of measures provide a natural framework for reviewing the existing literature on trust: individual attributes, behaviors, situations, and institutional arrangements.

One of the more well-known streams of trust research includes studies of *trust as an individual attribute*. This approach focuses on an individual's trust in the motives of others (e.g., how much they believed others in the absence of clear-cut reasons to disbelieve (Rotter 1967, 1971, 1980)). This approach also involves studies of individual characteristics associated with being perceived as trustworthy (Bies 1987; Butler and Cantrell 1984; Gabarro 1978; Rotter 1980; Schlenker, Helm and Tedeschi 1973). Attributions of trustworthiness are based on interpersonal interaction history (e.g., personal experiences in interacting with another person who has acted in a trustworthy or untrustworthy manner) or on social/demographic characteristics (e.g., gender, age, family background, education) which serve as a proxy for personal experience (Barber 1983, Zucker 1986). For example, recent research on impression management suggests that individuals sometimes attempt to frame "images that are projected" (Schlenker 1980, p. 6) so as to appear more trustworthy (Greenberg 1990).

Scholars who focus on *trust as a behavior* conceptualize high trust behavior as cooperation and low trust behavior as competition. This approach is dominated by the work of Deutsch (1958), who examines trust from a game theory perspective and spawned a number of studies of the determinants of cooperation and competition (Axelrod 1984; Deutsch 1960, 1962; Deutsch and Krauss 1962; Loomis 1959; Matthews, Kordonski, and Shimoff 1983). Other researchers have studied trust behavior in terms of trust-related interactions between partners, focusing on patterns of mutual openness and cooperation over time (Argyris 1982, Gabarro 1978, Golembiewski and McConkie 1975, Swinth 1967, Zand 1972). For example, Butler (1983) finds that personality traits and perceptions of others are not significant predictors of trusting behavior, but that reciprocal trust from the other party is. The primary finding that emanates from this research is that relational trust behaviors tend to spiral upward (i.e., to higher levels of mutual trust) if reciprocated, and downward if not.

Research on *trust as a situational feature* suggests that trust is only necessary under conditions of: interdependence, uncertainty that hinges on the choices made by others, and consequentiality (Deutsch 1962, Larzelere and Huston 1980). Interdependence is an essential trust-related feature because expectations about another's trustworthiness only become relevant when the completion of one's own consequential activities depend on the prior actions or ongoing cooperation of another person (e.g., Deutsch 1958, 1960; Deutsch and Krauss 1962; Lindskold 1978; Loomis 1959; Matthews and Shimoff 1979). For example, Kee and Knox (1970, pp. 358–9) define "a trust situation [as involving] two parties which are to a certain extent interdependent with respect to the outcomes defined by their joint choices and one of the parties is confronted with the choice between trusting or not trusting the other."

Finally, *trust as an institutional arrangement* reflects the use of contracts, sanctioning capabilities, or legalistic procedures as formal substitutes for interpersonal trust. Fox (1974), Granovetter (1985), Shapiro (1987), and Zucker (1986) suggest that when the interpersonal roots of trust are no longer available (e.g., when high levels of mobility decrease interpersonal transaction history or when personal contact is not feasible), trust will take the form of institutional arrangements (e.g., through formal certification of expertise or performance binding). This approach focuses on the use of formal (often legalistic) mechanisms that serve as administrative or symbolic substitutes for trust that can enhance the legitimacy of an otherwise suspect arrangement (e.g., Zucker 1986).

Extending Ideas About Trust

The literature also suggests that attempts to "remedy" trust violations legalistically frequently fail because they paradoxically reduce the level of trust rather than reproducing trust. The adoption of legalistic "remedies" (i.e., institutionalized mechanisms that mimic legal forms and exceed legal/regulatory requirements) imposes a psychological and/or an interactional barrier between the two parties that stimulates an escalating spiral of formality and distance (Granovetter 1985, Homans 1974, Larson 1992, Zucker 1986) and leads to a need for more rules (Fox 1974, Peachey and Lerner 1981, Shapiro 1987). And so the process is perpetuated.

Edelman's (1990) study of the institutionalization of civil rights reform in the United States provides an illustration. Many nonunion organizations responded to the Civil Rights Act of 1964 by adopting formal due process procedures that were not legally required because organizations were under considerable pressure (from both the executive branch and civil rights groups) to demonstrate support for civil rights in the workplace. Highly formalized procedures were adopted because they "resemble[d] the formal protections that characterize the public legal order" (p. 1406) and would therefore convey the appearance of legitimacy and responsiveness. Adoption of these procedures was largely symbolic "with no real benefit to employees" (p. 1436).

The existing literature does not fully explain why legalistic mechanisms have the effects that they do. The distancing explanation offered by Granovetter (1985), Zucker, (1986), Shapiro (1987) and others would be adequate if legalistic "remedies" uniformly led to failure and escalation—however, institutional scholars find that these mechanisms are sometimes quite effective in warding off the threat of reduced trust (e.g., Meyer 1983, Meyer and Zucker 1989).

We suggest that legalistic responses are more or less effective depending on the specific nature of the expectations that have been violated. They can restore trust expectations effectively when violations are specific to a particular context or task (e.g., the use of contractual product-specific quality standards (Williamson 1975)). However, when fundamental values are violated, and perceived trustworthiness is undermined across contexts, then legalistic remedies are ill-suited to restoring lost trust—and can exacerbate the problem due to their effect on perceived interpersonal distance. We will refer to the former situation as "violated trust" and to the latter as "distrust"—and we will examine this distinction as providing the foundation for explaining the limited effectiveness of legalistic remedies.

Our perspective—while a sharp departure from much of the literature on trust—is consistent with the frameworks, terminology, operationalizations, and concepts used in that literature. For example, Zucker (1986, p. 59) suggests that disruptions of trust arise when either "background expectations" (i.e., common world understandings) or "constitutive expectations" (i.e., context-specific understandings) are violated. However, this approach to trust is challenged by Zucker herself (1986, p. 102): "distrust only emerges when the suspicion arises that the disruption of expectations in one exchange is likely to generalize to other... interactions or exchanges, at least of a particular type," an assertion that is more consistent with our conceptualization.

Other scholars provide additional support. Barber (1983, p. 165) distinguishes two types of trust that reflect "two more specific kinds of expectations... technically competent performance and direct moral responsibility." Gabarro (1978) distinguishes "functional or specific competence" from "character" (i.e., broad dispositional attributes that could affect many situations) as two bases of trust. Kee and Knox (1970) distinguish "subjective" versus "manifest" trust in terms of ascribed motives versus observed competence. Even Deutsch distinguishes trust from suspicion (Deutsch 1958, 1960) and acknowledges that trust-based relations (cooperatively oriented bargainers, in his terms) and distrust-based relations (competitively oriented bargainers, in his terms) may have different determinants (Deutsch and Krauss 1962). Perhaps the closest approach to the one we are advocating is Fox's (1974) analysis of the relationship between trust, discretion, and control in work settings. Fox separates low-trust conditions from high-trust conditions and suggests that the circumstances underlying each represent distinct configurations of beliefs, interaction processes, and causal dynamics.

Distinguishing Trust and Distrust

Based on our analysis of the extant work on trust, we have proposed an alternative way of thinking about trust and distinguishing it from distrust. Before we can apply this approach to explaining the use and effects of legalistic remedies for trust/distrust, we need to develop more fully our conceptualization of trust and distrust. Thus, in this section, we will clarify our use of trust and distrust.

Trust is violated to the extent that expectations about context-specific task reliability are not met. Under such conditions, a judgment must be made as to whether the violation is an isolated event (e.g., a contract proposal missed a deadline because a Federal Express airplane crashed) or is more typical of that particular person's behavior in a specific context (e.g., a generally outstanding employee who does not work well under tight deadlines and always misses them). We suggest that, to the extent that a violation is judged to have been an isolated or random event, attributions of individual trustworthiness will remain unaffected (Kelley 1967, McArthur 1972). However, to the extent that a violation is attributed to an individual's typical context-specific behavior and there is a perception that similar violations may recur within the same context, trust will be disrupted.

Distrust is engendered when an individual or group is perceived as not sharing key cultural values. When a person challenges an organization's fundamental assumptions and values, that person may be perceived as operating under values so different from the group's that the violator's underlying world view becomes suspect (Gabarro 1978, Lindskold 1978) and the threat of future violations of expectations arises because the person is now seen as a cultural outsider—as one who "doesn't think like us" and may, therefore, do the "unthinkable." As a result, an individual may be branded as "untrustworthy" in a global sense—that is, they may come to be distrusted.

Stigmatization illustrates our conceptualization of perception-based generalization. When a person has one stigmatized attribute or behavior s/he is often perceived as being generally "different" and presumed to violate basic cultural values. As Jones, Farina, Hastorf, Markus, Miller and Scott (1984) note, stigmas are attributed to the basic disposition of the individual and, thus, can spoil his/her overall identity. We suggest that violations associated with stigma are an example of the type of violations that would engender distrust because they are perceived as generalized value incongruities.

Clarifying the Distinction Between Trust and Distrust

Table 1 shows our conception of the effect of violated expectations on trust and distrust. Two factors are critical. First, have expectations concerning value congruence or task reliability been violated? Second, is the violation perceived as context-specific and localized—or is the violation perceived as representing a more generalized and pervasive problem? When the type of violation and its perceived pervasiveness are consistent (see Cells 2 and 3 in Table 1), we propose that the effect on trust/distrust is clear and predictable: trust will be reduced when a task reliability violation is perceived as localized (i.e., context-specific), and distrust will be engendered when a value-related violation is perceived as generalized. When the type of violation and its perceived pervasiveness are not consistent (i.e., Cells 1 and 4 in Table 1), the effect on trust and distrust is indeterminate.

Generalized Value Congruence Condition. If an individual holds even a single key value that is different from the dominant group's, the influence of schematized stereotypes and the desire for cognitive consistency will make it more likely that all of the person's values will be perceived as different. This tendency to

Table 1. Hypothesized Effect of Violations of Expectations on Trust and Distrust

	Perceived Pervasiveness of Violation	
	Context-Specific	Generalized
Value Congruence	Value violations rarely perceived as localized (indeterminate effects)	Distrust engendered
Type of Violated Expectations	CELL 1	CELL 2
	CELL 3	CELL 4
Task Reliability	Trust reduced	Multi-domain task reliability rarely perceived as generalized (indeterminate effects)

over-generalize and taint the individual's entire identity is likely to be exacerbated when the differences involve that which is stigmatized (Page 1984, Sutton and Callahan 1987)—and to engender distrust.

Context-specific Task Reliability Condition. We hypothesize that, unless core values of the organization are violated, individual instances of task unreliability will be perceived as context-specific, rather than generalizable. Even if an individual's task violations spread to other types of tasks or contexts, there are several processes that are likely to impede the perception of generalized threat. Context-specific violations of trust can be viewed as isolated exceptions because they do not challenge "general world understandings" (Zucker 1986). Even repeated violations of trust can be excused as personal quirks as long as the violations are confined to a particular domain and are not interpreted as threatening to "spill over" into other domains. For example, as observers become more familiar with an individual's strengths, these can compensate for their unreliability (e.g., an employee always arrives late to meetings, but makes good contributions once arriving). Over time, to accommodate increasingly diverse instances of unreliability (e.g., the employee isn't only late to early morning meetings, but is now always late for meetings) observers can develop more encompassing cognitive categories (e.g., it's just meetings that are a problem, since they always seem to get their other work done on time), thus delimiting the perceived generalizability of the violation—and affecting trust.

Perceptions concerning what constitutes the boundaries of a "domain" are crucial here, since the notion of context-specificity can be influenced by whether a domain is defined broadly (thus making it less likely that "spill-over" will occur) or narrowly (thus making even very similar violations appear to be drawn from different domains). Specificity may in some cases be rather clear, such as when an incident has only very local implications and occurs only once. To the extent that the number of violations or their diversity increases, it becomes increasingly difficult to perceive a person's violations as isolated.

Mixed Conditions. However, when the type of violation and its perceived pervasiveness do not coincide, the effect on trust/distrust is hypothesized to be more indeterminate, hinging on the observer's perceptions and the specifics of the situation. In this paper, we will focus on Cells 2 and 3 and will not address cases of context-specific value incongruence or generalized task unreliability (which are unlikely to be prevalent in practice). However, we will revisit these cases in discussing the implications of our approach for future research.

These arguments suggest that violations of task reliability expectations are likely to continue to be perceived as isolated incidents, whereas comparable violations of value expectations are likely to be perceived as manifestations of general incongruities.

The Role of Legalistic Remedies in the Production and Reproduction of Trust

A Theoretical Model of the Determinants and Effects of Using Legalistic Remedies for Trust/Distrust

Our reconceptualization of trust has broad implications for how we theorize about the determinants and effects of trust and distrust. Figure 1 provides a graphic depiction of the distinctions between trust and distrust and the effects of using legalistic mechanisms to "remedy" trust violations and distrust.

The model assigns the term "trust" to refer to belief in a person's competence to perform a specific task under specific circumstances and the term "distrust" to refer to the belief that a person's values or motives will lead them to approach all situations in an unacceptable way. When trust is disrupted or distrust is engendered, organizations often rely upon legalistic mechanisms to reproduce trust (Fox 1974, Granovetter 1985, Shapiro 1987, Zucker 1986), using such time-honored bureaucratic techniques as formalization (e.g., using written time records) and standardization (e.g., of output requirements). In many cases, these techniques will become institutionalized by attaining a rule-like, objective status (Zucker 1977) and in some cases will become legalistic as they mimic legal forms and move beyond legal/regulatory requirements (Sitkin and Bies 1993).[2]

While legalistic mechanisms are often effective in ameliorating context-specific reliability problems, they are less effective in dealing with generalized value incongruence. As shown in the model, trust violations can be halted by legalistic interventions, but distrust is escalated by increasing perceived interpersonal distance and by failing to address the tendency of perceptions of value incongruence to generalize beyond the immediate situation.

Legalistic Remedies and the Restoration of Trust

In the model, we have defined "trust" as a context-specific expectation of employee reliability. When an employee violates these expectations, we suggest that managers will respond by using legalistic approaches such as formalization and standardization for enhancing reliability (Blau 1972, Durkheim 1949, Taylor 1911). Such remedies (e.g., contracts, job descriptions, and leave policies) are appropriate when task requirements are understood well enough to identify and codify reliability-related inputs, transformation procedures, and/or outputs (March and Simon 1958, Perrow 1967). Under these conditions,

Sim B. Sitkin and Nancy L. Roth

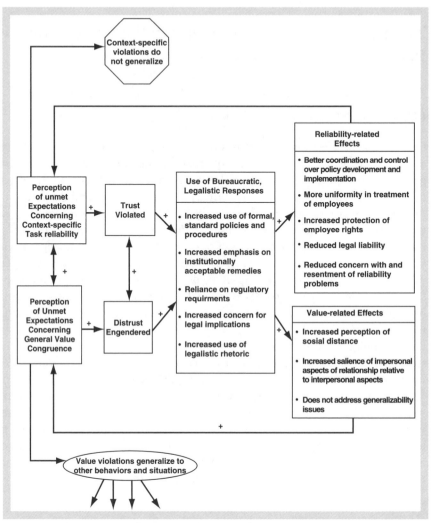

Fig. 1. Model of the Determinants and Effects of Using Legalistic Remedies for Trust/Distrust.

legalistic mechanisms can serve as substitutes for the capacity to directly monitor organizational activities (Williamson 1975), thus reducing the need to rely upon interpersonal bases of trust.

Although they are by no means a panacea, legalistic remedies can promote reliability in several ways (Sitkin and Roth 1993). First, they foster coordination and control to minimize implementation-related problems. Second, through the use of standards and compliance, they can reduce discrimination by insuring that employees will be treated more uniformly and that their rights will be protected. Finally, the collective impact of these effects is to reduce an organization's legal liability and to minimize reliability-related resentment and concern.

Legalistic remedies are likely to be more effective in promoting reliability when they address context-specific problems because the narrower the domain, the easier it is to anticipate and specify relevant contingencies (Arrow 1974). To the extent that the requirements of a task can be specified in formal rules or procedures, legalistic mechanisms can restore reliability-based trust (e.g., Fox 1974, Williamson 1975) within that specific setting. This idea receives support from several different schools represented in the literature. For example, control theorists (e.g., Eisenhardt 1985, Ouchi 1979) and agency theorists (e.g., Arrow 1974, Williamson 1975) offer a range of conditions under which contractual or legalistic specifications can be effective in assuring the trust needed for coordinated action to take place. Additionally, game theorists show that explicit situational constraints can be quite effective in fostering trusting behavior (Deutsch and Krauss 1962, Matthews and Shimoff 1979). For example, in a series of experiments concerning the effect of contextual constraints on trust, Matthews, Kordonski and Shimoff (1983, p. 276) find "little evidence for the development of 'generalized' interpersonal trust that might be maintained independently of situational contingencies."

Legalistic Remedies and the Reduction of Distrust

The question of whether legalistic remedies are effective in situations characterized by distrust, as defined here, is not even raised in previous research.[3] While Deutsch (1958) suggests the importance of formal remedies (procedures or sanctions) in fostering cooperative (i.e., trusting) behavior, he distinguishes "suspicion" from "trust" and focuses solely on trust. While Zucker (1986) briefly notes the distinction between trust and distrust, and Granovetter (1985) and Shapiro (1987) highlight the limitations of legalistic remedies in situations of trust violation, none of them considers the use of legalistic remedies in situations of distrust. To address this theoretical gap, our suggestion that distrust rests on perceptions of generalized value incongruence provides a theoretical framework for focusing on the question of whether the adoption of formal legalistic mechanisms of control can restore value congruence, once the presence of shared values has been questioned.

Our approach addresses the issue in two ways. First, it can help to explain why legalistic remedies might be adopted to "remedy" distrust. Since value-based distrust is engendered when basic social values are violated by individuals or groups who are unfamiliar with or unaccepting of them, rules, regulations, standard procedures, and other legalistic mechanisms of control may be adopted to symbolize cultural unity (i.e., widely shared values) and to articulate and enforce communal norms and customs (Barber 1983, Edelman 1990, Selznick 1969, Zucker 1988). Second, our conceptualization of distrust and its role can help to explain the limited effectiveness of legalistic remedies on distrust. While legalistic remedies can symbolize legitimacy and value congruence (Meyer and Rowan 1977, Selznick 1969), their very explicitness undermines their effectiveness (Eisenberg 1984) in ameliorating distrust.

Institutional theorists (e.g., Zucker 1977) explain this phenomenon by noting that the power of institutionalized beliefs and practices is largely based on their being tacitly accepted and, therefore, remaining unexamined. According to Zucker (1977), once a previously tacit set of beliefs, values, or practices becomes formalized, its presumed legitimacy is inadvertently threatened by raising the question of whether the formalized approach is necessarily the only (or even the best) way to resolve the issue. That is, when a practice is formalized (written down or made official) this act of formalization may not only reflect the institutionalized status of the practice, but it also unintentionally begins the process of eroding that status.[4]

Our conceptualization of distrust provides three reasons why the adoption of legalistic "remedies" is likely to exacerbate the problem of distrust: they are impersonal, distance-enhancing, and context-specific. First, legalistic remedies can erode the interpersonal foundations of a relationship they are intended to bolster because they replace reliance on an individual's "good will" with objective, formal requirements. "They do not produce trust, but instead are a functional substitute for it ... they do not allow for the extent to which concrete personal relations and the obligations inherent in them discourage malfeasance" (Granovetter 1985, p. 489).

Second, when rules and procedures form the basis of continuing relations they can disrupt the "implicit agreements" that efficiently govern social interaction (Arrow 1974, p. 26) by interposing a structural barrier between the parties, making the relationship feel less direct and close. The more distant the relationship, the more likely it is that differences rather than similarities will be salient and that those differences will be construed as indicative of value incongruencies. Zucker (1986) and Shaprio (1987) stress that increases in physical and social distance lead to a decline in personal contact, transaction history, and familiarity—all of which reduce the potential for personal experience to serve as a basis for trust. Shapiro argues that formal procedures and other legalistic mechanisms tend to increase the perceived distance between parties because their relationships are no longer direct (i.e., they are mediated by laws, rules, and procedures). As Peachey and Lerner (1981, pp. 441 and 447) note: "Where direct social bonds among people are lacking, laws and legal mechanisms tend to be more prevalent ... More laws generate more enforcement and more enforcement leads to more perceived injustice, less faith in the system, and more laws ... " Thus, one paradoxical consequence of using legalistic substitutes for interpersonal trust is that they erode the more stable and renewable social foundation upon which trust is built (Granovetter 1985, Shapiro 1987).

Third, legalistic remedies typically are tailored to a specific context for which procedures or outputs can be specified (e.g., due process procedures that specify the details for handling hiring, firing, or other human resource decisions). The specificity and explicitness at the heart of legalistic remedies do not address the value incongruence that underlies distrust, and instead escalates distrust by focusing on minutiae. Fox (1974, pp. 104–105) describes an example, in which the escalating cycle of distrust is initiated when "subordinates ... try to limit the discretion of their superiors ... In so doing they manifest an institutionalized distrust of management, thereby strengthening a management belief in a divergence of goals which disposes it to manifest counterexpressions of distrust toward subordinates ... Further reciprocation ... by subordinates may impart another twist to the spiral ... The inclination is for each to measure both his own and the other's contribution with increasing precision."

In summary, our analysis provides an explanation for Shapiro's (1987) observation that the adoption of legalistic mechanisms to enhance trust were only partially successful: the reliability-oriented attributes of legalistic remedies may be effective in restoring trust, but are less successful in addressing the value-oriented basis of distrust. Although the trust/distrust distinction was notaddressed explicitly in previous research, earlier work provides support for our analysis. First, past research shows that formal control mechanisms are more effective in obtaining compliance with specifiable objectives than in obtaining commitment to a general value orientation (Ouchi 1979). Second, research that examines how organizations attain value congruence among members stresses the importance of informal and personal processes, rather than highly legalistic ones (e.g., Van Maanen and Schein 1979). Third, transaction cost economists and agency theorists suggest that formal specification of exchange relations can be effective only when requirements can be identified in sufficient detail a priori and violations can be observed (e.g., Arrow 1985, Eisenhardt 1985, Williamson 1975)—and these criteria are rather difficult to meet in specifying the degree to which tacit cultural values are shared.

....

The Disruption of Trust and Distrust: The Case of HIV/AIDS

This section of the paper applies our theoretical model of the effectiveness of legalistic remedies for trust/distrust to the case of organizational responses to employees with HIV/AIDS. The possibility that trust may be violated is raised by the medical aspects of the disease. With the advances in biomedical research of the last few years, people who have the HIV virus can be expected to live for ten or more years before they suffer from the debilitating symptoms of the opportunistic infections to which people with lowered immune functioning fall prey. When their immune functioning is reduced to this level, HIV-infected people are said to have AIDS, the final stage of the syndrome that is generally referred to as HIV/AIDS. At that stage, employees may become less reliable at work as they are often plagued by serious infections and fatigue. Our model labels such occurrences as context-specific trust violations because periodic absence from work or temporarily reduced productivity due to illness can be perceived as localized, short-term problems for an otherwise reliable performer—and, thus, would not be expected to generalize and taint the employee's entire relationship with the organization.

The possibility of distrust being engendered by the presence of employees with HIV/AIDS is raised by the stigmatized features of the syndrome (Sitkin and Roth 1993): (1) it is a deadly disease (fatality); (2) although it is known to be transmissible under clearly defined conditions, its causes and effects are perceived as uncertain (perceived uncertainty); (3) it involves groups and activities that are not fully accepted by mainstream society (attributed marginality); (4) the stigmas associated with HIV/AIDS are transmitted through behaviors that are engaged in voluntarily (voluntary behaviors); (5) the stigmas associated with HIV/AIDS are transmissible in the workplace, although the virus itself is not transmissible under ordinary workplace conditions (communicability). These features (which need not all be present to engender stigmatization) may raise questions in workplace settings concerning the extent to which infected employees hold values that are congruent with those of their coworkers. Our model suggests that perceived value incongruence will diffuse to other situations and behaviors in which the infected employee is involved, thus engendering generalized distrust of employees with HIV/AIDS.

Application of Proposed Model of Trust/Distrust to the Case of HIV/AIDS

Figure 2 depicts the application of our trust/distrust model to the case of organizational employees with HIV/AIDS. As shown in the figure, the medical characteristics of the illness are hypothesized to have their primary effect on perceptions of context-specific reliability and trust, whereas stigma-related characteristics are hypothesized to have their primary effect on perceptions of generalized value incongruence and distrust. The remainder of this section

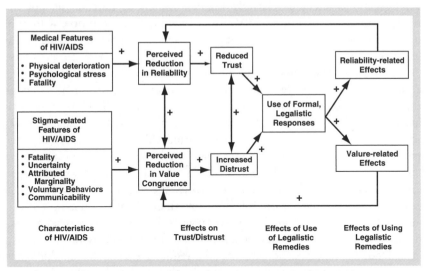

Fig. 2. HIV Characteristics and their Relationship to a General Model of the Determinants and Effects of Using of Legalistic Remedies for Trust/Distrust.

discusses in detail the application of our trust/distrust model to the case of HIV/AIDS and presents our hypothesis that legalistic responses to employees with HIV/AIDS will be more effective in addressing the reliability (trust) issues raised by employees with the disease, and less effective in dealing with the value congruence issues (distrust). We will suggest that the stigmatized features of the illness engender distrust which generalizes to such an extent that (1) employees with HIV/AIDS are perceived to be less reliable than they are; (2) the illness is perceived to be more communicable than it is in workplace settings; and (3) workplace responses are designed to address the less stigmatized reliability issues, thus ignoring the underlying value congruence problems and engendering an escalating spiral of distrust.

Effect of the Medical Features of HIV/AIDS on Perceived Reliability

Like other catastrophic illnesses, HIV/AIDS can have a substantial, if largely hidden, effect on workplace reliability due to the medical features of the illness. On a number of dimensions—ranging from lost productivity and absenteeism to the increased cost of benefit packages—the price of the increased incidence of any catastrophic illness within the workforce can be substantial, whether the illness affects an irreplaceable executive, a highly skilled technician, or a more easily replaced member of the workforce (Allstate Forum on Public Issues 1987).

Sim B. Sitkin and Nancy L. Roth

Although it has affected relatively few individuals to date, in its potential for organizational disruption HIV/AIDS has much in common with other catastrophic illnesses such as cardiovascular disease, lung cancer and alcoholism (Sitkin and Roth 1993).

Employees in the early stages of HIV infection show no ill symptoms because they have not yet developed AIDS-related opportunistic infections (Volberding, Lagakos, Koch, Pettinelli, Myers, Booth, Balfour, Reichman, Bartlett, Hirsch, Murphy, Hardy, Foeiro, Fischl, Bartlett, Merigan, Hyslop, Richman, Valentine and Corey 1990). During this pre-AIDS period (which may last as long as ten years—and may last longer in the future as drug therapies are improved,[5] these individuals are fully reliable as employees. However, task reliability often decreases as the disease progresses simply because a sick employee is often less reliable than a healthy one.

Reduced reliability is manifest in several ways that can have a cascading effect on the workplace. Production goals may be threatened, as the progressive illness leads to repeated hospitalizations, reduced energy levels, diminished productivity, and increased absenteeism (Koch 1989, Roth 1990). Bosses and coworkers have to cope with reduced employee reliability as the disease progresses and employees with HIV/AIDS succumb to opportunistic infections that their immune systems have become powerless to fight. Conflict, disruption, and unpleasant workplace interactions can result (e.g., James 1988), as even the most sympathetic of superiors or coworkers may feel burdened by having to assume additional responsibilities to compensate for the lack of reliability that can accompany serious illness (Puckett and Emery 1988).

This scenario of disease progression suggests how HIV/AIDS can undermine the reliability-related basis of trust, particularly in the final stages of the illness. This impact on workplace reliability is not unique to HIV/AIDS, as it is characteristic of a number of catastrophic illnesses that affect employees (Panem 1988, Perrow and Guillen 1990, Puckett and Emery 1988, Sitkin and Roth 1993, Sontag 1988). Although employees with HIV/AIDS present the organization with legitimate concerns about reliability, particularly in the final stages of the illness, we suggest that the stigmas associated with the illness bolster perceptions of unreliability. Employers may overestimate the future unreliability of employees with HIV/AIDS. Or perhaps employers are so loathe to address the stigmas associated with HIV/AIDS directly that they find it easier to handle employees with the illness as if reliability were the primary issue, rather than focusing on the stigmas that create discomfort. James (1988) documents several cases of employers overreacting to "reliability" issues associated with employees recovering from cancer and heart disease. Such employees are often fired, moved to less demanding positions, or refused positions altogether, even though in the case of heart disease "after the rehab program a lot of people are in better shape than they've been in for years." James (1988,

p. 14R) notes that "job discrimination against AIDS patients is especially virulent ... Even people who don't have full-blown AIDS suffer discrimination; just having the virus is enough." He cites an example of a pharmacist who was refused a position after it was disclosed that he had HIV, even though he was asymptomatic and chances of transmission of the virus under his work conditions were negligible.

A second key point is that this effect is not generalized—it is context-specific. HIV/AIDS (like other potentially debilitating physical ailments) has real physical limitations associated with it, but these limitations are often confined to the performance of specific tasks within specifiable domains. For example, just as a blind person is unable to perform tasks that require sight but is fully able to complete tasks when sight is not essential, so too the characteristics of HIV/AIDS have real but circumscribed effects.

Effect of Stigma-related Features of HIV/AIDS on Trust/Distrust

In addition to its potential effects on reliability, HIV/AIDS engenders organizational responses that cannot be explained by the medical features of the illness alone (Roth, Sitkin, and House in press). Employers have gone to court to argue their "right" to test potential employees for the virus as a condition of employment, claiming that HIV infection would reduce employee reliability. In contrast, despite growing attention to controlling corporate health costs, employers still rarely condition employability on smoking, alcohol consumption, or diet—despite their well-established links to cancer, heart disease, alcoholism and other illnesses that can affect absenteeism, turnover, and health costs (see Mann 1991, Sitkin and Roth 1993). Those with HIV/AIDS are much more likely to be perceived as both unreliable and "different" because the concerns their illness engenders are perceived as fundamental and potentially threatening. Cancer and heart disease lack the degree of stigmatization associated with HIV/AIDS (Roth, Sitkin, and House in press), and employees who are incapacitated by these diseases are much more likely to be perceived as "merely" unreliable when they are unable to work (and dealt with in terms of context-specific reliability requirements) than are employees with HIV/AIDS. Furthermore, disclosure that an employee has these illnesses does not set off the same type of fear reaction that is often seen when an employee discloses positive HIV status (Tillett 1989). This pattern of responses is important because it represents one condition under which value congruence is likely to be questioned and, thus, distrust is likely to be engendered.

Responses to employees with HIV/AIDS are more value-laden and evoke memories of the fear and ignorance associated with stigmatized epidemics and plagues of the past (Panem 1988, Sontag 1988). For example, a laborer who showed no symptoms but had taken several sick days told a company physician (after confidentiality was promised) about his HIV/AIDS status. Shortly thereafter he was dismissed because there were no "lighter" jobs available. In another case, a teacher who was hospitalized for pneumonia was asked, prior to returning to work, to certify that he was "free of infectious diseases." He soon received a threatening letter from a parent and was subsequently suspended without pay and then fired (AIDS Council of New South Wales 1991).

Perhaps it should not be surprising that HIV/AIDS evokes such responses, since that which does not fit into a society's everyday classification schemes— the uncertain, the marginal, and the transitional—is most likely to be stigmatized (Douglas 1966; Goffman 1963; Jones, Farina, Hastorf, Markus, Miller and Scott 1984; Page 1984). Nonetheless, stigmatization represents one condition under which value congruence is likely to be questioned and, thus, distrust is likely to be engendered.

The Effect of the Stigma of HIV/AIDS on Perceived Value Congruence. Of the five features associated with the stigmatization of HIV/AIDS, attributed marginality most clearly illustrates the effect of stigmatization on perceived value congruence. Value congruence in organizations rests to a large degree on the presumption of commonality among members (Schein 1985, Selznick 1957). The link between marginality and value congruence is reflected in Douglas' (1966) use of the term "marginal" to characterize groups that are shunned or rejected because their behavior, their characteristics, or their affiliations are seen as threatening dominant social norms. The mere presence of those labelled as marginal (i.e., "not like us") implicitly constitutes a direct challenge to the presumption of social similarity, shared values, and value congruence (i.e., that the people we work with are "just like us").

When attention is drawn to individual and subgroup differences, coworkers may begin to question whether shared values and priorities among colleagues can be assumed to exist and generalized suspicion can develop (Deutsch 1958, Douglas 1985). Those who are sick may be presumed to practice stigmatized behaviors or to be members of stigmatized groups and, therefore, supervisors and coworkers may wonder if they can be trusted to cleave to shared organizational values while holding different personal values.

The Effect of Stigmatization on Generalized Distrust. We have identified two factors that can fuel the effect of stigmatization on generalized distrust. First, people who have such nonobvious stigmas as homosexuality and intravenous drug use often do not disclose their stigmas and choose to "pass" as "normal." When they do disclose, they tend to tell people with whom they have strong interpersonal ties (e.g., parents and close friends) rather than people from whom they are more distant (e.g., coworkers) (Kleck 1968). When such disclosures are made, supervisors and close coworkers may feel betrayed by the sick employee because the "unfairness of his past silence" (Goffman 1963, p. 95) makes those who were "concealed-from" question whether they ever really knew the "concealer" and, therefore, whether they were lied to in other arenas as well (Tedlow and Marram 1991).

Second, although it has not been addressed in the literature, we propose that distrust can be generalized in another way—individuals can begin to distrust their own judgment, as they ask themselves, "how could I have been fooled?" The sudden revelation of health status and its association with stigmatized behaviors can introduce managerial suspicion of employees and divisiveness among coworkers. When individual members of an organization begin to distrust their colleagues or to distrust their own ability to recognize tainted information, this may be taken as evidence that the very basis of shared values has begun to erode (see Tedlow and Marram 1991).

Legalistic Organizational Remedies and HIV/AIDS

Prevalence of Legalistic Remedies. One implication of our analysis is that legalistic responses would be a common—and perhaps even predominant—reaction to the presence of an employee (or other member) with HIV/AIDS because HIV/AIDS is associated with both reduced trust and increased distrust. This assertion receives consistent support in previous research on organizational responses to HIV/AIDS. Advice given in the practitioner literature on human resource management (e.g., Banta 1988, Chapman 1987, Myers and Myers 1987, Waldo 1987) frequently suggests that clearly defined policies and procedures will "remedy" the problems associated with having employees with HIV/AIDS. Surveys (Masi 1987) provide evidence that by 1987 as many as 15 percent of the United States' Fortune 500 companies had developed HIV/AIDS-specific policies[6] and that scores of other firms were reviewing existing catastrophic illness policies to ensure that they would deal sufficiently with HIV/AIDS. Case study research (Kirp 1989, Puckett and Emery 1988) similarly emphasizes formal policies and procedures as remedies for the HIV/AIDS problem. In an experiment designed to compare how decision makers respond to employees with various diseases, Roth, Sitkin, and House (in press) report that the more stigmatized the disease, the more likely decision makers are to employ legalistic mechanisms rather than relying on informal norms or supervisor discretion. In addition, case studies like Kirp's (1989, Kirp, Epstein, Franks, Simon, Conway, and Lewis 1989) provide support for the notion that legalistic responses to issues such as hiring/firing, testing, promotions, assignments, benefits, privacy, and educational programs should include legalistic decision criteria, adversarial processes, and law-like rhetoric—as well as the adoption of formal policies and procedures.

Why Legalistic Remedies are Used. We have suggested that an employee with HIV/AIDS has the potential to destabilize organizations in two ways: by disrupting the coordination of interdependent tasks that depend upon employee reliability and by challenging deeply held organizational values and beliefs. Reliability problems can be illustrated in the case of an employee on whom others depend because of his or her unique knowledge or skills. If that person becomes less reliable (due to low energy, poor concentration, or unplanned hospitalizations), they can critically disrupt the work of those who depend upon them. For example, if a person is known to have an advanced case of HIV/AIDS, it may not be sensible to assign them to direct an important long-term project. Value congruence problems are illustrated when an employee violates tacit organizational values simply by having a disease (i.e., HIV/AIDS) that is often associated with being gay. For example, consider the case of an organizational member who is an active participant in company sports teams, socializes with other company employees and is accepted as a cultural insider in the firm's "macho" culture, but is then suddenly shunned when coworkers find out that he has AIDS and is gay.

Organizations often adopt legalistic mechanisms to "remedy" the reliability and value incongruence problems associated with having an employee with HIV/AIDS. Legalistic remedies can have two distinct functions that map directly on the dual organizational effects of having an employee with HIV/AIDS. The first function is strictly administrative—to handle the reliability issues. The second function is largely symbolic—to demonstrate that the organization is acting responsibly, to show that the problem has been "remedied," and to suggest that addressing the reliability issues eliminates the need to address the value incongruence issues (often without acknowledging the presence of value incongruence at all).

The administrative function of legalistic mechanisms is to ensure that coordinated operations will be minimally disrupted by the presence of an organizational member with a serious illness (e.g., HIV/AIDS), to protect the rights of all employees to be treated in a fair and even-handed way, and to address the fears of coworkers. Administrative policies can focus on a variety of issues including: nondiscrimination in hiring and firing, sick leave, medical confidentiality, short- and long-term disability, reasonable accommodation of employees whose abilities have changed due to illness, cross training, job sharing, availability of slack resources, and workplace education programs. Such formal policies serve to enhance the trust of the organization and coworkers in the continuing capability of the organization to perform reliably with an employee with HIV/AIDS and the trust of employees that the organization will take care of their needs (Allstate Forum on Public Issues 1989; Banta 1988; Chapman 1987; Letchinger 1986; Rowe, Russell-Einhorn and Baker 1986; Susser 1987).

Legalistic remedies can also fulfill the second, more symbolic institutional function. For example, by promulgating written policies and procedures for handling employees with HIV/AIDS, the organization sends the message to employees that having a coworker with HIV/AIDS is a routine matter that can be dealt with in a standardized, formal, familiar way (i.e., legalistically). This can also reassure employees that should they become ill, they will receive appropriate health benefits and that their rights concerning nondiscrimination and confidentiality will be protected. Formal policies also give organizations (and their members) a way of communicating about HIV/AIDS that shields them from the embarrassment of discussing the issues associated with it directly. Simply having a policy can give the impression that the problem has been adequately addressed (Meyer and Rowan 1977).

Such policies can also address the fears of external publics (Kirp, Epstein, Franks, Simon, Conway, and Lewis 1989) who may be concerned that the presence of employees with HIV will make the organization less reliable, will pose a health threat to consumers, or will pose a threat of stigma to those associated with an organization that has an employee with HIV/AIDS. They can reassure external audiences that standards are being maintained, that the "damage" caused by the ill employee will be contained, and that the stigma will not diffuse. Thus, such policies can signal to all who are concerned that the issue has been dealt with responsibly and that interactions can continue undisturbed. In so doing, they serve both to enhance the organization's legitimacy and to reduce the threat of litigation.

In theory, legalistic mechanisms alone should be able to address the problems associated with employees with HIV/AIDS. However, the response of Pacific Bell to employees with HIV/AIDS shows how legalistic mechanisms can be used to preserve organizational trust but cannot remedy distrust problems without the help of some nonlegalistic actions (see Kirp 1989). Early in the epidemic, Pacific Bell responded to employees with HIV/AIDS in its traditional, highly formalized way. They framed the problem as an everyday supervisory and benefits administration issue. In terms of our model, they only acted to address the problems of trust violation by focusing on reliability concerns.

As the epidemic continued, various managers found that addressing trust-related reliability issues was not sufficient—dealing with workers' fears about being exposed to HIV through casual contact required that management go beyond traditional, legalistic responses. Management and the union cooperated closely in developing education programs to address employee fears directly. Most importantly, the company, which had been in "open warfare" with

San Francisco's gay community, saw the HIV/AIDS issue as an opportunity to redress previous wrongs (for example, their exclusionary hiring policies had led to the largest ever settlement in a gay discrimination case—$3 million). As a result, Pacific Bell went beyond the legalistic by becoming publicly associated with the disease by funding and promoting an educational video about HIV/AIDS in the workplace. By going beyond the merely legalistic, this willingness to address publicly all of the uncomfortable issues associated with HIV/AIDS—homosexuality, drug use, sex, death—sent a symbolic message that the company was changing. It also began to remedy the distrust that had been engendered by its discriminatory hiring practices that could have escalated (in terms of externally initiated litigation and internal employee relations) had Pacific Bell not addressed directly the stigmas associated with HIV/AIDS.

Legalistic responses can promote trust by creating human resource policies aimed at assuring minimal levels of employee benefits are provided and to facilitate better coordination and planning. In addition, less legalistic organizational "remedies" can reduce distrust by making it clear that sick employees are "part of the same family" (to increase perceptions of shared values) or by educating coworkers about the disease (to reduce the degree to which fear increases perceived social distance and stigmatization).

Relative Effectiveness of Legalistic Remedies for Trust and Distrust. As the Pacific Bell example illustrates, we anticipate that use of legalistic "remedies" would be relatively effective with respect to the reliability-related problems created by HIV/AIDS, but would be ineffective or even counterproductive with respect to the value-related problems associated with HIV/AIDS.

While legalistic responses are designed to address reliability issues (Banta 1988; Gray 1989; Kirp 1989; Kirp, Epstein, Franks, Simon, Conway and Lewis 1989; Myers and Myers 1987), they appear to be less effective in altering perceptions of distrust or the view that persons with HIV/AIDS are (and will remain) cultural outsiders (see Illingworth 1990; Kirp, Epstein, Franks, Simon, Conway and Lewis 1989; O'Malley 1989; Rowe, Russell-Einhorn and Baker 1986; Shilts 1987). Legalistic remedies are more likely to be effective to the extent that the issue to be addressed is context-specific because the narrower the domain, the easier it is to anticipate and specify relevant contingencies. The presence of an employee with HIV/AIDS is likely to violate trust as the employee's disease progresses and he or she is less reliable at work because of absenteeism, reduced ability to concentrate, or lowered productivity. Formal rules and procedures can be designed to specify the amount of sick leave and short-term disability to which employees are entitled, the extent to which they can be accommodated when they become unable to perform certain tasks and the methods that will be used to protect the confidentiality of sick employees if they desire. Within that narrow domain, such remedies are expected to be fairly effective.

On the other hand, we would expect legalistic mechanisms to be less effective in addressing value incongruence problems associated with having an employee with HIV/AIDS that can engender distrust. Our model suggests that legalistic mechanisms would be more likely to exacerbate rather than ameliorate distrust because they are impersonal, distance enhancing, and context-specific. People with catastrophic illnesses are often lonely, scared, and angry (Kubler-Ross 1969), but employees with HIV/AIDS face the additional fears and pains associated with having an illness that is stigmatized in so many ways (Sontag 1988). In addition to needing reassurance that their jobs will be there when they recover sufficiently to work, many such employees also need the reassurance that their coworkers will continue to treat them as a "member of the team." Impersonal policies and procedures cannot legislate the familial aspects of organizational interaction (Held 1990).

In some cases legalistic "remedies" increase the distance between employees. By developing policies devoted to HIV/AIDS, organizations call attention to the issue and suggest that it is different from other illnesses that might affect employees. The sense of difference created by singling out the syndrome may give both sick employees and their coworkers a sense that people who have it are outsiders—a response that is opposite to the one that was originally intended.

Finally, legalistic "remedies" are typically tailored to a specific context. The specificity and explicitness at the heart of legalistic remedies cannot address the general sense of untrustworthiness that is associated with an employee who has HIV/AIDS, independent of an individual's context-specific actions. Employees with HIV/AIDS are often viewed as less reliable than they really are because of the stigmas associated with the illness. Furthermore, even though the illness is not transmitted in ordinary workplace settings, people with HIV/AIDS are often viewed as a threat to the health of coworkers because of the stigmas associated with the illness. This suggests that stigmas are not addressed effectively by formal policies and procedures because coworkers' fears cannot be alleviated by simply issuing a policy that declares that HIV cannot be transmitted under ordinary workplace circumstances.

Escalating Cycle of Distrust. Legalistic "remedies" can also fuel escalating cycles of distrust. This effect is illustrated by one of the most important and frequently cited HIV/AIDS issues for which legalistic remedies are used—confidentiality in handling employee information (Allstate Forum on Public Issues 1987; Rowe, Russell-Einhorn and Baker 1986). Formal systems are adopted by organizations to ensure the confidentiality that sick employees need to protect their vulnerable interests (Comptroller General's Task Force on AIDS in the Workplace 1987, Stein 1987) because employees with HIV/AIDS are justifiably concerned about threats to insurance coverage, employment status, social relations, and personal reputations.

Formalizing how HIV/AIDS information is handled can foster a sense of openness and sharing, can comfort employees with HIV/AIDS and their fearful coworkers, and can also minimize the conflict and disruption that can arise from HIV/AIDS-related concerns. In contrast, we have identified three reasons why legalistic remedies that are adopted to protect confidentiality may exacerbate the very problems they are intended to mitigate. First, by shielding information an emphasis on confidentiality can maintain the ignorance of those who have unfounded fears concerning coworkers with HIV/AIDS. Second, it can also increase the perceived distance between sick employees and their coworkers by erecting a veil of secrecy between them. Third, it can convey to sick employees that their illness is so stigmatized and shameful that it cannot even be discussed. Taken together, these factors can reinforce suspicions that the other group is somehow "different" and therefore to be distrusted (Goffman 1963, Illingworth 1990, Shilts 1987). Although all parties might agree on the value of openness, it would be naive to ignore the discrimination and distrust that frequently result from the disclosure of HIV/AIDS information.

Discussion

In this section, we provide an agenda for further research in three related domains: our conceptualization of trust/distrust and its implications for organizations, the effects of stigma on decision making in organizations, and a theoretical framework for conceptualizing responses to HIV/AIDS in the workplace.

We have provided a theoretical framework for understanding the effects of organizations adopting legalistic mechanisms to remedy trust problems. Building on a substantial body of earlier work (Barber 1983, Deutsch 1962, Fox 1974, Gabarro 1978, Rotter 1980, Shapiro 1987, Zand 1972, Zucker 1986), we have defined trust as an expectation. However, we have departed from previous work by suggesting that the specific nature of the expectation will distinguish among types of trust. We have identified two types of expectations: expectations concerning context-specific task performance (trust) and expectations concerning generalized value congruence (distrust).

We have suggested that the effectiveness of legalistic mechanisms in restoring trust/distrust in organizations will depend in part on the nature of the expectation being violated. Thus, we build on and extend the work of Dimaggio and Powell (1983), Meyer (1983), and Zucker (1977, 1988) by explaining *why* legalistic mechanisms can function effectively both administratively and symbolically—that is, because they are relatively more effective in addressing trust violations and less effective in reducing distrust. We extend the work of Fox (1974), Granovetter (1985), and Shapiro (1987) by explaining why, in situations of distrust, adopting legalistic mechanisms may not only fail to restore trust, but may lead to an escalating spiral of formality and distance that increases distrust.

In addition, by applying our theoretical framework to the case of organizational responses to employees with HIV/AIDS, we have been able to provide a theoretical framework that can guide future research on this timely and significant organizational issue. In the case of HIV/AIDS, we have shown the relative efficacy of legalistic mechanisms in dealing with reliability problems associated with sick employees that violate trust and their relative ineffectiveness in handling distrust grounded in the value incongruence issues that are raised by the stigmas associated with the syndrome.

Distinguishing Trust and Distrust. Two basic propositions developed in this paper are new to the literature on trust. First, we conceptualized trust and distrust as distinct constructs and theorized about why trust and distrust might be expected to have different determinants and effects. Further research is needed to test whether trust and distrust can be empirically differentiated, both in terms of individual perception and in terms of causal relations. For example, the recent work of Levin and Chapman (1990) on the effect of the insider/outsider distinction could be applied to the trust/distrust distinction.

Second, the notion that trust and distrust differ in the degree to which they are context-specific or generalized can be tested empirically. While we were able to show that the extant evidence in the case of HIV/AIDS is consistent with our theory, the evidence should be considered suggestive at best. Task reliability as an exemplar of violations of context-specific expectations should be examined empirically, as should our proposal that value (in)congruence is the organizational equivalent of generalizability of expectations. This kind of distinction may be especially relevant to scholars who study organizational culture, socialization processes, and value and belief systems.

In our emphasis on stigmatization as a violation of value congruence, we have examined only a small subset of the possible conditions that could engender distrust. While we did this in order to focus on an extreme example (HIV/AIDS) that might clarify the distinction, it is likely that much more subtle cultural violations can also engender distrust. Therefore, future research—both theoretical and empirical—could fruitfully examine other, nonstigmatized issues that might engender distrust. For example, recent experimental studies (Levin and Chapman 1990; Roth, Sitkin, and House in press) have begun to identify factors that could identify the distinguishing characteristics of and boundaries between stigmatized and nonstigmatized conditions and responses.

In addition, future research should conceptually and empirically explore situations of localized value incongruence and generalized unreliability. We speculate that localized value incongruence might result in an employee's being more closely watched for future value incongruities—a concept which is consistent with the notion of "markability" in the stigma literature (Jones et al. 1984). In contrast, responses to generalized unreliability may be more susceptible to situation specifics. For example, a long-term employee who has an established record of loyalty and diligent effort may have established sufficient idiosyncrasy credits to offset a lack of reliability. Another potentially important contingency factor is the balance between the resources the employee does contribute to the organization (e.g., they may perform some critical activities reliably) and the degree to which their unreliability threatens core operations (Miceli and Near 1992, Pfeffer and Salancik 1978).

The Effect of Trust and Distrust on the Use of Legalistic Remedies. We have argued that both reduced trust and increased distrust will be associated with the increased use of legalistic remedies, although these hypothesized relationships have not yet been subjected to field or experimental studies of any kind. There are a number of avenues that researchers could pursue to test the proposed relationships. First, it has not been established empirically that both relationships exist. Although Zucker used historical data to support her contention that the disruption of trust fosters increased use of formal organizational mechanisms, Zucker did not clearly differentiate trust from distrust and thus it is unclear which construct is causally responsible in her study. Second, even if both trust and distrust have the hypothesized causal relationship with legalistic responses, the relative strength of their influence is as yet unexamined. Third, there are a number of distinguishable components that are included under the general rubric of the term "legalistic response," including formal policies and procedures, institutionally legitimated responses, reliance upon regulatory requirements, adversarial processes, attention to the threat of litigation, and the use of legalistic rhetoric (Sitkin and Bies 1993). Another line of fruitful research could examine systematically the extent to which trust and distrust are independently or jointly associated with the use of each of these forms of legalistic response.

A number of scholars and practitioners have pointed to the transformation of organizations toward structures and processes increasingly characterized as flatter, decentralized, client-focused, self-organizing, and learning oriented (see Lewin and Stephens 1992 for a recent review). A tacit—but unexamined—assumption underlying these new organizational forms is that employees can be trusted to operate with increased autonomy and that conveying to employees that they are trusted will enhance their sense of responsibility and performance. Some elements of these design innovations, such as increased informality in supervisor/subordinate relations, would appear to support trust-related assumptions. However, other elements may inadvertently undermine trust and increase distrust (e.g., the use of highly formalized and detailed quality standards or the formalization of rules concerning the management of a diverse workforce).

Thus, one potentially important theoretical and practical implication of our analysis is that increased concern with diversity, justice, and other highly charged issues can fuel increased "legalization" in a way that directly undermines the assumptions underlying these emergent organizational forms. This suggests that explicit attention to the causes and effects of trust and distrust are fundamental (and currently overlooked), and must be considered in efforts to increase empowerment and create autonomously operating groups (Dumain 1991, Huber 1984, Lewin and Stephens 1992). Similarly, to create organizations that are capable of effective experimentation and learning (Argyris and Schon 1974, Senge 1990, Sitkin 1992) or bridging traditional organizational boundaries (Larson 1992, Miles and Snow 1986, Powell 1990), it is critical that scholars and practitioners develop an enhanced understanding of how trust/distrust interact with the use of potentially rigid legalistic procedures.

The Effects of Legalistic Remedies. We have proposed a theoretical explanation for Peachey and Lerner's (1981) and Shapiro's (1987) insight that legalistic responses seemed to be ineffective in addressing the problems they were intended to remedy, but were very effective in promoting an escalating cycle of what Meyer (1983) referred to as organizational "legalization." Future work could directly test the degree to which legalistic remedies that have effectively addressed concerns for reliability are inadequate nonetheless in addressing problems associated with value incongruence, and whether unresolved value incongruence leads to escalating legalization.

Stigmatization in Organizations. Earlier research concerning stigma by Goffman (1963) and Page (1984) provides useful guidance concerning the personal attributes that lead to stigmatization and suggests that mere association with a stigmatized individual may, in turn, stigmatize others. Sutton and Callahan (1987) draw upon Goffman's concept of "courtesy stigma" to apply this work to organizational processes, showing how organization-level stigmatization can taint individuals who are associated with those organizations. Although it is not the central point of this paper, our examination of the stigmatization of HIV/AIDS and its effect on organizational responses extends previous work by switching the diffusion process examined by Sutton and Callahan. Where Sutton and Callahan looked at how an organization's attributes can threaten to affect individuals in the organization (i.e., corporate executives), we examined how an individual's attributes can threaten the organization. Perhaps one reason that Sutton and Callahan's work has not stimulated subsequent attention to stigma in organizations is that stigma is more likely to transfer from individuals to organizations than vice versa because most of the attributes that foster stigmatization occur at the individual level. Thus, the process we have described may provide a basis for increased attention by organizational scholars to the role of stigma in organizations.

In addition, the factors that underlie the stigmatization of HIV/AIDS (fatality, uncertainty, attributed marginality, voluntary behaviors, and communicability) can lead to the identification of other possible sources of stigmatization in organizations. Responses to issues ranging from handling toxic chemicals, workplace sex, drug use, gender and race relations, cigarette smoking and other personal health habits, and corporate illegal activity may be usefully conceptualized in terms of responses to that which is stigmatized. By focusing attention on the effects of stigmatization on trust/distrust and on legalistic responses, a broader range of potential effects are available for future work by scholars interested in the effects of stigmatization on organizational behavior.

HIV/AIDS in the Workplace. Although the rising incidence of HIV/AIDS in the workplace has drawn a great deal of attention in the managerial literature and among scholars with a primary interest in regulatory or legal issues, organizational scientists have largely ignored the phenomenon. One explanation for this gap is that there have been no theoretical frameworks through which to fruitfully examine the HIV/AIDS phenomenon. One contribution of this paper is to draw on prior research about trust and stigmatization to outline several conceptual foundations upon which future work on HIV/AIDS can be built. Because we have examined HIV/AIDS within an organizational context (rather than the personal, interpersonal, or legal contexts that have dominated past work), we have been able to identify two important issues that have been largely overlooked in earlier studies. First, HIV/AIDS can be examined in the context of other organizational stigmas to further our understanding of how the stigma of HIV/AIDS affects employees with the virus, their coworkers, and the responses of their employers. Second, scholars who have studied HIV/AIDS have not focused on the effect of HIV/AIDS on trust and distrust and, as we have shown, this is indeed a promising lens through which to examine responses to HIV/AIDS. Thus, this paper not only has been able to use the phenomenon of HIV/AIDS to illustrate several broad theoretical propositions, but, as a result, has provided a theoretical springboard for further conceptual and empirical research on HIV/AIDS in the workplace. Using trust/distrust and stigmatization as a basis, perhaps future work on HIV/AIDS can move beyond prescriptive argumentation or anecdotal detail to help us understand more systematically the determinants and effects of organizational responses to HIV/AIDS.

Acknowledgements

The authors wish to thank Robert Bies, Janet Dukerich, and Arie Lewin, and three anonymous reviewers for their helpful feedback on earlier versions of this paper. Both authors contributed equally to the preparation of this paper. We also acknowledge the support of the Graduate School of Industrial Administration, Carnegie Mellon University (where the first author was a visiting faculty member) and the National Centre in HIV Social Research, University of New South Wales (where the second author was a visiting postdoctoral research fellow) while portions of this paper were prepared.

Notes

1. The distinction between the "production" and "reproduction" of trust was developed by Zucker (1986) and Shapiro (1987) to reflect the idea that trust is grounded in interpersonal relationships and that attempts to use control mechanisms to foster trust are actually an effort to "reproduce" an otherwise naturally occurring social phenomenon.
2. See Sitkin and Bies (this issue) for a discussion of legalistic organizational responses that serve both administrative and symbolic functions.
3. Although it is not misleading even in this extreme form, this statement is not literally true. For example, Arrow (1974) does recognize limitations in the use of formal institutional arrangements to enforce a generalized morality. Deutsch (1971, p. 47) also implicitly raises this issue in his outline of the preconditions for the effective resolution of disputes, in which two (of nine) preconditions include the following statements: that "there have been no serious ideological incompatibilities" and that "neither party ... has adopted a legalistic approach." However, Deutsch neither elaborates on these points, nor does he link them.
4. To highlight the difference between our approach and Giddens' (1979) emphasis on the emergent construction of institutional arrangements, one might label this erosion process "destructuration."
5. In fact, progress in medical technology suggests that in the not-too-distant future, HIV/AIDS may become a manageable long-term illness (like diabetes) and, thus, move out of its current status as a "catastrophic" illness.
6. While the literature on HIV/AIDS in the workplace suggests that relatively few business firms had adopted formal human resource policies that are specific to HIV/AIDS by the late 1980s (e.g., Masi 1987, Myers and Myers 1987), this does not imply a lack of legalistic organizational responses to the handling of HIV/AIDS. To the contrary, many organizations appear to be following Puckett and Emery's

(1988) advice of responding to HIV/AIDS under existing formal policies and procedures for handling catastrophic illnesses (see also Myers and Myers 1987) so as to provide a basis for claiming that employees with HIV/AIDS are treated the same as others who have catastrophic illnesses.

....

References

AIDS Council of New South Wales (1991), *HIV/AIDS Related Discrimination*, Sydney, New South Wales, Australia: ACON.

Allstate Forum on Public Issues (1987), *AIDS: Corporate America Responds*, Chicago, IL: Allstate Insurance Company.

Anderson, J. C., and J. A. Narus (1990), "A Model of Distributor Firm and Manufacturer Firm Working Partnerships," *Journal of Marketing*, 54, January, 42–58.

Argyris, C. (1982), "How Learning and Reasoning Processes Affect Organizational Change," in Goodman, P. S. (Ed.), *Change in Organizations*, San Francisco: Jossey-Bass, 47–86.

—— and D. A. Schon (1978), *Organizational Learning*, Reading, MA: Addison-Wesley.

Arrow, K. J. (1974), *The Limits of Organization*, New York: Norton.

—— (1985), "The Economics of Agency," in J. W. Pratt and R. J. Zeckhauser (Eds.), *Principals and Agents: The Structures of Business*, Boston: Harvard Business School, 37–51.

Axelrod, R. (1984), *The Evolution of Cooperation*, New York: Basic Books.

Banta, W. F. (1988), *AIDS in the Workplace: Legal Questions and Practical Answers*, Lexington, MA: Lexington Books.

Barber, B. (1983), *The Logic and Limits of Trust*, New Brunswick, NJ: Rutgers University Press.

Barnard, C. I. (1938), *The Functions of the Executive*, Cambridge, MA: Harvard University Press.

Beyer, J. M. (1981), "Ideologies, Values and Decision Making in Organizations," in P. C. Nystrom and W. H. Starbuck (Eds.), *Handbook of Organizational Design, Volume 2*, London: Oxford University Press, 166–202.

Bies, R. J. (1987), "The Predicament of Injustice: The Management of Moral Outrage," in B. M. Staw and L. L. Cummings (Eds.), *Research in Organizational Behavior, Volume 9*, Greenwich, CT: JAI Press, 289–319.

Blau, P. M. (1968), "Social Exchange," in *International Encyclopedia of the Social Sciences, Volume 7*, New York: Free Press, 452–457.

—— (1972), "Interdependence and Hierarchy in Organizations," *Social Science Research*, 1, 1–24.

Browning, L. D., and R. Folger (in press), "Communication under Conditions of Litigation Risk: A Grounded Theory of Plausible Deniability in the Iran Contra Affair," in S. B. Sitkin and R. J. Bies (Eds.), *The Legalistic Organization*, Newbury Park, CA: Sage.

Butler, J. K., and R. S. Cantrell (1984), "A Behavioral Decision Theory Approach to Modeling Dyadic Trust in Superiors and Subordinates," *Psychological Reports*, 55, 19–28.

——— (1983), "Reciprocity of Trust Between Professionals and Their Secretaries," *Psychological Reports*, 53, 411–416.

Chapman, F. S. (1987), "AIDS and Business: Problems of Costs and Compassion," *Fortune*, September 15, 122–127.

Comptroller General's Task Force on AIDS in the Workplace (1987), *Coping with AIDS in the GAO Workplace: The Task Force Report*, Washington, DC: U.S. Government Accounting Office.

Cyert, R. M., and J. G. March (1963), *A Behavioral Theory of the Firm*, Englewood Cliffs, NJ: Prentice Hall.

Deutsch, M. (1958), "Trust and Suspicion," *Journal of Conflict Resolution*, 2, 4, 265–279.

——— (1960), "The Effect of Motivational Orientation upon Trust and Suspicion," *Human Relations*, 13, 123–139.

——— (1962), "Cooperation and Trust: Some Theoretical Notes," in M. R. Jones (Ed.), *Nebraska Symposium on Motivation*, Lincoln, NE: University of Nebraska Press, 275–320.

——— (1962), "Trust, Trustworthiness, and the F Scale," *Journal of Abnormal Social Psychology*, 61, 138–140.

——— (1971), "Conflict and Its Resolution," in C. G. Smith (Ed.), *Conflict Resolution: Contributions of the Behavioral Sciences*, Notre Dame, IN: University of Notre Dame Press, 36–57.

——— and R. M. Krauss (1962), "Studies of Interpersonal Bargaining," *Journal of Conflict Resolution*, 6, 1, 52–76.

Dimaggio, P., and W. W. Powell (1983), "The Iron Cage Revisited: Institutional Isomorphism and Collective Rationality in Organizational Fields," *American Sociological Review*, 48, 147–160.

Douglas, M. (1985), *Risk Acceptability According to the Social Sciences*, New York: Russell Sage Foundation.

Dumain, B. (1991), "The Bureaucracy Busters," *Fortune*, 123, 36–51.

Durkheim, E. (1949), *Division of Labor in Society*, Glencoe, IL: Free Press.

Edelman, L. B. (1990), "Legal Environments and Organizational Governance: The Expansion of Due Process in the Workplace," *American Journal of Sociology*, 95, 1401–1440.

Eisenberg, E. M. (1984), "Ambiguity as Strategy in Organizational Communication," *Communication Monographs*, 51, 227–242.

Eisenhardt, K. M. (1985), "Control: Organizational and Economic Approaches," *Management Science*, 31, 134–149.

Etzioni, A. (1965), "Organizational Control Structure," in J. G. March (Ed.), *Handbook of Organizations*, Chicago, IL: Rand McNally, 650–677.

Fox, A. (1974), *Beyond Contract: Work Power and Trust Relations*, London: Faber Ltd.

Gabarro, J. J. (1978), "The Development of Trust, Influence, and Expectations," in A. G. Athos and J. J. Gabarro (Eds.), *Interpersonal Behavior: Communication and Understanding in Relationships*, Englewood Cliffs, NJ: Prentice-Hall, 290–303.

Garfinkel, H. (1963), "A Conception of, and Experiments with, "Trust" as a Condition of Stable Concerted Actions," in O. J. Harvey (Ed.), *Motivation and Social Interaction: Cognitive Determinants*, New York: Ronald Press, 187–239.

Giddens, A. (1979), *Central Problems in Social Theory*, Berkeley, CA: University of California Press.

Goffman, E. (1963), *Stigma: Notes on the Management of Spoiled Identity*, Englewood Cliffs, NJ: Prentice-Hall.

Golembiewski, R. T., and M. McConkie (1975), "The Centrality of Interpersonal Trust in Group Processes," in C. L. Cooper (Ed.), *Theories of Group Processes*, London: John Wiley & Sons, 131–185.

Granovetter, M. (1985), "Economic Action and Social Structure: The Problem of Embeddedness," *American Journal of Sociology*, 91, 3, 481–510.

Gray, A. (1989), "The AIDS Epidemic: A Prism Distorting Social and Legal Principles," in P. O'Malley (Ed.), *The AIDS Epidemic: Private Rights and the Public Interest*, Boston: Beacon Press, 227–249.

Greenberg, J. (1990), "Looking Good vs. Being Fair: Managing Impressions of Organization Justice," in B. M. Staw and L. L. Cummings (Eds.), *Research in Organizational Behavior, Volume 12*, Greenwich, CT: JAI Press, 111–157.

Held, V. (1990), "Mothering versus Contract," in J. J. Mansbridge (Ed.), *Beyond Self-interest*, Chicago: University of Chicago Press, 287–304.

Homans, G. C. (1974), *Social Behavior: Its Elementary Forms*, New York: Harcourt Brace Jovanovich.

Huber, G. P. (1984), "The Nature and Design of Post-industrial Organizations," *Management Science*, 30, 928–951.

Illingworth, P. (1990), *AIDS and the Good Society*, London and New York: Routledge.

James, F. E. (1988), "Office Pariahs: Sometimes the Stigma of Serious Illness Hurts More than the Disease Itself", *Wall Street Journal*, April 22, 13R–14R.

Jennings, E. E. (1971), *Routes to the Executive Suite*, New York: McGraw-Hill.

Jones, E. E., A. Farina, A. H. Hastorf, H. Markus, D. T. Miller, and R. A. Scott (1984), *Social Stigma: The Psychology of Marked Relationships*, New York: W. H. Freeman and Co.

Kee, H. W., and R. E. Knox (1970), "Conceptual and Methodological Considerations in the Study of Trust and Suspicion," *Journal of Conflict Resolution*, 14, September, 357–366.

Kelley, H. H. (1967), "Attribution Theory in Social Psychology," in D. Levine (Ed.), *Nebraska Symposium on Motivation, Volume 15*, Lincoln, NE: University of Nebraska Press, 192–241.

Kirp, D. L. (1989), "Uncommon Decency: Pacific Bell Responds to AIDS," *Harvard Business Review*, May/June, 140–151.

—— S. Epstein, M. S. Franks, J. Simon, D. Conway and J. Lewis (1989), *Learning by Heart: AIDS and Schoolchildren in America's Communities*, New Brunswick, NJ: Rutgers University Press.

Kleck, R. (1968), "Self Disclosure Patterns of the Nonobviously Stigmatized," *Psychological Reports*, 23, 1239–1248.

Koch, J. J. (1989), "Hiring Workers with AIDS," *Recruitment Today*, Fall, 30–33.

Kubler-Ross, E. (1969), *On Death and Dying*, New York: Collier Books/Macmillan.

Larson, A. (1992), "Network Dyads in Entrepreneurial Settings: A Study of the Governance Exchange Relationships," *Administrative Science Quarterly*, 37, 76–104.

Larzelere, R. E., and T. L. Huston (1980), "The Dyadic Trust Scale: Toward Understanding Interpersonal Trust in Close Relationships," *Journal of Marriage and the Family*, August, 595–604.

Letchinger, R. S. (1986), "AIDS: An Employer's Dilemma," *Personnel*, 58–63.

Levin, I. P., and D. P. Chapman (1990), "Risk Taking, Frame of Reference, and Characterization of Victim Groups in AIDS Treatment Decisions," *Journal of Experimental Social Psychology*, 26, 421–434.

Lewin, A. Y., and C. U. Stephens (1992), "Designing Post-industrial Organizations: Theory and Practice," in G. P. Huber and W. H. Glick (Eds.), *Organizational Change and Redesign*, New York: Oxford University Press.

Lewis, J. D., and A. J. Weigert (1985), "Trust as Social Reality," *Social Forces*, 63, 4, 967–985.

Lindskold, S. (1978), "Trust Development, the GRIT proposal, and the Effects of Conciliatory Acts on Conflict and Cooperation," *Psychological Bulletin*, 85, 4, 772–793.

Loomis, J. L. (1959), "Communication and the Development of Trust," *Human Relations*, 12, 305–315.

Luhmann, N. (1979), *Trust and Power*, Chichester: Wiley.

Macaulay, S. (1963), "Non-contractual Relations in Business: A Preliminary Study," *American Sociological Review*, 28, 55–67.

Mann, J. (1991), "Commentary on: 'A Case of AIDS,'" *Harvard Business Review*, November/December, 14–25.

March, J. G., and H. A. Simon (1958), *Organizations*, New York: Wiley.

Masi, D. A. (1987), "AIDS in the Workplace: What Can Be Done?," *Personnel*, July 57–60.

Matthews, B. A., W. M. Kordonski, and E. Shimoff (1983), "Temptation and Maintenance of Trust: Effects of Bilateral Punishment Capability," *Journal of Conflict Resolution*, 27, 2, 255–277.

—— and E. Shimoff (1979), "Expansion of Exchange: Monitoring Trust Levels in Ongoing Exchange Relations," *Journal of Conflict Resolution*, 23, 3, 538–560.

McArthur, L. A. (1972), "The How and What of Why: Some Determinants and Consequences of Causal Attribution," *Journal of Personality and Social Psychology*, 22, 171–193.

Meyer, J. W. (1983), "Legalization in Education," in J. Meyer and W. R. Scott (Eds.), *Organizational Environments: Ritual and Rationality*, Beverly Hills, CA: Sage.

—— and B. Rowan (1977), "Institutionalized Organizations: Formal Structure as Myth and Ceremony," *American Journal of Sociology*, 83, 340–363.

Meyer, M. W., and L. G. Zucker (1989), *Permanently Failing Organizations*, Newbury Park, CA: Sage.

Miceli, M. P., and J. P. Near (1989), *Blowing the Whistle*, Lexington, MA: Lexington Books.

Miles, R. E., and C. E. Snow (1986), "Organizations: New Concepts for New Forms," *California Management Review*, 28, 62–73.

Myers, P. S., and D. W. Myers (1987), "AIDS: Tackling a Touch Problem Through Policy," *Personnel Administrator*, April, 95–108.

O'Malley, P. (Ed.) (1989), *The AIDS Epidemic: Private Rights and the Public Interest*, Boston: Beacon Press.

Ouchi, W. G. (1979), "A Conceptual Framework for the Design of Organizational Control Mechanisms," *Management Science*, 25, 833–848.

—— (1980), "Markets, Bureaucracies and Clans," *Administrative Science Quarterly*, 25, 129–141.

Page, R. M. (1984), *Stigma*, London: Routledge and Kegan Paul.

Panem, S. (1988), *The AIDS Bureaucracy*, Cambridge, MA: Harvard University Press.

Parsons, T. (1951), *The Social System*, Glencoe, IL: Free Press.

Peachey, D. E., and M. J. Lerner (1981), "Law as a Social Trap: Problems and Possibilities for the Future," in M. J. Lerner and S. C. Lerner (Eds.), *The Justice Motive in Social Behavior: Adapting to Times of Scarcity and Change*, New York: Plenum Press.

Perrow, C. (1967), "A Framework for the Comparative Analysis of Organizations," *American Sociological Review*, 32, 194–208.

—— (1984), *Normal Accidents: Living with High-Risk Technologies*, New York: Basic Books.

—— and M. Guillen (1990), *The AIDS Disaster: The Failure of Organizations in New York and the Nation*, New Haven, CT: Yale University Press.

Pfeffer, J., and G. R. Salancik (1978), *The External Control of Organizations*, New York: Harper & Row.

Powell, W. W. (1990), "Neither Market nor Hierarchy: Network Forms of Organization," in B. M. Staw and L. L. Cummings (Eds.), *Research in Organizational Behavior, Volume 12*, Greenwich, CT: JAI Press, 295–336.

Puckett, S. B., and A. R. Emery (1988), *Managing AIDS in the Workplace*, Reading, MA: Addison-Wesley.

Roth, N. L. (1990), *Calendars on the Wall: The Influences of Sexuality, Disability, and Time on Provider/client Communication about HIV/AIDS*, Unpublished Ph.D. Dissertation, University of Texas at Austin.

—— S. B. Sitkin, and A. House (in press), "Stigma as a Determinant of Legalization," in S. B. Sitkin, and R. J. Bies (Eds.), *The Legalistic Organization*, Newbury Park: Sage.

Rotter, J. B. (1967), "A New Scale for the Measurement of Interpersonal Trust," *Journal of Personality*, 35, 651–665.

—— (1971), "Generalized Expectancies for Interpersonal Trust," *American Psychologist*, 26, 443–452.

—— (1980), "Interpersonal Trust, Trustworthiness, and Gullibility," *American Psychologist*, 35, 1, 1–7.

Rowe, M. P., M. Russell-Einhorn, and M. A. Baker (1986), "The Fear of AIDS," *Harvard Business Review*, July-August, 28–36.

Schein, E. H. (1985), *Organizational Culture and Leadership*, San Francisco, CA: Jossey-Bass.

Schlenker, B. R. (1980), *Impression Management: The Self-concept, Social Identity, and Interpersonal Relations*, Belmont, CA: Brooks/Cole.

——— B. Helm and J. T. Tedeschi (1973), "The Effects of Personality and Situational Variables on Behavioral Trust," *Journal of Personality and Social Psychology*, 25, 3, 419–427.

Scott, W. R. (1987), "The Adolescence of Institutional Theory," *Administrative Science Quarterly*, 32, 493–511.

Selznick, P. H. (1957), *Leadership in Administration: A Sociological Interpretation*, New York: Harper and Row.

——— (1969), *Law, Society, and Individual Justice*, New York: Sage Foundation.

Senge, P. M. (1990), *The Fifth Discipline: The Art and Practice of the Learning Organization*, New York: Doubleday.

Shapiro, S. P. (1987), "The Social Control of Impersonal Trust," *American Journal of Sociology*, 93, 3, 623–658.

Shilts, R. (1987), *And the Band Played On: Politics, People, and the AIDS Epidemic*, New York: St. Martin's Press.

Sitkin, S. B. (1992), "Learning through Failure: The Strategy of Small Losses," in B. M. Staw and L. L. Cummings (Eds.), *Research in Organizational Behavior, Volume 14*, Greenwich, CT: JAI Press, 231–266.

——— and R. J. Bies (1993), "The Legalistic Organization: Definitions, Dimensions, and Dilemmas," *Organization Science*, 4, 3, 345–351.

——— ——— (in press), "The Legalization of Organizations: A Multitheoretical Perspective," in S. B. Sitkin and R. J. Bies (Eds.), *The Legalistic Organization*, Newbury Park, CA: Sage.

——— and N. L. Roth (1993), "Legalistic Organizational Responses to Catastrophic Illness: The Effect of Stigmatization on Reactions to HIV/AIDS," *Employee Responsibilities and Rights Journal*, 6, 4, in press.

Sontag, S. (1988), *AIDS and Its Metaphors*, New York: Farrar, Straus, and Giroux.

Stein, R. E. (1987), "Strategies for Dealing with AIDS Disputes in the Workplace," *The Arbitration Journal*, 42, 3, 21–29.

Stone, C. D. (1975), *Where the Law Ends: The Social Control of Corporate Behavior*, New York: Harper & Row.

Susser, P. A. (1987), "AIDS and Employment: Few Answers, Many Questions," *Employee Relations Today*, Summer: 160–163.

Sutton, R. I., and A. L. Callahan (1987), "The Stigma of Bankruptcy: Spoiled Organizational Image and Its Management," *Academy of Management Journal*, 30, 405–436.

Swinth, R. L. (1967), "The Establishment of the Trust Relationship," *Journal of Conflict Resolution*, 12, 335–344.

Taylor, F. W. (1911), *The Principles of Scientific Management*, New York: Norton.

Tedlow, R. S., and M. S. Marram (1991), "A Case of AIDS," *Harvard Business Review*, November/December, 14–25.

Tillett, G. (1989), *AIDS and the Workplace: A Practical Approach*, New South Wales, Australia: CCH Australia Ltd.

Van Maanen, J., and E. H. Schein (1979), "Toward a Theory of Organizational Socialization," in B. M. Staw and L. L. Cummings (Eds.), *Research in Organizational Behavior, Volume 1*, Greenwich, CT: JAI Press, 209–264.

Volberding, P. A., S. W. Lagakos, M. A. Koch, C. Pettinelli, M. W. Myers, D. K. Booth, H. H. Balfour, R. C. Reichman, J. A. Bartlett, M. S. Hirsch, R. L. Murphy, W. D. Hardy, R. Foeiro, M. A. Fischl, J. G. Bartlett, T. C. Merigan, N. E. Hyslop, D. D. Richman, F. T. Valentine, L. Corey, and the AIDS Clinical Trials Group of the National Institute of Allergies and Infectious Diseases (1990), "Zidovidine in Asymptomatic Human Immunodeficiency Virus Infections: A Controlled Trial in Persons with Fewer Than 500 CD4-positive Cells per Cubic Millimeter," *New England Journal of Medicine*, 322, 14, 941–949.

Waldo, W. S. (1987), "A Practical Guide for Dealing with AIDS at Work," *Personnel Journal*, 66, 8, 135–138.

Weber, M. (1947), *The Theory of Social and Economic Organization*, New York: Free Press.

Williamson, O. E. (1975), *Markets and Hierarchies: Analysis and Antitrust Implications*, New York: Free Press.

Yudof, M. G. (1981), "Law, Policy and the Public Schools," *Michigan Law Review*, 79, 4, 774–791.

Zand, D. E. (1972), "Trust and Managerial Problem Solving," *Administrative Science Quarterly*, 17, 229–239.

Zucker, L. G. (1977), "The Role of Institutionalization in Cultural Persistence," *American Sociological Review*, 42, 726–743.

—— (1986), "Production of Trust: Institutional Sources of Economic Structure, 1840–1920," in B. M. Staw and L. L. Cummings (Eds.), *Research in Organizational Behavior, Volume 8*, 53–111, Greenwich, CT: JAI Press.

—— (1988), *Institutional Patterns and Organizations*, Cambridge, MA: Ballinger.

Trust and Breach of the Psychological Contract

Sandra L. Robinson

In light of trends toward globalization, restructuring, and downsizing, psychological contracts are playing an increasingly important role in contemporary employment relationships. Organizations, under pressure to make rapid and constant changes, have had to alter employment relationships and the psychological contracts that underlie them. Psychological contracts refer to employees' perceptions of what they owe to their employers and what their employers owe to them. In this climate of change, the traditional contract of long-term job security in return for hard work and loyalty may no longer be valid (Sims, 1994), and employees and employers alike are now reconsidering their mutual obligations. More importantly, these changes have increased the likelihood of psychological contract breach. Organizations must now repeatedly manage, renegotiate, and alter the terms of the employment agreement continually to fit changing circumstances (Tichy, 1983; Altman and Post, 1996) and thus may be less willing or less able to fulfill all of their promises. In addition, constant contract change means increased opportunities for employees and employers to misunderstand the agreement and to perceive a contract breach even when an actual breach did not occur. It should not be surprising, therefore, that the majority of employees currently believe their employer has breached some aspect of their employment agreement (Robinson and Rousseau, 1994).

Given the apparent prevalence of perceived contract breach, it is imperative that we develop a solid understanding of this phenomenon. Unfortunately, empirical study of psychological contract breach remains in its infancy. Prior research has thus far demonstrated that psychological contract breach and violation is relatively common (Robinson and Rousseau, 1994) and that it is associated with various negative outcomes such as a decrease in perceived obligations to one's employer, lowered citizenship behavior, and reduced commitment and satisfaction (Robinson, Kraatz, and Rousseau, 1994; Robinson and Rousseau, 1994; Robinson and Morrison, 1995). A fundamental and important unanswered question is what role trust plays in the experience and effects of psychological contract breach. Rare is the theoretical paper on psychological contracts that does not mention the word trust or note its central role in psychological contracts (e.g., Rousseau, 1989; Rousseau and McLean Parks, 1994; Morrison and Robinson, 1997). Despite the repeated mention of trust in the psychological contract literature, however, there has been virtually no theoretical explication or empirical examination of trust in relation to the experience of psychological contract breach. This lapse of systematic attention to the function of trust is found not only in the study of psychological contracts but in organizational science in general (Mayer, Davis, and Schoorman, 1995). As Gambetta (1988: unnumbered foreward) suggested, "scholars tend to mention (trust) in passing, to allude to it as a fundamental ingredient or lubricant, an unavoidable dimension of social interaction, only to move on to deal with less intractable matters." The purpose of this study is to develop and test a relatively parsimonious theoretical model of the role of trust in the psychological contract breach experience by exploring the multiple roles played by past and current trust in influencing the detection, interpretation, and impact of psychological contract breach.

Psychological Contracts Defined

The psychological contract is defined as an individual's beliefs about the terms and conditions of a reciprocal exchange agreement between that person and another party (Rousseau, 1989). Although the psychological contract was originally defined by Argyris (1960), Levinson (1962), and Schein (1980) to characterize the subjective nature of employment relationships, the present conceptualization focuses on individuals' beliefs in and interpretation of a promissory contract. Unlike formal or implied contracts, the psychological contract is inherently perceptual, and thus one party's understanding of the contract may not be shared by the other.

Psychological contracts, comprising perceived obligations, must be distinguished from expectations, which are general beliefs held by employees about what they will find in their job and the organization. For example, a new manager may expect to receive a high salary, to be promoted, to like his job, or to find the walls of his office painted a neutral color. These expectations emanate from a wide variety of sources, including past experience, social norms, observations by friends, and so forth. Psychological contracts, by contrast, entail beliefs about what employees believe they are entitled to receive, or should receive, because they perceive that their employer conveyed promises to provide those things. Thus only those expectations that emanate from perceived implicit or explicit promises by the employer are part of the psychological contract. For example, if a new manager believes she was promised pay commensurate with performance at the time of hire, it creates an expectation, but it also creates a perceived obligation that is part of the psychological contract. Although psychological contracts produce some expectations, not all expectations emanate from perceived promises, and expectations can exist in the absence of perceived promises or contracts.

Psychological Contract Breach and Trust

Psychological contract breach is a subjective experience, referring to one's perception that another has failed to fulfill adequately the promised obligations of the psychological contract (Rousseau, 1989). Psychological contract breach can and does occur in the absence of an actual breach (i.e., whereby one party deliberately reneges on another party's contract and that fact can be determined by a neutral third party) (Morrison and Robinson, 1997). It is an employee's belief that a breach has occurred that affects his or her behavior and attitudes, regardless of whether that belief is valid or whether an actual breach took place. Thus the focal point of interest in this study is not actual breach, but employees' perception of a breach, and subsequent use of the term psychological contract breach in this study refers to employees' perceptions of contract breach, not actual breach. In this study, psychological contract breach is operationalized as an employee's perception of the extent to which the employer has failed to fulfill the following promised obligations: high salary, promotions and advancement, pay based on performance, long-term job security, sufficient power and responsibility, training and career development.

Psychological contract breach is a subjective experience based not only (or necessarily) on the employer's actions or inactions but on an individual's perception of those actions or inactions within a particular social context. Thus the experience of psychological contract breach should depend on social and psychological factors specific to the employment relationship in which it occurs (Morrison and Robinson, 1997). One such factor of particular importance is that of trust and, more specifically, trust in one's employer. Integrating various definitions of trust found in the literature (e.g., Frost, Stimpson, and Maughan, 1978; Barber, 1983; Gambetta, 1988), trust is defined here as one's expectations, assumptions, or beliefs about the likelihood that another's future actions will be beneficial, favorable, or at least not detrimental to one's interests. As a social construct, trust lies at the heart of relationships and contracts, influencing each party's behavior toward the other (e.g., Deutsch, 1958; Blau, 1964; Zand, 1972). As a general positive attitude toward another social entity, trust acts as a guideline, influencing one's interpretation of social behaviors within a relationship. Trust is thus likely to play a significant role in the subjective experience of psychological contract breach by one's employer: Trust in one's employer may influence an employee's recognition of a breach, his or her interpretation of that perceived breach if it is recognized, and his or her reaction to that perceived breach.

Prior Trust as Cause of Psychological Contract Breach

As a prior positive attitude, trust in one's employer at the time of hire may influence psychological contract breach by reducing the likelihood that a contract breach will be perceived. A long history of research on cognitive consistency and attitude change has found that people act in ways that preserve their established knowledge structures, perceptions, schemata, and memories (Greenwald, 1980). Cognitive consistency is maintained through selective perception, by seeking out, attending to, and interpreting one's environment in ways that reinforce one's prior knowledge, beliefs, and attitudes (Fiske and Taylor, 1984). A rich body of empirical evidence has identified a variety of encoding and decoding biases that tend toward confirming, rather than disconfirming, prior beliefs (Snyder and Swann, 1978; Lord, Ross, and Lepper, 1979). Greenwald (1980) reviewed much of this literature, citing evidence of confirmation bias in responding to persuasion (e.g., Hovland, Janis, and Kelley, 1953; Greenwald, 1968; Petty, Ostrom, and Brock, 1981), in information search (e.g., Mischel, Ebbesen, and Zeiss, 1973; Snyder and Swann, 1978), in memory and recall (Mischel, Ebbesen, and Zeiss, 1973; Snyder and Uranowitz, 1978), and in the effects of first impressions (review by Schneider, Hastorf, and Ellsworth, 1979).

One aspect of selective perception is that of selective attention. People tend to seek out and focus on information that confirms prior cognitions, and they tend to avoid or ignore information that disconfirms them (Cohen, Brehm, and Latane, 1959; Olson and Zanna, 1979; Eagly and Chaiken, 1993). In psychological contract breach, selective attention could operate such that prior trust in one's employer will influence the likelihood that an employee will perceive a breach by his or her employer. Thus an employee with low prior trust is more likely to look for, find, and remember incidents of breach, even in the absence of an objective breach, because it is consistent with his or her low prior trust. Conversely, an employee with high prior trust will be less likely to perceive a breach when one does not occur and more likely to overlook, forget, or not recognize an actual breach when it does occur. Thus, the first hypothesis is as follows:

Hypothesis 1: *An employee's initial trust in his or her employer (at Time 1) will be negatively related to perceiving a contract breach by his or her employer (at Time 2).*

Outcomes of Psychological Contract Breach

Consistent with prior studies finding psychological contract breach to be negatively correlated with various work behaviors (e.g., Robinson and Rousseau, 1994; Robinson and Morrison, 1995), it is likely that employees who experience a psychological contract breach will reduce their subsequent contributions to the firm. Katz (1964) identified several distinct forms of employee contributions, all of which are important to an organization's well-being: (1) performing prescribed roles as part of one's job; (2) engaging in innovative and spontaneous behaviors that are not specified by job requirements but that facilitate organizational effectiveness; and (3) joining and remaining in the organization. Thus, the second hypothesis is as follows:

Hypothesis 2: *Psychological contract breach (at Time 2) will be negatively related to all three types of employees' contributions to the organization (at Time 3).*

Subsequent Trust as a Mediator of the Breach-outcome Relationships

Although prior studies have reported relationships between psychological contract breach and employees' negative behavioral reactions, no one has examined why psychological contract breach has the effects that it does. I argue here that the impact of psychological contract breach comes about as a result of two psychological dynamics: unmet expectations and a loss of trust, both of which mediate the relationships between psychological contract breach and employees' behavioral reactions. The unmet-expectations research has repeatedly demonstrated that when employees fail to receive something they had expected to receive, they experience "reality shock," a sense of discrepancy, and thus dissatisfaction with the current situation, which in turn lowers performance and increases turnover (for a review, see Wanous et al., 1992). When an employee experiences psychological contract breach, he or she recognizes that something expected was not received, which in turn reduces his or her contributions to the organization. Thus, the following hypothesis is offered:

Hypothesis 3: *A sense of unmet expectations will mediate the relationship between psychological contract breach (at Time 2) and employees' contributions to the firm (at Time 3).*

Critics of the contract paradigm contend that the sole psychological mechanism underlying reactions to psychological contract breach is the sense of unmet expectations. Thus the effects of psychological contract breach can be reduced to unmet expectations alone. If it is true that psychological contract breach has its effects solely through unmet expectations, it suggests that prior empirical research on the effects of psychological contract breach has merely replicated the research on the effects of unmet expectations and hence it adds little value to the literature.

Psychological contract theorists, however, contend that the effect of psychological contract breach involves more than unmet expectations because it entails not only a loss of something expected but also an erosion of trust and the foundation of the relationship between the two parties. As Rousseau (1989: 129) stated, "the intensity of the reaction [to violation is directly attributable not only to unmet expectations of specific rewards or benefits, but also to more general beliefs about respect of persons, codes of conduct and other patterns of behavior associated with relationships involving trust."

Prior writings have posited that trust plays a key role in mediating the effects of psychological contract breach, but thus far, this role has not been explicated. I argue here that trust plays a mediating role because psychological breach undermines two conditions leading to trust—judgments of integrity and beliefs in benevolence—that in turn reduce employees' contributions. Trust comes, in part, from judgments about integrity that are based on the perceived consistency of another's actions and the extent to which another's actions are congruent with his or her words (Mayer, Davis, and Schoorman, 1995). In this sense, trust is cognitively established, in that one builds probabilistic beliefs about another's future actions based on rational reasons, such as the past behavior of or experience with that other party (Lewis and Weigert, 1985; Good, 1988). When an employee perceives a contract breach by the employer, he or she perceives an inconsistency between the employer's words and actions. As a result, the employee loses confidence that the contributions made today will be reciprocated, as promised, by the employer in the future. The link between performance and outcomes is undermined, and the employee's motivation to contribute to the firm declines (Katz, 1964; Porter and Lawler, 1968).

Another condition leading to trust is belief in benevolence, whereby the trustee is believed to want to do good to the trustor because of the specific attachment they share (Mayer, Davis, and Schoorman, 1995). Trust comes not from a cognitive calculus of how a particular party will act but, rather, from the relational bonds between the parties (Lewis and Weigert, 1985) and the implicit assumptions that others in one's social relationships have respect and concern for one's welfare (Barber, 1983; Gambetta, 1988). These implicit assumptions are largely taken for granted and unacknowledged until violated (Garfinkel, 1963; Luhmann, 1979; Zucker, 1986). When a psychological contract breach occurs, however, it may throw into conscious question the validity of these assumptions, which in turn undermines the foundation of the relationship itself. Trust is an essential ingredient for any stable social relationship (Blau, 1964; Simmel, 1978). When promises are broken, this trust is shattered, and as the relationship dissolves, the employee pulls away from it, less willing to invest further in the relationship and less willing to act in ways that serve to maintain it. The above arguments clarify how psychological contract breach may undermine an employee's trust in his or her employer and lead an employee to reduce his or her future contributions to the firm. Consistent with logic explicated above, the following hypothesis is offered:

Hypothesis 4: *A loss of trust will mediate the relationship between psychological contract breach (at Time 2) and employees' contributions to the firm (at Time 3).*

Prior Trust as a Moderator of the Relationship between Breach and Trust

As previously noted, prior trust may cause psychological contract breach because of the cognitive consistency bias of selective attention: Because people tend to seek out information that confirms their prior beliefs and avoid information that disconfirms them, employees with high prior trust will be less likely to perceive breaches than employees with low prior trust. A similar cognitive consistency bias, known as selective interpretation, suggests that prior trust may also moderate the relationship between psychological contract breach and subsequent trust by influencing the interpretation of a breach, if one is perceived.

Selective interpretation is another way to maintain cognitive consistency. It refers to the tendency of individuals to interpret information in ways that confirm their prior attitudes and beliefs (for reviews, see Fiske and Taylor, 1984; Eagly and Chaiken, 1993). A primary function of attitudes is to serve as an appraisal heuristic, enabling individuals to assess objects and events in their environment efficiently and make sense of their world (Smith, Bruner, and White, 1957; Pratkanis, 1989; Pratkanis and Greenwald, 1989). In this capacity, an attitudinal heuristic uses a stored evaluation of an object as a guide for understanding the actions of that object (Pratkanis and Greenwald, 1989). Research shows that people tend to make incoming information fit with their prior attitudes, rather than the reverse (Fiske and Taylor, 1984). They also readily generate causal explanations of events (Nisbett and Wilson, 1977; Wilson and Nisbett, 1978), typically ones that reinforce and maintain their prior theories and hypotheses. For example, individuals attribute an actor's behavior to internal causes when it is consistent with their attitudinal expectations, but they attribute it to external causes when it is inconsistent with those attitudes (Regan, Straus, and Fazio, 1974).

This literature suggests that when an employee perceives that his or her contract has not been completely fulfilled by his or her employer, the employee's prior trust in his or her employer will guide or influence the employee's interpretation or understanding of that transgression. An employee with high prior trust will tend to perceive the breach in ways consistent with that prior trust, and thus interpret it in relatively neutral or positive terms (e.g., viewing it as an unintentional event, a misunderstanding, a temporary lapse, or outside the responsibility of the employer). As a result, the employee will be able to maintain a relatively high level of trust in the employer, despite the perceived transgression. In contrast, an employee with low prior trust will tend to perceive the breach in ways consistent with low prior trust and to interpret it in a more negative light (e.g., as a deliberate dishonest act or as intentional betrayal or violation by the employer). Hence, the low-prior-trust employee will actually lose the most trust in his or her employer following a perceived contract breach. Thus, the final hypothesis is as follows:

Hypothesis 5: *Prior trust will moderate the relationship between psychological contract breach and subsequent trust such that those with low prior trust (at Time 1) will experience a greater decline in trust (at Time 3) after a perceived breach (at Time 2) than will those with high prior trust (at Time 1).*

....

Method

Sample

Participants were 125 alumni of a midwestern graduate business school. Thirty-four percent were women. The average age of the participants at the end of the study was 30 years (S.D. = 2.01), their average full-time work experience was 6.29 years (S.D. = 1.78). Average salaries were $69,200, ranging from $25,000 to $160,000. The respondents worked in a wide variety of industries: consulting (23.5 percent), financial services (18.6 percent), food and kindred products (17.5 percent), chemicals and allied products (13.7 percent), machinery (5.5 percent), electronic equipment (3.3 percent), transportation equipment (3.3 percent), wholesale and retail trade (2.7 percent), petroleum and energy products (2.7 percent), and others (9.2 percent).

Procedure

I surveyed participants three times over a 30-month period. I gave the first survey, at Time 1 (T1), to 264 graduates of a master's of business administration (MBA) program who had recently accepted a job offer. They were given the opportunity to win a cash prize in return for their participation. Two hundred and eighteen responded, yielding an 83 percent response rate.

The second survey, at Time 2 (T2), was mailed 18 months later to the 218 respondents of the first survey. I asked participants to mail the completed surveys to me in self-addressed, stamped envelopes. I sent a follow-up letter two weeks later and a hand-written note, encouraging participation, four weeks later. One hundred and eighty-four completed surveys were returned and six were returned as undeliverable due to address changes (response rate of 87 percent).

The third survey, at Time 3 (T3), was mailed 12 months after the second survey to the remaining 184 participants. Again, I sent a follow-up reminder two weeks after the survey was mailed and handwritten notes, encouraging participation, four weeks later. In total, 165 respondents returned completed surveys; four were returned as undeliverable due to address changes. The response rate for the third survey was 92 percent.

Only those participants who had remained with their employer across the three time periods ($N = 125$) were included in the analysis because the dependent variables were measured in the third time period. The one exception to this rule was for an analysis examining the relationship between psychological contract breach at T2 and turnover at T3. In this analysis, the sample ($N = 140$) comprised those who had remained with their employer at all three time periods and those who had voluntarily left their employer between T2 and T3.

Measures

Psychological contract breach. Psychological contract breach was measured in the following way. At T1, participants were asked to indicate the extent to which their employer was obligated to provide a set of items to them. The instructions read, "Employers make promises to give employees certain things in exchange for their contributions to the organization. Using the scale below, please indicate the extent to which you believe your employer will be obligated or owe you based on an implicit or explicit promise or understanding, the following: . . . ." Participants were provided with a five-point Likert-type scale, ranging from "not at all obligated" to "very obligated," along with a list of the following employer obligations: promotion and advancement, high pay, pay based on current level of performance, training, long-term job security, career development, and sufficient power and responsibility. Thus a high score indicated high perceived obligation, and a low score indicated little or no perceived obligation on the part of the employer to provide these things. These obligations were drawn from Rousseau's (1990) measure of psychological contracts. Rousseau interviewed human resource managers from 13 engineering, accounting and manufacturing firms and identified these obligations as those most commonly promised by employers to MBA graduates during the recruitment process. I found additional support for Rousseau's measure in a survey of full-time employed, evening MBA students. One set of students ($N = 75$) were asked to describe what they were obligated to provide to their employer and what their employer was obligated to provide to them in return. Based on their open-ended responses. I compiled a list of the most commonly reported obligations and gave it to another set of students ($N = 79$) who reported the extent to which these obligations were promised to them at the time of hire. Results showed that the seven obligations used in Rousseau's (1990) measure were those most frequently reported as belonging to the employment contracts of this sample.

At T2, participants were asked to indicate the degree to which their employer had fulfilled each of the seven obligations measured at T1. The instructions read, "Employers make implicit and explicit promises during recruitment which obligate them to give certain things to their employees in exchange for their employees' contributions to the organization. Employers vary in the degree to which they subsequently fulfill those promises and obligations to their employees. Read over the following items listed below. Think about the extent to which your employer made implicit or explicit promises to provide you with these items. Then think about how well your employer has fulfilled those promises. Using the scale below, please indicate the extent to which your employer has fulfilled the following obligations." They were provided with a five-point Likert-type scale, with anchors ranging from "not at all fulfilled" to "very well fulfilled."

The measure of psychological contract breach was created as follows. The degree to which each item was fulfilled at T2 was subtracted from the degree to which it was obligated at T1. For example, if an item was perceived to be highly obligated at T1 (a score of 5) and was perceived to be not fulfilled at all at T2 (a score of 1), it resulted in a high breach discrepancy ($5 - 1 = 4$). Conversely, if an item was perceived to be not obligated at T1 (a score of 1) yet well fulfilled nonetheless at T2, it resulted in a high fulfillment discrepancy

$(1 - 5 = -4)$. As a final example, an item not perceived promised at T1 (a score of 1) and not fulfilled at T2 (a score of 1), yielded no discrepancy $(1 - 1 = 0)$.

These differences between obligations and fulfillment were then aggregated. The aggregated score ranged from -4 to $+4$, such that a -4 score indicated a strong sense of psychological contract fulfillment and a $+4$ score indicated a strong sense of psychological contract breach. I used this measure for several reasons. First, because it takes into account both perceived fulfillment and perceived breach of the contract, rather than just perceived breach, it captures the full range of variance in this variable and does not artificially truncate it. Second, aggregating the perceived fulfillment and perceived breach of specific items captures the sense of psychological contract breach in a way that is consistent with the theoretical focus of this paper and with the literature's conceptualization of psychological contract breach. The sense of psychological contract breach emanates from a culmination of perceptions about how specific terms of the psychological contract have been fulfilled. This general perception takes into account breach discrepancies (perceptions that the employer has failed to fulfill specific obligations), fulfillment discrepancies (perceptions that the employer has provided some terms beyond what the employer was obligated to provide), and no discrepancies (perceptions that the employer has fulfilled specific obligations as promised). Coefficient alpha for this scale was .78.

In addition to the above quantitative measure of the degree of breach, I also obtained a qualitative measure of the interpretation of the perceived breach from a subset of the participants $(N = 33)$. These participants were asked, at T2, to indicate why their employer had failed to fulfill their contract. These responses were then coded in terms of the degree to which the participant perceived the employer to be responsible for the contractual transgression. This coding was done by three judges, blind to the purpose of the study, using a scale ranging from 1, "not at all the employer's fault," to 5, "very much the employer's fault." I aggregated the responses of the judges to create a measure of the interpretation of the psychological contract breach, in this case, the degree to which the psychological contract breach was perceived to be the fault of the employer.

Trust. Trust was measured at T1 and T3. I used a seven-item trust scale that reflects the dimensions of trust identified by Gabarro and Athos (1976). Items included in this scale were the following: "I believe my employer has high integrity"; "I can expect my employer to treat me in a consistent and predictable fashion"; "My employer is not always honest and truthful"; "In general, I believe my employer's motives and intentions are good"; "I don't think my employer treats me fairly"; "My employer is open and upfront with me"; "I am not sure I fully trust my employer." Participants used a five-point

Likert-type scale, with anchors ranging from "strongly disagree" to "strongly agree." Coefficient alpha for the T1 measure was .82; for T3, it was .87.

Unmet Expectations. Unmet expectations was measured with two global items at Time 3: "To what extent have your initial expectations (at the time of hire) been met regarding what you thought you would get from your job?" and "Have your initial expectations, what you thought you would get from your organization when you joined, been met?" Participants answered both questions using a five-point Likert-type scale, with anchors ranging from "not at all met" to "very well met." The correlation between these two items was .81, and they were thus aggregated into a single index.

Employee Contributions

Performance. I assessed performance at T3 by asking participants to answer two questions: (1) How would you rate your own work performance? and (2) How would your employer probably rate your work performance? Participants used five-point Likert-type scales, with anchors ranging from "poor" to "excellent." These two items were highly correlated ($r = .84$) and hence were combined into a single index.

Organizational Citizenship Behavior: Civic Virtue. Organ (1988) identified five distinct dimensions of organizational citizenship behavior (OCB): altruism, conscientiousness, courtesy, sportsmanship, and civic virtue. This study focused on the civic virtue form of OCB, which is defined as "behavior on the part of an individual that indicates that he/she responsibly participates in, is involved in, or is concerned about the life of the company" (Podsakoff et al., 1990: 115). I selected civic virtue for attention because, compared with other types of citizenship behavior, it is usually directed at the organization and more likely to be a purposeful contribution to the organization by an employee. Altruism, sportsmanship, and courtesy, in contrast, are typically directed at individuals within the organization, and conscientiousness, although it can be targeted at the organization, is often targetless (Organ, 1988). Thus, although all forms of OCB are contributions to the organization and thus may be influenced by psychological contract breach, civic virtue is the most direct contribution and thus should be most influenced by perceived breach.

On the third survey, civic virtue was assessed using a measure designed by Podsakoff et al. (1990). Participants were asked to indicate how characteristic each of four statements was of their behavior at work. Responses were on a five-point Likert-type scale, with anchors ranging from "very uncharacteristic" to "very characteristic." Sample items included "I attend functions that are not required, but that help the agency/company image" and "I attend meetings that are not mandatory, but are considered important." The coefficient alpha of this measure was .67.

Intentions to Remain. Intentions to remain with one's employer was measured at T1 and at T3. At T1 and T3, participants were asked, "How long do you intend to remain with your current employer?" (in years). At T3, participants were also asked four Likert-scaled questions, borrowed from Chatman (1991): (1) To what extent would you prefer a job other than the one you are in? (2) To what extent have you thought about changing firms since you began to work for your firm? (3) If you had your way, will you be working for your firm 3 years from now? and (4) How long do you intend to remain with your firm? These items were combined into a single measure. Coefficient alpha was .86.

Turnover. Actual turnover was measured at T2 and T3 by asking participants how many employers they had worked for since graduation. To calculate turnover, I dummy coded this information ($0 =$ still with first employer; $1 =$ had left first employer). To distinguish between voluntary and involuntary turnover, I also asked participants the following question: "If you are no longer with the firm you joined right after graduation, please indicate the reason(s) why (check all that apply): (1) I was laid off (e.g., due to economic conditions, restructuring, etc.) (2) I was fired (e.g., due to poor performance, personality clashes, etc.) (3) I quit because (please specify) and (4) Other (please specify)." By T2, 22 (14 percent) had resigned, and by T3, a total of 39 (24 percent) had left their employer; two reported having been fired, and the remaining 37 claimed to have left voluntarily. Thus, 15 respondents had voluntarily resigned from T2 to T3.

Control Variables

Several additional variables were controlled for in the analyses to rule out alternative explanations. For all of the analyses, trust in one's employer (T1), years of work experience, and intentions to remain (T1) were controlled for, because trust, tenure, and intentions to remain with the organization may influence employees' contributions to the firm by increasing their attachments and vested interests in the success of the organization. Further, the absolute number of pay raises received by T3 and the absolute number of promotions received by T3 were controlled for in all of the analyses because they represent common rewards that should strongly influence managerial performance. By demonstrating that psychological contract breach (including perceived breach of promises of pay and promotions) has its effects on subsequent performance beyond that accounted for by the absolute number of pay raises and promotions actually received, one shows that it's not just the amount of these rewards received that matters but, rather, the extent to which the employee received those rewards commensurate with what was perceived to be promised and obligated to be provided by the employer.

Results

Table 1 reports the means, standard deviations, and zero-order intercorrelations of the measures. The three dependent variables were reasonably independent, with the highest correlation existing between performance and civic virtue ($r = .41$, $p < .01$). Trust (T1) ranged from moderate to high, with a mean of 4.12, suggesting that these new employees entered the employment relationship with at least some degree of trust in their new employer. An examination of initial obligations at the time of hire reveals that these employees believed that their employer was obligated to fulfill the following conditions (mean level of obligation in parentheses): pay based on current level of performance (4.36); career development (3.93); sufficient power and responsibility (3.63); training (3.61); promotion and advancement (3.55); high pay (3.02); and long-term job security (2.46). Hierarchical regression was used to test hypothesis 1, that initial trust in one's employer would be negatively related to perceiving a contract breach. In the first step, psychological contract breach was regressed on several control variables: intentions to remain (T1), initial obligations, and work experience. When trust (T1) was entered into the equation, it produced a significant beta ($-.19$, $p < .05$), indicating that it explained unique variance in psychological contract breach that was not accounted for by the other variables, which supports hypothesis 1.

Hypothesis 2, predicting that psychological contract breach would be negatively related to employees' contributions, was tested with several sets of hierarchical regressions, one for each dependent variable. For each equation, the control variables were entered first, followed by psychological contract breach. As Table 2 reveals, after controlling for number of promotions received, number of pay increases received, trust (T1), intentions to remain (T1), and work experience, psychological contract breach was found to be negatively related to performance, civic virtue, and intentions to remain with one's employer (T3). Relatedly, those who had voluntarily left their employer between T2 and T3 had reported significantly more psychological contract breach (mean = 4.85) than did those who had not left their employer (mean = .82, $t = 3.00$, $p < .001$). These results taken together indicate that

Table 1 Means, Standard Deviations, and Zero-Order Correlations of Measures ($N = 125$)

Variable	Mean	S.D.	1	2	3	4	5	6	7	8	9	10	11	12	13	14	15	16	17	18
1. Promotions	1.04	.72																		
2. Pay increases	2.37	.80	.25**																	
3. Trust (T1)	4.12	.57	.09	.02																
4. Intent to remain (T1)	15.91	9.95	-.12	-.08	.13															
5. Work experience	6.14	1.61	-.08	-.01	.04	.13														
6. Unmet expectations	2.66	1.10	-.10	-.20*	.04	-.01	.13													
7. Overall breach (T2)	.16	.83	-.09	-.09	-.18*	-.09	-.16	.30												
8. Breach-promotion	-.02	1.50	-.06	-.11	-.03	-.11	-.13	.22*	.65**											
9. Breach-high pay	-.26	1.41	.04	.04	-.07	-.08	-.20*	.15	.63**	.48**										
10. Breach-perf. based pay	1.01	1.24	.09	-.06	-.14	-.01	-.10	-.31**	.61**	.33**	.54**									
11. Breach training	.45	1.33	-.07	-.04	-.04	.02	-.04	.34**	.66**	.19*	.28**	.38**								
12. Breach-job security	-.87	1.32	-.08	-.08	-.01	-.18*	-.01	.03	.49**	.23*	.07	-.00	.18							
13. Breach-development	.51	1.16	-.19*	-.05	-.01	-.03	-.07	.30**	.66**	.35**	.18*	.32**	.50**	.41**						
14. Breach-responsibility	-.03	1.27	-.06	.03	-.02	-.09	-.09	.14	.67**	.35**	.28**	.20*	.35**	.31**	.40**					
15. Intent to remain (T3)	2.98	1.42	-.04	.09	-.15	-.11	.15	-.31**	-.38**	-.21*	-.21*	-.28**	-.33**	-.00	-.30**	.32**				
16. Trust in employer (T3)	3.40	.84	.01	.08	.34**	.02	.02	-.29**	-.29**	-.10	-.11	-.29**	-.26**	-.05	-.26**	-.24**	.60**			
17. Civic virtue	4.04	.57	.13	-.10	.16	.22*	.04	-.08	-.25**	-.11	-.20*	-.15	-.21*	-.06	-.24**	-.16	.38**	.32**		
18. Performance	4.45	.57	.18	-.04	.09	.13	-.05	-.26**	-.18*	-.04	-.12	-.09	-.08	-.15	-.25**	-.11	.30**	.41**	.41**	
19. Turnover	n/a	n/a	n/a	n/a	-.11	.12	n/a	n/a	.20*	.24**	.06	.00	-.06	.15	.15	.31**	n/a	n/a	n/a	n/a

*$p < .05$; **$p < .01$.

Table 2. Hierarchical Regressions Predicting the Impact of Breach on Employee Contributions at Time 3 ($N = 125$)

Variables	Performance		Civic virtue		Intent to remain (T3)	
Promotions	.17	.18**	.20*	.18*	.07	.04
Pay increases	−.02	−.04	−.13	−.15	.12	.09
Trust (T1)	.05	−.04	.07	−.06	.05	−.03
Intent to remain (T1)	.15	.14	.23**	.21**	.09	.16
Work experience	−.17*	−.19*	−.07	−.09	−.05	−.08
Step 2: Predictor						
Breach (T2)		−.18*		−.22**		−.35**
$R2$	.06	.09	.09	.14	.03	.15
F	1.56	1.96**	2.36*	3.07**	.75	3.23**
(d.f.)	(5.115)	(6.113)	(5.115)	(6.113)	(5.115)	(6.113)
Change in $R2$		.03		.05		.12

*$p < .05$; **$p < .01$.

psychological contract breach was negatively related to employees' contributions to the firm, and thus hypothesis 2 was supported.

Hypotheses 3 and 4 predicted that the above relationships between psychological contract breach and employees' contributions would be mediated by unmet expectations and trust (T3), respectively. To test these hypotheses, I followed Baron and Kenny's (1986) recommendations for examining mediating effects in regression. They argued that mediation is demonstrated if three conditions are fulfilled: The first condition stipulates that the independent variable and the proposed mediator must each be significantly related to the dependent variable when considered separately. The preceding analyses demonstrated that the independent variable (psychological contract breach) was significantly related to the three dependent variables (performance, civic virtue, and intentions to remain), independent of the proposed mediators (trust and unmet expectations). To determine whether the proposed mediators were related to the three dependent variables, the correlation matrix in Table 1 was examined. Trust (T3) was significantly related to performance, civic virtue, and intentions to remain (T3), and trust (T3) therefore met the first condition as a mediator for all three variables. Unmet expectations was also significantly related to performance and intentions to remain (T3), but it was not related to civic virtue. Thus, unmet expectations fulfilled the first condition as a potential mediator for two of the dependent variables, but not as a mediator for the relationship between psychological contract breach and civic virtue.

The second condition requires the independent variable to be significantly related to the proposed mediator. This condition was tested by separately regressing trust (T3) and unmet expectations on the control variables and psychological contract breach. As Table 3 reveals, psychological contract breach was significantly related to both trust (T3) and unmet expectations. Hence, both of the proposed mediators met the second condition.

Table 3. Hierarchical Regressions Predicting the Impact of Breach on Employee Trust and Unmet Expectations at Time 3 ($N = 125$)

Variable	Unmet expectations		Trust	
Promotions	−.04	−.01	−.01	−.03
Pay increases	−.19*	−.17*	.07	.05
Trust (T1)	−.03	−.01	.28**	.27**
Intent to remain (T1)	.01	.04	−.02	−.05
Work experience	.18*	.22**	−.09	−.12
Breach		.33**		−.26**
R^2	.08	.18	.09	.16
F	1.86	4.22**	2.36*	3.57**
(d.f.)	(5.115)	(6.113)	(5.115)	(6.113)
Change in R^2				

* $p < .05$; ** $p < .01$.

The last condition stipulates that the relationship between the independent variable and the dependent variable should be weaker or nonsignificant when the proposed mediator is in the regression equation than when the proposed mediator is not in the equation. To test this last condition, several regressions were performed for each dependent variable, with and without each of the potential mediating variables. Table 4 shows the results.

When performance was regressed on psychological contract breach, number of promotions received, number of pay increases received, trust (T1), intentions to remain (T1), and work experience, psychological contract breach was found to be significant and negatively related to performance. In step 2, unmet expectations was added to the equation, and un-met expectations was significant, while psychological contract breach was no longer significant. In step 3, unmet expectations was removed from the equation and trust (T3) was added in. Trust (T3) was found to be significant, and psychological contract breach was no longer significant. In step 4, both trust (T3) and unmet expectations were entered into the equation together and both were found to be significant, although trust (T3) explained more variance, and psychological contract breach was not significant. Taken together, these results indicate that both trust (T3) and unmet expectations each separately fully mediated the relationship between psychological contract breach and performance; that each mediator explained unique variance unaccounted for by the other mediator; and that trust (T3), in comparison with unmet expectations, played a stronger mediating role.

When civic virtue was regressed on psychological contract breach, number of promotions received, number of pay increases received, trust (T1), intentions to remain (T1), and work experience, psychological contract breach was found to be significant and negatively related to civic virtue. Next, when trust (T3) was added to the equation, it was found to be significant, whereas psychological contract breach was no longer significant. Thus, trust (T3) fully mediated the relationship between psychological contract breach and

Sandra L. Robinson

Table 4. Hierarchical Regressions Examining the Mediating Effects of Unmet Expectations and Trust on the Breach-Contribution Relationships ($N = 125$)

Variable	Performance				Civic virtue		Intent to remain (T3)			
Promotions	−.18*	−.21*	−.24**	−.26**	.18*	.18*	.04	.04	.06	.05
Pay increases	−.04	−.08	−.05	−.08	−.15	−.16	.09	.04	.06	.03
Trust (T1)	.04	.03	−.07	−.07	.06	.01	.03	.02	−.12	−.12
Intent to remain (T1)	.14	.16	.17	.18*	.21*	.22**	.06	.07	.09	.09
Work experience	−.19*	−.15	−.17*	−.14	−.09	−.06	−.08	−.02	−.02	.03
Breach	−.18*	−.08	−.08	−.02	−.22**	−.16	−.35**	−.24**	−.20**	−.13
Unmet expectations		−.22*		−.22*				−.27**		−.24**
Trust (T3)			.30**	.33**		.23**			.56**	.53**
R^2	.09	.16	.20	.24	.14	.19	.15	.22	.41	.46
F	1.96*	2.94**	4.01**	4.38**	3.07**	3.60**	3.23**	4.51**	11.18**	11.58**
(d.f.)	(6.113)	(7.112)	(7.112)	(8.110)	(6.113)	(7.112)	(6.113)	(7.112)	(7.112)	(8.110)
Change in R^2		.06	.11	.04	.05	.04	.12	.07	.26	.24

* $p < .05$; ** $p < .01$.

civic virtue behavior. As previously noted, since unmet expectations was found to be unrelated to civic virtue, it precluded the possibility of unmet expectations serving as a mediator for the relationship between perceived breach and civic virtue.

Finally, regressing intentions to remain (T3) on psychological contract breach, number of promotions received, number of pay increases received, trust (T1), intentions to remain (T1), and work experience, psychological contract breach was found to be significant and negatively related to intentions to remain (T3). When unmet expectations was added to the equation, it was significant, but psychological contract breach also remained significant, although its beta weight decreased. Conversely, when trust (T3) was added to the equation, it was significant, but psychological contract breach also remained significant, although its beta weight decreased. The beta weight of psychological contract breach decreased more when trust (T3) was entered into the equation than when unmet expectations was entered into the equation. When both unmet expectations and trust were added to the first equation, both mediators were significant, although trust (T3) explained more variance than unmet expectations, and psychological contract breach was no longer significant. Taken together, this set of regression equations indicates that trust (T3) and unmet expectations (T3) each separately partially mediated the relationship between psychological contract breach and intentions to remain (T3); together the two mediators fully mediated the relationship; and trust (T3), compared with unmet expectations, was a stronger mediator.

Thus the relationship between psychological contract breach and performance was fully mediated by unmet expectations and by trust, although trust explained more variance than unmet expectations. The relationship between psychological contract breach and civic virtue was fully mediated by trust only and not at all mediated by unmet expectations. Finally, the relationship between psychological contract breach and intentions to remain was partially mediated by unmet expectations and by trust, although trust played a stronger mediating role than unmet expectations, and fully mediated by both unmet expectations and trust together. The results show considerable support for the third and fourth hypotheses, which predicted that unmet expectations and trust would mediate the negative relationships between psychological contract breach and employee contributions.

Hypothesis 5 posited that trust (T1) would moderate the relationship between psychological contract breach and trust (T3), such that those with low prior trust should experience a greater decline in trust following a psychological contract breach than those with high prior trust. To test this hypothesis, moderated regression was performed. The interaction terms used in this approach are likely to correlate with the variables from which they were created. To reduce this multicollinearity, Aiken and West (1991) and Cronbach (1987) recommended that the independent variables first be centered around zero, subtracting each variable from its respective mean. This transformation does not affect the correlations among the variables, and it allows for a better estimate of the interaction term. In the first step, the centered dependent variable was regressed on the independent variable along with the control variables. In the second step, the interaction term was added to the equation.

As Table 5 shows, the interaction term was significant for the relationship between psychological contract breach and trust (T3). As would also be expected, it was not significant for the relationship between psychological contract breach and unmet expectations. To interpret the effect of the interaction term, I followed Aiken and West's (1991) recommendations. First, the regression equation was restructured algebraically to express the regression of

Table 5. Hierarchical Regressions Examining the Moderating Influence of Prior Trust ($N = 125$)

Variable	Unmet expectations		Trust (T3)	
Promotions	−.01	−.01	−.03	−.03
Pay increases	−.15	−.16	.03	.04
Intent to remain (T1)	−.04	.04	−.04	−.07
Work experience	−.21*	.21*	−.09	−.09
Trust (T1)	.01	.01	.27**	.22**
Breach	.30**	.30**	−.22*	−.17
Trust (T3)	−.12	−.12		
Unmet expectations			−.13	−.11
Trust (T1) × Breach		−.02		.19*
R^2	.20	.20	.17	.21
F	3.97**	3.45**	3.33**	3.53**
(d.f.)	(7,112)	(8,110)	(7,112)	(8,110)
Change in R^2		.00		.03

*$p < .05$;   **$p < .01$.

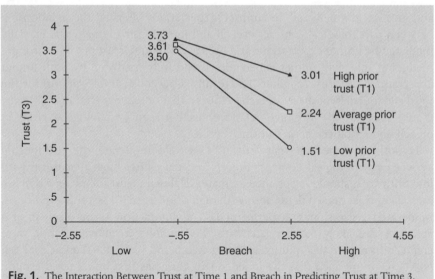

Fig. 1. The Interaction Between Trust at Time 1 and Breach in Predicting Trust at Time 3.

trust (T3) on psychological contract breach at different levels of prior trust (T1): $Y = (b_1 + b_3Z)X + (b_2Z + B_0)$, where b_1 = the unstandardized regression coefficient for psychological contract breach, b_2 = the unstandardized regression coefficient for prior trust (T1), b_3 = the unstandardized regression coefficient for the breach × prior trust interaction, and b_0 = the constant. Next, a series of simple regression equations were derived by substituting in three different values of prior trust, as recommended by Cohen and Cohen (1983): the mean of prior trust as a centered variable (.00), one standard deviation above the mean (.57), and one standard deviation below the mean (−.57). These simple slopes and their corresponding equations are presented in Figure 1. Next, t-tests for each of the simple slopes were computed to determine whether each of the slopes differed from zero and each other.

As Figure 1 illustrates, the direction of the interaction effect is consistent with hypothesis 5: those with low prior trust experienced a greater decline in trust following a psychological contract breach than did those with high prior trust. When prior trust is relatively high, the relationship between psychological contract breach and trust (T3) is not significant; when prior trust is moderate, the relationship is significant and negative; when prior trust is relatively low, the significant negative relationship between psychological contract breach and trust is even stronger.

The above interaction effect was expected on the basis of the rationale that the lower an employee's prior trust, the more likely he or she will be to perceive or interpret the contractual transgression in a negative light and the more his or her subsequent level of trust will be affected. To test this argument further, I conducted an analysis of participants' written explanations for why the perceived breach occurred, which had been provided by a subset of the sample ($N = 33$). Consistent with the above argument, trust (T1) was found to be negatively related to holding the employer responsible for the perceived breach (beta $= -.34$, $p < .05$), and holding the employer responsible for the perceived breach was found to be negatively related to trust (T3) when controlling for prior trust (T1) (beta $= -.33$, $p < .08$).

Discussion

It has been suggested that the traditional employment relationship of long-term job security in return for loyalty is becoming extinct (e.g., Altman and Post, 1996) and that employees are now cynical and unwilling to trust the promises of their employers in this era of downsizing and organizational change (Kanter and Mirvis, 1989). The results of this study, however, do not support these claims: New hires in this study reported relatively high initial trust in their employers, and they reported that their employers made promises obligating them to provide a variety of traditional benefits and rewards in return for the employees' contributions to the firm. Moreover, these employees believed in the promises of their employer, reacting strongly when those promises went unfulfilled.

Psychological contract breach was found to be negatively related to three forms of employee contributions: performance, civic virtue behavior, and intentions to remain with the organization. The results reported here are surprisingly strong when one considers several facts. First, the reports of employee contributions were obtained one year after the occurrence of the psychological contract breach. Thus, the effects of psychological contract breach may be enduring. Second, employees reported their contributions to their firm in the same survey that they reported the number of promotions and pay raises they had received since joining the firm. Despite the fact that they were required to contemplate and report on pay, promotions, and contributions at the same time, and despite the fact that pay and promotion are central motivators of performance, neither the absolute number of pay raises or promotions obtained explained as much variance in employee contributions as did psychological contract breach one year earlier.

These findings both confirm and extend the few prior studies that have found negative relationships between psychological contract breach and employee behaviors, such as citizenship behavior (Robinson and Morrison, 1995), intentions to remain (Robinson and Rousseau, 1994), and decreases in employees' perceived obligations to their employer (Robinson, Kraatz, and Rousseau, 1994). This study, however, has several significant unique strengths. It entailed a more comprehensive examination of the relationship between psychological contract breach and employee contributions because it considered three different facets of employee contributions. Second, this study used a validated, multi-item measure of psychological contract breach, whereas most prior studies have relied on a single-item, global measure. Finally, it was longitudinal, rather than cross sectional, and it statistically controlled for alternative explanatory variables. This study thus provides stronger evidence than prior works that psychological contract breach causes decreases in the full range of employee contributions to the firm.

Trust as a Cause of Psychological Contract Breach

The primary contribution this study makes is that it explicates and empirically examines the roles of trust in the psychological contract breach experience. Much of the theoretical literature on psychological contracts mentions trust as an important related construct, yet virtually no attention has been devoted to understanding the relationship between trust and psychological contract breach. The first role of trust identified in this study was as a factor influencing the likelihood that psychological contract breach would be perceived. Initial trust in one's employer was found to be negatively related to psychological contract breach one year later. A simple explanation for this observed relationship is that employers who are not trustworthy are both less likely to be trusted by their employees and more likely actually to breach an employee's contract. An alternative explanation, however, is that this relationship is due to the bias of selective attention. A large stream of research demonstrates that people tend to seek out and recall information that confirms their prior beliefs and attitudes while ignoring, overlooking, or forgetting evidence that disconfirms them (Fiske and Taylor, 1984; Eagly and Chaiken, 1993). Employees with high initial trust in their employers may have overlooked or forgotten actual breaches by their employer, whereas employees with low initial trust may have actively searched for or remembered incidents of breach, even when no actual breach occurred.

Trust as a Mediator of the Relationship between Breach and Outcomes

Trust was also identified in this study as a mediator of the relationships between psychological contract breach and employees' subsequent contributions. Consistent with prior psychological contract theory, results showed that psychological contract breach led to a loss of trust, which in turn fully mediated the relationship between perceived breach and two employee contributions and partially mediated another. Unmet expectations, however, partially mediated two of the relationships between psychological contract breach and employee contributions and fully mediated another.

The above results on the mediating role of trust and unmet expectations have several important theoretical implications. The contract literature has repeatedly stated two assumptions: (1) that a loss of trust is the critical ingredient in the relationship between psychological contract breach and subsequent employee reactions and (2) that the impact of psychological contract breach comes from something more than just the loss of expected rewards and benefits. This study empirically supports these previously untested assumptions, and this is important for two reasons. First, it empirically demonstrates, for the first time, why psychological contract breach has the effects that it does on employee behavior, because it identifies the crucial mediating variables. Second, it validates the several prior studies on the effects of psychological contract breach. Until now, it was impossible to determine whether prior studies on the effects of psychological contract breach were demonstrating anything new beyond what is already known about the effects of unmet expectations. Even though it has been argued in the contract literature that psychological contract breach and unmet expectations were not synonymous and that the effects of psychological contract breach were something more than just the effects of unmet expectations, there were no empirical data to support these claims. The results of this study show that psychological contract breach produces unmet expectations but that unmet expectations alone cannot account for the effects of psychological contract breach. These results also suggest that although the constructs of psychological contracts and psychological contract breach are related to expectations and unmet expectations, they are in fact distinct. To date, the relationship between these constructs has been unclear, and the literatures on them have tended to remain separated. This study brings them together and suggests that these literatures do not compete with each other but, rather, complement one another.

Trust as a Moderator

Perhaps the most interesting finding of this study is that prior trust moderated the relationship between psychological contract breach and subsequent trust; employees with low initial trust in their employer experienced a greater decline in their trust following a perceived breach than did employees with high initial trust in their employer. This relationship can be attributed to the bias of selective interpretation; employees with high initial trust assimilate the evidence of an unfulfilled contract into their prior attitude of trust, such that the contractual transgression is interpreted in a positive light, whereas employees with low levels of initial trust are more likely to interpret the psychological contract breach in the most unfavorable light and thus confirm their prior attitude. Content analysis of written attributions for the perceived breach by a subset of the sample supports this argument. Employees with low prior trust were more likely than those with high prior trust to blame their employer for the perceived breach, and blaming their employer for the perceived breach was negatively related to subsequent trust. This finding is consistent with a long history of research on attitude function, cognitive consistency, and preservation of schemata (for reviews, see Fiske and Taylor, 1984; Eagly and Chaiken, 1993) that shows that beliefs and attitudes influence individuals' interpretations of reality such that they interpret it in ways consistent with those prior beliefs and attitudes. Even when faced with evidence that should disconfirm their prior beliefs, individuals are able to devise causal explanations for that evidence that allows the prior belief to remain intact (Nisbett and Ross, 1980).

This reported interaction effect between psychological contract breach and prior trust has several important theoretical implications. First, with the exception of Robinson and Rousseau (1994), we know nothing about factors that moderate the relationship between psychological contract breach and its effects. That prior trust in one's employer influences both one's recognition of a psychological contract breach and one's interpretation of that perceived breach demonstrates that the experience of psychological contract breach and violation does not occur in a vacuum but depends on the social and psychological context in which it occurs. Second, understanding the factors that moderate the relationship between breach and subsequent trust is important because psychological contract breach has its impact on employee contributions largely through a loss of subsequent trust.

The interaction effect reported here is especially interesting when compared with the findings of Brockner, Tyler, and Cooper-Schneider (1992), who found a similar interaction effect but one that worked in the opposite direction. They found that individuals with high prior commitment to an authority experienced a greater decline in their commitment after the authority was perceived to be unfair than did individuals with low prior commitment. The results of these two studies, which appear different on the surface, may actually be combined to reach an interesting conclusion. This study examined the interaction between an individual's prior positive attitude and the perceived occurrence of an action by an authority (e.g., the extent to which the authority fulfilled its promises), showing that employees' prior positive attitudes toward an employer will tend to mitigate the impact of perceived negative actions by that employer because employees will tend to interpret those actions in a way that is consistent with their prior positive attitude. Brockner and his colleagues, however, examined the interaction between an individual's prior attitude and the individual's judgment of fairness of an authority's action, which means that they measured not whether the employee perceived the employer's actions but, rather, the employee's interpretation of those actions that *were* perceived. Their study shows that if, despite an employee's positive prior attitude, the employer's actions are ultimately interpreted in a negative light by the employee, a contrast effect will result, and the employee's subsequent positive attitude will be strongly and negatively affected. An interesting avenue for future research would be to test this explanation and to identify the threshold of assimilation: At what point will disconfirming events be assimilated with one's prior positive attitudes and at what point will such events be seen as disconfirming one's prior positive attitudes?

Additional Implications

Demonstrating the relationship between trust and the effects of psychological contract breach bridges the gap between the emerging psychological contracts literature and the more established literature on organizational trust. Trust has been long associated with organizational effectiveness (e.g., Deutsch, 1958; Zand, 1972; Golembiewski and McConkie, 1975). The findings of this study reveal an additional way in which trust influences organizational effectiveness: by influencing employees' perceptions and interpretations of contract breach and their contributions to the firm after the perceived breach. Moreover, this study extends prior studies of trust by revealing an important potential cause of trust: psychological contract breach. Finally, this study lends empirical support to past and current theory on the development of trust. It has been repeatedly argued that trust begets trust, such that trust between two parties promotes trusting behavior, which in turn enables trust to develop further (e.g., Solomon, 1960; Zand, 1972). The findings reported here suggest that trust may beget trust not only by influencing the trusting behavior of each party but also by influencing each party's perceptions of the other's behavior.

Limitations

One limitation of this study may be the generalizability of the results. The relationship between psychological contract breach, trust, and employee contributions may be weaker or nonexistent in situations in which employees' behavior is much more constrained. Employees with high skills levels, mobility, and employment alternatives, such as those in this study, can afford to reduce their inputs. Situational constraints, however, could reduce the relationship between attitudes and behaviors (Schuman and Johnson, 1976; Pratkanis and Greenwald, 1989) and between trust and cooperation (Mayer, Davis, and Schoorman, 1995). Employees with job insecurity, few skills, or few employment alternatives may not change their contributions despite the experience of psychological contract breach.

There are also several possible limitations to the measure of psychological contract breach. First, this measure does not account for possible change in the psychological contract from Time 1, when the promises were made, to Time 2, when the breach was perceived. If the terms of the agreement have changed, this measure may have error that would have weakened the reported results. This limitation would be difficult to circumvent, however, because it requires one to be able to measure the perceived obligation of each contract term just before that particular term is perceived unfulfilled by each individual.

A second possible limitation of this measure is that it aggregated the degree to which specific terms were perceived to be breached and fulfilled, weighing perceived breaches and fulfillment equally. People may be more sensitive to perceived breaches, however, than to perceived fulfillment (or overfulfillment), and thus one may argue that the former should be weighted more heavily than the latter in the aggregation. Because it is very difficult to determine how much more weight should be given to perceived breaches than to perceived fulfillment, they were weighted equally, which produces the most conservative measure of psychological contract breach. A related limitation of this measure is that it does not take into account the possibility that some terms may be more personally important to specific employees than others and therefore should be weighted more heavily than others. A finer-grained measure may have produced stronger results.

Managerial Implications

This study highlights the practical importance of maintaining employees' perceptions of trust and contract fulfillment. Previous work implicating the role of contracts and contracting within organizations has centered around the importance of specifying optimal contracts to achieve a convergence between individual and organizational goals (e.g., Alchian and Demsetz, 1972; Williamson, 1975). This study suggests, however, that managing employees' perceptions of the employer and the employment contract may be as important as creating a specific type of contract in the first place.

The results showing the impact of prior trust on the recognition and interpretation of a breach offers a particularly interesting consideration for managers. If prior trust moderates the impact of psychological contract breach, it suggests that firms that actively establish and maintain trusting relationships with their employees may inoculate them from the negative effects of potential contractual transgressions. If employers can earn the trust of their employees early on, employees will be less likely to perceive a contract breach in the first place and more likely to retain their trust despite possible changes or breaches (perceived or actual) in the employment agreement.

Psychological contract breach, along with its negative consequences, is likely to remain common in organizations as long as trends toward globalization, restructuring, and downsizing continue. As this study shows, the likelihood of psychological contract breach, and its negative impact, can be offset if employees' trust in their employer remains high. If restructuring and downsizing continue to be facts of organizational life, then the challenge for managers is to learn how to navigate such changes in a way that preserves employees' sense of trust. By effectively managing employees' trust, organizations may be able to avoid the negative ramifications of psychological contract breach.

....

References

Aiken, Leona S., and Stephen G. West 1991. Multiple Regression: Testing and Intrepreting Interactions. Newbury Park, CA: Sage.

Alchian, Armen Albert, and Harold Demsetz 1972. "Production, information cause, and economic organization." American Economic Review, 62: 777–795.

Altman, Barbara W., and James E. Post 1996. "Beyond the social contract: An analysis of executives' views at 25 large companies." In Douglas T. Hall (ed.), The Career is Dead—Long Live the Career: A Relational Approach to Careers: 46–71. San Francisco: Jossey-Bass.

Argyris, Chris 1960. Understanding Organizational Behavior. Homewood, IL: Dorsey.

Barber, Bernard 1983. The Logic and Limits of Trust. New Brunswick, NJ: Rutgers University Press.

Baron, R. M., and David A. Kenny 1986. "The moderator-mediator distinction in social psychological research: Conceptual, strategic, and statistical considerations." Journal of Personality and Social Psychology, 51: 1173–1182.

Blau, Peter M. 1964. Exchange and Power in Social Life. New York: Wiley.

Brockner, Joel, Tom R. Tyler, and Rochelle Cooper-Schneider 1992. "The influence of prior commitment on reactions to perceived unfairness: The higher they are, the harder they fall." Administrative Science Quarterly, 37: 241–261.

Chatman, Jennifer A. 1991. "Matching people and organizations: Selection and socialization in public accounting firms." Administrative Science Quarterly, 36: 459–484.

Sandra L. Robinson

Cohen, Arthur, Jack Williams Brehm, and Bibb Latane 1959. "Choice of strategy and voluntary exposure to information under public and private conditions." Journal of Personality, 27: 63–37.

Cohen, Jacob, and Patricia Cohen 1983. Applied Multiple Regression/Correlation Analyses for the Behavioral Sciences, 2nd edn. Hillsdale, NJ: Erlbaum.

Cronbach, Lee J. 1987. "Statistical tests for moderator variables: Flaw in analyses recently proposed." Quantitative Methods in Psychology, 102: 414–417.

Deutsch, Morton 1958. "Trust and suspicion." Journal of Conflict Resolution, 2: 265–279.

Eagly, Alice H., and Shelly Chaiken 1993. The Psychology of Attitudes. New York: Harcourt Brace Jovanovich.

Fiske, Susan T., and Shelley E. Taylor 1984. Social Cognition. New York: Random House.

Frost, Taggart, David V. Stimpson, and Michol R. C. Maughan 1978. "Some correlates of trust." Journal of Psychology, 99: 103–108.

Gabarro, John J., and J. Athos 1976. Interpersonal Relations and Communications. Englewood Cliffs, NJ: Prentice-Hall.

Gambetta, Diego 1988. Trust. New York: Basil Blackwell.

Garfinkel, Harold 1963. "A conception of, and experiments with trust as a condition of stable concerted actions." In O. J. Harvey (ed.), Motivation and Social Interaction: Cognitive Determinants: 187–238. New York: Ronald.

Golembiewski, Robert T., and Mark McConkie 1975. "The centrality of interpersonal trust in group process." In Cary L. Cooper (ed.), Theories of Group Process: 131–185. London: Wiley.

Good, D. 1988. "Individuals, interpersonal relations and trust." In Diego Gambetta (ed.), Trust: 31–48. New York: Basil Blackwell.

Greenwald, Anthony G. 1968. "Cognitive learning, cognitive response to persuasion and attitude change." In Anthony G. Greenwald, Timothy C. Brock, and Thomas M. Ostrom (eds.), Psychological Foundations of Attitudes: 147–169. New York: Academic Press.

—— 1980. "The totalitarian ego: Fabrication and revision of personal history." American Psychologist, 35: 603–618.

Hovland, Carl I., Irving L. Janis, and Harold H. Kelley 1953. Communication and Persuasion. New Haven, CT: Yale University Press.

Kanter, Donald Lucky, and Philip H. Mirvis 1989. The Cynical Americans. San Francisco: Jossey-Bass.

Katz, Daniel 1964. "The motivational basis of organizational behavior." Behavioral Science, 9: 131–146.

Levinson, Harry 1962. Men, Management and Mental Health. Cambridge, MA: Harvard University Press.

Lewis, J. David, and Andrew Weigert 1985. "Trust as a social reality." Social Forces, 63: 967–985.

Lord, Charles G., Lee Ross, and Mark R. Lepper 1979. "Biased assimilation and attitude polarization: The effects of prior theories on subsequently considered evidence." Journal of Personality and Social Psychology, 37: 2098–2109.

Luhmann, Niklas 1979. Trust and Power. New York: Wiley.

Mayer, Roger C., James H. Davis, and F. David Schoorman 1995. "An integrative model of organizational trust." Academy of Management Review, 20: 709–734.

Mischel, Walter, Ebbe B. Ebbesen, and A. R. Zeiss 1973. "Selective attention to the self: Situational and dispositional determinants." Journal of Personality and Social Psychology, 27: 213–225.

Morrison, Elizabeth Wolfe, and Sandra L. Robinson 1997. "When employees feel betrayed: A model of how psychological contract violation develops." Academy of Management Review, vol. 22. no. 1 (in press).

Nisbett, Richard E., and Lee Ross 1980. Human Inference: Strategies and Shortcomings of Social Judgment. New York: Appleton-Century-Crofts.

Nisbett, Richard E., and Timothy DeCamp Wilson 1977. "Telling more than we can know: Verbal reports on mental processes." Psychological Review, 84: 241–259.

Olson, James M., and Mark P. Zanna 1979. "A new look at selective exposure." Journal of Experimental Social Psychology, 15: 1–15.

Organ, Dennis W. 1988. Organizational Citizenship Behavior: The Good Soldier Syndrome. Lexington, MA: Lexington Books.

Petty, Richard E., Timothy M. Ostrom, and Thomas C. Brock (eds.) 1981. Cognitive Responses in Persuasion. Hillsdale, NJ: Erlbaum.

Podsakoff, Philip M., Scott B. MacKenzie, Robert H. Moorman, and Richard Fetter 1990. "Transformational leader behaviors and their effects on followers' trust in leader, satisfaction, and organizational citizenship behaviors." Leadership Quarterly, 1: 107–142.

Porter, Lyman W., and Edward E. Lawler 1968. Managerial Attitudes and Performance. Homewood, IL: Irwin.

Pratkanis, Anthony R. 1989. "The cognitive representation of attitudes." In Anthony R. Pratkanis, Steven James Breckler, and Anthony G. Greenwald (eds.), Attitude Structure and Function: 71–98. Hillsdale, NJ: Erlbaum.

Pratkanis, Anthony R., and Anthony G. Greenwald 1989. "A sociocognitive model of attitude structure and function." Advances in Experimental Social Psychology, 22: 245–285.

Regan, D. T., Ellen Straus, and Russell H. Fazio 1974. "Liking and the attribution process." Journal of Experimental Social Psychology, 10: 385–397.

Robinson, Sandra L., Matthew S. Kraatz, and Denise M. Rousseau 1994. "Changing obligations and the psychological contract: A longitudinal study." Academy of Management Journal, 37: 137–152.

Robinson, Sandra L., and Elizabeth Wolfe Morrison 1995. "Psychological contracts and OCB: The effects of unfulfilled obligations." Journal of Organizational Behavior, 16: 289–298.

Robinson, Sandra L., and Denise M. Rousseau 1994. "Violating the psychological contract: Not the exception but the norm." Journal of Organizational Behavior, 15: 245–259.

Rousseau, Denise M. 1989. "Psychological and implied contracts in organizations." Employee Responsibilities and Rights Journal, 2: 121–139.

—— 1990. "New hire perceptions of their own and their employer's obligations: A study of psychological contracts." Journal of Organizational Behavior, 11: 389–400.

Rousseau, Denise M., and Judi McLean Parks 1994. "The contracts of individuals and organizations." In L. L. Cummings and Barry M. Staw (eds.), Research in Organizational Behavior, 15: 1–43. Greenwich, CT: JAI Press.

Schein, Edgar H. 1980. Organizational Psychology. Englewood Cliffs, NJ: Prentice-Hall.

Schneider, David J., Alex H. Hastorf, and Phoebe C. Ellsworth 1979. Person Perception. Reading, MA: Addison-Wesley.

Schuman, Howard, and M. P. Johnson 1976. "Attitudes and behavior." In Alex Inkeles, J. Coleman, and Neil Smelser (eds.), Annual Review of Sociology, 2: 161–207. Palo Alto, CA: Annual Reviews.

Sims, Ronald R. 1994. "Human resources management's role in clarifying the new psychological contract." Human Resources Management, 33: 373–382.

Simmel, Georg 1978. The Philosophy of Money. London: Routledge and Kegan Paul.

Smith, Mahlon B., Jerome S. Bruner, and Robert W. White 1957. Opinions and Personality. New York: Wiley.

Snyder, Mark, and William B. Swann 1978. "When actions reflect attitudes: The politics of impression management." Journal of Personality and Social Psychology, 34: 1034–1042.

Snyder, Mark, and Seymour W. Uranowitz 1978. "Reconstructing the past: Some cognitive consequences of person perception." Journal of Personality and Social Psychology, 36: 941–950.

Solomon, Leonard 1960. "The influence of some types of power relationships and game strategies upon the development of interpersonal trust." Journal of Abnormal and Social Psychology, 4: 367–392.

Tichy, Noel M. 1983. Managing Strategic Change. New York: Wiley.

Wanous, John P., Timothy D. Poland, Stephen L. Premack, and K. Shannon Davis 1992. "The effects of met expectations on newcomer attitudes and behaviors: A review and meta-Wanous analysis." Journal of Applied Psychology, 77: 288–297.

Williamson, Oliver E. 1975. Markets and Hierarchies. New York: Free Press.

Wilson, Timothy DeCamp, and Richard E. Nisbett 1978. "The accuracy of verbal reports about the effects of stimuli on evaluations and behavior." Social Psychology, 41: 118–131.

Zand, Dale E. 1972. "Trust and managerial problem solving." Administrative Science Quarterly, 17: 229–239.

Zucker, Lynne G. 1986. "Production of trust: Institutional sources of economic structure, 1840–1920." In Barry M. Staw and L. L. Cummings (eds.), Research in Organizational Behavior, 8: 53–111. Greenwich, CT: JAI Press.

12 Paranoia and Self-Consciousness

Allan Fenigstein and Peter A. Vanable

A series of studies by Fenigstein (1984) suggested that self-consciousness heightened the tendency to engage in seemingly paranoid inferences. Subjects who were high in public self-consciousness (i.e., who tended to focus on the publicly observable aspects of themselves; see Fenigstein, Scheier, & Buss, 1975), compared with those low on that dimension, were more likely, for example, to assume that an acquaintance who walked by without saying "hello," actually intended to avoid them, as opposed to simply not noticing them. In another study, subjects in a group experiment were faced with the possibility that the experimenter had chosen either the subject or another person who was present to participate in a demonstration. Public self-consciousness again strengthened subjects' beliefs that they, rather than the other person, had been volunteered for the demonstration. In both studies, self-consciousness increased the extent to which subjects perceived another's behavior as being intentionally directed toward them (labeled the *self-as-target bias*). Given that this bias is one of the defining characteristics of paranoid thought (see e.g., Greenwald, 1980). Fenigstein's (1984) research suggests the possibility that self-consciousness has important implications for paranoia. What follows is an attempt to more systematically develop that relationship, both theoretically and empirically.

The notion that self-consciousness and paranoia are related is far from novel. More than 70 years ago, Kraepelin (1915) recognized that heightened self-consciousness can be easily demonstrated in paranoid personalities. Similarly, Cameron (1943), in his seminal work on paranoia, described the paranoic woman whose preoccupation with how she looks creates a readiness to detect ridicule or criticism from others; in effect, her own self-consciousness leads her to incorrectly impute self-referent thoughts to others. More recent writings have echoed the same relationship. Shapiro (1965) noted the self-consciousness of many mildly paranoid people, suggesting that the simple awareness of attention from another person is capable of precipitating a personal feeling of exposure or vulnerability. Finally, Laing (1969) also argued that the self-conscious awareness of oneself as an object of the awareness of others leads to a heightened sense of being seen; as a result, self-conscious persons are susceptible to the paranoid feeling that they are the object of other people's interest more than, in actuality, is the case.

Essentially, these clinical observations suggest that (a) a central feature of paranoid ideation is the self-referent assumption that one is the object or target of another's thought or behavior, an assumption that is often unfounded and (b) these self-referential social inferences are related to self-consciousness (i.e., as a result of directing one's own attention toward the self, one may come to think that others are also directing attention toward oneself). Each of these points are elaborated in turn.

Paranoia and Self-Reference

In discussing paranoia, several cautions need to be introduced. Although *paranoia* is an accepted psychiatric diagnosis (American Psychiatric Association, 1987), the term has also become so much a part of today's vernacular, as in "don't be paranoid," that its actual meaning can be easily obscured. The present analysis begins with descriptions of psychopathology, but attempts to maintain a distinction between clinical paranoid syndromes and other forms of behavior that—although apparently normal—may best be characterized as paranoid. This potential confusion is compounded by the fact that clinicians recognize several different paranoid disturbances, although it may be suggested that many of these syndromes share similar characteristics. In particular, it is argued that almost all paranoid disorders involve personalistic or self-referent interpretations of others' behavior. For example, those with paranoid personality disorders are extremely mistrustful. Convinced that others are out to exploit them, their suspicion is manifested by a marked propensity to misinterpret seemingly innocuous events as personally threatening. Similarly, the delusional (paranoid) disorder, which is frequently characterized by persecutory or grandiose delusions, almost always involves the highly self-centered belief that others are taking special notice of one. Thus, in both syndromes, there is an exaggerated and unwarranted tendency to regard the behavior of others as if it were related to or targeted toward the self, so that, for example, innocent comments from others are taken as malevolent put-downs, or the continual appearance of a stranger on the street means that one is being watched or plotted against.

This conceptualization is by no means an attempt to reduce the complex syndromes of paranoia to simple errors of self-referent processing. However, the persistent misperception of oneself as the target of another's thoughts or actions, commonly known as an *idea* (or in extreme cases, as a *delusion*) *of reference*, has long been recognized as one of the hallmarks of paranoia (e.g., Cameron, 1943; Colby, 1977; Magaro, 1980; Maher, 1988; Millon, 1981; Oltmanns, 1988; Swanson, Bohnert, & Smith, 1970; Ullman & Krasner, 1969). Moreover, the identification of exaggerated self-referent processing as a prevalent distortion in the pattern of paranoid thought provides an intriguing link between paranoia and self-consciousness.

It needs to be emphasized that the present research is concerned solely with normal, nonpathological phenomena. One of the underlying assumptions of this research is that ordinary individuals, in their everyday behavior, manifest characteristics—such as self-centered thought, suspiciousness, assumptions of ill will or hostility, and even notions of conspiratorial intent—that are reminiscent of paranoia. Such behaviors are consistent with contemporary work in both social cognition and psychiatry, which questions the assumption of normative rationality and suggests that normal individuals engage in a variety of implausible interpretations or ideational distortions in attempting to explain events (e.g., Chapman & Chapman, 1988; Maher, 1988; Nisbett & Ross, 1980; Strauss, 1969; Tversky & Kahneman, 1974). Moreover, these behavioral occurrences within the normal population are frequently and casually referred to or described as *paranoid;* thus, the term has taken on meaning that is apparently independent of any indication of clinical disturbance. Because of the term's common usage, and because there is no obvious alternative that successfully captures the mode of thought and perception that is under investigation here, *paranoia*, despite its unintended clinical implications, is used throughout this article as a descriptive term.

Self-Reference and Self-Consciousness

The present analysis contends that self-consciousness, through activation and involvement of the self in the processing of social information, may contribute to the paranoid misperception of others' behaviors as being directed or targeted toward the self. Several studies have found that self-focused attention facilitates the processing of self-referent information by activating the general domain of self-knowledge during the encoding process (e.g., Agatstein & Buchanan, 1984; Hull & Levy, 1979; Hull, Van Treuren, Ashford, Propsom, & Andrus, 1988; Turner, 1978, 1980). Through this activation, or priming (e.g., Bargh &

Pietramonaco, 1982; Higgins, Rholes, & Jones, 1977; Wyer & Srull, 1981), of self-knowledge, new information is more likely to be interpreted using the primed category (i.e., perceived in self-referent terms). For example, previous research has shown that as a result of directing attention toward the self and increasing its accessibility, the self is more likely to be seen both as a causal agent (e.g., Duval & Wicklund, 1973; Fenigstein & Levine, 1984; Ross & Sicoly, 1979; Sandelands & Calder, 1984) and as a target of other's behavior (Fenigstein, 1984). Thus, to the extent that paranoia involves perceptions of the world that implicate the self to an excessive degree, self-consciousness may heighten the tendency to engage in paranoid inferences.

Study 1

Study 1 examines the relationship between dispositional self-consciousness and a measure of paranoia developed for a normal college population.

Method

Measurement of Self-Consciousness

Fenigstein et al. (1975) conceptualized self-focused attention in terms of relatively stable personality tendencies, termed *self-consciousness*, and constructed an instrument (the Self-Consciousness Scale) to measure these self-attentional dispositions. Factor analyses of the scale have consistently yielded two stable self-consciousness dimensions: Private and Public. The Private factor is defined by an awareness of the inner or personal aspects of self, such as one's private thoughts and feelings. The Public subscale involves an awareness of the self as a social object (i.e., as an entity that is the object of awareness of others). There is considerable evidence for both the construct and discriminant validity of these factors (Carver & Scheier, 1981; Fenigstein, 1987).

Public self-consciousness appeared to be particularly relevant to the present research, although initially, private self-consciousness was also examined. Publicly self-conscious persons (Fenigstein et al., 1975) are attentive to how they are viewed by others, and the essence of the self-referent thought that is characteristic of paranoid persons is a readiness to misperceive others' actions as somehow relevant to themselves. Laing's (1969) description of self-consciousness, in his discussion of paranoia, also focused on an awareness of oneself as an object of someone else's observation: a description virtually identical to what

Fenigstein et al. (1975) called *public self-consciousness*. In addition, previous research investigating the paranoid, self-as-target bias has identified public self-consciousness as a significant influence (Fenigstein, 1979, 1984).

Measurement of Paranoia

For purposes of the present research, a new measure of paranoia was developed for use with college students.

Selection of items. Following Zimbardo, Andersen, and Kabat (1981), who used several Minnesota Multiphasic Personality Inventory (MMPI)-based scales in their study of experimentally induced paranoia, the present study also measured paranoia with a questionnaire derived from the MMPI. Items were initially selected if they had been previously used in at least one of the following paranoid reaction scales, reported in Dahlstrom, Welsh, and Dahlstrom (1975): Comrey's Paranoia Factor Scale (p. 283); Horn's Paranoia Scale (p. 283); Baggaley and Riedel's Paranoid Tendency Scale (p. 283); Endi cott, Jortner, and Abramoff's Suspiciousness Scale (p. 288); and Watson and Klett's Paranoid Projection Scale (p. 293).

Because all of the above scales, as well as the MMPI itself, were intended primarily for a clinical population, several considerations guided the selection of items for use with a college population. Items had to relate to at least one of the following aspects of paranoia (taken from Magaro, 1980, and Millon, 1981): (a) a belief that people or external forces are trying to influence one's behavior or control one's thinking; (b) a belief that people are against one in various ways; (c) a belief that some people talk about, refer to, or watch one; (d) suspicion or mistrust of others' motives; and (e) feelings of ill will, resentment, or bitterness. Other MMPI items that were part of the earlier paranoia scales were not selected for the present questionnaire either because of their obscurity (e.g., "Everything tastes the same.") or because they were so obviously psychotic (e.g., "I commonly hear voices without knowing where they come from.") as to be inappropriate for the assessment of any moderate but presumably normal paranoid tendencies in college students.

These considerations led to the initial selection of 32 items to measure paranoia. Subjects were asked to respond to each item on a 5-point scale ranging from 1, *not at all applicable to me*, to 5, *extremely applicable to me*. Throughout the course of refining the questionnaire, a variety of different filler items were embedded among the paranoia items in an attempt to disguise the nature of the measure. (Use of different filler items had little effect on the basic psychometric properties of the paranoia inventory.) Pilot testing as well as subsequent administrations indicated that very few subjects were able to detect the purpose of the questionnaire or the aim of the research.

Allan Fenigstein and Peter A. Vanable

Pilot Testing. The 32-item scale was administered to 144 undergraduates, 86 women and 58 men. As a result of this pilot testing, the scale went through two additional revisions, involving a total of 186 students, in an attempt to eliminate items that had (a) low or ambiguous factor loadings, (b) extremely skewed distributions, or (c) poor correlations with the total scale. The final paranoia scale that emerged from these operations contained 20 items (see Table 1).

Reliability and Validity

The data presented in these analyses were provided by four separate samples of students who were tested between 1985 and 1988. All the samples (ranging in size from 119 to 180 subjects, with a combined N of 581) were administered the Paranoia Scale, together with a measure of social desirability (Crowne & Marlowe, 1964). In addition, different samples completed a number of different self-report instruments (described later).

Table 1. Paranoia Scale: Factor Structure and Internal Consistency

Items on the Paranoia Scale	Loadings on the first unrotated factor	Corrected item–total correlations
1. Someone has it in for me.	.46	.38
2. I sometimes feel as if I'm being followed.	.33	.27
3. I believe that I have often been punished without cause.	.47	.39
4. Some people have tried to steal my ideas and take credit for them.	.47	.40
5. My parents and family find more fault with me than they should.	.47	.39
6. No one really cares much what happens to you.	.49	.40
7. I am sure I get a raw deal from life.	.58	.50
8. Most people will use somewhat unfair means to gain profit or an advantage, rather than lose it.	.50	.42
9. I often wonder what hidden reason another person may have for doing something nice for you.	.60	.51
10. It is safer to trust no one.	.48	.40
11. I have often felt that strangers were looking at me critically.	.53	.45
12. Most people make friends because friends are likely to be useful to them.	.54	.46
13. Someone has been trying to influence my mind.	.43	.36
14. I am sure I have been talked about behind my back.	.56	.48
15. Most people inwardly dislike putting themselves out to help other people.	.45	.37
16. I tend to be on my guard with people who are somewhat more friendly than I expected.	.49	.41
17. People have said insulting and unkind things about me.	.55	.47
18. People often disappoint me.	.60	.51
19. I am bothered by people outside, in cars, in stores, etc. watching me.	.43	.35
20. I have often found people jealous of my good ideas just because they had not thought of them first.	.51	.43

Internal Consistency. Across the four samples, the coefficient alphas ranged from .81 to .87, with an overall alpha for the combined sample of .84. The corrected item–total correlations for the combined sample ranged from .27 to .51, with a mean item–total *r* of .42 (see Table 1). The alphas as well as the item–total correlations indicated a substantial degree of internal consistency.

Test–Retest Reliability. The scale was readministered, after 6 months, to 107 subjects from the original 1985 sample of 180. Despite the relatively long interval between testings, the test–retest correlation of .70 showed that the questionnaire had good stability.

Construct Validity. Because this research was using a scale made up of MMPI items, there was a need to establish the validity of the scale for normal college students, both to assure that it measured what it purported to measure and that it was appropriate for use with the present research samples. In addition to the tendency to read personal and hidden meanings into benign events, paranoia is characterized by a pervasive mistrust of others, a readiness to perceive others as threatening and to react with ill will and resentment, and a belief that others shape what occurs in the world, resulting in a corresponding need to determine events as one desires (American Psychiatric Association, 1987; Millon, 1981).

On the basis of these considerations, the relationships between paranoia and measures of trust, anger, and control beliefs were investigated, using a number of conceptually relevant inventories (independently developed, in large part, for use with college students): an assessment of Trust in Close Relationships by Rempel, Holmes, and Zanna (1985) and Rotter's (1980) Interpersonal Trust Scale; Siegel's (1985) Multidimensional Anger Inventory and the Anger Expression Scale of Spielberger et al. (1985); a scale of Control by Powerful Others developed by Levenson (1973); and Burger and Cooper's (1979) Desirability of Control Questionnaire.

....

Results

Validation Measures

As expected, on the basis of clinical descriptions of paranoid thought and behavior, the present measure of paranoia was negatively correlated with both interpersonal trust, $r(150) = -.30, p < .01$, and trust in close relationships, $r(119) = -.32, p < .01$, and positively correlated with anger, both in its experience, $r(180) = .45, p < .01$, and in its expression. Interestingly, paranoia was more closely associated with the tendency to express anger inwardly (e.g., boil inside, secretly criticize others), $r(132) = .51$, $p < .01$, than outwardly (e.g., strike out at others, lose one's temper), $r(132) = .18$, $p < .05$, consistent with characterizations of paranoids as very guarded and unrevealing in an attempt to maintain tight emotional control. Paranoia was also correlated with both a belief in the control of powerful others, $r(150) = .34$, $p < .01$, and a corresponding need for personal control, $r(180) = .29$, $p < .01$.

These results, which generally suggest a moderate amount of shared variance between paranoia and the other measures (mostly around 10 percent, but ranging up to 25 percent), can be taken as evidence for both convergent and discriminant validity: The present scale was significantly related to assessments of other psychological variables that are associated with paranoid symptomatology, but the amount of unshared variance between the constructs measured was considerable enough so as not to undermine the distinctiveness of the paranoia measure. (Additional evidence for the construct validity of the scale is provided in Studies 2 and 3, in which the scale is shown to be associated with a behavioral criterion of paranoia.)

Across all samples, paranoia was strongly and negatively correlated with social desirability, $r(581) = -.49$, $p < .01$. Consequently, correlations between the Paranoia Scale and previously cited validation measures were recalculated, controlling for social desirability. The resulting partial correlations showed that social desirability had little effect on the zero-order correlations reported earlier. The high negative correlation of paranoia with social desirability may be interpreted to mean that paranoia scores, rather than representing genuine self-characterizations, were motivated primarily by the need for social approval. This interpretation, however, fails to account for the relationships between paranoia and other socially disapproved characteristics, such as mistrust and anger, which remain significant even after controlling for social desirability. In addition, it may be argued that paranoia's negative correlation with social desirability is in fact quite predictable. Because paranoia has a clear quality of social disapproval, it is reasonable to expect that persons who identify themselves as having paranoid thoughts are unlikely to present themselves as having strong needs for social approval. It may also be argued that to the extent that paranoid responses are recognized as socially undesirable, the present scores may be regarded as a conservative estimate of underlying paranoid tendencies.

Norms

That paranoid responses were viewed as likely to be disapproved of was also indicated by the fact that the distribution of scores on the paranoia measure was clearly skewed toward the low end. Nevertheless, there was a surprising willingness on the part of subjects to endorse most of the paranoid items as self-descriptive. Combining across samples, 62 percent of the subjects, on average, endorsed a paranoid scale item as being at least slightly applicable to the self, and 33 percent endorsed the item as at least somewhat applicable. The mean (M) total score on the paranoia scale (on a range of 20–100) was 42.7 (standard deviation [SD] = 10.2), with men ($M = 43.5$, $n = 214$) scoring only slightly and nonsignificantly higher than women ($M = 42.3$, $n = 367$). There was apparently sufficient variation in scores to consider the instrument suitable for use with a college population.

Evidence of a General Factor

Factor analyses, together with the reliability data, offered strong evidence of a single, general factor. Given that the scale was constructed to tap an underlying homogeneous variable, the general factor should be reflected as the first unrotated factor. In each sample, every item loaded positively (at least .23) on the first unrotated factor derived from principal axes factor analysis, and for the combined sample, all of the items had loadings greater than .30 (see Table 1), the conventional cutoff to ensure that the loading is meaningful (e.g., Gorsuch, 1983; Nunnally, 1978). In comparison, only two items in the combined sample had a positive loading greater than .30 with the second unrotated factor, and there was almost no consistency in these items across the separate samples. For the combined sample of 581, the first unrotated factor accounted for 25 percent of the total variance in the scale, whereas the second factor accounted for only 7 percent of the variance; the amount of variance accounted for by the first 2 unrotated factors was very consistent across individual samples.

The relatively high interitem correlations (mean r of .21) for the scale items, the low number of negative correlations in the matrix of interitem correlations (less than 1 percent of the total), the strong reliability (alpha) coefficients, and the uniformly high loadings on the first compared with the second unrotated factor, all suggest that the scale items are related to a general factor measuring a unitary attribute (cf. Briggs & Cheek, 1988).

The present use of an unrotated factor solution may be justified in several ways. In measuring a limited domain personality construct, especially when a homogeneous factor may be involved, rotation to a simple structure may not provide an appropriate or meaningful solution to the data (e.g., Cattell, 1978; Hogan & Nicholson, 1988). In fact, for the present data, rotated factor analyses tended to yield different solutions across samples (regardless of whether oblique, varimax, or quartimax rotations were used), whereas the unrotated analysis yielded very consistent results.

In addition to the reliability and factor-analytic evidence, the existence of a general factor may also be argued conceptually. Shapiro (1965) suggested that the fundamental basis of paranoia is a pervasive and exaggerated view of the social world as threatening and untrustworthy. Viewed from this perspective, the criteria used in selecting items for the scale, although representing a variety of paranoid attributes (e.g., ideas of reference, suspicion or mistrust, a generally hostile outlook), may be seen as forming a coherent pattern in that they all relate to an everpresent concern for and expectation of threatening others.

Self-Consciousness and Paranoia

Given the extreme sensitivity of paranoid persons to the behavior of others (although not necessarily to their approval), and the highly social nature of paranoid ideas (e.g., Millon, 1981), it was expected that paranoia would be related to the public dimension of self-consciousness. The correlations between the Public Self-Consciousness Scale and the Paranoia Scale were very consistent across all four samples, ranging from .37 to .41, with a combined $r(581) = .40$, $p < .01$, suggesting a strong and stable association. Although the research was primarily interested in public self-consciousness, relationships with private self-consciousness were also examined. Because the two self-consciousness factors shared some variance (about 10 percent, on average, across samples; see also Fenigstein, 1987), a partial correlation between private self-consciousness and paranoia, controlling for public self-consciousness, was computed: The resulting $r(581) = .15$ was only marginally significant. However, the partial correlation between public self-consciousness and paranoia, controlling for private self-consciousness, remained strong, with the overall $r(581) = .35$, $p < .01$, indicating that the relationship between public self-consciousness and paranoia was relatively independent of private self-consciousness.

....

Discussion

These findings offered empirical support for the long-standing, but previously untested, clinical insight suggesting that self-directed attention, especially to-ward the self as a social object, is related to a number of paranoid beliefs. The correlational evidence does not allow for any conclusive causal inferences, but there are at least two possibilities. Consistent with the previously discussed self-reference effect, it may be that self-consciousness leads to paranoia. In addition to previously cited clinical examples, it has also been observed that adolescents, who are regarded as notoriously self-conscious, are especially prone to the feeling that everyone is looking at them, precisely because their own attention is focused on themselves (Elkind, 1967). However, one cannot rule out the possibility that chronic paranoid thoughts are likely to heighten one's self-consciousness. A belief system that construes others' behaviors in terms of the self may very well create a chronic state of self-focus. For the moment, both arguments await further research.

The present research also suggests that although paranoid thought has usually been regarded as a form of psychopathology, there are at least certain characteristics of paranoia that are not uncommon in normal college students. That is, just as the extensive experimental social-cognitive literature of the past two decades has shown that there are elements of depression in what is otherwise a clearly nonclinical population, so too the concept of paranoia may need to be extended to include the thought processes that characterize everyday life.[1] The present results tend to confirm what many of us recognize and what is reflected by the frequent use of the term *paranoia* in our language: that on various occasions, one may think one is being talked about or feel as if everything is going against one, often resulting in suspicion and mistrust of others, as though they were taking advantage of one or were to blame for one's difficulties. Moreover, these beliefs appear to be associated with a consciousness of the self as a social object.

Study 2

Study 1, relying exclusively on questionnaire measures, found a correlation between dispositional self-consciousness and paranoid thought. In Study 2, a behavioral measure of paranoia is introduced. The feeling of being watched or that others are taking special notice of one is a classical manifestation of a paranoid idea of reference (Laing, 1969; Magaro, 1980; Meissner, 1978; Millon, 1981). Consistent with the present analysis, it may be argued that this feeling of being observed derives from one's own self-directed attention. To the extent that publicly self-conscious persons are preoccupied with how they are seen by others, they may become susceptible to the belief that they are actually the object of observation by others.

In the present research, subjects were placed either in an empty room or in a room with a two-way mirror, and the extent to which they felt they were being observed was assessed. Although the mirror obviously suggested the possibility of being observed, it was hypothesized that the acceptance of that possibility would vary as a function of individual differences in self-consciousness. The present research also offered the opportunity to further validate the Paranoia Scale by examining whether responses to the scale were predictive of feelings of being watched.

Method

Subjects

The subjects were 19 male and 21 female undergraduates who participated individually in the research to earn extra credit in their introductory psychology course. Several weeks before the experiment, these participants had completed the Self-Consciousness Scale (Fenigstein et al., 1975) and the Paranoia Scale, as part of a battery of questionnaires. Because of the small number of subjects available, median splits were used to create groups of low- and high-public self-consciousness subjects and groups of low- and high-paranoia subjects. There were roughly equal numbers of men and women in all groups.

Procedure

Before the "real" experiment began, subjects were asked to leave their belongings with the experimenter and wait alone for 5 minutes in a "waiting room." Half the subjects were seated in a room across from what was obviously a two-way mirror, which was illuminated in such a way that they could only see themselves; however, no mention was made of the mirror, and there was no observer on the other side of the mirror. The other subjects were seated in a room containing no mirror. After 5 minutes, the subjects were taken out of the waiting room and asked to fill out a six-item questionnaire about their thoughts and feelings. The critical item on the questionnaire asked, "While you were waiting, did you feel you were being watched?," which was answered on a 10-point range from *not at all* to *definitely*.

In the next part of the experiment, the subjects engaged in an anagram task, purportedly as part of a study of problem solving, in a room different from the waiting room. Subjects who had previously waited in the mirrored room now did the anagrams in a nonmirrored room; subjects who had waited earlier in a bare room now completed the anagrams seated across from the two-way mirror in which they could see only themselves. Again, no mention was made of the mirror, but the experimenter did watch the subjects through the two-way mirror, without the subjects' knowledge. After working on the anagrams for 5 minutes, subjects were taken out of the room and again asked to fill out a new copy of the six-item questionnaire, with the critical item now asking, "While you were trying to solve the anagrams, did you feel you were being watched?"

Subjects were then questioned about their perceptions of the study, and the nature of the research was described. Although no subjects voiced any suspicion of the role of self-consciousness or self-attention in the research, 8 of the subjects raised questions about whether the mirror was a two-way mirror. In all cases, these were subjects who indicated on the questionnaire that they felt they were being watched through the two-way mirror, and so this question was reasonable and expected. Although the number of subjects involved was too small to warrant statistical analysis, 6 of the 8 subjects who asked were high in public self-consciousness, and so their suspicions were consistent with some of the major findings presented in the Results section.

Results

Mirror Presence, Mirror Order, and Gender

Subjects' feelings of being watched were measured in two situations: first, while they were waiting in a mirrored or nonmirrored room, and subsequently, while they were working on anagrams in a nonmirrored or mirrored room, respectively. Thus, for all subjects, paranoid notions of being observed were assessed in both the absence and presence of a two-way mirror, although the order of this sequence was varied. To test the mirror's effect as well as the order effect and the possibility of gender differences, subjects' responses were initially analyzed using a two-between (gender and order of mirror presentation) × one-within (nonmirrored or mirrored room) analysis of variance (ANOVA).

There were no main effects or interactions for gender in this analysis (nor in any subsequent analyses involving premeasured dispositions). Men and women did not differ in their sense of being watched in this research, and so gender is not further discussed. The sequence variable also had no significant main or interactive effects in this analysis. Feelings of being watched were apparently unaffected by the order in which subjects encountered the mirror; nor were subjects more likely to feel observed when they were engaging in an experimental activity as compared with merely waiting. These nonfindings also suggest the absence of a priming effect: Being asked about feeling watched in the prior waiting session had no effect on the report of such feelings in the next part of the study. Thus, the order in which subjects were exposed to mirror and nonmirror conditions was ignored in all subsequent analyses.

Allan Fenigstein and Peter A. Vanable

The presence or absence of the two-way mirror, not surprisingly, had a significant effect on the dependent measure, $F(1, 36) = 19.87$, $p < .001$. Subjects were much more likely to feel that they were being observed when there was a mirror through which they could be observed ($M = 5.30$) than in the absence of the mirror ($M = 2.80$). (In fact, every subject experienced at least some sense of being watched in the presence of the mirror, suggesting that the two-way mirror was a sufficiently prominent stimulus.)

Pretested Self-Consciousness and Paranoia

More relevant to the present investigation were the effects of the premeasured dispositions on feelings of being watched in the presence and absence of the mirror. On the basis of preliminary analyses, using both regression techniques and ANOVA, which showed significant effects for public self-consciousness and paranoia but not for private self-consciousness (consistent with the findings of Study 1), the latter variable was ignored in favor of analyses that concentrated on the former two.

Feelings of being observed were analyzed using a two-between (low or high public self-consciousness and low or high paranoia) × one-within (nonmirrored or mirrored room) ANOVA (see Table 2). In addition to the previously established mirror effect, there were significant main effects for both paranoia, $F(1, 36) = 8.10$, $p < .01$, and public self-consciousness, $F(1, 36) = 7.14$, $p < .02$. These dispositional measures did not interact with each other, but there was a significant interaction between the mirror and public self-consciousness, $F(1, 36) = 11.98$, $p < .01$. There were no other significant interactions.

The paranoia main effect offered evidence of construct validity: Persons scoring high on the Paranoia Scale showed a stronger tendency toward feelings of being watched than those scoring low on the scale. The correlations

Table 2. Feelings of Being Watched as a Function of Mirror Presence, Paranoia, and Public Self-Consciousness

Public self-consciousness	Mirror absent			Mirror present		
	Low paranoia	High paranoia	Row M	Low paranoia	High paranoia	Row M
Low	2.00	4.33	2.82	4.00	3.57	3.85
Cell n	13	7	20	13	7	20
High	1.71	3.37	2.78	6.00	7.15	6.75
Cell n	7	13	20	7	13	20
Column M	1.90	3.70	2.80	4.70	5.90	5.30
Column n	20	20	40	20	20	40

Note. Higher numbers indicate greater feelings of being watched.

between paranoia and feelings of being watched were significant both in the mirror, $r(40) = .27, p < .05$, and in the no-mirror conditions, $r(40) = .46, p < .01$. Thus, the pretest measure was predictive of a behavioral criterion of paranoia.

The effects of public self-consciousness were clearly influenced by the presence of a mirror. High-public self-conscious persons, as predicted, were more likely than the low-self-conscious group to feel they were being watched, but this effect was significant only when there was a mirror through which subjects could be seen, $F(1, 39) = 20.19, p < .01$; this pattern was confirmed by correlational analyses that yielded a significant relationship between public self-consciousness and feelings of being watched in the mirror's presence, $r(40) = .48, p < .01$, but not in its absence.

Because of the shared variance between the self-consciousness and paranoia measures, $r(40) = .51, p < .01$, covariance analyses were also performed. With self-consciousness as a covariate, the main effect for paranoia remained significant, $F(1, 37) = 6.61, p < .02$. Similarly, the main and interactive effects of self-consciousness remained significant, while controlling for paranoia, $F(1, 37) = 4.53, p < .05$, and $F(1, 37) = 9.19, p < .01$, respectively.

Discussion

The present research found that publicly self-conscious persons, as well as those predisposed toward paranoid thoughts, have a heightened sense of being observed. Paranoid subjects expressed this feeling, regardless of whether there was an obvious means (i.e., the mirror) through which they could be observed; that is, even when waiting in an apparently empty cubicle, persons prone toward paranoid ideas were subject to the feeling of being observed.

Publicly self-conscious subjects, however, were much more responsive to the presence of a two-way mirror. Only under these conditions were they likely to assume—relative to the low–self-conscious group—that there were persons on the other side of the mirror watching them, although they were given no information to that effect. It may be that the two-way mirror suggested the presence of others, and under those circumstances, public self-conscious persons are prepared to assume they are being watched; sitting alone in a nonmirrored room, however, may not be a sufficiently salient social situation for such persons.

Thus, when preoccupied with the way in which one is seen by others (i.e., when publicly self-conscious), persons are likely to exaggerate the extent to which others, who are or may be present, are watching or noticing them (see also Argyle, 1969; Elkind, 1967; Fenigstein, 1979). These findings also suggest an interesting reciprocal relationship: Just as an observing audience increases feelings of self-consciousness (Carver & Scheier, 1978; Scheier, Fenigstein, & Buss, 1974), so too, self-consciousness increases feelings of being observed. It is important, however, to note the orthogonal effects of public self-consciousness and paranoia: Although self-consciousness may be an important contributor to paranoid feelings, the two can operate independently of each other.

Study 3

Whereas Study 2 looked at the role of dispositional self-consciousness as it related to paranoid feelings of being watched, Study 3 examines the effects of experimentally manipulated self-attention on this dependent measure in an attempt to increase the plausibility and generalizability of a self-attention interpretation. Given the findings of the previous study, which suggested that issues of self-focused attention were especially salient in the presence of a two-way mirror, the mirror was again used as a background stimulus.

Attentional focus was controlled through a story-construction technique, developed and validated by Fenigstein and Levine (1984) and subsequently used in a number of laboratory studies of self-attention (e.g., Pyszczynski, Hamilton, Herring, & Greenberg, 1989; Pyszczynski, Holt, & Greenberg, 1987). This previous research has shown that subjects writing stories using self-relevant words experience greater self-focus than do subjects writing stories using other-relevant words. This technique has generally been regarded as a nonspecific self-attention manipulation, which is responsive to the particular cues of the situation. In the presence of a two-way mirror, it was assumed that at least some attention would be directed toward the self as a social object. Again, it was predicted that directing one's own attention toward the self, this time as a result of the story writing manipulation, would heighten feelings of being the object of attention of others.

Method

Subjects

Twenty-one undergraduate subjects (13 women and 8 men) participated in the study for optional course credit and were randomly assigned to experimental conditions. One female subject was dropped from the analysis because of procedural difficulties, leaving 10 subjects in each of two experimental conditions; gender was close to being equally distributed across both conditions. Pretest measures of self-consciousness and paranoia were available for all subjects.

Procedure

Subjects were seated in a room containing a two-way mirror, which was illuminated in such a way that subjects looking at it could only see themselves. In this study, subjects were seated facing away from the mirror. It was assumed that this positioning would reduce the self-focusing effects of the mirror, but leave unaffected the possibility of being observed. No mention was made of the mirror, but postexperimental interviews revealed that indeed virtually every subject was aware that someone could be watching them from behind the mirror. In fact, there was no hidden observer during the experiment.

The experimental self-attention manipulation, using the story-construction task (Fenigstein & Levine, 1984), was introduced as a task examining the use of language. Subjects were given a list of 20 words and asked to construct a story incorporating as many of the words as possible. For subjects in the high–self-attention condition, 5 of the words in the list were intended to direct the subject to construct self-referent stories: *I*, *me*, *my*, *mine*, and *myself*. For the other subjects, the corresponding third-person pronouns (appropriate to the subject's own gender) were used to direct the construction of an other-referent story. These key words were embedded among 15 other words (e.g., *afternoon*, *walk*, *park*), which were identical for all subjects. Subjects were given about 10 minutes to think about and write their stories, during which time the experimenter was out of the room. On returning, the experimenter asked the subjects to fill out a six-item questionnaire, which asked subjects about their stories as well as their thoughts and feelings during the writing task. Included among the questions was the major dependent variable: "While you were writing the story, did you feel as though you were being watched?"; and a manipulation check: "How much of the story that you wrote was about you?" All items were answered on a 10-point scale.

In the postexperimental session, no subject indicated any suspicion of the role of self-attention in the research or any awareness of the connection between the story-construction task and the dependent measure. As before, questions were raised about the two-way mirror, and again, consistent with predictions and with the findings presented in the Results section, this concern was more prevalent among high–self-attention subjects.

Results

Self-Attention

Preliminary analyses again indicated that gender had no significant effects in this research, and this variable was ignored in subsequent analyses. As expected, subjects in the self-referent word-story group ($M = 6.00$) rated the stories they wrote as being more about themselves than did subjects in the other-referent group ($M = 2.10$), $F(1, 19) = 13.82$, $p < .01$, indicating that the story writing manipulation was successful in directing attention toward the self.

A one-way ANOVA revealed a significant main effect for self-attention on feelings of being watched, $F(1, 19) = 10.2$, $p < .01$; subjects who were writing stories about themselves ($M = 6.40$) were much more likely to feel as though they were under observation than were subjects whose stories were less self-focused ($M = 2.80$).

The poststory questionnaire included other questions concerned with feelings of being challenged and being evaluated. The word–story manipulation had no effect on these measures, suggesting that the writing task was not perceived in motivational or evaluative terms. Rather, the effects of self-attention in this experiment appeared to be specific to feelings of being watched.

Paranoia

The primary interest in this study was on the experimental manipulation of self-attention, and so subjects were not preselected on the basis of their pretest scores. However, in the interests of replicating some of the findings of the previous study, it was possible to examine the correlation between pretested paranoia and the dependent variable. (A preliminary ANOVA found no interaction between paranoia scores and self-attention conditions on the dependent measure, thus justifying the correlational analysis.) Controlling for the contribution of public self-consciousness, a significant partial correlation was found between paranoia and a sense of being observed, $r(17) = .41$, $p < .04$, replicating part of Study 2 and again offering evidence for the construct validity of the paranoia measure.

General Discussion

The present research investigated the notion that self-attention, the awareness of oneself as an object of attention, may be related to paranoia. To see oneself as an object of attention, especially to others, may leave one susceptible to the idea that others are more interested in the self than in fact is the case; such self-referent perceptions of the behavior of others is one of the hallmarks of paranoid thought. On the basis of these arguments, it was expected that self-focused persons would tend to think in paranoid ways.

Study 1, after developing a measure of paranoia for use with a normal population, showed that persons high in public self-consciousness, compared with persons low on that dimension, were more likely to endorse certain beliefs and attitudes characteristic of paranoia, as defined by several clinical criteria. Study 2 offered evidence, replicated in Study 3, for the construct validity of the Paranoia Scale by showing that scale responses subsequently predicted the characteristically paranoid sense of being seen or observed.

Study 2 also found that in a potentially public situation, high–public self-conscious subjects were more likely than subjects low in public self-consciousness to assume that they were being watched. In some ways, this second study may be viewed as a conceptual replication of the earlier self-as-target research (Fenigstein, 1984), although in the present research, self-conscious subjects perceived themselves as the target of another's observation, rather than another's actions. To the extent that both ideas of reference and feelings of being watched are prominent features of paranoia, the two studies together offer convergent evidence for the notion that paranoid thoughts are related to dispositional public self-consciousness.

Study 3, by using an experimental manipulation, rather than a dispositional measure of self-attention, and again finding that self-focus is related to paranoid thoughts of being watched, suggests that this relationship is a robust one. Moreover, that both a stable self-consciousness attribute and a self-reflective experimental induction produced similar results offers converging evidence for an attentional explanation. The nature of the causal relationship between self-attention and paranoid thought is also clarified by Study 3. Causality could not be determined in Study 2, because self-consciousness was a non-manipulated individual difference. However, the results of the third study, in which self-attention was experimentally induced, clearly demonstrate that the sense of being watched by others was a function of self-attention. Given the similar paradigms for the two studies, it seems reasonable to infer that an analogeous causal sequence was operating in the second study.

Allan Fenigstein and Peter A. Vanable

The research presented has emphasized the relationship between self-consciousness and a tendency, known as *personalism* (Heider, 1958; Jones & Davis, 1965), to take things personally or to perceive events as if they were intentionally directed toward the self. Personalism, because it is associated with more extreme internal attributions for others' behavior, has some interesting implications for several different aspects of paranoia (see Kihlstrom & Hoyt, 1988). To the extent that one interprets others' behavior in terms of their dispositions or their personal intent, such attributions seem likely to result in suspicion and mistrust of others' motives, acute sensitivity to rebuff, and intensified hostility in reaction to perceived threats (e.g., Darley & Huff, 1990), characteristics that have all been associated with paranoia (American Psychiatric Association, 1987; Millon, 1981; Shapiro, 1965). Previous research has found in fact that persons high in public self-consciousness are especially sensitive to rejection (Fenigstein, 1979), and future research is planned to further explore the relationships among self-attention, personalism, and other elements of paranoid thought.

It has been argued that the relationship between self-attention and paranoid thought is mediated by the accessibility of self-relevant knowledge domains. In effect, self-consciousness, by activating self-knowledge, acts as a priming mechanism so that the self is likely to become involved, for example, as a target in the interpretation of others' behavior (cf. Johnson, 1988; Rogers, 1981). This argument offers a broadened view of the role of the self and self-attention in social perception. Specifically, it may be suggested that activation of the self-schema not only influences the dimensions along which others are judged and remembered (e.g., Higgins, King, & Mavin, 1982; Lewicki, 1984; Markus, Smith, & Moreland, 1985) and facilitates the encoding of information according to its self-relevance (e.g., Hull & Levy, 1979; Hull et al., 1988), but also actively biases the perception of others to make it appear as if their behavior, real or imagined, is somehow related to the self (e.g., that others are watching, thinking about, or perhaps even trying to influence the self).

Acknowledgements

Portions of this research were conducted as part of Peter A. Vanable's senior honor's thesis. Preparation of this article was supported by National Science Foundation Grant RII-8308033. We would like to thank Michael Levine, as well as several anonymous reviewers, for their thoughtful contributions to the research. Part of this article was written while Allan Fenigstein was on sabbatical at the University of Kent at Canterbury, England.

380

Notes

1. The parallel between depression and paranoia may be extended to the issue of continuity. Whether there is a continuum between mild depression and severe depression is still a matter of controversy, even after a great deal of research (see e.g., Hammen, 1987). Clearly, speculation about the continuity of paranoid phenomena, at this point, would be highly premature, although some theorists seem willing to make the case (e.g., Chapman & Chapman, 1988; Strauss, 1969). The present research, however, offers no basis for any attempt to generalize the present findings beyond the domain of normal, nonpathological phenomena.

References

Agatstein, F. C., & Buchanan, D. B. (1984). Public and private self-consciousness and the recall of self-relevant information. *Personality and Social Psychology Bulletin, 10,* 314–325.

American Psychiatric Association (1987). *Diagnostic and statistical manual of mental disorders* (3rd ed. rev). Washington, DC: Author.

Argyle, M. (1969). *Social interaction.* New York: Atheneum.

Bargh, J. A., & Pietramonaco, P. (1982). Automatic information processing and social perception: The influence of trait information presented outside of conscious awareness on impression formation. *Journal of Personality and Social Psychology, 43,* 437–449.

Briggs, S. R., & Cheek, J. M. (1988). On the nature of self-monitoring: Problems with assessment, problems with validity. *Journal of Personality and Social Psychology, 54,* 663–678.

Burger, J. M., & Cooper, H. M. (1979). The desirability of control. *Motivation and Emotion, 3,* 381–393.

Cameron, N. (1943). The development of paranoic thinking. *Psychological Review, 50,* 219–233.

Carver, C. S., & Scheier, M. F. (1978). Self-focusing effects of dispositional self-consciousness, mirror presence, and audience presence. *Journal of Personality and Social Psychology, 36,* 324–332.

Carver, C. S., & Scheier, M. F. (1981). *Attention and self-regulation: A control theory approach to human behavior.* New York: Springer-Verlag.

Cattell, R. B. (1978). *The scientific use of factor analysis in behavioral and life sciences.* New York: Plenum Press.

Chapman, L. J., & Chapman, J. P. (1988). The genesis of delusions. In T. F. Oltmanns & B. A. Maher (Eds.), *Delusional beliefs* (pp. 167–183). New York: Wiley.

Colby, K. M. (1977). Appraisal of four psychological theories of paranoid phenomenon. *Journal of Abnormal Psychology, 86,* 34–59.

Crowne, D. P., & Marlowe, D. (1964). *The approval motive.* New York: Wiley.

Dahlstrom, W. G., Welsh, G. S., & Dahlstrom, L. F. (1975). *An MMPI handbook: Vol. 2. Research applications*. Minneapolis, MN: University of Minnesota.

Darley, J., & Huff, C. W. (1990). Heightened damage assessment as a result of the intentionality of the damage-causing act. *British Journal of Social Psychology, 29,* 181–188.

Duval, S., & Wicklund, R. A. (1973). Effects of objective self-awareness on attributions of causality. *Journal of Experimental Social Psychology, 9,* 17–31.

Elkind, D. (1967). Egocentrism in adolescence. *Child Development, 38,* 1025–1034.

Fenigstein, A. (1979). Self-consciousness, self-attention, and social interaction. *Journal of Personality and Social Psychology, 37,* 75–86.

Fenigstein, A. (1984). Self-consciousness and the overperception of self as a target. *Journal of Personality and Social Psychology, 47,* 860–870.

Fenigstein, A. (1987). On the nature of public and private self-consciousness. *Journal of Personality, 55,* 543–554.

Fenigstein, A., & Levine, M. P. (1984). Self-attention, concept activation, and the causal self. *Journal of Experimental Social Psychology, 20,* 231–245.

Fenigstein, A., Scheier, M. F., & Buss, A. H. (1975). Public and private self-consciousness: Assessment and theory. *Journal of Clinical and Consulting Psychology, 43,* 522–527.

Gorsuch, R. L. (1983). *Factor analysis* (2nd edn.). Hillsdale, NJ: Erlbaum.

Greenwald, A. G. (1980). The totalitarian ego: Fabrication and revision of personal history. *American Psychologist, 35,* 603–618.

Hammen, C. (1987). The causes and consequences of attribution research on depression. *Journal of Social and Clinical Psychology, 5,* 485–500.

Heider, F. (1958). *The psychology of interpersonal relations*. Hillsdale, NJ: Erlbaum.

Higgins, E. T., King, G. A., & Mavin, G. H. (1982). Individual construct accessibility and subjective impressions and recall. *Journal of Personality and Social Psychology, 73,* 35–47.

Higgins, E. T., Rholes, W. J., & Jones, C. R. (1977). Category accessibility and impression formation. *Journal of Experimental Social Psychology, 13,* 141–154.

Hogan, R., & Nicholson, R. A. (1988). The meaning of personality test scores. *American Psychologist, 43,* 621–626.

Hull, J. G., & Levy, A. S. (1979). The organizational functions of self: An alternative to the Duval and Wicklund model of self-awareness. *Journal of Personality and Social Psychology, 37,* 756–768.

Hull, J. G., Van Treuren, R. R., Ashford, S. J., Propsom, P., & Andrus, B. W. (1988). Self-consciousness and the processing of self-relevant information. *Journal of Personality and Social Psychology, 54,* 452–465.

Johnson, M. K. (1988). Discriminating the origin of information. In T. F. Oltmanns & B. A. Maher (Eds.), *Delusional beliefs* (pp. 34–65). New York: Wiley.

Jones, E. E., & Davis, K. E. (1965). From acts to dispositions: The attribution process in person perception. In L. Berkowitz (Ed.), *Advances in experimental social psychology* (Vol. 2, pp. 219–266). San Diego, CA: Academic Press.

Kihlstrom, J., & Hoyt, I. P. (1988). Hypnosis and the psychology of delusions. In T. F. Oltmanns & B. A. Maher (Eds.), *Delusional beliefs* (pp. 66–109). New York: Wiley.

Kraepelin, E. (1915). *Psychiatrie: Ein Lehrbuch* [Psychiatry: A textbook] (7th edn.). Leipzig, Germany: Barth.

Laing, R. D. (1969). *The divided self.* New York: Pantheon Books.

Levenson, H. (1973). Multidimensional locus of control in psychiatric patients. *Journal of Consulting and Clinical Psychology, 41,* 397–404.

Lewicki, P. (1984). Self-schema and social information processing. *Journal of Personality and Social Psychology, 47,* 1177–1190.

Magaro, P. A. (1980). *Cognition in schizophrenia and paranoia: The interpretation of cognitive processes.* Hillsdale, NJ: Erlbaum.

Maher, B. A. (1988). Anomalous experience and delusional thinking: The logic of explanations. In T. F. Oltmanns & B. A. Maher (Eds.), *Delusional beliefs* (pp. 15–33). New York: Wiley.

Markus, H., Smith, J., & Moreland, R. L. (1985). Role of the self-concept in the perception of others. *Journal of Personality and Social Psychology, 49,* 1494–1512.

Meissner, W. W. (1978). *The paranoid process.* Northvale, NJ: Jason Aronson.

Millon, T. H. (1981). *Disorders of personality.* New York: Wiley.

Nisbett, R. E., & Ross, L. (1980). *Human inference: Strategies and shortcomings of social judgement.* Englewood Cliffs, NJ: Prentice-Hall.

Nunnally, J. C. (1978). *Psychometric theory* (2nd edn.). New York: McGraw-Hill.

Oltmanns, T. F. (1988). Approaches to the definitions and study of delusions. In T. F. Oltmanns & B. A. Maher (Eds.), *Delusional beliefs* (pp. 3–12). New York: Wiley.

Pyszczynski, T., Hamilton, J. C., Herring, F. H., & Greenberg, J. (1989). Depression, self-focused attention, and the negative memory bias. *Journal of Personality and Social Psychology, 57,* 351–357.

Pyszczynski, T., Holt, K., & Greenberg, J. (1987). Depression, self-focused attention, and expectancies for positive and negative future life events for self and others. *Journal of Personality and Social Psychology, 52,* 994–1001.

Rempel, J. K., Holmes, J. G., & Zanna, M. P. (1985). Trust in close relationships. *Journal of Personality and Social Psychology, 49,* 95–112.

Rogers, T. B. (1981). A model of the self as an aspect of the human information processing system. In N. Cantor & J. F. Kihlstrom (Eds.), *Personality, cognition, and social interaction* (pp. 193–214). Hillsdale, NJ: Erlbaum.

Ross, M., & Sicoly, F. (1979). Egocentric biases in availability and attribution. *Journal of Personality and Social Psychology, 37,* 322–336.

Rotter, J. B. (1980). Interpersonal trust, trustworthiness, and gullibility. *American Psychologist, 35,* 1–7.

Sandelands, L. E., & Calder, B. J. (1984). Referencing and bias in social interaction. *Journal of Personality and Social Psychology, 46,* 755–762.

Scheier, M. F., Fenigstein, A., & Buss, A. H. (1974). Self-awareness and physical aggression. *Journal of Experimental Social Psychology, 10,* 264–273.

Shapiro, D. (1965). *Neurotic styles.* New York: Basic Books.

Siegel, J. M. (1985). The measurement of anger as a multidimensional construct. In M. A. Chesney & R. H. Rosenman (Eds.), *Anger and hostility in cardiovascular and behavioral disorders* (pp. 59–82). Washington, DC: Hemisphere.

Spielberger, C. D., Johnson, E. H., Russell, S. F., Crane, R. J., Jacobs, G. A., & Worden, T. J. (1985). The experience and expression of anger: Construction and validation of an anger expression scale. In M. A. Chesney & R. H. Rosenman (Eds.), *Anger and hostility in cardiovascular and behavioral disorders* (pp. 5–30). Washington, DC: Hemisphere.

Strauss, J. S. (1969). Hallucinations and delusions as points on continua function. *Archives of General Psychiatry, 21,* 581–586.

Swanson, D. W., Bohnert, P. J., & Smith, J. A. (1970). *The paranoid.* Boston: Little, Brown.

Turner, R. G. (1978). Self-consciousness and speed of processing self-relevant information. *Personality and Social Psychology Bulletin, 4,* 456–460.

Turner, R. G. (1980). Self-consciousness and memory of trait terms. *Personality and Social Psychology Bulletin, 6,* 263–280.

Tversky, A., & Kahneman, D. (1974). Judgement under uncertainty: Heuristics and biases. *Science, 185,* 1124–1131.

Ullman, L. P., & Krasner, L. (1969). *A psychological approach to abnormal behavior.* Englewood Cliffs, NJ: Prentice-Hall.

Wyer, R., & Srull, T. (1981). Category accessibility: Some theoretical and empirical issues concerning the processing of information. In E. T. Higgins, C. P. Herman, & M. P. Zanna (Eds.), *Social cognition,* (Vol. 1, pp. 161–198). Hillsdale, NJ: Erlbaum.

Zimbardo, P. G., Andersen, S. M., & Kabat, L. G. (1981). Induced hearing deficit generates experimental paranoia. *Science, 212,* 1529–1531.

V. ORGANIZATIONAL TRUST IN CONTEMPORARY CONTEXTS

13

Secrecy, Trust, and Dangerous Leisure: Generating Group Cohesion in Voluntary Organizations

Gary Alan Fine and Lori Holyfield

As communitarians assert, participation in a voluntary organization encourages—perhaps demands—a sense of belonging (Bellah et al. 1992; Wolfe 1989, 1991). Within small-group research this "belongingness" or "we-ness" is labeled *group cohesion*. Although cohesion has numerous definitions, the standard views suggest that cohesion constitutes those forces which cause members to remain within a group (Festinger, Schachter, and Back 1950:164: Piper et al. 1983) and/or to resist centrifugal forces (Brawley, Carron and Widmeyer 1988; Gross and Martin 1952:553).[1] Cohesion is a variable intervening between characteristics of group life and outcome variables, notably the success of the group (e.g., survival of the group or stability of membership).[2] Cohesion is a property of social systems rather than individuals (Frank 1957), even though it is individuals who experience feelings of commitment on which this solidarity is based (Evans and Jarvis 1980; Kanter 1972: 72–73).

Although cohesion is often studied in the laboratory, it is important for understanding the processes by which natural groups or organizations provide satisfaction for members, thus increasing their stability (Hechter 1987). In our view, cohesion is linked to a set of cultural processes that regulate group life. Cohesion serves as a collective orientation that depends on social relations and produces a group "culture" (Eder 1988; Fine 1979; Owen 1985; Sherif et al. 1961) which organizes interaction and encourages continued participation (Shaw 1981:216–17).

Gary Alan Fine and Lori Holyfield

To explore the production of cohesion, we focus on voluntary organizations. Groups with the authority to enforce explicit social control over participants (e.g., the classroom or the shop floor) have less need to be concerned about affiliation than do voluntary groups. Specifically we examine leisure groups that involve some measure of risk, a feature which is linked experimentally to the presence of cohesion (Harrison and Connors 1984:68; Stokes 1983) and in which a status system among participants develops, implying competition.

Leisure groups, because force and moral compunction are absent, are ideal organizations for examining how affiliation arises in the face of individual interest. If individual interest is privileged, one might say, the need for solidarity is diminished except when it serves instrumental goals. Yet if this were true, voluntary groups would be far less stable than they are. Groups in which members engage in *dangerous* leisure, because of their subcultural character (i.e., sharing tasks beyond the skills of most outsiders) and because of the need for mutual aid in achieving desired ends and avoiding tragic outcomes, are particularly likely to encourage communal affiliation. Status within the group and satisfaction from the activity flow from individual achievement.

All leisure worlds depend for their survival on providing egoistic satisfaction (Irwin 1977; Stebbins 1992); they are grounded in self-interest. The need for cohesion is particularly salient in a society such as ours, which reveres self-interest and competition (Shils 1956:21; Turner 1987:96–104). Thus, the paradox: How is voluntary organization possible, given the tension between solidarity and individualism? As Erving Goffman remarked famously in his essay "Fun in Games,"

Games can be fun to play, and fun alone is the approved reason for playing them. The individual, in contrast to his treatment of "serious" activity, claims a right to complain about a game that does not pay its way in immediate pleasure and, whether the game is pleasurable or not, to plead a slight excuse, such as an indisposition of mood, for not participating. (1961:17)

Yet in this passage Goffman ignores the relational context in which many games occur. In leisure scenes an egoistic perspective is linked inextricably to a need for communal belonging. Relationships and social identity may be as important as the activity itself (Turner 1987:103): we often play without complaint even when we "don't feel like it." If a leisure group is to remain stable, it must develop benefits that begin with and then transcend the activity for which individuals join. Once participants become knowledgeable, many leisure activities can be performed outside the organizational order.[3] As a result, the activities by themselves do not necessarily bind actors to the group; other forces must provide that social glue.

One reason why people participate in leisure organizations is simple: they receive benefits that outweigh the costs of participation, and this ratio is more favorable than that for nonparticipation. To some degree, this simple model is true. People do not participate in organizations unless they "get something out of it." If this were the entire basis of participation, however, one might expect that leisure organizations would be very fragile, and that individuals would be neutral rather than emotionally committed to the group. Many leisure participants, particularly the active participants, have a long-term allegiance that transcends immediate benefits. The "groupness" of the scene is powerful (Stebbins 1979) and stabilizes individuals' attachment, thus building cohesion.

The successful leisure organization provides resources necessary to facilitate activities (planned outings, equipment, information) (Fine 1989; Hoggett and Bishop 1986), but these resources provide only a tenuous means of linking persons to the organization. By themselves, such resources do not create cohesion, short of the benefits the individual receives immediately in exchange for the expenses of belonging. To increase the tensile strength of organizational existence, cohesion is essential. The emotional investment and social identity inherent in voluntary organizations have a power that transcends the ostensibly voluntary character and raises the exit costs.

Aside from the content of their activities, many enthusiasts treasure the company of others. They choose to belong to an *organized group*, even though they could engage in these activities by themselves or by developing private dyadic or group relationships. Yet "sociable organizations" (Aldrich 1971) are valued; a group of persons with common interests magnifies the pleasures derived from doing the activity. These individuals select a social setting that motivates them to rely on, care about, and share with others. This situation leads to identity work (Snow and Anderson 1987) in which participants—through a sense of belonging—come to see themselves as characterized by the activity, rather than seeing the activity merely as something they do.

Generating cohesion in a social system that relies on individual interest demands a recognition of the interplay between integrating and centrifugal forces. To develop this recognition, we focus on two fundamental, seemingly oppositional forces, *trust* and *secrecy*, which often combine to create social integration, to stabilize leisure organization, and to provide a basis of communal allegiance.[4] Trust and secrecy operate by regulating information and building meaningful, extended relationships. An organization provides the environment in which relationships can flourish, and experiences and knowledge can be shared. This is particularly important in risky situations involving external dangers.[5]

To suggest that the combination of trust and secrecy provides the basis for the existence of voluntary organizations devoted to competitive, risky activities is to recognize a profound irony: that the tension between attachment (trust) and competition (secrecy) builds social order. Both attachment and competition require an arena to flourish: the leisure group provides this space.

What begins with the sharing or withholding of knowledge eventually becomes a basis for establishing tight-knit social connections, linked both to status claims and to emotional ties. The establishment of these connections, with their boundaries of legitimate information domains, creates organizational stability. Voluntary allegiance depends on the existence of both a public and a private sphere. In an effective organization, members have expectations about how much of their selves and knowledge to invest in the collective good, and how much to shelter. This play of persons and information constitutes the basis of collective attachment and personal satisfaction.

We begin this project with an ethnographic description of mushroom collection, a voluntary but risky social world. We describe how trust and secrecy are socially constructed in a mycological society, and argue that both depend on relationship status, allegiance, and social control; yet both contribute to the creation of group cohesion. We conclude by discussing the extent to which the core concepts of trust and secrecy can be generalized to other spheres of social life.

The World of Mushroomers

The first author conducted participant observation and in-depth interviews with mushroom collectors, a voluntary leisure community that relies on the existence of trust and secrecy. He focused on those groups which facilitate this environmental leisure activity. Members of mycological societies routinely place their welfare in the hands of others by accepting their judgments of edibility. Further, personal benefits accrue from accepting communal authority in that one's knowledge and the range of mushrooms one consumes are increased. The combined existence of costs and benefits underlines the critical role of trust. Yet secrecy, too, is crucial because of the members' competitiveness in finding mushrooms. This fact reveals their desire to achieve personal benefits to which all members are not entitled by membership alone.

The Minnesota Mycological Society,[6] founded in 1898, is the second oldest continuously active amateur mushroom society in the United States. In most major metropolitan areas, particularly in the northeast, the midwest, and the west, groups of amateurs have banded together for support and community. The club consists primarily of amateurs; although professional mycologists are welcome to join, none were active members of the Minnesota club during the period of observation.

As in many voluntary organizations, segmented interest groups exist under the rubric of the larger organization. Some of the approximately 200 members are interested primarily in examining mushrooms from a quasi-scientific perspective; these individuals sometimes are labeled *amateur mycologists*. Some enjoy compiling lists or collections of the mushrooms they find; others, known as *pot hunters*, collect mushrooms to eat (i.e., for the pot). For still others, photography is their first love. Although the members of the organization are friendly and mutually supportive, tension occasionally flares over the division of club resources among interest groups.

The Minnesota Mycological Society meets one evening a week for approximately two hours during the prime mushroom-picking months in Minnesota: May, June, September, and October. At these meetings the president describes the mushrooms that members bring and that the Identification Committee has identified. Members also describe their memorable mushroom finds and, in keeping with norms of secrecy, describe where and how their patches were discovered. At some meetings, members give talks (e.g., on cultivating mushrooms, mushrooms in other countries, or foreign travel) or show slides. In addition to these weekly meetings, the club organizes approximately a half-dozen forays to state and county parks and to private properties. Two of the forays last for a weekend. The club also holds a banquet in January, and has established a mycology study group that meets once a month to examine mushrooms with microscopes and chemicals. The first author attended most of the meetings, forays, and banquets during a three-year period, and wrote detailed field notes. These notes were supplemented by a questionnaire sent to all members (with a 66 percent response rate, $n = 129$) and by in-depth interviews with two dozen members of the group, lasting approximately 90 minutes each.

The first author also attended a national foray organized by the North American Mycological Association (NAMA) and two regional forays, one in the midwest and one in the northeast. Data on these forays are supplemented by copies of newsletters published by some two dozen mycological societies. The analysis does not examine all mushroom hunters, but only those who have chosen to join voluntary organizations for this purpose.

Organizing Trust

Group cohesion depends on making the existence of the group or organization *matter* to individuals, thus bolstering its voluntary character. One fundamental way of doing this is by establishing a cocoon to protect members from the risks of the activity. Trust refers to an actor's belief that a person or collectivity will perform actions (including providing information) that will prove helpful or not detrimental to him or her, thus permitting the establishment of a relationship of cooperation (e.g., Gambetta 1988:217). Yet this perspective, which emphasizes the cognitive, evaluative component of trust, is necessary but not sufficient. Interpretation is possible only in a world of cultural meanings, emotional responses, and social relations—a moral world that depends on what people ought to do, as well as what it is in their interest to do. One not only thinks trust, but feels trust. Although trust depends at first on information judged to be protective, in time it involves valuing the *relationship* in which trust is embedded as well as the information that is acquired (Good 1988; Lewis and Weigert 1985). First, the information is accepted as derived from organizationally validated sources. Subsequently the sources themselves are trusted (McNulty 1994); they are transformed from spokespersons for the group to personal acquaintances. Reputation is an important feature in relationships of trust: those with good reputations are likely to receive information (if they are novices) and to be asked for information (if they are veterans) (Kollock 1994).

The means by which trust commits individuals to an organization is most obvious in the secret society, where the existence of one's membership must be held in confidence. The hidden relations among members constitute the power of the group; breaching these relations threatens the group's existence (Bellman 1981). Yet although secret societies may be a dramatic example of the importance of investing confidence in others, such a connection is significant in any organization that provides protective information on which members rely. Simmel (1950:318) observed that confidence is one of the most important synthetic forces in group life.[7] It is an intermediate position between knowledge and ignorance, neither of which requires the presence of others. Confidence is social; it reflects *trust* in another or in a group of others. It emerges from the "objectification" of culture (i.e., the segmentation of the self into specialized roles) and from the growth of specialized knowledge, which requires us to rely on others for information necessary for achieving our ends (Giddens 1990:88–89).

We judge and evaluate information provided in socially meaningful contexts. Giddens (1991) writes of a "moving world of normalcy," maintaining that trust is "the outcome of the routinized nature of an uneventful world" and that it creates a protective "cocoon" which makes possible the enactment of the social world and the emergence of meaning. The metaphor of a protective cocoon is important, especially for social scenes, such as those discussed here, which are not routine. Trust is interactional, interpreted, and negotiated, not fully determined or calculating. Because of its grounding in interaction, trust depends on facework. Yet, insofar as it is institutionalized within an organization, it is also faceless: simultaneously fragile and robust, fluid and consequential (Giddens 1990:88–91).

The trust that participants place in others allows them to see the dangerous world at least as manageable, if not as routine (Donnelly 1994; Vester 1987). Members depend on organizations—and on those who make up the organizations—to provide relevant and protective information and to keep that information sheltered from those outside who are deemed to have no right or competence to know. Organizations structure the access points for trust (Giddens 1990:85). As trust in information becomes trust of persons, ties to the organization are strengthened[8] and lead to the potential for cooperation. Instrumental affiliation becomes emotional attachment.

The establishment of trust locates attachment in rapport and identification, not merely in common interest or spatial copresence. Trust, which originates in confidence in information provided by groups and individuals, and builds on personal commitment to the group (Kanter 1972:65–67), is translated into a "pure" relationship. This relationship, when generalized to the collectivity, produces organizational loyalty (Eisenstadt and Roniger 1984:6; Gellner 1988). Trust is a fundamental anchoring dimension of cohesion.

To address the dynamics of trust in organizational life, we examine the awarding, managing, and transforming of trust. Strong pressures are exerted on the new member of an organization to demonstrate regard for others by following their advice—demonstrating that they are trustworthy. As a result, the establishment of trustworthiness becomes critical. One must be socialized to risk and to competence, and the organization must establish procedures—formal or implicit—by which trustworthiness is created. Finally, trust changes over time, from an emphasis on meaning to a more subtle connection with the identity of others and one's relations with them.

Awarding Trust

Trust is particularly likely to be evident when external threats are present. Mycological organizations generate trust by supplying protective information to novices, who find themselves in an uncertain environment. Mushroom collectors must learn how to avoid the possibility of illness, or even death, from consuming "bad" mushrooms. Consequently, the practical question of trust emerges early and dramatically. The first question that novices wish to have answered by "experts" is "Can I eat it?" a blunter version of "What is this?" Not all mushroomers make consumption their central reason for joining a club, but few lack interest in the question.[9] Eating mushrooms is recognized as potentially dangerous, particularly in view of the publicity accorded the occasional death. Organizations provide both the resources to experience risk and the expertise to cope (Hewitt 1984).

Throughout organizational life, considerable social pressure exists to award trust to members of the group, thus validating the organization. This trust seems to be awarded easily. Novices first taste many species of mushrooms at social events where the mushrooms have been picked and identified by others. This situation poses a delicate problem of impression management for the novice, who cannot personally ascertain whether the species identification is accurate. Should the (often unknown) identifier be trusted? Typically the social pressures are strong enough to ensure consumption, however cautiously and anxiously. Persons who refuse to eat mushrooms prepared by others at a foray or banquet must justify this behavior lest it be assumed that they do not trust their comrades; such a significant affront could disrupt social relations. They must attest through their behavior that they accept identifications by others and acknowledge the legitimacy of a community of competence, even though they personally may be unsure about the proper identification.

At a club foray, a cook prepared a mushroom pate made with some *Amanita fulva* and some *Russulas* (not identified to species), identified by a knowledgeable club member. Both are edibles, but the *Amanita* is very rarely eaten because of its deadly genus-mates. Many who ate the pate were individuals who told me privately that they had no interest in eating any *Amanitas*, even if edible. The pate becomes a major topic of conversation. (field notes)

One fairly new club member who consumed the pate, without realizing at the time that it contained *Amanitas*, told me later that if she had known, "I don't think it would have stopped me from eating it, because I really have a lot of confidence in the group. And I just have the feeling that nobody is deliberately mixing something up that hadn't been proved edible." (personal interview)

The absence of an established personal relationship is striking. It emphasizes the extent to which novices will place their trust in the organization; this trust was established previously, but is made relevant by the situation. Such trust represents not only trust in individual expertise, but also, and more prominently, trust in a *system* of expertise.[10] New members are willing to consume potentially deadly mushrooms collected, identified, and cooked by strangers. As the second author, a novice rock climber, said after an energetic climb, "I suddenly realized that I was putting my life in the hands of someone whose last name I didn't even know."

The social psychological centrality of this trust is evident in anxious jokes made by veteran mushroomers about using new members as guinea pigs:

The oath taken on induction [into the International Mushroom Pickers Society] indicates their enthusiasm in the mycological pursuits: "I solemnly promise to cherish the brotherhood and good fellowship of my brother IMPS, even to the extent of willingness to serve as a mushroom taster of wild mushrooms for a probationary period of one year *without liability to our organization if rigor mortis sets in due to ingestion of nonedible fungi.*" (Rosen 1982: 18–19)

Jerry, the club president, jokes at a meeting about the birch polypore, which some field guides say is edible, but is tough and, according to some, is bitter: "I'd like to encourage someone else to try it and tell me." He adds: "By the way, new members, if you join, you're guinea pigs for the first year. [Laughter.] Not so at all. Just joking." (field notes)

The insistence on trust is found throughout leisure organizations, and thus legitimates the organization. To alleviate the concern about the universality of trust, organizations typically establish roles that are validated as deserving trust while maintaining the impression that the organization as a whole is trustworthy.

Managing Risk

To ensure that members can be trusted, socialization becomes essential. It is desired both by the participants, who voluntarily selected this domain, and by organizational leaders. Only through expertise can one achieve the rewards that attend belonging. Yet, once one belongs to the organization, how is competence to be socialized? Risks exist in sharing one's activities and organizational identity with the untutored. A tension exists between teaching and shunning a novice. As a result, competence and trustworthiness may be hard to acquire: experienced participants may find it more rewarding to share their leisure with other experts rather than to serve as teachers of novices, and thus perhaps to limit what they can accomplish.

A set of social and normative pressures encourages voluntary instruction. In practice, expert members teach novices because of the belief that one should repay one's own socialization with the socialization of others (a form of generational justice, crucial to parenting as well), the satisfaction of generating shared interest, the status rewards of contacts with less knowledgeable persons, and the claim that one's own community will be extended by creating other experts. The challenge for the novice is that to become expert, one must spend time with experts. Thus affiliation must develop, sometimes through collective events (forays) sponsored by the organization.

When mushrooms are to be consumed, particularly those with toxic counterparts, providers may be limited to those whose trustworthiness has been validated by the organization. At the national foray, for instance, only a small number of experienced mushroomers were selected to pick edible amanitas (*Amanita rubescens*) for the tasting session. These specimens, part of a family with deadly species, were reviewed carefully by a small, even more knowledgeable, identification committee.

For mushroomers, the protection against danger[11] is social: new members are advised to join a club, take a course, foray with an experienced participant, or ask another person to identify their mushrooms before cooking (e.g.,

Coombs 1986:23). Novices are encouraged to work initially with more experienced members who can teach "safety." To aid in the development of competence, training may occur at group meetings, or forays may be organized to train (and judge) new members. Novices are often encouraged to attend club meetings and lectures to gain practical information, and simultaneously to cement their attachment to the group. Trust in information provided by the organization and in the members of that community provides a bulwark against danger (Williams 1988).

Transforming Trust

An individual's experience of trust within a group is altered over time: the organization is transformed from an object of trust to an arena of trusting interactions. When joining an organization, most new members simultaneously express interest and ignorance. As a result, the first goal of membership is information, which is provided by group members. For a novice, organizational legitimation is crucial to trust. The group has awarded status to some members (by role or by reputation); the new member trusts these individuals, though perhaps not totally and not without some anxiety. Without trust, the urge to exit is strong. Over time, trust becomes based in shared experience, and evaluation depends on topics on which the judge has some measure of expertise. As the new member becomes more proficient, he or she develops standards of judgment by which to evaluate competence and award trust.

In practice, the novice at first assumes that "mere" membership in an organization bestows a "cloak of competence," just as we give those with professional credentials the benefit of the doubt. Because novices rarely begin with highly dangerous or difficult activities (Bryan 1977), the advice given, if in error, will likely be relatively inconsequential. For experienced members, who engage in riskier activities, trust must be earned. As in work situations (Haas 1974; Hughes 1971), participants must decide whether they can trust new colleagues; experienced members implicitly evaluate the new members' developing competence before accepting their advice and before developing long-term trusting relations:

One veteran collector tells me: "If someone I don't know really well comes up and offers me some mushrooms that he just picked, I know enough to know that I want to know what he picked. I know enough that I am not just going to eat anything that somebody hands me." (personal interview)

Testing occurs when experienced members judge the extent to which they should trust novices. One veteran recalled, "When we first joined our club we were watched by the long-time members for interest and consistency" (personal letter). In the words of another, "The society was filled with friendly people who shook my hand and welcomed me. Then they waited" (Norvell 1983-84:7).

The trust derives from the relationship where "knowing well" and "judging highly" combine to establish a zone of trust. Trust gained, however, can become trust lost. Should one identify a poisonous mushroom as an edible species, others would remain suspicious until competence had been demonstrated specifically. In most situations, credibility is lost only once (Hunt 1995; Stuller 1989:92) unless the mistake is defined as reasonable. In fact, those who have a reputation for consuming risky mushrooms, even if they know exactly what they are eating, are mistrusted and/or teased by more conservative members, who profess to avoid anything that those persons might prepare.

As one acquires knowledge, trust changes: the basis of trust is tranformed from organizational position to displayed competence. This change alters the role of the organization. At first the organization is itself a validator, an object of trust; later it becomes an arena in which trusting relations are enacted and organizational interaction serves as its own reward.

....

Organizing Secrecy

Trust, which is connected directly to mutual support, contributes to cohesion. In general, the more trust, the greater the degree of cohesion (Stokes 1983).[12] Secrecy is not implicated so obviously in the development of group feeling because, on the surface, it separates individuals. Trust depends on a willingness to share knowledge and experience. Secrecy, like trust, is linked to information and to relationships, but it privileges information (Luhrmann 1989) and implies that relationships will be competitive (Bellman 1981). Trust is one of the prime *synthetic* forces of a social system; secrecy, at first glance, is its *analytic* equivalent. Trust represents the midpoint between certainty and ignorance—sufficient knowledge to recognize what constitutes legitimate information and who provides it. Secrecy represents the two endpoints: keeping knowledge for oneself while keeping others in ignorance.

Secrecy, and the accompanying deception, may be necessary for smoothing social order (Nyberg 1993), for managing impressions (Goffman 1967), and as a means of social control (Luhrmann 1989; Redlinger and Johnston 1980; Wilsnack 1980). Even though concealment of information can impose heavy burdens on social systems and individuals (Bok 1983), raising questions of ethics and participation, secrecy also protects valued resources. Secret societies represent the institutionalization of secrecy (Erickson 1981), but secrecy is also endemic in many organizations embedded in systems of internal or external competition.[13] One can examine effects of organizational secrecy under two conditions: when members of organizations attempt to keep certain information from those outside the organization (external secrecy),[14] and when members of organizations keep information from other members (internal secrecy). We are concerned here with the latter.

Secrecy is particularly evident in those leisure worlds which operate in conditions of scarcity and competition, and in which comparison of participants is encouraged.[15] Despite the communal, subcultural features of leisure, and because of the potential scarceness of the prize and the zero-sum quality of the quest, mushrooming, like other competitive subcultures (e.g., Hummel and Foster 1986; Mitchell 1983:5; Stuller 1989), has an air of secrecy. Competitive social worlds are structured such that few see a contradiction between protecting information and establishing close bonds. For mushroomers, resources are scarce and certain kinds of knowledge contribute directly to obtaining these resources. Under these circumstances, transaction costs limit the information that individuals share voluntarily, unless the relational context outweighs the value of keeping information private.

How can secrecy both divide and unify? How does the existence of a robust and accepted class of secrets within a group—"a community of secret holders"—permit and even encourage continued allegiance? Part of the answer is found in what Bellman (1981: 21) terms "the paradox of secrecy." This paradox is the fact that secrecy is constituted by the procedures by which secrets are communicated; in other words, it is defined by the *telling* of secrets in "appropriate" contexts and relations. Secrecy is governed by implicit rules, and in this sense is normative. The telling of secrets on certain occasions builds community among members: when enough members privately communicate secrets, everyone eventually becomes a holder, a giver, and a recipient of secrets. As with trust, information leads to the development of relationships. An economy of secrets exists by virtue of their breach.

Not all secrets are transmitted, however. Community is built not only by the occasional spread of information, but also by keeping it. This secrecy depends on the assumption that over time, all members will have secrets which they will keep, and that none will lack the resources (e.g., places to pick mushrooms) necessary to succeed. The underlying assumption is that mushrooming need not be a zero-sum game: although particular specimens may be picked only once, numerous unpicked mushrooms await energetic collectors.

In practice, mushroomers describe their experiences in lengthy narratives ("treasure tales"); they merely exclude relevant details, thus preventing others from gaining access to the same locale (Rey 1994). When all participants operate in this way, a community of secret holders can share each other's triumphs and frustrations as well as a sense of comradely competition—

judging oneself against others. In such cases, relationships are based on the legitimation of privileged information.

Keeping Secrets

Secrecy, on its surface, opposes the assumption that all members of the group have the interests of others at heart (Richardson 1988:209). This centrifugal force is mitigated in those circumstances in which all participants keep secrets from others while sharing protective knowledge. This process has been observed in those occupations in which individuals strive for scarce resources but require a general sharing of information to protect themselves, such as commercial fishermen (Ellis 1986; Palmer 1990; Thorlindsson 1994). The voluntary segregation of knowledge among all members of a collectivity preserves relationships. The drawing of boundaries around one's own preserve of information is expected, and the friendly competition that results is recognized as part of the satisfaction ("fun") of sharing an avocation with people about whom one cares (Donnelly 1994).

The recognition of a paradoxical relationship between secrecy and secrecy and sociability is evident in humor, which reveals ambivalence about hiding information in a group that defines itself as a community. Joking permits the "processing" of this ambivalence:

Jerry, the club president, in adjourning a meeting at the end of morel season, jokes: "Why don't you share your favorite spots now that the season is over? We'll put them on slips and next year give everyone a slip. Don't give any bum spots." Of course, nothing is done about either of the suggestions; spots are used by members from year to year. (field notes)

The president may tease members about sharing, while knowing that it is precisely the absence of sharing which makes members interested in each other's experiences and narratives.

Members offer an ethical justification for the secrecy: they claim that they prefer the satisfaction of finding mushrooms for themselves, which provides a sense of personal accomplishment. As one member commented,

Something's worth as much trouble as it takes to get it. This is true of learning to find mushrooms. I've told people to do some searching, and have them put forth an effort so they'd appreciate more. (personal interview)

The assumption is that each member can or should discover spots; although spots are rarely shared, everyone finds mushrooms. This is not entirely true, however, particularly for new members who haven't found spots and may not even know where to look. As a result, most clubs sponsor forays that allow members to find morels, chanterelles, and other prime edibles; give longtime members the opportunity to identify and compare a wide range of mushrooms, as well as socialize with friends; and teach novices which habitats and natural indicators to look for (such as other plants that bloom concurrently), so they can develop their own "secrets." Aside from forays to public areas, novices quickly learn that they will not be given specific locations; rather, members share enough general information about indicators of edible mushrooms so that novices can discover mushroom spots themselves. Jokes effectively socialize novices to group expectations:

A novice collector asks Jerry where he should go to find morels. Jerry responds, "In the woods." Then he seriously describes indicators of morels, such as poison ivy, bedstraw, and prickly ash. (field notes)

Once burned, the initiate quickly learns to use similar mocking remarks (and helpful information) to train those who arrive later.

In some sense, finding mushrooms is ultimately a zero-sum game, even though the game can be expanded by the search for new spots. Yet if you pick a patch of mushrooms, no one else can find that same patch, at least in that fruiting. You "own" your spots, particularly because many species appear annually in the same location.[16] They are valuable resources. Morel spots in particular are "owned" and are not shared or given lightly, because of their scarcity, the short fruiting season, and their economic value. When I asked one mushroomer about his concept of secrecy, he referred to his morel spots:

[The morel grows] one particular time of the year for a very short time. It happens to be an edible and hard to find, and we work hard to find them. The reason you don't usually just give it to somebody else is the hours it took you to find it. I've put in some tough days. (personal interview)

If one shares the location of a patch of morels, the other person may reach that location first in the following year.

To maintain their spots, some collectors deliberately cover with leaves the stems of the mushrooms they have picked, so that others will not learn that mushrooms grew in the area. Others, recognizing this game, look for piles of leaves as a sign that mushrooms may be underneath (field notes). One mushroomer explained that although he tells others the direction from the Twin Cities where he finds morels (e.g., "east of here," "way up north," "by the Mississippi"), he will not name the *county* in which the mushrooms were found (personal interview).

The value of secrecy is underlined in the humorous attempts to make members divulge information. An intense joking culture flourishes among mushroomers in which they jocularly attempt to make others reveal the locations of their finds, particularly morels (Rey 1994). Mushroomers speak of a transitory hearing disorder that they label "morelitis":

Howard says that he found a lot of morels yesterday. Another club member asks where, and Howard doesn't answer at first, then jokes that he has "morelitis," adding "there is a temporary disease which we get called morelitis, which involves a temporary loss of hearing" (i.e., when someone asks where you found morels). He explains that he was northeast of Forest Lake, but won't be more specific than that. (field notes)

This discourse emphasizes shared understandings of mushroom etiquette. One must respect another person's informational preserve, thus building the relationship, as indicated by these joking remarks:

Helen and June are talking at the national foray about picking morels. Helen (from Minnesota) tells June (from Pennsylvania) that she finds morels right across from her house. June asks: "Where do you live?" (Both laugh) (field notes)

Jerry describes a foray that he plans to lead near his summer home: "I won't take you to my favorite [chanterelle] spots, but I will take you to [my friend's] favorite spots." (field notes)

This concern is also expressed seriously when one fears that the person one is addressing might get the wrong idea about the nature of the questioning:

Donna has brought some very large Sulfur Shelves, a prime edible. Dave asks: "Where did you find these?" Then he quickly adds: "On what kind of tree?" (Indicating that he is not asking their location). (field notes)

At the national foray Mary (who visits Philadelphia often) asks John (from Philadelphia) where he finds mushrooms: "Where do you go outside Philadelphia? You don't have to tell me specifically. I'm just curious." John tells her the small city near where he picks. (field notes)

The elaboration of these questions reflects "motive talk" (Hewitt 1989)— justifications and disclaimers—that ratifies the shared assumptions about appropriate informational preserves. Without these accounts, the listener could assume the questioner's social incompetence, either novice status or cultural marginality.

Sharing Secrets

On occasion, secrecy is explicitly abrogated; thus the legitimacy of secrecy in other circumstances is emphasized. Mushroomers occasionally share their spots with others; this sharing indicates the normative boundaries of secrecy. In some cases, sharing otherwise secret information is a group policy, as when a mycological society schedules a foray to a public place.[17] "Held" information also can be transmitted privately, however, and occur within a developed or developing relationship. The structural sharing of information over time becomes linked to relationships.[18] This sharing reflects a special act of friendship, cementing a social tie.

Mark tells me that he doesn't begrudge Jerry the 800–1000 morels Jerry finds on his father's property, because at the end of last season Jerry told him about one of his other morel spots he hadn't used. (field notes)

This mushroomer made the model of exchange explicit in the context of a relationship:

Mark tells me, "I must have found fifteen pounds of those things [Matsutakes]. It was one of the best mushroom-pickings of my life. It was like another world." After he told me he had given the spot to a friend, he added, "I returned an old debt. I had been picking his spots for a number of years." (field notes)

Sometimes spots are given privately to new members who seem enthusiastic— a symbolic gesture of acceptance and an indication that they are judged to be committed to the activity. In addition, spots may be shared when a mushroomer decides that he or she is no longer interested in picking a particular species or plans to leave the community. The gift indicates the "ownership" of the spot and the control over the resource. In the latter case, one's mushroom spots are labeled a "legacy" or an "heirloom" (Lonik 1984:10), which makes this leisure group analogous to a family. In the transfer of such knowledge, the recipient acknowledges the giver's status. As noted, such a gift ideally should be reciprocated through some exchange—for example, the trade of a morel spot for a spot where Hen of the Woods mushrooms are found or, as often in cases of status difference, an expression of respect. Occasionally a member invites another to a favorite spot to have companionship: such a "gift" implies some measure of reciprocity.

Members are not *entitled* to all information by belonging. Such entitlement is outside the legitimate privileges of participation, despite ideals of trust and communion; it represents an extra-organizational tie, although that tie depends on the organization to give it meaning. Occasionally the special relationship implied by the sharing of private information may provoke mild friction among members:

Jerry tells several members that he picks Hen of the Woods in Theodore Wirth Park. Jerry says that Dave "gave" him the trees one fall when Dave had stopped picking there. Harvey, an older man who lives near the park, is very interested, but when he asks Dave where he found the Hen of the Woods, Dave is noncommittal: "I just go around everywhere." Harvey tries to get him to be more specific, but Dave remains vague. (field notes)

The legitimacy of withholding information allows relationships within the club to retain their power rather than being reduced to homogenized sharing. In addition, there are limits on what can be done with the information that is provided. Sometimes members give others "limited" access to spots that they themselves still use, as when the other member is treated as a "guest." The information that is acquired from the invitation is "provisional" and should not be shared or used without permission.

Jerry tells me that he is annoyed with Howard. Jerry had shown Howard some of his chanterelle spots, and then the next week without telling him, Howard visited these spots. This particularly annoyed Jerry because it was on someone else's land: "I don't know why he did it. I asked him not to." (field notes)

The guest does not "own" and should not use the secret knowledge that has been acquired. Expectations related to the fair distribution of scarce resources dictate what information can be kept secret without affecting the trust that is part of the relationship. Sharing the secret exemplifies the trust among members; if relationships are to remain strong, the secret must not be abused. Personal information enters into a private relationship. In a stable, tight-knit organization, a network of such relationships collectively ties members to each other in a complex web. If secrets are localized in a few dyads or small groups, fragmentation or cliquishness may result.

Socialization to Secrets

Voluntary organizations must determine how to socialize novices to prescribed "moral" behavior. If new members wish to be viewed as competent, they must learn which knowledge they should reveal to others; the location of their "spots" should remain closely guarded. This norm contradicts an ideology of communion, suggesting that nothing should be held back from the "brotherhood." Many enthusiastic new members, embracing this perspective, wish to tell everyone what they found *and* where they found it. One mushroomer commented wistfully:

At first I wanted to share information, but no one else did, so [my wife and I] stopped. It was kinda sad, but it was like putting pearls before swine. (field notes)

Another described a personal experience that convinced her of the need for secrecy:

I now practice the same form [of secrecy], which I did not at first ... until I "learned better." I used to show anybody who was interested where and how to pick morels and other species ... until one day I showed a person my *Pleurotus ostreatus* log ... loaded ... I wanted to get a photo of this before harvesting and the person knew this ... but couldn't hold himself back long enough. He had cut off almost all the mushrooms before I had safely put the camera and lenses away—and the result was I got only a handful of mushrooms off "my own" (note I use a possessive phrase for a wild log) log. (letter to author)

This mushroomer is sensitive to the irony of considering public land as "her own." Even so, she accepts the validity of secrecy, given the structure of the leisure world. Although some individuals feel that the need for secrecy is unfortunate, its practical value is widely accepted.

Novices also wish to communicate their spots to others to demonstrate that they are competent. In fact, however, such sharing only announces their novice status and demonstrates their ignorance of cultural scripts.

Jerry, the club president, asks if anyone knows any place the club might foray. A woman in the audience responds: "I know a wonderful place for shaggy manes ... Literally thousands and thousands." Jerry jokes: "I'll give you my phone number [meaning he wants to keep the information for himself], ... You don't have to give us your best foray spots." The spot is not mentioned again (field notes).

When one returns from the hunt, it is bad form to tell anyone, even one's nearest and dearest, the precise location of a Real Find (should there be one). The location of a find may be offhandedly reported as somewhere within 60 miles of the precise spot. (Ms. Mushroom 1984: 29)

One should be able to describe the find for the enjoyment of one's colleagues, but should provide little information as to its location. Novices must learn not to share too much.

As is often the case, social control is communicated effectively and efficiently through humor (Seckman and Couch 1989). Socialization to secrecy is evident when a less sophisticated member asks a veteran where he or she found a patch of mushrooms. "Outside" is a frequent response. Secrecy seems to contradict the idea of leisure community, but novices must recognize quickly that the existence of secrecy does not suggest the absence of interpersonal and collective concern.

....

Cohesive Ties

In a study of Mensa, the organization for high-IQ individuals, Aldrich (1971) proposed the existence of a class of groups he terms "sociable organizations." These organizations provide settings in which voluntary "communities of rapport" develop (Hetherington 1994; Schmalenbach 1977). Groups that engage in serious leisure (Stebbins 1992) are particularly likely to form tight-knit organizations. These are groups that we join because we choose to do so. Unlike some voluntary organizations (notably marriage), sociable organizations allow us to choose how much time we wish to spend without serious complications. They are "ungreedy" institutions (contra Coser 1974).

Like Goffman's concept of fun in games, participating in a sociable organization must be rewarding over time; the lack of institutional reward justifies disengagement. The attitude toward the organization differs from that toward the activity itself, which typically has an elaborated rationale. The organization is viewed as the means to the activity, and few people would suggest that one should continue to participate in a sociable organization one did not enjoy. In theory the organization is tangential, while the activity is essential. How are such organizations stabilized? How is group cohesion generated in the face of forces, such as secrecy and the recognition of danger, that militate against continued involvement in group life?

First, a group must generate trust so that individual members facing danger are willing to leave life-and-death decisions in the hands of colleagues (or, in other leisure groups, willing to accept information that may be of economic or social consequence). Patterns of interaction must create confidence that the other members of the organization (and the organization itself, as reflected in the leadership) share interests and operate to support each other. Members must be trusted to provide protective information. This trust is evident even while members compete and hide information from each other. The information that is hidden would be available to all members if they wished to devote sufficient time and effort; the information that is shared exemplifies the process, though not the outcomes, of successful performance (information on *how* and *what* to collect as opposed to *where* to collect).

Secrecy, though it appears to be centrifugal, binds members together in providing for friendly competition—an arena of fun, reflected in narrative. That others care about their colleagues' successes and failures suggests that the relationships are meaningful. Secrecy provides ground rules for this game, given scarcity and the possibility of effort. To be competitive implies incorporating knowledge and skills that differentiate oneself from others. Participants enjoy this competition and the resulting secrecy; it permits them to judge themselves against group standards, incorporating the experiences of others. The group trains the novice to the point where he or she can find collecting spots without aid. This perspective on socialization assumes that locations for mushrooms need not be scarce, and are limited only by the effort one wishes to invest. (This is also assumed under most circumstances in a society that operates with the metaphor of a free market.) The model of a zero-sum game applies only when one believes that the number of sites cannot be expanded. Such a perspective is key in defining the organization.

In view of the importance of relationships and information preserves, trust in others and shielding of knowledge are compatible. The link between trust and secrecy supports group cohesion while leaving room for personal investment. Collective spheres of knowledge are compatible with private information, which in turn creates a satisfying competitive culture among those who are perceived as sharing interests. The community of secrecy depends on the recognition of trusting relations and on the fact that others can be trusted not to hold back information that might be protective. If one did not trust one's colleagues' claims as to how many mushrooms they collected from their secret spots (at least to a degree; "fish stories" are not unknown), much of the interpersonal satisfaction of competition would be lost.

Trust plays an important role because this case study involves some personal risk. In many or most voluntary worlds, however (and in many nonvoluntary worlds as well), members rely on others for information that will protect them from costs and embarrassments. A comparative analysis of dangerous and secure worlds may illuminate how trust operates similarly and differently in groups. Likewise, the types of secrecy found in competitive groups (e.g., hiding resources or not sharing techniques), mentioned above, certainly determine what information is shared. Competition is not antithetical to group cohesion; it provides a consensual basis for competence on which status is built. Members become friends over time, and although turnover occurs among peripheral members, the stability of core members is impressive.[19]

This analysis has taken mushroom collecting as a model for the relationship between trust and secrecy, but the relative influence of trust and secrecy may vary among groups. Groups grounded on competition and lacking dramatic consequences may give greater weight to secrecy than those in which consequences are real and omnipresent, and in which trust must continually be publicly displayed. The relationship structures within a group vary according to the salience of trust and secrecy. At the same time, each group may be a community grounded on personal commitment, which is translated in turn into group cohesion.

Conclusion

In this analysis we portray how the dialectic between individual and group interest can be resolved through the paradoxical compatibility of private action with collective concern. Trust and secrecy, in our view, are pervasive and necessary features of social order; they are present in virtually every situation in which interactants care about the doings of others.

Beyond voluntary groups that facilitate dangerous leisure, this linking of trust with competitive domains is part of culturally valued scripts. Contexts of open and closed awareness can coexist together (Glaser and Strauss 1967). In typical service encounters, for example, customers often do not share extra change with cashiers, and cashiers may be silent about items of poor quality. Within their relationship, however, each expects and trusts the other to avoid forgery, violence, gross harassment, and claims of financial dishonesty. Tact is based on trust and secrecy. In family life, children and parents are supposed to hide some doings, even while ensuring that their kin are able to pursue life, liberty, and happiness. Even the routine relationship between mugger and victim, although filled with surprises and hidden knowledge, often follows a script that parties should be able to trust. When we believe that this script is likely to be violated, the city becomes a much more frightening place for all parties. If routine interaction is to proceed, trust must exist in its routine basis, even though information may be withheld which permits parties to achieve their goals in the face of competition for resources. Trust and secrecy—and open and closed information systems—operate within the same social web.

No one doubts that people like to think of themselves in cohesive, communal terms, as trusting in each other, committed to the group, and accepting democratically adopted policies. In practice, however, access to information and relationships differs according to one's social position. The culturally valued scripts that allow for the simultaneous existence of trust and secrecy may not be fully available to all members of society. In fact, they may never be made explicit but may remain largely taken for granted. This situation protects the cultural framework from being contested or challenged and thereby preserves the cultural constructs of allegiance and initiative (Moscovici 1993).

In some ways, voluntary leisure worlds represent the larger society. Mushroomers feel no special *obligation* to share their resources with others, and permit some to go without; this perspective is often expanded to economic spheres. For instance, some individuals with material resources consider improper the demand that they provide for those with fewer resources; they assume that what is achievable for one should be achievable for all, with sufficient effort. The *means* by which success is attainable should be taught; the *results* should not be equalized. Friendly competition can become friendly fire. Not being expected to share, we preserve resources for those we perceive as having the motivation to achieve such goals, even while we accept the belief that we are tethered together. If trust and secrecy are to function together, a floor must be established, below which those without resources and the means to acquire them cannot be allowed to sink.

The link between communal allegiance and individual initiative is effective in voluntary scenes, in which few people question its legitimacy. Yet, we might question its effectiveness in those social systems in which membership is not voluntary and in which access to resources depends on the presence or absence of structural barriers. In an "information age," in which access to knowledge is power, this relationship between trust and secrecy may weigh more heavily on some (the resource-poor) than on others, preventing the development of relationships necessary for navigating in a complex, differentiated world.

The examination of leisure worlds is only a beginning. The analysis of trust and secrecy needs to be expanded to those groups which depend on explicit social control and on access to external resources, and in which the exit costs are far greater than those found in forests and fields.

....

Acknowledgements

The authors wish to thank Patricia and Peter Adler, William Andrews, Elizabeth Brumfiel, Douglas Harper, Sherryl Kleinman, Richard Lempert, Tanya Luhrmann, Neil Smelser, Robert Stebbins, Robert Sutton, Jim Thomas, and Leigh Thompson for comments on an earlier version. Portions of this paper were prepared while the first author was a fellow at the Center for Advanced Study in the Behavioral Sciences. He is grateful for financial support provided by National Science Foundation Grant SBR-9022192. Versions of this paper were presented at the meetings of The Society for the Study of Symbolic Interaction/Stone Symposium, held in Las Vegas in 1992, and at the University of Georgia, the University of North Carolina, the University of California, Los Angeles, and the University of Chicago. Fine can be reached at g-fine@north-western.edu. Holyfield can be reached at lholyfie@uark.edu.

....

Note

1. Kanter's (1972) model of individual "commitment," grounded in an analysis of nineteenth-century communes, distinguishes between continuance, cohesion, and control, important processes evident in voluntary total institutions. The social psychological literature on "cohesion" typically conflates the first two and sometimes incorporates the third, emphasizing not the individual's level of commitment but the group's level of cohesion. Commitment is an individual-level variable; cohesion operates collectively.

2. Social psychological research, in practice, has used cohesion either as an independent variable that produces outcomes on performance variables (e.g., Evans and Dion 1991; Wheelan 1994) or as a dependent variable that is a function of membership composition, feedback, or group structure (Drescher, Burlingame, and Fuhrman, 1985). Only rarely do researchers explore the variables mediating the effects of cohesion, such as the salience of social norms (Rutkowski, Gruder, and Romer 1983).

3. Stebbins (1992) observes that leisure activities differ in their collective character. Some, such as sports teams, theater troupes, or musical ensembles, demand group participation. In those cases, the organization provides for training and sharing interest; in addition, participation in the organization constitutes the "doing" of leisure. In contrast, we generalize from organizations that cater to individuals interested in activities that can be performed solo or in small groups outside the organization.

4. We do not make the extreme claim that all leisure groups have the same mix of trust and secrecy. Groups in which danger is recognized establish mechanisms for establishing trust. Groups that are grounded on the comparative ranking among members, which is based on achievement (competition), develop information preserves; they avoid sharing resources (mushrooms, caving routes) or keep private their styles of performance (parachuting, bungee jumping). Some risky groups may have relatively little secrecy, and vice versa, but we claim that groups involving risk typically have an achievement-based status hierarchy which involves protected information.

5. Some measure of trust is found in all organizations in which negative outcomes are possible. In stamp collection, for example, novices might trust others to inform them about stamp values or how to preserve their collections safely. Of course physical dangers, and the edgework that accompanies them, make the need for trust even more explicit (Lyng 1990).

6. There is only one mushroom club in the Twin Cities area. We believed it would be disingenuous to create a pseudonym that would not shield the identity of the group as a whole. Following standard ethnographic practice, we use pseudonyms for individuals except when quoting published materials.

7. Luhmann (1988:97–99) distinguishes between confidence and trust regarding whether potential negative consequences are considered (trust) or ignored (confidence). In English, at least, this distinction would seem to contradict the fact that the two words are often interchangeable, and the uncertainty as to whether danger is recognized consciously.

8. This assumes that the organization is viewed as unified. In some instances, trust (and loyalty) to individuals in factionalized organizations may weaken the organization while strengthening subgroups (Richard Lempert, personal communication, 1995).

9. Of the 129 members of the Minnesota Mycological Society who responded to my questionnaire, 94 percent said they had eaten wild mushrooms.

10. This point raises the delicate issue of relations among novices. Novices often announce their lack of expertise to others to avoid responsibility for expertise. This announcement, however, is voluntary, a novice potentially could harm others and thus weaken the bonds of trust. As a result, in most instances in which expertise is crucial, experts are assigned to monitor the information (and comestibles) that are distributed.

11. Mushroom fatalities in the United States are very few, typically no more than a half-dozen a year. Only two of 129 Minnesota mushroomers reported becoming so

ill from eating mushrooms that they had to be hospitalized. Only 15 percent had even become ill from eating mushrooms, however minor the discomfort.

12. A point may occur at which too much trust will not promote belonging because an independent contribution to the group would become impossible. With continued dependency, personal interest may not develop fully.

13. We recognize the fine line between information that is termed private and that which is secret (Bellman 1981; Shils 1956; Warren and Laslett 1977); secret information often refers to that which is valued negatively by those from whom the information is shielded. The knowledge discussed here might be defined as private, although mushroomers themselves refers to their shielded information as "secret." Because the information we will discuss is public *in principle*, and is information to which others wish access, we find it legitimate to designate the shielding as indicating secrecy. Our operational definition merely denotes the concealment of information to which others wish access, and which is potentially public.

14. In the most obvious and most acceptable context for secrecy, a group member encounters an outsider, and doesn't tell or misleads that person. The other, being a stranger, has no right to obtain information. The legitimacy of secrecy toward outsiders is evident in the stories that mushroomers tell about deceiving anonymous others as to what they are looking for and what they have found (see Fine 1987). These stories are relished when retold within the group.

> Diane mentions that one day she was picking morels. Exiting the woods, she met two well-dressed businessmen who were going into the woods to pick morels. Diane reports: "They asked, 'Did you find any?' and I said, 'No, there weren't any. This is a bad place.' And they got in their cars and left." Club members laugh loudly. (field notes)

Secrecy strengthens the organization by emphasizing its boundaries (Bales 1970), as is necessary for collective identity. The members shield secret information from those who are excluded, thus emphasizing their mutual allegiance.

15. Mushroomers compare the number of mushrooms (especially morels) that they have collected. As one collector told me, "You go out and think you've had a wonderful day, and you come back and find people have picked a hundred pounds. Sometimes it tends to be less for its own sake than for the sake of stashing away hoards of morels" (personal interview). Like fishers, mushroomers have bragging rights.

16. Because ownership is secret, it is possible that several people may have the same spot. This is a source of frustration when someone discovers that their spot has been picked.

17. This approach is taken by the Humboldt Bay Mycological Society:

> Beginning this year *Mycolog* will feature a regular article on what fungi are fruiting and where to collect them. This column will help novices follow the season and will provide "well-publicized" collecting places, for we know the old hands already have their secret spots (*Is It Mushrooming Yet?*" 1983).

18. I found little pooling of spots among friends (that is, spots to which two non-relatives have access). Mushroomers may invite close friends to visit their spots, but the spots belong to the sharer.

19. In comparing the 1981 and the 1982 membership lists, I found that 69 percent of members (64 of 93) who had been in the club at least two years in 1981 (i.e., were not new members) continued their membership; only 48 percent (20 of 42) of the new members continued their membership the following year. These figures, however, undercount the actual renewal rate because many members did not renew their membership until late in the year, although they continued to participate in club activities. By the end of most years, approximately 200 members had paid dues. Twenty-nine members in 1982 remained members in 1992—a real core, in view of mobility and morbidity.

References

Aldrich, Howard. 1971. "The Sociable Organization: A Case Study of Mensa and Some Propositions." *Sociology and Social Research* 55:429–41.

Bales, Robert Freed. 1970. *Personality and Interpersonal Behavior.* New York: Holt, Rinehart and Winston.

Bellah, Robert, Richard Madsen, William M. Sullivan, Ann Swidler, and Steven Tipton. 1985. *Habits of the Heart: Individualism and Commitment in American Life.* Berkeley: University of California Press.

Bellman, Beryl. 1981. "The Paradox of Secrecy." *Human Studies* 4:1–24.

Bok, Sissela. 1983. *Secrets: On the Ethics of Concealment and Revelation.* New York: Vintage.

Brawley, Lawrence R., Albert V. Carron, and W. Neil Widmeyer. 1988. "Exploring the Relationship between Cohesion and Group Resistance to Disruption." *Journal of Sport and Exercise Psychology* 10:190–213.

Bryan, Hobson. 1977. "Leisure Value Systems and Recreational Specialization: The Case of Trout Fishermen." *Journal of Leisure Research* 9:174–87.

Coombs, Don. 1986. "The 1, 2, 3, 4, 5 of Starting Out." *Mushroom* 4 (Spring): 174–87.

Coser, Lewis A. 1974. *Greedy Institutions: Patterns of Undivided Commitment.* New York: Free Press.

Donnelly, Peter. 1994. "Take My Word for It: Trust in the Context of Birding and Mountaineering." *Qualitative Sociology* 17:215–41.

Drescher, Stuart, Gary Burlingame, and Addie Fuhrman. 1985. "Cohesion: An Odyssey in Empirical Understanding." *Small Group Relations* 16:3–30.

Eder, Donna. 1988. "Building Cohesion Through Collaborative Narration." *Social Psychology Quarterly* 51:225–35.

Eisenstadt, S. N. and L. Roniger. 1984. *Patrons, Clients, and Friends.* Cambridge, U.K.: Cambridge University Press.

Ellis, Carolyn. 1986. *Fisher Folk.* Lexington: University of Kentucky Press.

Erickson, Bonnie. 1981. "Secret Societies and Social Structure." *Social Forces* 80:188–210.

Evans, Charles R., and Kenneth L. Dion. 1991. "Group Cohesion and Performance: A Meta-Analysis." *Small Group Research* 22:175–86.

Evans, Nancy J., and Paul A. Jarvis. 1980. "Group Cohesion: A Review and Reevaluation." *Small Group Behavior* 11:359–70.

Festinger, Leon, Stanley Schachter, and Kurt Back. 1950. *Social Pressures in Informal Groups: A Study of a Housing Project.* New York: Harper.

Fine, Gary Alan. 1979. "Small Groups and Culture Creation." *American Sociological Review* 44:733–45.

—— 1987. "Community and Boundary: Personal Experience Stories of Mushroom Collectors." *Journal of Folklore Research* 24:223–40.

—— 1989. "Mobilizing Fun: Provisioning Resources in Leisure Worlds." *Sociology of Sport Journal* 6:319–34.

Frank, Jerome D. 1957. "Some Determinants, Manifestations, and Effects of Cohesiveness in Therapy Groups." *International Journal of Group Psychotherapy* 7:53–63.

Gambetta, Diego. 1988. "Can We Trust Trust?" pp. 213–37 in *Trust*, edited by Diego Gambetta. Oxford: Basil Blackwell.

Gellner, Ernest. 1988. "Trust, Cohesion, and the Social Order." pp. 142–57 in *Trust*, edited by Diego Gambetta. Oxford: Basil Blackwell.

Giddens, Anthony. 1990. *The Consequences of Modernity.* Stanford: Stanford University Press.

—— 1991: *Modernity and Self-Identity.* Stanford: Stanford University Press.

Glaser, Barney G., and Anselm L. Strauss. 1967. "Awareness Contexts and Social Interaction." *American Sociological Review* 29:669–79.

Goffman, Erving. 1961. *Encounters.* Indianapolis: Bobbs-Merrill.

—— 1967. *Strategic Interaction.* Philadelphia: University of Pennsylvania Press.

Good, David. 1988. "Individuals, Interpersonal Relations, and Trust." pp. 31–48 in *Trust*, edited by Diego Gambetta, Oxford: Basil Blackwell.

Gross, Neal, and William E. Martin. 1952. "On Group Cohesiveness." *American Journal of Sociology* 57: 546–54.

Haas, Jack. 1974. "The Stages of the High-Steel Ironworker Apprentice Career." *Sociological Quarterly* 15:93–108.

Harrison, Albert A., and Mary M. Connors. 1984. "Groups in Exotic Environments." *Advances in Experimental Social Psychology* 18:49–87.

Hechter, Michael. 1987. *Principles of Group Solidarity.* Berkeley: University of California Press.

Hetherington, Kevin. 1994. "The Contemporary Significance of Schmalenbach's Concept of the Bund." *Sociological Review* 42:1–25.

Hewitt, John P. 1984. "Stalking the Wild Identity." Unpublished manuscript.

—— 1989. *Self and Society.* Boston: Allyn and Bacon.

Hoggett, Paul, and Jeff Bishop. 1986. *Organizing Around Enthusiasms.* London: Comedia Publications Group.

Hughes, Everett. 1971. *The Sociological Eye.* Chicago: Aldine.

Hummel, Richard, and Gary S. Foster. 1986. "A Sporting Chance: Relationships Between Technological Change and Concepts of Fair Play in Fishing." *Journal of Leisure Research* 18:40–52.

Hunt, Jennifer. 1995. "Divers' Accounts of Normal Risk." *Symbolic Interaction* 18:439–62.

Irwin, John. 1977. *Scenes*. Beverly Hills: Sage. "Is It Mushrooming Yet?" *1983. Mycolog*, 38 (September):2.

Kanter, Rosabeth Moss. 1972. *Commitment and Community: Communes and Utopias in Sociological Perspective*. Cambridge, MA: Harvard University Press.

Kollock, Peter. 1994. "The Emergence of Exchange Structures: An Experimental Study of Uncertainty, Commitment, and Trust." *American Journal of Sociology* 100:313–45.

Lewis, J. David, and Andrew J. Weigert. 1985. "Trust as a Social Reality." *Social Forces* 63:967–85.

Lonik, Larry J. 1984. *The Curious Morel*. Royal Oak, MI: RKT Publications.

Luhmann, Niklas. 1988. "Familiarity, Confidence, Trust: Problems and Alternatives." pp. 94–107 in *Trust*, edited by Diego Gambetta. Oxford: Basil Blackwell.

Luhrmann, T. M. 1989. "The Magic of Secrecy." *Ethos* 17:131–65.

Lyng, Stephen. 1990. "Edgework: A Social Psychological Analysis of Voluntary Risk Taking." *American Journal of Sociology* 95:851–86.

McNulty, Elizabeth W. 1994. "Generating Common Sense Knowledge among Police Officers." *Symbolic Interaction* 17:281–94.

Mitchell, Richard, Jr. 1983. *Mountain Experience*. Chicago: University of Chicago Press.

Moscovici, Serge. 1993. "The Return of the Unconscious." *Social Research* 60:39–93.

Ms. Mushroom. 1984. "Etiquette." *Mushroom*, 2 Summer, 28–29.

Norvell, Lorelei. 1983–1984. "Which Are You?" *Mushroom*, 2 Winter, 5–7.

Nyberg, David. 1993. *The Varnished Truth*. Chicago: University of Chicago Press.

Owen, William Foster. 1985. "Metaphor Analysis of Cohesiveness in Small Discussion Groups." *Small Group Behavior* 16:415–24.

Palmer, Craig T. 1990. "Telling the Truth (Up to a Point): Radio Communication among Maine Lobstermen." *Human Organization* 49:157–83.

Piper, William E., Myriam Marrache, Renee Lacroix, Astrid M. Richardsen, and Barry D. Jones. 1983. "Cohesion as a Basic Bond in Groups." *Human Relations* 36:93–108.

Redlinger, Lawrence J., and Sunny Johnston. 1980. "Secrecy, Informational Uncertainty, and Social Control." *Urban Life* 8:387–97.

Rey, Theresa. 1994. "The Stories Are as Good as Collecting Mushrooms." *Mushroom*, 12 Spring, 16–17.

Richardson, Laurel. 1988. "Secrecy and Status: The Social Construction of Forbidden Relationships." *American Sociological Review* 53:209–19.

Rosen, Samuel R. 1982. *A Judge Judges Mushrooms*, Nashville, TN: Highlander.

Rutkowski, Gregory K., Charles L. Gruder, and Daniel Romer. 1983. "Group Cohesiveness, Social Norms, and Bystander Intervention." *Journal of Personality and Social Psychology* 44:545–52.

Schmalenbach, Herman. 1977. *On Society and Experience*. Chicago: University of Chicago Press.

Gary Alan Fine and Lori Holyfield

Seckman, Mark, and Carl Couch. 1989. "Jocularity, Sarcasm, and Relationships." *Journal of Contemporary Ethnography* 18:327–44.

Shaw, Marvin. 1981. *Group Dynamics: The Psychology of Small Group Behavior.* 3d. ed. New York: McGraw-Hill.

Sherif, Muzafer, O.J. Harvey, B.J. White W. R. Hood, and Caròlyn Sherif. 1961. *Intergroup Conflict and Cooperation: The Robbers Cave Experiment.* Norman: Oklahoma Book Exchange.

Shils, Edward A. 1956. *The Torment of Secrecy.* Glencoe, IL: Free Press.

Simmel, Georg. 1950. *The Sociology of Georg Simmel.* New York: Free Press.

Snow, David and Leon Anderson. 1987. "Identity Work among the Homeless: The Verbal Construction and Avowal of Personal Identities." *American Journal of Sociology* 92:1336–71.

Stebbins, Robert A. 1979. *Amateurs.* Beverly Hills: Sage.

—— 1992. *Amateurs, Professionals, and Serious Leisure.* Montreal: McGill-Queen's University Press.

Stokes, Joseph Powell. 1983. "Components of Group Cohesion: Intermember Attraction, Instrumental Value, and Risk Taking." *Small Group Behavior* 14: 163–73.

Stuller, Stu. 1989. "Birding by the Numbers." *The Atlantic* (May): 88–94.

Thorlindsson, Thorolfur. 1994. "Skipper Science: A Note on the Epistemology and the Nature of Expertise." *Sociological Quarterly* 35: 329–46.

Turner, John C., with Michael A. Hogg, Penelope J. Oakes, Stephen D. Reicher, and Margaret S. Wetherell. 1987. *Rediscovering the Social Group: A Self-Categorization Theory.* Oxford: Basil Blackwell.

Vester, Heinz-Gunter. 1987. "Adventure as a Form of Leisure." *Journal of Leisure Research* 6:237–49.

Warren, Carol, and Barbara Laslett. 1977. "Privacy and Secrecy: A Conceptual Comparison." *Journal of Social Issues* 33:43–51.

Wheelan, Susan A. 1994. *Group Processes: A Developmental Perspective.* Boston: Allyn and Bacon.

Williams, Bernard. 1988. "Formal Structures and Social Reality." pp. 3–13 in *Trust,* edited by Diego Gambetta. Oxford: Basil Blackwell.

Wilsnack, Richard. 1980. "Information Control: A Conceptual Framework for Sociological Analysis." *Urban Life* 8:467–89.

Wolfe, Alan. 1989. *Whose Keeper?* Berkeley: University of California Press.

—— 1991. *America at Century's End.* Berkeley: University of California Press.

14

Swift Trust and Temporary Groups

Debra Meyerson, Karl E. Weick, and
Roderick M. Kramer

January 1, 1991. The Grand Kempinski Hotel, Dallas, Texas. 9.00 a.m. "Crew Call." About 35 people gather. Some are local. Some flew in overnight from here or there. Some drove in. The 35 encompass almost that many different technical disciplines. Many are meeting each other for the first time. Ten and one-half hours from now they will tape a two hour lecture (given by the author), which will become the centerpiece of an hour-long public television show. They'll tape it again the next day. Then they'll disperse, never again to work together in the same configuration.

Peters, *Liberation Management*
(1992, p. 190)

This is the "Dallas Organization." As Peters and others have noted, temporary groups of this sort are becoming an increasingly common form of organization (Kanter, 1989; Peters, 1992). In many respects, such groups constitute an interesting organizational analog of a "one-night stand." They have a finite life span, form around a shared and relatively clear goal or purpose, and their success depends on a tight and coordinated coupling of activity.

As an organizational form, temporary groups turn upside down traditional notions of organizing. Temporary groups often work on tasks with a high degree of complexity, yet they lack the formal structures that facilitate coordination and control (Thompson, 1967). They depend on an elaborate body of collective knowledge and diverse skills, yet individuals have little time to sort out who knows precisely what. They often entail high-risk and high-stake outcomes, yet they seem to lack the normative structures and institutional safeguards that minimize the likelihood of things going wrong. Moreover, there isn't time to engage in the usual forms of confidence-building activities that contribute to the development and maintenance of trust in more traditional, enduring forms of organization. In these respects, temporary groups challenge our conventional understandings regarding the necessary or sufficient antecedents of effective organization.

These observations come together in a fascinating puzzle. Temporary systems exhibit behavior that presupposes trust, yet traditional sources of trust—familiarity, shared experience, reciprocal disclosure, threats and deterrents, fulfilled promises, and demonstrations of nonexploitation of vulnerability—are not obvious in such systems. In this respect, temporary systems act as if trust were present, but their histories seem to preclude its development.

In the following discussion we argue that one way to resolve this puzzle is to look more closely at the properties of trust and of temporary systems. A closer look suggests that temporary groups and organizations are tied together by trust, but it is a form of trust that has some unusual properties.[1] In other words, we propose that the trust that occurs in temporary systems is not simply conventional trust scaled down to brief encounters among small groups of strangers. There is some of that. But as we will show, the trust that unfolds in temporary systems is more accurately portrayed as a unique form of collective perception and relating that is capable of managing issues of vulnerability, uncertainty, risk, and expectations. These four issues become relevant immediately, as soon as the temporary system begins to form. We argue that all four issues can be managed by variations in trusting behavior, and if they are not managed, participants act more like a permanent crowd than a temporary system. It is the configuration of these variations in behavior that accounts for the unique form that trust assumes in temporary systems, a form that we call *swift trust*.

The argument that swift trust is a useful concept for understanding the functioning of temporary systems will be developed in the following way. First, borrowing from Goodman and Goodman (1976), we describe social constraints and resources found in temporary systems that provide the context for trust and influence its form. Second, we describe three concepts of trust to explain referent situations other than temporary systems. Accompanying each description, we suggest how each concept could be adapted to the conditions of a temporary system and help us understand better how that system is held together and what effect these ties have on outcomes. Third, having discussed systems and trust separately, we interweave them to capture the unique configuration we call swift trust in temporary systems. Finally, we consider the social and cognitive mechanisms that may contribute to the resilience and fragility of swift trust. In doing so, we begin to grasp what makes for more and less successful temporary systems and we begin to gain a better understanding of how trust in general unfolds, builds, and dissipates in organized settings.

Temporary Systems

Goodman and Goodman were among the earliest investigators to think systematically about temporary systems—and among the few to do so. These authors based their ideas predominantly on the systems that formed around theater productions (Goodman, 1981, chap. 4; Goodman & Goodman, 1972), although they also examined auditing teams and research and development projects. They define a temporary system as "a set of diversely skilled people working together on a complex task over a limited period of time" (Goodman & Goodman, 1976, p. 494). Such a system differs from a more stable system in several ways. The tasks as well as the personnel are less well understood in a temporary system, which means they cannot be assigned in ways traditionally relied on to achieve the most effective use of resources. Furthermore, although a temporary system resembles an organic system (Burns & Stalker, 1961), it also differs because it includes "members who have never worked together before and who do not expect to work together again" (p. 495) and members who represent a diversity of functions or skills.

Goodman and Goodman suggest that four concurrent problems provide the context within which any temporary system forms and operates. The first problem, and the one that is most central in our analysis, involves interdependence. "The task is complex with respect to interdependence of detailed task accomplishment, so that it is not easy to define tasks clearly and autonomously. The members must keep interrelating with one another in trying to arrive at viable solutions" (1976, p. 495). This continuous "interrelating" keeps the issue of trust salient throughout the life of a temporary system. The other three components of context include the uniqueness of the task relative to routine procedures available in the organization, the significance of the task in that the organization is willing to create a new structure to deal with it, and the use of clear goals to define the task and impose a time limit for its completion.[2]

Examples of temporary systems described by Goodman and Goodman (1976, p. 495) include presidential commissions, Senate select committees, theater and architectural groups, construction, auditing, negotiating teams, juries, and election campaign organizations.[3] In thinking through the issues of trust and temporary systems, we have also considered film crews (Kawin, 1992), auctions (e.g., Clark & Halford, 1980), cockpit crews in planes (Weiner, Kanki, & Helmreich, 1993), paramedics (e.g., Mellinger, 1994), music composition in films (e.g., Faulkner, 1983), investment banking (Eccles & Crane, 1988), fire-fighting crews (e.g., Klein, 1993), diagnostic teams (e.g., Orr, 1990), nuclear power plant operators (e.g., Gaddy & Wachtel, 1992), and AIDS outreach work (e.g., Suczek & Fagerhaugh, 1991). Although these represent specific settings in which "a set of diversely skilled people work together on a complex task over a limited period of time," part of the impetus for this chapter has arisen from the observation that an increasing number of settings in all organizations involve temporary systems. Temporary systems have become common as a result of more subcontracting, fewer people to handle more diverse assignments, time compression in product development, more use of temporary workers, intensified competition that requires immediate adaptability, loss of valuable experience in response to early retirement programs, and more "network" organizations.

The characteristics of temporary systems, which have potential relevance for the formation of trust, include the following:

1. Participants with diverse skills are assembled by a contractor to enact expertise they already possess.
2. Participants have limited history working together.
3. Participants have limited prospects of working together again in the future.
4. Participants often are part of limited labor pools and overlapping networks.
5. Tasks are often complex and involve interdependent work.
6. Tasks have a deadline.
7. Assigned tasks are nonroutine and not well understood.
8. Assigned tasks are consequential.
9. Continuous interrelating is required to produce an outcome.

To convert the individual expertise of strangers into interdependent work, when the nature of that interrelating and work is not obvious, people must reduce their uncertainty about one another through operations that resemble trust. Interdependent strangers faced with a deadline also face the need to handle issues of vulnerability and risk among themselves. As we will see shortly, people handle these three issues by the ways in which they entrust their fate to others and the way they act when others entrust their fate to them. To trust and be trustworthy, within the limits of a temporary system, means that people have to wade in on trust rather than wait while experience gradually shows who can be trusted and with what: Trust must be conferred presumptively or *ex ante*.

In temporary systems, there is a premium on making do with whatever information is available in advance of close monitoring so that interdependent work is initiated quickly. Swift judgments about trustworthiness can't be avoided, because they enable people to act quickly in the face of uncertainty. People have to make consequential presumptions: no system, no performance. It's as basic as that. Which is not to say it's as simple as that. By no means is this conversion simple. But neither is it slow. To see some of what is involved, we turn next to three quite different accounts of trust, each of which helps us understand better what role trust plays in a temporary system and how that trust develops.

....

On Framing Swift Trust

In this section we examine three definitions of trust and suggest how swift trust might be represented using the imagery of each definition.

Trust and Vulnerability

The first set of definitions comes from Baier (1986). Her first approximation of a definition of trust is "accepted vulnerability to another's possible but not expected ill will (or lack of good will) toward one" (p. 235). Trust, in this view, is defined by two things: (a) the grounds for expecting that others will not take advantage of one's vulnerability and varieties of vulnerabilities and (b) the grounds for expecting that one will not be harmed by those who are entrusted with the valued items, even though they could derive from such diverse sources as the reality of the interdependence, implicit or explicit threats from the truster or from the network in which the activity occurs, norms in the setting, institutional and cultural categories, role clarity, inability of trustee to conceal harm-doing, and prospect of repeated interactions.

Vulnerability is defined in terms of the goods or things one values and whose care one partially entrusts to someone else, who has some discretion over him or her. Because self-sufficiency is rare in interdependent activities, divisions of labor, and complex tasks, vulnerability is common. Goods entrusted include reputations, conversation, health, safety, investments, political position, and music. Some of these goods are "intrinsically shared" (e.g., chamber music, conversation) and some rely on the behavior of others during certain situations (e.g., safety during fire-fighting missions, health during a serious illness). These situations require us to "allow many other people to get into positions where they can, if they choose, injure what we care about, since those are the same positions that they must be in order to help us take care of what we care about" (Baier, 1986, p. 236).

Given these ideas, the challenge is to see if swift trust can be singled out by the unique goods that are entrusted in these situations and/or the unique grounds that are invoked for expecting others to not take advantage of these vulnerabilities. In the case of the Dallas Organization, reputations are entrusted and the realities of task interdependence forestall intentional harm-doing to those reputations. The Dallas Organization forms around a task that cannot be executed by any one person. The organization is assembled by a "contractor" who may be the link pin (Likert) on which trust is focused (each of the 35 people trusts the contractor's selection criteria for the other 34). Thus, the contractor's reputation as much as the reputation of the performers is at stake—if the 35 or any significant subset foul up, future opportunities for the contractor to assemble an organization will dry up. In the Dallas Organization, individuals know that their specialty is crucial *and* worthless without links to other specialties. They also know of the implicit threat imposed on their own reputations if they don't perform. When all of these pieces are combined, they suggest the existence of vulnerabilities (e.g., reputations and outputs are at stake) and significant grounds for expectations of good will (e.g., threats, the reality of interdependence, and prospects for future interactions).

If membership in a temporary system is a one-shot event with little prospect of future interaction, and if there is low dependence on any one project for continuing work, as well as limited diffusion of information about the project outcomes outside the system, then little is at stake reputationally. Vulnerability is low, as is the need for trust. However, as the size of the pool from which members are selected gets smaller, talent becomes thinner, and information about per-formance diffuses more effectively, then reputations become vulnerable. In the words of one studio executive, "If someone in, say, makeup doesn't show up or shows up drunk to the set, they will be dead. They won't work for a very long time" (personal communication, 1993). Also, because the prospect of future interaction among the members within this limited labor pool is relatively high, grounds for expectations that members will not act with ill will increases.

Newcomers with fewer opportunities for work and those on the periphery of a network are more vulnerable than veterans who have more opportunities and are central. Well-positioned, high-status, seasoned individuals have more resili-ent reputations (and are therefore less vulnerable) and can withstand periodic failures or self-centered behaviors. This is a familiar pattern in Hollywood. And people who work in systems tied together by weak ties (acquaintances and contacts) have less control over the diffusion of their reputations and are more vulnerable than those in networks of *strong* ties (friendship and family). Net-works characterized by weak ties should result in wider dissemination of information because networks are less likely to overlap with one another. Here, an implicit threat of significant reputational damage imposed by the nature of the social network increases vulnerability, yet this threat can create the grounds for expecting trustworthy behavior among participants.

In general, we suggest that perceptions of the nature of the network and labor market available for temporary systems can have an impact on the form and incidence of trust in temporary systems through its effects on perceptions of vulnerability. People who are scarce freelance specialists and tied into minimally overlapping networks should perceive their position in temporary systems to be more vulnerable. Their reputation is entrusted to others who can do considerable damage in multiple networks. But in a situation of high interdependence, everyone is comparably vulnerable. Each controls the other's fate and thereby imposes the same threat. Although such a mutual threat may produce wariness, it could also lay the grounds for participants to expect and be receptive to trust and trustworthy behavior. In some temporary systems there is a high need to trust, partly because that is the only viable option. Overtures that address this need, such as short-term promises that are kept (Kouzes & Posner, 1987), should trigger reciprocal behavior.

If we assume that a condition of vulnerability is unsettling and people try to reduce it, then they can do so in one of three ways. First, they can reduce their dependence on others by cultivating alternative partners, projects, and networks. This is a form of "hedge," which we will discuss later. However, that avenue is often blocked, especially for newcomers. Second, because (inter) dependence may be inherent in the nature of the task, the vulnerability can be reduced by cultivating adaptability and the feeling of mastery that "I can handle anything they throw at me" (Faulkner, 1971, p. 136), coupled with "distancing" oneself (Faulkner, 1983, p. 153) from the settings. The feeling of mastery can be a cognitive illusion of sorts, which will also be discussed as a mechanism that can build resilience into the system. Third, one can presume that the other people in the setting are trustworthy. If one acts toward them in a trusting manner, the presumption of trust often acts like a self-fulfilling prophecy and creates the trusting behavior that was presumed to be there (Baier, 1985, chap. 15). The choice among these paths is driven as much by one's own social position, background expectancies generated by the context, and disposition as it is by any characteristics of one's associates. The nature of this choice is one way in which swift trust in temporary systems assumes a distinctive form.

When people in temporary systems entrust important things, such as reputation, to the care of others, they accept the possibility of ill will but usually do not expect it. This suggests that a closer look at the grounds of their expectations may give further clues regarding the shape of trust in temporary systems. We have already seen two possible reasons why people do not expect ill will even though they are vulnerable: implicit threats within the system (e.g., mutual fate control) and the prospect of future interaction. A third reason is role clarity. If people in temporary systems deal with one another more as roles than as individuals—which is likely because the system is built of strangers interacting to meet a deadline—then expectations should be more stable, less capricious, more standardized, and defined more in terms of tasks and specialties than personalities. Moreover, those roles are predicated, in turn, on a stable body of effective principles and practices. As Dawes (1994) noted,

We trust engineers because we trust engineering and believe that engineers are trained to apply valid principles of engineering; moreover, we have evidence everyday that these principles are valid when we observe airplanes flying. We trust doctors because we trust modern medicine, and we have evidence that it works when antibiotics and operations cure people. (p. 24)

What is ironic, if we set the issue of expectations up this way, is that people who enact roles (Fondas & Stewart, 1994) in an innovative, idiosyncratic manner could incur distrust. Because it is harder to draw boundaries around their apparent unpredictability, this could mean that this same unpredictability could extend to how they handle whatever one entrusts to them.

The scenario suggests that an increase in role clarity leads to a decrease in expected ill will, and an increase in trust presumes that roles in temporary systems are clear, that people act toward one another in terms of roles and have a clear understanding of others' roles. Change in any of these three variables should produce a change in trust. Again, we want to underline the general argument. What is often distinctive about temporary systems is that they form among people who represent specialties, and the relating in a temporary system is among roles as much as people. The content of any role description largely excludes expectations of "ill will" and highlights, instead, contributions that can legitimately be expected of the role occupant.

There are, of course, exceptions to this line of argument, and some of the most glaring ones occur in Hollywood. There is role clarity in film production, just as there is in other temporary systems, but with one big difference. The background expectancy among occupations within the industry is often one of expected ill will. Stories of hollow promises and backstabbing characterize the industry, as a conversation (paraphrased) with one Hollywood executive illustrates:

I have lots of friends in the industry, but these are friends because we have something to offer each other. I don't expect anyone to be my friend when things aren't going well or when I stop having something they want. I expect people to backstab me anytime and the only reason they don't is that I could backstab them back. (personal communication, 1993)

If people in Hollywood talk the talk of cooperation but walk the talk of competition and self-interest, then role clarity is a predictable mixture of hyperbole, euphemism, hollow promises, and side bets. Trust of sorts could still develop in this context, but it would require other grounds, such as network-based threats or prospects of future interactions, to mediate the background expectations of ill will. But trust based on mutual expectations of hype is likely to translate into distancing and hesitant interdependence, which means the temporary system is not really much of a system. Dubious credibility is especially likely when high expectations are institutionalized as part of the everyday rhetoric and uttered noncontingently in the context of budgets and deadlines by people who don't know what they are talking about (as one producer said, "Now, since this story is set in France, we should hear lots of French horns," Faulkner, 1983, p. 141). These are the realities of filmmaking.

More generally, expectations of ill will or good will form in temporary systems just as they do in other sites. Because there is insufficient time for these expectations to be built from scratch, they tend to be imported from other settings and imposed quickly in categorical forms. Expectations defined in terms of categories are especially likely because people have little time to size up one another (Fiske & Taylor, 1991). Categories invoked to speed up perception reflect roles, industry recipes, cultural cues, and occupational- and identity-based stereotypes. As Brewer (1981) has noted in her observations of the "minimal group paradigm," social categories, such as those derived from common membership in a social identity group,

can serve as a rule for defining the boundaries of low-risk interpersonal trust that bypasses the need for personal knowledge and the costs of negotiating reciprocity with individual others. As a consequences of shifting from the personal level to the social group level of identity, *the individual can adopt a sort of "depersonalized trust" based on category membership alone.* (p. 356, emphasis added)

These categorization effects appear to be quite robust, emerging even when the basis of social unit formation is arbitrary, transient, and objectively meaningless.

With some exceptions (such as in the film industry and stereotypes of some social identity groups), most social categories invoke expectations of good will rather than ill will from one's associates. Trust (or distrust) in temporary systems can develop swiftly because the expectations that are invoked most quickly tend to be general, task-based, plausible, easy to confirm, and stable, all of which implies that the care of valuable things can be entrusted to individuals who seem to fit these institution-driven categories.

We see that the fate of trust in temporary systems is disproportionately influenced by the context in which the system forms. Context defines vulnerability and expectations. And context affords or withholds the resources that encourage or discourage people from managing their vulnerability, quickly, with overtures of trust. Trust, in response to vulnerability, is mediated by conditions of the labor pool from which the system forms, and trust in response to expectations of ill will is mediated by background expectancies consisting of categorical assumptions and interpretive frames (Zucker, 1986, pp. 57–59) derived from the context of the temporary system.

Before moving to other formulations of trust, we want to highlight the quality of interdependence that may be found in temporary systems. Swift trust in temporary systems seems to flow from the nature and magnitude of the interdependence in the setting and the implicit threat that stems from this interdependence. We suspect that a key variable in temporary systems is the degree to which interdependence is in fact high. So far we have assumed that interdependence is high, which means that vulnerability of any one person is high because that person's contribution and reputation are affected by others, as are their contributions and reputations.

In temporary systems, interdependence is crucial. But it should not be extreme. Variations in interdependence affect the extent to which trust is a big deal. It is our hunch that swift trust occurs when the demands of interdependence are in line with the importance of what is being entrusted and the probability that others will care for what is entrusted with good will. There are no certainties anywhere in these calculations, only implicit probabilities. Modest interdependence leaves actors with sufficient control over their contributions, which means the actors are only moderately vulnerable to associates who probably will not take advantage of those vulnerabilities. That's enough to trigger trust. And to do so quickly. If modest dependence is sufficient, then vulnerability and expectations also will be manageable, as will the amount of trust that must be initiated to tie the setting together.

Trust and Uncertainty

A second portrait of trust is found in Gambetta (1988), who argues that

trusting a person means believing that when offered the chance, he or she is not likely to behave in a way that is damaging to us, and trust will *typically* be relevant when at least one party is free to disappoint the other, free enough to avoid a risky relationship, *and* constrained enough to consider that relationship an attractive option. (p. 219)

For Gambetta, trust is an issue of monitoring, as it often is for economists and game theorists:

Trust (or, symmetrically, distrust) is a particular level of the subjective probability with which an agent assesses that another agent or group of agents will perform a particular action, both *before* he can monitor such action (or independently of his capacity ever to be able to monitor it) *and* in a context in which it affects his own action. (p. 217)

Trust involves an estimation about whether the trustee will do something beneficial or detrimental before the truster can really know for sure. And the estimate itself is focused. It is a

threshold point, located on a probabilistic distribution of more general expectations [expectations expressing such things as the reputation of others], which can take a number of values suspended between complete distrust (0) and complete trust (1), and which is centered [*sic*] around a mid-point (0.50) of uncertainty. (p. 218)

Trust, in other words, is coincident with uncertainty. And uncertainty is coincident with temporary structures enacted to deal with transient events singled out from ongoing change. The uncertainty tends to focus on the ease with which others can disappoint our expectations.

If other people's actions were heavily constrained, the role of trust in governing our decisions would be proportionately smaller, for the more limited people's freedom, the more restricted the field of actions in which we are required to guess *ex ante* the probability of their performing them. (Gambetta, 1988, p. 219)

A ruler of a slave society, for example, only has to trust that slaves are not going to commit mass suicide. As coercion and power diminish from this point, there are more ways in which trustees can disappoint. As the number of different ways in which trustees can disappoint increases (i.e., their freedom of action increases), so too should the probability that one or more of these ways could be activated immediately (e.g., an actor may disappoint in numerous ways—by walking off the movie set, through inattention to the director's suggestions, failure to follow the producer's timetable, or failure to say the writer's scripted lines). Disappointments take varying spans of time to develop. If there is a preponderance of swift, immediate disappointments that could unfold in a relationship, then we would expect to find a more rapid development of trust (or distrust). What we would not expect to see is a postponement of choices involving trust. The open field of actions does not allow that luxury.

Gambetta contributes a simple but important insight to our emerging view of swift trust and temporary systems. Uncertainty on matters of trust is highest when there is a 50–50 chance ("a midpoint of uncertainty") that an unmonitored person will take advantage of our trust. This suggests at least two things. First, it suggests that people should be motivated to avoid the uncertainty of a .50 probability of harm, because this requires monitoring that uses up valuable information-processing capability (Brehmer, 1991, p. 196). In a temporary system with deadlines and specific goals, anything that subtracts from task performance, such as distracted attention, should be a glaring threat. Faced with high uncertainty, people should be inclined either toward complete trust (1) or complete distrust (0), both of which provide more certainty and use up less attention in monitoring. Swift trust, then, might occur when uncertainty is high and unacceptable and when some cues in the setting favor an interpretation of the other as trustworthy rather than as untrustworthy. That is, in an effort to avoid uncertainty, the person is likely to be more trusting or more distrusting than the data warrant, simply in the interest of reducing uncertainty and getting on with the task. Such acts reflect the necessary willingness to suspend doubt. In this way, temporary systems may be suggestible systems.

A second implication of Gambetta's analysis is that if people find it hard to resolve uncertainty quickly with a move toward either unwarranted trust or unwarranted distrust, then we would expect to see more idiosyncratic resolutions of trust uncertainty consistent with personality predispositions and a priori implicit theories of trust. There is widespread agreement that when faced with uncertainty and weak situations, people respond dispositionally. In particular, we would expect that a priori tendencies toward high or low trust (Rotter, 1980) would have a strong impact in determining the pattern of trust to be observed in a temporary system, especially when uncertainty is high. Furthermore, implicit theories of trust should exert more influence. Here we take our lead from Good (1988, p. 33), who argued that "trust is based on an individual's theory as to how another person will perform on some future occasion, as a function of that target person's current and previous claims, either implicit or explicit, as to how they will behave." As uncertainty increases, not only should implicit theories, predispositions, and categorical assumptions be more influential, but people should try more urgently to confirm them.

Thus, to understand swift trust in temporary systems is to appreciate the fact that relative strangers are uncertain caretakers of one's goods, especially when opportunities for early and continuous monitoring of their actions are negligible. To reduce this uncertainty, people fall back on predispositions, categorical assumptions, and implicit theories to move them toward the greater certainty of clear trust or clear distrust. Trust that flows from dispositions, assumptions, and theories is swift because to some extent it occurs independent of the object of perception. An individual's associates in a temporary system function essentially as a pretext to access over-learned tendencies and cognitive structures that provide guidelines for trust or mistrust.

Trust and Risk

The final suggestion of how to conceptualize trust, and by extension how to conceptualize swift trust, is Luhmann's (1988) rich distinction between confidence and trust. Luhmann argues that trust and confidence are different ways of asserting expectations that may lapse into disappointment. Trust and confidence are also different ways in which people gain a sense of self-assurance, or in Gambetta's terms, act in the face of uncertainty.

For Luhmann, trust is about risk, and risk is about the choice to expose oneself to a situation where the possible damage may be greater than the advantage that is sought (p. 98). This stipulation is crucial because, without it, whatever risks one faces are within the acceptable limits of rational choice, and trust plays no part in the decision to proceed. Luhmann alerts us to look more closely at risk in temporary systems.

The close relationship between trust and systems we are trying to work out is anticipated by Luhmann's (1988) observation that "a system requires trust as an input condition in order to stimulate supportive activities in situations of uncertainty or risk" (p. 103). Trust, which is a way people assert expectations, presupposes a situation of risk and the possibility of disappointment, which depends in part on our own previous behavior and choices. Luhmann pulls these strands together this way: Trust "requires a previous engagement on your part. It presupposes a situation of risk." You may or may not buy a used car that turns out to be a "lemon." You may or may not hire a baby-sitter for the evening and leave him or her unsupervised in your apartment; he or she may be a "lemon." You can avoid taking the risk, but only if you are willing to waive the associated advantages. You do not depend on trusting relations in the same way you depend on confidence, but trust also can be a matter of routine and normal behavior. The distinction between confidence and trust thus depends on perception and attribution. If you do not consider alternatives (every morning you leave the house without a weapon!), you are in a situation of confidence. If you choose one action in preference to others in spite of the possibility of being disappointed by the actions of others, you define the situation as one of trust. In the case of confidence, you will react to disappointment by external attribution and alienation. In the case of trust, trusting choice (pp. 97–98). Situations of confidence can turn into situations of trust if it becomes possible to avoid the relationship (p. 98), and trust can change into confidence if people lose their ability to influence the relationship. Trust, therefore, "is an attitude that allows for risk-taking decisions" (p. 103). Without trust, risk is avoided, innovative activities dry up, only routine actions are available for retrospective sensemaking, and uncertainty remains unresolved.

These observations about trust, in general, when adapted for temporary systems, alert us to several issues. To understand trust in temporary systems, one should not overrely on the fact that such systems are short-lived, transient, and fleeting. To do so is to miss the equally important point that in a temporary system, everything is risked, every time. It is rare for risks to be small and for disappointments to be a mere nuisance. Temporary systems form in the context of large risks where the damage incurred could outrun the advantages gained. Trust, rather than rational calculation, is necessary to deal with this imbalance. In film production, for example, the exact nuance needed from an actor may be given only once. If it is missed by the person running the camera, it is missed forever. Sidney Pollack noted that because movies are shot out of sequence, only the director knows where the emotional tone of the picture has to be at the moment any scene is shot. This is what creates the high stakes in the temporary system of film production. Nicholas Kent (1991, p. 170), citing a Pollack remark, shows how small moments can be monumental in filmmaking:

"In film, as opposed to theater, an actor doesn't have to understand at all how they did what they did or why they have to do what they do. You just have to do it once and the camera has to be rolling." The tragedy [for Pollack] is seeing an actor give him what he wants before he can capture the moment on film.

What all of this has to do with trust is that the potential for damaged reputations and failed investments is substantial in temporary systems devoted to filmmaking. This in turn suggests that something more than rational choice is necessary for success in such a system. That something more is trust—trust in the cinematographer, the actor's willingness to take direction, and the executives staying out of the editing suite while the film is being cut.

The more general point we want to make is that "temporary" does not mean "trivial." Typically, the formation of a temporary system signals the unavailability of any existing structure to handle what has become a significant but nonroutine issue that needs a novel set of specialists who can meet a deadline. Failure to handle the issue means big losses for the people who authorize the system and the people who run it. In Luhmann's terminology, the magnitude of potential damage is greater than the potential gain. So trust is an issue right from the start. The moment the system is envisioned, assessments of potential damage figure into its design: "Unless the system is formed things will get worse, but even if it is formed, there are no guarantees that we'll be better off" (Luhmann, 1988, p. 103). The system is formed in spite of these threats, which is itself an exercise of trust because the output could turn out to be a "lemon." The temporary system itself must comprise trust because it faces a future of potential disappointments and unstable collaboration among near strangers.

Luhmann's ideas about risk also point to a different aspect of temporary systems—namely, their preoccupation with action. Swift trust may be a by-product of a highly active, proactive, enthusiastic, generative style of action. This possibility comes about because risks, choices, actions, and trust have an unusual, self-reinforcing character, as suggested earlier. Luhmann puts it this way:

Trust is based on a circular relation between risk and action, both being complementary requirements. Action defines itself in relation to a particular risk as external (future) possibility, although risk at the same time is inherent in action and exists only if the actor chooses to incur the chance of unfortunate consequences and to trust. (1988, p. 100)

To act one's way into an unknown future is to sharpen the element of risk in that projected action, which gives character to the action and substance to the risk. Each creates the necessity for trust, the grounds to validate it, and the potential for invalidation and disappointment. All of this gets triggered basically because forceful action can never guarantee a specific outcome. That's the risk that is made tolerable by trust.

Our point is simply that as action becomes more forceful, the qualities of risk associated with that action become clearer, which then clarifies the action even more and adds to its forcefulness, which further sharpens perceptions of risk, and so on. As these "complementary requirements" build on one another, the person becomes more willing to incur the chance of unfortunate consequences and to trust. The more forceful the action, the greater the willingness to trust and the more rapidly does trust develop. Hence, temporary systems that are high in their capability to generate activity and whose cultures value the generation of activity could, by virtue of these tendencies, also heighten perceptions of risk, the willingness to take risks, and the willingness to trust.

Interweaving Trust and the Temporary

There is no shortage of claims that trust is indispensable to social life. Simmel (1978) is representative:

Without the general trust that people have in each other, society itself would disintegrate, for very few relationships are based entirely upon what is known with certainty about another person, and very few relationships would endure if trust were not as strong as, or stronger than, rational proof or personal observation. (pp. 178–179)

Relative to such abundant and strong claims about the importance of trust, our theories about it remain few and weak. As we said at the beginning of this chapter, our interest here is in the increasingly common collective known as a temporary system in which trust appears to flourish even though its usual antecedents seem to be missing. Having taken a closer look at properties of temporary systems and trust, we feel that trust does appear in temporary systems, but it does so in response to a different set of antecedents than investigators usually examine. Furthermore, because swift trust forms in response to a different set of antecedents, its development is also as different as is its effect on outcomes.

An inquiry into swift trust in temporary systems starts with propositions such as the following ones, which restate themes introduced earlier:

Proposition 1. The smaller the labor pool or network from which personnel in a temporary system is drawn, the more vulnerable the people who are drawn; the stronger the grounds for not expecting harmful behavior, the more rapidly will trust develop among people. The presumption here is that people in a small labor pool have a higher chance of interacting with one another again in the future, which means their reputations as competent or incompetent people whom others can trust or distrust will follow them and shape these future contacts. Reputations are implicitly threatened in any given project to the extent that chances of future interaction increase. In Axelrodian (Axelrod, 1984) terms, the "shadow of the future looms larger" in such groups. However, people in overlapping networks or networks of weak ties may face more reputational vulnerability because a damaged reputation would disseminate across a wider group of people.

Proposition 2. Role-based interaction leads to more rapid development of trust than does person-based interaction. This presumes that role expectations tend to be more stable, less capricious, more standardized, and defined more in terms of tasks and specialties, all of which diminish the anticipation of ill will and help reinforce and sharpen expectations.

Proposition 3. Inconsistent role behavior and "blurring" of roles will lead to a slower build of trust. This presumes that role blurring heightens uncertainty. People who exhibit inconsistent role behavior raise questions about what they will do with whatever is entrusted to them. Attempts to answer these questions slow the development of trust.

Proposition 4. People under time pressure in temporary systems make greater use of category-driven information processing, emphasizing speed and confirmation rather than evidence-driven information processing that is focused on accuracy. The presumption here is that interpersonal perception in temporary systems is subject to the same patterns in a speed-accuracy tradeoff as is perception in other kinds of systems. The time-limited nature of a temporary system tends to be reflected in perceptual tradeoffs that favor speed.

Proposition 5. Category-driven information processing in temporary systems is dominated by institutional categories that are made salient by the context in which the systems form. The presumption here is that categories imported to accelerate interpersonal perception disproportionately reflect local organizational culture, industry recipes, and cultural identity-based stereotypes. These categories affect expectations of good will or ill will and encourage swift trust or swift distrust. In some cases, trust may develop even more swiftly when imported categories also produce behavioral confirmation. When this happens, not only do perceivers look for data that confirm their initial categorization, but their behavior itself increases the likelihood that the target will behave in the manner anticipated. This combination of selective perception and behavioral confirmation produces data relevant to trust more quickly, which means trust itself is enacted sooner.

Proposition 6. Greater reliance on category-driven information processing in temporary systems, with its attendant pressure for confirmation, leads to a faster reduction of the uncertainty associated with trust but to a higher risk that subsequent action will disconfirm the trust and produce damage. The presumption here is that swift trust, especially in response to category-driven perception, overlooks a great deal. Although these oversights leave room for behavioral confirmation and self-fulfilling prophecies, they also allow for actions that disrupt trust (Zucker, 1986, p. 59) and for errors in misplaced trust.

Proposition 7. Swift trust is more likely at moderate levels of interdependence than at either higher or lower levels. The presumption here is that moderate interdependence creates moderate vulnerability, which can be handled with the moderately strong expectations of good will that flow from placement of a trustee in a salient institutional category. People who fit salient categories are to be trusted more so as the degree of trust needed is modest.

At higher levels of interdependence, conformity of action with expectations based on general categories alone is too little data for too high stakes. This combination represents a greater amount of perceived vulnerability than the data can address. Trust will be shaky rather than solid, slow rather than swift, and actions will be tentative rather than firm.

Although this sampler of propositions suggests something of the mind-set necessary to interweave trust and the temporary, it does not direct sufficient attention toward what we regard as a critical ingredient in the emergence and maintenance of swift trust in many temporary groups: the role of the contractor. Below, we focus briefly on the contractor and revisit this role in subsequent sections.

....

The Role of the Contractor in Temporary Systems

In discussing the teamwork necessary for film production crews to function productively, Kawin (1992) notes the following about the director:

Of all the people on the set, the director is the one who ought—who needs—to respect the contributions of every member of the production team. The director provides artistic and practical guidance—in a word, *direction*—for the project. The director's guiding vision can inspire the crew, can give them the sense that they are all working together on a good and worthwhile picture, not just putting in their time and building up their résumés. When a studio executive says "Trust me," there may be something in the voice that suggests piranha in the swimming pool. When a director says "It'll work" and it doesn't—when a stunt kills an actor, to take an extreme example—trust can be forfeited permanently. Most people know not to trust executives who say "Trust me," just as it is difficult to believe someone who keeps saying "To tell you the truth . . . ." But on the set, where time is money, nerves may be frayed, and reputations are at stake, the director and the heads of the production categories must be able to be trusted. (pp. 403–404)

Faulkner (1983) comes at the same setting from the other side when he remarks that the conflicts and uncertainties of filmmaking "are locked into a short-term contracting arrangement which places the filmmaker in a position of dependence on outsiders—freelance specialists—with the attendant risk of having to trust the professional judgments and craft instincts of these employees" (p. 121). Each party in filmmaking is dependent on the other, which creates vulnerability, uncertainty, and risk. The trust necessary to act in the face of vulnerability will be there quickly, depending on the perceptual categories that are imported for sizing up one another and the probability for good or ill will associated with the category. The reputation of the contractor and the expectation of good will on his or her part may be all that is necessary to create the general background expectation of good will, independent of information about the other participants.

....

Swift Trust: Fragile or Resilient?

An analysis that presumes swift trust plays a central role in the life of the temporary group should consider whether such trust is fragile or resilient. To be efficacious, swift trust should be resilient enough to survive those moments and incidents that occur during the life of a temporary group and call into question or threaten to disrupt trust. At the same time, swift trust must not be so resilient as to lead individuals to trust beyond the point where doing so is adaptive or sensible.

Researchers have generally argued that different forms of trust vary considerably in their fragility and resilience. For example, the trust associated with close personal relationships has generally been characterized as a "thick" form of trust that is relatively resilient and durable: Once in place, it is not easily disrupted, and once shattered, it is not easily restored (cf. Janoff-Bulman, 1992; Putnam, 1992). Other forms of trust, in contrast, have been characterized as fragile or "thin" because they are conferred gingerly and withdrawn readily. One might observe this kind of trust in a newly formed exchange relation or collaboration: Expectations are high, but so are reservations. One foot is in the water, but the other is braced firmly on solid ground.

The question of the thickness or thinness of trust that is appropriate in a given social or organizational context raises difficult and also revealing questions about how individuals initially calibrate and update their expectations about others' trustworthiness. With respect to temporary systems, this entails deciding, among other things, when there is a lesson to be learned from a specific experience with another group member and when there isn't. In other words, it includes knowing or deciding when one should suspend or rescind further trust and when one should put aside one's doubts for another day.

Most conceptions of how trust gets developed and updated have emphasized that trust is a history-dependent process (Lindskold, 1978; Rotter, 1980) in which individuals operate like Bayesian statisticians drawing inferences based on relevant but limited samples of experience. Boyle and Bonacich's (1970) characterization is typical: Individuals' "expectations about trustworthy or cooperative behaviors will change in the direction of experience and to a degree proportional to the difference between this experience and the initial expectations applied to them" (p. 130). According to such conceptions, trust builds incrementally and accumulates.

Such perspectives imply that, to the extent it entails expectations about the possible benefits of collaboration, along with attendant fears about vulnerability and exploitation, swift trust should thicken or thin as history unfolds. However, as noted earlier, temporary groups typically lack the requisite history on which such incremental and accumulative confidence-building measures are predicated. There is, quite literally, neither enough time nor opportunity in a temporary group for the sort of experience necessary for thicker forms of trust to emerge. It may be useful to consider, therefore, how history—or, more accurately, substitutes or proxies for history—might contribute to the development of trust in temporary systems.

There is substantial evidence that the "mere" process of group formation alone may provide an initial foundation for the emergence of a protean sort of swift trust. As suggested earlier, even when the basis for group formation appears arbitrary, a presumptive, depersonalized form of trust may emerge (Brewer, 1981).

The existence of such cognitive bases for conferring trust on other group members is augmented, of course, by other psychological mechanisms that reduce perceptions of vulnerability as well as expectations of disappointment in groups. First, and quite obvious, is the simple fact that the formation of a temporary group is neither arbitrary nor meaningless. Individuals enter such groups with a strong and reasonable presumption that the boundary that defines inclusion or exclusion is informative. Inclusion is presumed to imply selectivity on the part of the contractor, and these judgments, in turn, are presumed to be predicated on sensible and more or less conscious criteria.

Here, the credibility of the contractor—in terms of his or her reputation for creating and composing successful temporary groups—serves as a useful substitute for interpersonal history. For example, certain directors such as Woody Allen, John Cassavettes, and Francis Ford Coppola have established strong reputations for assembling remarkable and successful ensemble casts and crews. Based on such reputations, individual actors at the margin are often willing to "sign on" to their films, knowing very little about the concrete details of their projects. They simply trust things to work out.

We suspect further that, on top of whatever reputational capital such directors enjoy, they are skillful at conveying the criteria for inclusion and its legitimacy. In putting together a film crew for the making of *House of Games*, David Mamet chose a cast and crew that consisted only of close friends. Doing so allowed each member of the group to focus on the task at hand and not worry about problems of trust. "That energy (small or large, but inevitable)," he noted, "that is devoted to establishing bona fides in an artistic collaboration between strangers ('How much does this other guy know? Can I trust him, is he going to hurt me?') was in our movie devoted to other things" (cited in Kent, 1991, p. 164). By using such criteria—and using them explicitly—the contractor solves his or her trust dilemma. They also go a long way toward solving the trust dilemma that other group members confront when deciding whether to join a temporary group.

Other psychological mechanisms may help reduce initial perceptions of vulnerability, allowing swift trust to get a toehold. Recent research on positive illusions (Taylor & Brown, 1988), for example, identifies a number of psychological mechanisms that presuppose individuals toward trusting their environments and their experiences. In particular, research on illusions of control and perceived invulnerability suggests that most individuals have in place an array of cognitive strategies that help them maintain confidence that they will be masters rather than victims of their experience. Along similar lines, research on unrealistic optimism (Weinstein, 1980) has shown that individuals often expect their own futures to be significantly better and brighter than others. Even when they view the world as a place in which bad things might happen, they underestimate the likelihood such things will happen to them. Thus, even in a world in which they know trust can be violated, they tend, all else equal, to assume that others will be disappointed and not themselves (cf. Janoff-Bulman, 1992).

Recent research further suggests that these illusions of control, invulnerability, and optimism extend to individuals within group settings. Evidence suggests that individuals enter groups expecting better things to happen to them compared to the average group member. Moreover, they often feel, *ex post*, that they did better and got more from their participation compared to the average other group member (see Paulus, Dzindolet, Poletes, & Camacho, 1993; Polzer, Kramer, & Neale, 1993; Schlenker, Soraci, & McCarthy, 1976). These attributional tendencies should contribute to the resilience of swift trust in a temporary group.

There is also an important sense in which evidence of the reasonableness and appropriateness of swift trust (in terms of positive expectation of benefits and reduced risks from participation) is provided by the actions of the temporary group itself. In a temporary group, people often act *as if* trust were in place. And, because trust behaviors are enacted without hesitation, reciprocally and collectively, they may provide what Cialdini (1993) has termed *social proof* that a particular interpretation of reality is correct. Thus, by observing others acting in a trusting manner, individuals can infer that such a stance is neither foolish nor naive. In this respect, each individual enactment of swift trust in the group, no matter how small, contributes to the collective perception that swift trust is reasonable. In this sense, the individuals in the temporary group, especially early in its life, when expectations are still fragile and forming, resemble the bystanders at the scene of an emergency who look around at the impassive faces of other bystanders and decide not to act because the others act as if there is no emergency (Darley & Latane, 1968). This cognitive process serves as another trigger to self-fulfilling cycles that further increase the resiliency of swift trust.

These psychological orientations and social mechanisms are well-known and do not provide special insight into the dynamics of swift trust in temporary systems, other than to suggest the readiness with which individuals might be predisposed toward conferring trust swiftly, on relatively minimal grounds, and setting off cycles that build trust. There are, however, other bases for swift trust.

First, although the members of a temporary group may lack history with respect to previous contact with each other, there is a sense in which the temporary group itself is not without history. As suggested earlier, there is a collective presumption that each member's inclusion in the group is predicated on a rich and relevant history. Each member assumes that the contractor has either had the requisite experience with others, or, at the very least, that he or she has "asked around" and "checked them out." Thus, trust in the contractor's presumed care in composing the temporary group serves as a proxy for individual knowledge or experience with others' reliability or competence. In this sense, the relevant history of the temporary group resides outside the group: It is tacitly understood by all group members that the necessary experience and learning were gained elsewhere but are nonetheless in place and do not need to be verified or negotiated.

In this regard, the contractor's reputation for putting together the "right kind" of group to get the work of the temporary group done is similar in function to the sorts of institutional mechanisms, such as board certifications and professional degrees, that enhance trust in various professional encounters (Zucker, 1986). For example, we trust board-certified medical specialists because certification signals professional competence, as judged by other competent specialists. Such reputational proxies are quite effective in professional encounters and within industries such as filmmaking in that individuals are often willing to commit to joining a temporary group, knowing very little about what they are getting into and relying only on the judgment of another professional.[4]

Hedges also play an important role in the development and maintenance of swift trust. The aim of a hedge is to reduce the perceived risks and vulnerabilities of trust by reducing interdependence and thus its perceived costs. Hedges guard against or minimize the dangers of misplaced trust, when, in Baier's terms, the goods are of high value. Hedges imply an attitude that is somewhat equivocal: One trusts the other, but not completely. The existence of a hedge allows one to enter into a risky activity because the "worst-case" outcome is anticipated and covered. In this respect, hedges function much like the Best Alternative to a Negotiated Agreement (BATNA) in a negotiation. BATNAs free negotiators to press their case because they reduce the perceived downside should bargaining fail. The "backup" job offer has the same liberating effect in a job interview when it comes to pressing one's demand for a better salary.[5]

As a cognitive process, hedging entails the creation of psychological "failsafe" mechanisms that provide reassurance, reducing dependence and vulnerability to a moderate level. The posture of hedging is reflected in Weick and Roberts's (1993) observation, based on their research on accidents in flight operations off nuclear carriers, that people who avoid accidents in such situations live by the credo, "Never get into anything without making sure you have a way out" (p. 640). Having a way out allows one to act in a trusting manner because there is a way out. A simple example illustrates this approach. Most people would be very reluctant to trust someone with the sole copy of a manuscript. Creating a backup of the manuscript as a hedge enables one to trust others, even others with whom people have had little or no prior experience. Hedges imply an orientation that resembles the attitude of wisdom described by Meacham (1983) as a stance of simultaneously believing and doubting, understanding and questioning.

This initial trusting behavior can set off a familiar cycle in which trust becomes mutual and reinforcing: Trust allows one to engage in certain behaviors, and these behaviors, in turn, reinforce and strengthen members' trust in each other. There is, of course, a functional irony here in that hedges, which represent acts of partial distrust, allow cycles that enact and reinforce trust within groups to get started.

Although we view hedges as contributing significantly to the resilience of swift trust, we should note that the process of hedging is not without its own risks and disadvantages. First, if others discover that what they initially believed was an act of trust was, in actuality, predicated on a hedge or an act of partial distrust, the self-reinforcing cycle we described earlier may be undermined. In this respect, contractors and others who acquire a reputation for playing it *too* safe by covering all of their bases, including always having a backup, may not inspire much trust at all. Second, having a hedge may sometimes reduce or diminish commitment to the group. When the going gets a little rough, those with attractive alternatives may decide to act on them and go elsewhere. Hedged trust may be abandoned too readily precisely because it *can* be abandoned. This is the intuition behind behavioral self-management strategies that posit that decision makers who want to maximize their commitment to a course of action should "burn their bridges" so that retreat from commitment is not possible (see Schelling, 1984).

Additionally, hedges may contribute to a false sense of invulnerability and security by fostering an exaggerated confidence in one's ability to manage whatever problems are encountered during the life of the temporary group. If perceived risk and vulnerability decrease sufficiently, according to Luhmann, one becomes confident (and sometimes overconfident) and need not rely on trust. As Steven Bach's (1985) account of the making of the film *Heaven's Gate* documents, decision makers who *think* they have control over all of their risks and vulnerabilities may fail to protect themselves or question their confidence when it would be appropriate. Steven Bach and David Field, studio executives, continually underestimated their dependence on director Michael Cimino, thinking they could, at any time, call his bluff. They therefore felt inappropriately secure because they failed to realize the full extent to which they were, in fact, unable to control Cimino. Thus, their *perceived* hedge was not really a hedge at all.

Another potential danger associated with hedging is perhaps less obvious. The process of creating hedges requires anticipatory ruminations about things that might go wrong. Although intended as an adaptive form of preemptive pessimism (cf. Norem & Cantor, 1986), there is evidence that the cognitive strategy of engaging in such "worse-case" thinking can lead to unintended effects, such as unrealistically diminished expectations (e.g., see Kramer, 1994; Kramer, Meyerson, & Davis, 1990).

We have described several cognitive and social processes that contribute to the development of swift trust. The question of the fragility or resilience of swift trust also entails, however, questions about how trust is sustained throughout the life of the temporary group. Groups that have clear expectations and stable role systems would seem less vulnerable to problems of disruption of trust than those lacking such clarity and stability. However, by their very nature, the relatively "thin" expectations and role systems associated with the temporary group almost inevitably must lapse or break down on occasion. In temporary groups, such as filmmaking groups on location, many things happen or fail to happen, and they do so quickly and often. For this reason, we suspect that collective trust may be more resilient within those temporary groups in which members are skilled in the art and *attitude* of improvisation. The attitude of improvisation requires careful attention, listening, and mutual respect. In other words, truly competent role performance of the sort we have associated with behavior in temporary groups often entails doing something different when something different has to be done.

Although our argument here may seem somewhat tautological (i.e., swift trust allows for improvisation, which in turn predicts swift trust), our observation may be more revealing of a double interact than faulty logic. As Putnam (1992) noted, trust not only "lubricates cooperation," but "cooperation itself breeds trust" (p. 171). This "steady accumulation of social capital" plays a central role in the maintenance of collective trust.

Temporary systems engaged in filmmaking illustrate this point nicely. The ability of the director, cinematographer, lighting technicians, and others to improvise inspires confidence that unexpected but unavoidable setbacks, difficulties, and crises are surmountable and survivable. Examples of this dynamic abound in filmmaking lore, and Robert Altman, Francis Ford Coppola, and Steve Spielberg are among those reputed to have especially keen improvisational skills (and, equally important, skill at eliciting improvisations from others when needed!). For example, during the filming of *Raiders of the Lost Ark*, director Steven Spielberg had planned a marvelous fight scene between the whip-wielding Indiana Jones (played by Harrison Ford) and an Arabian swordsman (recounted in Taylor, 1992). He had carefully scripted this scene to be the best sword fight ever, "the most definitive whip versus sword fight in cinematic history" (p. 107). When the time came to shoot the scene on location in Tunisia, both Spielberg and Ford were suffering from heat exhaustion. In addition, Ford had developed gastroenteritis and was not up to the arduous physical demands of the proposed scene. On the spot, they improvised a scene in which Indiana Jones, confronted by the swordsman, simply pulls out his gun and shoots the swordsman. What was to become one of the most memorable scenes in the film was entirely improvised. The ability and *willingness* of the director to retreat from his original vision and discover a superior one, we suggest, can inspire a powerful kind of collective trust that things will work out, especially when they have to.

Another feature of temporary groups, we argue, may contribute to the maintenance of swift trust—a structural feature that, a priori, one might argue would hinder it. This is the constrained time a temporary group has to do its work. The pace at which activity unfolds in many temporary groups and the required focus of attention on the task at hand may obviate the chance for certain kinds of dysfunctional group dynamics to occur. Because time is short and concentration is crucial, there may be less opportunity in temporary groups for the kinds of corrosive interpersonal and group dynamics that often plague more enduring groups. All of the messy things that go along with "thicker" interpersonal relationships (conflicts, jealousy, misunderstandings, hurt feelings, revenge fantasies, and pursuit of hidden agendas) have less opportunity to surface and play themselves out in the life cycle of temporary social systems. There is simply not enough time for things to go wrong. In contrast, groups that have more time for their tasks also have more time to develop complex relations that could go sour. Thus, the bounded life of the temporary group may make the mind concentrate on the task at hand and thereby keep interpersonal relations out of trouble.

Because swift trust is often centered around and bounded by trust in each individual's competent and faithful enactment of a critical *role*, out-of-role behavior can breed distrust. Individuals' expectations surrounding their own and others' behavior in temporary groups, as we noted earlier, are predicated on what Barber (1983) has characterized as a form of fiduciary trust. The "expectation of technically competent role performance for those involved with us in social relationships and systems," he observes, reflects an "expectation that partners in interaction will carry out their duties" (p. 9). In this sense, the act of conferring swift trust entails rendering judgments more about other individuals' professionalism than their character. Deviations from or violations of group norms and presumptions about competent role behavior call into question the "professionalism" of the transgressor. Not only are they noted and frowned on, but they are likely to be punished.

Again, we suspect the contractor may play an important role here in being not only the architect and facilitator of swift trust but also its centurion. In talking about the highly effective and cohesive film production team he had put together, Alan Ladd, Jr. noted, "When it's your money, and someone isn't performing, you get rid of them, no matter how much you like them; you've got a responsibility to others, including yourself, and you can't afford to let a ship sink because one person can't pull his or her weight" (quoted in Barsh, 1982, p. 19). A contractor must be cooperative and forgiving but also provocable (Axelrod, 1984).

The net result of all of this is that, in an odd sort of way, the very lack of time, along with the collective impatience for lapses in role performance it necessitates, may work in favor of the temporary group's mission. Although such factors may hinder the development of thicker forms of trust, they may sustain swift trust.

As we have tried to suggest in this section, the development and maintenance of trust in temporary groups depend on a variety of subtle psychological processes and social mechanisms. To the extent that such factors operate convergently, swift trust is overly determined. In this regard, swift trust may be subtle, but it also may be rather resilient.

Conclusion

Our analysis suggests a rather rich and complex phenomenology associated with trust in temporary systems. In closing, we should note that what may be most distinctive about swift trust in temporary systems is that it is not so much an interpersonal form as it is a cognitive and action form. Trust work, in the preceding analyses, largely was tied to the level of interdependence. We suggested that swift trust is most likely when interdependence is kept modest through a combination of distancing, adaptability, resilience, interacting with roles rather than personalities, and viewing one's participation as partly voluntary (trust) and partly involuntary (confidence). In short, swift trust is less about relating than *doing*.

The portrait we have drawn of swift trust in temporary systems may be a little too "cool" for some people's taste. There is less emphasis on feeling, commitment, and exchange and more on action, cognition, the nature of the network and labor pool, and avoidance of personal disclosure, contextual cues, modest dependency, and heavy absorption in the task. That's what seems to give swift trust its distinctive quality. Swift trust is not surrender. But neither is it calculated aloofness. Instead, it is artful making do with a modest set of general cues from which inferences are drawn about how people might care for what we entrust to them. Those inferences are driven by generic features of the setting rather than by personalities or interpersonal relations. In this sense, swift trust is a pragmatic strategy for dealing with the uncertainties generated by a complex system concocted to perform a complex, interdependent task using the specialized skills of relative strangers. Given those complexities, unless one trusts quickly, one may never trust at all.

Ultimately, of course, knowing when to confer trust quickly, and when to withhold or withdraw it, may be crucial to the success of the temporary system.

Acknowledgement

We gratefully acknowledge comments and suggestions provided by Joel Brockner, Robert Cialdini, Jim March, Joel Podolny, Gene Webb, and Mayer Zald at various stages in the writing of this chapter. An earlier version of this work was presented at the conference on trust in organizations held at the Graduate School of Business Stanford University May 14–15 1994.

....

Notes

1. So much so that Robert Cialdini (personal communication, 1994) suggested that the form of trust-like behavior observed in temporary groups might more accurately be characterized as a sort of pseudo-trust or "trustoid" behavior. This is a provocative suggestion. However, for reasons that will become more obvious as our analysis unfolds, we regard trust in temporary groups as a very real form of trust and not merely trust-like.

2. Somewhat unexpected as a characteristic of such systems is the high probability that experience in temporary systems may *not* promote professional growth and learning and may, in fact, slow career progress. Because people are selected to apply their special knowledge to a specific problem, they tend to be selected "for their current capabilities rather than for any learning value the assignment may have for them" (Goodman & Goodman, 1976, p. 496). Repetition of what people already know is especially likely when the temporary system functions with a structure of clarified roles in which specialties interact with specialties. This contrasts with a system in which people interact, at least for some portion of the time, on the basis of blurred roles or changing expectations. High role clarity and stability of expectations are associated with an adequate performance that tends to be low on innovation and individual learning. A move toward more blurred roles, as when members interact in a manner more like Likert's participative system four (Goodman, 1981, pp. 7, 135; Goodman & Goodman, 1976, pp. 499–500), produces more innovation and learning.

3. There are a variety of spontaneous or "ephemeral" organizations and groups, such as improvisational jazz ensembles or pick-up basketball teams, in which swift trust seems to play an important role (Eisenberg, 1990; Lanzara, 1983; Weick, 1990; Weick & Roberts, 1993). However, we wish to focus in this chapter on temporary groups whose products or outputs are more consequential.

4. There is irony and danger here. As March (1994) notes, those who rise to positions of leadership, such as contractors, may do so on a history of accidental successes that, although giving themselves and others a sense of confidence, is predicated at best on shaky evidence and ambiguous performance.

5. There is an important asymmetry here, of course, in that most group members probably prefer that they have good alternatives in place themselves while preferring that others *don't*. They want others to have no choice but be *really* committed, and they prefer to hedge our own bets.

References

Axelrod, R. (1984). *The evolution of cooperation.* New York: Basic Books.

Bach, S. (1985). *Final cut: Dreams and disaster in the making of* Heaven's Gate. Beverly Hills, CA: Sage.

Baier, A. (1985). *Postures of the mind.* Minneapolis: University of Minnesota.

Baier, A. (1986). Trust and antitrust. *Ethics, 96,* 231–260.

Barber, B. (1983). *The logic and limits of trust.* New Brunswick, NJ: Rutgers University Press.

Barsh, J. (1982). *The Ladd company* (Harvard Business School Case 9-482-122). Boston: Harvard Business School Press.

Boyle, R., & Bonacich, P. (1970). The development of trust and mistrust in mixed-motive games. *Sociometry, 33,* 123–139.

Brehmer, B. (1991). Modern information technology: Timescales and distributed decision making. In J. Rasmussen, B. Brehmer, & J. Leplot (Eds.), *Distributed decision making: Cognitive models for cooperative work* (pp. 193–200). Chichester, UK: Wiley.

Brewer, M. B. (1981). Ethnocentrism and its role in interpersonal trust. In M. B. Brewer & B. E. Collins (Eds.), *Scientific inquiry and the social sciences.* San Francisco: Jossey-Bass.

Burns, T., & Stalker, G. M. (1961). *The management of innovation.* London: Tavistock.

Cialdini, R. (1993). *Influence.* New York: Morrow.

Clark, R. E., & Halford, L. (1980). Reducing uncertainty and building trust: The special case of auctions. In S. Fiddle (Ed.), *Uncertainty: Behavioral and social dimensions* (pp. 305–322). New York: Praeger.

Darley, J. M., & Latane, B. (1968). Bystander intervention in emergencies: Diffusion of responsibility. *Journal of Personality and Social Psychology, 8,* 377–383.

Dawes, R. M. (1994). *House of cards: Psychology and psychotherapy built on myth.* New York: Free Press.

Eccles, R. G., & Crane, D. B. (1988). *Doing deals.* Boston: Harvard Business School Press.

Eisenberg, E. M. (1990). Jamming! Transcendence through organizing. *Communication Research, 17,* 139–164.

Faulkner, R. R. (1971). *Hollywood studio musicians.* Chicago: Aldine.

Faulkner, R. R. (1983). *Music on demand.* New Brunswick, NJ: Transaction Books.

Fiske, S. T., & Taylor, S. F. (1991). *Social cognition* (2nd ed.). New York: McGraw-Hill.

Fondas, N., & Stewart, R. (1994). Enactment in managerial jobs: A role analysis. *Journal of Management Studies, 31,* 83–103.

Gaddy, C. D., & Wachtel, J. A. (1992). Team skills training in nuclear power plant operations. In R. W. Swezey & E. Salas (Eds.), *Teams: Their training and performance* (pp. 379–396). Norwood, NJ: Ablex.

Gambetta, D. (1988). Can we trust trust? In D. Gambetta (Ed.), *Trust: Making and breaking cooperative relationships* (pp. 213–237). Oxford, UK: Basil Blackwell.

Good, D. (1988). Individuals, interpersonal relations, and trust. In D. Gambetta (Ed.), *Trust: Making and breaking cooperative relations* (pp. 31–48). Oxford, UK: Basil Blackwell.

Goodman, L. P., & Goodman, R. A. (1972). Theater as a temporary system. *California Management Review, 15*(2), 103–108.

Goodman, R. A. (1981). *Temporary systems.* New York: Praeger.

Goodman, R. A., & Goodman L. P. (1976). Some management issues in temporary systems: A study of professional development and manpower—The theatre case. *Administrative Science Quarterly, 21*, 494–501.

Janoff-Bulman, R. (1992). *Shattered assumptions: Towards a new psychology of trauma.* New York: Free Press.

Kanter, R. M. (1989). *When giants learn to dance.* New York: Simon & Schuster.

Kawin, B. F. (1992). *How movies work.* Berkeley: University of California Press.

Kent, N. (1991). *Naked power: Money and power in the movies today.* New York: St. Martin's Press.

Klein, G. A. (1993). A recognition-primed decision (RPD) model of rapid decision making. In G. A. Klein, J. Orasanu, R. Calderwood, & C. E. Zsambok (Eds.), *Decision making in action Models and methods* (pp. 138–147). Norwood, NJ: Ablex.

Kouzes, J. M., & Posner, B. Z. (1987). *The leadership challenge.* San Francisco: Jossey-Bass.

Kramer, R. M. (1994). The sinister attribution error: Paranoid cognition and collective distrust in organizations. *Motivation and Emotion, 18*, 199–230.

Kramer, R. M., Meyerson, D., & Davis, G. (1990). How much is enough? Psychological components of "guns versus butter" decisions in a security dilemma. *Journal of Personality and Social Psychology, 58*, 984–993.

Lanzara, G. F. (1983). Ephemeral organizations in extreme environments: Emergence, strategy, extinction. *Journal of Management Studies, 20*, 71–95.

Lindskold, S. (1978). Trust development, the GRIT proposal, and the effects of conciliatory acts on conflict and cooperation. *Psychological Bulletin, 85*, 772–793.

Luhmann, N. (1988). Familiarity, confidence, trust: Problems and alternatives. In D. Gambetta (Ed.), *Trust: Making and breaking cooperative relations* (pp. 94–108). Oxford, UK: Basil Blackwell.

March, J. G. (1994). *A primer on decision making.* New York: Free Press.

Meacham, J. A. (1983). Wisdom and the context of knowledge: Knowing that one doesn't know *Contributions in Human Development, 8*, 111–134.

Mellinger, W. M. (1994). Negotiated orders: The negotiation of directives in paramedic-nurse interaction. *Symbolic Interaction, 17*(2), 165–185.

Norem, J. K., & Cantor, N. (1986). Defensive pessimism: Harnessing anxiety as motivation. *Journal of Personality and Social Psychology, 51*, 1208–1217.

Orr, J. E. (1990). Sharing knowledge, celebrating identity: Community memory in a service culture. In D. Middleton & D. Edwards (Eds.), *Collective remembering* (pp. 169–189). London: Sage.

Paulus, P. B., Dzindolet, M. T., Poletes, G., & Camacho, L. M. (1993). Perception of performance in group brainstorming: The illusion of group productivity. *Personality and Social Psychology Bulletin, 19*, 78–89.

Debra Meyerson et al.

Peters, T. (1992). *Liberation management*. New York: Knopf.

Polzer, J., Kramer, R. M., & Neale, M. (1993). *Individual and group illusions: Antecedents and consequences*. Unpublished manuscript.

Putnam, R. (1992). *Making democracy work*. Princeton, NJ: Princeton University Press.

Schelling, T. C. (1984). The intimate contest for self-command. In T. C. Schelling (Ed.), *Choice and consequence*. Cambridge, MA: Harvard University Press.

Schlenker, B. R., Soraci, S., & McCarthy, B. (1976). Self-esteem and group performance as determinants of egocentric perceptions in cooperative groups. *Human Relations, 29*, 1163–1176.

Rotter, J. B. (1980). Interpersonal trust, trustworthiness, and gullibility. *American Psychologist, 35*, 1–7.

Simmel, G. (1978). *The philosophy of money*. Boston: Routledge & Kegan Paul.

Suczek, B., & Fagerhaugh, S. (1991). AIDS and outreach work. In D. R. Maines (Ed.), *Social organization and process* (pp. 159–173). New York: Aldine De Gruyter.

Taylor, P. M. (1992). *Steven Spielberg*. New York: Continuum.

Taylor, S. E. (1989). *Positive illusions: Creative self-deception and the healthy mind*. New York: Basic Books.

Taylor, S. E., & Brown, J. D. (1988). Illusion and well-being: A social psychological perspective on mental health. *Psychological Bulletin, 103*, 193–210.

Thompson, J. D. (1967). *Organizations in action*. New York: McGraw-Hill.

Weick, K. E. (1993). Collective mind in organizations: Heedful interrelating on flight decks. *Administrative Science Quarterly, 38*, 357–381.

Weick, K. E., & Roberts, K. H. (1993). Collective mind in organizations: Heedful interrelating on flight decks. *Administrative Science Quarterly, 38*, 357–381.

Weiner, E. L., Kanki, B. G., & Helmreich, R. L. (Eds.), (1993). *Cockpit resource management*. San Diego: Academic Press.

Weinstein, N. D. (1980). Unrealistic optimism about future life events. *Journal of Personality and Social Psychology, 39*, 806–820.

Zucker, L. G. (1986). Production of trust: Institutional sources of economic structure, 1840–1920. In B. M. Staw & L. L. Cummings (Eds.), *Research in organizational behavior* (Vol. 8, pp. 53–111). Greenwich, CT: JAI.

15

Trust, Power, and Control in Trans-Organizational Relations

Reinhard Bachmann

Introduction

Today, a majority of practitioners and academic observers seem to agree that specific forms of long-term oriented co-operation between—in formal terms—independent forms imply important advantages which would neither occur simply on the basis of purely opportunistic behavior and short-term orientations nor would they arise from structures of central control and organizational integration. In the organizational and management literature of the past 15 years or so, many successful inter-firm relationships are described as being based on a *hybrid* form of co-operation where business partners are "neither friends nor strangers" (Lorenz 1988) and where the structure and quality of relations are constituted somewhere "between market and hierarchy" (Williamson 1985). "Strategic alliances" (Jarillo 1988; Child and Faulkner 1998) and "organizational networks" (Miles and Snow 1986; Sydow et al. 1995; Ebers 1997) are increasingly seen as a very promising form of trans-organizational relationships. The various reasons given for this view are built on the argument that this approach provides a balance between competition and co-operation and can avoid the primacy of one of these principles over the other (Dei Ottati 1994). It can, on the one hand, be conducive to reducing costs through specialization and competition. On the other hand, long-term oriented relationships allow for mutual flexibility, the joint use of technical and economic know-how as well as a collective bearing of risks associated with technological innovation (Loasby 1994). The possible problems connected to *hybrid* relations, such as the increased vulnerability of individual organizations or possible mutual blockages between them, particularly when fast decisions are needed, obviously rate low compared to the possible advantages, and are often altogether ignored in the literature.

Undoubtedly, the trend towards the establishment of close- and long-term oriented external relationships is strong and has also been confirmed by many contributions which in recent years discussed the characteristics of the system of inter-firm relations in Japan. Primarily drawing on the automobile and the electronics industry, the patterns of "obligational contracting" (Sako 1992) were viewed as the seed-bed of economic success and it was found that management in Europe and in North America were keen either to imitate Japanese business practices or to develop similar concepts on their own (e.g. Ackroyd et al. 1988; Oliver and Wilkinson 1988; Morris and Imrie 1992). Furthermore, the literature on so-called "industrial districts" (e.g. Keeble and Weever 1986; Sengenberger et al. 1990) has explained the economic success of geographical regions such as Baden-Württemberg and the Emilia Romagna by the long-term orientations which prevail in the relations between the predominantly small and medium-sized enterprises (SMEs) of these regions. Despite the fact that some of the prime examples referred to in this context lost part of their economic dynamism in the early 1990s, the thrust of the argument of several strands of organizational and socio-economic literature is unmistakable. Largely irrespective of the sector under review, there is a worldwide trend towards stable and tightly woven trans-organizational relations, both in vertical and horizontal co-operations. At the same time, short-term oriented opportunism, as one extreme, and complete organizational integration and central control, as the other, seem to have forfeited much of the attractiveness which they had in previous times. Obviously, the chances associated with *hybrid* forms of co-operation today are generally deemed much greater than the risk of buying-in the possibly detrimental side-affects of such relations.

Against the background of this observation, the issue of trust has moved centre-stage in many contributions to the analysis of trans-organizational economic activities. Under current macro-economic developments, trust is seen as becoming the central mechanism to allow for an efficient solution of the problem of co-ordinating expectations and interactions between economic actors. While hierarchical relations are mainly controlled by bureaucratic procedures and top-down mechanisms of co-ordinating interactions, market relationships between anonymous buyers and sellers are based on the idea that economic actors simply use their individual resources and market power to follow their idiosyncratic interests, irrespective of what damage they might impose upon others. In both cases, trust may play *some* role as a useful lubricant in avoiding extreme tensions, but only *hybrid* forms of co-ordinating interactions are seen as being based on trust as the *central* mode of controlling them. In other words, this—and only this—form of co-ordinating and controlling the structure and dynamics of relationships is constitutively dependent on the existence of a considerable amount of trust among economic actors. Thus, it is not by accident that, with the trend towards *hybrid* forms of co-operation, trust has been recognized as an extremely important mechanism in business relationships, although this does not mean that its potential as well as its risks are particularly well understood.

In recent years an impressive number of articles has been published which analyze specific empirical cases and suggest various classifications of trust such as "contractual trust" vs. "competence trust" vs. "goodwill trust" (Sako 1992) or "calculus-based trust" vs. "knowledge-based trust" vs. "identification-based trust" (Lewicki and Bunker 1995) (for an instructive overview of currently available classifications: see Möllering 1998). However, it is doubtful whether these classification schemes lead very far in coming to grips with the phenomenon itself. They can probably only be taken as a confirmation that trust has been recognized by many scholars as one of the most central issues when the structure and quality of relationships within and—particularly—between organizations are under consideration. Fruitful conceptual approaches to develop a deeper theoretical understanding of the phenomenon of trust are still very rare (for exceptions see Lane and Bachmann 1996 connecting to ideas developed by Niklas Luhmann within the theoretical paradigm of Systems Theory, and Sydow 1998 who draws heavily on Anthony Giddens' Structuration Theory) and much theoretical input is still needed to understand fully how trust works as a governance mechanism and what function it can fulfil in co-ordinating expectations and interactions within trans-organizational relationships.

Large parts of the existing literature on trust building on wider political and philosophical aspirations are inspired by a *harmonic vision* and the deep desire to see benevolence and altruism prevail in social relationships between economic actors. From their perspective, the growing importance of trust indicates that, after all, business relationships can transcend the Hobbesian state of *homo homini lupus*. It is even argued that capitalism might be seriously undermined by the increasing relevance of "socially-oriented trust" (Lyons and Mehta 1997) and the capitalist system might even collapse one day, due to an overdose of trust (Adler 1998). In contrast, critical analysts oriented towards a Marxist research perspective developed within the context of the Labour Process Debate of the 1970s (Braverman 1974) emphatically reject this view and argue that trust is simply a particularly sophisticated tool to exert power on weaker business partners (Knights and Willmott 1990; Bieber and Sauer 1991; Rainnie 1993; Sauer and Döhl 1994). Thus, it is argued, trust will help to sub-ordinate the business behavior of individuals under the imperatives of capitalism, rather than questioning them. Close and stable relations between independent buyer and supplier firms, for instance, are seen as allowing the stronger part—usually the bigger buyer firm—to minimize uncertainty within their environment and to systematically shift risk to the weaker side—usually the smaller supplier firm. The stronger the position of the firm, the argument goes, the easier it is for their management to "trust" business partners.

Both of these approaches mark the extreme ends of the mainstream of the current theoretical debate on trust, but none of them digs deeply enough into the complex social processes determining the logic of inter-firm relationships. Doing so would mean analyzing tensions and contradictions within and between the concepts of trust and power, rather than competing for the most simple explanation of the socio-economic world. The increased attractiveness of *hybrid* forms of co-operation, where trust plays a central role in the co-ordination of interactions, is neither fully explained by pointing to the pragmatic advantages such as pooling risks and resources etc., nor is it simply based on an ideology. It also appears to reflect a severe and deep-seated paradox to which firms are struggling to adapt their current strategies. Fierce competition, on the one hand, destroys trust which only seemed to be affordable "in the old days" while, on the other hand, trust-based relations with closely collaborating suppliers, customers and business partners seem to become more and more the most important resource for survival in the shark tank of contemporary capitalist competition.

Conventional economic theory, as is recognized widely today, is equally unlikely to provide a significant input in a theoretically informed and, at the same time, practically usable understanding of these issues. The argument which, for instance, is offered by Transaction Cost Economics (Williamson 1985), namely that the decision as to whether trust is invested in a relationship depends on "asset specificity" and is driven by the idea of reducing the costly effects of opportunistic behavior, seems too simple to explain recent economic developments and strategies. Even less capable of comprehending the complexity of trans-organizational relationships in terms of trust and power are other approaches within current economic theory. Game Theory (Axelrod 1990), for example, is based on the counter-factual assumption that actors' behavior is exclusively driven by calculation. This is not only an extremely simplified view of the socio-economic world but—no matter whether this is meant to be a heuristic device or an empirically testable hypothesis—from the beginning, it places itself much too far beyond the terrain of realistic empirical research perspectives.

This chapter will avoid such simplifications and will develop a conceptual argument which—in its main thrust—aims at overcoming the deficits of conventional economic theory. It suggests a more realistic understanding of economic behavior and a much wider analytical focus. In doing so, it will dig into basic *sociological theory* which will be necessary to gain a deeper understanding of trust and power as *social control mechanisms* in business relationships. To analyze the preconditions and consequences of economic decisions and interactions, a variety of different social factors which easily may come into conflict with each other, rather than a single abstract principle, are assumed to be relevant in constituting the qualitative aspects of trans-organizational relationships.

On the basis of this insight, the second section of this article will be concerned with a conceptual analysis of trust drawing on Systems Theory (Luhmann) as well as on several other strands of basic sociological theory (Structuration Theory, New Institutionalism and—with much more critical reservation—Rational Choice). In this context, power as a similar mechanism to co-ordinate and to control trans-organizational relations, will also be looked at and compared to trust with regard to the social functions both mechanisms can fulfil. With reference to the country-specific conditions of the social governance of inter-firm relationships, Germany and Britain will then be discussed (third section) as quite distinct examples of different modes of producing co-operation and controlling the dynamics of economic interactions. In this section, it will be demonstrated how the quality of trans-organizational relationships emerges in a dialectic process which involves the constitution of specific forms of trust and power. The concluding part of this article (fourth section) will check whether the proposed combination of sociological theory and comparative empirical studies in the institutional structure of business systems can be deemed an innovative and fruitful approach to reveal the social processes which constitute the quality of trans-organizational relations, as well as the functions that trust and power fulfil within this process.

....

Theoretical Considerations

Trust as a Means for Coping with Uncertainty

Luhmann's analysis of the origin and social function of trust starts with a mind experiment. Imagine a world in a—so to speak—*state of nature* which, in social terms, is completely unstructured and thus must appear ultimately complex to the individuals who inhabit it. This world cannot be described as a social system which is differentiated from its environment as it has no specific features or any form of internal organization. Within this world every conceivable action or reaction can be expected from any other actor, and thus it seems unlikely that two (or more) actors will actually manage to establish any kind of interactive process. On the basis of these conditions, social actors are confronted with a severe problem which they have little chance of solving. As the future behavior of other actors with whom they might want to interact is completely contingent, an unlimited number of possible (re-)actions would need to be taken into account which would simply exceed their psychological capacities. In this situation, no selection of likely (vs. unlikely) possibilities can be made, as the whole world appears uncertain and—in this sense—too complex for social actors to allow for any co-ordination of expectations and interactions (Luhmann 1979).

Of course, the *real* social world has little in common with this imagined world. Within the real world social actors obviously do cope with the problem of co-ordinating their interactions. From this observation Luhmann concludes that within the real social world there must be mechanisms at work which reduce uncertainty and complexity, and thus allow for expectations about other social actors' future behavior. Using a Kantian expression one could say that the existence of such mechanisms is "the precondition of the possibility" of the co-ordination of social interactions. In more evolutionary terms one could argue that at the origin of the social world lies the constitution of successful generalised forms of social practices induced by individuals' repeated decisions to co-operate with each other rather than remaining in isolation. In any case, such mechanisms are essential in regard to the constitution of differentiated social systems. Without these co-ordination mechanisms, the social world would simply not exist.

Further, to follow Luhmann, trust seems to be a prime example of these basic co-ordination mechanisms. Trust reduces uncertainty in that it allows for *specific* (rather than arbitrary) assumptions about other social actors' future behavior. Someone who considers to trust another actor finds it conceivable to offer a—for himself more or less costly or inconvenient—favor to someone as a *"Vorleistung"* (Luhmann 1989: 23), which means that he simply makes the assumption that the trustee will not opportunistically take advantage of his not being willing and/or able to insist on any guarantees or concrete, immediate and/or enforceable promises in exchange. On the basis of this assumption—which would by no means seem reasonable if there were any good alternatives!—the actors get into the position for starting to interact with each other. It is worth noting that in such a situation it is not only the trustor who can make specific assumptions about the trustee's behavior. The trustee can also single out a small number of (re-)actions that he assumes the trustor will find preferable to all other possibilities of behavior. Thus systems of social interactions can emerge, because the reduction of diffuse complexity allows for establishing longer chains of co-ordinated social actions and reactions. The willingness to make one-sided commitments alone may not be sufficient to generate differentiated social systems, but it is a necessary precondition of many forms of social interaction. If there was no trust in the world, in the sense of *"Vorleistung"*, then actors would often find it impossible to even consider engaging in social activities with other actors.

Trust and Risk

Although trust is such a fundamental mechanism in all social reality, it also involves a problem which would be naive to ignore: Trust is a risky engagement (Luhmann 1979). It may be true that trust absorbs *uncertainty* and diffuses complexity, but, at the same time, it produces *risk*, as it is inevitable that a social actor who decides to trust another actor extrapolates on limited available information about the future behavior of this actor (Luhmann 1979: 26). In other words, trust can be disappointed and, then, appear to be misplaced, for in business (as well as in other fields of social life), one can be betrayed, and overly romantic assumptions can result in considerable losses. This is the risk that someone, when considering whether he should trust another actor or not, wants to *minimize*. If he could *exclude* it, trust would simply not be needed. Thus, risk seems to be an unavoidable feature of trust while, at the same time, trustors constantly try to find *good reasons* for believing that the risk they are prepared to accept is low. If they cannot find sufficient reasons for this assumption, they might well refrain from trusting, and either avoid social interaction all together or seek an alternative basis for it. One could say that, drawing on a universal disposition and the limitedness of social actors' psychological capacity to deal with complexity, a trustor *initially* offers a *"Vorleistung"* as a way of reducing uncertainty, and then *subsequently* seeks reasons for why he could deem the risk involved in his decision to be acceptable. Only if these reasons are found is trust likely to become the dominant control mechanism within social relationships between individuals or organizations.

As Luhmann suggests, the existence of *legal norms* is one of the most effective remedies for confining the risk of trust and thus for providing those *good reasons* which a potential trustor seeks before actually deciding to invest trust in a relationship. Legal regulation and the possibility of sanctions—if it comes to the worst—reduces the risk of being betrayed. It is, however, important to note that, as Luhmann clearly sees, legal norms do not fulfil their social function by actually being mobilized. According to his theory, the basic social function of legal norms is to be seen in their potential to direct the expectations of social actors to certain routes of behavior, long before sanctions are seriously considered by those who feel betrayed and might want to take recourse to legal action. Thus, legal norms and trust are more than compatible. In fact, legal regulation can foster the constitution of trust; but "the structure of the trust relationship requires that such calculation should remain *latent* (. . .), purely a reassuring consideration" (Luhmann 1979: 36). With reference to relationships between individual or organizational *economic* actors it can be assumed then, that *commercial* law can play a vital role in situations in which an actor needs to decide whether he should invest trust in the relationship with his business partner, or whether he should refrain from doing so. While, in the *first step*, an economic actor might—for no reason other than his psychological disposition—be inclined to offer a *"Vorleistung"* to his customer, supplier or business partner, the existence and *latent* influence of the legal system may—in a *second step*—actually lead him to decide to engage in a trust-based relationship.

Interestingly, this is an insight which openly contradicts the traditional mainstream of socio-legal studies (Macaulay 1963; Beale and Dugdale 1975). In this body of literature, the influence of legal norms on the quality of business relationships is seen as marginal at best, and trust is described as a phenomenon which, if it emerges, does so irrespective of whether legal norms exist or not. Referring to the legal code by, for instance, detailed contracts is seen as more likely to be detrimental than conducive to the constitution of trust. Some newer contributions from the organizational literature continue to suggest this view (e.g. Sitkin and Roth 1993), largely ignoring the difference between practices of confirming standard legal norms by routinely repeating them in small letter appendices and fierce "battles of contracts" (Sako 1992) where both contractors try to force their one-sided advantages upon the other. In the latter case—but only then!—trust and law would indeed be difficult to reconcile.

Further along the lines of Luhmann's argument, commercial law and practices of contracting can be understood as *one* important element within the wider institutional framework (Deakin et al. 1994; Lane and Bachmann 1996) in which trans-organizational business relationships are embedded. Besides legal regulation, there are other elements of the institutional arrangements of socio-economic systems which need to be taken into account when the process of trust building is under review. The role of trade associations, for example, which may or may not represent the collective interests of a whole industry, the structures of the specific financial system, the more or less coherent system of technical norming and standardization of products and production processes, and the economic policy of the relevant political administration also belong to the institutional environment which determines the quality of interactions between firms. One of the central functions of such an institutional framework, which differs between regions and nation states, is to be seen in their potential to generate *shared* economic, technical, cultural and social knowledge and to produce collectively accepted norms of business behavior. Through this potential of institutions, rather than through their ability to mobilize sanctions, the risk that can never be ruled out completely when a social actor decides to trust his business partner can at least often be reduced to a level that he might find tolerable. Thus, the existence of a tightly knit framework of institutions can be seen as minimizing the risk of trust. The common experience of living within the same world of institutional structures orientates the expectations and (re-)actions of social actors towards specific patterns of behavior. For this reason, it can be assumed to be less likely that a supplier, customer or horizontally co-operating business organization will behave in an unforeseen manner and that their individual representatives are inclined to cheat when the institutional framework in which their interactions are embedded is strong and coherent. Of course, exceptions are always possible.

Reconstructing the Link between Action and Institutions

Luhmann's theory of trust, on the one hand, fundamentally differs from conceptualizations which raise moral claims for *altruistic behavior* (Lyons and Mehta 1997). On the other hand, Luhmann rejects the notion that social actors base their decisions and behavior necessarily and exclusively on *egoistical motives*. In doing so, his theory is clearly opposed to central assumptions of Rational Choice Theory, which suggests that trust can be sufficiently understood as a strategy of rational actors to maximize their individual interests. Coleman (1990), for instance, represents precisely this view and argues that social actors calculate the gains and losses which might result from their decision to trust or not to trust another social actor before they actually make their decision. This view, however, is connected to assumptions as unrealistic as those which can be found in the literature based on moral postulates and social romanticism. Moreover, Coleman's formalistic approach goes astray, because, by the very nature of trust, it is impossible to quantify either the propensity for defection or the extent of potential gains and losses. At the same time, however, it is only these situations in which trust might become relevant at all. If, in a given situation, the social actors involved are in a position to assess the consequences of their decisions in very exact and reliable terms, trust will no longer be needed.

Interestingly, there are also ideas which Coleman and Luhmann have in common. Both, for instance, assume that *institutions* generally play an important role in the problem of assessing the risk which is implied when a social actor decides to invest trust. Similar to Luhmann, Coleman recognizes "social structures in which it is in the potential trustee's interest to be trustworthy" (1990: 111). However, this is not to overlook the fact that institutions, from a Rational Choice point of view, are only seen as *parameters* within social actors' rational calculations (Deakin and Wilkinson 1998). In contrast, Luhmann, who rejects the concept of solipsistic and solely calculation-oriented actors, suggests that institutions are to be understood as reducing risk by providing patterns of social behavior which in a *non*-deterministic manner orient social actors' expectations and decisions. In Luhmann's view, the first and very basic problem with which social actors need to cope is not how to identify profitable opportunities for trust investments, but how to reduce uncertainty. Given that social actors in a *first step* reach a state of being willing to consider trust as a means to coordinate their interactions, the institutional framework of the business system in which their relationships are embedded provides—according to Luhmann's theory—the basis for the *second step* to trust, as it largely decides how much risk social actors will have to accept if they actually invest trust in a specific exchange relationship. It is only at the latter point that Rational Choice Theory enters the debate, with the argument that elements and characteristics of the institutional framework will be subject to rational consideration by calculating individuals. This assumption, however, seems highly unrealistic as is shown, not only by Luhmann, but also by much of other sociological theory and empirical evidence. Institutions—as already pointed out with reference to the legal system—tend to do their job in a *latent* manner, which makes them more effective and helps to avoid a permanent overcharge of social actors' abilities to always ground their decisions, as well as to engage in social conflict. There are exceptions to this rule, of course, but not enough of them to carry a whole theory of social interaction.

In a number of respects, Luhmann's theory comes closer to New Institutionalism (Powell and DiMaggio 1991; Scott 1995) than to concepts based on Rational Choice. Both theoretical approaches, Luhmann's Systems Theory and New Institutionalism, agree on the argument that background beliefs and *tacit knowledge* are much more important in determining social actors' behavior than explicit calculation over potential gains and losses associated with specific decisions. On the basis of *phenomenological premises*, Neo-Institutionalists—who share these assumptions with Luhmann—explain the functioning of social institutions by the more subtle processes which control the patterns of social interactions. The fact that the institutional influences on individuals' and organizations' interactions are often withdrawn from their consciousness is actually viewed not only as accidental, but as the central precondition of institutions being able properly to fulfil their function of stabilizing social actors' mutual expectations and patterns of interaction. This is not to say, however, that the given socio-economic order is unalterable under conditions of concerted social action (Thelen and Steinmo 1992).

Giddens' Structuration Theory (Giddens 1976, 1984) also connects quite closely to this view on the *micro–macro link* within social systems. Giddens agrees with Systems Theory and New Institutionalism that institutions are to be seen as relatively enduring patterns of social practices which shape social actors' behavior. In this process, expectations and interactions between actors are *channelled* in a relatively loose—though not arbitrary!—manner. Since social actors themselves are assumed to produce and to reproduce the institutional order in which they live, they are in principle also free to change its structures. However, according to Giddens, they cannot avoid permanently orienting their behavior towards the *existing* institutional arrangements, unless they accept that their actions are meaningless to others. As a consequence of these referencing processes, the institutional arrangements of a given social system tend to be confirmed *under normal circumstances* rather than challenged, which explains why institutions are *relatively* stable over time. The New Institutionalist (Zucker 1986; Powell 1996) as well as the Structurationist understanding of trust between individuals and organizations (Giddens 1990; Sydow 1998) thus focus on reconstructing the role of institutions in a way that has little in common with what Rational Choice suggests. Although Coleman acknowledges that institutions are important in whether social actors find reasons to trust or not to trust each other, his explanation of this fact is based on a simple *input–output model* of individual cognition. Luhmann, Zucker and Giddens, in contrast, base their reconstruction of institutionally-based trust production on genuine *sociological theory* which provides a much wider framework of analysis.

Against the background of the latter issues, one can understand how institutional arrangements such as, for instance, the specific type of commercial law and the specific role of trade associations, which might be powerful or weak in a given business system, shape the quality of trans-organizational patterns of interaction. Stable institutions reduce the risk of being betrayed, in that they constitute a "world in common" (Harold Garfinkel) with shared norms and solid standards of behavior. Seen from a Neo-Institutionalist as well as from a Structurationist point of view, this process appears to be very similar to what Systems Theory suggests. In all three of these perspectives, trust is constitutively based on a *fuzzy logic* of shared beliefs, rather than on calculation. Structuration Theory and New Institutionalism are highly compatible with Luhmann's theory in placing the problem of how to cope with uncertainty at the starting point of their argument. Thus, trust is viewed as a mechanism which—in a very basic sense—allows for social interaction, and it is not seen as a (potential) result of rational calculation. In that trust reduces uncertainty, at the same time, it unavoidably produces risk with regard to the potential trustor's specific decision problem, and it is an intrinsic feature of trust that this risk is inaccessible in precise terms, due to the limited knowledge available to the potential trustor. For this reason, it does not make much sense to describe social actors' decisions to trust or not to trust as a 'bet' on the basis of precise information, as Coleman suggests (1990). It may well be that social actors *occasionally* consider the risk of trust in a calculating manner, which then presupposes precise—though not necessarily complete—knowledge (Bachmann 1998: 301–303). However, this is an exceptional step out of everyday-practice and routine, which can destroy the ground on which a trustor walks. In most cases, potential trustors need, and get, *good reasons* instead of precise data for their decisions. In this context, it is important to see that bearing the risk of trust in a specific issue is only a *subsequent* problem, which would not arise if social actors had not already developed a disposition to make a *"Vorleis-tung"* in a *first impetus* which—in a *circular* process—confirms itself in a *second impetus* in the light of institutional arrangements likely to reduce the risk of trust. Rational Choice is blind to the *first impetus* to trust and has no understanding of the circularity of trust production and the self-hightening process that can be found in a fertile institutional environment.

System Trust and Personal Trust

Luhmann (1979) as well as Giddens (1990) are primarily interested in what they call *system trust*. They contrast it with trust which is likely to develop when individual actors frequently have face-to-face contact and become familiar with each others' personal preferences and interests without substantially taking recourse to institutional arrangements—i.e. *personal trust*. Here again, they closely connect with Zucker (1986), who suggests that highly differentiated socio-economic systems presuppose that *system trust* or—what she calls *insti-tutional-based trust*—is produced in sufficient quantity and in a reliable manner. Luhmann's core idea of law as a means to reduce risk most directly refers to the concept of *system trust* or, if Zucker's expression is preferred, *institutional-based trust*. Thus it seems worth inspecting this concept a bit closer and analyzing the associated issues.

A classic example which is often referred to in the context of *system trust* is the trust economic actors have in the universal usability of money which can be seen as a precondition for the existence of large and efficiently working economic systems. Money as a medium to symbolize the transfer of material resources works, to a large extent, independently of whoever uses it, for whatever purpose and in whichever particular circumstances the payments are made (Simmel 1978). To this extent, one can say that the existence of a stable monetary *system*—which might include common practices of money lending and a central reserve bank acting as a "third party guarantor" (Cole-man 1990: 182)—produces the amount of trust needed to enable modern socio-economic systems to function efficiently. Like other elements and sub-systems of the institutional framework in which business relations are embedded, the abstract rules of the monetary system provide a means to control actors' expectations collectively, and thus facilitate coordinated interaction between them. In such a manner, trust—i.e. *system trust*—can be produced without this process being dependent on individual sympathy and/or long-standing personal experiences that actors might or might not have with each other.

Trust, Power, and Control in Trans-Organizational Relations

Undoubtedly, *personal trust* once fulfilled a pre-eminent role in business relationships. Today however, Zucker (1986) argues, *personal trust*—or what she calls *process-based trust*—is by no means sufficient to produce the quantity of trust that is needed in highly differentiated socio-economic systems. With reference to the American economy of the 19th and early 20th century, she explains the limits of a mode of trust production which is constitutively based on personal contacts and familiarity. The problem with this form of trust is that it takes tremendous amounts of time and effort to establish it and thus cannot be deemed a very efficient way of co-ordinating economic transactions within complex socio-economic systems. According to Zucker (1986), face-to-face contacts may still be extremely important in many situations, but they cannot serve any longer as the main, or even less so, the only mode of trust production. In other words, today, trust based on individual actors' integrity can only fulfil a supplementary function, compared with trust produced by institutional arrangements. It appears that this argument could be confronted with the assumption that although *system trust* might be seen as the result of an *advanced form* of trust production, *personal trust* or *process-based trust* would still be essential as the *starting point* for a relationship. Notwithstanding that much of the more superficial organizational literature on trust, which is not much bothered about cultural differences that may be influential here, indeed generally argues along these lines, it is not too difficult to see that—as is illustrated, for example, by the monetary system—*system trust* is not only most central to the functioning of *modern* socio-economic systems, but is also—if not particularly—in the starting phase of inter-firm relationships under these conditions. Luhmann's analysis of the role of the legal system in relation to *system trust* is based on exactly the same premise, and with reference to Giddens and Zucker this assumption can be exemplified even more clearly.

According to Giddens' (1990) theory of trust, the functioning of abstract systems, such as the monetary system, the legal system or the air traffic control and safety system, which Giddens himself suggests as an instructive example of *system trust* (Giddens 1990: 85f), presupposes that social actors, whether they are friendly smiling stewardesses on airliners or lawyers in black gowns, play a different role compared to the constitution of *personal trust*. They appear at the 'access points' of the systems which they represent and by 'face–work commitments' assure potential users or clients that these systems can be deemed trustworthy. In this way, face-to-face contacts *help* to absorb risk. These contacts thus seem to be quite important to the constitution of trust, but as such, they are by no means sufficient to produce *system trust*. Giddens leaves no doubt that stable and anonymously working institutional arrangements, standards of expertise, rules and procedures which are represented by these individuals, are the central source of *system trust*. Transferring these considerations to the world of trans-organizational business relations contributes to the insight that a *commonly acknowledged* system of legal regulation, financial arrangements, and interests organized by trade associations, etc., makes it much more likely that economic actors will behave more trustworthily than would be the case if there was nothing to rely on but face-to-face experiences with individuals more or less representing the interests of their organizations of co-operating firms.

The Dialectics of Trust and Power

Trust generally may be seen as an efficient means of co-ordinating trans-organizational relations, but it also has severe disadvantages which at least could lead to the question of whether there are alternative mechanisms to substitute for it. The risk associated with the decision to invest trust in a relationship may, in certain circumstances, be seen as intolerably high, and social actors might not be able to find enough *good reasons* to base a relationship on the assumption that a potential trustee will behave trustworthily. If this is the case, trust is unlikely to develop between social actors. However, this is not the only problem that can occur with trust. Even if trust has been established successfully in a relationship, it always remains a fragile mechanism. Irrespective of how likely it is, it is an intrinsic feature of trust that it *can* turn out to be misplaced, and the risk of a sudden breakdown of trust can never be excluded. When this happens, considerable consequences, not only in emotional terms, are to be expected. Business organizations, for instance, who realize that their main suppliers, customers or horizontally co-operating partners are beginning to cheat on them might overnight find themselves in a situation which challenges their mere existence.

Fortunately, trust is not the only way to reduce complexity and uncertainty. Another mechanism to co-ordinate expectations and to control the dynamics of a social relationship is power. In many respects, but not all, power is equally efficient, and at the same time it is more robust and the risks of misplacement or unforeseen breakdowns do not usually result in situations as dramatic as when trust is involved. Both mechanisms, trust and power, largely seem to operate on the basis of the same principle. Power works in that it "influence(s) the selection of actions in the face of other possibilities" (Luhmann 1979: 112). In this regard, there is no difference in how trust does its job. Both mechanisms allow social actors to link their mutual expectations with each other and to co-ordinate (re-)actions between them. However, there is also a slight difference between trust and power as regards the mode of selection of expectations. While in the case of trust, the actor who considers to invest trust in his assumptions selects the possibility that the potential trustee will behave the way be prefers, the powerful actor selects a possibility of behavior which he suggests to the subordinate actor as an undesirable behavior that should be avoided. In other words, the powerful actor does not simply make the assumption that the subordinate actor will comply with what he wants him to do. He prefers to construct an undesirable hypothetical possibility regarding the subordinate actor's future behavior and connects it with a threat of sanctions. In that sense, one can say that trust works on the basis of *positive* assumptions about *alter ego's* willingness and ability to co-operate, while power is constitutively based on the selection of a *negative* hypothetical possibility regarding *alter ego's* (re-)actions, and this is presented to the subordinate actor by the powerful actor as being in neither of their interests.

In many fields of social conduct, the identification of an undesired possibility of how social actors might behave in the future can reduce complexity sufficiently. Thus, power—similar to trust—can be seen as another mechanism for co-ordinating social interactions efficiently and for allowing relatively stable relationships to develop between co-operating social actors. It often suggests itself as a serious alternative to trust, but it should not be overlooked that the usability of power depends greatly on whether or not the threat of sanctions which is implied is realistic and has a good chance for being acknowledged by the subordinate actor. The more the latter starts to doubt that the threat of sanctions would ultimately be used against him, the weaker is the position of the powerful actor. Thus, there are no reasons to assume that power, unlike trust, cannot break down, if it is massively challenged. However, the damage is usually not quite as severe and a relationship may be continued more easily in this event, as power does not carry the same emotional weight that trust does. At the same time, power is anything but a simple trial-and-error game. Like trust, power has its risks as well as its safeguards but although it may not exclude risk entirely, it can reduce it considerably. As argued above, in the case of trust, the social actor who considers investing in it has *good reasons* to assume that the risk associated with the decision to actually trust another actor is relatively low. In the same sense, one could say that a social actor who considers using power can usually refer to "authoritative" and "allocative" resources (Giddens 1984) which can be deemed likely to find recognition by the subordinate actor. Otherwise, it would seem silly, or at best naive, to rely on the mechanism of power, just as would be the case when a social actor offers *blind trust* to another social actor.

In contrast to trust, power does not enjoy a very high reputation in day-to- day praxis, nor is it much valued by mainstream political philosophy. In both perspectives, it is often classified as an unacceptable means to control social communication (Foucault 1972; Habermas 1984; 1987). Luhmann, however, questions this view and suggests that power should be seen as a mechanism which has a high capacity for co-ordinating interactions and for controlling the dynamics of social relationships. Although it may not always carry the seal of legitimacy, Luhmann (1979) argues, it should not be overlooked as an important medium of communication which highly differentiated societies simply cannot afford to renounce. Whether power is used to *confirm* authority and hierarchy or whether it is used to *challenge* such structures is a subsequent empirical question which has little to do with the primary social function of power itself. Giddens (1984), remarkably, is one of the few "critical" sociologists who not only agrees with Luhmann's analytical, rather than political, concept of power, but even uses this understanding of power as one of the central premises of his Theory of Structuration.

On closer inspection, most social relationships are based on a mixture of both trust and power. Since both of these mechanisms are limited in their capacity to control the structure and dynamics of relationships, a combination often seems to be the only way to ensure that the co-ordination of expectations and interactions is satisfactorily achieved. However, as trust and power can produce very different qualities of relationships and are not equal in terms of what harm or benefits they can produce for the social actors on both sides, it is important to know on which of these mechanisms a specific relationship is *predominantly* based. In that sense, one can speak of two *alternatives* between which social actors can choose, although this is certainly not an arbitrary choice. As with trust, social actors usually have *good reasons* when they consider the use of power. If it is true that the risk of trust can be reduced by strong and coherent institutional arrangements which make it easier for a potential trustor to actually decide for trust to be the dominant co-ordination mechanism within a relationship, the reverse conclusion seems to be unavoidable: If the institutional order of a business system is patchy or cannot be deemed very reliable, potential trustors are more inclined to use power (if that they have access to corresponding resources) as the primary co-ordination mechanism within their trans-organizational relations, because, in these circumstances, they will often find it easier to bear the risk of open conflict than the risk of misplaced trust. Power may generally be the second best choice, but it is a good choice if trust seems not affordable.

A more detailed analysis of how trust and power do their jobs reveals that both mechanisms of social control, on the one hand, can be seen as *alternative* means of fulfilling the same social function, which do not exclude each other but occur in combination in many cases. On the other hand, however, it seems that the relationship between trust and power is more complicated and that what has been argued so far only applies when the focus of analysis is confined to the *micro* level of social interaction. As soon as the focus of analysis is widened and different forms of trust and power are taken into account— including those emanating from the institutional framework, in which social interactions between economic actors are embedded—power often appears as a *precondition* rather than an *alternative* to trust.

Only under conditions in which the institutional order of a socio-economic system is weak and patchy, where trust is mostly *personal trust* rather than *system trust,* and where power solely depends on individually attributed resources, might an individual social actor be seen as being confronted with a simple choice between basing a relationship more on trust or more on power. In this situation, however, as has been touched upon already, the risk of trust is likely to be intolerably high for a potential trustor who will then have *good reasons* to favour power instead of trust, provided that he has the necessary resources to draw upon. Where these are not available, he is more likely to meet other social actors who will exert power *on him* than he will have the chance to offer or be offered trust. Thus, in social systems which are based on a low level of institutional regulation, power is more often chosen as the dominant mechanism to co-ordinate expectations and to control social relationships between individuals and organizations. In circumstances of a strong and coherent institutional framework where trust is produced on an institutional basis, i.e. in the form of *system trust,* and the risk of betrayal can be deemed relatively low by someone considering either power or trust in a specific relationship, individual power resources will have a relatively low value and will often remain unused. Instead, *system trust* is likely to be the prevailing social co-ordination mechanism under these conditions. At the same time, however, one should see that power is not generally absent in this case. Rather, it appears as *system power* in the form of law, powerful trade associations, inflexible business practices, technical standardization, and rigid structures of hierarchy. It is precisely this de-personalized form of power—or *"Herrschaft"* to use Weberian terminology—which can "mass-produce" trust and thus can be seen as the central *precondition* of, rather than an *alternative* to *system trust.*

....

Patterns of Social Control in Trans-Organizational Relations: Germany and Britain Compared

The Functioning of Trust and/or Power within Specific Structures of Governance

The literature which analyzes empirical features of national business systems widely agrees that the British socio-economic system is characterized by a relative lack of co-operative mechanisms to solve the problem of co-ordinating social actors' expectations and interactions. In contrast, the German system is often described as being built on governance mechanisms which balance individual interests with collective goals and allow for long-term perspectives in business relationships (Stewart et al. 1994; Lane 1995; Lane and Bachmann 1996; Bachmann and Lane 1997). Although neither system is in itself homogenous as, for instance, sectoral differences can play an important role (Arrighetti et al. 1997), and despite the observation that in the face of globalization Germany today seems to be moving closer towards the Anglo-countries' business model (rather than the other way round), the British and the German business systems still differ significantly in their basic features. Thus, the socio-economic systems of these two countries can be deemed good examples to put the theoretical conceptualizations presented above to test and to examine empirically the conditions and consequences of different forms of trust within each framework of institutional order. In particular, in the following paragraphs of this section, it will be shown that the two mechanisms for co-ordinating expectations and interactions in business relations—trust and power—take on specific forms in Germany and Britain, and appear in specific relationships to each other within the given institutional context. Thus these mechanisms, it will be argued, constitute quite distinct patterns of social control in trans-organizational exchange relationships and, to a very large extent, also determine the quality of relationships between interacting firms.

The available comparative empirical studies generally confirm that in patchy and incoherent institutional environments with a relatively weak form of embeddedness of social interactions into these structures, trust is neither produced in large quantity, nor of very reliable quality. While, in both countries, trust is highly valued as an efficient means of coping with uncertainty, in the British socio-economic system, which is a prime example of extensive de-regulation (Lane 1995; Lane and Bachmann 1997), trust is a much more scarce resource than in the German business environment, which is still characterized by tight regulation and a strong institutional order. When trust occurs in the British system, it is likely to be *personal trust* constituted on the basis of individual experiences, rather than *system trust* produced by reference to the institutional framework. In both systems, inter-personal contacts between gatekeepers of business organizations are highly important in fostering the development of trust, but the difference seems to be that, in the British case, these contacts tend to result in trust in the integrity of the interacting individuals themselves, while in the German case, the personal level of communication between firms indeed tends to be only symbolic "face work" at the "access points" of organizations (Giddens 1990). In other words, German businessmen trust each other as representatives of their organizations which are embedded in highly regulated socio-economic systems, rather than as more or less sympathetic and potentially dangerously idiosyncratic individuals who merely by accident represent firm A instead of firm B, the latter being the case when *personal trust* is concerned. Thus, Giddens' concept of *system trust* and the process of re-embedding abstract systems and organizational structures into social praxis by individual social actors is particularly well illustrated by the social constitution of trans-organizational relationships within the German institutional framework, and only to a lesser extent does it apply to business relationships in Britain.

Empirical evidence also confirms that—as has been argued at the theoretical level—modern socio-economic systems are far too complex to be dominantly controlled by the trust that manifests itself in gentlemen's agreements and other forms of *personal trust*. As *system trust*, however, is not produced in sufficient quantity in the British system, due to a lack of collectively binding norms and standards of business behavior, it is not surprising to see that, under these conditions, businessmen are more inclined to consider their individual resources of power to control the dynamics of their relationships instead of trust. Compared to the German socio-economic system, in the British system there is a significantly reduced chance of efficiently co-ordinating social actors' expectations and interactions in business relationships by means of trust. Comparative analyses of the British and the German systems also widely support the theoretical assumption which has been developed earlier in this chapter, namely that the *genuine form of power* draws on *individual* resources rather than institutions but can, in functional terms, do a job similar to trust in situations where, as is characteristic of the British system, institutional arrangements are not strong enough to serve as a basis for producing trust in a fast and reliable manner. At least in today's world of business, *trust in its genuine form* is a systemic form of trust, i.e. *system trust*, since the constitution of trust, much more than the availability of power, relies on the existence of coherent and strong institutions. To a large extent, this explains the different qualities of trans-organizational exchange relationships between firms in Germany and in Britain. It would either presuppose too much time and effort or it would be too risky for British businessmen to base their relations extensively on trust. Provided that a social actor has resources of power available to draw on, making use of them often seems to be the better choice.

Clearly, this is not to say that British businessmen are only disadvantaged and that the 'mass-production' of *system trust* in Germany has no negative sides at all. In the light of empirical evidence, it could be argued that the absence of strong forms of *system trust* at least results in a greater awareness of the development of *personal trust* which allows for specific and very valuable forms of flexibility including an increased chance of building trust-based relationships across the boundaries of the domestic institutional system. German firms' limited ability of developing trust-based relationships in their foreign activities seems to be closely connected to the dominance of the institutional-based mode of trust production in this system, for if trust relies so heavily on the existence of highly generalized rules guaranteed by the institutional system, it is not surprising that trust finds no ground when there is no shared world of institutional arrangements, which can be assumed to be the case in most international business relationships. Here, *personal trust* is often indispensable. This, to a large extent, explains why British firms generally tend to find it easier to deal with foreign business partners than their German counterparts do.

Differences between the Institutional Frameworks

The differences between both countries are deeply rooted in ancient traditions which concern the role of the state and the relationship between state and civil society (Lane 1995). While, for instance, in the German tradition, the authority and neutrality of commercial law is guaranteed by the state and is not meant to be questioned by an individual who only pursues his own interest, this hardly matches Anglo-Saxon views where law is seen as a means for protecting individual interests against collective pressures and political dictate. Thus, according to the tradition of English law, it is left much more up to personal discretion as to how the individual wishes to engage in business relationships and under what conditions. If it comes to legal disputes, British lawyers tend to react very cautiously when investigating private business and, at best, in forming a judgement, refer to the letters of the contract, even if these seem to have been imposed by the stronger individual or organization on the weaker side. German lawyers, in contrast, apply highly generalized legal rules. They draw on a very detailed legal code which implies sometimes *fuzzy*, but always strictly binding, guidelines of business behavior such as, for example, the notion of "good faith" (Arrighetti et al. 1997). These rules override whatever individuals may agree in their contracts and it is common practice of law that courts seek to resolve legal disputes by suggesting (re-)balancing individual interests according to these rules. Thus it can be concluded that, within the German system, legal regulation, as part of the overall institutional framework, is strong and can efficiently reduce risk. In the sense of Luhmann's argument presented above, it guides economic actors' expectations and is highly influential on their behavior, long before disputes actually arise and cases are taken to court. In Britain, legal disputes are generally more likely, while it is less likely that a solution for these, acceptable for both sides, can be found. The German system of legal regulation helps to prevent opportunisitc strategies of the stronger side. It tends to encourage re-negotiations between the contractors and thus facilitates *system trust* in trans-organizational relations. In the British system, almost the opposite holds true.

Trust, Power, and Control in Trans-Organizational Relations

How elements of the institutional framework of the socio-economic system such as commercial law translate into relationships between social actors is well illustrated by the differences in using contracts in both countries. Within the British system, detailed written contractual arrangements are often the result of a fierce 'battle of contracts' (Sako 1992) in which each side tries to force its conditions upon the other. Thus, contracts in Britain—as has been argued, for example, by Beale and Dugdale (1975)—can, indeed, frequently be seen as a sign of distrust, rather than as being conducive to the constitution of trust in trans-organizational relations. In Germany, in contrast, contracts and trust are not contradictory to each other at all, which strikingly shows the limitations of traditional socio-legal studies. Seeking the reason for this difference between both countries reveals that, within the German system, contracts are used in a way quite different to what can be observed in Britain. German businessmen have long and detailed contracts because they repeat many standard legal norms which are found in the legal code and would apply anyway. This practice simply has the function of *re-assuring* each other of the common legal principles within a *shared world* of institutional order, and thus can foster trust in a semi-conscious manner.

While different concepts of commercial law and legal practice are based on very old traditions, in the past 15 years or so de-regulation policy has further weakened the institutional framework of the British socio-economic system. A good example of these developments is the changed role of trade associations, which in the post-war decades had achieved at least some importance within the system. Today, British trade associations are small, and many of them compete with each other in the same sector. Almost none of them represents the majority of their industry and thus can neither speak for it, nor can they be seen as organized interest groups with which the political administration can discuss matters of state-initiated economic policy. They are privately owned consultants who sell their services to *customers* and, thus, can hardly be compared to their German counterparts. Within the German socio-economic system, powerful trade associations truly stand for their industry. These trade associations are self-organized by their *members* who take an active interest in the representation of collective strategies within their industry. In work groups, economic and technical knowledge is frequently exchanged between the member firms and this is highly conducive to generating and monitoring the rules and standards of business behavior within the sector (and beyond). Thus, German trade associations can also function as transmitters of state policy and their advice on economic policy is much valued by the political administration (Bachmann and Lane 1997).

British trade associations cannot be understood as a relevant element within a strong institutional framework since they lack the capacity to provide general guidelines of behavior. Consequently, they hardly contribute to reducing risk and producing *system trust* in trans-organizational relationships. The German socio-economic system, in contrast, illustrates particularly well what the role of trade associations can be regarding the constitution of trust. In Germany, trade associations, in which membership is almost compulsory for firms active in a given industry, are an efficient tool of self-organized monitoring of the behavior of individual firms. The idiosyncratic and opportunistic behavior of individual managers or organizations is largely prevented in that these trade associations execute a threat of social sanctions, which often is *latent*, but fully sufficient to *channel* economic actors' expectations and interactions into stable and predictable patterns. In that sense, it can be said that they are an important element of the institutional framework and through their *system power* they produce *system trust* at a high level.

The link between the constitution of trust and the quality of the institutional order—as has been analyzed in the theoretical section of this article—can be widely confirmed by comparative empirical studies. These also give no indication that the British business system is only based on institutions different from those which can be found in Germany. There is simply a lower level of institutional regulation in the British system, and the embeddedness of individual interaction into the collectively accepted institutional order is equally weak. Under these conditions, power-based relationships often seem to be the only way to effectively co-ordinate economic interactions between firms. This conclusion is also supported by the British understanding of what business, in general, is all about. Contrary to what many German businessmen would freely admit, the British concept of business leaves no doubt that making high *individual* profits is the ultimate goal of all business. Within this context, the co-ordination of expectations and interactions by drawing on individual resources of power—even if this implies relatively aggressive behavior—is not observed suspiciously, particularly when it is obvious that the inter-personal mode of trust production would be too slow and inefficient. The British example confirms that the use of power is not always an inappropriate means of controlling the dynamics of relationships. It is to be seen rather as an efficient co-ordinator of mutual expectations which allows for swift decisions and reactions. However, compared to trust, power is less capable of producing goodwill as well as a certain type of flexibility which can—as has been argued in the introductory section of this article—save costs and foster the preparedness to engage in collective strategies.

Trust or/and Power as an Embedded Decision

Empirical research also confirms that economic actors frequently find themselves in situations in which they actually need to *decide* whether they want to base a specific relationship more on trust or more on power. In that sense, both mechanisms can be understood as *alternative options*. Further, along the lines of the theoretical analysis given above, it holds true that, in the vast majority of cases, these decisions are not based on rational calculation. Social actors in Britain and Germany usually have *good reasons* either to invest trust or to rely more on their resources of power—assuming that the latter are available to them. In the German business system, the risk that trust might be betrayed seems generally low. In contrast, the risk a British businessman is prepared to run when he considers trusting an unknown supplier, customer or horizontally co-operating organization is relatively high. Within the context of a strong institutional system which provides a close monitoring of the conformity of social actors' behavior, one can assume that, in most cases, it would not pay off to cheat. If the institutional environment is patchy and/or weak, the chances that social actors will consider such a behavior are significantly greater.

In neither of the two systems is the risk of trust usually assessed in formal terms. It simply seems that the risk is considerably higher when businessmen have to interact within an environment which has few and weak institutional safeguards. If, as the German case shows, *good reasons* can be found, such as tight legal regulation of contractual relationships or the existence of powerful trade associations, the likely decision to trust a potential business partner will be built on a *fuzzy*, but nevertheless *strong*, basis. Within the German governance system, a potential trustor could hardly quantify the chance that the trust he offers to another social actor will not be betrayed and what precisely it is that may make his business partner appear to be trustworthy. He simply tends to find the risk of trust tolerable when he perceives the co-operating organization's (re-)actions as being embedded in the institutional framework of a coherent business system constituted and guaranteed by the political administration, by latent threats of social and legal sanctions, as well as by hierarchical structures of self-control within the industry. In the British case, the same logic can be reconstructed with regard to the use of power. Within this business system, the risk of trust often seems intolerably high, and businessmen in many situations can find *good reasons* to consider their resources of power. Such a decision is, as in the case of trust, equally grounded in a *fuzzy* basis of knowledge and, again, is anything but arbitrary.

Also, empirical evidence confirms that the alternative between trust and power is usually not very clear-cut. The important questions concern the *proportions* of trust and power which together govern a trans-organizational relationship and what *forms* of trust and power become relevant to engage in specific relationships to each other. Thus, it corresponds to theoretical considerations presented above, that although the level of trust is high in trans-organizational relationships in Germany, businessmen, at the same time, draw widely on *system power* in that they insist on practices such as detailed written contracts, regular checks of product quality or seniority rules as to who, for instance, is entitled to claim privileged treatment from trade associations, state-run agencies of economic development, banks, etc. Within this system, both trust and power are cushioned in generalized rules and routine practices which sometimes veils the fact that there are decisions to be made at all. In Britain, in contrast, trust and power are more likely to be seen as contradictory to each other. Mixtures of both mechanisms—occurring in their personal forms, i.e. as *personal trust* and *personal power*—are nevertheless also the normal case in British trans-organizational relations.

Comparative empirical analyses strongly support the theoretical assumption that power embodied in rigid institutional structures constitutes the possibility that trust can be produced quickly and efficiently between socio-economic actors who are personally unknown to each other. The German business system illustrates particularly well that power can appear as a *condition* of, rather than an *alternative* to trust, but it is most important to note that the form of power which is concerned here is not *personal power* but *system power* which is anonymous and is carried out through the structures of hierarchy and the authority of institutions. This form of power may not be neutral to individual actors' interests (Berger and Luckmann 1966) but it can hardly be (mis-)used by them for opportunistic strategies. Thus, it can provide generally acknowledged guidelines of behavior, and for this reason, *system power* can foster the efficient production of a high level of trust in trans-organizational relations. No matter how strongly social actors may be inclined to offer a *"Vorleistung"* as a *first step*, they will take this form of power as an effective means to reduce the risk of betrayal and thus, in a *second step*, will develop a general preference to base their business relationships on trust, i.e. *system trust*, rather than making references to their *individual resources of power*. At the same time, however, it should not be overlooked that the existence of this form of power also restricts individual creativity and the ability to speed-up decision processes. The latter is directly linked with the German innovation crisis, which, under conditions of rapidly changing global markets, became evident recently (Kern 1997, 1998).

Conclusion

As has been shown in this article, a theoretically and empirically fruitful approach to analyzing the constitution of trans-organizational relations needs to draw substantially on genuinely sociological concepts such as trust and power, and to thoroughly examine how both co-ordination mechanisms are linked into each other within the specific socio-economic order. With reference to these categories, a wider focus of analysis can be established and the limitations of purely economic explanations of what constitutes the quality of trans-organizational relations can be transcended. Besides greater theoretical comprehensiveness, the approach proposed in this article also provides a more realistic view and a deeper conceptual understanding of empirical reality than is possible solely by reference to conventional economic theory.

The theoretical framework presented above is based on the assumption that, within the economic sub-system of society, social actors build their decisions on *good reasons* rather than on calculation or idiosyncratic preferences. These are constitutively drawn from structural contexts and institutional arrangements in which their expectations and patterns of interaction are embedded. In other words, neither a mysterious logic of structural processes nor arbitrary decisions of individuals are assumed to be the ultimate driving force of social processes. Rather, it has been argued, social actors inevitably build their expectations and shape their interactions *in the light of* institutional contexts. The micro—macro link between the level of institutional structure and the level of inter-personal interactions is thus seen as a loosely coupled connection within which intermediary mechanisms such as country-specific patterns of employing trust and/or power play a vital role in the social constitution of trans-organizational relations. Within this context, trust, power and the possible combinations of both can be studied in terms of their efficiency, and the intrinsic *fuzzy logic* of trust can be described in precise analytical terms.

In the empirical part of this article two distinct patterns of the social coordination of economic activities were reconstructed with reference to the British and the German business systems. Trust and/or power were suggested to be central mechanisms which—depending on the institutional framework of economic interaction—take on specific forms and engage in specific relationships to each other. While in a less strongly regulated system, such as the British business environment, social actors, to a large extent, need to secure the effectiveness of the co-ordination of their mutual expectations and interactions on the basis of individual experiences and resources, the same is neither necessary nor a promising strategy—as can be studied with reference to the German example—when the business system is built on a strong institutional framework of governance structures. In the first case, trust and power are likely to appear as *personal trust* and *personal power* between which—provided that suitable resources are available and thus power is an option at all—social actors need to decide. Given these conditions, they indeed often prefer the latter. Under conditions of "mass-production" of *system trust*, however, trust is constitutively based on *system power* embodied in collective practices and routines, hierarchical forms of social order, and formal rules of business behavior. In these circumstances, social actors are much less confronted with the need to make an explicit decision between trust and power, preferring to buy *system trust* and *system power* in a package. Thus, generally, the quality and dynamics of trans-organizational relations can be reconstructed as being controlled by patterns of *trust and/or power mechanisms* which are characteristic of the specific arrangements of institutional regulation in which business activities are embedded.

Against the background of this approach to analyzing the constitution of business relationships, it becomes apparent why simplistic explanations of the quality of trans-organizational relations must fail. As has been shown in the theoretical and empirical sections of this article, the quality of inter-firm relations is constituted by a social process much more complex than can be captured by one-dimensional economic approaches. These seem to be ignorant of the most important mechanisms which, in specific combinations and in specific circumstances, shape the form and quality of relationships. At the same time, it is not sufficient merely to describe the phenotypical phenomena found. The identification of, for instance, *hybrid* forms of co-ordination of expectations and interactions as a way to overcome the shortcomings of purely market-based relationships, on the one hand, and hierarchically integrated relationships, on the other hand, may draw on empirical observations and plausible conceptual assumptions such as the notion that long-term oriented forms of close co-operation allow for the pooling of risks or knowledge flows across organizational boundaries. However, these well-known arguments are usually not based on a sufficiently deep understanding of social reality. The theoretically grounded analysis proposed in this article, in contrast, is designed to dig below the surface of what can be observed at first sight. With the conceptual tools provided by this article, the problem of why *hybrid* forms of co-operation and the notion of trust today are so much embraced—particularly in low trust systems such as the British business environment which, however, lack the institutional preconditions of producing a high level of trust and encourage aggressive competition as well as the use of individually accessible resources of power instead of trust—can be analyzed quite fruitfully. At the same time, these conceptual insights allow for reconstructing the problem of 'over-embeddedness' (Uzzi 1997: 58) of trans-organizational relations in high trust systems such as Germany, and provide an indication as to what kind of trust is needed under these conditions to increase individual willingness to take risks associated with technical and economic innovation. To harvest the advantages of *hybrid* and flexible relations within this business environment seems to require an approach quite different from what is often suggested with reference to the Anglo-countries.

Comparative analyses of business systems quite clearly show that current mainstream debates are misled in basing their central arguments on the assumption that it all depends on the abstract question of whether market and hierarchy can be balanced in such a way that none of these principles is predominant in business relationships. If the problem was only to find the most effective *mixture* of the two ingredients—individual autonomy and institutional regulation—it would not seem too challenging to agree on a solution. However, as the Anglo-German comparison presented above shows, it is vitally important to gain a deeper understanding of how the specific socio-economic system under review works and how the relevant mechanisms of co-ordination of interactions between firms are constituted. Only if the logic of the specific business system can be revealed may it be possible to reconstruct the patterns in which these mechanisms decide upon the quality of business relationships.

Analyzing the social constitution of trans-organizational relations in the way proposed in this article makes evident that neither Marxist, nor Neoclassical, nor harmonistic views on socio-economic processes can contribute much to understanding and solving the current problems of advanced business systems. The Marxist view, which was and still is taken by Labour Process Theorists, assumes that there is "a constant threat of *collapsing trust into control*" and that trust is nothing more than a "sub-type of generic power" (Reed 1998: 7). As has been shown in this article, however, the relationship between trust and power is much more complicated, and varies according to the institutional framework of the specific business environment. Within the British and the German business systems, both mechanisms divide into specific forms and build up specific *trust/power control patterns*. At the same time, the notion that the growing importance of trust could lead to the end of capitalist profit-maximizing can equally not be confirmed by the analysis presented above. The fact that today many firms have developed a strongly increased interest in flexible *hybrid* relationships is as much a consequence of intensified competition on globalized markets as it is a trend often sharply questioned by the same developments. This paradoxical situation leads to different strategies of co-operation with specific conditions and consequences within the prevailing *trust/power control patterns*. One of the most important questions to answer in this context is whether, and in what circumstances, this paradoxical situation can be taken as a force to foster performance and innovativeness, rather than a hindrance to both. To find well-grounded solutions to real-world problems of this kind, the employment of sociological theory has been shown in this article to be useful. In contrast, formal models based on counter-factual assumptions—such as the idea of an exclusively calculating economic actor—seem to be historically exhausted today. It is high time to re-introduce society in economics (Ortmann et al. 1997) and to lay the ground for a theoretically informed and empirically interested approach to come to grips with contemporary problems of socio-economic systems.

Reinhard Bachmann

Acknowledgement

I am thankful to Steffen Albrecht, Arndt Sorge and three anonymous referees for their assistance and extremely helpful advice.

References

Ackroyd, Stephen, Gibson Burrell, Michael D. Hughes, and Alan Whitaker 1988. 'The Japanization of British industry?'. *Industrial Relations Journal* 1: 11–23.

Adler, Paul 1998. 'Market, hierarchy and trust: The knowledge economy and the future of capitalism'. Paper presented at the U.C. Berkeley Forum on Knowledge and Firms, September 1997.

Arrighetti, Alessandro, Reinhard Bachmann, and Simon Deakin 1997. "Contract law, social norms and inter-firm cooperation". *Cambridge Journal of Economics* 21: 171–195.

Axelrod, Robert 1990. *The evolution of cooperation*. London: Penguin.

Bachmann, Reinhard 1998. 'Trust—conceptual aspects of a complex phenomenon' in *Trust within and between organizations. Conceptual issues and empirical applications*. Christel Lane and Reinhard Bachmann (eds.), 298–322. Oxford: Oxford University Press.

—— and Christel Lane 1997. 'Vertrauen und Macht in zwischen-betrieblichen Kooperationen—zur Rolle von Wirtschaftsrecht und Wirtschaftsverbänden in Deutschland und Großbritannien' in *Managementforschung 7*. Georg Schreyögg and Jörg Sydow (eds.), 79–110. Berlin and New York: Walter de Gruyter.

Beale, Hugh, and Tony Dugdale 1975. 'Contracts between businessmen: planning and the use of contractual remedies'. *British Journal of Law and Society* 2: 45–60.

Berger, Peter L., and Thomas Luckmann 1966. *The social construction of reality*. Garden City, NY: Doubleday.

Bieber, Daniel, and Dieter Sauer 1991. ' "Kontrolle ist gut. Ist Vertrauen besser?" Autonomie und Beherrschung in Abnehmer—Zuliefer-beziehungen' in *Zulieferer im Netz—zwischen Abhängigkeit und Partnerschaft. Neustrukturierung der Logistik in der Autozulieferung*. Hans G. Mendius and Ulrike Wendeling-Schröder (eds.), 228–254. Köln: Bund Verlag.

Braverman, Harry 1974. *Labor and monopoly capital: the degradation of work in the 20th century*. New York: Monthly Review Press.

Child, John, and David Faulkner 1998. *Strategies of cooperation: Managing alliances, networks and joint ventures*. Oxford: Oxford University Press.

Coleman, James S. 1990. *Foundations of social theory*. Cambridge, MA: Belknap Press.

Deakin, Simon, and Frank Wilkinson 1998. 'Contract law and the economics of interorganizational trust' in *Trust within and between organizations. Conceptual issues and empirical applications*. Christel Lane and Reinhard Bachmann (eds.), 146–172. Oxford: Oxford University Press.

Deakin, Simon, Christel Lane, and Frank Wilkinson 1994. ' "Trust" or law? Towards an integrated theory of contractual relations between firms'. *Journal of Law and Society* 21: 329–349.

Dei Ottati, Gabi 1994. 'Cooperation and competition in the industrial district as an organization model'. *European Planning Studies* 2: 463–483.

Ebers, Mark, (ed.) 1997. *The formation of inter-organizational networks.* Oxford: Oxford University Press.

Foucault, Michel 1972. *The archeology of knowledge.* New York: Pantheon.

Giddens, Anthony 1976. *New rules of sociological method.* London: Hutchinson.

—— 1984. *The constitution of society.* Cambridge: Polity.

—— 1990. *The Consequences of modernity.* Stanford: Stanford University Press.

Habermas, Jürgen 1984/1987. *The theory of communicative action.* 2 vols. Cambridge: Polity.

Jarillo, J. Carlos 1988. 'On strategic networks'. *Strategic Management Journal* 9: 31–41.

Keeble, David, and Egbert Weever, (eds.) 1986. *New firms and regional development.* London: Croom Helm.

Kern, Horst 1997. 'Vertrauensverlust und blindes Vertrauen. Integrationsprobleme imökonomischen Handeln' in *Differenz und Integration. Die Zukunft moderner Gesellschaften. Verhandlungen des 28. Kongresses der Deutschen Gesellschaft für Soziologie,* Vol. 1. Dresden, 7–11 Oct. 1996. Stefan Hradil (ed.), 271–282. Frankfurt and New York: Campus.

—— 1998. 'Lack of trust, surfeit of trust: Some causes of the innovation crisis in German industry' in *Trust within and between organizations. Conceptual issues and empirical applications.* Christel Lane and Reinhard Bachmann (eds.), 173–202. Oxford: Oxford University Press.

Knights, David, and Hugh Willmott 1990. *Labour process theory.* London: Macmillan.

Lane, Christel 1995. *Industry and Society in Europe: Stability and change in Britain, Germany and France.* Aldershot: Elgar.

Lane, Christel, and Reinhard Bachmann 1996. 'The social constitution of trust: Supplier relations in Britain and Germany'. *Organization Studies* 17/365–395.

—— —— 1997. 'Cooperation in inter-firm relations in Britain and Germany: the role of social institutions'. *British Journal of Sociology* 48: 226–254.

—— —— (eds.) 1998. *Trust within and between organizations. Conceptual issues and empirical applications.* Oxford: Oxford University Press.

Lewicki, Roy J., and Barbara B. Bunker 1995. 'Trust in relationships: A model of development and decline' in *Conflict, cooperation and justice.* Barbara B. Bunker and Jeffrey Z. Rubin (eds.), 133–173. San Francisco: Jossey-Bass.

Loasby, Brian J. 1994. 'Organizational capabilities and inter-firm relations'. *Metroeconomica* 45: 248–265.

Lorenz, Edward H. 1988. 'Neither friends nor strangers: Informal networks of subcontracting in French industry' in *Trust: Making and breaking of cooperative relations.* Diego Gambetta (ed.), 194–210. Oxford: Blackwell.

Luhmann, Niklas 1979. *Trust and power.* Chichester: Wiley.

—— 1989. *Vertrauen. Ein Mechanismus zur Reduktion sozialer Komplexität.* 3. print. Stuttgart: Enke.

Lyons, Bruce, and Judith Mehta 1997. 'Contracts, opportunism and trust: Self-interest and social orientation'. *Cambridge Journal of Economics* 21: 239–257.

Macaulay, Stewart 1963. 'Non-contractual relations in business: a preliminary study'. *American Sociological Review* 45: 55–69.

Miles, Raymond E., and Charles C. Snow 1986. 'Organizations. New concepts for new forms'. *California Management Review* 28: 62–73.

Morris, Jonathan, and Robert Imrie 1992. *Transforming buyer–supplier relations: Japanese style industrial relations in a western context.* London: Macmillan.

Möllering, Guido 1998. 'Trust across borders: Relative rationality and relative specificity in the context of international co-operation and emerging markets'. Paper presented at the Academy of International Business Annual Conference, London, 3–4 April.

Oliver, Nick, and Barry Wilkinson 1998. *The Japanization of British industry.* Oxford: Blackwell.

Ortmann, Günther, Jörg Sydow, and Klaus Türk, (eds.) 1997. *Theorien der Organisation. Die Rückkehr der Gesellschaft.* Opladen: Westdeutscher Verlag.

Powell, Walter W. 1996. 'Trust-based forms of governance' in *Trust in organizations. Frontiers of theory and research.* Roderick M. Kramer and Tom R. Tyler (eds.), 51–67. Thousand Oaks: Sage.

Powell, Walter W., and Paul J. DiMaggio, (eds.) 1991. *New institutionalism in organizational analysis.* Chicago: Chicago University Press.

Rainnie, Al 1993. 'The reorganization of large firm subcontracting: Myth and reality'. *Capital and Class* 49: 53–75.

Reed, Michael 1998. 'Organization, trust and control: A realist analysis'. Paper presented at the 14th EGOS Colloquium, University of Maastricht, Netherlands, July 9–11.

Sako, Mari 1992. *Prices, quality and trust. Inter-firm relations in Britain and Japan.* Cambridge: Cambridge University Press.

Sauer, Dieter, and Volker Döhl 1994. 'Arbeit an der Kette. Systemische Rationalisierung unternehmensübergreifender Produktion'. *Soziale Welt* 45: 197–215.

Scott, W. Richard 1995. *Institutions and organizations.* Thousand Oaks: Sage.

Sengenberger, Werner, Gary Loveman, and Michael Piore 1990. *The re-emergence of small enterprises: Industrial restructuring in industrialised countries.* Geneva: International Institute of Labour Studies.

Simmel, Georg 1978. *The philosophy of money.* London: Routledge.

Sitkin, Sim B., and Nancy L. Roth 1993. 'Explaining the limited effectiveness of legalistic 'remedies' for trust/distrust'. *Organization Science* 4: 367–392.

Stewart, Rosemary, Jean-Louis Barsoux, Alfred Kieser, Hans-Dieter Ganter, and Peter Walgenbach 1994. *Managing in Britain and Germany.* London: Anglo-German Foundation.

Sydow, Jörg 1998. 'Understanding the constitution of interorganizational trust' in *Trust within and between organizations. Conceptual issues and empirical applications.* Christel Lane and Reinhard Bachmann (eds.), 31–63. Oxford: Oxford University Press.

Sydow, Jörg, Arnold Windeler, Michael Krebs, Achim Loose, and Bennet van Well 1995. *Organisation von Netzwerken*. Opladen: Westdeutscher Verlag.

Thelen, Kathleen, and Sven Steinmo 1992. 'Historical institutionalism in comparative perspective' in *Structuring Politics*. Sven Steinmo, Kathleen Thelen and Frank Longstreth (eds.), 1–32. Cambridge: Cambridge University Press.

Uzzi, Brian 1997. 'Social structure and competition in interfirm networks: the paradox of embeddedness'. *Administrative Science Quarterly* 42: 35–67.

Williamson, Oliver E. 1985. *The economic institutions of capitalism*. New York: The Free Press.

Zucker, Lynne G. 1986. 'Production of trust: Institutional sources of economic structure'. *Research in Organizational Behaviour* 8: 53–111.

Index

Index

Index

Index

Index